Galician Villagers
and the
Ukrainian National Movement
in the
Nineteenth Century

Galician Villagers
and the
Ukrainian National Movement
in the
Nineteenth Century

by
John-Paul Himka

in association with
Canadian Institute of Ukrainian Studies
University of Alberta

First published 1988

Published by
THE MACMILLAN PRESS LTD
Houndmills, Basingstoke, Hampshire RG21 2XS
and London
Companies and representatives
throughout the world

Printed in Hong Kong

British Library Cataloguing in Publication Data
Himka, John-Paul
Galician villagers and the Ukrainian
national movement in the nineteenth century.
1. Galicia (Poland and Ukraine)—Politics
and government
I. Title
320.947'718   DK4600.G36
ISBN 0–333–45795–1

Для Михайлика і Евочки.
Щоб Ви знали
Чия правда, чия кривда,
І чиї ми діти.

Contents

List of Illustrations ix
List of Maps xi
List of Tables xiii
Preface xv
Acknowledgments xvii
Introduction xxi
    Statement of the Problem xxi
    The Geographical and Chronological Setting xxii
    The Methodology xxv
    Some Technical Matters xxvii
Abbreviations.. xxxv
1. Serfdom and Servitudes 1
    The Nature of Serfdom 1
    The Enforcement of Serfdom 10
    The Resistance to Serfdom 16
    The Revolution of 1848–9 26
    Servitudes 36
    A Case in Point: The Events in Dobrotvir 40
    The Servitudes Struggle and Its Lessons 48
    The Memory of Serfdom in the Late Nineteenth Century 56
2. The Cultural Revolution in the Village: Schools, Newspapers and
   Reading Clubs 59
    Education and the School System 59
    The Newspaper Batkivshchyna 66
    The Correspondence in Batkivshchyna 80
    Reading Clubs 86
    Opposition to the Reading Clubs 92
    Generations and Gender in the Reading Clubs 97
3. Village Notables as Bearers of the National Idea: Priests, Teachers,
   Cantors 105
    What Was Notable about the Notables? 106
    Notables before the National Movement 117
    In the National Movement 123
    Tensions between Priest and Peasant 133
4. The Awakening Peasantry 143
    Who Were the Peasant-Activists? 143
    Commune and Manor 145
    The Money Economy and Its Representatives 158
    The Challenge to Traditional Authority in the Commune 175

    The Transformation of Peasant Culture 189
    Class and Nation 204
Conclusions 217
Appendices 223
    I. Archival Sources 225
    II. Corpus of Correspondence 239
    III. Correspondence by Occupation of Authors 251
    IV. List of Activists 255
    V. Activists by Occupation 319
Bibliography 329
Index 345

List of Illustrations

Vasyl Nahirny 77
Mykhailo Pavlyk
Iuliian Romanchuk

Sylvester L. Drymalyk 256
Kyrylo Genyk
Amvrosii de Krushelnytsky
Antin Rybachek
Danylo Taniachkevych (younger)

List of Maps

The Crownlands of Austria-Hungary, 1914 xxxi

The Circles of Eastern Galicia, 1867 xxxii

The Districts of Eastern Galicia, 1868 xxxii

The Districts of Eastern Galicia, 1910 xxxiv

The Oblasts and Raions of Former Eastern Galicia
    in the Ukrainian SSR, 1972 xxxv

List of Tables

1 Illegal Servitude Actions in Eastern Galicia and Northern Bukovyna, 1850–1900..50

2 Number of Inhabitants per School in Galicia, 1830–1900.....................61

3 Public Elementary Schools in Galicia: Total, With Ukrainian Language of Instruction, and Bilingual (Ukrainian-Polish), 1869–1900.................62

4 Percentage of School-Age Galician Children Actually Attending School, 1830–1900..64

5 Growth of Ukrainian Periodical Press in Galicia, 1850–1910................67

6 Press Run and Frequency of Ukrainian Political Periodicals in Galicia, 1880 and 1885...68

7 Press Run of *Batkivshchyna*, 1879–85..70

8 Confiscations of *Batkivshchyna*, 1879–96 71

9 Reasons Given for Confiscation of *Batkivshchyna*, 1879–81 72

10 Editors of *Batkivshchyna*, 1879–96..76

11 Correspondence to *Batkivshchyna* and Occupation, Summary...............85

12 Literacy and Illiteracy in Reading Club Memberships, 1897–1910........88

13 Reading Club Officers, 1884–5, by Occupation.....................................89

14 Growth of Prosvita Membership, 1868–1908 91

15 TsDIAL, 146/64–64b (Servitudes Commission):
Holdings Consulted 227–8

16 TsDIAL, 156/1 (Supreme State Prosecutor's Office in Lviv, Illegal Servitude Actions):
Holdings Consulted 230

17 TsDIAL, 168/1–2 and 488/1 (Indemnization Commission):
Holdings Consulted 232–4

18 TsDIAL, 348/1 (Prosvita, Reports from Reading Clubs):
Holdings Consulted 236

Preface

The conception of this book can be located and dated with precision. It was conceived in the library of the University of Lviv in February 1976. At that time I was researching my doctoral thesis on the socialist movements in Galicia, and needed to consult a newspaper for the Ukrainian peasantry entitled *Batkivshchyna*. I noticed immediately that there were two types of article appearing in the paper. There were the earnest, lucid, somewhat dull and paternalistic articles contributed by the editor and other highly educated people in the city, explaining the world to the peasants and exhorting them to vote correctly, establish reading clubs and cooperative stores and acquire an education. And then there were the other articles, enlivened by exaggeration, dialect-laden and juicy language and a rustic humour. These talked of a different world, inhabited by hard-pressed church cantors, tyrannical village mayors, good and bad priests, grasping Jewish tavern-keepers, righteous country school teachers and drunk and sober, ignorant and educated, opportunistic and self-sacrificing peasants. The setting and origin of these articles were the Ukrainian villages of Galicia. The authors were in large part peasants, but also village notables ranging from the lowly cantor to the pastor. They wrote about the progress of the national movement and the conflicts it engendered in particular villages. They boasted, lamented, praised, slandered and described.

The articles fascinated me. I ordered almost all the issues of *Batkivshchyna* in the university library and scanned the items of correspondence from the countryside. I began to see certain patterns emerging and decided then that I would return to this source in the future to study the grass-roots national movement. The return resulted in the present study.

The present study also represents part of a larger project conceived in the course of my doctoral research and may be regarded as another installment in a series of works interpreting the rise of social and national consciousness in Austrian Galicia from the perspective of social history. The earlier installments are the doctoral thesis, and later book, on the Polish and Ukrainian socialist movements, 1860–90, and a series of shorter studies on such topics as the priest-peasant relationship and naive tsarism. In the future

I hope to continue work on this broad theme, turning next to an examination of the Greek Catholic church and nation-building.

Something remains to be said about the structure of this book. Its methodology demands a focus on details and an investigation of matters and personages that have historical relevance only when understood as a collectivity. This focus on minutiae, which was indispensable to the method of investigation, complicates the presentation. It is difficult not to force the reader to wade through much the same swamp of detail as the investigator had to. I have tried to alleviate this problem by confining the greater part of the details to the appendices, which constitute a lengthy section of the book. But it has been neither possible nor entirely desirable to remove all the minutiae from the text.

Acknowledgments

Three institutions funded the research for this monograph. The Canadian Institute of Ukrainian Studies awarded me a grant in 1978, which allowed me to employ two research assistants, Yarema Kowalchuk and Nestor Makuch. The Institute, especially its former director, Dr. Manoly R. Lupul, also encouraged this project while I was on staff in 1978–81 and while I was Neporany Postdoctoral Fellow in 1982–4. Dr. Bohdan Krawchenko, the current director, has been most solicitous in bringing this work into print. The Institute also put at my disposal the skills of Peter Matilainen, who gave technical asssistance with computer wordprocessing, and Lida Somchynsky, who typed part of the manuscript. Myroslav Yurkevich of the Institute read the manuscript and proposed valued improvements. The International Research and Exchanges Board (IREX) gave me emergency support in 1982 which allowed me to conduct research in Vienna. In 1983 IREX not only provided me with a generous stipend, but also arranged for my wife and me to spend six months in the Ukrainian SSR. I especially appreciated the conscientiousness and interest in my work displayed by programme officer Oksana Stanko. The Canadian Foundation for Ukrainian Studies awarded me the Neporany Postdoctoral Fellowship, which gave me twelve months to devote to research and writing in Canada, 1982–4.

The Ukrainian Academy of Arts and Sciences in the US, particularly Dr. Eugene Lashchyk, invited me to present a series of five lectures based on this study at its annual seminar in Hunter, New York (August 1984); the seminar led to the clarification and revision of parts of the manuscript. Students and auditors of my course "Topics in Ukrainian History" at the University of Alberta (fall 1986) critically read and discussed chapter three and other parts of this work. Anonymous reviewers for the Social Science Federation of Canada offered valuable criticisms.

Libraries and archives at which I worked (and staff members to whom I am especially indebted) are the Cameron and Rutherford libraries at the University of Alberta, in Edmonton (Alan Rutkowski); the John Robarts Library at the University of Toronto, especially the Peter Jacyk Collection of Ukrainian Serials; the Widener Library at Harvard University, in Cambridge, Massachusetts (Oksana Procyk); the Austrian National Library

(G *Österreichische Nationalbibliothek*) in Vienna; the Scientific Library of Lviv State University (U *Naukova biblioteka Lvivskoho derzhavnoho universytetu*); the V. Stefanyk Lviv Scientific Library of the Academy of Sciences of the Ukrainian SSR (U *Lvivska naukova biblioteka im. V. Stefanyka Akademii nauk URSR*), especially its manuscript division (director Ie.M. Humeniuk and Petro Hryhorovych Babiak) and branches on vul. Radianska and vul. Lysenka; the Central State Historical Archives of the Ukrainian SSR in Lviv (U *Tsentralnyi derzhavnyi istorychnyi arkhiv URSR u m. Lvovi*) (director Nadiia Fedorivna Vradii and senior archivist Ivanna Volodymyrivna Zahrai); the State Archives of Lviv Oblast (U *Derzhavnyi arkhiv Lvivskoi oblasti*); and the Central Scientific Library of the Academy of Sciences of the Ukrainian SSR (U *Tsentralna naukova biblioteka Akademii nauk URSR*) in Kiev, especially its newspaper division.

Credit for the maps belongs to the Department of Geography of the University of Alberta, Cartographic Division, Geoffrey Lester, Supervisor; the maps were drawn by Stephanie Kucharyszyn. The four maps of Galicia are used by permission of Alberta Culture.

Some parts of the text have been previously published or are scheduled for publication. An early version of the first sections of Chapter 1 appeared as "Serfdom in Galicia" in the *Journal of Ukrainian Studies* 9, no. 2 (winter 1984): 3–28. Parts of Chapter 4 are included in two contributions to conference proceedings, which will be published by the Canadian Institute of Ukrainian Studies (Edmonton): "Ukrainian-Jewish Antagonism in the Galician Countryside during the Late Nineteenth Century," in *Jewish-Ukrainian Relations in Historical Perspective*, ed. Howard Aster and Peter J. Potichnyj; and "Cultural Life in the Awakening Village in Western Ukraine," in *Continuity and Change: The Cultural Life of Alberta's First Ukrainians*, ed. Manoly R. Lupul. Both the latter contributions also contain material not included in this book.

The scholars who assisted me most along the way were Iaroslav Romanovych Dashkevych, formerly of the Central State Historical Archives in Lviv, who followed my research in Ukraine with genuine interest and guided me to many of the sources I consulted and avenues I explored; Patricia Kennedy Grimsted, of the Ukrainian Research Institute at Harvard University, who put her expertise on Ukrainian archives at my disposal; Bohdan Klid, graduate student at the University of Alberta, who read and commented on portions of the manuscript; H.I. Kovalchak, Feodosii Ivanovych Steblii and Stepan Mykolaiovych Trusevych, of the Institute of Social Sciences in Lviv, who afforded me an opportunity for a collective consultation; Dmytro Denysovych Nyzovy, of the Chair of the History of the Ukrainian SSR at Lviv State University, who was my official advisor in Lviv and answered many questions about old Galicia; Omeljan Pritsak, of the Harvard Ukrainian Research Institute, who made several suggestions about methodology that I adopted; the late Ivan L. Rudnytsky, of the Department of History of the University of Alberta, with whom over the years I had discussed many problems of Ukrainian history, including some of the ideas developed in the pages that follow; and Franz A.J. Szabo, of Bishop's University, who read the section on serfdom and offered valuable suggestions.

Other individuals who facilitated my work include my wife, Chrystia Chomiak, herself a historical researcher, who served as the first sounding board for many of the notions developed in this study and then read the manuscript very carefully; David Evans, of the Press and Cultural Section of the US Embassy in Moscow, who helped my wife and me throughout our stay in the USSR; my father, John Himka, who read parts of the manuscript and encouraged my work; and Mykhailo Viktorovych Maidanov, of Lviv State University, who arranged access to libraries and archives, living quarters, visas and other matters during six months' research in Lviv.

To all these institutions and individuals I am deeply grateful.

Introduction

Statement of the Problem

Few historians of Eastern Europe would dispute that the single most important occurrence in that region from the Age of Enlightenment until World War I was the diffusion of national consciousness to the primarily rural masses of the population. It was this process that laid the foundations for the emergence of independent East European states after the Great War and that made the national antagonisms in the region so explosive during the first half of the twentieth century.

The European peasantry entered the nineteenth century without a national consciousness. As a Polish village mayor confessed in 1912, "I . . . did not know that I was a Pole till I began to read books and papers, and I fancy that other villagers came to be aware of their national attachment much in the same way."[1] This lack of a national consciousness was by no means limited to Eastern Europe. A celebrated recent study has shown that the peasants of France did not turn into Frenchmen until the eve of the First World War.[2]

This is not, of course, to suggest that peasants lacked ethnicity (they were, in Eastern Europe at least, the very repository of the traits that made an ethnos); nor is it to suggest that peasants did not view themselves as ethnically distinct from the representatives of other nationalities with whom they came into contact. But they did not think and act politically along national lines. (Indeed, they did not think politically at all.)

Yet by the early twentieth century, we find a very heightened political consciousness, with both social and national dimensions,[3] among many of the

---

[1] Slomka, *From Serfdom to Self-Government*, 171. Full bibliographical data for works cited in the footnotes are provided in the bibliography.

[2] Weber, *Peasants into Frenchmen*.

[3] "In Europe, the formation of modern social consciousness, genetically connected with the development of the social and political emancipation of the plebeian classes and groups, took place on two main planes: the class plane and the national plane. The feeling of class solidarity became the foundation of integrating processes on the horizontal plane, while national ties played the role

peasantries of Eastern Europe. The rise of this new consciousness went hand in hand with the formation of a network of rural institutions linked with the national movement: reading clubs, credit unions, cooperative stores, choirs, insurance agencies, volunteer fire departments and gymnastic societies.

This monograph studies that penetration of the national movement into one region of rural Eastern Europe. It is not concerned with the first stage of national movements, in which "the historical legends, folksongs, and other lore of a given people"[4] were collected by a small number of intellectuals generally based in cities. During this initial phase of the national movement, often referred to as the national "awakening" or "revival," the village played an entirely passive role. Highly educated enthusiasts descended upon it, to be sure—in order to learn the language of the peasants and record their songs, sayings and stories—but these activities basically left the village unchanged. Rather, this monograph is concerned with the second phase (Miroslav Hroch's "Phase B"),[5] in which the national movement assumed organizational forms and developed a mass constituency. In the second phase the countryside was crucial, for it was here that the overwhelming majority of almost all East European nations lived. Indeed, very many East European nations, of the "submerged" or "nonhistorical" category,[6] had only a minimal representation in the urban centres on their own territory.

National movements during this second phase, in which they spread to the countryside, can be studied either from the perspective of the urban-based national leadership, working to develop and expand a network of institutions under its command, or else from the perspective of the local cadres of the movement in the countryside itself. This monograph proceeds from the latter perspective, which I believe is more appropriate to the general problem of this second phase and certainly richer material for social history. Attention is focussed here on village society, how the national movement found such a resonance in it and how it changed under the movement's impact. The goal of the monograph is to present as ramified and accurate of an account as possible of the social dynamics involved in the case of one rural national movement, that of the Ukrainians of Galicia.

The Geographical and Chronological Setting

Galicia was the northeasternmost part of the Austro-Hungarian empire, accounting for over 10 per cent of the empire's area and about 15 per cent of its inhabitants. It was part of Austria (Cisleithania) rather than Hungary and accounted for a quarter of Austria's area and population. It shared a long

---

[3](continued) of a binding agent in vertical (national) integrating processes." Chlebowczyk, *On Small and Young Nations*, 11.

[4] Magocsi, "Nationalism and National Bibliography," 82.

[5] On the significance of Phase B, see Hroch, *Die Vorkämpfer*, 25.

[6] I deal with the distinction between "historical" and "nonhistorical" nationalities in *Socialism in Galicia*, 4–7. See also the stimulating debate over this distinction between Ivan L. Rudnytsky and George G. Grabowicz: *Harvard Ukrainian Studies* 5, no. 3 (September 1981): 358–88.

border with the Russian empire to the north and east; most of its southern flank bordered Hungary. In the extreme west it touched Prussia and the Austrian crownland of Silesia. In the southeast it bordered the Austrian crownland of Bukovyna. Its largest cities were Lviv,[7] now in the Ukrainian SSR, and Cracow, now in the Polish People's Republic. The Carpathian mountains ran along its southern border and the narrower western part of Galicia was also hilly. The rest of the crownland was an extension of the great Ukrainian steppe.

Galicia was primarily inhabited by Poles and Ukrainians, who each constituted over 40 per cent of the population in the late nineteenth century. Jews made up over 10 per cent of the population and Germans most of the rest. Exact determination is impossible, since the imperial Austrian censuses did not record nationality as such, but only religion and colloquial language (G *Umgangssprache*). Moreover, the refusal of the census bureau to recognize Yiddish as a language meant that the sizable Jewish minority disappeared in the language statistics, artificially inflating the number of Germans (toward the middle of the century) and Poles (toward the end of the century). In 1880 Galicia had a total population of 5,958,907. Roman Catholics, who were overwhelmingly Poles, with a very small German and Ukrainian (U *latynnyk*) minority, accounted for 46 per cent of the population. The Greek Catholics were almost exclusively Ukrainian, by ethnic origin if not always by consciousness; they made up 42 per cent of the population. Jews accounted for 12 per cent and Protestants, who were almost exclusively German, for less than 1 per cent. By colloquial language, the Galician population was composed 52 per cent of Polish-speakers, 43 per cent of Ukrainian-speakers and 5 per cent of German-speakers.[8]

The Poles lived primarily in Western Galicia, although they also constituted a significant minority (numerically and otherwise) in Eastern Galicia. In the east they formed the overwhelming majority of the landlord class, the majority of the bureaucracy and a plurality of the urban population. Polish peasant communities were mainly in Western Galicia. The two and one-half million Ukrainians (1880) lived in Eastern Galicia, mainly in the countryside. The Jews were dispersed over the whole of Galicia, but more densely in Eastern Galicia. Most of them lived in towns and cities, but 40 per cent lived in villages (1880).[9] The Germans lived both in the cities, where they worked in the bureaucracy, and in Evangelical agricultural communities in the countryside.

This study has not one, but three chronological frameworks: 1772–1914, 1867–1900 and 1884–5. The first of these frameworks, 1772–1914, represents the actual chronological limits of the material included in the text. In the year 1772 Austria acquired Galicia as its share of the first partition of Poland. Even in a study primarily devoted to the post-emancipation village, it

---

[7] R *Lvov*, P *Lwów*, G *Lemberg*.

[8] *Rocznik Statystyki Galicyi*, 3 (1889–91): 1–2.

[9] Lestschinsky, *Dos idishe folk in tsifern*, 98.

has proven necessary to give an account of and refer back frequently to the
era of serfdom (1772–1848). Serfdom had to be described, not only because it
had a formative impact on the Ukrainian village, but also because it provides
a frame of reference for appreciating the transformation of the village in the
late nineteenth century under the impact of the national movement. The two
decades following emancipation from serfdom in 1848 were dominated by a
struggle between landlords and peasants over the question of "servitudes," i.e.,
rights to forests and pastures. As we will see, the servitudes struggle had a
profound influence on the political consciousness of the peasantry, both by
creating a stratum of peasant leaders dispersed throughout Galicia who would
later play a role in the national movement and by teaching masses of the
peasantry an important lesson about the need to educate themselves and their
children. By the year 1914 the process of nation-building described in this
monograph had already been completed, but I have studied certain patterns
in the development of the rural national movement through that year.
Although Austrian rule in Galicia only ended in 1918, the outbreak of World
War I and the Russian occupation of Galicia in 1914 changed the historical
situation completely.

The second framework, 1867–1900, represents the actual chronological
period in which the Ukrainian national movement penetrated rural Galicia,
and so it is the period with which this investigation is most concerned. In
1867 the Habsburg empire was restructured so that Hungary acquired formal
autonomy under the actual rule of the Magyar nobility and constitutional,
representative government was introduced in Austria. Following the example
of the Magyars, the Poles in Galicia won informal autonomy for the
crownland in 1868. Galician affairs thereafter came under little scrutiny from
the central government in Vienna and real political authority locally was in
the hands of the viceroy's office,[10] the diet,[11] the crownland administration,[12]
the district captaincies[13] and the crownland school council.[14] All these
institutions were dominated by Polish nobles. This situation, which placed the
Ukrainian movement at a great disadvantage, pertained until the First World
War. However, the all-Austrian constitution mitigated the Ukrainians'
disadvantages. It guaranteed freedom of association, which allowed the
formation in 1868 of the Ukrainian national movement's society for
propagating enlightenment, Prosvita, as well as the establishment on the
local, village level of reading clubs and other institutions. It also introduced
an elected parliament, which forced the national intelligentsia in the city to
undertake an effective propagation of the national idea among the newly
enfranchised Ukrainian masses in the countryside. A number of indicators

---

[10] U *namisnytstvo*, P *namiestnictwo*, G *Statthalterei*.

[11] U *soim*, P *sejm*, G *Landtag*.

[12] U *kraiovyi viddil*, P *wydział krajowy*, G *Landesausschuss*.

[13] U *starostva*, P *starostwa*, G *Bezirkshauptmannschaften*.

[14] U *Kraiova shkilna rada*, P *Krajowa Rada Szkolna*, G *Landesschulrat*.

show that by 1900 the national movement had established such a strong base
in the countryside that we can consider the second phase in the development
of the national movement completed.[15] The choice of the year 1900 as the
closing date was also motivated by the decision to leave out of consideration
here the great agrarian strikes of 1902 and 1906, as well as the strike of 1900
in Borshchiv district. These strikes clearly belong to another set of problems
(the coordinated activities of the organized village) and another era.

Finally, the third framework, 1884–5, represents a focal point required by
some aspects of the methodology. Although this study investigates the whole
period 1867–1900, it has proven fruitful also to stop the flow of history at one
moment and examine that moment in detail. This methodological technique is
all the more justified when we consider that the penetration of the national
movement into the countryside was a cumulative process, encompassing
different villages at different times. Thus at any moment in the 1870s–1890s,
there would have been some villages that had not yet been drawn into the
movement, others that would have just started the process of integration into
the nation and others still that would have had flourishing national
institutions. The fixing of a moment, then, does not greatly hinder the understanding of the phases and process of development of the national movement
locally. The choice of the years 1884 and 1885 has been motivated partly by
their almost exact correspondence to the centre of the time-span 1867 to 1900
and partly by other considerations connected with the methodology.

The Methodology

An obstacle to studying the diffusion of national consciousness among the
peasantry has been the lack of appropriate sources. As Eugen Weber
compained, while grappling with the problem of understanding rural France
in the late nineteenth century, peasants left too few written accounts of their
concerns; they were "inarticulate, that is, on those particular levels that provide most of the records on which historians rely."[16] This study of Galicia,
however, is based on sources written by the peasantry itself as well as by
rural strata close to it. The sources express the peasants' views on the
national question and describe at first hand their participation in the national
movement.

In 1879 the leaders of the Ukrainian national movement in Lviv began
publishing a newspaper, *Batkivshchyna*, that was specifically intended to
carry the national idea to the peasantry. One feature of the paper was a section entitled "Visty z kraiu" (News from the Crownland) that carried items
of correspondence[17] from activists in villages and small towns. These are the
sources on which this study primarily relies. I have examined in detail the

[15] I have argued this in a series of earlier works, particularly Himka, "Priests and Peasants,"
9–10. Himka, "Hope in the Tsar," 135–6. Himka, "Young Radicals," 233–5. Himka,
"Background to Emigration," 21–3. Himka, *Socialism*, 172, 178.

[16] Weber, *Peasants into Frenchmen*, xiii.

[17] U *dopysy, korespondentsii, pysma*.

"Visty z kraiu" section of *Batkivshchyna* for 1884 and 1885. After eliminating a few items of correspondence originating outside Galicia (Vienna and Bukovyna), I was left with 281 items. These form the *corpus of correspondence*, abbreviated as *CC*. A complete list of the 281 items of correspondence, with full bibliographical information, is contained in Appendix II, "Corpus of Correspondence."

The corpus of correspondence has been used to produce a *list of activists*, abbreviated as *LA*. The list, which contains 368 entries, includes all authors of items of correspondence whom it has been possible to identify by name, as well as all officers of reading clubs and other activists mentioned in the correspondence. Biographical information on the activists is presented in Appendix IV, "List of Activists."[18]

Both the corpus of correspondence and the list of activists are devices that allow quantitative generalization. It is possible to investigate what percentage of the items of correspondence dealt with a certain theme and what percentage of the authors, reading club officers or activists in general were of a certain occupation or background. This affords clearer insights into the inner workings of the national movement in the village.

It was necessary to choose only a sample of the c. 1,500 items of correspondence that appeared in *Batkivshchyna* in 1879–96 to allow a closer examination of those chosen. I settled on the years 1884 and 1885 largely through force of circumstance. For a long time these were the only two years of *Batkivshchyna* available on the North American continent, where I began work on this project. Fortunately, the two years proved to be quite suitable. They were removed enough from 1879, when the paper first appeared, so that the editors could rely on a steady flow of correspondence from authentic local activists, yet earlier than 1890, when *Batkivshchyna* (but not the national movement in the village) began a serious decline. Furthermore, they included the parliamentary election year of 1885, which meant that the important electoral struggle would be reflected in the correspondence. There were also drawbacks to the choice of 1884–5. No popular assembly (U *viche*) was held in those years, and the small-town intelligentsia still played a much smaller role than it would even a decade later. (On these two aspects, see the Conclusions.)

Although the study interrogates most closely the corpus of correspondence of 1884–5, it also employs a wide range of secondary literature and other sources, including items of correspondence from other years, in order to put the information from 1884–5 into the context of the wider trends discernible in the period 1867–1900. Thus the synchronic, restricted source base is complemented by a diachronic, open source base to provide a many-sided analysis of the penetration of the Ukrainian national movement into the Galician village.

---

[18] Unfortunately, when this manuscript was essentially completed, I discovered that the list of activists had omitted by oversight two individuals: Antin Vasylevsky and Oleksa Shkliar, founders of the reading club in Berezhnytsia, Stryi district (mentioned in *CC* 236). The omission is of negligible significance.

Although the focus of this book is Ukrainian Galicia, it is intended as a case study with implications, *mutatis mutandis*, for the history of the rest of Eastern Europe as well. Explicit comparisons with other regions of Eastern Europe are drawn repeatedly in the footnotes, and the study is placed in a general East European context in the Conclusions.

Some Technical Matters

Terminology, transliteration, place names. In general I have attempted to find English equivalents for most of the technical terms employed in this study. Upon first usage the original Ukrainian, Polish and German terms are given either in the footnotes or, if only a single term is involved, in the text itself in parentheses. The Ukrainians of Galicia in the late nineteenth century called themselves *rusyny*; Poles called them *Rusini* and Germans called them *Ruthenen.* I will use the term "Ruthenian" to render this historical name for the Ukrainians, employed chiefly in translations from sources.

Transliteration follows the Library of Congress system as simplified by the Canadian Institute of Ukrainian Studies.

For place names I also follow the guidelines established by the Canadian Institute of Ukrainian Studies. In brief these are: common English equivalents are used where they exist (thus Kiev, Cracow); otherwise place names appear in the language of the country in which they are currently located (thus Lviv, Przemyśl); for localities situated on traditional Ukrainian ethnic territory, but outside the Ukrainian SSR, the Ukrainian equivalent is given in parentheses on first mention.

Dates. From 1 March 1700 there was an eleven-day difference between the new, Gregorian calendar and the old, Julian calendar; from 1 March 1800 a twelve-day difference; and from 1 March 1900 a thirteen-day difference. Sometimes Ukrainians in Galicia used the Gregorian calendar, particularly in relations with non-Ukrainian society, and sometimes the Julian, usually in internal communication and always in church affairs. Unfortunately, I have not always been able to determine with certainty which calendar was in mind when dates were adduced in the sources. Therefore I have refrained from converting the dates in the text to a single calendar and have decided instead to mark each date N.S. (new style, Gregorian) or O.S. (old style, Julian) as I think probable. In cases where two dates are given, e.g., 25 December (7 January), the earlier date is Julian and the later its Gregorian equivalent (when Orthodox Christians celebrate Christmas on what is the seventh of January by the secular, Gregorian calendar, their church calendar—which is Julian—reads the twenty-fifth of December). I have not considered it necessary to specify the calendar for dates appearing as part of the bibliographical information in citations of periodicals.

Measurements. I have not converted units for measuring area from the Lower Austrian system used in Galicia to the metric system, since this would have complicated many calculations in which only the relative, and not absolute, size of landholdings was significant. The basic units of land area were the (G) *Joch* (U and P *morg*) and the square (G) *Klafter*.[19] I have decided to use the German terms, since these were all-Austrian units of measurement. One *Joch* equals 0.575 hectares (somewhat more than an acre) or 1600 square *Klafter*. One square *Klafter* equals 3.596 square metres.

Currency. Until 1857 one (G) gulden[20] contained 60 (G) kreuzer.[21] Beginning in 1857, one gulden contained 100 kreuzer. In 1892, a new currency was introduced, while the old one remained in circulation. In the new currency one crown[22] contained 100 hallers.[23] From 1892 until 1900, when the old currency was withdrawn from circulation, one gulden equalled two crowns and one kreuzer two hallers.

Administrative-territorial divisions. From 1772 until 1867 Galicia was divided into circles.[24] Of the eighteen circles existing by the mid-1840s, twelve with a Ukrainian majority formed Eastern Galicia. In 1867 the circles were replaced by seventy-four smaller units, districts.[25] Forty-eight of these were in Eastern Galicia. In 1876 the capital of Bircza (Bircha) district was transferred to Dobromyl. Near the turn of the century some new districts were created. Pechenizhyn district became separate from Kolomyia district shortly before 1900. Zboriv district became separate from Zolochiv district in 1904. Radekhiv and Skole districts were created c. 1906. When Husiatyn was destroyed in 1914 at the beginning of the First World War, the district capital was moved to Kopychyntsi.[26]

---

[19] U *sazhen, siazhen*; P *sążeń*.

[20] U *zolotyi rynskyi*, P *złoty ryński* or *reński*.

[21] U *kraitsari, kreitseri*; P *krajcary*.

[22] G *Krone*, U and P *korona*.

[23] G *Haller*, U *helery*, P *helerzy*.

[24] U *okruhy*, P *cyrkuły*, G *Kreise*. The translation of these terms by the English word "circle" finds justification in the *Oxford English Dictionary*; definition 22 of "circle" is: "A territorial division of Germany under the Holy Roman Empire. Also a secondary division in certain German and Slavonic Provinces. (G. *Kreis*, F. *cercle*)."

[25] U *povity*, P *powiaty*, G *Bezirke*.

[26] For further information on these technical matters, see Himka, "A Researcher's Handbook," and Ihnatowicz, *Vademecum*.

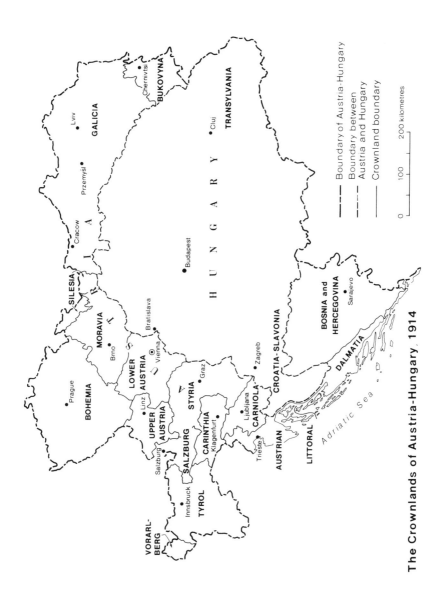

The Crownlands of Austria-Hungary, 1914

Boundary of Austria-Hungary

Boundary between Austria and Hungary

Crownland boundary

0   100   200 kilometres

GALICIA

Chernivtsi

BUKOVYNA

Lviv

TRANSYLVANIA

Przemysl

Cluj

Cracow

SILESIA

A

L

E

S

I

HUNGARY

Budapest

MORAVIA

Bratislava

Brno

LOWER AUSTRIA

Vienna

BOSNIA and HERCEGOVINA

Sarajevo

CROATIA - SLAVONIA

Zagreb

Prague

BOHEMIA

STYRIA

Graz

Linz

UPPER AUSTRIA

CARNIOLA

Ljubljana

DALMATIA

Salzburg

SALZBURG

CARINTHIA

Klagenfurt

AUSTRIAN LITTORAL

Trieste

Adriatic Sea

Innsbruck

TYROL

VORARL-BERG

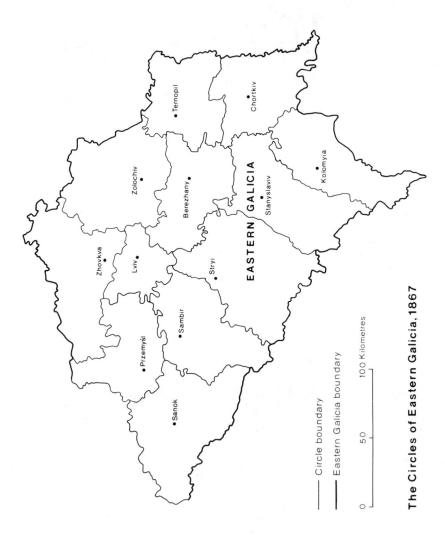

The Circles of Eastern Galicia, 1867

- District boundary
- Boundary of Eastern Galicia

0   50   100 Kilometres

The Districts of Eastern Galicia, 1868

District boundary
Boundary of Eastern Galicia

0   50   100 Kilometres

The Districts of Eastern Galicia, 1910

Enlarged area

UKRAINIAN SSR

Black Sea

Sokal

Radekhiv

Nesterov
Kamianka-Buzka

Shumske

Iavoriv

LVIV OBLAST

Busk

Brody

Kremenets

Mostyska

Horodok

⊙ Lviv

Zolochiv

Lanivtsi

Pustomyty

Peremyshliany

Zboriv

Zbarazh

Staryi Sambir

Sambir

Mykolaiv

Berezhany

Kozova

⊙ Ternopil

Pidvolochysk

Drohobych

Zhydachiv

Rohatyn

TERNOPIL OBLAST

Turka

Stryi

Halych

Terebovlia

Skole

Kalush

Monastyr-yska

Husiatyn

Dolyna

Ivano-Frankivsk ⊙

Buchach

Chortkiv

Rozhniativ

IVANO-FRANKIVSK
OBLAST

Bohorodchany

Tlumach

Zalishchyky

Borshchiv

Nadvirna

Horodenka

Kolomyia

Sniatyn

Kosiv

Verkhovyna

——— Raion boundary

——— Oblast boundary

**The Oblasts and Raions of Former Eastern Galicia
in the Ukrainian SSR, 1972**

Abbreviations

CC Corpus of Correspondence (Appendix II).

G German (language).

L Latin (language).

LA List of Activists (Appendix IV).

Lev1 Levytsky, Ivan Em. *Halytsko-ruskaia bybliohrafiia XIX stolitiia s uvzhliadneniem ruskykh izdanii poiavyvshykhsia v Uhorshchyni i Bukovyni (1801–1886).* 2 vols. Lviv: Stavropyhiiskii instytut, 1888–1895.

Lev2 Levytsky, Iv. Em. *Ukrainska bibliografiia Avstro-Uhorshchyny za roky 1887–1900.* 3 vols. (and first 16 pages of unfinished fourth volume). Materiialy do ukrainskoi bibliografii, Bibliografichna komisiia Naukovoho tovarystva imeny Shevchenka, 1–3. Lviv: NTSh, 1909–11.

Lev3 Levytsky, I.O. "Materialy do ukr[ainskoi] bibliohrafii Avstro-Uhorshchyny, 1894." LNB AN URSR, Viddil rukopysiv, fond I.O. Levytskoho, sprava 6, papka 2.

Lev493 Levytsky, I.O. "Materialy do biohrafichnoho slovnyka." LNB AN URSR, Viddil rukopysiv, fond 1 (NTSh), sprava 493.

LNB AN URSR Lvivska naukova biblioteka im. V. Stefanyka Akademii nauk URSR.

LODA Lvivskyi oblasnyi derzhavnyi arkhiv.

N.S. New style (Gregorian calendar).

NTSh Naukove tovarystvo imeny Shevchenka.

od. zb. odynytsi(a) zberezhennia.

O.S. Old style (Julian calendar).

P Polish (language).

R Russian (language).

Schem. Leop. Schematismus universi venerabilis cleri Archidioeceseos Metropolitanae graeco-catholicae Leopoliensiis pro anno Domini.... Lviv: E typographia Institutio Stauropigiani, various years. (Title varies.)

Shem. Lviv. *Shematyzm vsechestnoho klyra Mytropolytalnoi arkhidiietsezii hreko-katolycheskoi lvovskoi na rik....* Lviv: Iz typohrafii Stavropyhiiskoho instytutu, various years. (Title varies.)

Spec. Orts-Rep. 1880 *Special-Orts-Repertorien der im oesterreichischen Reichsrathe vertretenen Königreiche und Länder.* Herausgegeben von der k.k. statistischen Central-Commission. Bd. XII: *Galizien.* Vienna, 1886.

Szem. kr. Gal. *Szematyzm Królestwa Galicyi i Lodomeryi z Wielkim Księstwem Krakowskiem na rok....* Lviv: Publishers vary, various years.

TsDIAL Tsentralnyi derzhavnyi istorychnyi arkhiv URSR u m. Lvovi.

U Ukrainian (language).

1. Serfdom and Servitudes

Nothing so stamped the character of the Galician countryside as the long experience of serfdom. For a hundred years after its abolition in 1848, the basic elements of the Galician village—from landholding arrangements and the layout of buildings to the categories of inhabitants and relations among them—all remained fundamentally as they had taken shape during the previous centuries of serfdom. Even though the national movement did not, and could not, reach the peasantry under serfdom, nothing is as essential to understanding the emancipated peasantry's embrace of that movement as an understanding of serfdom. It was first in the throes of liberation from serfdom, during the revolution of 1848–9, that peasants entered the national movement and that, as a corollary, the national movement began to enter that crucial second phase in which it developed a mass constituency. Although during the final struggle over the terms of emancipation, the servitudes conflict that dominated the 1850s and 1860s, the national movement was once again largely absent from the countryside, this struggle too contributed to the national movement's popularity in the village after the 1860s.

The Nature of Serfdom

> Ta iak tiazhko na tu horu kamin
> vykotyty—
> Oi tak davno bulo tiazhko
> panshchynu robyty.
> —Ukrainian folk song[1]

Under serfdom, Galician peasants paid rents in labour, kind and money to the lord of the manor, the state and the church. According to the land cadastre of 1819–20, peasants paid out 84.7 per cent of their net annual income in rents. The lion's share of rents went to the landlords (80.0 per cent), the rest to the state (16.1 per cent) and church (2.8 per cent). The

---

[1] "As hard as it is to roll a boulder up a hill, that's how hard it used to be to do corvée labour." "Na panskii roboti," in *Khodyly opryshky*, 45.

greater part of feudal rents was paid in labour (83.2 per cent in 1845) and
much less in kind (10.8 per cent) and money (6.0 per cent).[2] The tithe in kind
(G *Zehent*) was uncommon in Galicia.[3]

The primary labour rent was the corvée,[4] unpaid labour on the lord's
estate. The corvée was reminiscent of slavery,[5] but not identical with it. The
slave was nothing more than an instrument of production for his master; the
serf, however, was a self-sustaining producer who worked a certain number of
days on the lord's estate and a certain number of days on his own farm,
which produced his means of subsistence. All the slave's labour belonged to
his master, while the serf's labour was divided in two, with a clear separation
in time and space.[6]

Under old Poland, serfs were sometimes forced to perform corvée labour as
many as four, five or even six days a week. The enlightened Austrian
government, however, prohibited imposing more than three days a week on
any Galician peasant.[7] The number of days of corvée required annually varied
from village to village and was recorded in a document known as the
inventory (G *Stockinventar*). The number of days of corvée required of
individual serfs in a particular village depended on the stratum to which they
belonged, which in turn was determined by the size of their farm.[8] Thus the
inventory for Mechyshchiv, Berezhany circle, compiled in 1773, specified that
serfs with more than 12 *Joch* of land would be considered half peasants;[9] serfs
with less than 9 *Joch* would be considered gardeners[10] (half peasants and
gardeners were the only strata defined in the Mechyshchiv inventory).[11]
So-called full peasants[12] were obliged to perform the maximum corvée in the
village. For example, full peasants in Ivachiv Dolishnii, Ternopil circle, owed

---

[2] Steblii, "Peredmova," *Klasova borotba*, 10. See also Rosdolsky, *Stosunki poddańcze*, 1:262–3;
Rosdolsky, *Die grosse Steuer- und Agrarreform*, 44–50, 93–8, 192, 195; and Rosdolsky, "The
Distribution of the Agrarian Product," 247–65. In general in Austria the peasant retained 30
per cent of his net income. Blum, *Noble Landowners*, 71.

[3] Blum, *Noble Landowners*, 75.

[4] U *panshchyna*, P *pańszczyzna*, G *Robot*.

[5] Kaunitz in 1772 referred to Galician serfdom as "the most profound slavery." Rosdolsky, *Die
grosse Steuer- und Agrarreform*, 12. Pre-partition Polish jurists themselves equated serfdom with
Roman slavery. Mises, *Entwicklung*, 15.

[6] Rosdolsky, *Stosunki poddańcze*, 1:121, 129–30. Labour rent "is not only directly unpaid
surplus-labour, but also appears as such." Marx, *Capital*, 3:790.

[7] Rosdolsky, *Stosunki poddańcze*, 1:174–5. The limitation on corvée labour was part of a
longer-range plan to convert all labour rents to money rents. See Vilfan, "Die Agrarsozialpolitik,"
8–11.

[8] The relation of the size of peasant tenure to the obligations required from individual households
is clearly explained in Blum, *Noble Landowners*, 68–9. See also Mises, *Entwicklung*, 23–5.

[9] P *półgruntowi, półrolnicy*; G *Halbbauern*; L *semi-cmethones*.

[10] U *zahrodnyky, horodnyky*; P *zagrodnicy, ogrodnicy*; G *Gärtlern*; L *hortulani*.

[11] TsDIAL, 168/1/228, p. 81v.

[12] U *tsilogruntovi*; P *całogruntowi, kmieci, rolnicy*; G *Ganzbauern*; L *cmethones*.

133 days of corvée a year, while half peasants owed 81 and quarter peasants[13] as well as gardeners owed 52.[14] The corvée was rendered either with draught animals provided by the peasant[15] or without draught animals ("pedestrian corvée").[16] Generally, full peasants did corvée labour with two draught animals, half peasants with one and the lower strata of the peasantry with none. For this reason, full, half and quarter peasants were also known respectively as "paired" peasants,[17] "single" peasants[18] and "pedestrians."[19]

Joseph II's limitation of the number of weekly corvée days to three alarmed Galician landlords. One writer has even compared the Galician nobility after the reform to "ants, whose ant hill has been destroyed"; the nobility "threw itself into a flurry of activity ... to reinstitute, as far as possible, the status quo ante, and its efforts in this regard in fact comprise the entire content of its economic activity."[20] Some landlords demanded that their serfs compensate them in money for the abolished labour days, threatening to confiscate land or cattle from serfs who did not pay; but the Austrian government prohibited such compensation.[21] Other landlords resorted to imposing piece-work on the serfs to increase the number of labour days.[22] A serf would be assigned a certain task, such as to plough a specified area of field, and, no matter how long the task took in reality, it would be counted as one day of corvée. Through this device the manor of Kunashiv, Berezhany circle, in the 1840s managed to extract 5,688 pedestrian and 3,600 draught corvée days beyond what was legally required of the serfs.[23]

The manor's most important mechanism for multiplying labour days, however, was the institution of the so-called "auxiliary days."[24] Amidst the

---

[13] U *chertovyky*; P *ćwierciogruntowi, ćwierciorolnicy*; G *Viertelbauern*.

[14] TsDIAL, 488/1/613, pp. 50v–53v.

[15] U *tiahla panshchyna*, P *pańszczyzna ciągła*, G *Zugrobot*.

[16] P *pańszczyzna piesza, robota ręczna*; G *Handrobot, Fussrobot*.

[17] P *parowi*, G *Zweispannigen*.

[18] P *pojedynki*, G *Einspannigen*.

[19] P *piesi*, G *Handfröhner*. There were also other, less popular, designations for the same system of stratification. In Vynnyky, Zhovkva circle, the serfs were divided into strata according to the number of days of corvée they owed each week. Thus there were three-day peasants, two-and-a-half-day peasants, etc. (P *III Dniowi*, etc.). TsDIAL, 168/1/571. In Volytsia, Stryi circle, the serfs were simply divided into first-class and second-class peasants (G *I Classe Bauern, II Classe Bauern*). TsDIAL, 488/1/62, p. 1v.

[20] Terletsky, *Znesenie panshchyny*, 98.

[21] Rosdolsky, *Stosunki poddańcze*, 1:177–8.

[22] Terletsky, *Znesenie panshchyny*, 107.

[23] The illiterate serfs kept track of the illegal days by putting notches in their rafters. The circle authorities recognized the legitimacy of their grievances *after* serfdom was abolished in 1848 and imposed a hefty fine on the manor. But in 1852 the peasant commune still had not been able to collect any of the money it was owed. TsDIAL, 146/64b/3213, pp. 114–15v; TsDIAL, 146/64b/3214, pp. 109–10v.

[24] U *dopomizhni dni*, P *dni pomocne*, G *Lohnhilfstage*.

clamour of Galician nobles protesting that the three-day limitation on corvée
would bring them to ruin, Emperor Joseph II decreed in 1786 that serfs who
were not obliged to work free three days a week on the estate could be required to work up to the full three days for wages.[25] Thus, for example, a
quarter peasant with the inventory obligation of one day of corvée a week
could also be made to work for pay on the estate another two days. Since
compulsion was still involved and the wages were fixed and very low,[26] the
auxiliary days differed little from serfdom from the point of view of either the
landlord or the peasant. Joseph II's intention and the letter of the law were
that the auxiliary days could only be demanded during haymaking and the
harvest. Hence they were also known as the "summer auxiliary days." In
practice, however, the seasonal character of the auxiliary days was ignored.
An official of Ternopil circle complained to the governor of Galicia in March
1846 that the auxiliary days were being used "to keep [peasants] on corvée
day after day throughout the entire year—and not only during haymaking
and harvests." In Chortkiv circle in 1838 peasants were compelled to work in
distilleries in fulfillment of their auxiliary days. As low as the wages were,
some landlords depressed them further either by luring peasants into debt and
having them work off usurious interest as auxiliary days or by paying the
serfs not in money but in tokens that could be redeemed solely at the
landlord's tavern.[27] The auxiliary days, so hateful to the peasantry, were only
abolished by the imperial patent of 13 April 1846, in the wake of a bloody
peasant uprising in Western Galicia.[28]

Landlords could raise labour rents not only by increasing the number of
labour days but also by expanding the number of hours in the working day.
In some districts there had been the custom of working only half a day on
corvée or of starting the working day at eight or nine o'clock in the morning.
In response to the three-day-limit, landlords universally replaced these shorter
working days with days that lasted from dawn to dusk. An imperial patent of
16 June 1786 (N.S.) limited the corvée working day to twelve hours in
summer (from 1 April through 30 September) and to eight hours during the
rest of the year (winter). These working days included a two-hour rest period
in summer and one hour in winter. Only during the harvest could the work
day legally be extended for one or two hours.[29] However, the legal situation
did not correspond to the reality.[30] In Chortkiv circle, as gubernial councillor
F. Hannsmann reported to the crownland presidium in 1838, landlords were
making serfs work twenty-four hours in the demesnal distilleries and counting

---

[25] Similar legislation applied to the Czech lands. Blum, *Noble Landowners*, 184.

[26] A day's work with a scythe was remunerated at 15 kreuzer; with a sickle at 12; less demanding
work at 8. Rosdolsky, *Stosunki poddańcze*, 1:201–2.

[27] *Klasova borotba*, 217–21, 291.

[28] *Istoriia selianstva URSR*, 1:344.

[29] Rosdolsky, *Stosunki poddańcze*, 1:177–8, 191.

[30] Terletsky, *Znesenie panshchyny*, 107, 161.

the twenty-four hours as one day of pedestrian corvée.[31] When in April 1846 an imperial patent reiterated the limits to the length of the working day, it came as news to the peasantry. Serfs, reported a Przemyśl (Peremyshl) circle authority to Lviv, had been working on estates from early morning until late evening, and sometimes late into the night. Awareness of the limits awakened an interest in time-keeping among the peasantry, since "no one now wants to be on corvée one minute longer than the labour time established by the patent." For the first time, peasant communities began investing in clocks.[32]

There were many, many other (for the most part illegal) ways for the inventive landlord to increase corvée labour. Just one gubernial document (from 2 January 1802) listed the following: drawing up a new inventory with augmented labour dues whenever there was a change in the person of the landlord; using deceit, threats and violence to acquire peasant signatures on a new inventory with increased obligations; requiring double days of pedestrian labour in place of draught labour; postponing the collection of winter corvée to the summer; collecting fines for trespassing peasant cattle in labour rather than money; and demanding payment of tavern debts in labour rather than money.[33]

The peasants' own crops suffered because of corvée obligations. As Tadeusz Wasilewski, a critic of the existing form of serfdom, wrote in the 1840s: "...The peasant who must perform corvée labour goes to his own field not when he has to, but when they allow him. How many times has his own grain demanded the sickle, but he performs corvée labour on Monday, Tuesday and Wednesday, while the grain is dropping from his own crops. He is lucky if on Thursday rain does not prevent him from harvesting."[34] In one of his short stories, set in 1846, the Galician-born writer Leopold von Sacher-Masoch described a moonlight harvest, necessary because the peasants had spent the days harvesting their lord's grain.[35]

Landlords also collected lesser labour rents in addition to the corvée. These included obligations to repair and make roofs for manorial buildings, to perform guard duty and sometimes even to gather mushrooms and nuts for the lord's kitchen. Almost universally serf women were obliged to spin a certain quantity of thread for the manor.[36] The imperial patent of 16 June 1786 abolished a number of forms of labour rent then existing in Galicia (L prohibita generalia), such as transporting the manor's grain to Gdańsk

---

[31] Klasova borotba, 221.

[32] Ibid., 322.

[33] Terletsky, Znesenie panshchyny, 106–10; see also p. 103.

[34] Cited in ibid., 161. A similar point had been made by Galician officials in 1781. Mises, Entwicklung, 27 note 3.

[35] Sacher-Masoch, "Der Jesuit: Erzählung eines polnischen Emissairs von 1846," Galizische Geschichten, 97–120.

[36] TsDIAL, 168/1/1222, p. 2v; 488/1/613, pp. 50v–53v.

(without this being counted as corvée) and netting all the fish in the lord's ponds, cleaning out the silt and stocking them again with fish.[37]

Labour dues to the state (aside from military service) included road work[38] and transport obligations.[39] In 1821 Galician peasants worked 1.6 million days on road construction and repair for the state; in that same year they worked 31.5 million days of corvée on the estates.[40] Corvée labour on behalf of the church, unless the church figured as owner of an estate, was not sanctioned by law, but in some parishes serfs were expected to work free on the priest's land[41] (U *daremshchyna*). Peasants were, however, legally required to provide labour to construct and repair churches and parish buildings;[42] this was not particularly onerous, since, once built, a church could stand for a century or longer.

Rents in kind to the manor usually included grain and poultry. In Polove, Zolochiv circle, full peasants gave the manor 4.5 "bushels"[43] of fodder oats, a capon and six chickens.[44] In Ivachiv Dolishnii full peasants gave 1 "bushel" (123 litres) of wheat and 2 "bushels" of oats; half peasants gave half that amount and quarter peasants a quarter. Full peasants, or rather their wives, also gave 2 capons, 2 hens and 20 eggs, while half and quarter peasants gave proportional quantities.[45] In some villages peasants also paid a tithe in sheep.[46] Rents in kind to the state consisted of irregular deliveries of provisions for soldiers. Rents in kind to the church, when they existed, were established by local custom or what the pastor could successfully impose. In Dubno, Rzeszów circle, the Greek Catholic pastor demanded 1,800 sheaves of grain annually from his parishioners in the 1840s.[47]

Collection of money rents by the manor was irregular. In some villages, such as Ivachiv Dolishnii, all peasants paid the manor a tax on their farms, with full peasants paying 6 gulden, half peasants 3 and quarter peasants 1.5. In other villages no taxes were paid on farms. Some serfs, especially craftsmen and peasants in state-owned villages, paid all their rents in money.[48] It was the custom in nearly all villages for bee-keeping serfs to pay a money tax on their hives to the manor.[49] The state, of course, was the largest

---

[37] Rosdolsky, *Stosunki poddańcze*, 1:195–200.

[38] U *sharvarok*, P *szarwarek*, G *Scharwerk*.

[39] U *forshpan*, P *forszpan*, G *Vorspann*.

[40] *Ibid.*, 1:262.

[41] See *Klasova borotba*, 515; and Adriian, *Agrarnyi protses*, 62.

[42] Klunker, *Die gesetzliche Unterthans-Verfassung*, 1:297–8.

[43] U *kortsi*, P *korcy*, G *Koretz*; 553.5 litres.

[44] TsDIAL, 168/1/1222, pp. 1v–2v.

[45] TsDIAL, 488/1/613, pp. 50v–53v.

[46] Rosdolsky, *Stosunki poddańcze*, 1:200. Mises, *Entwicklung*, 20.

[47] *Klasova borotba*, 515. Mises, *Entwicklung*, 20–1, mentions tithes in grain to the pastor.

[48] U *chynshovi*, P *czynszownicy*, G *Zinsler*.

[49] P *oczkowe*, G *Bienenzins*. See TsDIAL, 168/1/1222, p. 3v; 488/1/613, pp. 50v–53v.

collector of money dues, in the form of taxes. The Austrian central government collected four times as much in taxes as had the prepartition Polish government.[50] In fact the principal aim of Joseph II's agrarian reform legislation was to increase the taxability of the countryside by alleviating the lot of the peasantry.[51] However, since the landlords did everything in their considerable power to nullify the effect of the Austrian reforms, the increased state taxes were a great burden on the peasantry.[52] The main form of money rent to the church were the fees collected by priests for performing baptisms, marriages and funerals. These sacramental fees were deeply resented by the peasants, who felt they were paying taxes on their very births and deaths.[53]

What did the peasants receive in return for all the feudal rents they paid? From the church they received certain civilizational benefits and from the state some protection against their landlords. But what did the landlord, who collected 80 per cent of their rents, give to the peasants? After serfdom was abolished in 1848, the Austrian government made a list of all feudal obligations in every Galician village. For the village of Polove we have seen what the peasants owed the landlord. In the list of obligations there was also a rubric for the landlord's obligations vis-à-vis the peasants.[54] In the Polove list, which was typical of dozens of others consulted, the landlord's obligations were described with a single German word: *Keine*, i.e., none.[55]

Actually, by Austrian law landlords did have one obligation vis-à-vis their subjects: to lend them seed grain and food in times of distress. This obligation, legally imposed from 1772 to 1848, proved extremely difficult for the government to enforce, and strong pressure had to be brought to bear on landlords before they fed starving serfs.[56] In 1847, while the great potato famine raged not only in Ireland but also in Galicia, the senior police

---

[50] *Historia Polski*, vol. 2, pt. 1, p. 223. Austrian, as well as Prussian, civil servants were amazed at how little the old Commonwealth had demanded in taxes. Rosdolsky, *Stosunki poddańcze*, 1:28.

[51] Rosdolsky, *Die grosse Steuer- und Agrarreform*, esp. 9–24; Rosdolsky, *Stosunki poddańcze*, 1:12–15, 28. See also Vilfan, "Die Agrarsozialpolitik," 30–1. For a good discussion of cameralist theory and the role of taxation in Maria Theresia's agrarian reforms, see Liebel-Weckowicz and Szabo, "Modernization Forces," esp. 304–8.

[52] See the moving case of the aptly named Havrylo Neporadny, of Kunashiv, Berezhany circle, who was unable to sow his land, let alone pay his taxes in 1825. He fled from the village, but found no refuge and eventually returned. He was arrested and lost his land and horses. TsDIAL, 146/64b/3212, pp. 46–7.

[53] A folk song from 1846 lamented: "*Popy takzhe nas derut, / Za pokhoron hrosh berut, / Urodytsia—tra platyty, / Uzhe trudno v sviti zhyty.*" ("The priests also fleece us. They take money for funerals. If a baby is born, one has to pay. It's getting difficult to live in the world.") *Klasova borotba*, 345.

[54] P *powinności wzajemne prawodzierżcy*, G *Gegenleistungen des Berechtigen*.

[55] TsDIAL, 168/1/1222, pp. 17v–42v. Describing the situation in 1773, Kaunitz stated that "on the one side are only rights, on the other there are nothing but obligations." Rosdolsky, *Die grosse Steuer- und Agrarreform*, 12.

[56] Rosdolsky, *Die grosse Steuer- und Agrarreform*, 141 note 64. Rosdolsky, *Stosunki poddańcze*, 1:38, 223–4.

commissioner in Przemyśl was worried that the widespread hunger would lead to unrest; he felt this could be avoided "if every landlord were humane enough to help his suffering serfs, as his means allowed; but such humanity, unfortunately, is lacking."[57] Even when landlords did provide grain subsidies to their peasants, this was not necessarily done out of humanitarian motives. In Chortkiv circle in the late 1830s landlords were lending grain to poverty- or disaster-stricken peasants so that they could later demand repayment in labour, in the form of extra auxiliary days.[58]

In addition to appropriating the peasants' surplus through feudal rents, landlords in the early nineteenth century also expropriated peasant land, both the so-called rustical land, which the peasants tilled as their individual farms, and the communal land, largely forest and pasture, which the peasants used collectively. (Communal land will be examined later, in the sections on servitudes.) The landlords' interest in peasant land was the result of their fear, awakened by Joseph's reforms,[59] that serfdom would be abolished. In that event, the manors wanted to have in their possession sufficient land to compensate for the loss of labour obligations. The encroachment of the manor on rustical land was forbidden by numerous decrees (in 1781, 1786, 1787, 1789, 1798, 1804, 1811 and 1827); that the legal prohibition had to be re- peated so often says much about its effectiveness.[60] A more important brake on the manors' invasion of peasant land was that a landed peasantry was a fundamental requirement of Polish-style serfdom, based on labour rents.[61] Landlords throughout Galicia took 342,659 Joch of rustical land away from their serfs from 1789 to 1847; this was almost 6 per cent of all rustical land registered in 1789. Most (over 80 per cent) was taken before the land survey of 1820,[62] i.e., in the immediate aftermath of the Josephine reforms. Landlords used the survey to claim as their own empty rustical plots (U pustky). They might themselves have emptied the plots in the first place. By illegally denying a peasant in need the loan of seed grain, the manor could force the peasant to abandon his land. By encouraging a peasant to drink liquor on credit or through usurious lending, the manor could also eventually remove him from his land.[63] Landlords also forced peasants to exchange

---

[57] *Klasova borotba*, 357.

[58] *Ibid.*, 218. The same abuse was recorded in a gubernial document of 2 January 1802, cited in Terletsky, *Znesenie panshchyny*, 110.

[59] "It was first under Austrian rule that the demesnes began to appropriate peasant lands.... " Mises, *Entwicklung*, 17.

[60] *Ibid.*, 57, 64–6. Terletsky, *Znesenie panshchyny*, 99–100.

[61] Mises, *Entwicklung*, 17, 21. This brake did not work very well in Hungary, where about 60 per cent of the peasantry was landless on the eve of emancipation. Kann and David, *The Peoples of the Eastern Habsburg Lands*, 236, 239, 241. However, in Hungary rents in nature, the so-called (G) *Neunte* or (L) *nona*, played a much larger role in the traditional feudal system. Blum, *Noble Landowners*, 75–6.

[62] Rosdolsky, *Wspólnota gminna*, 49–50.

[63] All these methods were used by landlords in the mid-1840s in Ternopil circle. *Klasova borotba*, 291–2.

rustical for demesnal land, giving their serfs plots of a smaller size and inferior quality.[64]

No survey of the feudal system in Galicia, however brief, can dispense with an account of the extra-economic aspects of the landlord-peasant relationship.[65] In old Poland the relations of personal dependence between landlord and serf were similar to those existing elsewhere between master and slave. Landlords could kill serfs on their own authority[66] and could sell them without the land to which they were in theory attached.[67] Austrian legislation made the Galician peasant a subject of the law and not, as formerly, beyond any law,[68] but the landlord's power over him remained great. Manorial officials could punish disobedient serfs. If peasants had complaints against the manor, they had first to bring them to the manor itself. In spite of Joseph II's prohibition of displays of servility, Galician peasants doffed their caps within three hundred paces of the manor.[69]

The feudal system, with the landlord's unbridled or barely bridled domination of the peasant, even affected the most intimate spheres of life. Until 1782 Galician serfs had to receive the lord's permission to marry. Serfs had also been required to pay a marriage tax to the lords, but Maria Theresia and Joseph II, who wanted to increase the population—especially the agricultural population—by removing all obstacles to marriage and

---

[64] Peasants of the Komarno region, Sambir circle, complained to the emperor in 1822: "...the lords have taken good land from us, and given us in exchange absolutely bad and small plots." *Ibid.*, 133. This was forbidden by laws of 1787, 1805 and 1825. Terletsky, *Znesenie panshchyny*, 100–1.

[65] Of course, if feudalism (or even serfdom) is understood primarily as a system of juridical relations, and not—as in this study—a mode of production, then what follows, rather than what preceded, is the crucial aspect. Those who consider feudalism/serfdom primarily as a juridical category consider it abolished in Galicia by the Josephine suspension of personal servitude (G *Leibeigenschaft*) on 5 April 1782 (N.S.). See Mises, *Entwicklung*, 42–6.

[66] L *ius vitae necisque, ius gladii.*

[67] Rosdolsky, *Stosunki poddańcze*, 1:127–32. Mises, *Entwicklung*, 12–14. Even during the first decades of Austrian rule Galician landlords rented out their serfs' corvée labour to other landlords. This was forbidden by laws of 1800 and 1801. Gubernial order of 2 January 1802, cited in Terletsky, *Znesenie panshchyny*, 108.

[68] Rosdolsky, *Stosunki poddańcze*, 1:260. "In the days of old Poland the landlord was the sole owner of all land in the village and the autocratic master of his peasants.... No one dared to interfere in his relations with his peasants; no one dared to restrict his almost limitless power over them and over their land; there was no state power and control over his conduct." Terletsky, *Znesenie panshchyny*, 98–9. "The protection of the law, which the absolutist state accorded, extended to both sides. For the serfs it meant more effective protection vis-à-vis the landlords, but the landowning class was also protected by the state vis-à-vis the serfs. But since the landowners had hitherto been in a by far stronger position than their subjects, the new protection of state law meant rather a gain for the peasants." Vilfan, "Die Agrarsozialpolitik," 29.

[69] *Klasova borotba*, 418. "...Our peasant takes off his cap from afar before the landlord,...he bows down almost to his feet...." Tadeusz Wasilewski, writing in the mid-1840s, cited in Terletsky, *Znesenie panshchyny*, 158.

procreation, abolished this ancient custom in 1777.[70] In spite of this
legislation, some manors refused to allow peasant lads to marry until they
had paid a tax.[71] By his patent of 5 April 1782 (N.S.), Joseph II prohibited
the landlords' practice of taking serf children to work in the manor
(G *Zwangsgesindedienste*), but the prohibition was not entirely effective. As
late as 1847 Count Bąkowski, lord of Ustie Zelene, Stanyslaviv circle, took
serfs' daughters to serve in the manor. A gubernial document of May 1847
reported that Bąkowski forced the daughters "in a manner grossly offensive to
public morality and enraging to human feeling to satisfy his lusts." Bąkowski
also dumped the dead body of one of his male servants, Fed Kostiv, into the
Dniester River before an autopsy could be performed. The gubernial acts
speak of forty rapes perpetrated by Bąkowski on serfs. But in the end, the
severe justice of feudal Galicia caught up with him and, blind to his exalted
position, banished him from his own estate for six years (1847–52).[72]

The case of Count Bąkowski illustrates that it was not possible simply to
legislate away the abuses of serfdom. Its abuses could only disappear with the
abolition of the entire system.

The Enforcement of Serfdom

> The peasantry . . . delights in
> violence and dreams about it.
> —A Galician official, 1847[73]

The feudal system rested on violence, not the violence *of* the peasantry, but
violence *against* the peasantry. There was no positive incentive for the serf to
work on the lord's estate, and all that could move him was coercion. A critic
of the 1840s, who argued that hired labour would be more efficient on the
demesnes, correctly summed up the situation when he declared that the only
motive forces in Galician serfdom were "threats on the one hand and fear on
the other."[74] The manorial authorities, particularly the mandator[75] and
steward,[76] made peasants compliant by beating them and locking them up in
the manorial prisons. Joseph II had limited the right of the manor to inflict

---

[70] Rosdolsky, *Stosunki poddańcze*, 1:94–5, 138–9. See also Mises, *Entwicklung*, 11–12.

[71] In villages belonging to the Bohorodchany manor, Stanyslaviv circle, peasants who wanted to
marry were required to pay 61.5 litres of wheat or a monetary equivalent (1799). *Klasova
borotba*, 61.

[72] Rosdolsky, *Stosunki poddańcze*, 1:137–8. The situation was much the same in Russia. Even
Richard Pipes, who feels that "it is particularly important to be disabused concerning alleged
landlord brutality toward serfs," admits: "Sexual license was not uncommon; there are enough
authenticated stories of landlords who staffed regular harems with serf girls." *Russia under the
Old Regime*, 152–3. See also *Istoriia selianstva URSR*, 1:318.

[73] *Klasova borotba*, 373.

[74] Tadeusz Wasilewski, cited in Terletsky, *Znesenie panshchyny*, 163.

[75] U *mandator, mandatar*; G *Mandatar*.

[76] U *ekonom, okonom*.

corporal punishment on serfs in 1775 and abolished it completely in 1788; but Franz I renewed that right in 1793.[77] Even so, the manor was not permitted to have peasants beaten with cudgels (U *kyi*; the cudgel was the prerogative of the circle authorities or their delegates). The efficacy of this prohibition was such that the government felt obliged to repeat it in 1805, 1818, 1821, 1828 and 1841.[78]

Some insight into the punitive measures applied to enforce serfdom can be gained by looking at the individual case of Hrynko Liush, a peasant from Kunashiv, Berezhany circle, who brought his complaints against the manor to the circle authorities in 1848. Liush's grievances dated back to Easter 1835, when he spent eight days in the manorial prison. At that time the manor had expropriated some bush-covered land from the peasant commune,[79] and the commune was protesting this. The commune eventually won its land back, but Liush—simply for carrying the commune's grievance to the circle authorities—was imprisoned by the manor. In August 1836 Liush was made to work two days of corvée in one week instead of the one and one-half days he was actually obliged by the inventory. In protest, he refused to work a third, auxiliary day. For this insubordination he spent two days in chains in the manorial prison and received twenty blows with a cudgel. He spent only two days in prison then because his labour was needed during the harvest. When the exact same conflict between Liush and the manor was repeated after the harvest in 1836, he was chained and imprisoned for eight days.[80] In the winter of 1837 the leaseholder (U *posesor*) of the estate, Suchodolski, tried to make Liush do corvée on a Ukrainian holy day. For his refusal, Liush spent another eight days in prison. In April 1837 Liush harnessed four oxen to a plough and ploughed the estate for a day and a half. Considering how many animals he used, he thought his labour should be counted for more than two days of corvée. For insisting on this he spent another four days in chains in prison. Later that same year Liush wanted to rent some pasture from the manor, but was refused. He therefore put his four oxen out to pasture in a neighbouring village. But soon thereafter the leaseholder demanded that Liush perform draught corvée. Liush pleaded for pedestrian work, since his oxen would die in the fields if he took them so soon from their grazing. His pleas cost him eight more days in chains in prison. After the harvest in 1837 Liush was ordered to make a two-day trip. Since he had no bread just then and no fodder for his horses, Liush requested that the order be postponed for one day. The leaseholder struck Liush several times in the face, neck and other parts of his body, and then put him in prison for eight days. Liush's trials did not end here. He was punished again in 1838, 1839, 1840, 1842, 1846 and 1847. Altogether in 1835–47, Liush spent 88 days in

---

[77] Steblii, "Peredmova," *Klasova borotba*, 7, 10. *Istoriia selianstva URSR*, 1:339.

[78] Terletsky, *Znesenie panshchyny*, 111.

[79] U *hromada*, P *gmina*, G *Gemeinde*.

[80] A landlord could not imprison a serf for more than eight days without permission from the circle authorities. Vilfan, "Agrarsozialpolitik," 27.

the manorial prison, many of them in chains. In 1846 he was beaten until he could no longer stand.[81]

Liush was obviously a stubborn individual. There were also stubborn communes. In 1780 the peasants of the small town of Stoianiv, Belz circle, refused to perform corvée labour beyond what was specified in the inventory. The manorial officials responded brutally. "Wherever they catch us," complained the peasants to the circle authorities, "they beat us, cripple us, murder us, attack our houses and frighten our children. They beat our women, causing miscarriages and endangering life." One day a serf, Demko Huliuk, was conscripted by soldiers to transport wood to Komarno and was unable to show up for corvée labour. For failing to appear, the demesnal authorities "twisted his neck, ripped the hair from his head and gave him 28 or 30 lashes without his shirt." He showed up for corvée labour the next day, but "as soon as ... the steward saw him there, he instantly, like some fury, pounced on him, grabbed him by the forelock and tossed the man back and forth; and then he ordered him to be laid out and flayed as the greatest felon."[82]

When the violence of the demesnal authorities did not suffice to enforce serfdom, the manor appealed to the circle officials for aid. The circle officials were not (heaven forbid!) cruel. Before they beat a particular peasant, a doctor would estimate how many blows that peasant could endure without crippling or killing him. For example, in Dorozhiv, Sambir circle, in 1846, the doctor told the circle commissioner that two peasants could each endure fifty blows with a cudgel. After the fifty blows were administered, the two peasants still refused to make up the auxiliary days they owed the manor. The commissioner ordered that the recalcitrants only be imprisoned, because—to use his own words—"it would have been cruel to punish them further on that same day."[83]

In documents emanating from the circle authorities themselves, there is never a description of the cudgel that they used on serfs. But a peasant document from 1848 (Turie, Zolochiv circle) describes one cudgel as "an oak stick covered with lead."[84]

When the violence of the circle authorities proved insufficient, they called in the military.[85] The serfs were made to quarter and pay the soldiers who

---

[81] TsDIAL, 146/64b/3214, pp. 27–8.

[82] *Klasova borotba*, 41–2.

[83] *Ibid.*, 328.

[84] *Ibid.*, 407. Whips were favoured by the manorial authorities. A Russian traveller to Galicia in the 1860s heard a description of a manorial whip from a peasant who drove him in a cart: "...like my horsewhip, only the handle was very, very short, and the strap was long, about the length of a man's body, plaited, with a knot at the end." Kelsiev, *Galitsiia i Moldaviia*, 106. "The whip, wielded by estate supervisors, played a formidable role in forcing peasants to work. Estate officials in Bohemia and Moravia-Silesia were called *karabáčník* by the peasants, for *karabáč* is the Czech word for whip." Blum, *Noble Landowners*, 186.

[85] When a peasant commune refused to perform corvée obligations, "the military was brought in and the peasants were beaten until they were willing to do corvée; and there have been some

were sent in to quell them. From mid-October 1847 until January 1848, 250 infantrymen and 65 cavalrymen were stationed in several communes in Zolochiv circle that refused to fulfill what they considered excessive corvée obligations. We have a peasant description of how the soldiers behaved:

> Urged on by the manor, these soldiers bullied us as much as they wished. They ordered us to catch flies and fry them in butter. Then they threw [peasants] on dung-heaps. They forced the women to make prostrations in the roads. One woman was beaten to death, another had a miscarriage as a result of a beating. Even officers brought in several skinny horses, fattened them up on oats they took from people and then sold the horses.[86]

Violence against peasants, particularly beatings, was an absolutely indispensable component of the feudal system. This was eloquently argued by a Przemyśl circle commissioner, Mikołaj Pobóg-Rutkowski. In a letter dated 18 December 1783 (N.S.), the noble Rutkowski pleaded with the higher circle authorities to allow him to beat every tenth peasant in the village of Vyshatychi:

> For the local peasant, who lives in gross ignorance and has no concept of honour, there is no better threat than the threat of corporal punishment. The local peasant is as stupid as he is stubborn, and the cudgel will instruct him more quickly than hunger or imprisonment. I was born on this land and I have observed the local peasants since I was a child. It is not without foundation that I can affirm that the local peasant can be corrected more quickly with ten blows than with ten days in prison.... Nothing but corporal punishment can make the local peasant obedient. Any other punishment will make the peasant still more stubborn and fresh.[87]

Rutkowski's conviction that the peasants were little better than beasts and that, as other beasts of burden, they needed to be beaten,[88] was shared by other noblemen. Johann Christoph von Koranda, who headed up Galicia's tax department, wrote in 1781 that the serfs were "regarded as cattle" by the Polish nobility.[89] A radical Polish democrat in the 1830s wrote: "The peasant in the eyes of a magnate was not a man, but an ox, destined to work for his comfort, whom it was necessary to harness[90] and thrash with a whip like an

---

[85](continued) cases in which peasants have received the last rites on the bench, under the blows of the cudgel." This is the testimony of a spokesman *for* the Polish nobility in 1848. *Die Revolutionsjahre*, 13.

[86] *Klasova borotba*, 488–9.

[87] *Ibid.* 52.

[88] "The beating of enserfed peasants by landlords and manorial officials was in essence an inseparable attribute of the system of serfdom, without which it did not at all seem possible to maintain the discipline of corvée labour. The psychological counterpart of this fact was...the conviction of the nobility that it was necessary to beat the peasant just like a draught animal...." Rosdolsky, *Stosunki poddańcze*, 1:77.

[89] Mises, *Entwicklung*, 43 note 1.

[90] On the harnessing of peasants, see below, 28.

animal."[91] The image of peasants as beasts is also explicit in a letter from an official of Stanyslaviv circle to the crownland presidium (September 1846): "... In the hill peasants of this circle those features that distinguish people from animals are but little developed."[92] In this case, the official was not interested in beating the peasants; he just wished to emphasize how ignorant they were.[93]

In fact, the peasants' ignorance was almost as important as violence in maintaining the feudal system. Rutkowski, for example, in the same letter where he justified beating peasants because they were "stupid" and denizens of "gross ignorance," also asked the circle authorities to think of some "special form of punishment" for one of the peasants of Vyshatychi, the mayor Ivan Beheka. Rutkowski felt that Beheka was the leader of the commune's resistance to corvée and road-work. Not only was Beheka "importunate and stubborn," but "he can read and write and knows some Latin."[94] As Rutkowski implied, an educated peasant was a dangerous peasant.

Landlords frequently had educated peasants sent to the army,[95] and did what they could to prevent the peasants from becoming educated. In 1825 the priest Stefan Hryhorovych founded a parish school in Zaluche, Kolomyia circle. At first he himself instructed the village youth in the school, teaching them reading and writing in Ukrainian as well as basic arithmetic. Eventually he turned the task over to a cantor, but the landlord had the cantor drafted into the army. (Military service then lasted fourteen years.) The same story repeated itself with a second cantor, and with a third. In 1840 the peasants of Zaluche appealed to the Greek Catholic school inspector in Horodenka: "We hear that they teach the deaf and dumb to read, but we are neither deaf nor dumb and we pay for the school ourselves. We do not understand what it means that our school is so disliked." In the end, Father Hryhorovych himself had to return to teaching and persisted in this work, despite persecution by the manor, until his death in 1845.[96] The landlord of Kunysivtsi, Kolomyia circle, expropriated the lumber that peasants had set aside to build a school in the mid-1840s.[97]

Landlord opposition to peasant education was not confined to placing obstacles in the way of individual peasants and individual schools on the

---

[91] Cited in Terletsky, *Znesenie panshchyny*, 8.

[92] *Klasova borotba*, 348.

[93] The Galician peasantry was called "hoc genus hominum pertinacissimum, quamvis stupidum" in a memorandum of the Estates Administration (P *Wydział Stanowy*), 10 November 1784. Rosdolsky, *Stosunki poddańcze*, 2:214. A court chancery memorandum of 1781 said that "laziness and stupidity" made the Galician peasant "unfeeling"; hence "only the most extreme hard treatment" could "awaken him from his inactivity."

[94] *Klasova borotba*, 52–3.

[95] Kachala, *Shcho nas hubyt*.

[96] Pavlyk, "Pro rusko-ukrainski narodni chytalni," 429. *Klasova borotba*, 229. Vozniak, *Iak probudylosia*, 151–2.

[97] *Klasova borotba*, 474.

village level. The entire political influence of the Galician nobility was used to hinder the development of popular education. In 1840 the Greek Catholic bishop of Przemyśl, Ivan Snihursky, proposed in the Galician estates diet that more elementary schools be founded in the countryside. He was almost unanimously voted down.[98] The noble Kazimierz Krasicki argued that public schools

> do not have a good influence on the mass.... For the mass suffice little church schools where it will be a holy, spiritual obligation to inculcate in the people an understanding of religion, morality, the individual's obligations from the perspective of society, the duties placed on him by his estate and a love for work and order.[99]

In 1842 only 15 per cent of Galician school-age children attended school, while in Bohemia 94 per cent attended and in all of Austria excluding Galicia 75 per cent attended.[100] When Galician peasants finally gained a political representation, during the revolution of 1848–9, the peasant deputies in the Austrian parliament (G *Reichstag*) made the expansion of education one of their foremost demands. Their programmatic statement of 3 September 1848 (N.S.) affirmed: "We consider it of the utmost necessity that schooling begin in every commune so that many persons of the lower estate can leave the darkness for the light."[101]

Lack of education put the peasantry at a great disadvantage during the feudal conflict with the landlord. When the nobles voted down Snihursky's proposal to found more schools in 1840, they derisively asked: Should we establish more schools so that the peasants can write more complaints against us to the circle authorities?[102] They were right, of course. An illiterate peasantry could not itself formulate any of the documents necessary to prevent landlords from extracting extra days of corvée, closing off pastures and forests and conscripting peasant girls for service in the manor. Ignorance also meant that the peasants had difficulty understanding the work of government commissions dispatched to resolve disputes between them and the manor; this was especially true if the commission's proceedings were deliberately conducted in German, as was the case in Horoshova, Chortkiv circle, in the 1840s. The peasants of Horoshova complained to the Supreme Ruthenian Council (U *Holovna ruska rada*) in 1849 that "at such investigations everything is carried on in German, and we can neither understand it nor read it; therefore we generally end up cheated."[103] Finally, the

---

[98] S.B., "O prawach włościan w Gallicyi," *Biblioteka Warszawska*, no. 4 (1843): 134.

[99] Cited in Zabrovarny, "Sotsialna svidomist," 284; also in Terletsky, *Znesenie panshchyny*, 134.

[100] *Tafeln zur Statistik ... 1842* (unpaginated).

[101] *Klasova borotba*, 427. See also Vozniak, *Iak probudylosia*, 151, for another example of peasant demands for education in 1848.

[102] S.B., "O prawach włościan," 143.

[103] *Klasova borotba*, 500. See also below, 30. The Hungarian nobility preferred Latin to both German and Magyar precisely because it was so difficult for the common people to understand. Rosdolsky, *Die grosse Steuer- und Agrarreform*, 157–8.

peasantry's ignorance was used as a pretext to keep it from exercising an influence over its own affairs. For example, Joseph II wanted to have peasants work on his famous land survey to make up for a shortage of trained engineers. Civil servants, however, protested (in vain) that "often in an entire commune one cannot find an individual who can write a single letter of the alphabet, read or even count beyond fifty." In fact, though, Joseph was correct: the peasants did very good work during the land survey. The bureaucracy's objections were rooted in its feudal outlook.[104]

The Resistance to Serfdom

> Oi ne budu, khlop molodyi,
> panshchynu robyty,
> Ia utechu v Voloshchynu i tam
> budu zhyty.
> Oi ne pidu na panshchynu, ne pidu,
> ne pidu,
> Koly bude temna nichka zrobliu
> panu bidu.
> Ne boiusia ia ni viita, ani ekonoma,
> Ia ne pidu na panshchynu, budu
> sydiv doma.
> —Ukrainian folk song[105]

In spite of all the force used against them, in spite of the servility inculcated by the frequent beatings[106] and in spite of their great ignorance, Galician peasants waged an impressive struggle against serfdom and the landlords throughout the period of Austrian rule and eventually succeeded in forcing the abolition of serfdom in 1848.

---

[104] Rosdolsky, *Die grosse Steuer- und Agrarreform*, 34 (and 35–7, 39–41).

[105] "I, a young man, will not do corvée labour. I'll flee to Wallachia and live there. I will not do corvée labour. I will not, I will not. In the dark of night I will do the lord harm. I am not afraid of the mayor or the steward. I will not do corvée labour. I will sit at home." "Na panskii roboti," in *Khodyly opryshky*, 45.

[106] The psychological effect of beating on the peasants was "the view, full of slavish submissiveness and resignation, held by the peasants themselves, that one must endure without murmur the lashings and floggings administered by the landlords, stewards and manorial bailiffs, simply because one had the misfortune to be born a peasant. And none of the negative aspects of the system of serfdom—with the one exception perhaps of the promotion of drunkenness by manorial tavern-keepers—had such a fatal, destructive influence on the peasant psychology as well as on the entire 'character' of that class as the continual corporal punishment meted out by the manorial authorities." There was even a *Ukrainian* proverb to the effect that sparing the rod spoils the peasant (U *Khlopa ne byi, khlop bude hnylyi*). Rosdolsky, *Stosunki poddańcze*, 1:77. Corporal punishment so permeated social relations that even herdboys after emancipation chose one of their number to be the "mayor" of the pasture "and he used a whip on the disobedient." Slomka, *From Serfdom to Self-Government*, 123–4.

The resistance to serfdom took many forms. By far the most common was the submission of complaints against the manor. The complaints did not bring into question the institution of serfdom itself, but only abuses, such as the augmentation of rents beyond what was specified in the inventory or by Austrian law, the seizure of rustical or communal land by the manor and excessive or cruel physical punishment of serfs (and *any* corporal punishment from 1788 to 1793).

The submission of complaints demanded literacy. Not only did grievances have to be presented in written form, but the peasants had to know what constituted an abuse, i.e., they had to know what was written in the inventory and what was written in imperial patents regulating serfdom. Since literacy was so rare among the peasantry, the peasants largely relied on nonpeasants to formulate their grievances. These nonpeasants were the so-called corner-scribes.[107]

Corner-scribes were the outlaw intelligentsia of feudal Galicia. They were a diverse group, including the educated dissenters that every oppressive society produces, the marginal elements that had received an education but no corresponding position in society, as well as unscrupulous hucksters out to take advantage of the ignorance of the peasantry. They were renegade petty officials, such as "the notorious" Adalbert Giżejewski, who lost his post in connection with a suit against Count Komorowski of Nestanychi, Zolochiv circle, and thereafter made his miserable living writing complaints for peasants. They were the sons of such officials, like the younger Giżejewski, who carried on the profession of corner-scribe after his father was arrested and imprisoned in 1846.[108] They were young burghers like Piotr Majbek, "without parents, without profession," who ran his business from a tavern in Ternopil and paid for his formulation of grievances by conscription into the military.[109] They were teachers, tavern-keepers, former manorial officials and, more rarely, petty leaseholders.[110]

Government and manorial officials as well as the landlords themselves considered them the cause of all unrest in the Galician village.[111] According to nobles like Count Jan Kanty Stadnicki, Kazimierz Badeni and Ignacy Poniatowski, who "well know the character of the peasants," only "restless heads" could provoke the serfs to "erroneous actions." Therefore, the

---

[107] U *pokutni pysari*, P *pisarzy pokątni*, G *Winkelschreiber*.

[108] *Klasova borotba*, 339, 356, 536 note 64.

[109] *Ibid.*, 204–6.

[110] Rosdolsky, review of Grynwaser, *Przywódcy i burzyciele włościan*, 356–61.

[111] *Klasova borotba*, 73, 82, 91, 121–2, 139–40, 187, 192, 196–8, 313, 321, 330, 360, 367. There is also an exceptional report by gubernial councillor Hannsmann that contains the truth about corner-scribes. Sent to investigate widespread unrest in Chortkiv circle in 1838, Hannsmann reported back to Lviv: "...Nowhere did I notice that so-called corner-scribes influence the peasants seditiously. The complaints that have been submitted are formulated without passion and contain nothing but a simple description of the oppression that the communes, in their view, experience." *Ibid.*, 213. For aversion to corner-scribes at the highest, imperial, level, see Vilfan, "Die Agrarsozialpolitik," 29.

presidium of the Galician estates diet begged the gubernium in 1822 to apply the sternest measures against corner-scribes.[112] Numerous laws prohibited the existence of corner-scribes and men who risked engaging in that profession faced unremitting persecution. Where it proved possible to eradicate corner-scribes, it became difficult, if not impossible, for peasants to register any formal, legal protest against feudal abuses.[113]

When grievances involved not individual peasants, but the entire commune, as was most frequently the case,[114] the commune elected one or more of its members to represent it. These plenipotentiaries[115] were often singled out for persecution by the manor, as was Hrynko Liush, whose repeated imprisonment and occasional thrashing has already been described. Ivan Smytsniuk, plenipotentiary of Iamnytsia, Stanyslaviv circle, was so importunate that the circle authorities decreed in 1835 that he could no longer represent the commune; but he continued in this role into the early 1840s. In 1836, to discourage Smytsniuk further, his son was conscripted into the army. Smytsniuk travelled to Vienna twice to bring his commune's grievances to the emperor; when he set off a third time in 1843 he was murdered by hirelings of the manor.[116] The plenipotentiaries of Smarzowa, Tarnów circle, in Western Galicia, suffered diverse persecutions at the hands of their landlord: imprisonment, confiscation of produce, expropriation of land and numerous beatings. One of the Smarzowa plenipotentiaries was Jakub Szela, who later led the savage peasant revolt in Western Galicia in 1846.[117] Plenipotentiaries also led the less violent peasant unrest that encompassed Eastern Galicia in that same year.[118] The primary function of these peasant leaders, however, was to carry the commune's grievances through the various levels of government until the commune had received satisfaction.

The right of Galician peasants to submit grievances against their landlords certainly represented an improvement in their situation compared to the lawlessness of old Poland.[119] The enlightenment of the Habsburg emperors in this regard is all the more striking when we recall that a neighbouring enlightened absolutist, Catherine II of Russia, issued legislation in 1767 stipulating that any landlord's serf who registered a grievance against his landlord was to be punished with hard labour (R *katorga*).[120] Nonetheless, the grievance procedure in Galicia was an instrument of very limited efficacy.

---

[112] *Klasova borotba*, 136.

[113] Rosdolsky, *Stosunki poddańcze*, 1:152.

[114] " . . . It was the rare peasant who dared to fight the manor 'in a duel.'" *Ibid.*, 1:146.

[115] U *povnomochnyky, upovnovazheni*; P *pełnomocnicy*; G *Bevollmächtigen*.

[116] *Klasova borotba*, 181–5, 228, 533 note 35.

[117] Rosdolsky, "Do historii 'krwawego roku,'" 410. In his dreadful account of 1846, Norman Davies identifies Szela as "an irascible peasant from Smorzowy [sic], famed for his successful litigations against wealthy landowners." *God's Playground*, 2:147.

[118] *Klasova borotba*, 323–4, 330–1.

[119] For some of the sixteenth-century legislation prohibiting serfs from complaining to the royal authorities about their landlords, see Mises, *Entwicklung*, 7 (see also 12–13).

[120] Wójcik, *Dzieje Rosji*, 291.

Until 1846[121] grievances had first to be brought to the manor for consideration, unless they involved expulsion from rustical land or corporal
punishment. The effect of this regulation was to warn the landlord that the
peasants were bringing charges against him and to allow him the opportunity
to attempt to stifle their complaint. According to a gubernial document of 2
January 1802, "some manors, their officials and leaseholders . . . use all sorts
of methods and tricks to hinder the peasants in submitting grievances, to
frighten them off from seeking to redress their injury in the circle captaincy
and in higher offices, and, if nonetheless the peasants demand recompense for
injuries endured, to threaten them with further exploitation and injury. . . . "[122]
If the peasants remained firm in their intention to pursue their grievance,
they could appeal to the circle authorities after the manor had informed them
of its decision. Appeals could later be made by both sides to the gubernium
and to the imperial court chancery.[123] In the appeals beyond the manorial
level, peasants were entitled to the gratuitous services of a subject's advocate
(G Untertansadvokat), a government-appointed legal councillor. Although
this was certainly the law under Maria Theresia and Joseph II,[124] it is
difficult to find evidence of the advocates' activity in the sources.

The circle and gubernial authorities, especially during the reign of
Joseph II, were inclined to side with the peasants, particularly if the
legitimacy of their grievance was convincingly documented or if the grievance
concerned an abuse of unusual enormity. Some Austrian civil servants,
especially in the 1770s and 1780s, distrusted the Polish nobility and sought to
alleviate the plight of the peasantry.[125] From the landlords' point of view, the
Austrian bureaucracy "took the side of the peasants," "provoked them to
[submit] unending, unfounded grievances against the manor" and "incited
serfs who were hitherto peaceful and obedient."[126] In 1846 some estate owners
complained that "many peaceful landlords say that they fear the coming of a
government official as much as the coming of a communist emissary."[127] From
the peasants' point of view, however, government officials were not so
favourably disposed to them. In 1822 the peasants of the Komarno region,
Sambir circle, complained to the emperor that circle officials sent to
investigate their grievances "appeared at night and quietly settled their affairs

---

[121] Blum, *Noble Landowners*, 228.

[122] Cited in Terletsky, *Znesenie panshchyny*, 105.

[123] Rosdolsky, *Stosunki poddańcze*, 1:144–7.

[124] Link, *The Emancipation of the Austrian Peasant*, 119–20. Vilfan, "Die Agrarsozialpolitik,"
25–6.

[125] But cf. Rosdolsky, *Die grosse Steuer- und Agrarreform*, 158–9, 169–71.

[126] *Klasova borotba*, 111–12, 145. These statements date from 1820 and 1824.

[127] Blum, *Noble Landowners*, 229. Much of the Galician gentry believed or pretended to believe
that the peasant insurrection of 1846 had been instigated by the Austrian bureaucracy. This false
interpretation has also dominated Polish historiography of the jacquerie. See Simons, "The
Peasant Revolt of 1846."

with the lords. . . . Even if there was any investigation of the injustice against
us, this was done only superficially, for appearances' sake, and always in
favour of the lords."[128] The peasants of Horoshova, Chortkiv circle, were not
surprised that the circle authorities always sided with their landlord, since the
circle captain[129] was a good friend of the mandator and enjoyed hunting on
the Horoshova estate.[130] A Ukrainian folk song from 1846 summed up the
peasants' attitude: "The circle sides with the lords / And does not care about
our injuries. / Complain—it doesn't help. / O God, grant us patience."[131]

Failing to find justice among the lords and officials, peasants took their
grievances to the emperor, whom they regarded as their protector.[132] Like
many other peasantries, the Galician peasantry viewed the monarch as a
stern, but just and benign, ruler who curbed the nobility and officials
whenever he became aware of the injustices they perpetrated or tolerated.
This view of the emperor was not only an ideological consequence of the
isolation and dispersement of the small peasant proprietors,[133] but also a reflection of the historical experience of the Galician peasants, of the
improvement in their lives when Emperor Joseph II reformed the conditions
of Galician serfdom.[134] The naive monarchists of rural Galicia sent
plenipotentiary after plenipotentiary on the long journey to Vienna, certain
that only the local officials were blind to the justice of their grievances. What
the plenipotentiaries' audience with the emperor was like has been vividly
described by the Serb awakener Vuk Karadžić:

---

[128] *Klasova borotba*, 133.

[129] U *okruzhnyi starosta*, P *starosta cyrkulowy*, G *Kreishauptmann*.

[130] *Ibid.*, 499.

[131] *"Tsyrkul z panamy trymaie, / O kryvdy nashi ne dbaie. / Uskarzhysia—ne pomozhe. /
Terplyvosti dai nam, Bozhe." Ibid.*, 345.

[132] " . . .'I'll go to the Emperor, for there I shall get justice!' The belief was that no one could
deal out such justice as the emperor himself, and men said 'everywhere else there is only
corruption!'" Slomka, *From Serfdom to Self-Government*, 159–60.

[133] "In so far as millions of families live under economic conditions of existence that separate
their mode of life, their interests and their cultural formation from those of other classes and
bring them into conflict with those classes, they form a class. In so far as these small peasant
proprietors are merely connected on a local basis, and the identity of their interests fails to
produce a feeling of community, national links, or a political organization, they do not form a
class. They are therefore incapable of asserting their class interest in their own name, whether
through a parliament or through a convention. They cannot represent themselves; they must be
represented. Their representative must appear simultaneously as their master, as an authority
over them, an unrestricted governmental power that protects them from other classes and sends
them rain and sunshine from above." Marx, "The Eighteenth Brumaire of Louis Bonaparte,"
Surveys from Exile, 239.

[134] "It was the agrarian and peasant reforms carried out by the enlightened absolute rulers that
spread royalist feelings among the populace, especially among peasants. . . . In time, the
stereotyped presentation of Joseph II as a benign, severe but just monarch gave way to a myth of
the peasants' emperor, a myth which was handed down from generation to generation in an
increasingly idealized form. During the following decades this myth exerted a strong influence on
the attitudes and social behaviour of the peasantry throughout the entire monarchy."
Chlebowczyk, *On Small and Young Nations*, 64.

When I entered the private office at 7 in the morning, there were 100 men and women waiting in one room. I imagined we'd all have our fixed time for talking to the Kaiser, and I thought that we'd go in one by one, as to a priest for confession. Then we went into a big reception room, and stood in order all round, when all of a sudden a whisper began to be heard: "Is that the Kaiser?" I looked, and there he was going from one to another, taking the petitions from each and asking what it was about.... When the Kaiser came to me, I gave him my petition, but what could I say to him with such a crowd listening: (I suppose that the whole thing has been arranged so that people can't beg of him personally and reveal all their troubles). When he took my petition, he said that I'd get what I wanted.... [135]

Some plenipotentiaries returned with the overly optimistic news that they had spoken with the emperor and that he had seen that the manor and local government were in the wrong.[136] It is not difficult to reconstruct the motivation of such false reports by the plenipotentiaries. They may have been deluded, by themselves or others, including the weak-minded emperor; they may have lacked the heart to confess to the commune that they had not received an audience with the emperor or that he had given them a noncommittal answer; or they may have lied in order to bolster the resistance of the commune to the manor.

The naive monarchism of the peasants, in Galicia as elsewhere in the eastern Habsburg lands,[137] was an important component of their ideology of resistance throughout the late eighteenth and first half of the nineteenth century. When in January 1784 Przemyśl circle commissioner Rutkowski read peasants the imperial patent of 1 October 1781 reforming serfdom, they told him that part of the patent was indeed composed by the emperor but the part that obliged them to do corvée and road work was written by the landlords.[138] In 1819 the peasants of Komarno refused to give fodder, chickens and capons to the lord until they heard from the emperor. "When the emperor writes to us in response to our petition, then will we do and give whatever he tells us."[139] In 1847 the peasants of Turie, Zolochiv circle, also refused to give rents in kind to their lord, falsely believing that the emperor had abolished them and that only "the circle authorities in league with the manor" demanded them.[140] The truth of the matter was, however, that the emperor—like the gubernial and circle authorities—protected the institution

---

[135] Cited in Wilson, *The Life and Times of Vuk Stefanović Karadzić*, 121. When Emperor Ferdinand finally did get the opportunity to give everyone what they wanted, in 1848, he did!

[136] For example, Fedir Chubei was sent to Vienna by the commune of Babyntsi, Chortkiv circle, in 1838. Here is how the circle authorities described his activities after returning: "He is deceiving the peasants that he spoke with his majesty the emperor, that he received money and a written order which frees them from corvée labour." *Klasova borotba*, 193.

[137] Verdery, *Transylvanian Villagers*, 99–103.

[138] *Klasova borotba*, 50.

[139] *Ibid.*, 90; see also p. 110.

[140] *Ibid.*, 355.

of serfdom, and necessarily many of its abuses, until constrained to abolish it in 1848.

Justice for the peasantry was not only uncertain but slow. The manor had a month to respond to a grievance before the commune was entitled to appeal to the circle authorities. Once the grievance reached the circle level, the commune would be fortunate if its grievance was reviewed within months and not years.[141] Franz Stadion, the governor of Galicia, took circle authorities to task on the eve of the 1848 revolution: "While the government is always willing to give the manors indispensable [military] assistance to collect rents from the serfs or in the event of a refusal to perform corvée labour, often many years pass before the serf can receive satisfaction in connection with the oppression against which he registers a complaint. This exasperating circumstance makes him, and not without reason, distrustful of the government."[142] If the circle authorities finally decided that the peasant commune was in the right, the landlord could, and usually did, appeal to the gubernial authorities. At this level of appeal as well as at the highest, the imperial court chancery, the case could also rest for a long time. During the entire process, peasants were obliged to be obedient to their landlord until their grievance was proven legitimate in the final instance.[143] Thus, the landlord could impose an extra day of corvée on the peasants and extract that day for years while the peasants, with the aid of a hounded corner-scribe, pursued their complaint down legal channels. If the peasants refused at any time to perform the extra day of corvée, the military would be sent in to beat and bleed them into submission. And if, in the end, the peasants were found to be right in their protest and the lord had to reimburse them in money for the extra days of labour, it could prove very difficult to extract the required payment from him.[144]

In this situation, it is hardly surprising that peasants also resorted to illegal measures in their struggle against feudal oppression. Most frequently, these took the form of refusing to fulfill feudal obligations. In its mildest incarnation, the refusal appeared as the shirking common to every system based on forced labour: working just hard enough to avoid the lash, bobbing up and down during harvesting while not actually cutting, spending more time sharpening than using a scythe, keeping inferior tools and animals precisely for use during corvée labour and so on.[145] A more forthright form of refusal on the part of an individual was flight, often to Bukovyna or Moldavia, where feudal dues were at first—at least through the end of the eighteenth century—less burdensome than in Galicia. At the outset of the

---

[141] Rosdolsky, *Stosunki poddańcze*, 1:144–7.

[142] *Klasova borotba*, 379.

[143] Rosdolsky, *Stosunki poddańcze*, 1:147.

[144] See above, note 23.

[145] Tadeusz Wasilewski, cited in Terletsky, *Znesenie panshchyny*, 162.

Austrian period, serfs were prohibited by law from leaving their masters,[146] but the Josephine reforms gave them the largely formal right to buy their way out of serfdom and move elsewhere. Few peasants could afford to pay the required quitrent and there was little opportunity for a former peasant to find employment. Near the middle of the nineteenth century, peasants felt that "running away would have done no good, for elsewhere it was no better."[147]

Communally, the refusal to fulfill feudal obligations took the form of a strike. Feudal strikes were often sparked by the authorities' delay in investigating a specific communal grievance, but also by false rumours that the emperor had abolished or severely curtailed serfdom. In the course of such a strike, communal solidarity played a key role. In Vyshatychi, Przemyśl circle, the peasants told the circle commissioner in the winter of 1783–4: "We have all unanimously made a compact that even if they lock us all in chains as well as our plenipotentiaries and even if they drive us off our farms as they are threatening, even then we will not perform [feudal] obligations or road-work."[148] In Perehinsko, Stryi circle, in 1817 a peasant threatened a potential strike-breaker with these words: "If you do not stand up for the commune and do not join with the commune, then the commune will hang you. The commune is a higher authority than the lord."[149] In Chortkiv circle in 1838 the commune of Melnytsia took an oath in the church to maintain solidarity. With candles burning and the gospel book raised above them, the peasants knelt down and swore that "one would not allow injury to another and one would stand up for the other completely."[150] In 1847 the peasants of Turie, Zolochiv circle, refused to give rents in kind to the manor. Their resistance was extremely difficult to break, as the circle commissioner reported, "because of the collectivity of their erroneous idea, which is manifested in the response that rose simultaneously from hundreds of throats: 'If the commune gives [the rents], then so will I.'" The commissioner chose twenty of "the loudest and most arrogant shouters" and had them flogged to the limit suggested by an attending surgeon. "The stubbornness of those punished grew into fanaticism; supported, on the one hand, by entreaties and demands to stand firm, and frightened, on the other hand, by threats from . . . the crowd in the event of a binding declaration [to give rents], the

---

[146] See the order of Count Anton Pergen, governor of Galicia, issued on 16 November 1772 (N.S.), in *Klasova borotba*, 39; the same text, in the original, is in Rosdolsky, *Stosunki poddańcze*, 2:65–6. For the situation on the eve of Austrian rule, see Mises, *Entwicklung*, 10–11 (on the early years of Austrian rule, 31–2).

[147] Slomka, *From Serfdom to Self-Government*, 15. See also above, 7 note 52. As Kann and David have noted in reference to a reform act passed by the Hungarian diet of 1839-40, which permitted peasants to buy their way out of serfdom: "It was clear that the impecunious peasantry could not be emancipated in this way. The device had failed a generation before under Joseph II." *The Peoples of the Eastern Habsburg Lands*, 233.

[148] *Klasova borotba*, 49–50.

[149] *Ibid.*, 76–7.

[150] *Ibid.*, 187, 199–201.

majority bore their punishment with stoic resignation. They considered themselves martyrs for the happiness of the entire commune.... ”[151] But no matter
how much solidarity the individual commune or several communes displayed,
until the refusal to render feudal dues threatened to encompass all of Galicia
in 1848 the use of military force always succeeded in crushing the peasants'
resistance.

Given the violent context of the enforcement of serfdom, it is
understandable that the peasants also resorted at times to violent forms of
struggle in their resistance to serfdom. Arson, directed against manorial
property (e.g., the manorial prisons) and sometimes against strike-breaking
peasants, was fairly common,[152] in spite of the dangers it posed for the
entirely wood structures of the commune itself. Social banditry
(U *opryshkivstvo*) was also prevalent, especially in the Carpathian mountains
in the late eighteenth and early nineteenth centuries.[153] Other manifestations
of violence emerged only sporadically in Eastern Galicia under Austrian rule.
Here there were no counterparts to the Ukrainian Cossack and *haidamak*
uprisings of the seventeenth and eighteenth centuries or to the Galician Polish
peasant revolt of 1846.

This is not to say that there were not isolated instances of large-scale or
particularly intensive peasant unrest. In the Komarno region of Sambir circle
in 1819 several thousand peasants were in open revolt. They occupied a
tavern at an important crossroads, thus interrupting communications for the
ludicrously undermanned government commission sent to pacify them. They
also captured circle officials and held them hostage in the tavern. In a
moment very characteristic of the serf mentality, they took away all the
documents from the circle commissioner and forced him to write new
documents guaranteeing that they would never be forced to do corvée labour
again.[154]

In the summer of 1838 a great wave of unrest swept Chortkiv circle,
inspired by events in neighbouring Bukovyna.[155] Thirty-nine villages took part
in strikes and other forms of protest before the disturbances were quelled by
the military in September. The leaders of the unrest were arrested and many
participants punished with the cudgel.[156]

The slaughter of the landlords that took place in Western Galicia in
1846[157] also had repercussions in Ukrainian villages. In 1846 in Horozhanna,

[151] *Ibid.* 355–6.

[152] *Ibid.*, 136, 141, 143, 269, 281, 292–3, 295, 335, 358.

[153] *Ibid.*, 91–3. There is a large literature on Ukrainian and Carpathian social banditry. See the
bibliography in Magocsi, *Galicia*, 91; also *Khodyly opryshky*; Hobsbawm, *Primitive Rebels*,
13–29; Sacher-Masoch, "Magass der Rauber," *Galizische Geschichten*, 1–53.

[154] *Klasova borotba*, 101, 104, 106, 110.

[155] *Ibid.*, 185–227.

[156] *Radianska Entsyklopediia Istorii Ukrainy*, sv. "Chortkivske selianske zavorushennia 1838" by
Iu.H. Hoshko.

[157] Galician, mainly Polish, peasants killed 728 noblemen and destroyed 474 manors in 1846.
Istoriia selianstva URSR, 1:344.

Sambir circle, where the military had put down peasant unrest in 1833,[158] the hated mandator and other manorial representatives and nobles tried to win the serfs over to the Polish insurrection against Austria. Instead of joining the noble insurgents, however, the peasants killed them.[159] In that same "bloody year," the peasants of Bilka, Lviv circle, were heard to be singing a song that started with a description of the evils of serfdom and ended with a summons to butcher the landlords.[160]

More peaceful, but also more ominous for the future of feudal relations, were other repercussions of 1846. The ill-starred Polish noble insurgents had hoped to win the peasants to their side by proclaiming the abolition of serfdom. This was the first time that peasants heard the nobles themselves speak of such a thing. Even though the peasants distrusted the insurgents and their promises, they realized that the end of the feudal system was at hand. For their loyalty to the Austrian state during the insurrection, the serfs expected to receive from the emperor what the rebel nobles had promised them: the end of the corvée and other feudal dues. When the emperor abolished the auxiliary days to alleviate peasant unrest in the spring of 1846, he only exacerbated the situation. The peasants were convinced that the emperor had abolished the corvée, and not just the auxiliary days as the manorial and circle officials informed them. The refusal to do corvée spread throughout Eastern Galicia and the villages had to be placed under military siege.[161]

Peasant resistance to serfdom spanned the entire period from 1772 to 1848, but it was particularly acute in the aftermath of the Napoleonic wars (when social banditism was also most rife)[162] and, much more so, in the decade preceding emancipation.[163] The latter period was marked by an intensification of opposition to serfdom not only in Ukrainian Galicia, but also in Polish Galicia (the 1846 uprising) and in Ukrainian Bukovyna (the uprising led by Lukian Kobylytsia). The accumulation of resistance made it impossible not to abolish serfdom after revolution broke out in Austria in March 1848.[164]

---

[158] *Klasova borotba*, 178–80.

[159] *Ibid.*, 279–81. Rosdolsky, "Do historii 'krwawego roku,'" 411–16. For another incident of violent peasant unrest in a Ukrainian village in 1846, see Hladylovych, "Spomyny," 1–20.

[160] "*[1] Pany kazhut, zhe my svyni, / Zhe ne znaiem, shcho to nyni, / Tilky panshchynu robyty, / I tym maiem v sviti zhyty. / [2] Pan nas kazhe vyhaniaty, / a okonom daie baty, / A iak vyidesh na panshchynu, / 'Roby,—krychyt—sukyi synu!' /.... [10] Ale to vso ne pomozhe, / Boronim zhe sia, nebozhe. / A zheby iuzh spokii maty, / Treba paniv vyrizaty.*" *Klasova borotba*, 344–6.

[161] *Ibid.*, 287–349.

[162] *Istoriia selianstva URSR*, 1:341–2.

[163] A very rough gauge of the intensity of peasant resistance is the number of documents from various decades in the collection *Klasova borotba*. For the decades between 1778 and 1817 there are from 3 to 6 documents each; from 1818–27 there are 44 documents; from 1828–37 there are 7; and from 1838–47 there are 128.

[164] "The unsettled conditions in the countryside continued until the spring of 1848 when the news

The Revolution of 1848–9

> The events of 1848 had a very
> pernicious influence on the
> peasantry.
> —Galician governor Agenor
> Gołuchowski to Austrian interior
> minister Alexander Bach, 1850[165]

The all-European revolution of 1848–9 had a tremendous effect on Ukrainian society in Galicia. The Ukrainian national movement, which had hitherto been a cultural movement embodied in grammar books and collections of folk songs and verse penned by priests and seminarians, emerged for the first time as a mass movement with a political dimension. In May 1848 educated Ukrainians, primarily but not exclusively clerics, formed the Supreme Ruthenian Council, which established affiliated Ruthenian Councils throughout Eastern Galicia.[166] The Council formulated the first political demands of the Ukrainian movement, particularly the division of Galicia along ethnic lines into two separate provinces.

The revolution left in its wake a nationally conscious intelligentsia, both clerical and secular, and a liberated peasantry that had already had its first exposure to politics and the national movement. A very thin stratum of Ukrainian secular intelligentsia was just emerging in the 1840s. The revolution crystallized its formation, partly because of a deliberate and far-sighted policy of the Greek Catholic clergy to give disproportionate prominence to laymen. Two of five places in the presidium of the Supreme Ruthenian Council were reserved for secular figures, and a *numerus clausus* was imposed on clergy in the Council's branches outside Lviv. The revolution also marked a turning-point for the clergy. Before 1848 most of the lower clergy and seminarians were not only linguistically Polonized, but some had assimilated Polish political ideals. Although individual churchmen had been the initiators of the Ukrainian cultural movement prior to 1848, it was only as a result of the revolution that Ukrainian national consciousness became

---

[164](continued) of the March Days in Vienna swept through the Monarchy. Then all factions realized that the peasants held the balance of power, and that that party would win out which could attract and hold the peasantry to its side." Blum, *Noble Landowners*, 232.

[165] *Klasova borotba*, 522.

[166] The affiliated Ruthenian Councils were organized territorially to correspond to the deaneries of the Greek Catholic church. By 1 October 1848 there were forty-three councils, in Berezhany, Bibrka, Bohorodchany, Bolekhiv, Brody, Buchach, Chortkiv, Drohobych, Halych, Horodok, Hrushiv, Iavoriv, Jarosław (Iaroslav), Kalush, Khodoriv, Kolomyia, Komarno, Lubaczów, Lviv, Naraiv, Olesko, Perehinsko, Pidhaitsi, Przemyśl, Rohatyn, Rozdil, Sambir, Sanok (Sianik), Stryi (lesser Council), Stryi (circle Council), Terebovlia, Ternopil, Turka, Uhniv, Utishkiv, Zaliztsi, Zarvanytsia, Zbarazh, Zboriv, Zhovkva, Zhuravno and Zolochiv. *Ibid.*, 435. This list is incomplete, unless the Vysotsko Ruthenian Council, constituted in June 1848, no longer existed by October. See *ibid.*, 409–10.

hegemonous in the Greek Catholic clergy as a whole.[167] A consequence of the revolution, therefore, was the production of a critical mass of intelligentsia, secular and clerical, in whom the Ukrainian national idea resided. It would be the Ukrainian intelligentsia forged in 1848 that would ultimately integrate the Ukrainian peasantry into the nation.

For the peasantry the major result of the 1848 revolution was emancipation from serfdom, which was announced on 22 April 1848 (N.S.) and became effective on 15 May.[168] The sundering of servile relations was a precondition for the participation of the peasantry in national politics. Without personal emancipation and mobility and without the weakening of the manor's power in the village, the national movement could never have penetrated among the peasantry.

Already in 1848 the newly emancipated peasants received their first introduction to politics. They took part in elections to the constituent Austrian parliament and sent dozens of Galician peasants to Vienna as their deputies.[169] The peasant deputies were the plenipotentiaries of the feudal era, only writ much larger. They came into parliament with the same devotion to the emperor and hatred for the landlords that had fueled them in their resistance to serfdom.[170] And they bore all the marks of newly emancipated serfs: their primitive ways sent civilized Vienna into titters and their weak or, in some cases, nonexistent knowledge of German made it difficult for them to follow and participate in the proceedings. To overcome their handicaps, the peasant deputies, both Ukrainian and Polish, collaborated closely with the representatives of the Supreme Ruthenian Council.[171]

The peculiar political constellation of revolutionary Austria in 1848 put the Galician peasant deputies in the camp of the reaction. The revolutionary forces of German Austria had entered into an alliance with the Magyar and Polish nobility, whose national struggles were directed against the imperial forces. The presence in the revolutionary camp of the nobility that oppressed them made the peasants, especially of the so-called "nonhistoric peoples," align themselves against the revolutionaries.[172] The traditional naive royalism of the peasants and the influence of the pro-imperial Greek Catholic hierarchy in the Supreme Ruthenian Council drew the peasants and their deputies

---

[167] Himka, "Greek Catholic Church," 436–7.

[168] *Klasova borotba*, 391. Kravets, *Selianstvo*, 14–15.

[169] The peasant deputies in the Vienna parliament in 1848–9 are the subject of an admirable study by Roman Rosdolsky (*Bauernabgeordneten*).

[170] "The only feeling that governed them, aside from their loyalty to the emperor, was a passionate hatred for the Polish nobles. Even in the parliament there were moments when one could read in their eyes that they were ready to let loose against the noblemen and frock-Poles [nonpeasant Polish deputies] and bash their skulls in." Kudlich, *Rückblicke*, 2:27.

[171] See the letter of parliamentary deputy Iuliian Velychkovsky to the Supreme Ruthenian Council, 21 August 1848, in *Klasova borotba*, 419–20.

[172] The social and national contradictions of the Austrian revolution are analyzed exceptionally well in Rosdolsky, *Zur nationalen Frage*.

even closer to the camp of reaction. But the peasant deputies were very revolutionary reactionaries. We have already seen that they d..nanded an expansion of elementary education, and later we will see that they also took an anticlerical stance. However, their most radical demands concerned servitudes (discussed later in this chapter) and the question of compensation to the landlords for the abolition of corvée labour.

The compensation question was heatedly debated in the parliament.[173] Almost all of the nonpeasant deputies felt that the landlords deserved some form of compensation for the loss of the corvée. Even the deputies representing the Supreme Ruthenian Council thought that compensation of the landlords was a moral obligation. They realized, however, that this position endangered their alliance with the peasant deputies: "We must either lose the confidence of our peasants and offend the radical Germans or vote against our conscience. One spoils our cause, the other is a sin."[174] The peasant deputies were entirely opposed to any form of compensation to the landlords. Their position was most eloquently expressed by the Ukrainian Ivan Kapushchak in his speech of 27 August 1848 (N.S.):

> The landlords had the right by law to demand corvée labour from us. This is indisputable. But were they satisfied with this? No and once again no! If we had to work 300 instead of 100 days [a year], if we had to work three or four days or an entire week and the landlord counted it as only one day, then I ask you, gentlemen: Who has to pay compensation, the peasant or the landlord?
>
> "But," they say, "the landlord treated the peasant kindly." That's the truth. But who considers it kind treatment if the peasant, after working the entire week, is "hosted" by the landlord on Sundays and holy days, that is, if the peasant is clapped in irons at the landlord's order and thrown into the stable, so that next week he would be more diligent about showing up for corvée labour? And for this the landlords should receive compensation?
>
> Then they say: "The noble is humane!" And that too is the truth, because he encouraged the exhausted peasant with lashes. If someone complained that his draught animals were too weak and he could not perform draught corvée, what did he hear in reply? "You and your wife step into the yoke!"[175] ...

---

[173] See Rosdolsky, *Bauernabgeordneten*, 105–45.

[174] Letter of deputy Hryhorii Shashkevych to the Supreme Ruthenian Council, 28 August 1848, in *Klasova borotba*, 422.

[175] The harnessing of serfs to the plough in fulfillment of draught corvée obligations was also practiced in the region of Right-Bank Ukraine where the Ukrainian poet Taras Shevchenko grew up. (Marian Jakóbiec, "Wstęp," in Shevchenko, *Wybór poezji*, xix.) This is why the image of peasants harnessed to ploughs occurs so frequently in Shevchenko's works: *"Liudei zapriahaiut / V tiazhki iarma.... Syny serdeshnoi Ukrainy! / Shcho dobre khodyte v iarmi, / Shche luchche, iak batky khodyly."* ("I mertvym, i zhyvym, i nenarozhdennym," in Shevchenko, *Kobzar*, 256, 259–60.) *"'Aby faida v rukakh bula, / A khlopa iak toho vola, / U pluh holodnoho zapriazhesh.'"* ("Mezh skalamy, nenache zlodii," *ibid.*, 365.) *"...Skriz na slavnii Ukraini / Liudei u iarma zapriahly / Pany lukavi...Hynut! Hynut! / U iarmakh lytsarski syny."* ("I vyris ia na chuzhyni," *ibid.*, 369.) In Left-Bank Ukraine as well peasants were yoked as draught animals. The poet Ivan Kotliarevsky, in his *Eneida*, imagined landlords tortured in hell because *"liudiam lhoty ne davaly / I stavyly ikh za skotiv."* (Cited by M.O. Maksymovych in *Ivan Kotliarevsky u dokumentakh*, 194.) The yoking of peasants was also known in Eastern Europe outside Ukraine. Verdery, *Transylvanian Villagers*, 262.

Then they say: "The manors protected the rights and property of the peasants." That's also the truth! But the manors took a bit of farmland away from one peasant and a bit of pasture away from another. Should we perhaps pay them compensation for these privileges? No!

...If a poor peasant wanted to climb the steps of the [manor] house, he was told to wait in the yard, because he would dirty the palace, because the peasant stinks and the lord cannot bear this [stench] in his living quarters.

For all this abuse are we now supposed to pay compensation? My opinion is: no. The whips and scourges that they used on our heads and on our exhausted bodies—yes, these we can leave them. Let these be their compensation.[176]

Kapushchak's speech made such an impression that it was reported in a number of European newspapers, including the *Neue Rheinische Zeitung* edited by Marx and Engels.[177] It represented the authentic voice of the Galician peasant, the "beast" that learned to speak in 1848. Other peasants felt exactly the same as Kapushchak: "They [the landlords] haven't compensated us for what we did: we worked for them for centuries day and night, more than once while we were hungry, and we destroyed our health and property on account of them. Therefore they are not entitled to any compensation." Moreover, "there will be no prosperity in the country until the nobleman walks behind a plough."[178]

In spite of the peasants' demonstrative opposition, the parliament and the emperor decided to compensate the nobility. The compensation, which extended to all of Austria, was particularly onerous in Galicia. The peasants here paid compensation until 1898, and most of what they paid was interest on the loan the Galician government took out to settle the landlords' claims. By 1898 the peasants of Eastern Galicia had paid over 50 million gulden for compensation proper and almost 62 million as interest.[179]

The new, political profile the peasantry exhibited in 1848 had important national ramifications. Pre-emancipation peasants did not yet display national consciousness in their grievances against the manor.[180] In fact, one finds in the

---

[176] Rosdolsky, *Bauernabgeordneten*, 136–8. *Klasova borotba*, 416–18. *Die Revolutionsjahre*, 12. The latter source also (pp. 12–14) reprints the response of the spokesman for the Polish nobility, Marian Dylewski.

[177] Rosdolsky, *Zur nationalen Frage*, 66–7.

[178] These are the words of anonymous peasants of Zagórze (Zahirie), Sanok circle, as reported by the priest Andrii Karpinsky to the Supreme Ruthenian Council, 15 February 1849, in *Klasova borotba*, 465.

[179] Sviezhynsky, *Ahrarni vidnosyny*, 14. See also Himka, "Background to Emigration," 12–13, 24 note 5.

[180] There is a deceptive document from Horozhanna, Sambir circle, dated 7 April 1846. The commune appealed to the circle authorities to transfer Horozhanna to state ownership "because Polish lords have been flaying us and oppressing us by various means." The same petition refers several times to "Poles" and "Polish lords." *Klasova borotba*, 300. This is a unique instance of a Ukrainian serf document (written, of course, in Polish) which identifies the landlords as Poles. However, this identification does not really represent national self-consciousness on the part of the peasants, who do not identify *themselves* by nationality in the document. In stating that the

documents of their struggle against serfdom passages that suggest oblivion to national concerns. For example, in 1819 the Ukrainian peasants of the Komarno region refused to allow the circle commission to record its proceedings in German and demanded that *Polish* be used instead.[181] It never occurred to them to ask that their own language be used. In 1822 the peasants of the town of Potik, Stanyslaviv circle, requested permission to settle in another "nation" (G *Nation*) to escape oppression from their landlord. The "other" nation they had in mind was Ukrainian-inhabited Bukovyna.[182] This national indifference characteristic of the pre-1848 peasantry was shattered by the revolution.

Had the Austrian revolution been able to confine itself to barricades in the cities and the expulsion of unpopular politicians and even the monarch, the peasantry might have remained relatively indifferent to the doings of the fractious gentlemen. But this was impossible two years after 1846. The Polish landlords feared another, even more terrible jacquerie[183] and faced a practically universal refusal on the part of the peasantry to perform corvée labour. For their part, the imperial authorities feared lest the vulnerable Polish nobility abolish serfdom on its own initiative, thus repeating the attempt of the radical Polish democrats of 1846 to win the peasantry to the Polish cause. In this inflammable situation, emancipation from serfdom could not be postponed; governor Franz Stadion announced it on 22 April 1848 (N.S.), a little over a month after the revolution broke out in Vienna and months before serfdom would be abolished throughout Austria.[184] Almost from the start, therefore, the revolution commanded the attention and participation of the Galician peasantry. The abolition of serfdom left unresolved two issues of great import to the peasantry: Would the peasants have to pay high taxes so that the lords might be compensated? Would the lords or the communes own the forests and pastures? The peasantry had to take what cognizance its ignorance permitted of the political situation in Galicia. It saw two contending forces in the crownland: the Polish National Council and the Supreme Ruthenian Council. In the former council were the hated landlords, in the latter their pastors. The Polish council took unabashedly pro-landlord positions on every issue of concern to the peasants. The Ruthenian council, though soft on compensation, supported the peasantry

---

[180](continued) nobles who oppressed them were Poles, the peasants were merely underscoring that their landlords were outlaws in the emperor's eyes, supporters of the abortive Polish insurrection of 1846.

[181] *Ibid.*, 112–13.

[182] *Ibid.*, 137. The Ukrainian peasants in Bukovyna returned the compliment. Their name for Galicia was *Liadchyna*, i.e., Poland. *Narysy z istorii Pivnichnoi Bukovyny*, 117. In the 1860s a Galician Ukrainian peasant referred to Right-Bank Ukraine as "Muscovy." Himka, "Hope in the Tsar," 128.

[183] Even the Polish mob in Lviv was panic-stricken in late March 1848 over rumours that Ukrainian peasants were ready to march on the city and slaughter its inhabitants. Vozniak, *Iak probudylosia*, 127–8.

[184] For a detailed discussion, see Kieniewicz, *Pomiędzy Stadionem a Goslarem.*

completely on servitudes and also posed, not without justification, as the
champion of peasant interests. It is hardly a cause for wonder, then, that the
Ukrainian peasants of Galicia, like the Ukrainian and Polish peasant deputies
in parliament, aligned themselves with the Supreme Ruthenian Council.[185] By
doing so they not only took their first steps into the Ukrainian nation but also
endowed the nation with unexpected force.

The power of the Ukrainian movement during the revolution of 1848–9
truly appears as something anomalous. Anyone familiar with the meager
achievements of the Ukrainian national awakening of the 1830s and early
1840s[186] can only be astounded by the creative energy unleashed by the
revolution. Although Ukrainian awakeners before 1848 had toyed with the
idea of a Ukrainian periodical, it was only late in 1847, under the pressure of
the intensifying revolutionary atmosphere, that concrete steps were taken in
this direction, and even then at governor Stadion's initiative. The periodical
remained in the planning stage until the outbreak of the revolution made its
appearance imperative. The first issue of the newspaper *Zoria halytska* came
out on 15 May 1848 (N.S.), and it exceeded any expectations entertained before the revolution. Its first issues had a press-run of 4,000, and after a few
months it had over 1,500 subscribers.[187] During the course of the revolution it
doubled its frequency, from weekly in 1848 to semiweekly in 1849. In these
same two years it was joined by six other Ukrainian periodicals.[188] The
revolutionary years also saw other phenomena that would have been difficult
to imagine in the previous decades, including a congress of ninety-nine
Ukrainian scholars, which convened in Lviv in October 1848, and the
formation of a Ukrainian national guard. Moreover, those Polish-speaking
clergymen with at most a romantic attachment to things Ukrainian were
transformed into Ukrainian *politicians*, capable of promoting their own goals
in the Vienna parliament, at the Prague Slav Congress and in the backrooms
of imperial ministries and the crownland administration. No one who knew
them from the 1830s and early 1840s would have imagined them
entertaining, let alone effectively pursuing, so political a plan as the division

---

[185] The Supreme Ruthenian Council also enjoyed a good reputation among peasants in regions
neighbouring Eastern Galicia. Polish peasant deputies asked the Council to publish a newspaper
in Polish for the peasants of Western Galicia. *Klasova borotba*, 419–20. Peasants in
Russian-ruled Right-Bank Ukraine envied the Galicians their "good priests who freed [them]
from serfdom." Himka, "Hope in the Tsar," 128.

[186] For example, when the greatest of the Galician Ukrainian awakeners, Markiian Shashkevych,
died in 1843, his friend Mykola Ustiianovych could find no outlet in which to publish an
obituary. The obituary had to wait until 1848 to appear. Vozniak, *Iak probudylosia*, 109.

[187] *Ibid.*, 122–5, 148–9.

[188] Ihnatiienko, *Bibliohrafiia ukrainskoi presy*, 32–5. A similar flourishing of the periodical press
was evident among the other Austrian Slavs during the revolution. The Czechs quadrupled the
number of their periodicals, from 13 on the eve of the revolution to 52 during it. The Slovenes
had one periodical in 1847 and six in 1848. The Slovaks and Croats also increased the number of
their periodicals during the revolution, although not so dramatically. Pech, "The Nationalist
Movements of the Austrian Slavs in 1848," 347.

of Galicia into two provinces, Polish and Ukrainian. When their Polish rivals in 1848 denounced the Ukrainian movement as the mere invention of Stadion, they were not merely trying to slander their opponents, but were also trying to explain to themselves the inexplicable force that confronted them.[189]

The unforeseen intensity of the Ukrainian movement in 1848 was due partly to the political freedom accompanying the revolution, but also to the engagement of the peasantry. The Supreme Ruthenian Council became the focus not only of the national ideals hesitantly developed by the Ukrainian intelligentsia in the 1830s–40s, but also of the social struggle of the Ukrainian peasantry, which had accelerated in the same period. With the peasants harnessed to the national cause, the cause was propelled forward by an elemental power.[190]

Peasants joined local Ruthenian Councils. In Vysotsko, Sambir circle, for example, peasants accounted for ten of the Council's thirty members and a peasant was even elected president.[191] The peasants also signed, with crosses, petitions drafted by the Supreme Ruthenian Council.[192] Thanks to peasant support, by the end of January 1849 the Council was able to collect over 200,000 signatures on a petition to divide Galicia into two provinces.[193] The meaning of the petition was explained by a peasant, Andrus Protsian, to other peasants who did not know whether or not they should sign:

> I was there myself on 3 August 1848 [O.S.] at the meeting in the circle capital of Stryi and I heard with my own ears how they declared that the Ruthenian

---

[189] The anomaly of 1848 is also evident by comparison with what immediately followed. The Ukrainians did not publish a twice-weekly newspaper again until 1861, when *Slovo* appeared. (Ihnatiienko, *Bibliohrafiia ukrainskoi presy*, 44.) In 1880 *Slovo* had a press-run of 850 and its national populist rival *Dilo* had a press-run of 550. (TsDIAL, 146/7/4149, pp. 406–7.) In 1885 the respective press-runs were 600 and 1,300. (TsDIAL, 146/7/4352, p 129.) The social structure of the Ukrainian movement exhibited in 1848, with its significant secular components, was not to emerge again until the late 1860s-early 1870s. See the comparison of the social compositions of the Supreme Ruthenian Council (1848), the subscription list of the almanac *Zoria halytskaia* (1860) and the popular educational society Prosvita (1868–74) in Himka, "Polish and Ukrainian Socialism," 136.

[190] Much the same was true in Romanian Transylvania: "...The significance of 1848 for Romanians is precisely the crucial chance it offered for political socialization, for Romanian intellectuals and peasants. Leaders took from the mass meetings a new awareness of the possibilities for a broadly based social movement. Peasants both saw that their social grievances were at last being taken seriously by important people—lawyers, bankers, gentlemen—and also perceived the importance of nationalist politics. Romanian intellectuals and peasants had certainly recognized these aspects of their situation before; but in 1848 they formulated for the first time a specific platform containing both nationalist and social-reformist planks, thereby uniting and systematizing in a single national movement objectives that different groups had been pursuing piecemeal." Verdery, *Transylvanian Villagers*, 189–90.

[191] *Klasova borotba*, 409–10.

[192] See *ibid.*, 392–3.

[193] Kozik, *Między reakcją a rewolucją*, 113. Polish politicians claimed that the peasants were unaware of what they were signing and that the petition therefore did not represent the authentic will of the people. Florian Ziemiałkowski proposed in parliament that the government "send to Galicia a commission which would ask the peasant whether he knew what he had signed." *Die Revolutionsjahre*, 21.

people is eminent, great and powerful, that it is the original inhabitant and numerous in Galicia, that, although until now we have been scorned and humiliated, this is a Ruthenian land and more of us Ruthenians live here than Poles. Therefore it is correct that there should be a Ruthenian gubernium here and that petitions submitted in the Ruthenian language should be answered by the authorities in that same Ruthenian language. Why should the Ruthenian people be so abased that its language can be heard neither in the schools nor in government offices, but only on the lips of a poor peasant?[194]

The peasants supported the Supreme Ruthenian Council "because they have the hope that through it they will see all their desires, wishes and needs brought to a better result."[195] The peasants sent the Council numerous concrete grievances concerning landlords who oppressed them and stole their land. They beseeched the Council to intercede for them to obtain justice. What is striking about these grievances, otherwise so similar to the grievances brought to the circle authorities and the emperor before 1848, is that *for the first time* the landlord-peasant conflict is formulated as a Polish-Ukrainian conflict. The expression of the fact that the landlords were Polish in Eastern Galicia and the peasants Ukrainian was an innovation of the revolution.[196] Before the revolution, as Hryhorii Shashkevych noted during it, the words "landlord" and "Pole" were synonymous in the peasant's consciousness, "but he was unable to make the distinction, and moreover he never even had a reason or occasion to do so."[197] But he had reason and occasion enough in 1848–9.

Thus the peasants of Pidhorodyshche, Berezhany circle, now referred to the beatings they had received under serfdom as blows "to the bodies of the Ruthenian people."[198] The peasants of Semyhyniv, Stryi circle, after explaining to the Council how the landlord and the mandator have abused them and how all appeal to the circle authorities has been fruitless, urged the Council to intercede and asked it rhetorically:

---

[194] Unfortunately, the lease-holder overheard Protsian's conversation and had the mandator lock him up for five days without food, water or the opportunity of relieving himself outside his small cell. "From the stench and from hunger he lost his strength and, as he tells it, by Friday he was no longer really conscious. He asked to be confessed, but this kindness was not allowed him." When the mandator realized that Protsian was in danger of death he released him. *Klasova borotba*, 425–6.

[195] Report from the Horodok Ruthenian Council to the Supreme Ruthenian Council in Lviv, 31 August 1848, in *ibid.*, 423.

[196] The Polish nobility was also aware of the close connection between nationality and class in Eastern Galicia in 1848. They referred to the Ukrainians as "the population belonging exclusively to the agricultural class," while the Poles represented "intelligence and great property." The creation of a separate Ukrainian province of Eastern Galicia would above all hurt "the landlords and all members of the wealthier and more intelligent class of society." *Die Revolutionsjahre*, 59, 69.

[197] Cited in Vozniak, *Iak probudylosia*, 134.

[198] *Klasova borotba*, 456.

How long will our enemies oppress us on our own land? How long must we await justice? And where can we find it, when it's not in the circle authorities? As soon as a Ruthenian deviates [from the law] in the slightest, the dragoons are called in.... [199]

The Council received a request to protect the rights to wood and pasture of the inhabitants of the town of Nyzhniv, Stanyslaviv circle, located "in a Ruthenian land, Galicia."[200] The inhabitants of the town of Oleshnychi, Zhovkva circle, also wanted the Council to help them regain their rights to use the forest: "If our national council aids us, we will see it as an authority, sanctioned authority, and we will shout 'Hail!' to our Ruthenians many times, until it echoes from shore to shore."[201] Peasants of Derzhiv, Stryi circle, compained of "injury received from the Poles [U *liakhy*]" when hayfields were appropriated by the manor.[202] The commune of Hryniv, Berezhany circle, asked the Council to protect its land from expropriation by the demesnal administration: "Our poverty forces us, the whole commune, to place ourselves under the protection of the honourable council and [to request] a defence of the Ruthenian nationality of Galicia against the difficulties and injuries caused us in our farms and pastures by the demesnal representatives of Count Potocki.... We, in such misfortune, ask [you] to recognize the justice of what we have described, so that such foes, the enemy Poles [U *liakhy*], would now finally stop mistreating us.... "[203] The peasants of Trościaniec (Trostianets), Przemyśl circle, complained to the Council about hayfields stolen by "the Poles" (U *liakhy*), i.e., the manor; "and although they are in the wrong they defend their action, and it is no wonder—for such is their Polish nature" (U *bo to liakhivska ikh taka pryroda*).[204] For the peasants of Ozerianka, Zolochiv circle, regaining a pasture taken by the manor was nothing less than "our cause, the Ruthenian cause."[205] Expropriations of land in Horoshova, Chortkiv circle, were "crying abuses against poor and faithful Ruthenians."[206] The peasants of Mylkiv, Zhovkva circle, would have taken their land back from the manor by force, "but since we are neither Poles [U *poliaky*] nor the Tatars of old, but Ruthenians by birth, this is not fitting.... "[207]

---

[199] *Ibid.*, 460.

[200] *Ibid.*, 465.

[201] *Ibid.*, 471.

[202] *Ibid.*, 475.

[203] *Ibid.*, 475–6.

[204] *Ibid.*, 478. Close to this in sentiment was a statement by Ivan Kapushchak in parliament. Defending the existence of a separate Ukrainian nationality in Galicia, Kapushchak explained that Poles and Ukrainians differed in language, religion and customs. The latter point he jokingly elaborated as follows: "They also differ in customs...the Poles like to rule over the other nationality." *Die Revolutionsjahre*, 20.

[205] *Klasova borotba*, 487.

[206] *Ibid.*, 499.

[207] *Ibid.*, 518.

These first expressions of national consciousness among the Galician Ukrainian peasantry are strikingly concrete. The Ukrainian national cause was identified in the peasants' minds with immediate, local, socio-economic grievances. Crucial to the emergence of even this simple identification with the Ukrainian national movement was the existence of a concrete embodiment of the movement in the form of the Supreme Ruthenian Council. The Council was viewed as a protector of peasant interests.

Not surprisingly, the ultimate ineffectiveness of the Council in defending the peasantry's interests undermined its popularity and authority. What the peasantry expected of the Council was nothing less than a reversal of the relationships existing in Eastern Galicia so that the peasants dominated the landlords. The Polish nobility, sensitive to the socioeconomic aspirations of its former serfs, perceived that ultimately the Ukrainian movement would have to propose "the division of demesnal property among the villagers."[208] Such a radical social transformation proved beyond the power and vision of the Council. By the summer of 1849 the Council realized that it was not powerful enough to retain the allegiance of the peasantry. On 15 June 1849 (O.S.) the Brody Ruthenian Council reported to Lviv that priests with grievances against the manor were not receiving a proper hearing in the Zolochiv circle government. This has "removed the confidence that the people formerly placed in their clergymen," the local representatives of the Council. "Now [the people] see the ineffectiveness of their clergy in giving them aid, which is ultimately and singularly what they hoped to obtain from them; they see the priests too are just as impotent as they are themselves.... "[209] On 17 July 1849 (N.S.) the Supreme Ruthenian Council appealed to the Austrian ministry of justice to respond quickly and justly to the many peasant grievances it had passed on to the ministry. Otherwise the peasant could easily be led astray by "the enemies of authority, who will daily tempt him with [visions of] a better future once the government is overthrown."

> ... And the Supreme [Ruthenian] Council will not be able to counteract this, because the negative response to the petitions it has submitted will deprive it of any influence and authority.
> Up to now the peasant has heard from the Supreme [Ruthenian] Council only appeals to perform obligations that are in the state's interests, to join the corps of free riflemen [national guard], that is, he has heard appeals to give everything, but, notwithstanding so many petitions [submitted by the peasant], he has yet to hear about any decisions in his favour. The settlement of these grievances, which concern the essence of private and public prosperity in Galicia, cannot be dragged out any longer.[210]

An indication of the waning confidence in the Council was that in May and June of 1849 the peasants began to take the settlement of their grievances into their own hands, reclaiming by force property that the manor

---

[208] *Die Revolutionsjahre*, 69.

[209] *Klasova borotba*, 481–2.

[210] *Ibid.*, 497–8.

had appropriated from them. The seizure of demesnal property affected "truly the whole crownland," "localities in each of the circles."[211] This extra-legal movement, so characteristic of the preceding, antifeudal struggle, was crushed by military intervention.

Servitudes

> Who doesn't know how little our
> peasantry holds sacred someone
> else's forest property?
> —A Galician landlord before a
> servitude commission, 1859,
> explaining why peasants' testimony
> must be disregarded[212]

Servitudes[213] were the rights of peasant communes and individual peasant households to take wood for fuel and construction from the forest and to graze their livestock in pastures.[214] In the theory of the landlords, these were rights that the serfs enjoyed in the *manorial* forests and pastures by virtue of their servitude. In fact, before the Austrian period peasant communes owned their own woods and pastures which they used collectively. But throughout the late eighteenth and first half of the nineteenth century, landlords appropriated these as their private property, allowing the peasants only "servitude" rights to wood and pasture. One aspect, then, of the servitudes dispute between landlords and peasants in Galicia was the question of ownership of the forests and pastures. Moreover, sometimes before and almost universally after 1848, the landlords denied the peasants even their servitude rights and demanded payment in labour or money for access to the forests and pastures. This was the second aspect of the servitudes dispute: the question of access, irrespective of ownership.

The manorial appropriation of communal land began with the very onset of Austrian rule in Galicia. The Austrian agrarian reforms, placing so many limitations on serfdom, seemed to the landlords a form of economic persecution as well as the first steps toward the complete abolition of serfdom. Driven by fear of the collapse of the feudal system, landlords sought to cushion the blow by augmenting their property holdings. They appropriated individual peasant farms in comparatively small number, since as long as serfdom continued to exist the estates demanded landed peasant labourers. But because communal land did not present the same obstacle, it was taken in much greater quantity.

---

[211] Galician governor Agenor Gołuchowski to Austrian interior minister Alexander Bach, 17 March 1850, in *ibid.*, 524; see also p. 525.

[212] TsDIAL, 146/64/198, p. 35v.

[213] U *servituty*; P *serwituty, służebnictwa*; G *Servituten*.

[214] Norman Davies's definition of *"serwituty"* as "minor feudal services not involving labour" is entirely a product of his vivid imagination. *God's Playground*, 2:187.

The forest legislation of Maria Theresia and Joseph II, which was motivated by concern over deforestation, provided the original pretext for landlords to assume control of communal land. An imperial patent of 28 January 1773 (N.S.), regulating royal forests only, forbade peasants to cut wood for construction or sale and allowed them only to gather dead wood for fuel. Although the law was not intended for private estates, the nobles immediately began to enforce similar rules in the villages' woods. The crucial piece of legislation, however, was the forest law of 20 September 1782 (N.S.) which placed all nonroyal woodland under the *supervision* of the manors. The intent of the law was to prevent the devastation of forests by regulating access to wood. Peasants were still entitled by law to use their forests, but they could do so only on certain days of the week and with the landlords' permission. The effect of the law was that landlords began to treat the woods as their own property and to consider the peasants' access to wood as their rights of servitude. Moreover, very many landlords immediately denied peasants any free use of the forest. They recognized that control of the forest was a way of obviating the three-day limit on corvée labour: if the peasant wanted to heat his home in the winter or repair a fence, let him pay for the required wood with extra labour on the estate. The state rejected this manorial interpretation of the patent and attempted to restore peasant rights to wood by the patent of 12 January 1784, which forbade nobles from abolishing customary forest rights, even including the right of cutting wood for sale where this practice had been established by custom. But the damage had been done: control, and ultimately ownership, of forests passed to the landlords, and even access to wood became problematic.[215] Landlords took advantage of the land surveys of 1789 and 1820 to formalize this arrangement, having the forests, and pastures as well, recorded as their own.

Of course, the manorial aggression against communal land was bitterly contested by the feudal peasantry, which submitted thousands of grievances in protest and suffered many a military incursion while defending its traditional lands and rights. But the conflict over servitudes became extremely acute with the abolition of serfdom in 1848.

Within the first days of the Austrian revolution, on 19 March 1848 (N.S.), a group of Galician landlords, who had already reconciled themselves to the fact that serfdom was soon to be abolished, submitted a proposal to the governor of Galicia on the way in which emancipation should be implemented. Their proposal included, as the governor expressed it, "a regulation of landholding, that is, a better rounding-off of demesnal lands" (the appropriation of more peasant land), as well as a long delay before the actual cessation of corvée obligations. Servitudes played a key role in their proposal. The abolition of the peasants' obligations vis-à-vis the manor, i.e., of all the corvée and other feudal rents in labour, nature and money, would be accompanied by the abolition of the manor's obligations vis-à-vis the peasants,

---

[215] Rosdolsky, *Stosunki poddańcze*, 1: 218–19. Kravets, *Selianstvo*, 97 note 3.

specifically of servitudes,[216] i.e., the peasants' rights of access to what were formerly their own forests and pastures. The abolition of servitudes would mean that the forests and pastures would become the completely private property of the landlords, unencumbered by the traditional rights of the peasants. This would allow the landlords to retain cheap, almost feudal labour for their estates, because the formally emancipated serfs would be unable to survive without wood and pastures.

The text of the gubernial circular announcing the abolition of serfdom had stated that "the existing servitudes remain in force, but in the future they will be redeemed."[217] In spite of this, landlords throughout Galicia began implementing the aforementioned proposal, that is, simultaneously with the abolition of serfdom and completely on their own authority, they abolished the servitudes, barring peasants from the forests and pastures.[218] Now they demanded payment in money or labour before allowing customary access. In the Kalush region landlords were demanding 300 and more days of labour a year even from small communities to continue their traditional use of forests and pastures.[219] In Monastyryska and neighbouring villages in Stanyslaviv circle, the peasants complained that their landlord not only denied them traditional access in 1848, but appropriated as-yet-unappropriated communal hayfields, pastures and fallow land. Thus, they said, "the favour of the most illustrious emperor, which for millions of his subjects has become a remedy, for us has become a poison, hastening us to our political [sic] grave.... " The peasants explained that their lord had only acquired an estate within the last three years and felt cheated by the abolition of serfdom: "he cannot live without serfdom and by various most unworthy methods he tries to reintroduce it." The landlord "acts as his stony heart tells him, as if there were no power over him, no authority on earth and no judgment after death."[220]

By abolishing servitudes the landlords were compensating themselves for the abolition of corvée labour. The peasants understood this well and were enraged to see the lords arguing in parliament for legally sanctioned pecuniary compensation, while simultaneously compensating themselves generously and illegally with forest- and pasture-land in the villages. One of the arguments against pecuniary compensation advanced by the peasants of

---

[216] *Klasova borotba*, 383, 536 note 70. The proposal of March 1848 repeated the main thrust of a petition of the Galician Estates of 1845: "...A study should be made to determine what methods [of commutation and redemption] are most suitable, and what arrangements are needed for a proper consolidation of the land of both lord and peasant; and for peasant land alone, determination of what is needed for the most expeditious promotion of the division of the commons and the abolition of the harmful servitudes." Cited in Blum, *Noble Landowners*, 220. In fact, the idea of exchanging servitudes for corvée labour went back to the late eighteenth century. Rosdolsky, *Die grosse Steuer- und Agrarreform*, 149. Mises, *Entwicklung*, 68.

[217] *Klasova borotba*, 391.

[218] See, for example, TsDIAL, 146/64/39; 146/64/40, pp. 3–3v; 146/64/41, p. 4; 146/64/198, p. 13v.

[219] *Klasova borotba*, 393–4.

[220] *Ibid.*, 457–8.

Zagórze, Sanok district, was that the landlords "are already giving themselves compensation for the abolished corvée, because they don't want to give us so much as a stick from the forest, but tell us we have to pay."[221] Peasants from Stryi circle said that the landlords "would like to take all the communal fields, pastures and forests [for the abolition of feudal rents]; they don't remember that they [already] received compensation for serfdom.... [If this continues,] the peasants will come to ruin and the abolition of serfdom will be paid for with the blood of poor peasants."[222]

The political representatives of the peasantry took a firm stand on the issue of servitudes. The Galician peasant deputies demanded that the rights of the communes to forests and pastures remain intact.[223] The Supreme Ruthenian Council was inundated with petitions from villages asking it to protect their ownership of and access to forests and pastures.[224] Local Ruthenian Councils also asked the Supreme Council in Lviv to take an active role in the defence of servitudes and communal land ownership.[225] On several occasions, the Supreme Ruthenian Council appealed to the imperial ministries on the servitudes issue.[226] Its strongest statement was in a petition to the ministry of justice, submitted 17 July 1849 (N.S.). The Council pointed out that it had appealed many times to the higher authorities to look into the grievances of the peasantry concerning servitudes and the ownership of communal land. These appeals, however, were completely ignored, and this, the Council argued, "impedes any positive influence on the peasantry." The peasantry had stopped heeding the Council's pleas for patience and legality; it was taking wood and pastures without sanction. In this, said the Council, the peasantry was only following the example of the landlords, who were also taking the law into their own hands by "continuing to take away rustical land and to deprive the peasants of their servitude rights.... " The Council noted with regret that the circle authorities were quick to send in soldiers when the peasants broke the law, but procrastinated when it came to investigating the crimes of landlords. The Council called on the ministry to enforce the law equally for lords and peasants and to establish unbiased commissions to settle the individual servitude disputes.[227]

Servitude commissions for all of Austria were established in accordance with the imperial patent of 5 July 1853. They were divided into local commissions, which carried out the preparatory work of gathering facts and making initial recommendations, and crownland commissions, which made

---

[221] *Ibid.*, 464–5.

[222] *Ibid.*, 521–2.

[223] *Ibid.*, 427–9.

[224] *Ibid.*, 455–8, 465–7, 469–71, 475, 477–80, 487, 498, 501, 515–19, 521–2.

[225] *Ibid.*, 393–4, 434.

[226] See, for example, its letter to the ministry of the interior, 28 October 1848, in *ibid.*, 451–2.

[227] *Ibid.*, 492–8.

decisions that could only be appealed to the ministry of the interior.[228] The crownland servitudes commission for Galicia was officially activated on 26 November 1855 (N.S.)[229] and remained in existence until 24 March 1895 (N.S.), when servitude issues were transferred to the courts and political authorities.

The patent of 5 July 1853 established three methods for settling servitude disputes: 1) the landlord could buy the servitudes from the commune or individual peasants; 2) he could compensate them for the lost rights by giving them an "equivalent," i.e., some forest- or pasture-land; or 3) he could allow the servitude rights, as regulated by the commission, to remain in existence. It was usually most convenient for the landlord to purchase the peasants' servitudes. He could pay in promissory notes with a nominal interest of 5 per cent; in circulation, however, the notes were discounted. The commission estimated the monetary worth of servitudes not on the basis of prices then current, but on the basis of the much lower prices of 1836–45. Thus a cartful (U *pidvoda*) of wood was valued at 8.5 kreuzer for redemption purposes, while a peasant might have to pay as much as 2 or 3 gulden for that same quantity of wood after emancipation.[230]

By the end of 1893 the Galician servitudes commission prided itself on having settled 30,571 disputes and having awarded the peasants of Galicia over 1.2 million gulden and 278,374 *Joch* of land as compensation for the loss of servitudes. These awards may seem to be high. Not, however, if they are understood in context. The several million peasants of Galicia received for the abolition of servitudes about forty times less in money than the several thousand landlords received for the abolition of serfdom. The peasants received in land less forest and pasture than the amount of rustical, primarily arable, land taken from them by the landlords just between 1789 and 1820. What could 1.2 million gulden mean to a peasantry that had spent 15 million gulden on lawyers, scribes, court fees, fines and other expenses directly related to the servitudes struggle? And what could 278,374 *Joch* mean to a peasantry that lost over 3.6 million *Joch* of forest and pasture in the course of that struggle?[231] These numbers mean that the peasants were to spend the next few decades after the abolition of serfdom in a fruitless and frustrating struggle to regain their rights to forests and pastures.[232]

A Case in Point: The Events in Dobrotvir

Dobrotvir (today Staryi Dobrotvir) was a small town in Kaminka Strumylova district. In 1880 it had a total population of 2,887, largely

---

[228] Kravets, *Selianstvo*, 96.

[229] TsDIAL, 146/64/1, pp. 9, 10v.

[230] Kravets, *Selianstvo*, 96.

[231] Figures not derived from those already mentioned in this chapter are taken from *ibid.*, 102.

[232] Here is how Norman Davies summarizes the servitudes struggle: "Unfortunately, *in the haste of the moment*, the landlords' title to woods and meadows was upheld. . . . " *God's Playground*, 2:187. Emphasis added.

Ukrainian (2,163 Greek Catholics, 2,231 Ukrainian-speakers) with Jewish and Polish minorities of about equal size (379 Jews, 333 Roman Catholics, 643 Polish-speakers) and a very small German colony (13 German-speakers, 12 Protestants). In the town proper lived 1,877 inhabitants and the rest lived in villages attached to the town: Dolyna (479), Rohale (376) and Rokyty (155).[233] Part of the town had retained its own communal pasture.[234] Another part, however, together with the small villages, had lost its communal land by 1848, in spite of petitions to the government protesting the appropriation. (References to Dobrotvir in the remainder of this section concern only that part which had lost its communal land.)

The servitudes commission came to Dobrotvir in the mid-1850s and gathered testimony and documentation to establish what rights the commune enjoyed by custom. It decided that the forest was not communal as the peasants held, but manorial, and that the peasants had only servitude rights to cut wood and graze cattle in the forest. It estimated the needs of the peasants and recommended that the manor cede the commune 77 *Joch* 698 square *Klafter* of forest as an equivalent for the abolished servitude rights. The peasants still thought the entire forest was rightfully theirs, especially since many had built their homes in the forest. They fought the commission's recommendation through their plenipotentiaries and brought their case before every court of appeal. However, the viceroy's decisions of 5 October 1867 and 10 March 1870, as well as the Austrian ministry of the interior's decisions of 24 January 1870 and 2 November 1871 (all dates in this section N.S.), confirmed the commission's recommendation, and the commune was legally bound to accept the equivalent and refrain from grazing livestock or cutting wood in the rest of the forest.

On 5 January 1872 the viceroy's office ordered the district authorities to send surveyors to measure and mark off the equivalent. They finished their

---

[233] *Spec. Orts-Rep. 1880*, 177.

[234] This account is based on fragmentary documentation from 1872–3 preserved among the records of the supreme state prosecutor's office in Lviv: a report of the Zolochiv prosecutor Julian Garbowski to the supreme state prosecutor's office in Lviv, 1 July 1872 (TsDIAL, 156/1/62, pp. 2–3v); a copy of a report of Zolochiv judge Modest Piasecki to the Zolochiv circuit court, 22 July 1872 (TsDIAL, 156/1/62, pp. 5–10v); an inquiry from the Zolochiv prosecutor's office to the supreme state prosecutor's office in Lviv, 14 September 1872 (TsDIAL, 156/1/62, pp. 12–12v); a report of the Lviv prosecutor Johann Reiner to the supreme state prosecutor's office in Lviv, 10 October 1872 (TsDIAL, 156/1/62, pp. 13–20); an appeal of the Galician viceroy Agenor Gołuchowski to the supreme state prosecutor's office in Lviv, 25 January 1873 (TsDIAL, 156/1/59, pp. 2–3); and two reports of the Zolochiv prosecutor Julian Garbowski to the supreme state prosecutor's office in Lviv, 7 February 1873 (TsDIAL, 156/1/59, pp. 6–9v) and 18 September 1873 (TsDIAL, 156/1/59, p. 16). The information in these documents is often repetitive and sometimes contradictory. It is unfortunate that I did not have access to the relevant papers of the Zolochiv prosecutor's office, which may not have been preserved, and to the documents of the servitude commission concerning Dobrotvir, which should be preserved in TsDIAL, fond 146, opys 64, 64a or 64b. To identify government officials I have used *Szem. król. Gal. 1873*.

work five months later, on 8 June. Boundary markers were erected and ditches dug to separate the equivalent from the rest of the forest. In the presence of witnesses, the equivalent was legally transferred to the commune, and the district commissioner, Erazm Zaremba, informed the commune that as of this day its rights to wood and pasture in the manorial forest had expired.

Although the officials had spoken their final word, the peasants of Dobrotvir would not reconcile themselves to the loss of their forest. They held secret meetings about what to do. Some proposed destroying the boundary markers and filling in the ditches separating the little equivalent from the mass of the forest. In the end they decided to appeal the case once more and registered a provisional grievance[235] with the district court in Kaminka Strumylova.

A number of peasants, probably delegated by the commune, continued to graze their cattle in the forest. They knew they were risking the confiscation of their cattle and perhaps fines and imprisonment, but they also knew from the proceedings and questions of the servitudes commission in the previous two decades that without the continuous exercise of customary rights the rights would be considered expired. The peasants broke the ban on grazing cautiously. They first took their cattle onto the equivalent and then led them where the boundary ditches had not yet been completed. They crossed the boundary here and let their cattle graze in the area outside the equivalent. The manor sent a complaint to the district authorities, who immediately dispatched the district adjunct Wiktor Hałajkiewicz. On 14 June Hałajkiewicz arrested several dozen peasants, fined them and warned the commune never again to trespass outside the equivalent. The offending peasants promised obedience, as did several other members of the commune.

Around this same time several peasants from Dobrotvir travelled to the district capital, Kaminka Strumylova, and spent Sunday in the tavern.[236] Here the peasants from Dobrotvir listened to the public reading of a letter that understandably electrified them. The letter was from Fedko Shyshka, a soldier in the imperial guard in Vienna, to his brother in the small village of Hrushka, located in Zhovkva district, but very close to Kaminka Strumylova. Shyshka said that numerous peasant deputations were travelling daily to see the emperor and that the emperor was responding favourably to their petitions. Shyshka urged his brother to inform the peasant communes of Hrushka and vicinity to send delegations to the emperor immediately if they had any grievances against the manor. The grievances had to be submitted to the emperor before the end of June, when new laws were otherwise supposed to abolish all traditional communal rights. Shyshka wrote that the delegations should contact him upon arrival in Vienna and he would counsel them.

---

[235] P *skarga prowizorjalna*, G *Provisialklage*.

[236] Until the coming of the national movement the tavern was a strategic centre for peasant resistance (*Klasova borotba*, 101–4, 237, 351–2, 378–9) and one of the few institutions that allowed peasants from different villages to exchange information about issues of concern to them as a class.

When the Dobrotvir peasants returned home and told the rest of the villagers what they had heard in the tavern, two peasants were immediately sent to Hrushka to find the letter and bring back the original or a copy. The peasants found the letter in nearby Batiatychi, in the possession of a cantor. They copied the letter and took it home to Dobrotvir, where a special meeting of the village council was called to discuss it. The main spokesmen at the meeting were Petro Maik, who was a plenipotentiary for the commune in servitude affairs, and Datsko Khymka,[237] a former soldier who had served in Vienna. Maik may at one point have signed his name to an agreement to accept the equivalent and seems to have opposed sending a delegate to the emperor. Khymka represented the view of the overwhelming majority of Dobrotvir peasants, who gave the letter full credence and hoped that now they would have their rights to ownership of the forest restored. He argued that the commune could not give up its rights, but should send him to bring its case before the emperor. He had contacts in Vienna from his years in the service and these would help him obtain an audience with his majesty.

Khymka convinced the villagers to send him to the imperial capital. He collected 100 gulden for the journey and took with him two documents to support the commune's claims: a very old document stating that the forest was the property of the commune and a favourable decision by the circle authorities in 1844. Almost as soon as he arrived in Vienna he was able to send a telegram to the mayor of Dobrotvir, Ivan Batiuk, saying that he was scheduled for an audience with the emperor on 20 June. The telegram raised the expectations of the commune to new heights. Franz Joseph did receive Khymka, as scheduled, on 20 June; he gave him a warm reception and promised him that within two weeks he would have an answer to his petition. Following the interview, Khymka returned to Dobrotvir, arriving on 23 June.

The peasants of Dobrotvir plied their representative with questions about his reception by the emperor. Everything Khymka said seemed to confirm the hopes that the letter had awakened. No sooner had he arrived in Vienna than the emperor received him. From the cordial reception he was accorded it was clear that the emperor favoured their obviously just cause. From the speedy settlement that the emperor promised it was certain that justice would soon be theirs. The peasants wanted to renew pasturing their cattle in the forest immediately. Khymka cautioned them against it, since the emperor had not actually promised to decide the dispute in their favour. Nonetheless, on that same day, 23 June, the peasants Dmytro Bratash, Mykhailo Koshakivsky and Oleksa Khymka drove their cattle out of the equivalent and onto the territory of the legally manorial forest. Following their example, all the inhabitants of Dobrotvir drove their cattle into the forest. They also began chopping wood. Apparently Datsko Khymka was soon won over to the majority view, because the events of the next two weeks show that someone with military experience was directing the other peasants; this is also confirmed by subsequent events.

---

[237] The author is descended from the Khymkas (Himkas) of Dobrotvir.

For the next few days the peasants of Dobrotvir pastured their cattle in the forest. There was nothing that the manorial forest wardens dared do to prevent this, because the herders were accompanied by groups of peasants armed with cudgels. The wardens could not confiscate the trespassing cattle; they could not even approach them without being chased off by peasants swinging cudgels and shouting threats. All they could do was report the trespassing to Felix Sosnicki, the administrator of the estate, who in turn reported it to the district authorities.

To restore order in Dobrotvir, the district authorities once again sent adjunct Hałajkiewicz to the town, this time in the company of four gendarmes. On 26 June, on the way to Dobrotvir, Hałajkiewicz and the gendarmes twice came upon bands of cudgel-bearing peasants grazing their cattle in the forest. At Hałajkiewicz's command, the peasants immediately chased their cattle onto the equivalent.

Hałajkiewicz then called a meeting of the town council in the communal chancery. He ordered the commune to desist from its illegal actions once and for all. But the council said that it could not enforce this in the commune. Several peasants explained that their houses were located within the boundaries of the forest and that accepting the equivalent would force them to abandon their homes. Others said that their rights to the forest were traditional and inviolable; this was where their cattle had grazed in the past, would graze in the future and were grazing at this very moment.

This last remark spurred Hałajkiewicz to return to the forest. He took with him the four gendarmes; the forest wardens, whom he deputized; Sosnicki; and Batiuk, the mayor. They came upon a clearing in the forest where peasants were watching over several hundred head of cattle. When Hałajkiewicz ordered them to disperse, they only drove their cattle more tightly together and deeper into the forest. Sosnicki and Hałajkiewicz then instructed the forest wardens to begin confiscating the trespassing cattle. As the wardens approached, the herders began yelling "*Gvalt!*" and hundreds, perhaps a thousand, peasants sprang from concealment—men, women and children, most of them armed with cudgels. The mayor was the first to take to his heels. Hałajkiewicz and the others also withdrew, while the peasants ridiculed and insulted them.

In the days following, the peasants not only continued to have the run of the forest, but liberated cattle that the manor had confiscated earlier. They also attacked the forest wardens, who had to go into hiding. The district captain himself, Mateusz Mauthner, came to Dobrotvir to restore order, but the peasants boycotted the public meeting he called.

The authorities had no choice but to send in the military, which was very busy that year putting down similar outbreaks of unrest. A squadron of cavalry arrived in Dobrotvir at the beginning of July. Mauthner himself joined the squadron commander on a patrol of the forest. They came upon the peasants, this time gathered in greater number than ever before and once again armed with their cudgels. The peasants let out a fearsome cry and brandished their weapons. Before the squadron could catch up with them, they drove their cattle onto ground so marshy that the horses could not follow them. They also formed tight phalanxes. The squadron commander informed the head of the district that the only way to dislodge the peasants would be to shoot at them with rifles, in which case many would be killed. Mauthner refrained from implementing so drastic a measure and appealed to Lviv to send reinforcements.

On 5 July a company of infantry arrived in Dobrotvir. Three days later Mauthner, accompanied by the entire small army he had sent for, once again patrolled the forest. He found peasant cattle there, but this time only under the protection of herders. The forest wardens confiscated the cattle and the herders fled, without shouting for help from other peasants. The cattle were paraded through the streets of Dobrotvir, but the peasants offered no resistance.

In the meantime, an investigative commission had been formed to look into the events in Dobrotvir. It was headed by Modest Piasecki from the circuit court in Zolochiv. Normally the case would have gone to the investigative court in Busk, but, considering the gravity of the case and that the Busk court had a backlog of over a hundred pending investigations, the case was turned over to the Zolochiv prosecutor's office. Piasecki arrived in Dobrotvir on the same day that Mauthner finally pacified the rebels, i.e., 8 July. Within his first few days in the town, Piasecki ordered a number of arrests. He ordered the arrest of Datsko Khymka, but was told that Khymka had gone off again to Vienna to see the emperor. Piasecki found his task very difficult. He had so many charges he wanted to bring against the peasants that he had difficulty sorting them all out and following any one of them through. It also seemed to him that the peasants' resistance had been so carefully planned that none of the forest wardens or officials had approached close enough to identify individual peasants engaged in illegal actions (more likely, the wardens feared for their life and property and pretended not to have recognized anyone). Moreover, the peasants refused to talk. Before Piasecki could even finish asking a question, he would be told: "I know nothing." And when peasants did talk, they gave him only confusing and contradictory information. Although Dobrotvir was comparatively quiet during the second week of July, the peasant commune had not formally renounced its resistance and individuals were still venturing into the forest and assaulting the wardens.

In mid-July the viceroy's office communicated to the commune that its petition had been answered by the emperor in the negative. This was a crushing disappointment for the peasants, who believed that all they had to do was hold out a little longer and the just emperor would give them back their forest. On 16 July the town council held a meeting to decide whether or not to abandon the struggle, accept the equivalent and request that the soldiers be removed from Dobrotvir.

As the council debated in the chancery, throngs of peasants gathered outside to listen to the proceedings. The pastor, Iosyf Kalechynsky, spoke to the council for two hours, pleading for obedience to the law and an end to resistance. The councilmen were inclined to agree with him. However, not all the peasants approved. Stefan Prots, who was reportedly quite tipsy at the time, circulated among all the other peasants present and expressed his disagreement with the priest. He also denounced the council, particularly those councilmen who had served as plenipotentiaries at the time that the servitude commission had made its original unfavourable decision. He accused Petro Maik, councilman and plenipotentiary, of having sold the commune's rights. Although, as later events would bear out, Prots's views were widely shared in the commune, a majority of the council voted to abandon resistance and to request that the military forces be removed from the town. On 21 July the commune of Dobrotvir formally submitted this request to the district officials. The district passed the request on to the viceroy's office, which had reserved to itself the right to terminate the military presence in Dobrotvir. By the second half of July, therefore, it seemed that the peasants of Dobrotvir had been subdued.

For the rest of the summer the government carried on its investigation into the incident. Judge Piasecki arrested Stefan Prots and Datsko Khymka as the main instigators of the trouble. Khymka, it turned out, had not gone to Vienna at all, but had been hiding in the store-house (U and P *komora*) of Panko Maik. He was discovered and arrested on the night of 16 July, probably when someone went to inform him how the council meeting had turned out. Piasecki also had Panko Maik arrested, for aiding the fugitive Khymka, and Mykola Ladyshevsky, for "public violence." On 6 August the Zolochiv court decided to refer the case to the Lviv criminal court and on 3 September the Lviv prosecutor, Johann Reiner, began studying it. He came to the conclusion that there was insufficient evidence to convict any of the accused individuals. On 26 October the Lviv criminal court dismissed the case and, after more than three months in prison, Datsko Khymka and the others were released.

Immediately upon Khymka's return to Dobrotvir, the commune elected him its plenipotentiary in servitude matters. He decided that an educated man, a lawyer, was needed to defend the commune's rights. He therefore hired a certain Johann Schön, who introduced himself as a lawyer. In reality, Schön was no lawyer; he had been a secretary in the district government until he was fired and thereafter supported himself as a corner-scribe, one, it seems, of the more unscrupulous variety. He sold his services dearly to the peasants of Dobrotvir, taking 50 gulden in cash and 450 gulden in a promissory note from Khymka. When the district authorities got wind of what Schön was charging and of how he had misrepresented himself as a lawyer, they had him arrested for fraud. All this occurred within the first week of Khymka's release from prison.

Before Schön could be prosecuted, however, a cholera epidemic broke out in Busk, where he was incarcerated. The Busk court decided to release him, lest he fall victim to the epidemic, and to suspend proceedings against him. The supreme state prosecutor's office in Lviv ordered the Busk court to renew its investigation and prosecution on 31 December, but by then Schön was already at liberty. Early in January of 1873 he made his way to Dobrotvir. It was probably not difficult for Schön to regain the confidence of Khymka and the commune. If he had said that the district authorities were only persecuting him for helping the peasants of Dobrotvir to regain their rights (which may, in fact, have been the case), the peasants should have found this explanation entirely plausible. With the return of this educated ally, the peasants of Dobrotvir were ready to renew their struggle.

Their first step was to take control of the local government. On 10 January 1873 the town council met in the chancery to review the communal accounts for 1872 and to establish the budget for 1873. The mayor, Ivan Batiuk, let it be known that the meeting was public and that all were invited to come and be convinced of the council's good management. The opposition to the council, led by Datsko Khymka, Pavlo Mudryk and others, turned up in force at the meeting. They behaved politely until the expenditures for 1872 were read aloud. Then Mudryk began to shout that the council did not look out for the welfare of the commune and that its budget consisted of superfluous and fictitious expenditures. "You vagabonds!" he shouted at the councilmen, "why have you come here?" (P *Wy wakabungy, pocości tu przyszli*). When one council member tried to respond to him, Mudryk waved his clenched fist at him and said: "I'll punch your face if you say a word" (P *Dam ci wpysk, jak będziesz co gadał*).

After this exchange, Khymka took the floor. He said that the council was doing no good for the commune. As plenipotentiary in servitude matters, he objected that the council stood by quietly while the manor felled wood on land that belonged to commune members. He demanded that the manor be prevented from cutting any more wood. Mayor Batiuk replied that the question of servitudes had already been settled definitively. But Khymka said that the council was deliberately procrastinating on the issue and that the commune had to elect a new council, mayor and scribe. After Khymka proposed that the assistant teacher[238] Petro Kostruba be appointed scribe, the incumbent scribe, Andrei Nakryiko, resigned. Then one by one the councilmen slipped out of the chancery in order to avoid additional accusations, and after two hours had passed only the opposition, consisting of about sixty peasants, was left.

The opposition transferred its meeting to Mudryk's house, where Johann Schön was waiting. After the peasants resolved to depose the current government and hold new elections, they sent for mayor Batiuk. He was informed that now the office of the communal government would be here, where Mudryk and the new scribe, Kostruba, lived. Khymka requested that Batiuk give the government's papers to Kostruba. Batiuk obeyed. He was later to justify himself before the authorities by saying that, although Khymka's demand was phrased in the form of a request, he was afraid to oppose it; also, since Nakryiko had resigned as scribe and he himself was illiterate, it made sense to give the papers to Kostruba.

---

[238] P *pomocnik nauczycielski*, G *Lehramtsgehülfe*.

This coup in the local government might have escaped the notice of the higher authorities had not Rudolf Kurzweil arrived in Dobrotvir on 14 January. Kurzweil was a retired manorial steward sent from Kaminka Strumylova to confiscate property from the peasants of Dobrotvir as payment for overdue taxes. Kurzweil needed some information from the town government and sought out Batiuk and Nakryiko. Batiuk told him that he could give him no information, since he did not have the council's papers. But Nakryiko advised Batiuk to go to Kostruba and get what the tax-collector needed. When Batiuk entered Mudryk's house to speak with Kostruba, he found about twenty peasants there as well as Schön. Kostruba refused to return the council papers and Batiuk went back to the chancery, where Nakryiko and Kurzweil were waiting for him. However, all who had been assembled at Mudryk's house followed Batiuk back to the chancery. Batiuk locked the chancery door to keep the rebels out. They demanded the key, saying that Schön had now been appointed scribe and needed access to the chancery; moreover, they wanted to elect a new council in the chancery. Batiuk refused to give them the key.

Khymka, Mudryk, Schön and the others then went to the tavern, where Schön made a speech. He stated that he was a certified Austrian lawyer and that he would win back Dobrotvir's rights to the forest. He accused both Batiuk and Nakryiko of being in league with the manor and of deceiving the commune. He insulted Kurzweil and declared that he had no business being in Dobrotvir. The speech won the approval of all who were gathered in the tavern, and they appointed him scribe by acclamation.

On the next day Batiuk travelled to Kaminka Strumylova and reported all that had transpired to the district authorities. The latter sent commissioner Erazm Zaremba to restore the legally elected town council to authority. Kostruba handed over the council's papers without resistance. The district authorities also informed viceroy Agenor Gołuchowski of the latest events in Dobrotvir. Gołuchowski recommended the matter to the attention of the supreme state prosecutor's office in Lviv, "because this is the sort of case that demands swift and energetic investigation as well as exemplary punishment of the guilty, especially since the commune in Dobrotvir has already several times given proof of its obstreperous and turbulent disposition."

In the end only two of the rebels, Mudryk and Schön, faced trial. The prosecutor asked that Schön be sentenced to six years of severe incarceration (G schwerer Kerker) and Mudryk to one month of imprisonment. But the court only sentenced them, on 28 August 1873, to four months of severe incarceration and eight days of imprisonment respectively.

Here the documentation on which this account has been based stops.

The Servitudes Struggle and Its Lessons

The conflict in Dobrotvir was not untypical of Eastern Galicia in the second half of the nineteenth century. About three thousand communes in Eastern Galicia—more than three-quarters of the total—were involved in legal disputes with the manor over servitudes.[239] Most of these conflicts were fought out before the servitude commissions and courts without recourse to the sort of mass, illegal action that broke out in Dobrotvir. Yet between 1850 and 1900 illegal servitude actions encompassed 984 villages and towns in the Ukrainian-inhabited portions of Galicia and Bukovyna (see Table 1). Eastern Galicia alone seems to have accounted for almost 90 per cent of these localities (c. 880).[240] Allowing for the repetition of illegal servitude actions in the same locality in different years (est. 10 per cent) and adding to the number of village communes in Eastern Galicia the number of small towns,[241] we can conservatively estimate that one in five communes in Eastern Galicia resorted to illegal mass action to defend its forest and pasture rights.[242]

The illegal servitude actions have been studied extensively by the Soviet historian M.M. Kravets. He counted how many such actions occurred in Eastern Galicia and Northern Bukovyna, and how many localities took part in these actions, in every year from 1850 to 1900. The results of Kravets's count are reproduced in Table 1. The table can be viewed as a barometer of the intensity of the peasants' involvement in the servitudes struggle.

The table shows that the servitudes issue was most heatedly contested in the early 1850s and continued to be important until about 1870; thereafter it declined in intensity. The illegal action in Dobrotvir in 1872 came at the end of a large wave of peasant unrest.

The greatest number of illegal actions occurred in 1850–2, in the aftermath of the revolution of 1848–9, as a direct continuation of the peasantry's seizure of manorial lands in the spring and summer of 1849; these actions also occurred before the imperial patent of 5 July 1853 and before the activity of the servitude commissions provided the peasants with legal channels for the pursuit of their rights to forests and pastures. The relative decline of illegal servitude actions in the period 1853–9 is directly attributable to the peasantry's faith in the imperial patent and the conflict's change of venue to the legally established servitude commissions.[243]

Beginning in 1860, however, there was a striking resurgence of illegal actions in the Galician countryside, which was to remain turbulent throughout the decade. Three factors account for the intensity of the servitudes

---

[239] Kravets, "Dzherela," 63. There were 3,734 village communes in Eastern Galicia in 1902 and 1,906 Greek Catholic parishes in all of Galicia in 1900. Bujak, *Galicja*, 1:48, 139.

[240] According to Kravets, "Servitutne pytannia," 66–72, illegal servitude actions took place in 109 villages and towns in Eastern Galicia in 1867–9; according to Table 1, in both Galicia and Bukovyna during the same years such actions broke out in 122 localities.

[241] Eighty-three in 1910. Rosenfeld, *Die polnische Judenfrage*, 79.

[242] The total number of communes is calculated on the basis of official statistics from 1900–10. The number of communes was smaller in 1850–70, when the majority of illegal servitude actions took place. There were not 3,500 village communes in the first half of the nineteenth century. *Istoriia selianstva URSR*, 1:335. The total number of illegal servitude actions, which is based on what one scholar could discover from surviving historical documentation, understates the extent of illegal resistance.

[243] Kravets, *Selianstvo*, 153.

TABLE 1 Illegal Servitude Actions in Eastern Galicia and Northern Bukovyna, 1850–1900

	Number			Number	
Year	Of Actions	Of Towns and Villages Involved	Year	Of Actions	Of Towns and Villages Involved
1850	88	103	1876	6	6
1851	46	51	1877	8	8
1852	46	56	1878	8	8
1853	32	39	1879	7	7
1854	15	24	1880	7	7
1855	24	30	1881	5	5
1856	17	21	1882	5	5
1857	25	31	1883	4	4
1858	36	38	1884	0	0
1859	27	29	1885	4	4
1860	42	54	1886	4	4
1861	22	26	1887	7	7
1862	27	27	1888	2	2
1863	38	41	1889	1	1
1864	46	51	1890	4	4
1865	35	37	1891	3	3
1866	26	27	1892	3	3
1867	41	45	1893	4	4
1868	28	33	1894	3	3
1869	36	44	1895	2	2
1870	17	19	1896	5	5
1871	15	16	1897	2	2
1872	16	16	1898	2	2
1873	9	9	1899	3	3
1874	8	8	1900	3	3
1875	7	7	Total:	871	984

SOURCE: Kravets, *Selianstvo*, 151 table 20 (based on the materials of LODA and Chernivetskyi oblasnyi derzhavnyi arkhiv and the press).

struggle in the 1860s. Firstly, by 1859 the servitude commissions had proposed settlements for most of the disputes and the peasantry recognized that it was being cheated, absolutely legally, of its cherished traditional rights. Secondly, the peasants were spurred to illegal action by the constitutional changes in Austria. Just as under serfdom the peasantry interpreted various patents limiting corvée labour to mean that corvée labour was being greatly curtailed or even abolished, so for the first decades after emancipation it interpreted laws extending political freedom to mean that its rights to the forests and pastures were being restored. The particular intensity of the conflict in the years of the two constitutions, 1860 and 1867, bears this out. Thirdly, in the 1860s, in connection with the abolition of serfdom in the Russian empire and the defeat of the Polish insurrection of 1863, many peasants abandoned their traditional naive loyalty to the Austrian emperor and put an equally, in fact even more, naive hope in the Russian tsar.[244]

In Dobrotvir traditional naive monarchism had remained intact into the early 1870s and even served as the ideological justification for the peasants' struggle. In many other villages, however, the unjust settlements of the servitude conflicts destroyed the peasants' faith in the justice of their emperor. Before the national movement took hold of the Galician countryside, the ideological vacuum created by the collapse of traditional naive monarchism was filled by a radical variant of this ideology that displaced all the peasants' hopes to a foreign monarch, namely the Russian tsar. From contact with the peasants of Russian-ruled Right-Bank Ukraine, Galician peasants learned that the Russian tsar had abolished serfdom in 1861, at the same time that it seemed serfdom was being reintroduced in Galicia through the loss of rights to forests and pastures. Also, the tsar brutally crushed the Polish nobility's insurrection in 1863–4, while the Austrian emperor was sanctioning the Polish nobility's plunder of communal land in Galicia. Moreover, in reaction to the Polish rebellion the tsar in 1864 stipulated terms of emancipation for Right-Bank Ukraine that were punitive to the local Polish nobility and seemed more favourable to the Ukrainian peasantry there than the terms of emancipation in Austrian Galicia. The importance to Ukrainian peasants in Austria of the Right-Bank agrarian reform of 1864 is corroborated by the large number of illegal servitude actions in that year: 46, a number that had not been surpassed since 1850 or equalled since 1852 and would never be achieved again.

Expressions of naive tsarism appeared almost throughout Eastern Galicia in the period. For example, in 1863 in Vyzhnie Synevidsko (Verkhnie Syniovydne), Stryi circle, peasants, armed with pikes and stones, attacked gendarmes who had confiscated their cattle for grazing in the forest. One of the peasants declared to a gendarme: "What are you doing and what do you want? You side with the lords, so you are thieves just as they are. And your emperor is a thief and a highwayman. If only the Russians[245] would come,

---

[244] This phenomenon is discussed in detail in Himka, "Hope in the Tsar," 125–38. See also Tarnavsky, *Spohady*, 52–4. Naive tsarism was by no means limited to the Ukrainian-inhabited regions of Austria. Also in Polish Western Galicia, during the mass peasant unrest of 1886, the peasants "praise Russia because Polish peasants are very well off there." "Zavorushenia posered Mazuriv," *Batkivshchyna* 8, no. 16 (23 [11] April 1886): 94.

[245] Kravets has put the passage into modern Ukrainian and uses the word *moskali*. It seems probable to me that the original read *moskal*, in the singular, and referred to the Russian tsar. Kravets may not have been aware of the specific meaning of the word *moskal* or, as would not be unusual in Soviet historiography, he may have wished to mute the naive monarchism as such and emphasize general pro-Russian feeling.

then we would slaughter all [of you][246] to the last man."[247] In May 1867, when the Borshchiv district authorities officially transferred a disputed pasture to the manor, the peasants of Kudryntsi crossed the river Zbruch into Russian territory and appealed to the local people to help them.[248] In April 1873, in Verbytsia, Rava Ruska district, an angry crowd of peasants prevented a surveying commission from measuring the equivalent and marking off its boundaries. One peasant told the commission: "If there is no justice in Vienna, then we will find it in the *Moskal*," that is, the Russian tsar.[249]

Naive tsarism, then, was born in the servitudes conflict in the early 1860s and continued to exist as an ideological component of many of the illegal servitude actions thereafter. It is no coincidence that when Austro-Russian tension flared up over the Balkans in 1887 and naive tsarism took on new life (see *LA* 33),[250] the number of illegal servitude actions also increased temporarily (see Table 1).

The intensity of the servitude struggle declined after the 1860s, especially after 1872. From 1872 on, illegal servitude actions were confined to actions by a single commune, while previous actions had sometimes involved more than one commune. Still, even at a lower intensity, the servitudes struggle lingered on into the twentieth century. Illegal servitude actions did not even stop in 1900, as our table does. In 1901, for example, peasants were shot in Monastyrets, Lisko district, in the course of a dispute with Count Krasicki over ownership of the pasture.[251]

The relative decline of the servitudes struggle after the 1860s coincided, by no means accidentally, with the rise of the national movement in the countryside. The national movement, whose cadres were often veterans of the servitudes struggle,[252] took over the defence of peasant interests and conducted it in a new, political style.

---

[246] Similarly, Kravets may have substituted the "[of you]" (U *vas*) for what was more commonly said in such circumstances: "landlords (or Poles) and Jews" (U *paniv [liakhiv] i zhydiv*).

[247] Kravets, *Selianstvo*, 161.

[248] *Ibid.*, 164.

[249] TsDIAL, 156/1/99, p. 3v.

[250] The abbreviation *LA* stands for Appendix IV, "List of Activists," the number for the specific activist's biography.

[251] Levytsky, *Istoriia politychnoi dumky*, 1:347.

[252] It proved possible to identify in the list of activists five peasants (*LA* 89, 90, 207, 299, 343) and one cantor-scribe (*LA* 328) as former servitude plenipotentiaries. Another peasant had been plenipotentiary before the indemnization commission (*LA* 287) and it is reasonable to assume that he had also served as such before the servitudes commission. One peasant had been fined and imprisoned for his part in an illegal servitudes action (*LA* 111). Other peasants came from families with a history of involvement in the servitudes conflict (*LA* 19, 215; probably 202). Priests had also been engaged in the struggle, since the manors encroached on parochial lands and rights. Three priest-activists had been involved in servitude disputes (*LA* 93, 112, 323) and one was the Lviv archeparchy's commissioner of servitude affairs (*LA* 70). This list is far from complete. I only had access to acts of the servitudes commission referring to less than one-ninth of the localities in which the sample of 368 activists of 1884–5 lived; it was possible to obtain some information from other sources, but unsystematically and very incompletely. I estimate that about a quarter of all the national activists had some direct or family connection to the servitudes

The question naturally arises: where was the national movement in the 1850s and 1860s when the servitudes struggle dominated the East Galician countryside? Why was there not a political and national face to the peasant in struggle for forests and pastures? For the 1850s, the answer is clear. This was a decade of reaction that precluded political representation by anyone in Austria, let alone by the Ukrainian peasants of Galicia. In the 1850s the organized Ukrainian movement, like so many of the creatures of 1848, went into hibernation. The government dissolved the already quite moribund Supreme Ruthenian Council in 1851 and what little national leadership survived was concentrated in the intimidated Greek Catholic metropolitan consistory in Lviv. With the predawn of the constitutional era in 1860 appeared some harbingers of the future. Galician peasants elected peasant deputies to the diet and placed great hopes in their ability to push through a satisfactory solution to the servitudes issue; this accounts for the relative ebb in illegal servitude actions in 1861–2 (see Table 1).[253] Ukrainian parliamentary deputies, who were inundated with peasant petitions much as the Supreme Ruthenian Council had been, presented strong statements on servitudes to the emperor on 11 May and 1 August 1861 (N.S.).[254] The political conjuncture, however, did not allow the Ukrainians in the imperial parliament and Galician diet any real influence.

Characteristic of the position of the Ukrainian movement during the early 1860s are the contents and fate of a brochure written by Iosyf Lozynsky, a priest and one of the early grammarians and national awakeners of Galician Ukraine. In 1862 Lozynsky published a nineteen-page brochure on the servitudes question entitled "Reflections on Property." The work was written in the vernacular in a popular style and was clearly aimed at the peasantry. Lozynsky argued that communal rights to forests and pastures were "natural and eternal" and necessary for the very existence of the peasantry.[255] Some said that the demands of the peasant communes display an appetite for others' property[256] and infection with communism, "but this is a vain and senseless cry, because the communes are not encroaching on someone else's, but claiming their own *property*, to which they had a right and which has passed into the hands of the large landowners illegally."[257] Even if the manors had managed to acquire the legally formulated consent of the peasant

---

[252](continued) struggle as presented in the listing above. If one were also to include all members of communes that had engaged in a servitudes dispute, then the vast majority of peasants in the list of activists could be considered veterans of the servitudes struggle.

[253] Kravets, *Selianstvo*, 159.

[254] "Nove podane nashykh poslov Dumy derzhavnoi z dnia 1. Avhusta s.h.," *Slovo* 1, no. 54 (5 [17] August 1861): 1; no. 55 (9 [21] August 1861): 1; no. 56 (12 [24] August 1861): 1–2; no. 57 (16 [28] August 1861): 1–2; no. 58 (19 [31] August 1861): 1.

[255] Lozynsky, *Hadky*, 7.

[256] See above, 36.

[257] Lozynsky, *Hadky*, 15.

communes to abandon these rights, this consent was obtained under duress and was therefore invalid. Under serfdom, "the peasant became the *slave* of his master, who denied him his natural rights, denied him any property, any right to land, to pasture, to forest, which rights belonged to him by nature and eternally."[258] The servitude commissions awarded such poor compensation for the suspension of rights to forests and pastures that the communes could not be satisfied. Lozynsky recommended that servitude disputes be settled on the basis of how land had been registered in 1789. A comparison of the Josephine land cadastre of 1789 with the Franciscan cadastre of 1820 would show that many forests and pastures registered as communal in the first cadastre appear as demesnal in the second. Since, as he correctly pointed out, this cadastre already reflected the unlawful acquisition of communal land by the manors, it represented a compromise on the part of the peasantry. He concluded his brochure with a plea to the communes "to await the settlement of their cases in patience and peace and without any illegal measures."[259]

Lozynsky's brochure was in the mainstream of the Ukrainian national movement's view on the servitudes issue. It staunchly defended the Ukrainian peasants' rights, but tendered a compromise to the nobility and supported exclusively legal action. The Greek Catholic metropolitan consistory recommended the brochure's distribution to the rural clergy.[260] However, the brochure was suppressed by the viceroy's office as liable to incite the peasantry and was therefore never circulated.[261]

Thus the Ukrainian national movement could not assume leadership of the peasants' struggle over servitudes, since there was insufficient political freedom to permit it to make its ideas known. Censorship was only one of the disadvantages under which the movement laboured at the height of the servitudes struggle. The lack of freedom of association also precluded the emergence of organizations that would mediate between the peasantry and the leadership of the national movement. Without a relatively free press, such as existed in 1848–9 and would exist again after 1867, and without rural organizations, such as the local Ruthenian Councils of the revolutionary years and the reading clubs of the constitutional era, a linkage between the national movement and the class struggle of the peasantry was simply impossible.

In spite of this mutual isolation, the national movement was to gain a great deal from the peasants' bitter experience during the servitudes conflict. The peasants learned important lessons: that their ignorance and illiteracy were severe drawbacks and that they required allies in the educated strata of society. Consider the case in Dobrotvir where, after the failure of petitions and force, the peasants sought their salvation in an educated man, albeit the corner-scribe Johann Schön. Throughout Galicia the peasants saw that the

---

[258] *Ibid.*, 11.

[259] *Ibid.*, 19.

[260] TsDIAL, 146/4/1307, p. 3.

[261] I have used a copy preserved in *ibid.*, 50–9.

literacy of the landlord gave him the upper hand in the courts and commissions. Most communes had no written proof that they owned the forests and pastures. Their submissions to the servitude commissions frequently said: "from time immemorial we remember" or "our fathers and grandfathers told us and our forefathers told them" that the forest or pasture was communal property. They had only oral tradition on which to base their claim. The landlords had documents. These could be receipts from the 1780s—little slips of paper signed with crosses, saying that the undersigned peasants had received wood from the manorial forest. Did those peasants know when they made their marks in order to receive indispensable construction materials that they were signing away the rights of their descendants?[262] When a commune picked plenipotentiaries to defend its rights in the commission, it picked its best members; some of them were even able to read and write. When the landlord picked a plenipotentiary, he chose someone with a good education and experience in the ways of the world, a lawyer if need be or a veteran estate official. The legal contest was hardly equal.

The peasantry, then, left the servitudes struggle with a heightened appreciation of the power of education. When the national movement founded reading clubs in the villages and urged the peasantry to build schools and otherwise educate itself, it struck a responsive chord in those far-sighted peasants who had learned the lessons of the struggle for wood and pasture. It is entirely understandable that precisely in the wake of the most intense period of the servitudes conflict, reading clubs and newspapers heralded the advent of the national movement in the countryside.

In looking back on the servitude disputes, peasants active in the national movement condemned the ignorance that had impeded their struggle. Mykhailo Pikh (*LA* 259), a peasant or cantor turned merchant in Stariava, Mostyska district, surely expressed the view of many other local activists in an item of correspondence sent to *Batkivshchyna* in 1886. Pikh censured the naive tsarism, violence and, above all, ignorance characteristic of the servitudes struggle. When "communes, Ruthenian and Mazurian [i.e., Polish], could not comprehend the loss of their property, they said: 'Things will not be right until the White Tsar comes.' But, dear brothers, such talk is sinful, on the one hand, and foolish, on the other."[263] His own village, Stariava, was once very rich, with about a thousand *Joch* of forest and pasture.

> Today it is poorer than all the surrounding villages. It has neither forest nor pasture, but only many sandy wastelands totalling 182 *Joch*. Whoever reads this will be amazed and will ask: what is the reason for such a change? To this there is only one answer: the main reason, aside from others, is ignorance.... During that time full of grief [i.e., before the abolition of serfdom] the commune of

---

[262] Hence the intense aversion of peasants to signing documents of any sort. See Rosdolsky, *Die grosse Steuer- und Agrarreform*, 127–8, and Adriian, *Agrarnyi protses*, 57–8.

[263] Mykhailo Pikh, "Pysmo z Mostyskoho povitu," *Batkivshchyna* 8, no. 39 (8 October [26 September] 1886): 233.

Stariava lost all its pastures and forests. How? Just listen! During the reign of Emperor Joseph II of blessed memory, on 20 September 1782, a law, i.e., an imperial patent, was issued that put communal forests under the supervision of the landlords so that wood would be cut properly without allowing thoughtless people to destroy the forests. The commune of Stariava, after having used [its rights] for a long time, was forced to sue for its forest. It received the following resolution: the landlord supervised the forest, hence it must be the landlord's forest. They [the peasants of Stariava] sued for forests, pastures and meadows for several decades, but they did not conduct the case intelligently. Forty years ago [c. 1846; 1849?], probably incited by some dishonest corner-scribe, they wanted to take back their property through rebellion and assaulted the manorial servants when the latter tried to chase the commune's cattle from the disputed pasture. The rebellion was reported, and hussars came and beat all without exception. They gave 25, 50 and 90 blows with a cudgel to whomever they could catch—men, women and even children. And many were also put in prison, where some died. The people were so terrified that they never defended anything again. They retreated, with only a heavy sigh, from every piece of land that the manorial servants forbade them. Did not similar things happen in very many villages? And now that it's too late, everyone weeps over the loss.

Let's tell ourselves the straight truth: was not cursed ignorance the cause of the misfortune and poverty of the commune?[264]

The replacement of desperate rebellion with rational political action, the eradication of ignorance through popular education and the formation of an alliance against the Polish landlords with educated conationals in the cities—these ideals of the national movement held a powerful attraction for a peasantry that had run the gauntlet of serfdom and servitudes.

The Memory of Serfdom in the Late Nineteenth Century

As the folk who knew this system and remembered it used to tell of it, no worse punishment could be found for men and women than serfdom was. People were treated worse then than cattle are today. They were beaten both at work and at home for the merest trifle. It is unbelievable how men could thus torture their fellows.
—Jan Słomka, mayor of Dzików in Western Galicia, 1912[265]

---

[264] *Ibid.*, 232–3. Very similar sentiments are expressed in Slomka, *From Serfdom to Self-Government*, 158.

[265] Slomka, *From Serfdom to Self-Government*, 14–15.

In the late nineteenth century when the national movement was penetrating the Galician Ukrainian village, the servitudes issue was more than a memory, since peasants were still contesting their rights to forests and pastures in the courts. Serfdom, however, was merely a memory, but a very powerful one. It continued to be, as a Polish anthropologist has observed, "one of the factors mobilizing the [emancipated] peasant masses in their struggle for social and political emancipation."[266] It was the power of this memory that moved the peasants of Iamnytsia, Stanyslaviv district, to erect a monument in 1905 to their martyred plenipotentiary Ivan Smytsniuk.[267] Numerous other villages erected crosses in commemoration of serfdom's abolition. The crosses stood as a reminder of the past oppression until the Soviet authorities tore many of them down, as religious symbols, after the Second World War.

In the second half of the nineteenth century the Ukrainian national movement initiated the custom of celebrating the abolition of serfdom every year on its anniversary, 3 (15) May. The peasants, dressed in their festive clothes, would gather in the village church. If several villages celebrated together, the peasants from the peripheral villages would march in procession to the designated church. Here they would celebrate a solemn liturgy and a memorial prayer service for Emperor Ferdinand I, who emancipated them. After the service, the peasants would march in procession to the cross commemorating the abolition of serfdom. The cross would be decorated with garlands and ribbons, and the procession would be accompanied by religious songs, the ringing of the church bells and shots from mortars. At the cross another prayer service would be held, to commemorate those who died under serfdom, and water would be blessed. The priest would then speak on the significance of emancipation. This would be followed by more singing and a picnic at the cemetery (*CC* 84, 94).[268]

A particularly revealing account of the commemorative ceremony and the emotions it evoked has been left by a *latynnyk*, i.e., a Ukrainian-speaking peasant of the Latin rite. He had first heard of the existence of the commemoration from his pastor, who denounced it as a "schismatic holy day." But by chance he travelled to the nearby village of Roznoshyntsi, Zbarazh district, on the very day of the celebration. He arrived to the roar of mortars being set off near the church "so that the village was shaking." He

---

[266] Dobrowolski, "Peasant Traditional Culture," 293.

[267] See above, 18. There is a photograph of the monument in *Klasova borotba*, 182; see also p. 533, note 35. In the summer of 1984 I met in Hunter, New York, a gentleman born in Iamnytsia. He spoke of Smytsniuk as part of the living tradition of his village (which he left during the Second World War).

[268] The abbreviation *CC* stands for Appendix II, "Corpus of Correspondence"; the numbers refer to specific items of correspondence. This composite picture of the ritual of commemorating the abolition of serfdom is also based on Tam[oshnii], " . . . vid Rozhnitova," *Batkivshchyr*   no. 23 (6 June [30 (sic) May] 1884): 140, and Vasyl Iakubiv *et al.*, "Pysmo z Brodskoho," *Batkivshcyna* 10, no. 22 (1 June [20 May] 1888): 135.

looked for the weaver he had come to see and found him bustling about a mortar.

I went into the cemetery and asked someone what was going on. I was answered by an old, grey-haired man: "Aren't you a peasant just like us? Didn't the landlords beat you with cudgels and whips as they did us Ruthenians? Didn't you go out every day at dawn for corvée labour as we Ruthenians did? Didn't you spend every Sunday and holy day in the mandator's prison as we Ruthenians did? Didn't your livestock perish beneath the landlord's burden as our Ruthenian livestock did? Didn't your wives spin thread, bleach linen, grind millet, give capons, eggs, fodder, hens and chickens [to the lord] as our Ruthenian wives did? Or maybe they didn't take your children by force to the manor, as if into Egyptian slavery under King Pharaoh, as they did our Ruthenian children? Don't you know what day this is?"

By then I had already guessed myself that on this very day serfdom had been abolished. The words of that old man sent a chill and a fire through my body. And then they once again rang all the bells and set off the mortars, and my body for some reason just shook with joy (CC 94).

2. The Cultural Revolution in the Village: Schools, Newspapers and Reading Clubs

In the late 1860s Austria embarked on a series of reforms with immense repercussions for the Galician peasantry. Among the reforms were the introduction of compulsory education and of relative freedom of the press and association. In Galician conditions, i.e., under the hegemony of the Polish nobility, none of these reforms could be thoroughly implemented. The school system in particular was not as well developed as elsewhere in Austria and the censor's handiwork was much in evidence in the Ukrainian press. Even so, the proliferation of schools, newspapers and voluntary associations in the Galician countryside engendered change significant enough to warrant the use of the term "cultural revolution" in the title of this chapter. We will return to the problem of culture in chapter four. Here we concentrate on those cultural innovations that laid the foundations for the emergence of a rural national movement.

Education and the School System

In 1886, in a front-page editorial of the Ukrainian pedagogical newspaper *Shkolna chasopys*, the educator and journalist Kyrylo Kakhnykevych compared the progress of education in Galicia with the situation in Bohemia, a crownland with about as many inhabitants: " ... Galicia has [proportionately] well nigh the most illiterates in Cisleithania, namely 4,835,283 illiterates among a population of six million (in Bohemia, with a population of 5,560,000, there are only 1,255,000 illiterates); there are 2,939 elementary schools (Bohemia has 16,000); there are 709,000 children of mandatory school age (926,000 in Bohemia), but only 380,000 attending school (890,000 in Bohemia).... "[1] Ten years later, according to Siegfried Fleischer, secretary of the Oesterreichisch-Israelitische Union, the situation

---

[1] [Kyrylo Kakhnykevych,] "Oplata shkilna i materialne stanovyshche uchyteliv narodnykh," *Shkolna chasopys* 7, no. 13–14 (8 [20] August 1886): 97. The figures were collected by Natal Vakhnianyn in an effort to have the Lviv city council petition the Austrian ministry of education to take measures to alleviate the situation.

was still scandalous: "An official statement of the Galician crownland school council shows that in 1896 there were four million illiterates in Galicia, three thousand communes without any school, two thousand communes that had to close down classes because of a lack of teachers and a thousand teachers without qualification."[2]

Galicia's proportion of illiterates was only exceeded by the crownlands of Bukovyna and Dalmatia. In Galicia in 1880 only 17.3 per cent of the men and 10.3 per cent of the women could read and write (the corresponding all-Austrian percentages were 61.9 and 55.13). Another 8.5 per cent of the men and 9.8 per cent of the women in Galicia could read but not write, leaving 74.2 per cent male and 79.9 per cent female illiteracy (in all of Austria, 32.6 and 36.1 per cent respectively).[3] In 1890 64.9 per cent of Galicia's population was illiterate, as was 75.5 per cent of Bukovyna's. Illiteracy was concentrated in the Ukrainian portions of the crownlands. Over 90 per cent illiteracy could be found in 34 districts of Eastern Galicia and in the Ukrainian-inhabited districts of northern Bukovyna (excluding the city of Chernivtsi).[4] In 1900, 63.8 per cent of Galicia's population was still illiterate and in 1910—58.7 per cent (41 per cent if children under nine years of age are excluded).[5]

Literacy varied from village to village. Some villages boasted nearly total literacy: "Our people [in Utishkiv, Zolochiv district] are already quite enlightened; starting from a forty-year-old peasant and ending with seven-year-old boys, all are literate. It pleases one's soul to enter our church and see how everyone, small and big, even women and girls, pray from books" (*CC* 216). "In our village [Zhulychi, Zolochiv district] all the youth, girls as well as boys, and even a majority of the older people are able to read and write..." (*CC* 224). In other villages there was barely any literacy. In Novosilka Iazlovetska, Buchach district, according to *CC* 48, there were only about ten literate people (the commune had a population of 1,055 in 1880).[6] As the correspondence cited above implies and the statistics on literacy in 1880 confirm, males tended to be more literate than females. Literacy was also, as the correspondence suggests, more prevalent among the youth than among older peasants. This is confirmed by an item of correspondence from 1882 concerning Dobrivliany, Drohobych district: "...In this village a school was established only about eighteen years ago, and thus only a small part of the people—and this exclusively from the younger generation—could learn

---

[2] Siegfried Fleischer, "Enquete über die Lage der jüdischen Bevölkerung Galiziens," in *Jüdische Statistik*, ed. Nossig, 217.

[3] *Rocznik Statystyki Galicyi* 3 (1889–91): 2.

[4] Kravets, *Selianstvo*, 135.

[5] Najdus, *Szkice*, 1:48. Sirka (*Nationality Question in Austrian Education*, 79) gives the following illiteracy rates for Galicia: 1880—77 per cent, 1890—68 per cent and 1900—56 per cent.

[6] *Spec. Orts-Rep. 1880*, 66.

how to read a bit. Among the older people, who hold all the offices and more prominent positions in the commune, absolutely none is literate."[7]

The low level of literacy in Galicia reflected the poor development of the school system. The crownland school council, created by an imperial resolution of 25 June 1867 (promulgated by the viceroyalty on 6 July 1867),[8] took responsibility for the development of the educational system. The council was composed of "civil servants and persons without much connection to schooling,"[9] i.e., Polish nobles and priests. Elementary-school teachers of any nationality and Ukrainians[10] had little influence over the council. The nobles on the council continued the policy of their forefathers of the feudal era: they kept the peasants ignorant.

The number of schools relative to the size of the population remained relatively constant from the mid-1840s to the beginning of the 1880s, when it began to increase very slowly (see Table 2). In 1880 Galicia had 2,847 elementary schools and 5,958,907 inhabitants; thus there was one school for

TABLE 2   Number of Inhabitants per School in Galicia, 1830–1900

Year	Number of Inhabitants per School
1830	2,603
1835	2,520
1840	2,310
1845	2,098
1850	1,968
1859	2,015
1865	1,709
1870	2,199
1875	1,942
1880	2,089
1885	1,990
1890	1,887
1895	1,785
1900	1,754

SOURCE: *Rocznik Statystyki Galicyi* 3 (1889–91):101 (for 1830–85); *Oesterreichisches statistisches Handbuch* 10 (1891):68 (for 1890); *ibid.* 15 (1896):83 (for 1895); *ibid.* 20 (1901):109 (for 1900).

---

[7] [Hryhorii Rymar,] "Pysmo z pid Drohobych," *Batkivshchyna* 4, no. 7 (1 April 1882): 54.

[8] Grzybowski, *Galicja 1848–1914*, 75. Bartel, *Zur Geschichte des galizischen Landesschulrates*, 347.

[9] Jan Dobrzański, "Szkolnictwo i działalność oświatowa," in *Historia Polski*, vol. 3, pt. 1, p. 806.

[10] One Greek Catholic priest sat on the council. A law of 1905 established that one Ukrainian would be included among the council's three representatives from the crownland administration. Bartel, *Zur Geschichte des galizischen Landesschulrates*, 349.

every 2,093 inhabitants.[11] In the rest of Austria in the same year there was a school for every 1,216 inhabitants. In 1899 Galicia had one school per 1,724 inhabitants. Only Bukovyna made a poorer showing, with one school per 1,923 inhabitants. The corresponding figure for all of Austria (including Galicia) was 1,351; for Bohemia 1,136; and for the crownland of Tyrol and Vorarlberg 565.[12] The Galician elementary school system only really expanded on the eve of the First World War: between 1868 and 1904 2,080 new elementary schools were founded, while from 1905 until 1914 1,444 were founded.[13]

Ukrainian education was particularly underdeveloped. Although for part of the late nineteenth century there were more schools with Ukrainian-language instruction than schools with Polish-language instruction in Galicia (see Table 3), much fewer pupils attended Ukrainian schools than Polish schools and the Ukrainian schools were of a much inferior quality. In the 1888–9

TABLE 3 Public Elementary Schools in Galicia: Total, With Ukrainian Language of Instruction, and Bilingual (Ukrainian-Polish), 1869–1900

Year	Total	Ukrainian Language of Instruction	Percentage	Ukrainian-Polish	Percentage
1869	2,476	1,293	52.2	67	2.7
1871	2,412	572	23.7	787	32.6
1883	3,126	1,537	49.2	na	na
1888–9	3,586	1,853	51.7	90	2.5
1890	3,685	1,803	48.9	na	na
1895	3,653	1,787	48.9	na	na
1900	3,938	1,900	48.2	0	0.0

SOURCE: Sirka, *Nationality Question in Austrian Education*, 75 (for 1869–71); *Oesterreichisches statistisches Handbuch* 3 (1884):59 (for 1883); *Rocznik Statystyki Galicyi* 3 (1889–91): 105 (for 1888–9); *Oesterreichisches statistisches Handbuch* 10 (1891):67 (for 1890); *ibid.* 15 (1896):82 (for 1895); *ibid.*, 20 (1901):108 (for 1900).

school year, for example, although over half of the schools were Ukrainian, only about one-third (35.3 per cent) of all elementary school pupils attended them; the majority (61.7 per cent) attended schools where Polish was the language of instruction.[14] The Ukrainian schools were very rudimentary, one-classroom affairs. In 1900 the 2,000 Polish schools in Galicia had a total of 5,671 classrooms, thus an average of 2.8 classrooms per school; the 1,864

---

[11] The slightly different figure in Table 2 is taken from another source.

[12] *Oesterreichisches statistisches Handbuch* 1 (1882): 1, 78; *ibid.* 19 (1900): 95.

[13] Bartel, *Zur Geschichte des galizischen Landesschulrates*, 351.

[14] *Rocznik Statystyki Galicyi* 3 (1889–91): 109.

Ukrainian schools had 2,368 classrooms, an average of 1.3 per school.[15] The difference in the number of classrooms in Polish and Ukrainian schools reflected the difference between urban schools, where three and four classrooms were common, and rural schools, where one and two classrooms prevailed.[16]

Compulsory elementary education, lasting eight years, was introduced in most of Austria in 1869. In Galicia it was introduced in 1873.[17] In the one-classroom schools that were typical of the Ukrainian village there were four grades; children were supposed to spend two years in each grade. At the urging of the Galician Polish deputies, the Austrian parliament enacted a law allowing individual crownlands to reduce the number of years of compulsory education and to lower educational standards (law of 2 May 1883). The Galician diet subsequently passed legislation (confirmed by the emperor on 7 February 1885) limiting the number of years of compulsory education for Galicians to six. After completing their six years of compulsory education, children were supposed to attend auxiliary lessons (by law at least four hours a week) for another two or three years. This legislation remained in effect from 1885 until 1895.[18]

In spite of the legislation on compulsory elementary education, Galicia had a very low frequency of school attendance (see Table 4). In 1880 only about half[19] of Galicia's school-age children actually attended school, while in the rest of Austria 95 per cent attended.[20] In 1899, when just over two-thirds of Galicia's children were attending school, Galicia had the lowest frequency in Austria (in all of Austria, including Galicia, which brought down the percentage considerably, the frequency was 87.8 per cent).[21] Nonattendance was particularly acute in the southern districts of Eastern Galicia. In 1901–2, when 72.9 per cent of Galicia's children were attending school, only 57.5 per cent were attending school in Turka district, 56.2 per cent in Kosiv district, 53.5 per cent in Sniatyn district, 52.5 per cent in Zalishchyky district and 42.1 per cent in Pechenizhyn district.[22] All five of these districts were overwhelmingly Ukrainian in population. In fact, Turka, Pechenizhyn and

---

[15] Najdus, *Szkice*, 1:76. Different, but similar figures are given by Kravets (*Selianstvo*, 133) for the 1900–1 school year: 4,250 classrooms in Polish schools, 2,250 classrooms in Ukrainian schools.

[16] Homola, "Nauczycielstwo krakowskie," 114.

[17] Sirka, *Nationality Question in Austrian Education*, 76. Tadeusz Mizia and Józef Miąso, "Oświata i szkolnictwo," in *Słownik Historii Polski*, 836.

[18] Grzybowski, *Galicja*, 84. "Novi ustavy shkolni," *Batkivshchyna* 7, no. 9 (27 [15] February 1885): 67. Najdus, *Szkice*, 1:50.

[19] 49.1 per cent according to *Rocznik Statystyki Galicyi* 3 (1889–91): 101; 53.1 per cent according to *Oesterreichisches statistisches Handbuch* 1 (1882): 81.

[20] *Oesterreichisches statistisches Handbuch* 1 (1882): 81.

[21] *Ibid.* 19 (1900): 95.

[22] Najdus, *Szkice*, 1:49.

TABLE 4 **Percentage of School-Age Galician Children Actually Attending School, 1830–1900**

Year	Percentage of School-Age Children Attending School
1830	9.7
1835	12.7
1840	13.1
1845	16.8
1850	14.0
1855	15.4
1859	21.5
1863	25.1
1869	43.1
1875	40.9
1880	49.1
1885	54.2
1890	57.9
1895	65.6
1900	71.0

SOURCE: *Rocznik Statystyki Galicyi* 3 (1889–91):101 (for 1830–85); *Oesterreichisches statistisches Handbuch* 10 (1891):68 (for 1890); *ibid.* 15 (1896):83 (for 1895); *ibid.* 20 (1901):109 (for 1900).

Kosiv had the smallest Polish minorities (3.1 to 4.4 per cent) of all forty-nine districts of Eastern Galicia in 1900.[23]

There are a number of factors responsible for the poor school attendance in Galicia, especially in Ukrainian Galicia. One obvious reason is that there were simply too few schools in the crownland. There was a correlation between the number of inhabitants served by each school and the percentage of school-age children attending school. In the 1888–9 school year the four districts in Galicia with under 1,000 inhabitants per school had a frequency of attendance ranging from 67.0 to 93.6 per cent. In the three districts (excluding the cities of Lviv and Cracow) in which each school served over 2,500 inhabitants, the frequency ranged from 39.5 to 46.2 per cent.[24] The all-Austrian educational statistics for 1899 also show a correlation between the number of schools relative to the size of the population and the frequency of attendance. Thus in those crownlands with over 90 per cent frequency, there were from 6.2 to 17.7 schools per 10,000 inhabitants; in those crownlands with under 90 per cent frequency, there were from 5.2 to 6.7

---

[23] Zalishchyky district ranked thirty-seventh in the size of its Polish minority (13.8 per cent) and Sniatyn forty-fifth (7.0 per cent). Głąbiński, *Ludność polska w Galicyi Wschodniej,* 74–5.

[24] *Rocznik Statystyki Galicyi* 3 (1889–91): 106–7, 114–15.

schools per 10,000 inhabitants.[25] Schools in Galicia were distant for many peasant children and overcrowded. A correspondent from Kulachkivtsi, Kolomyia district, complained that the children of his village had to walk three and one-half kilometres over almost impassable roads to get to the school in Hvozdets, which served no less than six communes. The situation was so unsatisfactory that several peasants pooled their funds to hire a private teacher for their children. Although the district school authorities had not provided adequate facilities for the school-age children of Kulachkivtsi, they did not hesitate to fine forty peasants in the village for not sending their children to school (*CC* 138).

The low frequency of attendance also derived in part from the economic circumstances of the Ukrainian peasantry. Every pair of hands on the farm made a difference, and many hard-pressed, traditionalist peasants were reluctant to send young workers to schools.[26] Peasants throughout Europe had resisted the education of their children. In late-nineteenth-century Germany, for example, "the peasantry, particularly in the Catholic south, put up deter-mined opposition to the extension of schooling (enforcement of attendance, raising the school leaving age, reforming the curriculum, and so on), which seemed to threaten the patriarchal authority of the peasant family and undermine the system of child labour."[27] Undoubtedly, the poor quality of the schools only served to reinforce such attitudes. However, one should be careful not to ascribe an opposition to education to the Galician peasantry generally. It is quite possible that in Galicia peasants had *less* against schooling than elsewhere in Europe. Many had learned the lesson of the servitudes struggle and wanted their children to receive the education they had not. Some had even managed to acquire an education outside the school system. For example, in Morozovychi, Sambir district, most peasants were literate, even though there was no school in the village. In the early 1860s, a period of heated struggle over servitudes, the villagers had hired a youth of noble origin to teach their children to read and write. They paid him 2 gulden for each boy he taught and fed him alternately at each villager's house. Instruction was conducted in the homes. After the first generation of literates was produced, older children spent the winter teaching younger children (*CC* 133).

Even where schools were in existence and where children were attending them, it was difficult at first to implant literacy. After attending school for half a dozen years, the peasant child frequently went out into an environment that did not foster the retention of literacy. Until there was a developed popular press in Ukrainian, there was little occasion for practice in reading. A few years out of school and the young peasant could forget what he once knew. As a correspondent from Perviatychi, Sokal district, complained: "We

---

[25] *Oesterreichisches statistisches Handbuch* 19 (1900): 95.

[26] See the related discussion below, 92–9.

[27] Eley, "State Formation, Nationalism and Political Culture," 284.

have a school... but so what? Only when a child is attending school can he read and write, and when he finishes he forgets it all, because here people don't like to read much" (*CC* 87).

The Newspaper Batkivshchyna

The Ukrainian-language periodical press emerged in Austria during the revolutionary years 1848–9, but only one of the seven periodicals founded at that time survived the decade of reaction. The lone survivor, *Vistnyk*, came out in Vienna. In Galicia the Ukrainian press disappeared by 1860 (see Table 5).[28] It reemerged with the dawn of the constitutional era. The most significant periodical of the 1860s was the newspaper *Slovo*, which had a Russophile orientation[29] after its first few years of publication. Founded in 1861, it appeared twice a week until 1873, when it began to appear three times a week; it ceased publication in 1887.[30] In spite of the relative freedom of the press in the late 1860s and 1870s, The Ukrainian press did not grow significantly during those years.

The flourishing of the periodical press began in the 1880s as Ukrainian periodicals developed a mass audience. In 1880 the national populists[31] founded their own newspaper, *Dilo*, which started as a twice-weekly publication, but became a daily in 1888.[32] Beginning in the mid-1880s, the number of Ukrainian periodicals published in Galicia increased at the rate of about one a year.

---

[28] Ihnatiienko, *Bibliohrafiia ukrainskoi presy*, 32–44. Ihnatiienko mistakenly lists the almanach *Zoria halytskaia* under the year 1860 as though it were a revival of the newspaper *Zoria halytska*.

[29] Russophilism held that the Ruthenians of Galicia were part of one large Russian nation that included the Great, White and Little Russians. The version of Ruthenian that the Russophiles wrote was a mixture of Church Slavonic and Galician Ukrainian vernacular, with some Russianisms. Their orthography was etymological, and this seemingly minor point won them many adherents from among the more traditionalist veterans of the national movement, who were not otherwise pro-Russian. The Russophiles, supported by funds from the tsarist government and pan-Slavic societies, had a pro-tsarist political orientation. Although they tried to conceal their pro-Russian sympathies behind a show of loyalty to the Austrian emperor, a number of prominent Russophiles were prosecuted for high treason in 1882. In religious questions they favoured purging the Ukrainian rite of Latin accretions; some advocated conversion from Greek Catholicism to Orthodoxy. The Russophile movement was the strongest trend among Ukrainians in Galicia until the political trial of 1882, when it began a rapid decline in popularity, but not simply as a result of the trial. At the turn of the century younger Russophiles developed a more consistent and uncompromising brand of Russophilism and used the Russian language in their publications.

[30] *Ibid.*, 44–5.

[31] National populism was the strongest current among Galician Ukrainians from the mid-1880s through the 1920s. The national populists considered the Ruthenians of Galicia to be a part of the Ukrainian nation, the majority of whose members lived in Ukraine under Russian rule. Like the Ukrainian movement in the Russian empire, from which it drew inspiration and with which it was allied, national populism defended the existence of a Ukrainian nation separate from both Poles and Russians. It used the Ukrainian vernacular, spelled phonetically, in its publications.

[32] *Ibid.*, 67.

TABLE 5 Growth of Ukrainian Periodical Press in Galicia, 1850–1910

Year	Number of Ukrainian Periodicals
1850	2
1855	3
1860	0
1865	6
1871	9[a]
1875	8[a]
1880	18
1885	16
1890	20[b]
1895	25[b]
1900	30[b]
1906	38
1910	43[b]

SOURCE: Ihnatiienko, *Bibliohrafiia ukrainskoi presy*, 36–8, 42, 44, 47–8. *Oesterreichisches statistisches Handbuch* 1 (1882):86. *Rocznik Statystyki Galicyi* 3 (1889–91):120. *Oesterreichisches statistisches Handbuch* 10 (1891):70. *Ibid.*, 14 (1895):87. *Ibid.* 19 (1900):97. *Ibid.* 25 (1906):91. *Ibid.* 29 (1910):93.

[a]Figures for all of Austria.
[b]Includes 1 periodical in the Russian language.

Not only did the number of Ukrainian periodicals increase beginning in the 1880s, but so did their circulations and periodicity. Of six Ukrainian political periodicals published in Galicia in 1880, two came out more frequently by 1885 and three had more than doubled their press runs (see Table 6). If we multiply the issues per year by the press run of all Ukrainian political periodicals in 1880, we find that 236,000 issues were printed. In 1885 about 600,000 issues were printed[33] and in 1889—834,450.[34] By 1905 just the four Ukrainian daily newspapers in Lviv accounted for over two million issues.[35] The dynamic growth of the Ukrainian press at the turn of the century shows that the press, and the national movement behind it, had found a mass constituency.

The first Ukrainian popular periodicals, aimed at the peasantry, appeared in 1863. The poet-awakener and priest Ivan Hushalevych published *Dom i shkola* in 1863–4. It came out three times a month and was subtitled "a

---

[33] According to the data in Table 6: 630,000. According to the Crownland Statistical Bureau: 573,325. *Rocznik Statystyki Galicyi* 3 (1889–91): 124.

[34] *Rocznik Statystyki Galicyi* 3 (1889–91): 124.

[35] *Dilo* had a press run of 2,600; *Narodna chasopys* 2,400; *Halychanyn* 2,200; and *Ruslan* 350. TsDIAL, 146/8/462, p. 14.

periodical devoted to schools and the village people."[36] More lasting was
Pysmo do hromady, which came out in 1863–5 and 1867–8 (irregularly in
1863, weekly in 1864–5 and fortnightly in 1867–8).[37] The editor, Severyn
Shekhovych, complained in August 1863 that the periodical had less than a
hundred subscribers and that no one wrote for it except his relatives.[38] The
real breakthrough in Ukrainian popular literature came in 1868 with the
founding of Prosvita, a national populist society devoted to publishing popular
booklets and fostering village reading clubs. Prosvita at first neglected
periodicals and limited its publication efforts to booklets for the peasantry.
One of the earliest of these, Father Stefan Kachala's *Shcho nas hubyt a
shcho nam pomochy mozhe*, went through three editions (1869, 1872 and
1874) with a total press run of nine or ten thousand copies.[39]

TABLE 6 **Press Run and Frequency of Ukrainian Political Periodicals in Galicia,
1880 and 1885**

	1880		1885	
Periodical	Issues per Year	Press Run	Issues per Year	Press Run
Batkivshchyna	24	600	52	1,500
Dilo	104	550	156	1,300
Myr	—	—	156	1,000
Nauka	12	100	12	600
Nove zerkalo	—	—	24	450
Novyi prolom	—	—	104	600
Ruska rada	24	800	24	800
Slovo	156	850	156	600
Strakhopud	24	500	—	—

SOURCE: TsDIAL, 146/7/4149, pp. 380, 406–7. TsDIAL, 146/7/4352, pp. 127, 129.

The success of the national-populist Prosvita spurred the Russophiles to
engage in similar work. *Slovo* in 1869–70 published an irregular supplement
for the peasantry entitled *Slovo do hromad*.[40] Shekhovych published
Hospodar in 1869–72, a fortnightly with practical advice about agricultural
technique.[41] The most important Russophile popular periodicals were those

---

[36] Ihnatiienko, *Bibliohrafiia ukrainskoi presy*, 46.

[37] *Ibid.*

[38] Pavlyk, "Pro rusko-ukrainski narodni chytalni," 480.

[39] *Ibid.*, 494, 526. For an analysis of the contents of this brochure, see Himka, "Priests and
Peasants," 6; see also below, 125.

[40] Ihnatiienko, *Bibliohrafiia ukrainskoi presy*, 54. Pavlyk ("Pro rusko-ukrainski narodni
chytalni," 488) writes that *Slovo do hromad* appeared weekly.

[41] Ihnatiienko, *Bibliohrafiia ukrainskoi presy*, 53.

founded by Father Ivan Naumovych in the district capital of Kolomyia in 1871: *Nauka*, a fortnightly and later monthly magazine, and *Russkaia rada*, a fortnightly newspaper.[42] Both periodicals appeared in the vernacular Ukrainian language and had the largest circulation of all Ukrainian periodicals in the 1870s. In their first years of publication they came out in press runs of 1,000–1,500 copies[43] and around 1876 *Nauka* was published in over 2,000 copies.[44] However, as the national-populist movement gained strength in the 1880s, the press runs of these two Russophile publications decreased (see Table 6).

It was not until October 1877 that the national-populist Prosvita society began publishing a monthly popular newspaper entitled *Pysmo z "Prosvity."* It came out through the summer of 1879[45] and was then replaced by the newspaper *Batkivshchyna*, "indisputably the best of all popular periodicals for the people that ever appeared."[46]

Batkivshchyna took its name from the Ukrainian word with the double meaning of "patrimony" and "fatherland." When Galician officials translated the title into German, they chose the latter meaning (G *Die Heimat*).[47] Peasants, however, used the word to mean "patrimony" (*CC* 110, 136; *CC* 222 uses the word *vitchyna* to mean fatherland). As is clear from the first editorial statement of *Batkivshchyna*, the founders of the newspaper deliberately played on this double meaning in order to make the more abstract, patriotic concept of *batkivshchyna* comprehensible in terms of the more concrete and familiar concept:

> ... The Ruthenian people is in extreme exigency: in its own country, on its own *batkivshchyna*, it works hard as a slave of someone else's pocket, in hunger and cold and rustling its rags, until all that will be left of its *batkivshchyna* will be a mendicant's staff and beggar's bag.... Our enemies ... *fleece us of everything we have, of our entire* batkivshchyna, *our land, our cattle, our housing, our clothing, our faith and our language—and we then have no choice but to perish!*[48] .... Let us save ourselves, let us save the precious remains of our *batkivshchyna!*[49]

The decision to establish *Batkivshchyna* was a direct result of the disastrous outcome of the parliamentary elections of 1879. In the 1873 elections sixteen Ukrainian deputies had been sent to parliament, but in 1879

[42] *Ibid.*, 55–6.

[43] Pavlyk, "Pro rusko-ukrainski narodni chytalni," 497.

[44] Dei, *Ukrainska revoliutsiino-demokratychna zhurnalistyka*, 119.

[45] Ihnatiienko, *Bibliohrafiia ukrainskoi presy*, 62. Pavlyk, "Pro rusko-ukrainski narodni chytalni," 545.

[46] Olesnytsky, *Storinky*, 1:150.

[47] For example, Galician viceroy Filip Zaleski in a report to Austrian prime minister Eduard Taaffe, 25 January 1885, in LODA, 350/1/4916, p. 104.

[48] Emphasis in original.

[49] Vid redaktsii "Batkivshchyny," "Do dila!" *Batkivshchyna* 1, no. 1 (1 October 1879): 1–2.

only three.[50] Even the popular writer Ivan Naumovych received only one vote in his home district of Skalat in 1879.[51] The dismal results of the election reflected the success of the Polish gentry by the mid-1870s in both consolidating their rule in the crownland and mastering the techniques of electoral chicanery, particularly the technique of bribing and pressuring peasant electors to vote against their own interests. The need for political work among the peasantry became apparent to the leadership of the Ukrainian national movement. Because Prosvita's statutes did not permit it to engage in directly political action, the national populists closed down *Pysmo z "Prosvity"* in 1879 and replaced it with the overtly political *Batkivshchyna*, which was formally independent of Prosvita.[52]

TABLE 7 Press Run of *Batkivshchyna*, **1879–85**

Year	Quarter			
	First	Second	Third	Fourth
1879	—	—	—	600
1880	450		600	
1881	400			600
1882	300		450	500
1883	700		700	
1884				1,500
1885	1,500	1,000	855	

SOURCE: TsDIAL, 146/7/4149, pp. 201, 241, 407. TsDIAL, 146/7/4220, p. 112. TsDIAL, 146/7/4240, pp. 20, 25, 42. TsDIAL, 146/7/4276, pp. 36, 237. TsDIAL, 146/7/4278, p. 367. TsDIAL, 146/7/4352, pp. 45, 129, 241, 278.

Batkivshchyna came out from October 1879 until December 1896, at first as a fortnightly (1879–82), then as a weekly (1883–92), and finally as a fortnightly alternating with another fortnightly, *Chytalnia* (1893–6). Annual subscriptions cost a modest 4 gulden when *Batkivshchyna* was a weekly and 2 gulden when it was a fortnightly.[53] The press run of the paper ranged from 300 to 1,500 in the period 1879–85, reaching its height at the end of 1884 and the beginning of 1885 (see Table 7), when it had the largest press run of any Ukrainian periodical (see Table 6). At the end of 1888 it had about 570 subscribers, who owed, however, nearly a thousand gulden for their

---

[50] Fifty-seven Polish deputies were elected in 1879. Rudnytsky, "Ukrainians in Galicia," 37 note 31.

[51] Olesnytsky, *Storinky*, 1:149–50. According to Pavlyk ("Pro rusko-ukrainski narodni chytalni," 545), Naumovych did not receive a single vote in Skalat district.

[52] Olesnytsky, *Storinky*, 1:149–50. Pavlyk, "Pro rusko-ukrainski narodni chytalni," 545.

[53] *Batkivshchyna*, 1879–96. Lev1–3. Ihnatiienko, *Bibliohrafiia ukrainskoi presy*, 64.

subscriptions.[54] Since many of the subscribers to *Batkivshchyna* were reading clubs and other voluntary organizations and since many individual subscribers passed their copies on to other readers, each copy of the newspaper may have served several dozen readers.

The Polish nobility that controlled the Galician government tried to hinder the development of a popular political newspaper for the Ukrainian peasantry by frequent confiscations. A third of the issues of *Batkivshchyna* published in 1879, a quarter in 1880 and 1881, and over 40 per cent in 1882 were confiscated by the authorities. Thereafter, with the exception of an election year (1885), a year of intense peasant unrest (1887) and the year of the founding of the Ruthenian-Ukrainian Radical Party (1890),[55] the authorities left *Batkivshchyna* in relative peace (see Table 8). The reason most frequently given for the confiscation of the paper was that it preached contempt for

TABLE 8 **Confiscations of** *Batkivshchyna*, **1879–96**

Year	Issues Confiscated (No.)
1879	5, 6
1880	1, 2, 4, 13, 15, 19
1881	1, 4 (twice), 11, 16, 17, 19
1882	1 (twice), 2, 4, 6, 8, 12, 13, 20, 21 22
1883	18, 19, 29, 36
1884	—
1885	6, 19, 22, 29, 32, 40
1886	15 (not confirmed by court), 16
1887	1, 25, 30, 43
1888	29 (not confirmed by court), 48 (twice)
1889	24
1890	7, 10, 40, 43, 46
1891	48
1892	—
1893	—
1894	2
1895	—
1896	2

SOURCE: Lev1–3. *Batkivshchyna*, 1895–6. TsDIAL, 146/7/4220, pp. 72–87. TsDIAL, 146/7/4240, pp. 89–97. TsDIAL, 146/7/4278, pp. 116–25, 315–20. TsDIAL, 152/2/14789–90, 14898–903, 15007–13. TsDIAL, 156/1/545, pp. 2–4, 11–12, 17–19, 30–2, 39–41, 50–1, 54–5, 71–2, 102–4, 107–16, 125–6.

---

[54] Pavlyk, *Perepyska*, 5:275.

[55] Radicalism was similar to national populism in national orientation, but the radicals were socialists. Their mentor was Mykhailo Drahomanov, the outstanding Ukrainian political thinker of the nineteenth century. Their hallmark, aside from an agrarian variant of socialism, was a strident anticlericalism. Radicalism first emerged in the mid-1870s.

the government and its representatives (see Table 9).[56] Issues were also suppressed for disseminating hatred of other religions and nationalities, particularly Jews,[57] but also Poles.[58] The Austrian and Galician authorities also considered *Batkivshchyna* somewhat anticlerical in the mid-1880s,[59] but I have been unable to determine whether the paper was ever confiscated for this reason.

The founder of *Batkivshchyna* and its actual editor for many years (until 1887)[60] was the prominent national populist Iuliian Romanchuk (1842–1932).

TABLE 9 Reasons Given for Confiscation of *Batkivshchyna*, 1879–81

Preaching Hatred of or Contempt for

Confiscated Issue	Government and Officials	Jews	Poles	Nobility
1879: no. 5	X	X		
no. 6	X	X	X	
1880: no. 1	X	X		
no. 2	X	X		
no. 4	X			
no. 13	X			
no. 15	X			
no. 19		X		
1881: no. 1	X			
no. 4	X			
no. 4 (2nd ed.)	X			
no. 11	X			
no. 16	X			X
no. 17	X			
no. 19	X		X	implied

SOURCE: TsDIAL, 152/2/14789–90, 14898–903, 15007–13.

---

[56] This was also the reason given for confiscating *Batkivshchyna* 1882, no. 20, and 1883, no. 29. TsDIAL, 146/7/4278, pp. 116–25.

[57] The attitude of *Batkivshchyna* to the Jews is explored in Himka, "Ukrainian-Jewish Antagonism."

[58] *Batkivshchyna* 1883, no. 36, was also confiscated for an anti-Polish article; *Batkivshchyna* 1885, no. 40, for an anti-Polish and anti-Jewish article. TsDIAL, 146/7/4278, pp. 315–20. "V spravi konfiskaty ch. 40 Batkivshcyny," *Batkivshchyna* 7, no. 46 (13 [1] November 1885): 320.

[59] See the correspondence between the Galician viceroy's office and Austrian ministry of the interior, 1885, in LODA, 350/1/4916, pp. 105, 114.

[60] Pavlyk, "Iz perepysky M.P. Drahomanova. III. Lysty M.P. Drahomanova do Oleksandra Borkovskoho, redaktora 'Zori'. (1888–1889)," *Zhytie i slovo* 5 (1896): 455, 455–6 note 1. See also Olesnytsky, *Storinky*, 1:150, and Pavlyk, *Perepyska*, 3:499–500.

Romanchuk, the son of an elementary school teacher, taught gymnasium in Lviv from 1863 until 1900. He was a deputy to the Galician diet (1883–95) and to the Austrian parliament (1891–7, 1901–18). He was among the founders of the national-populist organizations Prosvita (1868) and the Shevchenko Society (1873) as well as of the Ukrainian National Democratic Party (1899), which he headed until 1907.[61] During the years he edited *Batkivshchyna*, Romanchuk belonged to the socially more radical wing of the national populists and used *Batkivshchyna* to develop a policy independent of his more clerically oriented and conservative rival in the national populist leadership, Volodymyr Barvinsky, the editor of *Dilo*.[62]

Although Romanchuk was the actual editor of *Batkivshchyna* from 1879 until 1887, other editors were announced to the public. While the announced editors usually did work on the paper, it was Romanchuk who determined policy. The first announced editor was the gymnasium teacher Markil Zhelekhivsky, who also figured publicly in the editorial boards of *Pravda* (1878) and *Dilo* (1880) and who had been active in the Ukrainian artisan association Pobratym (1872–5).[63] Zhelekhivsky only figured as editor for the first nine issues of *Batkivshchyna*, after which he was replaced by Volodymyr Podliashetsky.

Podliashetsky, a legal clerk (U *advokatskyi kontsypiient*) by profession, was the announced editor of *Batkivshchyna* from February 1880 until October 1885. He eventually proved an embarassment to the national populists. He served on a committee set up by the latter in 1884 to help peasants who had borrowed money from the Rustical Bank, which had collapsed that year. Peasants sent money directly to the committee to help settle their debts. In 1885 Podliashetsky absconded with several thousand gulden of the peasants' money, left the country and was never heard of again.[64]

After Podliashetsky, the announced editor of the paper was Vasyl Nahirny (1848–1921), who later became the actual editor of the paper (briefly in 1887,[65] for the whole second half of 1889[66] and probably for most of 1890). Nahirny's parents were relatively prosperous peasants, but with four siblings among whom the land had to be divided and with the death of his mother while he was still a small child, Nahirny was to struggle with poverty for

---

[61] *Entsyklopediia Ukrainoznavstva*, s.v. "Romanchuk Iuliian" by I. Sokhotsky.

[62] Pavlyk, "Iz perepysky," 455–6 note 1.

[63] Pavlyk, "Pro rusko-ukrainski narodni chytalni," 516. Levl, nos. 1860–1, 2113. Himka, "Voluntary Artisan Associations," 184–5, 191.

[64] "Nasha neopytnost," *Novyi prolom* 4 (6), no. 381 (25 October [6 November] 1886): 1.

[65] Pavlyk, *Perepyska*, 5:187.

[66] *Ibid.*, 5:402.

most of the time that he acquired his education. His education, formidable by Galician Ukrainian standards, was due to an accident. Nahirny broke his leg as a child, and his father and grandmother decided not to have it set, primarily so that the boy would never be drafted. His right leg remained lame all his life. Since, as an invalid, he could never become a farmer, he was sent off to be educated. He first attended a school run by the cantor in his native village of Hirne, and then, in 1859, he began to attend the normal school (G *Normalschule*)[67] in nearby Stryi. From 1866 until 1870 he attended the real school (G *Realschule*) in Lviv,[68] after which he enrolled in the technical academy in the same city. In 1872 he did what few Galician Ukrainians ever did, let alone those of peasant origin: he went abroad to acquire a higher education. From 1872 to 1875 he studied architecture at the academy in Zurich, and then from 1875 to 1882 he worked as an architect in Switzerland. While in Zurich he was a founder of the Russian and Ukrainian student club Rus[s]kii kruzhok and later head of the society Slavia. When Nahirny returned to Galicia in the fall of 1882, he was a valuable asset to the national populists: an educated man who had seen more of the world than they had (and in 1883 he travelled to Kiev to study Eastern church architecture); who knew Russian and Eastern Ukrainian culture first hand from contacts with the students in Zurich; and who, moreover, knew the Galician peasantry from the inside, as their offspring.

Immediately upon returning to Galicia Nahirny took an active role in the Ukrainian movement, especially its economic aspects. He was a founder of the wholesale cooperative Narodna torhovlia in 1883 and a leader of the second Ukrainian artisan association in Lviv, Zoria (founded 1884). His work as an architect, with a specialization in village churches, brought him into direct contact with many local activists and potential activists of the Ukrainian movement throughout Galicia. He designed churches in a number of localities that later figured in the correspondence of *Batkivshchyna*.[69] Evidently, Nahirny used his meetings with the clergy, cantors and church committees (brotherhoods) not only to discuss designs for churches, but also to recruit correspondents for the newspaper he nominally edited.[70]

---

[67] A higher quality elementary school.

[68] A four-grade technical school.

[69] For example, Nahirny designed the churches in Perehinsko, Dolyna district, where *CC* 257 and *CC* 258 originated; Ostriv, Sokal district, where *CC* 279 (which describes the consecration of the new stone church) originated (perhaps this was written by Nahirny himself); and Olesko, Zolochiv district, where *CC* 154 originated and which is mentioned in *CC* 262. I have not compared the complete list of churches and parts of churches designed by Nahirny, 1882-90, with all the locations connected with the correspondence of 1885-90. I have used only a partial list of ten churches and checked them only against the correspondence of 1884-5.

[70] This account of Nahirny's life is based on Lev493, N-7. See also: Nahirny, *Z moikh spomyniv*. Curiously, neither in his autobiographical letter to Ivan Levytsky nor in his published memoirs does Nahirny write about his involvement with *Batkivshchyna*. This silence probably stems from the unpleasant auspices under which he began his nominal editorship, Podliashetsky's swindle, and from its unpleasant ending, the break with Mykhailo Pavlyk and the Ukrainian radicals (to be described below).

In 1887 Romanchuk resigned as actual editor of *Batkivshchyna* and handed the paper entirely over to Nahirny. Nahirny quickly passed the actual editing on to the insurance clerk, former editor of *Myr* (1885–7) and eminent bibliographer of Galicia, Ivan Omelianovych Levytsky (1850–1913).[71] Levytsky had the reputation of being efficient and hard-working, but politically unstable and conceptually vacuous. During his short stint as actual editor he came once a week to *Batkivshchyna*'s office and did whatever Nahirny instructed him to do; he also proofread the issues.[72]

By September 1888 at the latest[73] *Batkivshchyna* had a new actual editor (and owner): Oleksander Borkovsky (1841-1921), the editor (1886–97) of the leading national populist literary journal, *Zoria*. Borkovsky apparently had his hands full with *Zoria*, because he soon began looking for someone else to take over *Batkivshchyna*. He was to turn to the radical Mykhailo Pavlyk.

The radicals had long been interested in *Batkivshchyna*, as the organ of the national populist movement that demonstrated the most concern for the Ukrainian masses. Although Pavlyk had criticized it strongly in 1880, from his anarchist-socialist perspective,[74] by late 1881 both he and the radicals' mentor, Mykhailo Drahomanov, began to discern in *Batkivshchyna* an evolution toward a more compatible ideology. They wrote to Romanchuk on 8 November 1881 (N.S.), urging him to call public assemblies of Polish, Ukrainian and Jewish workers and peasants with the aim of forming a populist organization on the order of the Austrian *Bauernvereine*. They offered their literary and financial support to such an undertaking. Effectively, this was a proposal to merge the radical movement with the more peasant-oriented wing of the national populists. Romanchuk replied on 25 December 1881 (N.S.), in a letter co-signed by Podliashetsky as editor of *Batkivshchyna*, that he could not accept the radicals' proposal, because ideological differences with the radicals remained too great, the work proposed was beyond the capacity of the Ukrainian movement and "it would be even more beneficial to the cause if we do things completely separately."[75]

Although not open to so far-reaching an alliance with the radicals, the national populists around *Batkivshchyna* were interested in making use of the talents and dedication of Pavlyk and the radical poet Ivan Franko, both of whom contributed to the paper in the mid-1880s.[76] In 1884 the national

[71] Pavlyk, *Perepyska*, 5:187. On Levytsky, see Magocsi, "Nationalism and National Bibliography," esp. pp. 83–5.

[72] Pavlyk, *Perepyska*, 5:187, 196.

[73] *Ibid.*, 5:241.

[74] Dei, *Ukrainska revoliutsiino-demokratychna zhurnalistyka*, 341–2.

[75] Pavlyk, *Perepyska*, 3:499–501, 515. See also M. Pavlyk, "Novynky z Avstriiskoi Ukrainy," *Hromada* 5, no. 2 (1881): 229.

[76] In 1886 Pavlyk published in *Batkivshchyna* articles on Bulgarian peasants ("Khliboroby v Bolharii") and Italian workers ("Robitnyky v Italii"). Pavlyk, *Perepyska*, 5:75. In 1884 Franko, in the name of the Ethnographic-Statistical Circle (a student organization), published an article on reading clubs and church brotherhoods. Moroz, *Ivan Franko. Bibliohrafiia*, no. 1907.

TABLE 10 Editors of *Batkivshchyna*, **1879–96**

Announced Editor	*Issues Edited*	*Actual Editor*
Markil Zhelekhivsky	1879–1880, no. 3	Iuliian Romanchuk, 1879–87
Volodymyr Podliashetsky	1880, no. 4–1885, no. 40	
Vasyl Nahirny	1885, no. 41–1890, no. 35	Vasyl Nahirny, before late July 1887; Ivan Levytsky, at least late July and August 1887; Oleksander Borkovsky, at least from September 1888; Mykhailo Pavlyk, 1889, nos. 1–24; Vasyl Nahirny, at least through the end of 1889
Volodymyr Levytsky	1890, nos. 36–52	
Kost Levytsky	1891–1892, no. 1	
Kost Pankivsky	1892, nos. 2–51	
Mykhailo Holeiko	1893–1895, no. 12	
Mykhailo Strusevych	1895, no. 13–1896	

SOURCE: *Batkivshchyna*, 1879–96, and Lev 1–3 (for announced editor and issues edited); text (for actual editor).

populists made overtures to Franko[77] and also, it seems, to Pavlyk[78] to assume the editorship of *Batkivshchyna*. The choice of Pavlyk as editor of *Batkivshchyna* was also considered in 1886 and 1887, and of Franko in 1887. Pavlyk was eager for the position in 1886–7, but the national populists were hesitant to begin any formal discussion with either of the radicals.[79]

---

[77] Kurhansky, *Maisternist Franka-publitsysta*, 47–8).

[78] See Pavlyk, *Perepyska*, 5:378, 383.

[79] *Ibid.*, 5:113, 187, 194, 196.

Василь Нагорный.

Vasyl Nahirny

Mykhailo Pavlyk

Iuliian Romanchuk

However, after Borkovsky, already busy enough with *Zoria*, became editor of *Batkivshchyna*, he began formal negotiations with Pavlyk in September 1888. By mid-November they had agreed that Pavlyk would immediately begin helping in the editorial office of *Batkivshchyna* and would edit the paper on his own from the beginning of 1889.[80] When the first issue under Pavlyk's editorship appeared, the national populists were shocked by the radical tone Pavlyk introduced, especially his anticlericalism and feminism. Nahirny was particularly upset, since he figured publicly as the paper's editor. He therefore insisted, at a meeting of the national-populist leadership with Pavlyk (22 January 1889 [N.S.]), that he replace Borkovsky as the national-populist "censor" of Pavlyk's work. To strengthen his position, he bought *Batkivshchyna* from Borkovsky in May 1889.[81] Throughout the half-year that Pavlyk edited *Batkivshchyna*, he and Nahirny were in constant conflict over the paper's orientation. As Nahirny and other national populists saw it, Pavlyk's social radicalism could alienate the more prosperous peasants; his anticlericalism could alienate the hierarchy as well as the parish priests, whom the national populists considered their strongest allies in the villages; and his advocacy of women's liberation could alienate and confuse the male peasantry as a whole. Therefore Nahirny became an increasingly severe censor, while Pavlyk continued to smuggle in his radicalism however he could. The only reason Nahirny kept Pavlyk on as editor was that Nahirny did not himself want to assume complete responsibility for the paper and the work this would entail. The final break between Pavlyk and Nahirny was precipitated when Pavlyk published in *Batkivshchyna* the text of a telegram sent to Rome by himself, Franko and several Polish progressives in connection with the unveiling of a monument to Giordano Bruno. The Greek Catholic metropolitan, Sylvester Sembratovych, was so offended that he forbade the faithful to read *Batkivshchyna* and brought pressure to bear on Nahirny to fire Pavlyk. As a result, Nahirny gave Pavlyk an ultimatum: either he edit the paper completely in line with the national populists' moderate orientation or he leave.[82] Pavlyk chose the latter course and resigned from *Batkivshchyna* on 2 July 1889 (N.S.), after having edited twenty-four issues.[83]

The expulsion of Pavlyk proved to be the turning point in the fortunes of *Batkivshchyna*. In the view of many, the national populists had behaved incorrectly. They had hired as editor a man well known as a principled radical, who had sat in prison more than once for his convictions; and then they expected him to edit the newspaper in a way opposed to his principles. Nahirny's ultimatum, according to the Polish daily *Kurjer Lwowski* (owned by the populist Bolesław Wysłouch), was "extremely uncouth and nonsensical, clearly characterizing *the low level of political and moral development* at

[80] *Ibid.*, 5: 241, 274–5, 368. Iashchuk, *Mykhailo Pavlyk*, 98.

[81] Pavlyk, *Perepyska*, 5:326, 329–30, 353, 358, 369–70.

[82] Hornowa, *Ukraiński obóz postępowy*, 96.

[83] Mykhailo Pavlyk, "Zaiava," *Batkivshchyna* 11, no. 25 (23 June [5 July] 1889): 332.

which the *leaders of Rus'* stand today."[84] Within six months of his dismissal from *Batkivshchyna*, Pavlyk was to begin editing, together with Franko, an openly radical newspaper, *Narod* (1890–5). In October 1890 the radical party was to emerge and in subsequent years it was to publish popular newspapers that were radical versions of *Batkivshchyna: Khliborob* (1891–4) and *Hromadskyi holos* (1895–1939, with interruptions). The radical movement immediately found a resonance in the village. Its popular newspaper, which started with a press run of 200 in 1891, had attained a press run of 1,000 by 1895.[85] So much for Nahirny's fears that radicalism would alienate the village; in fact, it proved to be a serious competitor with national populism for the loyalties of the peasantry. In 1891 *Batkivshchyna* was moved to publish a long series of front-page editorials opposing the ideas of radicalism.[86]

The rise of radicalism corresponded with the decline of *Batkivshchyna*. After Pavlyk left the paper, Nahirny edited it himself, at least through 1889.[87] He probably edited the paper through early 1890, when a new editor was announced. From 1890 through 1896, when *Batkivshchyna* ceased publication, there were six different (announced) editors. One, Mykhailo Holeiko, was so careless in his work that in 1895 he forgot to change the year printed on the paper; thus the first twelve issues of *Batkivshchyna* for 1895 are all dated 1894! The paper became blander in tone and was hardly confiscated at all from 1891 to 1896 (see Table 8). In 1891 the paper became much thinner and in 1893 it began coming out at fortnightly intervals instead of weekly, alternating with another popular fortnightly, *Chytalnia*.[88] At the beginning of 1896 the editor of *Batkivshchyna* announced that the paper would continue to appear, since "the task that our newspaper has assumed is great and still not even one per cent completed."[89] But at the end of 1896, *Batkivshchyna* announced that both it and *Chytalnia* would cease publication

---

[84] Emphasis in original. "Z prasy ruskiej," *Kurjer Lwowski*, no. 183 (8 July 1889): 3. Although Pavlyk's comrade Franko worked for *Kurjer Lwowski*, this article is not attributed to him in the exhaustive bibliography of his works compiled by M.O. Moroz (*Ivan Franko. Bibliohrafiia*, see pp. 215–25).

[85] Dmytruk, *Narys z istorii ukrainskoi zhurnalistyky*, 133.

[86] [Kost Levytsky], "Shcho ie radykalizm," *Batkivshchyna* 13 (1891), nos. 15–22, 27, 31, 33, 35, 37, 39.

[87] Pavlyk, *Perepyska*, 5:402.

[88] "Vid vydavnytstva 'Batkivshchyny'," *Batkivshchyna* 15, no. 1 (1 [13] January 1893): 8. The idea of publishing *Chytalnia* had been in the air since 1886, when Romanchuk was considering it as a popular monthly that would appear *in addition* to the weekly *Batkivshchyna*. In 1888, while Pavlyk was negotiating entry into *Batkivshchyna*, plans were made, but not carried through, to publish *Batkivshchyna* as a fortnightly in alternation with another fortnightly, *Narodna chytalnia*. The advantage to alternating two similar fortnightlies, instead of publishing one weekly, was that weeklies had to pay a high press tax (300 gulden annually in the case of *Batkivshchyna*) as well as leave under bond a large surety (3,000 gulden); fortnightlies were much less costly. (Pavlyk, *Perepyska*, 5: 113, 274.) Thus the ultimate change to the alternating-fortnightly pattern in 1893 probably indicates that *Batkivshchyna* was having financial difficulties.

[89] "Vid redaktsii," *Batkivshchyna* 18, no. 1 (1 [13] January 1896): 1.

and be replaced by a new weekly.[90] *Batkivshchyna*'s successor, *Svoboda*, was
to last, with one interruption (1920–1), from 1897 to 1939. It is interesting
that a number of its editors in the early period were renegade radicals.[91]

The Correspondence in Batkivshchyna

The editors of *Batkivshchyna* in Lviv were linked with their readers in the
countryside through items of correspondence submitted to the section of the
paper entitled "Visti z kraiu" (News from the Crownland). When the paper
first got off the ground and had not yet built up a network of contacts with
local Ukrainian activists in the villages, it published few items of
correspondence. The same was true of the 1890s, when links with both
readers and contributors were degenerating. But in the heyday of
Batkivshchyna, in the mid-1880s, it received more submissions from the
countryside than it could publish without creating a backlog.[92]

The editors promised to publish all submissions signed by an author known
to them.[93] They were hesitant to publish anonymous items of correspondence,
because these were usually denunciations of individuals in a particular village
and the editors had no guarantee that they were justified. On one occasion,
after receiving a number of anonymous submissions on the alleged collapse of
the reading club in Rudno, Lviv district, the editors decided to publish one of
the items (*CC* 240) to provoke a response from their known contacts in
Rudno (the response was published in *CC* 243).

Submissions to *Batkivshchyna* were edited to conform to the political
profile of the paper. Criticism of priests, although by no means absent in the
correspondence, was toned down. For example, *Batkivshchyna* published only
part of an item of correspondence (*CC* 167) that censured some priests for
indifference to the work of enlightenment in the village. The editorial note
accompanying the item explained that "now is not the time to come forth
with accusations and quarrels among the Ruthenians themselves." The editors
also said that for the same reason certain submissions from Kolomyia, Skalat,
Zhydachiv and other districts were not being published. Anticlerical
sentiments in the correspondence were also suppressed by Vasyl Nahirny (as
Pavlyk's censor) in 1889. Nahirny also eliminated parts of one item of
correspondence that were socially radical and pro-Jewish.[94] The editorial
tampering with the submissions lessens their value as historical sources

---

[90] "Vid vydavnytstva," *Batkivshchyna* 18, no. 24 (16 [28] December 1896): 185.

[91] Volodymyr Okhrymovych was editor in 1900 and publisher in 1907; Ievhen Levytsky was
editor in 1902; and Viacheslav Budzynovsky was editor and publisher in 1903–6. Ihnatiienko,
Bibliohrafiia ukrainskoi presy, 110.

[92] Redaktsiia Batkivshchyny, "Novynky i vsiachyna," *Batkivshchyna* 6, no. 23 (6 June [30 May]
1884): 139.

[93] *Ibid.* "Perepyska redaktsii," *Batkivshchyna* 6, no. 13 (28 [16] March 1884): 80.
"Sprostovania," *Batkivshchyna* 6, no. 21 (23 [11] May 1884): 131. Editorial comment to
CC 254.

[94] Pavlyk, *Perepyska*, 5: 355–6, 367. See Himka, "Ukrainian-Jewish Antagonism."

expressing rural attitudes, but does not completely negate it. The editors at least refrained from adding their own passages to the correspondence. Thus the correspondence reflects authentic attitudes of local activists of the Ukrainian movement, even if one-sidedly.

The correspondence was important for the editors of *Batkivshchyna* and for the Ukrainian national movement as a whole because it allowed the city-based national movement to keep informed of the mood of the countryside. The correspondence played a much more important role, however, in the villages from which it emanated. Here the items of correspondence broke down the traditional isolation of the Ukrainian village. "In our reading club we find out from newspapers and books what is happening in other villages, in our whole crownland, in our monarchy and, in fact, in the entire world" (*CC* 41). "We should inform ourselves about each other, because in that way we will be able to become better acquainted and recognize our needs" (*CC* 25).

The correspondence allowed each village to compare itself with other villages, and such comparisons are found frequently in the corpus of correspondence.[95] An important point of comparison was the progress of institutional development. The national populists had a series of institutions that they felt should be introduced in all villages, including reading clubs, schools, Ukrainian-run stores, loan funds, community halls, communal granaries and choirs.[96] A typical comparison was made by a correspondent from Tetevchytsi, Kaminka Strumylova district. His village, he admitted, "is not...such a very famous village, as are some of the other villages I read about in *Batkivshchyna*, but, as they say, it's not the worst. It has a communal granary, loan fund and choral singing. The people...are sober, hard-working and moral" (*CC* 214).

The correspondence nurtured a sense of village pride and, where it seemed warranted, shame. For example, a peasant from Ternopil district lamented: "From your dear *Batkivshchyna* I am finding out that other communes are introducing new institutions [U *novi poriadky*] for their own and their children's good: they are founding reading clubs, communal funds and other things. Only in our unfortunate communes of Ivachiv Dolishnii, Ivachiv Horishnii and Plotycha is everything the same as in the past" (*CC* 77). Villages began to care for their reputations. When the Russophile popular paper *Russkaia rada* printed an item of correspondence stating that the village of Trostianets could serve as a model for Ilyntsi, Sniatyn district, a native of the latter village was moved to submit an item to *Batkivshchyna* describing the loan fund, widespread sobriety, literacy and interest in Ukrainian publications in Ilyntsi (*CC* 24). Damage to a village's reputation in *Batkivshchyna* could make inhabitants of that village uncomfortable when

---

[95] *CC* 10, 16, 35, 36, 77, 155, 214.

[96] See the list in Vasyl Nahirny, "Iak maie vyhliadaty uporiadkovana hromada," *Batkivshchyna* 14, no. 29 (17 [29] July 1892): 145–6.

they went to the marketplace, as this item of correspondence from Iamnytsia, Stanyslaviv district, demonstrates:

> Mister editor!
> You have no idea what trouble you caused us by writing about us, saying that our communal council in Iamnytsia rented the communal store to a Jew. Peasants from neighbouring villages read that, and now whenever one of them meets someone from Iamnytsia, he immediately starts an argument about that store. We had the most trouble at the market in Stanyslaviv: the peasants from neighbouring villages reproved us strongly and one peasant from Poberezhzhia even wanted to beat up some of our people, he was so angry (*CC* 86).[97]

The publication of items of correspondence from other villages encouraged activists to submit items concerning their own villages. "Mister editor! We too read your periodical *Batkivshchyna*, which is dear to us and which is found in every honourable Ruthenian commune, and we find in it very many items of correspondence about various communes, but no one so far has mentioned our famous Chortovets [Horodenka district]. Therefore please publish these few words" (*CC* 2). "Forgive me, mister editor, that in writing my first letter to you, I do not write it as fluently and finely perhaps as your more intelligent correspondents. I am a simple man and I have never written to a newspaper, but reading your dear *Batkivshchyna* for a whole year has filled me too with a desire to write, and if you permit me, I will frequently report on our life [in Vynnyky, Zhovkva district], our reading club and other local matters" (*CC* 5). "I have been very pleased to learn from *Batkivshchyna* what is going on in our crownland, and therefore I am writing about our village too, Vyspa near Rohatyn" (*CC* 61). "When I keep reading about the institutions that have been introduced in various villages, I regret that nothing is heard here about my village [the author had been a cantor in Piznanka Hnyla, Skalat district, but was now working as a custodian at the Greek Catholic seminary in Lviv]. It, after all, is not worse than other villages, and it is fitting that the world should hear about it" (*CC* 85). "I read in your *Batkivshchyna* about all sorts of interesting and beneficial things and about reading clubs, and now the desire has seized me to report something from our neighbourhood [Spasiv, Sokal district] as well" (*CC* 87).

The correspondence also generated further correspondence as points of view expressed in one item were rebutted in another. For example, a peasant from Strilkiv, Stryi district, complained that the members of the reading club were reluctant to pay their dues (*CC* 34). The pastor of Strilkiv wrote back to *Batkivshchyna*, saying that dues were paid gladly (*CC* 40).[98] In this way the newspaper became an outside forum for airing differences within the village.

The correspondent, especially the peasant correspondent, was an intellectual pioneer in an environment that traditionally resisted innovations

---

[97] It should be noted that antagonism between villages, which "often passed into open brawls," was also a feature of traditional peasant life before the penetration of the national movement. Dobrowolski, "Peasant Traditional Culture," 294.

[98] For other examples of correspondence submitted as a response to earlier correspondence, see *CC* 109; 121; 240 and 243.

and pioneering. The point made by William Thomas and Florian Znaniecki with reference to the Polish village applies equally well to the Ukrainian village:

> The general unwillingness with which a conservative peasant group usually greets the appearance of intellectual interests in any one of its members can probably be best explained by its aversion to individualization in any form. A man who reads in a non-reading community has interests which the community does not share, ideas which differ from those of the others, information which others cannot obtain; he isolates himself in some measure from his environment, lives partly in a sphere which is inaccessible to others—and what is worse—strange and unknown to them; thus, he in certain respects breaks away from social control.[99]

The correspondent, dissociated to some degree from the rest of the village, was the yeast of the countryside. By corresponding with the world of newspapers, reporting on his own particular village, he entered decisively into a wider community to which he usually referred as "the world" or "the whole world" (U *svit* or *tsilyi svit*). He was able to reprimand his fellow villagers for their contempt of learning or ignorant disregard of their own best interests. The publication of the isolated peasant's correspondence gave him psychological assurance of the support of the wider community. Publication, furthermore, helped to legitimize the correspondent in his own village, because "the individual who has any connection with the press obtains direct recognition from his immediate milieu on the ground of his supposed recognition by the wider community."[100] Not only did the individual correspondent receive legitimation in the press, but so too did the point of view he expressed in print.

Correspondents frequently and deliberately used their writings to censure certain individuals in their villages who, they felt, held up progress. A peasant from Liubycha Kameralna, Rava Ruska district, took his village government to task for corruption and drunkenness. At the end of his item of correspondence, he addressed the village officials: "You might be angry at me that I have disgraced you before the world; but I am concerned with the good of our children, and anything that anyone does against that good I will denounce before the world" (*CC* 49).

Often correspondents used the tactic of first denouncing perceived enemies of the national movement without mentioning their names, and then threatening to write a second installment that would reveal the names of offenders who did not in the meantime reform. Thus a member of the reading club in Vynnyky, Zhovkva district, complained that some peasants in his community preferred the tavern to the reading club. "I would like," he wrote, "to record the names of all those peasants who have so shamed themselves; let the whole world know and read about it. But for now I will still remain silent; if, however, they don't repent of their sin, then let your newspaper publish

---

[99] Thomas and Znaniecki, *The Polish Peasant*, 2:1361.

[100] *Ibid.*, 2:1391.

them to their shame" (*CC* 5). Other drinkers were also threatened with publication of their names by correspondents (*CC* 155, 192). The same tactic was used to discourage enemies of the reading club (*CC* 84) and peasants who visited fortune-tellers and practitioners of folk medicine (*CC* 78). The threat to reveal names could extend beyond the peasant community. A peasant from Skalat district accused some Ruthenian landlords of using liquor to get peasants to work on Sunday. "I don't want to write too much or mention who exactly they are. I hope that this brief mention will suffice to make them repent and reform, because if not, I will write more" (*CC* 251). Another peasant, from the Carpathian foothills, felt that many educated people were refraining from enlightenment work among the common people because they were afraid of the landlords and leaseholders and had contempt for the peasantry. "I myself know many such people, but I don't want to reveal their names just yet; perhaps they will still reform!" (*CC* 47).

Very similar was the tactic of simply threatening to write more should enemies of the Ukrainian movement not change their ways. Thus a member of the reading club in Stopchativ, Kolomyia district, wrote that "the mayor Onufrii Zaiachuk, from the very beginning to this day, has shown himself an implacable opponent of the reading club.... We reserve to ourselves the right to write about mayor Onufrii Zaiachuk at length some other time. For now we only advise him not to make war against the reading club and enlightenment" (*CC* 263). The same type of threat was made against the village government of Olesha, Tovmach district, also for opposing the reading club (*CC* 60), and against the peasants of Rivnia, Kalush district, who did not want to have a school and spent their time in the tavern (*CC* 228).

Who were the correspondents to *Batkivshchyna*? To answer this question, we will use two devices: an analysis of the corpus of correspondence from 1884–5 and the biographies of 56 authors (correspondents) who have been identified in the list of activists.[101]

From the corpus of correspondence it has proven possible to identify by occupation the authors of 100 items (35.6 per cent of the total of 281 items). The detailed results of this analysis are presented in Appendix III, "Correspondence by Occupation of Authors," and summary results in Table 11. Of the 56 authors in the list of activists, 48 have been identified by occupation. Fifteen were peasants[102] and six others were peasants who had at least one other occupation.[103] Nine were cantors[104] and seven others were

---

[101] *LA* 1, 3, 4, 17, 26, 29, 39, 44, 75, 78, 87, 95, 99, 101, 118, 125, 128, 132, 137, 142, 151, 157, 161, 165, 177, 185, 189, 193, 194, 199, 200, 203, 215, 219, 220, 222, 231, 250, 256, 258, 259, 264, 266, 282, 286, 293, 298, 321, 324, 328, 331, 334, 359, 361, 364, 368.

[102] *LA* 1, 4, 78, 101, 125, 157, 161, 177, 194, 199, 203, 220, 250, 286 and 321.

[103] *LA* 75, 215 (and cantor); 3 (perhaps cantor); 137 (and cobbler); 231 (and soldier); 331 (and cantor and scribe).

[104] *LA* 26, 39, 118, 142, 151, 219, 222, 264 and 282.

cantors with at least one other occupation.[103] Seven were teachers[104] and five were priests.[105] One was a full-time scribe (*LA* 193) and three others were scribes with more than one occupation.[106] Two were merchants (*LA* 128 and 259). When one compares the data from the corpus of correspondence and from the biographies of the 56 authors in the list of activists (Table 11), it becomes clear that the list of 56 authors underrepresents the participation of the most plebeian elements (peasants and burghers) in the correspondence. The plebeian elements preferred anonymity. Therefore it is safe to assume that many items of correspondence that were unsigned or unidentifiable by the occupation of the author were contributed by peasants and burghers. We may thus assume that peasants contributed more than half the items of correspondence in *Batkivshchyna*, and that cantors, burghers, teachers and priests accounted for most of the rest.

TABLE 11 Correspondence to *Batkivshchyna* and Occupation, Summary

Occupation	Percentage of Identified Items of Correspondence in *CC*	Percentage of Identified Authors in *LA*
Peasants	45.0	37.1
Cantors	16.7	25.7
Teachers	11.5	14.6
Priests	10.0	10.4
Scribes	3.3	4.9
Merchants	3.0	4.2
Artisans/Burghers	10.5	0.5
Others	—	1.0

SOURCE: Appendix IV, Correspondence by Occupation of Authors; Appendix V, List of Activists.

Note: If an item of correspondence had more than one author of different occupations or if an author had more than one occupation, the occupation has been counted fractionally.

The correspondents were linked with the nuclear organizations of the national movement in the Galician village, the reading clubs (to be discussed later). Of the total of 281 items of correspondence in our corpus, 55 (19.6 per cent) have been identified as emanating from members of reading clubs.[109]

---

[105] *LA* 3, 75, 215 (and peasant); 266, 328 (and scribe); 368 (former, and custodian); 331 (and peasant and scribe).

[106] *LA* 17, 29, 87, 165, 256, 293 and 334.

[107] *LA* 44, 95, 185, 298 and 324.

[108] *LA* 266, 328 (and cantor); 331 (and peasant and cantor).

[109] *CC* 4, 5, 6, 10, 12, 14, 15, 22, 40, 41, 42, 46, 49, 52, 53, 67, 73, 76, 84, 92, 100, 105, 108, 122, 131, 137, 142, 143, 145, 146, 153, 154, 162, 173, 191, 192, 194, 210, 219, 235, 236, 237, 241, 243, 246, 248, 252, 255, 260, 263, 268, 271, 275 and 277.

Undoubtedly, many more items, probably the vast majority, were written by members of reading clubs, even though positive identification has not been possible. Of the 56 authors in the list of activists, it has proven possible to establish that 26 (46.4 per cent) held office in a reading club in 1884–5.[110]

Some items of correspondence were contributed by representatives of the village government: only one by a mayor (*CC* 243), but several by councilmen[111] and by scribes.[112] Of the 56 authors in the list of activists, one has been identified as a mayor (*LA* 199), one as a councilman (*LA* 334) and three as scribes (*LA* 266, 328, 331). A significant proportion of the 56 author-activists (23, i.e., 41.1 per cent) also published something outside the corpus of correspondence.[113] All the correspondents were male.

Reading Clubs

If the Ukrainian national movement had had to rely entirely on the education provided by the crownland school council, it would have had great difficulties penetrating the village. The national movement required a better educated peasantry. It needed a peasantry that it could reach through the press, a peasantry that could vote on the basis of informed judgments, a peasantry that would not be cheated and deceived by anyone who wore a suit and knew something of the wider world. To this end it fostered the establishment of reading clubs, institutions that provided popular adult education with a national orientation. The reading clubs created an environment in which reading was prestigious, complemented the education received in the schools, and also brought education, if not always literacy, to the illiterate.

Ivan Franko defined reading clubs as "houses [U *khaty*] where people gather to read books and newspapers or to listen as others read aloud, to discuss and to deliberate about all sorts of necessary, especially educational, activities."[114] The effect these clubs had on the educational level of the peasantry has been well described by the teacher Hryhorii Tymchuk (*LA* 334):

> The permanent teacher Hryhorii Tymchuk has been concerned with the school [in Kolodribka, Zalishchyky district] since 1865, but in spite of all his zeal, when the young people finished school and devoted themselves to the hard work of farming, they gradually became unaccustomed to books and learning and in

---

[110] *LA* 17, 215, 266, 298 (presidents); 44 (president and member of administration); 87, 321, 328, 334 (vice-presidents); 78 (vice-president and auditor); 231 (vice-president and member of administration); 99, 142, 185, 286, 331 (secretaries); 75 (secretary and librarian); 199 (treasurer); 4, 194, 250, 256 (librarians); 157, 161 (members of administration); 1, 101 (deputy members of administration).

[111] *CC* 13, 23, 24, 35, 67, 73, 76, 92.

[112] *CC* 14, 81, 162, 191, 192, 210.

[113] *LA* 17, 26, 29, 39, 44, 95, 118, 125, 142, 165, 193, 199, 203, 215, 220, 231, 256, 259, 264, 293, 324, 331, 368.

[114] Ivan Franko, "Choho khoche 'Halytska robitnytska Hromada'?" *Tvory,* 19:52.

the end forgot everything they had learned. Now it's different. The school-age youth hurries to the reading club in days free from work, listens attentively to intelligent discussion and [public] reading and reads books and newspapers on its own. Thus the young people develop a growing taste for reading and learning, and it is not so easy for them to forget what they learned in school. This is a great boon to the school, a strong and lasting foundation for the enlightenment and education of the youth. And even adult peasants, encouraged by this, are quicker and more diligent in sending their children to school for an education. In fact, there are even some older peasants in the village who have learned on their own initiative how to read and to write a bit as well; in the main they have learned from their children, who are pupils in the school (*CC* 76).

The reading clubs not only encouraged literacy,[115] but also disseminated learning among the illiterate through public readings in the reading clubs. Generally, priests, teachers and cantors were the ones who read aloud to the assembled reading club members.[116] Thus members of reading clubs did not have to know how to read, though reading on one's own was encouraged. About a quarter of the members of reading clubs were illiterate (see Table 12).

The opening of a reading club was a major event in the village and was marked by appropriate ceremonies. This, along with the commemoration of the abolition of serfdom, was one of several secular festivals introduced into the Ukrainian village by the national movement. The inauguration of a reading club generally entailed the invitation of guests from outside, such as delegations from neighbouring villages, a choir from another reading club and a prominent representative of the intelligentsia who lived in the vicinity. The festivities began with a religious service, a solemn divine liturgy or vespers. One of the members of the reading club would later host everyone in his home, appropriately decorated for the purpose (with periwinkle wreaths, religious and national pictures and a display of books and periodicals). The pastor and either the teacher or the educated guest would make speeches about the importance of the reading club. Dinner, a concert, verse recitals and the shooting of mortars or rifles would also solemnize the day. The reading club would have its first official business meeting, during which the statutes were read aloud, new members (often attracted by the pageantry of the inauguration) were registered and officers elected.[117] Subsequent annual meetings would repeat on a lesser scale the festivities of the opening day.

The officers generally elected in the reading clubs were a president (U *holova*) and vice-president (U *zastupnyk holovy*), a secretary (U *pysar*),

---

[115] In Svarychiv, Dolyna district, 50 of 73 members of the reading club could read, "including some who remembered the alphabet and writing only after the opening of the reading club, but now they read fluently." "...z Dolynskoho," *Batkivshchyna* 6, no. 27 (4 July [22 June] 1884): 168.

[116] Mykhailo, "Spravy ruskykh chytalen. I," *Batkivshchyna* 6, no. 47 (21 [9] November 1884): 295.

[117] This composite picture is based on *CC* 53, 59 and 63.

TABLE 12 Literacy and Illiteracy in Reading Club Memberships, 1897–1910

Year	Literate	Illiterate	Percentage of Literate	Number of Reading Clubs Considered
1897	46	6	88.5	2
1898	108	54	66.7	3
1899	91	38	70.5	4
1901	108	20	84.4	4
1902	16	4	80.0	1
1903	329	96	77.4	9
1904	113	29	79.6	2
1905	118	26	81.9	2
1906	134	49	73.2	4
1908	28	0	100.0	1
1909	71	50	58.7	2
1910	295	111	72.7	6
Total	1,457	483	75.1	

SOURCE: TsDIAL, 348/1/1297, pp. 28, 31, 36; 1319, pp. 13–14; 1479, pp. 11–12, 14; 1498, pp. 47, 51, 57–8, 60; 1627, p. 7; 2448, pp. 3, 37–9; 2846, pp. 48, 52–4; 2900, pp. 3, 34–6, 42; 3031, pp. 25, 59; 4921, pp. 26–31; 5874, pp. 37, 40, 42, 46; 6127, pp. 62, 64, 66, 68–9.

Note: Information for reading clubs in the following localities (arranged in alphabetical order by districts) and years is incorporated in the table: Brovary, Buchach district, 1901, 1903, 1910; Svarychiv, Dolyna district, 1899, 1909; Khorostkiv, Husiatyn district, 1903–4, 1906, 1910; Iabloniv, Kolomyia (later Pechenizhyn) district, 1898–9, 1901, 1903, 1906; Kovalivka, Kolomyia (later Pechenizhyn) district, 1901–3, 1906, 1910; Vysloboky, Lviv district, 1897, 1899, 1903, 1908–9; Briukhovychi, Peremyshliany district, 1897–8; Korelychi, Peremyshliany district, 1898, 1910; Volytsia, Sanok district, 1903; Vydyniv, Sniatyn district, 1903, 1905, 1910; Kiidantsi, Zbarazh district, 1899, 1901, 1903, 1906; Zhulychi, Zolochiv district, 1903–5, 1910.

a librarian (U *bibliotekar*) and a treasurer (U *kasiier*). Aside from these members of the administration proper (U *viddil*), deputy members of the administration (U *zastupnyky viddilu*) were also elected. Some reading clubs had more officers, such as auditors (U *kontroliery*).

The majority of officers in the reading clubs were peasants, or burghers in clubs located in towns. Together, these plebeian elements made up over three-quarters of the officers in reading clubs. Priests made up about a tenth of the officers, and teachers and cantors each about a twentieth (see Table 13).

Priests in the reading clubs tended to be presidents. Of a total of 43 presidents identified in the list of activists, 26 were priests (60.5 per cent of the presidents; 86.7 per cent of the priests who were officers). Teachers were concentrated in the presidency (3 teachers), vice-presidency (4) and

TABLE 13 Reading Club Officers, 1884–5, by Occupation

Occupational Category	Number	Percentage
Peasants	162	65.1
Priests	30	12.0
Burghers and Artisans	28	11.2
Teachers	12	4.8
Cantors	10	4.0
Others	7	2.8
	249	

Note: Those reading club officers who had more than one occupation have been counted fractionally.

Peasants: *LA* 1, 4, 5, 6, 9, 10, 12, 15, 16, 18, 20, 22, 23, 25, 32, 34, 36, 37, 45, 46, 49, 51, 52, 57, 61, 63, 64, 65, 68, 74, 76, 77, 78, 79, 82, 86, 89, 90, 92, 97, 101, 102, 106, 111, 115, 121, 122, 126, 127, 130, 131, 134, 138, 141, 145, 147, 152, 153, 155, 156, 157, 158, 160, 161, 163, 166, 169, 172, 175, 180, 181, 182, 186, 190, 192, 194, 196, 197, 199, 201, 204, 208, 209, 210, 211, 212, 216, 217, 218, 221, 223, 227, 229, 230, 233, 235, 236, 238, 239, 240, 242, 249, 250, 251, 252, 254, 257, 260, 261, 262, 263, 265, 267, 269, 270, 272, 274, 277, 278, 279, 283, 284, 285, 286, 288, 289, 292, 297, 299, 302, 305, 307, 310, 311, 312, 313, 316, 319, 320, 321, 326, 327, 329, 335, 338, 339, 343, 350, 351, 352, 354, 355, 356, 357, 358, 362, 367.

Burghers and Artisans: *LA* 28, 30, 31, 33, 58, 72, 88, 103, 113, 139, 140, 144, 149, 150, 173, 174, 187, 188, 226, 253, 268, 291, 341, 342, 347, 360.

Priests: *LA* 13, 24, 38, 41, 44, 56, 60, 66, 71, 93, 109, 116, 120, 146, 148, 162, 164, 183, 185, 191, 195, 198, 213, 234, 243, 244, 298, 332, 333, 346.

Teachers: *LA* 11, 14, 17, 42, 48, 87, 105, 133, 136, 256, 290, 334.

Cantors: *LA* 54, 81, 100, 142, 170, 266, 304.

Others: *LA* 67 (physician); *LA* 53, 303 (scribes).

With More than One Occupation: *LA* 75, 215, 306, 344 (peasants and cantors); *LA* 328, 331 (cantors and scribes); *LA* 119, 366 (peasants and artisans); *LA* 19, 317 (peasants and merchants); *LA* 348, 349 (artisans and scribes); *LA* 231 (soldier and peasant); *LA* 246 (peasant and scribe).

secretarial posts (2) (altogether, 9 of the 12 teachers who were officers; 75 per cent). Secretaries of reading clubs were frequently literate notables rather than peasants. Of 38 secretaries, 4 were cantors, another 4 part-time cantors or scribes, and 2 scribes (together with the teachers, these *ex officio* literates accounted for 31.6 per cent of the secretaries, while they accounted for only 11.8 per cent of all reading club officers). All the officers in the reading clubs were male.

Although Franko defined the reading clubs as "houses," i.e., buildings, reading clubs rarely had their own separate premises in the mid-1880s. Many

reading clubs met in private homes (e.g., *CC* 36, 53), although this was not
the best place for them to meet. As a teacher from Buzhok, Zolochiv district,
noted: "Our man does not go gladly to such a [private] house, because he is
afraid lest he disturb the owner; to the tavern, by contrast, he goes boldly,
because he says to himself: the tavern is open to everyone" (*CC* 42). Reading
clubs also met in village council buildings (*CC* 32), schools (*CC* 34),
community halls (*CC* 42), empty cantors' residences (U *diakivtsi*) (*CC* 44,
83) and even outdoors (*CC* 73). They generally met on Sundays and
holidays,[118] although occasionally a reading club would also be open on another day or other days of the week (e.g., the reading club in Vynnyky,
Zhovkva district, was open on Thursdays and Saturdays as well; *CC* 5).
Reading club members paid dues ranging from 50 kreuzer to 1 gulden 20
kreuzer a year, collected annually, monthly or weekly.[119] One reading club
had differential dues, charging 1 gulden a year for richer peasants and 50
kreuzer for poorer peasants (*CC* 271). The dues went toward the purchase of
books and subscriptions. The number of members in reading clubs varied
from about fifteen to over a hundred, but generally reading clubs averaged
from forty to sixty members. In the mid-1880s there were about 400
Ukrainian reading clubs in Galicia.[120] By 1914 there were well over 3,000.[121]

The reading clubs were connected with larger, umbrella organizations, the
national populist Prosvita and the Russophile Kachkovsky Society
(U *Obshchestvo im. Mykhaila Kachkovskoho*). Prosvita was founded in Lviv
on 8 December 1868. In its first years (1868–74), Prosvita had 277 members
(275 individuals and 2 reading clubs). Over a quarter of the members (27.6
per cent) lived in Lviv, about a fifth in other Galician cities (19.4 per cent)
and a little less than half (46.6 per cent) in villages and small towns (another
6.5 per cent of the membership lived in cities outside Galicia). Exactly a
third of the members were priests and most of the rest belonged to the
secular intelligentsia (educators accounted for 20.3 per cent of the membership; lawyers for 17.2 per cent; secondary-school and university students for
10.0 per cent; government employees for 7.7 per cent; and other sectors of the
secular intelligentsia for 6.9 per cent). The participation of peasants in
Prosvita in these early years was negligible. The priests were based mainly in
the countryside (91.7 per cent), while the secular intelligentsia was based in
the cities (ranging from 100 per cent in the case of the students to 63.6

[118] *CC* 34, 75, 76, 161, 188.

[119] *CC* 34, 76, 100, 105, 107, 224, 271.

[120] In 1884 the ethnographic-statistical student club recorded 359. Mykhailo, "Spravy ruskykh
chytalen. I," 295. The crownland statistical bureau recorded 461 in 1886, 422 in 1888 and 421 in
1889. *Rocznik Statystyki Galicyi* 3 (1889–91): 180.

[121] The national populist Prosvita was the patron of 2,944 reading clubs in 1914. In the same
year the Russophile Kachkovsky Society was the patron of about 300 clubs. *Entsyklopediia
Ukrainoznavstva*, s.v. "Obschchestvo im. Mykhaila Kachkovskoho" and "Prosvita." There were
also some reading clubs independent of either society.

per cent in the case of the lawyers).[122] Thus, in its early years, Prosvita was urban-based and intelligentsia-led, with priests forming its advance guard in the countryside.

TABLE 14 Growth of Prosvita Membership, 1868–1908

Years	Average Annual Recruitment of New Members
1868–74	39
1875–80	207
1881–5	267
1886–90	398
1891–5	624
1896–1900	1,098
1901–5	1,113
1906–8	1,416

SOURCE: Lozynsky, *Sorok lit diialnosty "Prosvity"*, 35–6.

Starting in the late 1870s Prosvita membership expanded, with the peasantry and peasant institutions forming the majority of new recruits. In mid-1876 Prosvita had 323 members, in March 1877—604 and in June 1878—1,024.[123] Information on the composition of new membership is available for the mid-1880s. At the end of 1883 Prosvita had about 900 *dues-paying* members (actual membership was much larger). Of 313 new members recruited in that year, 164 were peasants and burghers (52.4 per cent), 42 were reading clubs (13.4 per cent) and 9 were church brotherhoods. At the end of 1884 Prosvita had 2,525 members. Of the 392 members recruited in 1884, 130 were reading clubs (33.2 per cent) and 2 church brotherhoods. Of 324 members recruited in 1885, 99 were peasants (30.6 per cent), 94 were reading clubs (29.0 per cent), 30 were burghers and 5 were church brotherhoods (29 priests and 14 elementary school teachers also joined).[124] By 1914 Prosvita had 36,500 members, and reading clubs associated with Prosvita had 197,000 members.[125] Table 14 shows the growth of the Prosvita membership from its establishment in 1868 until 1908.

Prosvita had branches (U *filii*) in smaller cities outside Lviv to serve reading clubs regionally. There were four such branches in 1880–90 and

---

[122] This is a summary of the results of my study on the membership of Prosvita in "Polish and Ukrainian Socialism," 126–42.

[123] Pavlyk, "Pro rusko-ukrainski narodni chytalni," 532, 545.

[124] "Diialnist Prosvity v rotsi 1883," *Batkivshchyna* 6, no. 4 (25 [13] January 1884): 21. "Diialnist Prosvity v rotsi 1884," *Batkivshchyna* 7, no. 5 (30 [18] January 1885): 34. "Tovarystvo Prosvita v rotsi 1885," *Batkivshchyna* 8, no. 4 (29 [17] January 1886): 21.

[125] *Entsyklopediia Ukrainoznavstva*, s.v. "Prosvita."

seventy-seven in 1914.[126] The branches distributed printed drafts of reading club statutes, counselled peasants on how to set up reading clubs and dispatched educated speakers to reading-club events (*CC* 44).

The Russophiles did not have their own organization analogous to Prosvita until 1874, when they founded the Kachkovsky Society in Kolomyia.[127] While Prosvita remained a largely nonpeasant organization until the late 1870s, the Kachkovsky society, largely through the efforts of Ivan Naumovych, immediately gained a following in the villages and established a network of reading clubs. In the period 1871–8 the national populists founded only six reading clubs; the vast majority of the 171 clubs founded in those years were Russophile in allegiance.[128] Within the first few years of its existence, the Kachkovsky Society had over five thousand members.[129] The Kachkovsky Society declined, however, as Prosvita won more of the countryside and as the Russophile movement as a whole declined. By 1914 the Kachkovsky Society was only about a tenth the size of Prosvita.[130]

Outside the formal structures of Prosvita and the Kachkovsky Society, Galician Ukrainian students took annual hikes through the countryside, at least in the years 1883–8,[131] visiting the reading clubs and offering lectures and concerts as they went.

Opposition to the Reading Clubs

The reading clubs were not introduced into the villages without resistance and opposition from some conservative peasants. A correspondent from Mshana, Zolochiv district, has described the sort of internal resistance in the peasant community that local proponents of the enlightenment movement encountered. He also answered his critics' arguments against reading newspapers. A reading club had not yet been founded in Mshana, but several

---

[126] *Ibid.*

[127] The founding meeting was held either 20 or 21 August 1874 (N.S.). "Novynky," *Pravda*, no. 13 (1874): 568. *Nauka*, no. 5 (1874): 193–7. The latter source contains the draft of the society's statutes.

[128] Pavlyk, "Pro rusko-ukrainski narodni chytalni," 499–500.

[129] According to Pavlyk (*ibid.*, 497), the society had 1,645 members in 1875, 4,791 in 1876 and 6,123 in 1877. Other sources give different figures. The city statistical bureau of Lviv registered 3,496 members in 1875. *Wiadomości Statystyczne o Mieście Lwowie* 3 (1877): 66, 70. A memorial book of the society confirms Pavlyk's figure for 1875, but states that there were 3,338 members on 8 January 1876. Monchalovsky, *Pamiatnaia knyzhka*, 21, 23. An official Austrian statistical publication mentions 7,253 members in 1877. *Statistische Monatsschrift* 4 (1878): 526.

[130] *Entsyklopediia Ukrainoznavstva*, s.v. "Obshchestvo im. Mykhaila Kachkovskoho."

[131] "Vandrivka ruskoi molodizhy i viche ruskykh akademykiv," *Batkivshchyna* 6, no. 30 (25 [13] July 1884): 186. *Prohramy vechernyts.* TsDIAL, 146/4/7653a, pp. 30–6. Vid komytetu vandrivnychoho, "IV. vandrivka akademych. molodezhy," *Dilo* 7, no. 48 (1 [13] May 1886): 2. Vandrivnyk, "Dopysy 'Dila'. Z Zolochivskoho," *Dilo* 8, no. 94 (25 August [6 September] 1887): 2. Vid komytetu vandrivky, "Vandrivka ruskoi molodizhy akademychnoi," *Dilo* 9, no. 147 (4 [16] July 1888): 2.

proprietors, the priest and the village government had put together enough money for a subscription to *Batkivshchyna*.

So now we have a community newspaper. But what does it profit us, if such darkness still reigns in our village that only a few—I don't know if it's even a dozen or so—proprietors can be found who are interested in knowing what's happening in God's wide world? The rest avoid listening to [the reading of] a newspaper. In fact, they even agitate among the others, saying: "Brother, don't contribute money for the newspaper, because times are tough as it is. Don't crawl over to listen when they read, because that's treason: our fathers didn't read and didn't listen to newspapers and they lived, so we don't have to [read and listen].[132] And you know that recently some people were imprisoned and taken before the courts for newspapers. Do you want us, too, to be arrested? Whoever's stupid, let him go listen, but we don't need it!" Then they each hide behind the other, pull their caps low over their brows, put their hands in their pockets and go as fast as they can to Iankel [i.e., the tavern-keeper]. There they brag even more about how they are supposedly wiser, while the stupider people remained to listen to the newspaper.

Shame on you, gentlemen, that you are so ignorant! You appeal to the example of your fathers and grandfathers, that somehow they lived, even though they didn't read newspapers. Why in those days there weren't even any schools, there were no telegraphs and no railways, and people ploughed with a *sokha* [hooked plough, harrow] or simple plough (U *pluh*). But today everything has changed, because the world does not stay in one place, but moves forward, and whoever doesn't move forward with it will fall by the wayside. Why are Czech and German peasants so much better off than we are? Because they are all literate and enlightened; each of them, either by himself or together with someone else, receives a newspaper; and it is very rare to find a house without a newspaper or booklets. So know and remember that newspapers and books are put out by intelligent people, who sincerely want to help you, who wish you well and want to enlighten and instruct you. Today more and more people in our land are beginning to read newspapers and books. Before long they'll be laughing at anyone who doesn't read, just as they would laugh at someone who today wanted to plough with a *sokha*! (*CC* 123).

In sum, this correspondent listed three reasons why some peasants opposed reading: the costs involved, the break with the tradition of illiteracy and the fear of arrest. All three reasons were also mentioned in other items of correspondence.

The opposition to the reading clubs claimed that the clubs demanded an expenditure (dues) that provided no immediate economic benefit. The rich

---

[132] This argument is strikingly similar to that put forward by some Ukrainian settlers in Canada at the turn of the century. When a school district was being established in Pobeda, Alberta, in 1908, it was opposed by "individuals, who considered education as a waste of time and money. They had never attended school themselves and they felt that their children could get along without any education just as their forefathers had done." Cited in Martynowych, *The Ukrainian Bloc Settlement*, 207. When the Czechoslovak government expanded the school system in Transcarpathia after World War I it encountered similar arguments from the Ukrainian peasantry, e.g., "Grandfather could not read nor write and he still went on living." Magocsi, *Shaping of a National Identity*, 170.

mayor of Fytkiv, Nadvirna district, refused to join the reading club because "I won't be eating bread from it" (*CC* 58). Similarly, a burgher from Mykulyntsi, Ternopil district, dropped out of the reading club at his wife's instigation, "because he wouldn't get bread from the reading club" (*CC* 175). In the Kolomyia region, complained a nonpeasant correspondent, peasants were unwilling to spend money on booklets and newspapers, saying: "Will newspapers and booklets feed me or quench my thirst? It's a waste of money" (*CC* 164). In Perviatychi, Sokal district, peasants who boycotted the printed word said: "...I prefer...to bring home a gallon of liquor, then at least I can have a good drink, but what will I get from a newspaper?" (*CC* 87). In Briukhovychi, Peremyshliany district, peasants did not want a reading club "because they fear the costs" (*CC* 241). In Berezyna, Zhydachiv district, a literate peasant opposed the reading club and used the argument of costs to discourage other peasants from attending; after one reading club member had paid his dues, the literate opponent asked him whether he had already bought himself a horse (*CC* 28). Such arguments were countered with the thesis that although newspapers and reading clubs brought no immediate economic benefit, they would in the long term contribute to the material prosperity of the peasantry. This, clearly, was an argument with greater appeal for younger peasants, whose lives were still before them, than for older peasants, who were more interested in the short term.

The second argument against reading clubs was that they were innovations. Vasyl Chernetsky (*LA* 44), a country priest who founded about a dozen reading clubs himself, wrote that "there is no reason to be surprised that our village people, being little enlightened, do not understand the benefit of reading clubs for their enlightenment, and being conservative, they find it difficult to accustom themselves at first to something that has not been in the village for ages past."[133] Among the arguments the rich mayor of Fytkiv used for not joining the reading club was: "What my father did, that I also will do" (*CC* 58). When Danylo Saikevych (*LA* 282) proposed founding a reading club and other institutions of the national movement in Radvantsi, Sokal district, his opponents told him: "That has not been done here and will not be done" (*CC* 106). In Rudno, Lviv district, there were some "older peasants" who disapproved of the reading club because "their grandfather and father didn't know this and they lived, so they too can now live without the reading club" (*CC* 240). Partly this traditionalist opposition to the reading club was a legacy of serfdom. To the extent that peasants had internalized, under the lash and cudgel, the feudal understanding of their station in life as ignorant, labouring animals, they considered education a distinguishing characteristic of an alien and oppressing class. This attitude was well expressed by an opponent of the reading club in Perviatychi: "Am I a lord that I should read a newspaper?" (*CC* 87). The same sort of traditionalist opposition was directed not only against reading clubs, but also against other institutions

---

[133] Vasyl Chernetsky [V. z Sokalshchyny], "Chomu upadaiut u nas dekuda chytalni?" *Dilo* 7, no. 16 (11 [23] February 1886): 1. See also Dobrowolski, "Peasant Traditional Culture," 287.

fostered by the national movement such as loan funds (*CC* 237) and Ukrainian-run stores.[134]

The third argument against reading clubs mentioned by the correspondent from Mshana was that reading clubs led to trouble with the law. A correspondent from Kiidantsi, Kolomyia district, also wrote that opponents of the reading club said: "For this (the reading club) there will be police investigations, prison terms" (*CC* 181). In part this reflected the well-grounded distrust of government inherited from the era of serfdom. Many peasants were simply convinced by experience (and surely the older the peasant, the stronger his conviction) that any attempt of the peasantry to better its lot would be repressed by the officials. However, there was a more concrete reason for fearing that reading clubs could lead to prison terms: in the late 1870s and mid-1880s radical Ukrainian peasants had been arrested in Galicia for reading forbidden socialist literature.[135] Since this was a novelty—the arrest of *peasants* for reading—word of it spread through the villages. It was not hard for some of the older peasants, who remembered the robbery of servitudes and the military enforcement of corvée labour, to interpret these sensational stories to mean that peasants could only read at the risk of punishment. Certainly it was difficult for many peasants to understand that some newspapers were forbidden and others allowed, since newspapers were a strange and new guest in the peasant cottage.

Other, related reasons for opposing the reading clubs were mentioned in the correspondence. Closely connected to the traditionalist argument was the argument that reading clubs required a certain level of literacy and education to begin with and that that level had not been reached. Thus, among the reasons why the peasants of Briukhovychi decided not to establish a reading club was that "there are few who know how to read" (*CC* 241). In Kiidantsi, Kolomyia district, where a reading club had been founded, opponents argued that none of its members was qualified to enlighten anyone else: "For this one needs an educated [U *'adykovanyi'*] man, and we don't have one." Other opponents ridiculed the "good-for-nothings" (U *laidaky*) who proposed to instruct established farmers (U *gazdy*) (*CC* 181). This attitude represented an acquiescence to and sanctioning of ignorance very similar to that displayed by those who wanted to stay illiterate because their fathers and forefathers had been so.

In Dobrostany, Horodok district, a radical version of the traditionalist argument was raised against the reading club. Here it was charged that the reading club was part of a conspiracy to reestablish serfdom and Poland and that the dues paid to the reading club were new taxes for this purpose. The opponents forbade their children to join the reading club. It may seem that the foes of the reading club in Dobrostany were using a very far-fetched argument to justify their opposition, but on closer inspection we can discern

---

[134] Traditionalist opposition to loan funds and Ukrainian stores is discussed in Himka, "Ukrainian-Jewish Antagonism." See also below, 171–2, 185.

[135] Himka, *Socialism*, 124–38.

the rational significance of their charges. For one thing, the opposition in Dobrostany was hardly alone in giving credence to rumours that the lords were planning to reinstitute serfdom and Poland. Such rumours surfaced in the mid-1880s not only in Ukrainian Galicia[136] but in Polish, Western Galicia as well.[137] The rumours frequently appeared in connection with naive tsarism, although this does not seem to have been the case in Dobrostany. The notion that the landlords wanted to restore Poland came, of course, from experience with the Polish insurrectionary movements of the 1830s, 1840s and 1860s. The idea that the lords wanted to reestablish serfdom was, as we have seen, widespread among the Galician peasantry when it was being deprived of its traditional rights to forests and pastures. The peasants of Dobrostany had had a particularly bitter struggle with the manor over servitudes.[138] They were so alienated by their servitudes experience that they boycotted all extracommunal institutions. Into the mid-1880s they preferred to pay regularly imposed fines rather than elect a municipal council or set up a school in the village, regarding even these innovations as tainted at the source (the nonpeasant, officials' and lords', world). It was an innovation—the abolition of servitudes—that ruined them, and it was the nonpeasant world—the officials, the servitudes commission, the landlord, the gendarmes and the soldiers—who had imposed this innovation on them. The peasants of Dobrostany stood by their traditional rights to the forest and elevated tradition itself to a holy principle. Thus the opponents of the reading club in Dobrostany viewed that institution too as an innovation from the nonpeasant world, just like schools, councils and servitude "equivalents." The reading club was seen as a deviation from and challenge to a proud tradition of independence sanctified by struggle and toil. Hence to join the club meant, in the assessment of the old guard in Dobrostany, objective support for the lords in their endeavour to restore Poland and serfdom. The reading club dispute became so heated in Dobrostany that opponents of the club attacked members with cudgels (CC 245).

---

[136] See Himka, "Ukrainian-Jewish Antagonism," and Himka, "Hope in the Tsar," 134.

[137] "National consciousness ... matured slowly, and up to our own day there were still those who only got angry and cursed when the name of Poland was mentioned. They would say that only the gentry could want Poland back, so that the masses would work for them as under serfdom. It was hard to explain to them that the evil days were gone and would not return. They wouldn't hear about Poland, in fear that the 'lords' would get the upper hand and bring back serfdom." Slomka, From Serfdom to Self-Government, 172–3. See also Brodowska-Kubicz, "Wizja Polski," 23. In 1885–6 the Polish peasants of Western Galicia engaged in massive unrest, fearing that their landlords were about to launch another insurrection to restore serfdom and Poland. Rosdolsky, Zur nationalen Frage, 140. "Zavorushennia posered Mazuriv," Batkivshchyna 8, no. 16 (23 [11] April 1886): 94. Kupchanko, Die Schicksale der Ruthenen, 157–76. Rich source materials on the subject are in the Austrian State Archives, Haus-, Hof- und Staatsarchiv, Informationsbüro, 1886/67, no. 1336, 1351, 1374, 1377, 1401, 1562. Polish historians have written little or nothing on the subject.

[138] The servitudes conflict in Dobrostany is described in Adriian, Agrarnyi protses (pp. 56–7 mention the commune's belief in 1881 that the lords were seeking to restore Poland and serfdom).

I

It remains to be noted that several items of correspondence implied that the opponents of the reading clubs were those peasants who often frequented the tavern (*CC* 87, 123, 240). The reading club and tavern were rival institutions. They competed for the peasants' time, loyalties and, to some extent, money. In the view of the Ukrainian national movement, the reading club was the temple of enlightenment, the tavern a place for stultification; the reading club was Ukrainian, the tavern Jewish; the reading club was a genuinely peasant institution, the tavern was owned by the landlord; the reading club preached sobriety, the tavern encouraged drunkenness; the reading club would teach its members to farm better and in the long run improve their material condition, but the tavern in the long run would only ruin them.[139] During both the struggle against serfdom and the struggle over servitudes, the tavern was a peasant stronghold. In the era of the national movement, however, this was no longer true; in fact, the tavern became alien territory and peasants who spent time there were considered turncoats by the activists of the national movement.

The above remarks do not exhaust the topic of opposition to the reading club. Although generational conflict over the reading club has already been implied, it will be discussed in more detail in the following section. Opposition to the reading club on the part of priests and village governments will be treated in subsequent chapters. I have already, elsewhere,[140] discussed the opposition of village Jews to the reading club.

Generations and Gender in the Reading Clubs

Peasants of different ages joined the reading clubs. There were adult men who had already come into possession of land;[141] adult, married women;[142] lads who still worked on their fathers' farms;[143] and unmarried girls (U *divchata*). For example, the reading club in Novosilky Kardynalski, Rava Ruska district, had 60 members in 1884, of whom 27 were men, 19 lads, 4 women and 10 girls (*CC* 74). In Vynnyky, Zhovkva district, the membership in 1885 consisted not only of adult men, "but also [of] women, lads and girls" (*CC* 153). Data from 1897–1910[144] show that about a quarter (26.7 per cent) of the membership of reading clubs consisted of youth, i.e., lads and girls, with little tendency to change over time (youth accounted for 28.8 per cent in 1897–1903 and for 24.7 per cent in 1904–10).[145]

---

[139] The rivalry between the tavern and the reading club is discussed in Himka, "Ukrainian-Jewish Antagonism."

[140] *Ibid.*

[141] U *hospodari, gazdy.*

[142] U *zhinky, hospodyni, gazdyni.*

[143] U *parubky, molodtsi.*

[144] Reports of local reading clubs to the central office of Prosvita in Lviv; a complete list of the reports consulted is included in Table 18 (Appendix I: Archival Sources).

[145] The slight drop in youth participation in the later period stems from the sharper decline in girls' participation, to be discussed below.

Although youth, narrowly defined as lads and girls, only accounted for about a quarter of the reading clubs' memberships, it was above all younger peasants who were attracted to reading clubs. This has already been suggested in the discussion of the opposition to reading clubs by traditionalist, presumably older, peasants. Very typical was the situation in Radvantsi, Sokal district, where Danylo Saikevych (*LA* 282) had been agitating "for sobriety, for loan funds, for a communal granary, for a reading club, for [choral] singing [from notes]." The established peasants in the village dismissed him, but "there were those who paid attention, mostly from among the younger peasants, both girls and boys" (*CC* 106).

Karl Mannheim has argued that there are no significant generational differences in peasant society, because of the lack of social change in the peasant community.[146] This view rests on the false premise that peasant society is changeless. Even if peasant society, considered in the general historical spectrum, is static, it was certainly not so in late-nineteenth-century Galicia. Here and at this time the penetration of the national movement created a generational difference and a "new type" of peasant.[147]

The generational differences in the Galician Ukrainian peasantry stand out when we examine reading clubs that were composed almost exclusively of young peasants. Typically, this type of reading club was especially prone to conflict with older peasants and the village establishment. The reading club members in Kiidantsi, Kolomyia district, for example, were exclusively "younger people." The correspondent from Kiidantsi explained that only the youth joined the reading club, because the older peasants were worthless. "More than one of our older peasants would sell his father for liquor, but he doesn't have the least desire to do anything good." Significantly, not only did the older peasants boycott the reading club, but so did the nonpeasant notables. The older peasants made fun of the "good-for-nothing" youth in the reading club, who presumed to teach the older peasants (*CC* 181). The correspondent from Kiidantsi also related a story about generational conflict over the reading club in one family. The father was an uncompromising opponent of the reading club. His son, however, was curious and attended

---

[146] "The importance of the acceleration of social change for the realization of the potentialities inherent in a generation location is clearly demonstrated by the fact that largely static or very slowly changing communities like the peasantry display no such phenomenon as new generation units sharply set off from their predecessors by virtue of an individual entelechy proper to them; in such communities, the tempo of change is so gradual that new generations evolve away from their predecessors without any visible break, and all we can see is the purely biological differentiation and affinity based upon difference or identity of age." Mannheim, "The Problem of Generations," *Essays on the Sociology of Knowledge*, 309.

[147] With the penetration of revolutionary ideas into the Russian village "there appeared a new type—the conscious young peasant. He had contacts with 'strikers,' he read newspapers, he told the peasants about events in the cities, he explained to his village comrades the significance of political demands, he summoned them to struggle against the great landowner-nobles, against the priests and the bureaucrats." V.I. Lenin, *Povne zibrannia tvoriv*, 30:298, cited in Assonova, *Sotisialistychni pohliady*, 23.

some club meetings, eventually joining and even donating 30 kreuzer to it. He tried to do all this without his father's knowledge, but it is hard to keep a secret in a village. One day when the son came home, his father grabbed him by the hair and held him while his mother beat him with a poker. Later the father went out into the village and boasted: "My Iakym also got a craving for those reading clubs, but my wife and I beat him and beat him. You'll see that my Iakym will never enter the reading club again" (*CC* 183).

In Volia Iakubova, Drohobych district, the reading club was also composed almost solely of youth. It came into conflict with the older, established peasants (U *starshi gazdy*), the village government, the church committee, two priests and eventually the law.[148] The reading club in Olesha, Tovmach district, was composed "almost exclusively of young proprietors" (*CC* 60). It, and especially its leading activist (*LA* 53), came into conflict with the mayor (see also *CC* 78, 118). In the late 1890s the reading club in Vysloboky, Lviv district, was dominated by youth (in 1897 the membership consisted of 9 men, 16 lads and 10 girls; in 1899, 10 men, 15 lads and 20 girls).[149] The pastor considered the members of the reading club "radicals, atheists and unbelievers."[150]

It has already been mentioned that there were no women among the correspondents to *Batkivshchyna* or officers of reading clubs in 1884–5; there are also no women included in our list of activists. However, from the previous discussion of age differences in the reading clubs, it is clear that women did participate in them.

Female membership in reading clubs was very poorly developed in the last third of the nineteenth and first decade of the twentieth centuries. Mykhailo Pavlyk, who was interested in both the women's question and the development of reading clubs, could find only one case in the 1870s in which females were members of a reading club: the reading club in Hodiv, Zolochiv district, founded in 1872, had a membership comprising 33 lads and 19 girls. Aside from this, women participated in dances sponsored by the reading clubs in Vilshanytsia, Stanyslaviv district (1872), and Litynia, Drohobych district (1876).[151]

In the mid-1880s, as our corpus of correspondence indicates, there was more female participation in the reading clubs. A priest who was a guest at the opening of the reading club in Ozeriany, Borshchiv district, was pleased to note the presence of women, lads and girls; earlier he had attended the opening of the reading club in nearby Lanivtsi, where only adult men were present (*CC* 97). "Widows" joined the reading club in Kovalivka, Kolomyia district (*CC* 260). Married women (U *gazdyni*) joined in Darakhiv, Terebovlia district (*CC* 82), and women and girls in Vynnyky, Zhovkva

---

[148] See *LA* 215; *CC* 92, 145, 219; and Himka, *Socialism*, 130–8.

[149] TsDIAL, 348/1/1498, pp. 47, 51.

[150] Letter of M. Zeleny, teacher and secretary of the reading club in Vysloboky, to the Prosvita administration in Lviv, 12 October 1896, in *ibid.*, p. 46.

[151] Pavlyk, "Pro rusko-ukrainski narodni chytalni," 520.

district (*CC* 153). A woman was mentioned among the twelve proprietors who founded the reading club in Nakvasha, Brody district (*CC* 201), and girls recited poetry in reading clubs in Berezyna, Zhydachiv district (*CC* 28), and in Zakomarie, Zolochiv district (*CC* 29). Nonpeasant females also participated in the reading clubs in the mid-1880s (which they did not do in the 1870s):[152] the daughter of the pastor signed the statutes for the reading club in Briukhovychi, Peremyshliany district (*CC* 57), and a group of noblewomen, including the lady of the manor, formally joined the reading club in Horodyshche, Ternopil district (*CC* 41). The percentage of females in the reading clubs of the mid-1880s could only be ascertained in two instances: in Novosilky Kardynalski, Rava Ruska district, 4 women and 10 girls made up 23.3 per cent of the membership (*CC* 74), and in Piznanka Hnyla, Skalat district, 4 women (3 of whom had the same last names as men in the reading club's administration) accounted for 8.0 per cent of the membership (*CC* 238). It is impossible to say, for the mid-1880s, what percentage of the reading clubs had female members and what percentage of the overall reading club membership was female.

It is possible, however, to answer these questions for a later period, 1897–1910, using the reading clubs' reports to Prosvita's central office in Lviv. The reports to which I had access (see Table 18 in Appendix I) provided information on the sexual composition of 13 reading clubs. Of these, 5 had no female membership at all, 2 had a female membership of under 3 per cent, 4 had a female membership of 3–5 per cent and 2 had a female membership of between 25 and 35 per cent.[153] Females accounted for 4.9 per cent of the total membership of reading clubs in 1897–1910 (108 out of 2,193).

The female membership in the reading clubs exhibited several peculiar tendencies. For one thing, the females in the reading clubs were overwhelmingly girls rather than adult women. Women accounted for only 23.7 per cent of the female membership and girls for 76.3 per cent. This was almost the exact inversion of the situation in male membership, where men accounted for 73.8 per cent and lads for 26.2 per cent. Also, there was a tendency for female participation to decline over time. In the period 1897–1903 females accounted for 7.3 per cent of the total membership of the reading clubs, but in 1904–10 for only 2.7 per cent. Furthermore, female membership in the reading clubs was ephemeral. In the 11 reading clubs for which the membership data encompass more than a single year, 4 never had any women members. Of the 7 that had some female membership, 3 had female membership in less than half of the years for which the data exist, 2

---

[152] *Ibid.*

[153] For most of these reading clubs, membership figures were available for more than one year; here I am referring to summary membership over time. The reading clubs with the largest female memberships were the ones in Vysloboky, Lviv district, which, as we have seen, was a youth-dominated reading club, and in Volytsia, Sanok district, the data for which are limited to one year.

had female membership in half the years, 1 had female membership in more than half the years and only 1 (Vysloboky, Lviv district) had female membership in all years. Female membership tended to disappear early. Of the 6 reading clubs with female membership in some but not all years, 3 had female membership in the first year for which data exist; but in none of these 3 did female membership survive through the last year. In only 1 of the 6 cases was the female membership present in the last year for which data exist.[154] An example of the ephemerity of female membership can also be found in the corpus of correspondence. In Dobrostany, Horodok district, "many women and girls declared their desire... to sign up as members" of the reading club in 1884 (*CC* 100), but a year later there were no females in the reading club (*CC* 245).

Thus female membership in the reading clubs was small, proportionally declining (in 1897–1910) and ephemeral. Unfortunately, the social history of Ukrainian women has not been written,[155] and without this context it is impossible to do more than venture some tentative hypotheses of why this might have been so.

Much certainly depended on the subordinate position of women in Ukrainian peasant society in the late nineteenth and early twentieth centuries. Women were not the equals of men, legally, economically or in the men's popular conception. They were, for example, excluded from participation as officers or electors in the village government,[156] and their wages as agricultural labourers were considerably lower than those of men.[157] Ukrainian men traditionally considered them inferior in intellectual matters. Thus when one correspondent to *Batkivshchyna* alluded to women having "a short mind" (U *rozum korotkyi*), he was thinking of an old Ukrainian proverb about women having long hair, but short intellects (*CC* 104).[158] As second-class citizens in the commune, women were also second-class members of reading clubs.

---

[154] This was the reading club in Svarychiv, Dolyna district. The data only encompass two years. In the first, 1899, there was no female membership; in the second (and last), 1909, there was one female among the club's 99 members.

[155] The most serious contribution to the history of Ukrainian women is the altogether recent work of Martha Bohachevsky-Chomiak, who has been concentrating on the organizational and intellectual, rather than social, history of Ukrainian women. In addition to her "Feminism in Ukrainian History" and "Natalia Kobryns'ka," she has finished a book-length manuscript entitled *Feminists despite Themselves: Women in Ukrainian Community Life, 1884–1939*, to be published by the Canadian Institute of Ukrainian Studies in Edmonton.

[156] Galician women, along with children, criminals and foreigners, were also forbidden to join political societies. Bujwidowa, *Kwestya kobieca*, 5. The prohibition did not apply to membership in reading clubs, but it did prevent women from joining such related organizations of the national movement as the Russophiles' Russkaia rada (founded 1870) and the national populists' Narodna rada (founded 1885).

[157] Najdus, *Szkice*, 1:144–5. Hryniuk, "A Peasant Society," 70.

[158] The proverb can already be found in an early eighteenth-century collection in the form *U zhenshchyny volosy dovhy, da um korotok*. Zinoviiv, *Virshi. Prypovisti pospolyti*, 250.

Furthermore, peasant women were more bound by tradition than peasant men. They were less exposed to new ideas, since they saw less of the outside world (only men were drafted for military service) and fewer of them attended school (as their lower literacy rates indicate). Therefore it is not suprising that some women could be found among the traditionalist opposition to the reading clubs. "What causes the worst trouble nowadays for the reading club are the women (U *baby*) [here] in Trybukhivtsi [Buchach district]. The proverb says it well: where the devil can't do it, he'll send a woman (U *de chort ne mozhe, tam babu pishle*). Women find it impossible to fit in their heads what the reading club is for" (*CC* 104). In the town of Mykulyntsi, Ternopil district, a woman prohibited her husband from attending the reading club (*CC* 175).

Not only did their position in a patriarchal society and their traditionalist outlook tend to keep women out of the reading club, but the leadership of the national movement was quite indifferent to their presence there. On the local level, some priests were known to encourage female membership, as in Kutkivtsi, Ternopil district. Here the pastor and president of the reading club, Mykhailo Iasenytsky (*LA* 120), speaking at the celebration of the reading club's fifth anniversary, "turned to the women present and, indicating their importance in national (U *narodnyi*) life, urged them to take advantage of the reading club" (*CC* 69). As has already been mentioned, a priest expressed satisfaction at seeing females attend the opening of the reading club in Ozeriany, Borshchiv district (*CC* 97). However, the central leadership of the national movement in Lviv did not think female participation was important. The newspaper *Batkivshchyna* did not publish articles for or about women until Pavlyk became actual editor in 1889. He initiated a column entitled "From the Life and Work of Our Women" (U *Z zhytia i pratsi nashoho zhinotstva*).[159] The national populist leadership opposed this innovation. Demian Hladylovych, a founder of *Dilo* and the insurance company Dnister and head of the Shevchenko Society, told Pavlyk that the column was inopportune (U *ne na chasi*). Kyrylo Kakhnykevych said that Pavlyk exaggerated women's oppression and that a peasant reading the column would mix everything up in his head. Better, said Kakhnykevych, to teach peasant women how they should set the table (U *iak maiut stavyty horshky*).[160]

The national populists' hostility to raising the women's question was partly a reflection of the pervasive sexism of the Galician Ukrainian intelligentsia.[161] But it also stemmed from a certain practical concern. Only men were enfranchised. Inasmuch as the national movement was ultimately concerned

---

[159] The first installment was: Mykhailo Pavlyk [Redaktsiia], "Z zhytia i pratsi nashoho zhinotstva," *Batkivshchyna* 11, no. 1 (7 [19] January 1889): 10.

[160] Pavlyk, *Perepyska*, 5:328–9.

[161] The Dnieper Ukrainian Mykhailo Drahomanov was shocked by the attitudes toward women he encountered in educated Galician Ukrainian society. Drahomanov, *Literaturno-publitstystychni pratsi*, 1:409, 419–20; 2:202–3.

with the votes that would give it political power, the male voter was its primary focus. It is no coincidence that the development of a mass women's movement in Ukrainian Galicia occurred only after women received the right to vote after the First World War.

The factors mentioned above go some of the distance toward an explanation of the low participation of women in the reading clubs. They also help explain the ephemerality and decline of female membership. Women, when allowed in the reading clubs, probably felt out of place there and dropped out, and no effort was made to replace them.

The recruitment of females to the reading clubs required a more sustained and intensive effort than the recruitment of males, because the turnover of female membership was much faster. As we have noted, the females in the membership were overwhelmingly unmarried girls. Married women tended to leave the reading club, probably because both the traditional duties of wife and mother were so demanding and social attitudes militated against the presence of married women in the reading club. Thus while lads would go on to become men in the reading club, girls would leave the club when they became women. Males could be recruited at any age, but females practically only while they were young. Furthermore, males were lads longer than females were girls, since females generally married several years earlier than males. Hence the potential female recruit was almost exclusively a girl in her late teens and early twenties.[162] If a group of girl friends entered the reading club together, most of them would marry in the next year or so and all would then quit the reading club. If a new effort was not made immediately to replace the female members, the club would revert to an all-male institution. One can readily see how this dynamic discouraged males from recruiting females and females from entering the reading club. This generational aspect of female membership was undoubtedly a major cause of the ephemerality of female membership.

In light of the above it becomes easier to understand why female membership exhibited a tendency to decline in the period 1897–1910. In 1896 Prosvita initiated a major campaign to found new and revive moribund reading clubs. Within the next several years many clubs were opened or reopened and recruited females. Then the females left the club and little effort was made to recruit more. With time, the reading clubs expanded (the average size was 41 members per club in 1897–1903; 59 in 1904–10) as lads in the reading clubs became men in the reading clubs and new lads were recruited. The expansion of the size of the reading clubs by additional males further depressed the percentage of females in the membership.

---

[162] Most Galician women married in their late teens or early twenties, most men in their late twenties. Over a quarter of the brides (28.1 per cent in 1899; 27.9 per cent in 1904) were under twenty, while bridegrooms under twenty were very rare (0.1 per cent in both years). The majority of brides (60.1 per cent; 59.4 per cent) were under twenty-four, while the vast majority of bridegrooms (83.2 per cent; 83.9 per cent) were twenty-four years old or older. *Oesterreichisches statistisches Handbuch* 20 (1901): 8; *ibid.* 26 (1907): 15.

Thus the cultural revolution in the village, as represented by newspapers, schools and reading clubs, affected the peasantry differentially, with female and older peasants least affected, and male and younger peasants most affected.

3. Village Notables as Bearers of the National Idea: Priests, Teachers, Cantors

The inhabitants of East Galician villages were predominantly Ukrainian peasants. Poles, Jews and Germans also lived there, as well as nonpeasant Ukrainians: priests, teachers and cantors. As we have already seen, these Ukrainian notables participated in the rural national movement, accounting for 38.2 to 50.7 per cent of the identifiable correspondents to *Batkivshchyna* (Table 11) and 20.8 per cent of the officers of the reading clubs (Table 13). Of the activists in our list who have been identified by occupation (357), 53 were priests, 23 teachers and 29 cantors (Appendix V); together they account for 29.4 per cent of the activists.

Priests, teachers and cantors were greatly overrepresented in the national movement. In the mid-1880s there were about 2,200 Greek Catholic priests in Galicia,[1] 1,350 Ukrainian teachers[2] and 2,200 Greek Catholic cantors.[3] Together, the population of the Ukrainian notables came to about 5,750, which was a mere 0.2 per cent of the entire Ukrainian-speaking population of Galicia.[4] By contrast, there were about two and one-half million Ukrainian peasants in Galicia.[5] Thus the rural Ukrainian notables played a role in the national movement greatly disproportionate to their numbers.

In explaining this role, we must first examine what distinguished the notables from the peasants. Then, to place the notables' participation in the

---

[1] In 1880 there were 2,327; in 1887—2,161. *Rocznik Statystyki Galicyi* 3 (1889–91): 56.

[2] There were 4,573 teachers in Galicia in 1885. *Ibid.*, 100. In 1900 less than 30 per cent of the teachers were Ukrainian. Najdus, *Szkice,* 1:76.

[3] I have seen no statistics for cantors. Presumably, the number of cantors would be roughly the same as the number of Greek Catholic parishes and chaplaincies. In 1887 there were 1,873 Greek Catholic parishes and 390 chaplaincies in Galicia. *Rocznik Statystyki Galicyi* 3 (1889-91): 56.

[4] In 1880 there were 2,549,707 Ukrainian-speakers in Galicia. *Oesterreichisches statistisches Handbuch* 1 (1882): 12. In 1890 there were 2,835,674. "Die Ergebnisse . . . 1890," 171.

[5] In 1900, 93.7 per cent of all Galician Ukrainian-speakers were employed in the agricultural and forestry sector. Himka, *Socialism,* 6.

national movement in an illuminating historical context, we will survey their involvement in the struggles over serfdom and servitudes as well as in the revolution of 1848–9. After a general survey of the notables' role in the rural national movement, concentrating on their motivations and function as mediators between the urban leadership and peasant constituency, the chapter will conclude with a more detailed analysis of the complex and important relationship between priests and peasants in the national movement.

Before moving on to these questions, however, it is worth noting that the notability was overwhelmingly male. All priests and cantors were men, as was the great majority of Ukrainian teachers in the mid-1880s.[6] This may also partially account for the low participation of women in the reading club movement.

What Was Notable about the Notables?

The notables differed from the peasantry in five major ways: their vocation was intellectual rather than manual labour; their economic circumstances left them relatively free from the necessity to perform agricultural labour and therefore relatively free to devote themselves to the national movement; they were better educated than the peasants; they were more mobile than the peasantry and saw more of the world than did the latter; and they enjoyed exceptional prestige in the village community.

The first of these distinguishing characteristics is straightforward. The peasant, by definition, was a manual, agricultural labourer. The priest, however, preached, counseled and performed rituals; the teacher instructed children; and the cantor sang the responses in liturgical services. Of the notables, the teacher had the most exclusively intellectual work, the cantor the least.

The second, economic characteristic is somewhat more complicated. Although all the notables were relatively free from the need to perform agricultural labour, this freedom was only relative and not absolute. In a society newly emerged from serfdom, money relations had not become hegemonous to the extent of completely abolishing the natural economy in the payment of traditional notables. Thus priests received part of their income from a parochial farm, cantors and even teachers were traditionally provided with gardens as an endowment and cantors frequently had to combine their cantorial duties with full-scale farming or even with agricultural day labour.

Of the three notable strata, priests were by far the best off materially. The clergy was divided into four ranks. In descending order, in terms of status and income, they were: the pastor (U *parokh*), chaplain (U *kapelian*; similar to a pastor, except that his parish was smaller), administrator (U *zavidatel* or *admynystrator*; a priest who temporarily assumed the duties of a pastor) and assistant (U *sotrudnyk*; a priest who assisted a pastor). According to the

---

[6] In 1875 women constituted only 9.5 per cent of all Ukrainians studying in the teachers' seminaries in Galicia; by 1885 this percentage had risen to 21.2. *Rocznik Statystyki Galicyi* 3 (1889–91): 94.

schematism of the Lviv archeparchy for 1885,[7] 62 per cent of all priests were pastors, 16 per cent chaplains, 13 per cent assistants and 9 per cent administrators. Of the priests in the list of activists who have been identified by status (47), 60 per cent were pastors,[8] 17 per cent assistants,[9] 13 per cent administrators[10] and 11 per cent chaplains.[11] The activist-priests thus generally corresponded in status with priests as a whole. The slight discrepancies are easily explained. The underrepresentation of chaplains among the activists probably reflects the difficulty of establishing reading clubs or other national organizations in localities with a very small population. The overrepresentation of administrators and assistants among the activists is probably due to age. Younger priests were both more likely to be active in the national movement[12] and more likely to be administrators and assistants rather than pastors and chaplains.[13]

The income of pastors derived primarily from three sources: a salary paid by the government, the so-called (L) *congruum* (U *kongrua*); an endowment (U *dotatsiia*) of land; and sacramental fees, the so-called (L) *jura stolae*. Voluntary donations from parishioners[14] were rare.[15]

The pastor's salary or *congruum* originated in the Josephine reforms, when many church lands were nationalized and their incomes used to pay the clergy. The *congruum* was considered a supplement to the income from the parish farm endowment and pastors of different parishes received different *congrua* depending on the size of the endowment. Thus the pastor of a parish with no endowment received 254 gulden 21 kreuzer (*LA* 255), while the pastor of a parish with a huge endowment (293.5 square *Joch*) paid 30 gulden 51 kreuzer into the "religious fund" (*LA* 109). On the average (judging by our priest-activists), a pastor received 120 gulden 26 kreuzer as a *congruum* in the mid-1880s, before a new law, passed in 1885 and taking effect gradually over 1886–7, slightly raised the *congrua*. Under this new law,

---

[7] *Schem. Leop. 1885* (excluding Bukovyna).

[8] *LA* 21, 24, 40, 41, 44, 56, 60, 62, 70, 73, 93, 95, 109, 112, 120, 146, 164, 183, 191, 195, 213, 225, 234, 244, 247, 255, 332, 333.

[9] *LA* 13, 38, 110, 148, 185, 198, 314, 322.

[10] *LA* 66, 159, 162, 167, 296, 298.

[11] *LA* 94, 205, 323, 324, 346.

[12] The average year of birth of all priests in the Lviv Greek Catholic archeparchy was 1835. (Calculated from *Schem. Leop. 1885*.) The average year of birth of the priest-activists (46 identified by age) was 1839. Of all the priests in the Lviv archeparchy, 48 per cent were born by 1835; of the priest-activists, 35 per cent. Several items of correspondence indicate that nonpriest-activists expected younger priests to be more active in the national movement than older priests: *CC* 69, 114.

[13] Of the priest-activists, the average year of birth of pastors was 1832, of chaplains 1839, of administrators 1847 and of assistants 1853.

[14] U *stypendii manualni* or *datky "na bozhe"*.

[15] "Propamiatne pysmo pro nuzhdenne polozheniie hr.-kat. dukhovenstva v Halychyni i Bukovyni," *Dilo* 5, no. 20 (18 February [1 March] 1884): 1.

pastors in Lviv and Cracow were to receive 1,000 gulden annually as their total income (*congruum* plus income from endowment plus income from *jura stolae*); pastors in other cities with a population of over 10,000 were to receive 700 gulden; pastors in cities with a population of 5–10,000 and in resort areas were to receive 600 gulden; and pastors and chaplains in all other localities were to receive 500 gulden.[16] Until this reform the *congrua* had remained basically unchanged since the time of Joseph II, except for a minor reform in 1836 that increased the *congrua* for some poor parishes in the mountain regions.[17]

The endowments of parishes were basically fixed throughout the Austrian period. In the mid-1880s, the average endowment of a Greek Catholic parish (again, judging by our pastor-activists) was 117.6 square *Joch*. For comparison, the average size of a peasant farm in 1847–59 was 7.3 square *Joch*[18] and by 1902 it had declined to 4.5 square *Joch*.[19] Pastors preferred to hire agricultural labourers rather than work the land themselves.[20]

Since both the *congrua* and endowments were relatively fixed throughout the Austrian period, pastors could only increase their income by increasing the fees they charged for performing sacramental rites, such as baptisms, marriages and funerals; although illegal this was of necessity a universal practice. These fees or *jura stolae* were a sore point in the priest-peasant relationship.[21] According to the radical Ivan Franko, using a pastor's financial record books, the pastor of a parish with 636 members earned 835 gulden 96 kreuzer in *jura stolae* in one year (1876).[22] A priest in the mid-1880s estimated that a parish of 2,401 souls would produce 600 gulden in *jura stolae*; of 1,891 souls 450 gulden; of 1,513 souls 400 gulden; of 1,190 souls 300 gulden; and of 893 souls 160 gulden.[23]

The same priest also wrote that the real incomes of pastors varied greatly and could be divided into five classes: c. 1,500 gulden, c. 1,300, c. 800, c. 600, c. 300. The disparity of incomes among pastors is visible in the data on pastor-activists. Some parishes had the reputation of being lucrative (see *LA* 109), others poor (*LA* 332). Some priests had exceptional business acumen and made a fortune (*LA* 70), others had no practical sense and went deeply into debt (*LA* 324, a chaplain; see also *LA* 164 and 244).

---

[16] "Zakon konhrualnyi," *Dilo* 6, no. 33 (21 March [2 April] 1885): 1–2.

[17] "Propamiatne pysmo...."

[18] Steblii, "Peredmova," *Klasova borotba*, 9.

[19] Sviezhynsky, *Ahrarni vidnosyny*, 27.

[20] "Propamiatne pysmo...," *Dilo* 5, no. 22 (23 February [6 March] 1884): 1.

[21] A proverb had it that priests were insatiable (U *Ne hoden popa nasytyty, iak diriavoho mikha*). Cited in Martynowych, *The Ukrainian Bloc Settlement*, 99.

[22] Ivan Franko, "Dokhody i vydatky vbohoho sviashchenyka," in Nechytaliuk, *Publitsystyka Ivana Franka.... Seminarii*, 61. This study of a priest's budget was originally published in 1878.

[23] Sviashch. T.A.O., "Russkoie dukhovenstvo v Halychyni," *Novyi prolom* 4 (6), no. 359 (5 [17] August 1886): 1–2.

The economic situation of chaplains was similar to that of pastors, except that they were poorer. The average chaplain-activist had a *congruum* of 91 gulden 42 kreuzer and a parish endowment of 46.7 square *Joch*. Since chaplaincies were smaller than parishes, the income from *jura stolae* would be correspondingly less.

Administrators, who temporarily served in a parish before a pastor was appointed, were paid a fixed salary, depending on the size of the parish, of 60, 50, 40 or 30 gulden monthly (after the reform of 1885–7).[24] They were also entitled to the *jura stolae* of the parish.

Assistants, who had no rights to the endowment in land, earned 210 gulden annually before the *congruum* reform[25] and, depending on the size of the parish, 400, 350, 300 or 250 gulden after the reform.[26] It was customary for the pastor to give some of the income from *jura stolae* to the assistant. In some parishes the assistant received one-third, but no norm for the division had been established by the mid-1880s.[27]

Although the income of a priest was high by comparison to that of a peasant[28] or cantor, his expenditures were also greater, corresponding to his station and education. He had to subscribe to the press and donate to worthy causes;[29] he had to eat and dress himself and his family better than the plebeians.[30] One of his most burdensome expenses was his family. Unlike his Roman-rite counterpart, the Greek Catholic priest was generally married.[31] Unlike his notable colleague, the teacher, the priest could not indefinitely postpone marriage,[32] but had to be married before accepting ordination,

---

[24] "Spravy ruskoi tserkvy i dukhovenstva," *Batkivshchyna* 6, no. 9 (29 [17] February 1884): 51.

[25] "Propamiatne pysmo . . ." *Dilo*, no. 20 (1884): 1. It could be less. The assistant in Dobrostany, Horodok district, earned 179 gulden 80 kreuzer. *Shem. Lviv. 1884*, 59.

[26] "Spravy ruskoi tserkvy. . . . "

[27] Ot iepyskopskoho ordynariata, Stanyslavov, "Iepytrakhylnyi dokhody i prykhodski sotrudnyky," *Slovo* 26, no. 124 (3 [15] December 1886): 1.

[28] Proverbs expressed the peasants' view that the priest led a life as comfortable as a cat's and that he did not have to work to earn his living (U *Nikomu tak ne dobre iak popovy i kotovy*; *Ne robyv pip na khlib i ne bude*). Cited in Martynowych, *The Ukrainian Bloc Settlement*, 99.

[29] "Propamiatne pysmo . . . ," *Dilo*, no. 20 (1884): 2.

[30] In the priest's budget examined by Franko, 475 gulden 26 kreuzer went for food and 125 gulden 16 kreuzer for clothes. Franko, "Dokhody i vydatky," 63–4.

[31] In the Lviv archeparchy in the mid-1880s, 80.5 per cent of the priests were married, 17.9 per cent were widowed and only 1.6 per cent were celibate. (Calculated from *Schem. Leop. 1885*.) In the Przemyśl eparchy in 1900, 74.3 per cent were married, 21.3 per cent were widowed and 4.4 per cent were celibate. *Schematismus . . . dioeceseos gr.-cath. Premisliensis . . . 1900*, 202.) Among the priest-activists, 75.5 per cent were married, 17.8 per cent widowed and 6.7 per cent celibate. It is not surprising that the activists should contain a slightly higher percentage of celibates, but it must be noted that the absolute numbers are low (3 of 45).

[32] In 1880, 78 per cent of Cracow's teachers were single; in 1910, 66 per cent. Homola, "Nauczycielstwo krakowskie," 115.

generally in his mid-twenties.[33] Thus from early in his career, more or less at the same age as a male peasant, the priest was encumbered with a family. Unlike the peasant's family, the priest's family was not directly able to participate in the priest's work and so augment the family income (except for some help with the farm endowment). Moreover, the priest had to provide much more for his family than the peasant for his, since by the late nineteenth century the priest was expected to educate his children, particularly his sons. The education of their children was a large burden on the clergy,[34] which drove some of them into debt (*LA* 164, 324; see also *LA* 244). Similarly, where a peasant perforce let a family member die, the priest would consider it his duty to pay for physicians for an ill member of his family (*LA* 324). In sum, although the priest was, on average, the wealthiest Ukrainian in the village, his level of civilization demanded that he expend more of his relative wealth, to such an extent that the Greek Catholic clergy of Galicia considered itself poor.[35] And, indeed, hunger was not unknown in Greek Catholic clerical families (*LA* 324), especially in the first hard years after ordination.[36]

The income of teachers was less than that of priests. In the 1860s, 150 gulden a year was a good wage for elementary school teachers. In 1873 the crownland school council reformed teachers' wages so that village teachers, depending on their qualifications, earned from 200 to 300 gulden.[37] In the early twentieth century, unqualified teachers in the countryside earned 500 crowns (250 gulden in the old currency) annually, so-called temporary teachers (who had received a diploma [P *świadectwo dojrzałości*] but had not yet passed the qualifying exam) earned 600 crowns, and permanent, qualified teachers earned from 800 to 1,000 crowns. About half the villages' qualified teachers received 900 and another quarter 1,000 crowns.[38]

The income of a village school teacher in the mid-1880s was thus comparable to that of an assistant in a parish. The teacher did not receive an endowment in farmland, as did the priest, although sometimes the school was endowed with a garden. Two of the teacher-activists in our list (*LA* 280, 340)

---

[33] In our list of priest-activists, over half (56.5 per cent) were ordained at the age of 24, 25 or 26.

[34] In the priest's budget examined by Franko, 361 gulden 20 kreuzer went toward the education of one son in 1876. Franko, "Dokhody i vydatky," 64.

[35] This is the burden of "Propamiatne pysmo...." See also "Zizd dukhovenstva u Lvovi," *Batkivshchyna* 6, no. 4 (25 [13] January 1884): 21.

[36] Recalling his early years as an assistant, Fylymon Tarnavsky wrote: "...My domestic situation was very, very difficult. There was nothing to live from.... My wife and child and I simply went hungry sometimes. Some neighbour women, who saw our poverty, would bring us eggs from time to time, or milk, and groats; and we lived off this alone. Our living quarters were very bad, old and damp. My wife's health began to fail." Tarnavsky, *Spohady,* 159.

[37] Homola, "Nauczycielstwo krakowskie," 122. Hr[yhorii] Vr[etsiona], "Platnia narodnykh uchyteliv v Halychyni," *Shkolna chasopys* 6, no. 6 (16 [28] March 1885): 41.

[38] Najdus, *Szkice,* 1: 303–5. A new law in 1907 raised the wages of a permanent teacher in the village to 1,000–1,200 crowns, and another increase was implemented on the eve of the First World War. Homola, "Nauczycielstwo krakowskie," 123.

seem to have supplemented their income with bee-keeping and gardening. The endowment of a school with a garden was a tradition dating to the period before the regulation of teachers' salaries by the state; in fact, it was a tradition rooted in the natural economy of serfdom. Sometimes a school was also endowed with living quarters for the teacher, but usually it was not. Thus the teacher generally had one major expense more than the priest: the cost of a home[39] (the priest's home was provided by the parish). An important difference between the priest's and teacher's income was that a sizable portion of the former's came directly from individual peasants (the *jura stolae*). The teacher's salary was paid in part by the communal (municipal) government and in part by the district and crownland.[40] The teacher would therefore be less likely than the priest to come into conflict with the peasantry over economic matters.

Galician school teachers were among the lowest paid in the empire.[41] Some experienced great hardship (see, e.g., *LA* 165), and if the exceptional teacher was wealthy, it was not because he was a teacher (e.g., *LA* 83 was prosperous, but only because his father was the richest farmer in the village). Still, teachers received enough from their salaries to subsist without having to take up additional work. The same cannot be said of the last of the village notables, the cantor.

Before the educational reforms of the late 1860s and early 1870s, the posts of cantor and teacher were often combined. The cantor-teacher (U *diakouchytel*) was supported by the commune, which gave him a house (U *diakivstvo*) and garden as well as contributions in kind and in money.[42] With the reforms, however, the posts of teacher and cantor were made separate and the garden (and often the house) went to the school and the contributions to the educational fund.[43] This dispossessed cantors in a number of localities, wherever an endowed school had been established before 1868.

The reforms of the late 1860s, while regularizing the salaries of teachers, did nothing for the cantors. Throughout the late nineteenth century the amount paid a cantor and method of paying him varied from one village to

---

[39] Vretsiona,"Platnia narodnykh uchyteliv.... "

[40] [I . . . niv, podorozhnyi], "Z-pid Horodka," *Batkivshchyna* 9, no. 39 (30 [18] September 1887): 233. Hryniuk, "A Peasant Society," 132.

[41] Homola, "Nauczycielstwo krakowskie," 123. Najdus, *Szkice*, 1:305.

[42] For example, when a school was founded in Dobrianychi, Berezhany circle, in 1819, each household was obliged to pay the cantor-teacher 5 measures (P *garcy*) of rye, 5 of barley as well as 1 gulden 30 kreuzer in cash. In addition, the commune bound itself to provide him with labour for his garden (P *robocizna*). TsDIAL, 146/64b/2285, pp. 9–9v. Gubernial laws of 1806 and 1808 sought to assure that cantors received an adequate income, but left the method of payment to local custom. Klunker, *Die gesetzliche Unterthans-Verfassung*, 1:305–6.

[43] Iliia Boikevych, "Vidozva do ruskykh diakiv Halychyny i Bukovyny," *Batkivshchyna* 6, no. 35 (29 [17] August 1884): 213. V. Chernetsky, "Pysmo z Krystynopolia," *Batkivshchyna* 9, no. 7 (18 [6] February 1887): 41 (this is the text of a petition sent by the cantors to parliament in February 1887). On schools with gardens, 1890–1900, see Hryniuk, "A Peasant Society," 135.

the next. Some cantors still retained a house and garden.[44] Some still received contributions in kind from parishioners: e.g., in Baryliv, Brody district, each household gave the cantor ten sheaves of grain;[45] in Burkaniv, Pidhaitsi district, the cantor was paid in barley and cash (CC 99); and in Mylna, Brody district, each landed peasant gave the cantor a (U) *chvert* (a measure equal to 30.15 litres) of grain.[46] In many villages the cantor relied on a yearly payment, the so-called (U) *rokivshchyna*, collected from individual parishioners when they made their annual confession before Easter (CC 126, 152).[47] Like the priest with his *jura stolae*, cantors were also paid by individual parishioners for their role in sacramental rites (CC 99).[48] According to our correspondents, cantors earned very little. One correspondent swore that no cantor in the Zboriv deanery earned more than 20 gulden a year (CC 215) and another correspondent, the cantor of Burkaniv (LA 39), said he earned 10 gulden and 10 (U) *chverti* of barley a year (CC 99).

Economic insecurity provoked the cantors of Galicia to organize and lobby for the interests of their estate. Beginning in the mid-1880s, cantors petitioned the Greek Catholic consistories, diet and parliament for a reform of their situation. Among their demands were the restitution of houses and gardens for cantors (CC 152, 244),[49] and fixed, higher wages paid regularly, either monthly or quarterly, by the communal governments or the church committees (CC 126, 152).

The editors of *Batkivshchyna*, although supportive of the cantors' movement, did not feel that the cantors could achieve their goals and advocated instead that cantors improve their material conditions by taking on a second, auxiliary profession such as scribe, merchant or craftsman.[50] In this spirit, the cantors' school in Zavaliv, Pidhaitsi district, offered, in addition to training in music, instruction in cobblery, tailoring, blacksmithing and the wheelwright's trade.[51] Among the 29 cantors in the list of activists, 10 had at least one other occupation, usually peasant or scribe (Appendix V); another (LA 39) worked as an agricultural labourer to make ends meet and another (LA 81) later became an insurance agent. As the cantor-activist Ihnatii Polotniuk (LA 264) wrote at the turn of the century, "in many of our

---

[44] "Pershyi zbir diakiv i diakivska sprava v Halychyni," *Batkivshchyna* 6, no. 33 (15 [3] August 1884): 202.

[45] Kravets, *Selianstvo*, 94–5.

[46] "Pivets tserkovnyi," *Novyi prolom* 2, no. 127 (4 [16] April 1884): 4. Confiscated copy in TsDIAL, 146/7/4370, p. 48.

[47] The Roman Catholic organist in Western Galicia was paid in much the same way. See Slomka, *From Serfdom to Self-Government*, 142.

[48] The cantor of Mylna also received fees for specific services. "Pivets tserkovnyi."

[49] See also "Pershyi zbir. . . . "

[50] "Sprava diakivska" *Batkivshchyna* 7, no. 4 (23 [11] January 1885): 24–5, and no. 5 (30 [18] January 1885): 33.

[51] " . . . shkola diakivska," *Batkivshchyna* 6, no. 36 (24 August [5 September] 1884): 224.

communes cantors are also farmers, communal scribes, managers of stores. . . . "[52]

Thus of the three strata of village notables, the cantors alone were unable to live entirely from their profession. They also were the only notables without state regulation of their wages. Like the priest, but unlike the teacher, the cantor frequently depended for his income on the contributions of individual peasants.

In reviewing the economic situation of the village notables, several points can be made. The priest and teacher received a salary sufficient to allow for their complete devotion to intellectual work, which often had a direct relation to the educational and organizational goals of the national movement. This was only partially true of cantors, although cantors who became scribes or store managers were in a situation similar to that of priests and teachers. Although the village notables were not professional activists of the national movement, their positions allowed them to be nearly such if they so chose. None of the village notables formed a truly wealthy stratum and all contained impoverished elements, but they were nonetheless materially better off than the peasantry as a whole. Moreover, they were all more integrated into the money economy than the peasantry, since all received at least part of their income in money. The teacher was entirely paid in money, the priest and cantor partially.

The analysis of the economic circumstances of the three strata of the notability has revealed a hierarchy in which the priests were at the top, the teachers in the middle and the cantors at the bottom. This hierarchy was not limited to the economic sphere, but extended to the other areas in which the notables differed from the peasantry: education, mobility and prestige.

The priest was the most educated of the notables. He attended the theological faculty of Lviv University for four years and could attend some courses outside that faculty.[53] Some clergymen received part of their education outside Galicia (e.g., *LA* 44). All priests would study at least five languages: Ukrainian, Polish and German as the living languages of Galicia, and Latin and Old Church Slavic as the languages of theology and liturgy. Some priests knew other foreign languages (*LA* 164, 323). After ordination priests were expected to continue educating themselves[54] and some had the reputation of being quite well read (*LA* 164, 323, 346).

Teachers attended a teachers' seminary for four years.[55] Although some teachers attended or finished gymnasium (e.g., *LA* 14, 29, 83), this was not a requirement for admission to a teachers' seminary. All teachers were expected

---

[52] Ihnatii Polotniuk, "V dili nashykh diakov," *Halychanyn* 20, no. 200 (6 [19] September 1901): 2.

[53] Fylymon Tarnavsky, who studied for the priesthood in the mid-1880s, has left a memoir of the experience. Tarnavsky, *Spohady*, 99–105, 110–15.

[54] "Propamiatne pysmo . . . ," *Dilo*, no. 20 (1884): 1–2.

[55] The school law of 14 May 1869, supplemented 2 May 1883, reprinted in *Kalendarz Nauczycielski . . . 1885*, 59.

to know German (this was tested in the qualifying exam),[56] and Ukrainian teachers studied both Ukrainian and Polish.[57]

Unlike teachers and priests, cantors had no systematized educational requirements. The only real educational prerequisite to become a cantor was literacy, which, of course, was still a great advance over the educational level of the peasantry as a whole. There were cantors' schools in Zavaliv, Pidhaitsi district;[58] in Przemyśl (founded by bishop Ivan Snihursky in 1818);[59] in Shumiach, Turka district;[60] and in Khrystynopil, Sokal district, later transferred to Stanyslaviv (this school was directed by Ihnatii Polotniuk [*LA* 264]). Studies at a cantorial school, however, were not compulsory. Cantors could pass qualifying examinations administered by the Greek Catholic consistories,[61] but these were not compulsory either. Of our cantor-activists, it has only been possible to identify two who passed such an examination (*LA* 118, 264). The cantors' movement pressed unsuccessfully for the regulation of education and qualifying exams from the mid-1880s into the early twentieth century.[62]

A striking characteristic of the village notables, by comparison to the peasants, was their mobility. In Galicia as a whole in 1900, 78.4 per cent of the population lived in the commune of their birth.[63] The peasants in our list of activists generally lived in the same village as their ancestors had.[64] For the notables, however, it was very rare to finish their lives in the same communes where they were born. And in between birth and death, most notables necessarily lived in several localities and spent some years in an urban environment. Again, the hierarchy of the notables holds true for mobility, with priests being the most mobile, teachers nearly so and cantors somewhere between the upper notables and the peasantry.

---

[56] Homola, "Nauczycielstwo krakowskie," ll7.

[57] There were no exclusively Ukrainian-language teachers' seminaries in Galicia, although there were exclusively Polish-language seminaries. Ukrainian teachers generally attended one of three utraquist (bilingual Polish-Ukrainian) seminaries. "V spravi iazyka ruskoho v utrakvystychnykh semynariiakh," *Dilo* 7, no. 134 (27 November [9 December] 1886): l.

[58] "Uriad parokhiialnyi z Zavalova," *Batkivshchyna* 6, no. 40 (3 October [21 September] 1884): 248.

[59] Pelesh, *Geschichte der Union*, 2:956, 958–9. "V diakivskii bursi," *Batkivshchyna* 6, no. 36 (24 August [5 September] 1884): 224.

[60] "Shkolu diakiv," *Batkivshchyna* 7, no. 48 (27 [15] November 1885): 332.

[61] "Ispyt diakiv v mytropolychii konsystorii," *Batkivshchyna* 7, no. 26 (26 [14] June 1885): 195. Polotniuk, "V dili nashykh diakov."

[62] "Pershyi zbir . . . ," *Batkivshchyna*, no. 33 (1884): 202–3. *CC* 126, 154, 244. Polotniuk, "V dili nashykh diakov."

[63] Bujak, *Galicja*, 1:65. In 1880 the percentage for all of Galicia was 89.4, while in the overwhelmingly Ukrainian and rural region of Southern Podillia the percentage ranged from 91.8 (Husiatyn district) to 94.0 (Borshchiv district). Hryniuk, "A Peasant Society," 82.

[64] See *LA* 16, 18, 19, 20, 36, 51, 52, 79, 82, 84, 85, 92, 101, 106, 107, 108, 117, 119, 122, 154, 158, 160, 169, 197, 199, 202, 208, 212, 239, 246, 249, 261, 283, 284, 287, 299, 306, 321, 337, 354, 365.

Priests were usually born in villages. As the sons of other priests, they may well have moved from village to village as children. Before reaching adolescence, the priest-to-be would attend elementary school in a nearby small city and later a gymnasium in a larger city. He would spend four years in Galicia's capital studying theology. Courting would take the priest to a number of villages during his summer vacations. Following ordination at about 26 years of age,[65] the priest would spend the next ten to twenty-five years being transferred from parish to parish as an assistant or administrator,[66] until finally settling in one locality as a chaplain or pastor. Thus priests saw a great deal of the Galician countryside, knew the cities too and spent their formative twenties in the capital. They therefore would find it much easier to think in national, as opposed to communal, terms than would the peasants. Some priests travelled outside Galicia (LA 44), some to Vienna (LA 164, 324), and some even travelled abroad (LA 164; see also LA 176).

Teachers had a similar mobility profile. They were generally born in villages and small towns, of humbler origins than the priests, and may have received some elementary or secondary education in a city. Ukrainian teacher candidates spent four years at the utraquist seminaries in Lviv, Ternopil or Stanyslaviv.[67] Once they began teaching, they could expect frequent transfers, especially until they became permanent, qualified teachers (which generally took four to ten years).[68] Our teacher-activists were frequently transferred,[69] perhaps more so than most Galician teachers were. The school councils punished undesirable political action by transfers, and this especially affected teachers active in the Ukrainian national movement.[70] Teacher-activists, like priest-activists, had sometimes been outside Eastern Galicia (LA 14, 178) and some even travelled outside the empire (LA 29, 280; LA 280 only went abroad, as a peasant would, when he was in the army). One teacher-activist (LA 83) eventually emigrated to North America.

The least mobile and travelled of the notables were the cantors. There was no typical pattern of mobility for them. Some cantors were born in one village and then later worked in another or several other villages.[71] Other cantors

---

[65] This was the average age of ordination of our priest-activists.

[66] Of our priest-activists, it has been possible to determine that LA 21, 38, 44, 110, 112, 148, 164, 167, 185, 198, 205, 234, 296, 298, 314, 322, 324, 325 and 332 had been stationed in more than one locality. LA 164 had five known postings and LA 167 was described as an "administrator-wanderer." Among our priest-activists, the assistants were born between 1848 and 1858 and the administrators between 1839 and 1853, while the chaplains were born between 1817 and 1849 and the pastors between 1806 and 1848.

[67] "V spravi iazyka ruskoho...," Dilo, no. 134 (1886): 1.

[68] Homola, "Nauczycielstwo krakowskie," 119.

[69] LA 136 had at least six postings; LA 11, 248 and 280—four; LA 14, 29, 42, 104 and 340—three; and LA 48, 83, 105, 165, 214 and 256—two. Only LA 87, 133, 334 spent a long time at one post.

[70] See LA 340 and CC 211. Najdus, Szkice, 1:297–9.

[71] LA 39 and 264 worked in more than one locality. Many parishes had the custom of hiring cantors for one year at a time. The hiring was customarily done on the Sunday after Easter

were peasants who learned the cantor's art and stayed in their native village (*LA* 168, 215, 306). Probably the more professional a cantor was, the more likely he was to move from village to village. Also, the more professional cantor would probably seek either training or certification in the eparchial seats (Lviv, Przemyśl, Stanyslaviv). When cantors engaged in more distant travel, they generally did so as the peasants—in a soldier's uniform (*LA* 264, 295; *LA* 368 moved from a village to Lviv after abandoning the cantor's profession to become custodian at the seminary). All in all, cantors were a bit more mobile than the peasantry, just as they were a bit more educated.

The final characteristic of the village notability was the social prestige it enjoyed. Again, the hierarchy previously noted reasserts itself here. The priest enjoyed the most prestige, especially among the traditional peasantry. Evhen Olesnytsky, reflecting in his memoirs on the 1860s, wrote: "Peasants' sons who finished secondary schools went almost without exception into theology, because it was the ideal of a peasant who had sent his son for a higher education to see him become a priest. Generally in the village other occupations were considered less valuable and less respected."[72] The priest's high prestige among the peasantry is not difficult to understand: to some degree it reflected respect for the priest's relative wealth and education, but it also reflected the special status of the priest as a religious authority in traditional society.

The urban-based secular intelligentsia must also have held the priest in highest esteem among the village notables, and not merely because of his more proximate educational and material level. The Ukrainian secular intelligentsia—Olesnytsky himself, for example—was largely descended from the Greek Catholic clergy (also, e.g., *LA* 67). Moreover, the clergy had a long tradition as a notable stratum in the village, which the teachers—essentially innovations of the constitutional era—did not. Finally, the clergy was the notable stratum most likely to be elected to an extra-communal representative body.[73]

The social origins of the clergy were higher than those of the other notables. Most priests were themselves the sons of priests (*LA* 44, 164, 323, 324) and only a minority were of peasant origin (*LA* 176, a seminarian in the mid-1880s). Some priestly families were of noble origin (e.g., *LA* 164, 191). By contrast, teachers[74] and cantors[75] were largely of plebeian background.

---

[71](continued) (St. Thomas Sunday). *CC* 106. Ot iepyskopskoho ordynariata, Stanyslavov, "Prykhodnyky, diaky i tserkovnaia prysluha," *Slovo* 27, no. 35–6 (9 [21] and 11 [23] April 1887): 1.

[72] Olesnytsky, *Storinky*, 1:26.

[73] *LA* 44, 191, 300 and 325 were elected to the district government; *LA* 324 was elected to parliament. By contrast, one teacher (*LA* 83) and one cantor (*LA* 328) were elected to the district government.

[74] *LA* 14, 178 and 280 were of peasant origin; *LA* 29 was of peasant-burgher origin, although he claimed noble-clerical roots for his family; and *LA* 83 was of Ukrainian petty-gentry origin (U *shliakhta khodachkova*; see below, 212–15). See also Homola, "Nauczycielstwo krakowskie," 115.

[75] *LA* 215 was of peasant origin; *LA* 264 was also of peasant origin, but with a burgher background in the family; some cantors were probably the sons of cantors.

Teachers occupied an intermediary position in the notable social hierarchy. A good indication of their status was that they were allowed to marry into priestly families (*LA* 83, 256), a prerogative generally of university students and seminarians and normally out of the question for peasants and even cantors.

The lowest prestige, of course, fell to the cantor. Even the peasant had a low opinion of him, considering him an inveterate drinker (U *shcho diak, to piiak*),[76] lazy and, so went the stereotype, a lover of knishes (*CC* 99).[77] Yet the cantor did enjoy some prestige, as is evidenced by the disproportionate role he played in communal government, particularly as scribe (*LA* 266, 304, 328, 331), but also as councilman (*LA* 215, 264).[78]

Notables before the National Movement

In the century before the national movement began to penetrate the village, the Galician countryside was the arena of chronic class conflict between peasants and landlords. The village notables could not stand entirely apart from the contest and the stances they took, when compared with their later role in the national movement, reveal elements of both continuity and change.

Under serfdom, there were only two strata of notables in the Ukrainian village: the priests and the cantors (including the cantor-teachers). Of the two, the priests took the most ambiguous stance, sometimes completely supporting the peasantry in its struggle against feudalism and sometimes siding with the manor and government against the commune. There were cases where individual priests embodied this duality. For example, in 1808 the Greek Catholic priest in Pryslip, Sambir circle, was considered to be in sympathy with the insurgent commune. Therefore when a military unit and circle officials arrived in the village, one of the first things they did was confront the priest. In the words of a circle commissioner, "they convincingly reminded him of his obligations," and as a result the priest revealed to them where the insurgent peasants were concentrated. Then the soldiers and officials took the priest to the peasants, ordering him "to address the mob with an instructive speech and to call them to order and obedience with regard to the manor." After they made the priest speak a second time, the

---

[76] Nikolaievich, "V dili nashykh diakov. (Holos iz provintsii)," *Halychanyn* 20, no. 190 (25 August [7 September] 1901): 2.

[77] Among the opponents of the reading club in Volia Iakubova, Drohobych district, was "one knish-eating cantor (U *odyn knyshoid-diak*), who runs after knishes from three villages away and who often enough can be found 'lying so that the dogs came and licked his mug'" (*CC* 92). The cantor's reputation as a knish-lover was immortalized in a children's rhyme, "Tovchu, tovchu mak." *Dytiachyi folklor*, 385–6.

[78] See also Polotniuk, "V dili nashykh diakov," *Halychanyn*, no. 200 (1901): 2.

"mob" dispersed.[79] In short, the pastor of Pryslip changed sides under pressure from the authorities.[80]

There are other documented cases in which the priest stood firmly with the peasants.[81] A priest in Stryi circle in 1789 spread anti-feudal rumours among the peasantry and seems to have headed a conspiracy directed against the nobility. He was arrested, but released for lack of firm evidence. A local noble, apparently not yet accustomed to the new Austrian legal procedures, beat the priest up on his own initiative. The Stryi circle authorities wanted to investigate the assault on the priest, but they were too busy at the time—all the commissioners "were up to their neck in work in connection with enforcing overdue road-labour obligations" (U *sharvarok*).[82] Father I. Vyshnevsky of the Hutsul village of Zhabie, Kolomyia circle, was a radical defender of peasant interests. He took on the functions of a corner-scribe and lawyer in pursuing peasant grievances in the mid-1840s and in 1844 he even sheltered some of the fugitive leaders of the Kobylytsia uprising in Bukovyna. He was hated by the circle authorities and local nobility for his "passion against the manor."[83] In June 1846 a circle commissioner reported to Sambir that the pastor of Dorozhiv was "a drunk, who—it seems—is inciting the commune." The commissioner visited him "before eight o'clock in the morning" and "found him already in an intoxicated state." The priest told the commissioner (in the presence of serfs, as the latter indignantly noted) that the circle authorities, by forcing the peasants to make up auxiliary days, were violating the provisions of the imperial patent of 13 April 1846. "Although," wrote the commissioner in his report, "I suitably put the aforementioned vicar in his place, he would not be convinced." About a week later the priest, "tipsy, cursed out two soldiers who were walking by."[84] One need not give complete credence to the commissioner's remarks on the priest's alcoholism; the commissioner was probably looking for some vice that would explain behaviour so depraved, a servant of God siding with serfs.

Cases of priests objectively serving the government and manor are also documented. The political authorities certainly expected the clergy to be cooperative in maintaining the feudal order and called on it, for example, to help enforce the auxiliary days[85] and to preach against social banditism (U *opryshkivstvo*).[86] The authority of priests was sometimes used by the

---

[79] *Klasova borotba*, 66–8.

[80] For another example of ambiguous behaviour, see the material on Iosyf Levytsky in *ibid.*, 334–5, 535 note 60.

[81] See also Rosdolsky, *Die grosse Steuer- und Agrarreform*, 14 note 15.

[82] *Klasova borotba*, 57, 59.

[83] *Ibid.*, 245–6, 249–50, 533 note 40, 534 note 44.

[84] *Ibid.*, 329.

[85] *Ibid.*, 56.

[86] *Ibid.*, 74.

circle officials to help restore order in rebellious communes[87] and one Greek Catholic priest went so far as to inform the police about the "spirit of resistance to serfdom and even bloodthirsty thoughts" infecting the Ukrainian population in 1846.[88]

Priests' support of the feudal system brought reprisals from the peasantry. Perehinsko, in Stryi circle, was owned by the Greek Catholic metropolitanate; thus clergy and manor here were identical. During anti-feudal disturbances in Perehinsko in 1843 the peasants besieged the rectory and later tried to ambush the priest.[89] Insurgent peasants in Dyniv, Sanok circle, in 1846 looted both the manor and the church. They tied up two priests, beat them and then shot at them with pistols.[90]

The priests' participation on both sides of the class struggle under serfdom indicates that they had conflicting interests, that there were factors binding them to both the peasant and the landlord. Of the links with the peasantry, the strongest perhaps was that of the pastor with his parishioners. The landowner and state officials would normally be outside the Greek Catholic community, and it would be the oppressed peasantry that the priest baptized, married, confessed and buried. The sharing of these intimate moments unquestionably gave the priest a deeper insight into the nature and aspirations of the peasant than that possessed by the nobles and officials. One might even imagine in this early period some confessional, preternational sympathies with the Greek Catholic Ruthenian peasantry. Furthermore, the priest was versed in Christian teaching, which throughout the ages has been a double-edged sword. The edge that spoke of social justice, equality and the exaltation of the humble could also cut into the soul of a priest in a Galician village.

More manifold were the factors inclining the clergy to support the feudal system. One factor was that the Greek Catholic church was itself a large landowner,[91] and behaved much as other estate-owners did in Galicia. For example, the priest who managed the Perehinsko estate, owned by the Greek Catholic metropolitanate, ordered that every serf in the village be beaten during a strike in 1817.[92] Clearly, a priest could not develop a reputation as a champion of the peasants against the manor and expect to be advanced in his eparchy. Furthermore, as already noted,[93] individual priests sometimes imposed feudal rents on their parishioners. In addition to the feudal interests

---

[87] *Ibid.*, 111, 306–7.

[88] *Ibid.*, 294.

[89] *Ibid.*, 233–4, 238.

[90] *Ibid.*, 269. See also Hladylovych, "Spomyny."

[91] The Galician metropolitanate owned about ten villages in 1830. *Istoriia selianstva URSR*, 1:335. Steblii, "Peredmova," *Klasova borotba*, 6. In 1902 it still owned 30,991 hectares. Sviezhynsky, *Ahrarni vidnosyny*, 24.

[92] *Klasova borotba*, 74–5.

[93] See above, 6.

of hierarchy and clergy, i.e., of the church itself, the landlords' influence over the clergy could dissuade priests from siding with the peasants. Throughout the Austrian period, the "presentation" (U *prezent*), i.e., appointment, of a pastor was the prerogative of the manor. A priest could spend a very long time as an assistant or administrator if he was known for his anti-feudal proclivities. Also, the priest would tend to follow the government's lead in siding with the nobility, because Greek Catholic priests were thoroughly imbued with the ideals of Josephinism,[94] which linked pastoral activity with service to the state. Even had the Josephine ideals been weaker, the officials had ways of convincingly reminding priests of their obligations (the case of the priest of Pryslip), including putting pressure on the consistory to remove them.[95] Besides these external pressures on the priest, there was an internal barrier to his complete dedication to the cause of the peasantry: for both moral and intellectual reasons, he would generally be unwilling to support the peasants when they engaged in futile extralegal, especially violent, resistance to serfdom. Finally, at least in the 1830s and 1840s, the educated priests preferred to socialize with the estate officials (stewards, mandators and forest wardens) rather than with the peasants.[96]

Most of these circumstances distancing the clergy from the peasantry in the feudal era would be absent in the era of the national movement: serfdom would have been abolished, the main focus of the movement would have shifted away from the socio-economic struggle between landlords and peasants, the Josephine ideal of service to the state would have been transformed into the ideal of service to the nation and the national movement would work within the legal political system, not against it. Also, the links between the clergy and peasantry would be strengthened by the addition of a consciously national solidarity.

The cantors and cantor-teachers were not at all ambiguous on where they stood during the feudal era: they sided with the peasantry. They can be found formulating peasant grievances,[97] opening the church for a solemn oath of communal solidarity against the manor,[98] inciting rebellion[99] and spreading anti-feudal rumours.[100] The crucial role of the cantor as the bearer of anti-feudal ideology was well understood by the radical Polish revolutionaries of 1846, who hoped that cantors would carry their message of revolt from

---

[94] See below, 124–5.

[95] This was what was happening in the affair of the allegedly alcoholic pastor of Dorozhiv cited above.

[96] Vozniak, *Iak probudylosia*, 135. Anatol Vakhnianyn, "Pro zhytie pytomtsiv i dukhovenstva v litakh 1837 i 1838," *Ruslan* 12, no. 81 (8 [21] April 1908): 3.

[97] *Klasova borotba*, 79–80.

[98] *Ibid.*, 189.

[99] *Ibid.*, 233–4.

[100] *Ibid.*, 378.

village to village.[101] In addition to aiding peasant resistance, cantors—by teaching peasant children to read—loosened the fetter of ignorance on the serfs. They did so at great risk to themselves, since landlords tried to discourage education by sending cantor-teachers or their children into the army.[102] I have not come across evidence of cantors cooperating with the landlords against the peasants during the feudal era.[103]

Interposed between the struggles over serfdom and servitudes were the tumultuous years of revolution, 1848–9. The revolution was a foreshadowing of what would only be consolidated later, during the period of the development of the national movement in the countryside.

The abolition of serfdom and formation of the Supreme Ruthenian Council allowed for the emergence of the first close alliance between the clergy and the peasantry. The priests worked among the peasants, reading aloud to them the appeals of the Supreme Ruthenian Council as well as articles from the first Ukrainian newspaper, *Zoria halytska*. They also encouraged peasants to sign petitions for the division of Galicia and in general brought the national idea from Lviv to the villages.[104] It is no wonder that in countless petitions to the Supreme Ruthenian Council, peasants identified the council with "our honourable spiritual fathers" and "the Greek Catholic rite,"[105] and that enemies of the Council—whether Polish priests,[106] mandators[107] or Polish circle commissioners[108]—began agitating against the Ukrainian priests among the Ukrainian peasantry.[109] Not all the ties binding the priest to the landlords

---

[101] From an anonymous leaflet urging the peasants of Eastern Galicia to rise against the landlords and Austrian government: "The cantor must copy this appeal and immediately and secretly pass it on to the cantor from Ilemnia, who must then send it to the cantor in Hrabiv, and he to Spas and so on from village to village, so that in a week this appeal reaches Perehinsko. If this is not done, then the cantor through whose fault it stopped will be killed without hestitation." *Ibid.*, 273; see also 276–7.

[102] See above, 14. Also: Boikevych, "Vidozva do ruskykh diakiv...." Luzhnytsky, *Ukrainska tserkva*, 491.

[103] The Polish ethnographer Kazimierz Dobrowolski has observed: "...The great majority of peasants who became literate [under feudalism] took minor posts in the villages as the rectors of parish schools, vicars, church organists [the equivalents of the cantors in Polish peasant society], scribes in village courts, and accountants in large estates. It was from this group that the leaders of peasant movements and jacqueries were recruited as well as the originators of a rebel peasant ideology, searching in the gospels for a justification for peasant rights." "Peasant Traditional Culture," 296.

[104] From a report of the Zbarazh Ruthenian council to Lviv: "...In those villages where our priests are enjoying their slumber, the peasants still know nothing" about the petition drive. *Klasova borotba*, 444. See also Kozik, *Między reakcją a rewolucją*, 53.

[105] *Klasova borotba*, 474, 476, 487, 489, 502, 512–13. See also above, 31 note 185, 35.

[106] *Ibid.*, 424.

[107] *Ibid.*, 426, 482.

[108] *Ibid.*, 405, 450.

[109] Many Ukrainian priests received death threats in 1848. Vozniak, *Iak probudylosia*, 150.

were broken yet.[110] The governors of Galicia still felt they could rely on priests to quell communes in open rebellion and to convince the emancipated peasants to fulfill corvée obligations still owing from before the abolition of serfdom.[111] The nobles' prerogative of presentation was still in force, although the Galician peasant deputies to parliament—in their programmatic demands of 3 September 1848—wanted to have the commune choose the pastor.[112] Also, a minority of Greek Catholic priests (a minority which would effectively disappear over the next two decades) were still so attached to the higher, Polish culture that they sided with the Poles during the revolution.[113] If the priests' commitment to the alliance with the peasantry was not yet total in 1848, neither were the peasants completely willing to trust those who had wavered in the decades previous. In the parliamentary elections of 1848, the overwhelmingly peasant electors chose fifteen Ukrainian peasants and only eight clergymen to represent them. As the Polish historian Jan Kozik concluded, "this testified ... clearly to the peasants' loss of confidence in the Ukrainian clergy.... "[114] Still, for all the reservations on both sides, reservations that would never entirely disappear during the period of the national movement, the revolution of 1848–9 sparked the first close working alliance between the peasantry and the largest and most important stratum of the village notables.

As one might expect, the cantors were enthusiastic supporters of the Ukrainian and peasant side during the revolution. They also read national literature aloud to the peasants[115] and took an active part in the local Ruthenian councils.[116] Persecution by the manor did not cease during the revolutionary period either. A manorial official in Derzhiv, Stryi circle, said he would hang the cantor-teacher if he had the authority and called him a rebel because he read *Zoria halytska*.[117] In a manner very similar to what would happen later in the national movement, both local Ruthenian councils[118] and the Ukrainian peasant deputies in parliament[119] called for a regularization and increase of the cantors' income.

During the struggle over servitudes, the role of priests was transitional between that which they had played under feudalism and that which they would play after the constitutional era allowed the national movement to reach the

---

[110] A priest in the region of Zhovkva in 1848 decided to join the Polish National Council so as not to court the wrath of a landlord. *Ibid.*, 135.

[111] *Klasova borotba*, 454, 507.

[112] Rosdolsky, *Bauernabgeordneten*, 172.

[113] Himka, "The Greek Catholic Church," 436–7.

[114] Kozik, *Między reakcją a rewolucją*, 86–7.

[115] *Ibid.*, 53.

[116] *Ibid.*, 38. *Klasova borotba*, 409.

[117] *Klasova borotba*, 474–5.

[118] *Ibid.*, 434.

[119] *Ibid.*, 428.

village (and had played briefly in 1848–9). We have already seen, in our discussion of Iosyf Lozynsky and the national movement's position on the servitudes struggle,[120] that the general policy of the clergy was one of support for the restitution of peasant rights, with a compromise offered to the landlords (accepting the Josephine cadastre as a basis for settlement). We have also seen that this general policy could not be communicated effectively in the absence of constitutionally guaranteed freedoms of the press, association and assembly.

However, in surveying the materials of the servitudes commission (see Table 15), I found no evidence that priests played a role in helping peasants pursue their legal cases. Priests often had their own servitude claims on the manor, which were always settled separately from the peasants' claims. It can well be imagined that priests would have tended to keep aloof from the peasants' generally hopeless servitude cases in order not to jeopardize their own. As for illegal and violent servitude actions by the peasantry, parish priests would oppose them just as they had opposed illegal resistance to serfdom from 1772 to 1848. Characteristic here is the behaviour of the priest of Dobrotvir,[121] who urged his parishioners to abandon their resistance. Finally, the church's role as landowner meant that it would oppose peasant claims to its forests and pastures[122] just as under serfdom it had broken resistance to corvée labour on its estates.

As for cantors and teachers, if the cantor of Batiatychi[123] and the teacher in Dobrotvir[124] are representative, they did as the lower notables did before and after the servitudes struggle: they sided unequivocally with the peasants.

In the National Movement

The notables' participation in the national movement was motivated by factors common to all three strata as well as by factors specific to each. What they held in common, albeit in varying degrees, can be summarized as the possession of sufficient education and extracommunal consciousness to comprehend the ideology of the national movement and act in accordance

---

[120] See above, 53–4.

[121] See above, 45.

[122] The radical Ivan Franko visited the village of Lolyn, Stryi district, in 1876 and was witness to a visitation by Metropolitan Iosyf Sembratovych. The peasants hated the metropolitan and offered Franko the following explanation: "Look at him, so dry and holy, but he brought down misfortune on our commune! Our alpine meadows (U *polonyny*) border those of Perehinsko, and Perehinsko belongs to the metropolitan. Well, out of the blue the metropolitan—may God strike him!—began to take away the meadow, which has been ours forever, about 500 *Joch*! How much legal work we had to go through in pursuit of our claim! We spent more than 300 gulden on the case, but what could we poor people accomplish against such a [powerful person]? We lost. Now we can graze neither cattle nor sheep and cannot keep as much livestock as formerly, because he has taken from us our best meadow!" Ivan Franko [M—on], "Pisma iz Avstriiskoi Ukrainy," *Volnoe slovo*, no. 54 (1 February 1883): 4.

[123] See above, 43.

[124] See above, 47–8.

with its precepts. Both priests and teachers, who knew their Polish counterparts, also had the example, and felt the effects of, Polish nationalism.

The specific motivations of the Greek Catholic priest in the national movement included confessional, ideological, pastoral and socio-economic elements. The confessional link between the priest and the national movement was that the priest was, first and foremost, a representative of the Greek Catholic church and this religion (more properly, rite) was, along with language, one of the most important characteristics differentiating Ukrainians from Poles and other nationalities in Galicia. The Poles were Roman Catholic, the Germans Roman Catholic and Protestant, and the Jews, of course, had their own religion.

There were some Ukrainian-speakers of the Latin rite[125] and some Greek-rite Polish-speakers,[126] both of whom can be considered borderline cases and ethnic raw material for both the Polish and Ukrainian national movements. Otherwise, the designations "Greek Catholic" and "Ruthenian" were synonymous in Galicia. Thus when the Supreme Ruthenian Council was formed in 1848, membership was open to any Galician-born Ukrainian of the Greek Catholic church "admitting through his faith to the Ruthenian nationality."[127] Given the identity between religion and nationality, the priest participating in the national movement was furthering the interests of the coreligionists entrusted to his care.[128]

The general connection between pastoral duties and national obligations implied by the aforementioned circumstance was strengthened by the Josephine ideology pervasive in the clergy. Josephinism had a particularly strong impact on the Greek Catholic church in Galicia. The Austrian enlightened emperors had really shaped this church, given it its very name,[129] educated its clergy for the first time,[130] and in general ended the decades of overt and covert discrimination the church had suffered in the Polish Commonwealth.[131] But the influence of Josephinism was not simply a matter

---

[125] The so-called (U) *Iatynnyky*, to be dealt with below, 208–12.

[126] Primarily Polonized artisans of Ukrainian origin. See Himka, "Voluntary Artisan Associations," 187.

[127] Himka, "The Greek Catholic Church," 435.

[128] See Hroch, *Vorkämpfer*, 132.

[129] In 1772 the Ukrainian church was still referred to as the Uniate or Greek Uniate church, a constant reminder that it had long been in schism from the True Church of Rome and had only embraced union within the recent historical past. The term implied a certain inferiority vis-à-vis the real "Roman Catholics." In July 1774 Maria Theresia decreed that the term "Uniate" was to be banished from private as well as public usage and replaced by the term "Greek Catholic."

[130] Under old Poland, most Uniate priests had no formal seminary training. The Habsburgs established the crucial educational institutions for the clergy: the seminary for Greek Catholics attached to St. Barbara's church in Vienna (the so-called Barbareum), founded in 1774 and replaced by a general seminary in Lviv in 1783, and the imperial seminary residence (G *Convict*) for Greek Catholics, founded in Vienna in 1803.

[131] In June 1744 Maria Theresia announced her intention "to do away with everything that might make the Uniate people believe they are regarded as worse than Roman Catholics." Cited in Pelesh, *Geschichte der Union*, 2:623–4.

of the Greek Catholics' gratitude for the Josephine reforms. Josephinism also flowed into an ideological vacuum in the Greek Catholic church. The church was virtually without tradition, having been established in Galicia only in 1700; without a clear idea of where it stood in relation to Roman Catholicism, with which it was newly united, and to Orthodoxy, which it had abandoned; and without the educated cadres to develop an independent religious tradition. Into this darkness poured the enlightenment of imperial Vienna. Thus the Greek Catholic church was permeated in its most formative period by Josephine ideals. Josephinism had a conception of the role of the clergy as promoters of secular enlightenment and servants of the state; it implanted an ideal code of behaviour in Greek Catholic clergymen that admitted no contradiction or even sharp distinction between the propagation of the faith and of secular knowledge. The Josephine legacy of a service-oriented clergy was inherited by the Ukrainian national movement; the ideal of service to the state was to be transformed so as to include—and in some cases even to dissolve into—service to the nation.[132]

An even stronger link between national and pastoral activity was forged by the Greek Catholic priests themselves, who formulated their own clerical version of the national ideology for the village and specialized in activity that was quasi-national and quasi-religious. The ideology of the Greek Catholic priest-activist conceived of the national movement as the struggle of virtue against vice. Particularly, four pairs of virtues and vices were at issue: ignorance-enlightenment, drunkenness-sobriety, sloth-diligence and prodigality-thrift.[133] The classic formulation of this view was Father Stefan Kachala's *Shcho nas hubyt a shcho nam pomochy mozhe*, published by Prosvita in several editions in the late 1860s and early 1870s.[134] The brochure was written in the form of a conversation among peasants and a priest. At one point the priest summarized the previous discussion and offered his counsel:

> ...We have reflected on why our people are becoming impoverished and why the Jews are taking [peasant] lands, and we have discovered that ignorance is the reason. Ignorance leads to drunkenness, to sloth and prodigality.... My advice is: oppose drunkenness with temperance, sloth with diligence, and prodigality with thrift. Or, to put it briefly: education, work and thrift will save us from usury.[135]

The same themes were found in Galician sermons. For example, Iulian Hankevych's sermon on the anniversary of the abolition of serfdom expressed sentiments almost identical to those of Kachala:

---

[132] See Himka, "The Greek Catholic Church," 429–52.

[133] I have also dealt with this conception in "Priests and Peasants," 6, 10–11; *Socialism*, 50–1; and "The Greek Catholic Church," 450.

[134] See above, 68.

[135] Kachala, *Shcho nas hubyt*, 28–9.

It is not sufficient that our people have received material freedom, i.e., the liberation from serfdom; they must also rise from moral and spiritual slavery, i.e., from sloth and drunkenness. Through these two vices our people do much harm to themselves, become ever more impoverished. To spiritual slavery also belongs the ignorance and darkness in which our people remain.[136]

Preaching in the Greek Catholic cathedral of St. George on the feast of St. George, Aleksander Bachynsky identified three reasons for "the decline of our people": lack of piety, laziness and, above all, drunkenness.[137] Metropolitan Iosyf Sembratovych himself urged his priests "to convince and confirm [the faithful] in the virtues of piety, sobriety, industry and thrift."[138]

Thus, the priests modified the national ideology and shaped it into a pastoral-theological mold. This interpretation of the national movement found full expression in the priests' practice. To combat ignorance, they took a very active part, as we know, in reading clubs.[139] To promote thrift and diligence, they founded and led loan associations[140] and economic cooperatives.[141] There was nothing specifically clerical in these forms of activity; they were consistent with the secular ideology of the national movement, and teachers engaged in them as well. Peculiar to the priest-activists, however, was their campaign against alcohol.[142] Priests founded brotherhoods of sobriety in their parishes and urged the faithful to swear oaths never to drink liquor again.[143] They also staged extravagant anti-alcohol missions, such as one that took place in Kolodribka, Zalishchyky district, in 1881. The pastor invited two preachers who were famous for their sermons against drink (Rudolf Mokh and Iliia Mardarovych). In addition to the two "apostles of holy sobriety," as they were known, twenty-two other priests attended the mission, including two from Bukovyna. Two thousand peasants, some from villages thirty kilometres distant, flocked to Kolodribka for the mission. An open-air liturgy was concelebrated by eleven priests; the main celebrant was the dean. After the liturgy they erected an iron cross to commemorate the mission, "and underneath it they buried, to the sound of mortar blasts, the enemy of

---

[136] Hankevych, *Sluchainyi propovidy*, 120–1.

[137] A. Bachynsky, "Propovid o prychyni upadku nashoho naroda," *Ruskii Sion* 7, no. 17 (1 [13] September 1877): 530–8.

[138] Iosyf [Sembratovych], "V dilakh zavedeniia bratstv tverezosty," *Slovo* 5, no. 60 (5 [17] June 1875): 1.

[139] *CC* 9, 10, 15, 28, 29, 32, 34, 42, 46, 48, 52, 53, 55, 57, 58, 60 (but cf. *CC* 118), 63, 69, 70, 73, 76, 80, 83, 84, 97, 100, 108, 115, 121, 137, 149, 194, 201, 206, 207, 216, 238, 240, 245, 260, 263, 268, 271, 278; *LA* 13, 21, 24, 38, 41, 44, 56, 59, 60, 66, 70, 71, 93, 94, 109, 110, 112, 116, 120, 146, 148, 159, 162, 164, 167, 183, 185, 191, 195, 198, 213, 225, 234, 243, 244, 255, 296, 298, 300, 314, 322, 324, 332, 333, 346.

[140] *CC* 33, 48, 71, 80, 198, 201, 262; *LA* 24, 44, 93, 146, 148, 159, 185, 247, 322, 323, 324, 325.

[141] *CC* 31, 201; *LA* 62, 70, 93, 159, 323.

[142] *CC* 12, 33, 55, 67, 110, 201, 212; *LA* 93, 95, 205, 225, 323.

[143] On the sobriety movement, see also Himka, "Priests and Peasants," 6–7, and Himka, "Ukrainian-Jewish Antagonism."

humanity—liquor" (*CC* 67). The priests' promotion of the sobriety movement, although consistent with the general aims of the national movement, was specific to their station and represented an amalgam of pastoral and national action.

Finally, inclining the Greek Catholic priest to the national movement was his inferior position in Galician society as a whole, particularly discrimination experienced as a member of the Ukrainian nation.[144] Aside from the general discrimination experienced by Ukrainians of all classes (low prestige, limited use of the Ukrainian language in government and higher educational institutions), Ukrainian priests experienced socio-economic discrimination specific to their stratum. Although the noble prerogative of presentation affected Polish, Roman Catholic priests as well, the Ukrainian, Greek Catholic priests experienced it in a different manner and its consequences were also different. Experientially, the Polish pastor, who may himself have been of petty gentry origin, received his appointment from a coreligionist and conational, while the Ukrainian pastor received his from someone socially, religiously and nationally foreign. For the Ukrainian, but not for the Pole, the noble patron was an "other." More importantly, the patron could use his power to hamper the Ukrainian priest's activity. It was commonly believed in the 1880s and 1890s, by Ukrainian radicals and priests alike, that the Polish nobility's monopoly of presentation was the most serious restriction on the priest's ability to participate in reading clubs, assemblies and other manifestations of the Ukrainian movement.[145] While certainly dampening the enthusiasm of some priests for the national movement, in others it must primarily have awakened resentment, particularly if a priest believed he had received a parish incommensurate with his merit solely because of his activism. Also, in addition to the differential effect of presentation on Ukrainian priests, Ukrainian priests were poorer than their Polish counterparts, and not only because they had families: while the land endowment of a Greek Catholic priest generally ran from 20 to 150 *Joch*, the endowment of the Latin rite priest was in the range of 50 to 200 *Joch*.[146] The Ukrainian priest was thus more removed in his personal economic condition from the Galician ruling class than was the Polish priest.

The teacher's motivations for participation in the national movement were also partly ideological. The national movement's great emphasis on education,

---

[144] That the Polish gentry had prejudices against the Ukrainian clergy was admitted (and regretted) by Adam Mickiewicz in the early 1830s. Cited in Terletsky, *Znesenie panshchyny*, 39.

[145] Franko, "Perekhresni stezhky," *Zibrannia tvoriv*, 20:372. Vasyl Chernetsky [V. z Sokalshchyny], "Chomu upadaiut u nas dekuda chytalni?" *Dilo* 7, no. 16 (11 [23] February 1886): 1. "Pravo pryzenty [sic] sviashchenykiv," *Batkivshchyna* 17, no. 11–12 (16 [28] June 1895): 87.

[146] Franko, "Zemelna vlasnist u Halychyni," *Tvory*, 19:284. Iakiv Holovatsky had complained in 1846 that the Ukrainian clergy were much more poorly endowed than the Latin rite clergy. Vozniak, *Iak probudylosia*, 121. Polish nobles in 1848 were also aware that "as a rule" the Roman Catholic clergy had larger endowments than the Greek Catholic clergy. "Memoriale der Galizier an die Herren Minister in Betreff der Theilung Galiziens," *Revolutionsjahre*, 67.

in its own terminology "enlightenment," must have appealed to every teacher who took his professional ethic seriously. As we have already ascertained,[147] the reading clubs were excellent supplements to formal instruction and, by reinforcing a tenuous literacy, could insure that the teacher's efforts in the classroom were not wasted.

Aside from professional considerations, considerations of prestige could also attract the teacher to the Ukrainain movement. Here his role as an instructor of peasants was valued much more highly than it was in Galician society at large. Also, since the peasants' respect for him would be directly proportional to their respect for education, he could only welcome a movement that repeatedly told the peasantry how important education was. (The effect of the national movement on the prestige of the priest was, as we will see, almost the opposite.)

The national movement's attraction for teachers also stemmed in part from the amphibious nature of teachers as a social stratum; they had strong links both to the secular intelligensia-leadership of the national movement and to the peasantry-mass, i.e., to both the subject and object of the movement. Teachers formed the only stratum of village notables that was also a stratum, the lowest, of the secular intelligentsia. The village elementary school teacher was not the equal, but nonetheless a colleague, of the urban secondary school teacher, who played a full-fledged role in the leadership of the national movement. Their solidarity was confirmed by joint participation in institutions (the Ukrainian pedagogical press, the Ruthenian pedagogical association [U Ruske tovarystvo pedahohichne]) established within the framework of the national movement. But the village school teachers differed from the secular intelligentsia in the Ukrainian leadership in two ways: they were rural rather than urban, and they were of peasant-burgher rather than clerical social origin. These characteristics differentiating the village teachers from the secular intelligentsia were precisely what linked them to the peasantry. Teachers in the village could enjoy the company of the new, enlightened type of peasants who participated in the national movement without the condescension typical of priests, because they were not such a high cut above them. The teachers' social locus, then, was analogous to a position between the poles of a magnet, with the field of force being the national movement; it is only natural that the teachers became magnetized.

Finally, more evidently than priests, Ukrainian teachers suffered discrimination as Ukrainians. They too were paid less on average than their Polish counterparts. There was no official salary differential for the two nationalities, but since Ukrainian teachers more frequently taught in smaller settlements and since their advancement was slower, they were a poorer lot than the Polish teachers. Where discrimination was overt was in the matter of teachers' training. There was no purely Ukrainian-language teachers' seminary in Galicia, although there were six purely Polish-language seminaries (in the mid-1880s). In the three bilingual teachers' seminaries, the

---

[147] See especially the testimony of a teacher, already cited above, 86–7.

Polish language dominated over the Ukrainian language.[148] Like Ukrainian priests, Ukrainian teachers also suffered from the control of their possibility for advancement by persons socially and nationally alien. In the case of teachers, not individual Polish nobles but rather the Polish and noble-clerical crownland and local school councils appointed them to their positions.[149] The school councils were infamous persecutors of Ukrainian activism among teachers; several of our teacher-activists (*LA* 165, 280, 340) suffered for their role in propagating the Ukrainian national movement. Again, as was the case with the priests, such external pressure could restrain some teachers from taking part in the movement, but for others, whose promotion to a permanent position was delayed or who endured frequent transfers, the persecution of the school councils would only kindle animosity. Moreoever, since in this case (as opposed to the priest's) the conflict was with a political institution (and not with an individual representative of the ruling class), the animosity was more likely to develop a political colouring.

While both the priests and teachers had ideological as well as material motivations for joining the national movement, the cantors—the least intellectual of the notables—did not. What ideological motivations were at work among this most plebeian of the notable strata were the same as those which affected the more enlightened sectors of the peasantry. The only exception to this generalization was the attempt at the formulation of an ideology for the cantors' movement. Here a specific historical myth (with a kernel of truth) was created, of the cantor as the traditional guardian of enlightenment through the darkest night of serfdom, a martyr to the Ruthenian cause. His activity in the national movement was the natural continuation of his historical mission.[150] Unlike the ideological motivations of the other notables, this was not something intrinsic to the cantors' stratum independent of the national movement (as was the priests' Josephinism and the teachers' professional ethic); it was, rather, a *response* to the national movement, a new interpretation of the cantor within the terms of that movement.

Specifically cantorial motivations would have been connected with attempts to increase the cantors' prestige, security and material conditions. These were the main concerns of the cantors' movement proper, which was, so to speak, a welcome guest within the national movement. By accepting the movement's doctrine of sobriety and himself promoting temperance in the village, a cantor could break down the demeaning stereotype peasants had of him. A cantor who served as secretary of a reading club, read aloud to the illiterate and less literate or conducted a choral group acquired a new and prestigious function, transcending the routine duties of liturgical singing. Such participation reinforced the cantor's position as an intellectual labourer,

---

[148] "V spravi iazyka ruskoho v utrakvistychnykh semynariiakh," *Dilo,* no. 7 (1886): 1. Kravets, *Selianstvo,* 135. "C.k. seminarya nauczycielskie," *Kalendarz Nauczycielski . . . 1885,* 170.

[149] Homola, "Nauczycielstwo krakowskie," 116. Kravets, *Selianstvo,*135.

[150] See especially the programmatic statement of Iliia Boikevych, "Vidozva do ruskykh diakiv . . . ," *Batkivshchyna,* no. 35 (1884): 213–14.

a position that was otherwise the most tenuous of the notable strata. Furthermore, the assumption of these functions would make a particular cantor less replaceable in a village and therefore more secure in his tenure. At the urging of the national movement (*CC* 13, 141, 161), many cantors became scribes; this increased not only their prestige and security but also their income. Similarly, the national movement *created* new positions—in cooperatives, stores and insurance companies—which gave cantors an auxiliary occupation more lucrative and prestigious than subsistence farming. Finally, the cantors looked to the national movement as a whole for endorsement of their aspirations for certification, regulation of placement and regulation and increase of wages.

So much for the motivations specific to the three notable strata. Let us now look at the specificities of their roles as mediators between the urban national leadership and the peasantry.

The priest was considered the most important mediator between the national movement and the peasantry. As the editors of *Batkivshchyna* wrote in 1895:

> In recent times there has been some formation of a secular intelligentsia, comprised of lower-rank civil servants (because Ruthenians are not recruited for higher posts, or very rarely are), teachers, notaries, lawyers, doctors, merchants and so forth. But nonetheless no one can replace the priest, because other members of the intelligentsia do not have as much opportunity for contact with people in the village.[151]

This was why Vasyl Nahirny and the national populists objected to the anticlericalism introduced into the paper by the radical Mykhailo Pavlyk. As Nahirny expressed it: "through the intercession of the saints to God, through the intercession of the priests to the people."[152] A correspondent to *Batkivshchyna* wrote: "... No one meets as frequently with the people as a priest. At work in the field, at banquets in his house and at every occasion, [the priest] can explain to our man what he absolutely must know [about politics]" (*CC* 203).

In fact, the whole fate of the national movement in individual localities was considered to be dependent on the degree of involvement of the priest. A burgher from Ternopil explained that the progress of enlightenment varied from place to place.

> This depends mainly on our priests. Where a priest is good, zealous and cares about the well-being and reputation of his people and his Ruthenian rite, his church, there the people have it better. But where, on the contrary, the priest is drowsy, inactive or plays at being a Pole, ... there, in that village or town, there is still no order among the parishioners. Darkness reigns there, aliens hold sway there, and the Ruthenian people on its own Ruthenian land has neither justice nor power (*CC* 11).

---

[151] "Pravo prezenty sviashchenykiv," *Batkivshchyna*, no. 11–12 (1895): 87.

[152] Pavlyk, *Perepyska*, 5:357.

A peasant correspondent from the Carpathian foothills expressed a similar viewpoint:

> Where there is a good priest, a zealous and true lover of the people [U *narodoliubets*], there is enlightenment, there is a reading club and the electors from that village vote for the Ruthenian candidate. But where the priest is indifferent, an elector from that village will not only not aid but will damage the Ruthenian cause (*CC* 167).

No other stratum of the notability was considered so crucial. In this estimation of the priest's key mediating function are reflected the priest's superiority in most of the qualities that distinguished the notability from the peasantry: economic status, education, mobility and prestige among both the intelligentsia and peasantry. It might be argued that the teacher approximated the priest in these respects, but there were some important differences that made the priest more suitable than the teacher as the principal bearer of the national idea. Every Ukrainian community, no matter how small, isolated or backward, was served by a priest. But not all Ukrainian villages had a school; and not in every Ukrainian village with a school was the teacher a Ukrainian. Furthermore, the priest's prestige among the traditionally minded peasantry (the teacher's would be higher among the already enlightened) meant that the priest could more easily be the pioneer of the national movement in the village. And since the national movement in the countryside was in its pioneering stage in the late nineteenth century, the priest was its crucial instrument.

This is not to say that the other notables were unimportant. The teacher, as has already been pointed out, occupied a social locus between the urban leadership of the movement and its peasant objects. It was thus poised for a mediating role in some ways more effective than that of the priest. The priest bent the national ideology into a clerical mold, while teachers remained true to the fundamentally secular aspirations put forward by the urban intelligentsia. By the early twentieth century this produced some tension between priests and teachers in the village.[153] As part of the secular intelligentsia, teachers were more willing than priests and more capable than cantors of passing on the national idea unadulterated. That the teacher alone lived in the same intellectual-cultural world as the higher, urban intelligentsia is well demonstrated by examining the publications of the notables in our list of activists. If we exclude from consideration all publications in *Batkivshchyna* and its successor *Svoboda* as well as all publications of a purely professional character (i.e., dealing exclusively with sacerdotal, pedagogical and cantorial concerns),[154] we find that only three priests[155] and

---

[153] Ia., "Dukhovenstvo, a vchytelstvo," *Ruslan* 9, no. 185 (24 July [6 August] 1905): 1–2.

[154] By these criteria, I have excluded from consideration the publications of two priests (*LA* 56, 195), one teacher (*LA* 17) and nine cantors (*LA* 26, 39, 91, 118, 142, 264, 295, 331, 368).

[155] *LA* 44, 95, 324.

three cantors,[156] but nine teachers[157] were authors. If we look not simply at the quantity of authors among the three strata of notables, but at the diversity of output of the authors of each stratum, the teachers again stand out. Only the teachers (among our activists) wrote riddles and puzzles (*LA* 29), verse and fiction (*LA* 105, 178), historical operas (*LA* 256) and scholarly works (*LA* 165). Only the teachers published translations from foreign languages (*LA* 178) and contributed to the Polish-language press (*LA* 29). Only the teachers, in sum, were thoroughly assimilated to the culture of the urban intelligentsia. Of the village notables, they were the most accurate mouthpiece of the national leadership.

The other side of the teachers' amphibious position was their relative proximity to the peasantry. Even though this meant that teachers could not enjoy the prestige and authority which the priest's distance from the peasantry lent him, it did mean that teachers had an insider's understanding of the peasants and more ease in communicating with them.

The latter virtues were even more true of the cantor. Of all the notables, he was closest to the peasantry. The advantages of this intimacy were explained by several cantors on the pages of *Batkivshchyna*. Luka Tomashevsky, cantor of Novosilky Kardynalski, Rava Ruska district:

> A good cantor is like the right arm of a good priest, and he can also contribute quite a bit to the good of the people. A cantor circulates among the people more than a priest, and therefore by his example he can teach people much.... There are a number of places where a priest won't go, but a cantor will; there are a number of good things that a priest can't do, but a cantor will (*CC* 14).

Iosyf Byliv (*LA* 39), cantor of Burkaniv, Pidhaitsi district:

> The cantor, after the priest, is the second model for the people. He can contribute much to the enlightenment of the people, since the cantor too has influence and capabilities among the people, [he can intervene] even where it would not be suitable for a priest to act (*CC* 99).

Iliia Boikevych (*LA* 26), cantor of Rohatyn:

> Our people are generally illiterate, but willingly follow an example. They rarely take an example from the highly placed, because the latter for the most part are estranged from the people by their [way of] life, dress, knowledge, conceptions; and even in their language they are rarely able to adapt to the understanding of the people, so that the people do not always trust them. We [cantors], however, live the people's life, speak their language; they understand and know us very well, and we them, so they have more trust in us.[158]

Although the cantor was the notable closest to the peasant, he was still by virtue of his profession more educated. His superior understanding and ability to communicate with the peasant made him a natural leader in the reading

---

[156] *LA* 215, 304, 344.

[157] *LA* 14, 29, 83, 105, 165, 178, 256, 280, 293.

[158] Boikevych, "Vidozva do ruskykh diakiv...," *Batkivshchyna*, no. 35 (1884): 243.

club movement. The cantor "should read booklets and newspapers, explain what he reads to the people and incline others to reading and enlightenment" (*CC* 14). In Ilyntsi, Sniatyn district, peasants "who cannot read themselves go to others, and mostly to the cantor, and he reads to them and explains" (*CC* 24). Peasants in Kulachkivtski, Kolomyia district, wanted to found a reading club. "Our only problem is that aside from our cantor Ivan Symotiuk and [the peasant] Onufrii Proskurniak there are no others who would be able to explain what they read; there are, it is true, more [peasants who are] literate, but they are all still little practiced in the reading of books" (*CC* 138). The cantor's special task in the national movement was the public reading and interpretation of the printed word. If the priest was the university of the national movement in the countryside, the cantor was its elementary school.

Each stratum of the village notability had something unique to offer the national movement. The comparison of the priest and cantor is especially interesting. The priest's importance in the national movement derived from his exalted position and prestige, while the cantor's plebeian life style and simplicity allowed him to act at times more effectively than the pastor; the priest contributed to the national movement the benefits of his higher education, the cantor his lack of the same. Every strength within a stratum was accompanied by a weakness: prestige brought distance from the peasantry; too much education inhibited communication with the uneducated. The existence of three layers of notability, each with its own qualities of mediation as well as its own motivations, was a great boon to the development of the national movement in the countryside.

Tensions between Priest and Peasant

In spite of the large contribution the Greek Catholic clergy made to the progress of the rural national movement,[159] its relations with the peasantry were more strained than those of any other notable stratum. Some of this strain was traditional, with economic roots, and the rest was connected with the penetration of the national movement into the village.

The traditional, economic conflicts between priests and peasants revolved around traditional peasant rights and, especially, payment for sacramental rites (the *jura stolae*). A conflict between the pastor and his parishioners over traditional peasant rights was reported by a correspondent from Fraha, Rohatyn district. The pastor, Petro Savchynsky,

> gives himself airs and makes much of his dignity. If you come to him, you don't know how to speak, because he immediately becomes offended. He never appears in the communal chancery. He does not live in peace either with the commune or the church brotherhood ... And there are quarrels over berries and plums [picked by peasants from the priest's land], over [customary gleaning rights in the priest's post-harvest] stubble and over paths [through the priest's property], on which people have long walked to church and to get water, but

---

[159] Himka, "Priests and Peasants," 5–9. Hryniuk, "A Peasant Society," 415–17.

now the priest's servants do not allow people to pass through [the priest's] courtyard on the way to church, and if anyone goes for water, they [the servants] break [that person's] buckets. Later we hear it mentioned in the sermon (*CC* 132).

Disputes over sacramental fees were particularly acrimonious, with a long history reaching back into the era of serfdom[160] and continuing into the twentieth century.[161] During the revolution of 1848–9, the Ukrainian peasant deputy Ivan Kapushchak moved in parliament to abolish sacramental fees entirely,[162] much to the indignation of priests in the Supreme Ruthenian Council.[163] That the sacramental fees were often exploitative was recognized by secular leaders of the Ukrainian national movement[164] as well as by Polish officials.[165] Opponents of the Ukrainian movement used the issue of sacramental fees to undermine the peasants' confidence in their clergy. This was true in 1848[166] as well as in the 1880s.[167] In the correspondence to *Batkivshchyna* of 1884–5 the issue of sacramental fees was mentioned only twice, in each case as an argument used by opponents of the national movement (a Jew told a peasant during elections: "So you listen to the priests, but they fleece you" [*CC* 204]; traditionalist peasants, reluctant to vote for the Ukrainian candidate, justified themselves by saying: "The priests exploit us" [*CC* 182]).

The paucity of references to this issue in our corpus of correspondence and its presentation as an issue put forward solely by enemies of the Ukrainian

---

[160] *Pravda pro uniiu,* 94, 106. See also above, 7.

[161] During the Ukrainian revolution in Eastern Galicia (1918–20), there were instances of anticlerical disturbances over the issue of sacramental fees. *Ukraine and Poland,* ed. Hunczak, 1:99.

[162] Rosdolsky, *Bauernabgeordneten,* 171–2.

[163] *Zoria Halytska,* no.19 (1849), cited in Pavlyk, "Pro rusko-ukrainski narodni chytalni," 465–6.

[164] Olesnytsky, *Storinky,* 1:34.

[165] For example, the Zolochiv district captain, characterizing Danylo Taniachkevych (*LA* 324) for the viceroy's office in 1879, said he was unlike "other priests, especially of the Greek Catholic rite, who see in their parishioners only a source of income, from which they are free to draw until they reach the bottom." TsDIAL, 146/7/4149, p.182.

[166] Activists of the local Ruthenian council in Zbarazh complained of difficulties they encountered in convincing the peasantry to sign the petition for the division of Galicia: "...Those inimical to us have confused our people and turned them away from it [the petition] by various lies. They have been saying: 'You would not have to pay the priests anything either for a funeral, or a marriage or any other religious services, but if you do sign, you will have to pay even more.'" *Klasova borotba,* 443.

[167] In 1880 some self-styled "friends of the communes," with access to the printing press of *Dziennik Polski* and funding from a Polish noble, mailed out to various Ukrainian communes a Ukrainian-language leaflet containing the legally valid, but long outdated schedule of sacramental fees established by Joseph II. The "friends of the communes" added this commentary: "It is said that serfdom no longer exists, it has disappeared. Therefore the fear of it also no longer exists. But fees for baptisms, marriages and burials exist to this day, and in some regions they are very great. A number of Christians have fallen into Jewish hands through a conscienceless priest." TsDIAL, 146/7/4220.

movement cannot be considered entirely trustworthy testimony to peasant attitudes. Because the question of sacramental fees was in fact frequently raised by opponents of the national movement, the leaders of the movement, and thus the editors of *Batkivshchyna*, were reluctant to raise the question themselves and probably preferred to suppress references to it. Also, if the editors received an item of correspondence that criticized priests for exorbitant sacramental fees, they might suspect the author of being under a nationally alien ideological influence. As we know, the editors of *Batkivshchyna* did not want to alienate the clergy[168] and deliberately suppressed criticism of priests in both the correspondence[169] and editorial articles.[170] That the issue of sacramental fees was none the less important to the peasantry is shown by the subsequent success of radicalism in fanning priest-peasant conflict precisely over this issue. Although the national movement did not allow for the full expression of priest-peasant economic conflict, it is likely that the economic tension still played a role in the background of disputes over other issues that *were* within the framework of the national movement.

Another source of tension between priest and peasant was the transformation of the priest-peasant relationship under the impact of the national movement.[171] Much of the priest's traditional authority had rested on the cultural difference between the educated pastor and his ignorant flock. A primary aim of the national movement, however, was the elevation of the cultural level of the Ukrainian peasant; hence it reduced the cultural distance between priest and peasant. This meant that the enlightened peasant, the product of the national movement, did not regard the priest as uncritically as his forebears had done. The tension implicit in this modification of the priest-peasant relationship was magnified by the ideology that the Greek Catholic clergy brought to the national movement. It was not difficult for the awakening peasants to recognize the paternalism of the clergy's crusade for enlightenment, sobriety, diligence and thrift; some resented its implicit stereotype of the ignorant, drunken, lazy and spendthrift peasant. This is well captured in a story by Leopold von Sacher-Masoch, who put the following words into the mouth of one of his peasant characters: "In some books you can read that the peasant of this land is indolent, a poor worker but a diligent drunkard, and stupid. The cantor once read us something like this, but thank God it isn't true."[172] The same sentiment is echoed in one item of correspondence, from Volchukhy, Horodok district. The correspondent

---

[168] See above, 130.

[169] See above, 80.

[170] See above, 78.

[171] The same was true in Polish Western Galicia: "The clergy were held in high esteem, being thought of as God's chosen, as people who already on this earth counted as saints. Everyone turned to them in need, with full confidence. Not until the popular movement in politics began did this relation change somewhat. . . . " Slomka, *From Serfdom to Self-Government*, 142.

[172] Sacher-Masoch, "Das Erntefest," *Galizische Geschichten*, 171–2.

criticized the priest for neglecting his liturgical and catechetical duties and
letting the church buildings deteriorate. "And in addition to all this, our
priest yells at every parishioner: 'Peasant shirker!'" (CC 89).

Such criticism of priests by correspondents was a symptom of the
enlightened peasants' new view of the clergy. As reluctant as the editors of
Batkivshchyna were to print this criticism, much of it still appeared. The
economic topics were generally taboo, and the correspondents focussed their
criticism on other matters. In particular, they censured individual priests or
priests of a certain region for not living up to the ideal of a priest-enlightener.
The nationally conscious peasant was sitting in judgment of his social
superior, appealing to the authority of the national movement. Thus a
correspondent from Tsvitova, Buchach district, wrote:

> There are two things that we especially need: a good priest and a good mayor.
> Indeed we have nothing against our spiritual father, we only wish that he would
> help us [that is, the reading club], if not by deeds then at least by words, and
> that he would restrain people from evil (CC 16).

A correspondent from Vyspa, Rohatyn district, lamented that for four years
the commune had had no good example from either the priest or the mayor
(CC 61). Another, from Lysiatychi, Stryi district, was disappointed that an
assistant in the parish "was only engaged in church affairs"; although the
pastor sat on the administration of the reading club, he was indifferent to its
fate (CC 70). A peasant from Ivachiv Dolishnii or Horishnii, Ternopil
district, wrote:

> God gave other communes somewhere [else] zealous priests who strive after the
> well-being and enlightenment of their parishioners with all their
> strength.... [But in Ivachiv,] the priest only takes care of his own business and
> does not care about the enlightenment of the people. "You parishioners live as
> you like, continue to remain in ignorance as you did under slavery-serfdom"
> (CC 77).

A burgher from Mykulyntsi, Ternopil district, wrote:

> ...Our enemies will make use of the withdrawal from the reading club of such
> persons as our spiritual father and Mr. D., the adjunct of the court; not so much
> as a hair would fall from their head were they to look after the reading club
> and give us a good example (CC 96).

According to a peasant, the priests of the Sambir region "do not want to be
active in enlightenment, they do not care about the founding of reading clubs
and so forth" (CC 130). A nonpeasant from the Kolomyia region tried to represent the viewpoint of the local peasantry:

> It is sad that the people have come to the conviction that all need and lie in
> wait for them only on account of their money, in order to deceive and cheat
> them and snatch away their hard-earned [literally: bloodied] money.... Rarely,
> very rarely, can one hear a good word about a priest, even more rarely about a
> teacher. Jew, leaseholder, landlord, priest, teacher—almost throughout the
> Kolomyia region they are regarded as equal benefactors by the people. The
> people have grown lazy and poor, have declined very much, and this because of

the indifference of our leaders, because they keep themselves at a distance from the people, who have, in the majority, lost faith in them and make fun of them, while they themselves wander aimlessly (*CC* 164).

A peasant from the Carpathian foothills held that

Our peasants would never vote for an alien candidate if our intelligentsia [here priests are primarily meant] did not turn its back on the common man. But a significant part of our intelligentsia does not mingle with its own people and does not say almost anything [to them] except [the traditional greetings] "Glory to God" and "Glory forever" (*CC* 167).

The former pastor of Kiidantsi, Kolomyia district, according to another correspondent, "used to say that the people of Kiidantsi were thieves and regarded Kiidantsi as a nest of every sort of sin and evil." But no one had ever seen the priest "sincerely strive to reform his parishioners" (*CC* 169). A peasant from Terebovlia district related three instances of priests refusing to support or actively opposing the Ukrainian candidate to parliament. "Hey, spiritual fathers," concluded the peasant, "why do you not, as [priests do] elsewhere, try to lead our people? If you continue to withdraw [from national work] and force the people to get by without you, this will not be good for you" (*CC* 220). A correspondent from the region of Hrymaliv, Skalat district, wrote in connection with the elections to parliament in 1885:

... From Husiatyn [district] they appealed, wrote and begged: hold a pre-election assembly, strike a committee! But our spiritual fathers said: "it will be better not to make a din, it will be better to do things quietly." And they conducted things so quietly that their own electors abandoned them and in the very presence of their pastors, as if to scorn and ridicule them, they cast their votes for the Polish and landlords' candidate.... Also, no one here fosters or troubles his head about such trifles as reading clubs.... And you, spiritual fathers, do not become angry when I tell you: more, much more work [is needed].... (*CC* 221)

A peasant at the general meeting of the Russophile political organization Russkaia rada complained that "many priests, officials and teachers do not care about the people's rights and call the Ruthenian language a 'boorish' (U *khamskyi*) language" (*CC* 266).

As this long list of complaints demonstrates, some peasants were beginning to feel that they could demand a certain type of behaviour from priests, and judged them in terms of their contribution to the national cause. As the items cited also show, this new peasant criticism was not limited to priests, but encompassed teachers as well (see also *CC* 23, 92, 118, 214). The shorter cultural distance between the other notables and the peasants was also being reduced by the national movement.

The new criticism of the priest could evolve into criticism of religious traditions themselves. This is demonstrated by an item of correspondence from Morozovychi, Sambir district. Although the item may appear to be simply a naive disquistion into the causes of poverty, the identity of the author—Ivan Mikhas (*LA* 220), later a professed radical and already in the mid-1880s under radical influence—leaves no doubt that an attack on the church is intended:

> Why should one wonder that our people are often skinny and weak, slow to work, happy to lie behind the oven, greedy for liquor? Just look at our life. For half the year a man doesn't *have* anything to eat, because the floods come and the hail, too, and nothing grows; it is a long, hard time before the next harvest, and the chance of earning something is up to God's will. For the other half of the year there's lenten *fasting*. And the way it is with us during lent, a man's lucky if he eats something that's cooked: borshch, potatoes or cabbage; if there's milk, God forbid that one give it even to a small child! So half the year a man doesn't eat because there is nothing to eat, and half the year he doesn't eat because he considers it a sin to eat.
>
> Now where is one supposed to get the strength and desire to work? It is good if you can pass the day almost unconsciously; it is better yet if you can lie down all day with no one chasing you to work. And if you drink some liquor, it seems that somehow you don't feel so faint and your hunger is forgotten. It's all right for the gentlemen to fast, since even their lenten fare is tasty and nutritious, and, what is more, they wash it down with a little wine. It was once even all right for us to fast, a long time ago, when there were plenty of fish and mushrooms in the forest and honey in the meadow. But now there are no fish, and even if there are you have to catch them secretly [because ponds, like forests and pastures, usually belonged to the landlords]; there are no mushrooms because there are no forests [i.e., in the peasants' possession]; there is no honey. All that's left is *kysil* [a sour fruit soup], cabbage and potatoes, and you're lucky to have that. But our cattle, calves, pigs, eggs, butter, even our cheese and milk take off for parts unknown, even across the border. Far away people think: "What a rich land! It feeds itself and can still feed others." And surely no one there can guess that this land is weak from fasting and hunger, that those eggs and that milk are the savings possible because of the fasting even of infants who cannot yet talk! What sort of savings is this! It is a grave waste because from a child so fed no worker can grow, no soldier, no wife, no mother—at most a cripple. And how many people have died because after several weeks of difficult fasting, finally being allowed to eat, they have so greedily snatched at their food that they knew no moderation!
>
> I heard somewhere that the Hungarians, even during lent, are allowed to use pork fat; and our neighbours, the Poles, are allowed during lent to eat meat once a week and dairy products three times. Now, thank God, we have a third bishop [a reference to the appointment of a bishop for the Stanyslaviv eparchy in 1885]; isn't it high time that our spiritual authorities reflect and take counsel among themselves so as to free us too a little from these fasts, so that the priests would instruct people and warn them against such excessive fasting. Isn't it less of a sin even to drink milk on Friday and eat meat on Sunday than it is to get drunk on both Sunday and Friday? And it seems to me that with more nutritious and more tasty food liquor would have to lose a lot of its appeal (*CC* 273).

Given that the reading club could become the forum for peasant interests and that the peasants in the reading clubs were precisely the type disposed to be critical of the clergy, if not yet openly anti-clerical, it is not surprising that our corpus of correspondence reports antagonism between priests and reading clubs. An interesting example comes from the village of Volia Iakubova, Drohobych district. The case is untypical because of its extremity—the reading club here, composed entirely of young peasants, was unequivocally radical in its orientation[173] and the author of the correspondence describing it, Atanas Melnyk (*LA* 215), was soon to be arrested for blasphemy. However, in another sense, the case of Volia Iakubova can be regarded as typical: it brought into relief the most troublesome features of the priest-peasant relationship. Here economic conflict is expressed, and the enlightened peasants' sitting in judgment on the priest is vividly described. Here is Melnyk's story:

> But the most saddening thing is that among the enemies of the reading club one finds as well our spiritual father, who seemed to welcome it at first. The reason for this [change of attitude] is not known. Perhaps he was turned against the reading club mainly by his wife, who in fact runs everything but the liturgical services. It is true that the members of the reading club did not make special allowances for our spiritual father and on a number of occasions examined his several unjust actions vis-à-vis the commune. And there were incidents between the commune and our pastor such as the following: Every year our pastor would lease the meadow "Pastivnyk" [a microtoponym] to the Jew Khaim for 90–110 gulden and then the commune would have to rent it from the Jew and pay him 100 gulden more [thus 190–210 gulden in total]. The members of our commune assembled, paid their respects to the priest and asked him to rent Pastivnyk [directly] to the commune. Well, he rented it [to us] all right, but for 200 gulden! [Also,] for example, our priest does not give religious instruction in the school, except once a month; he preaches in the church that the people shouldn't drink, but during baptisms and weddings he tells [the hosts] to have liquor brought to him to his home. Bah, he even says that the *members of the commune are sheep, from whom he must have everything there is: the fleece and the cheese and the dung!*
>
> In consideration of the communal welfare, members of the reading club had to discuss such and similar actions of our spiritual father, and so he began to make war, vehement war, against the reading club (*CC* 92).

In a follow-up item of correspondence, Melnyk blamed the pastor for the economic decline of the villagers over the past two decades. Then he went on to describe how the priest opposed the reading club and other manifestations of the national movement:

> ... Our priest often speaks ... against the reading club, against its members and against other institutions. We used to have choral singing, which very much pleased the members of our own and other communes and attracted many members to the reading club. But our priest condemned it to death by locking up the choir loft. And when our people asked the reverend about this, he said that members of the reading club were carrying newspapers with them to the choir loft, and if they were carrying them, they would read them! And that he dissolved the brotherhood of sobriety is really most saddening. In our village there is still the custom of bringing a litre of liquor [to the priest] for baptisms!

---

[173] See Himka, *Socialism*, 129–38.

Once a member of the reading club read to people near the church from a newspaper, including, among other things, about the Stundists [a Protestant, clergyless sect] in Ukraine; our pastor immediately took him to court for this. Witnesses were interrogated in Drohobych and the court released the accused, adding that all are allowed to read what is written in newspapers. The priest then wrote a notation in that reading club member's birth certificate so as to have his [the reading club member's] appeal against being drafted into the army refused. When his [the reading club member's] father came to intercede, the priest told him: "Your son has become a thorn in my side. Let him go to the army. I'll teach him!" And in the end he added that he would do the same to every member of the reading club!

And the priest does a number of other spiteful things to reading club members....

In conclusion, we appeal to you, father! Do not be so stubborn in your behaviour, because it is only honourable to be stubborn in a good cause. Take example from neighbouring priests, from those who understand that they are supposed to be faithful servants of Christ's doctrine. As it is our commune is being very patient: other communes would long ago have appealed to the consistory and God knows where else. But we continue to wait. Will you change? (*CC* 145)

Other correspondents also wrote about clerical opposition to the reading club. One from Iamnytsia, Stanyslaviv district, wrote: "We will establish a reading club, even though the priest doesn't want it! But we pay no attention to this; we have to have a reading club even without him" (*CC* 86). The priest-reading club conflict in Iamnytsia had been described earlier in *Batkivshchyna* (but outside our corpus of correspondence):

...Several years ago the commune brought in wood for a reading club, but the priest said: "It would be sufficient if you read prayers in church!" Thus he frightened people away from the reading club.... Our pastor, to be sure, travels on [temperance] missions and preaches eloquently in the church about sobriety and piety, but he must also strive after the enlightenment of his parishioners, because an ignorant people is always easy for evil persons to exploit and will become a slave of aliens.[174]

As was the case in Volia Iakubova, some priests turned against the reading club after initially supporting it. This happened in Ternopil, where a priest left the reading club "because of some petty matters" (*CC* 69). In Olesha, Tovmach district, the pastor was originally elected president of the reading club (*CC* 60) and even urged the club to expand its activities by establishing a store (*CC* 78). Several months later, however, the priest was accused of being indifferent to the teacher's and mayor's campaign against the reading club (*CC* 118); soon the priest left the reading club entirely and joined forces with the mayor against the reading club's leading activist.[175]

---

[174] "...vid Stanislavova," *Batkivshchyna* 6, no. 22 (30 [18] May 1884): 132.

[175] "...z Tovmatskoho," *Batkivshchyna* 7, no. 1 (2 January 1885 [21 December 1884]): 6.

Conflict between priests and reading clubs is also documented in *Batkivshchyna* outside our corpus of correspondence.[176] It is documented too in a questionnaire Prosvita sent to affiliated reading clubs in 1910. Question 29 of the questionnaire read: "How does the local intelligentsia (clergy, teachers, youth [sic] and others) relate to national causes?" Of the eight answers to which I had access, four reported that the local notability, including the clergy, opposed the national movement. The answer to question 29 from Khorostkiv, Husiatyn district, was simply: "It is sad to say."[177] In Brovary, Buchach district, a barely literate peasant wrote: "Hostile, from the party of oinker-intelligentsia."[178] The youthful reading club in Vydyniv, Sniatyn district, responded that "the pastor is a clerical; he is hostile to everything that is secular. The women school teachers are Polish pestilences."[179] The scarcely literate response from Kovalivka, in Pechenizhyn district, was that "the clergy acts as Russophiles, because Father Trach is hostile to people. And the woman teacher is a Pole, so that there is no counsel from her."[180] A fifth response, from Zhulychi, Zolochiv district, was that "the intelligentsia, except for one teacher, a Pole, relates in a medium way" (U *vidnosytsia seredno)*.[181] Only three reading clubs reported the notability favourably disposed: in Korelychi, Peremyshliany district;[182] in Svarychiv, Dolyna district;[183] and in Vysloboky, Lviv district.[184] In the latter community, priest-reading club relations may have been fine in 1910, but fourteen years earlier the pastor had denounced the club from the pulpit and dismissed the church trustees who had joined it.[185]

In the above-cited responses to the Prosvita questionnaire, teachers were explicitly mentioned three times as indifferent or hostile to Ukrainian reading clubs. It is important to note that in all cases the teachers were also explicitly identified as Poles. Since Polish teachers were likely to be influenced by the Polish national movement, the chief rival of the Ukrainian national movement, it is understandable that they would have no use for the reading club. This may explain some instances in our corpus of correspondence where teachers are identified as opponents of the reading club (e.g., *CC* 118; and see

---

[176] For example: N[ykolai] K[ryvy], "...z Hlubichka Velykoho," *Batkivshchyna* 6, no. 21 (23 [11] May 1884): 132, in conjunction with "Z pid Ternopolia," *ibid.* 6, no. 34 (22 [10] August 1884): 212; Parokhiiane z Romanova, "Prosvitytel naroda," *ibid.* 12, no. 5 (26 January [7 February) 1890): 69; "Radist i neradist," *ibid.* 12 no. 12 (16 [28] March 1890): 165.

[177] TsDIAL, 348/1/5874, p. 47.

[178] TsDIAL, 348/1/1297, p. 37. The notion of "oinkers" (U *khruni*) is examined below, 152–3. Oinkers supported the landlords.

[179] TsDIAL, 348/1/1479, p. 15.

[180] TsDIAL, 348/1/2900,p. 4.

[181] TsDIAL, 348/1/2448, p. 4.

[182] TsDIAL, 348/1/3031, p. 60.

[183] TsDIAL, 348/1/4921, p. 32.

[184] TsDIAL, 348/1/1498, p. 65.

[185] *Ibid.*, p. 46.

LA 214)—they may not have been of Ukrainian nationality. In other cases, the reading club may have been too radical for any member of the notability to support comfortably (for example, the reading club in Volia Iakubova, which numbered the assistant teacher Pavlo Horutsky among its enemies; *CC* 92).

However, it was the Ukrainian priest, not the Ukrainian teacher, who was most frequently criticized by the correspondents for indifference or hostility to the reading club. And this criticism coexisted in the correspondence with recognition of the clergy's outstanding contributions to the reading clubs. What we have here is not contradictory evidence concerning the clergy's attitude to the rural national movement, but rather two distinct patterns: one of support, the other of indifference and antipathy. This duality is very reminiscent of the clergy's behaviour under serfdom, already examined, and analogous to that of the communal governments.[186] One can view the clergy's two patterns of relating to the rural national movement as chronologically distinct, with the clergy at first welcoming and then shying away from the movement. Although this chronological distinction is implied for individual priests in some items of correspondence cited above and although elsewhere I have argued why the clergy as a whole would first support and later refrain from supporting the national movement in its parishes,[187] this distinction should not be understood too rigidly. There were always, at any point between 1860 and 1914, priests who were proponents and priests who were opponents of the rural institutions of the national movement. This was a consequence of their ambiguous social position, so close to, but divorced from—and often economically antagonistic to—the peasantry. Yet the overall tendency must have been for parish priests to have been more fervent, and more naive, supporters of the rural national movement during its early phases, before they heard the voice of the peasant they had awakened.

---

[186] Examined below, 175–89.

[187] Himka, "Priests and Peasants," 9–13.

4. The Awakening Peasantry

The key to the development of a mass constituency for the Ukrainian national movement was the participation of the peasantry. This chapter examines the motivations of the peasantry in joining the national movement and also some of the changes wrought in the peasantry as a result. After a brief discussion of the social and cultural profile of the peasant activists, the chapter examines in some detail the socio-economic underpinnings of Polish-Ukrainian and Jewish-Ukrainian conflict in rural Galicia. The next two sections discuss the impact of the national movement on the political and cultural life of the village. The chapter concludes with an analysis of the relative weight of socio-economic and national factors in determining the peasantry's participation in the national movement.

Who Were the Peasant-Activists?

The peasants who took a leading role in the national movement were similar to the notables in that they seem to have been, on the whole, economically better off than the rest of the peasantry and better educated; we may presume that their material and cultural status also gave them prestige in the commune.

Information on the economic status of the peasant-activists is fragmentary. For 53 of the activists,[1] it has only been possible to determine that they were "proprietors," i.e., landed peasants. Except for 5 lads,[2] who were not yet of landowning age, none of the peasant-activists for whom we have economic information was landless.[3] Of 22 peasant-activists whose economic condition is

---

[1] *LA* 4, 12, 27, 35, 36, 45, 52, 55, 69, 74, 75, 79, 85, 89, 90, 97, 107, 108, 111, 125, 126, 153, 158, 161, 163, 166, 210, 224, 230, 236, 237, 265, 271, 272, 281, 289, 292, 309, 317, 318, 321, 330, 336, 337, 338, 344, 345, 350, 351, 353, 354, 355, 366.

[2] *LA* 180, 181, 196, 215, 231.

[3] It is impossible to say what percentage of Galician peasants were landless. Kravets (*Selianstvo*, 72) estimates that 25 to 30 per cent were landless in 1900, but offers no grounds for this estimate. The estimate does not seem altogether unreasonable, since in four villages for which I happen to have fairly complete information, 19 per cent of the households were gardeners and cottagers in the mid-1850s. (Balyntsi, Kolomyia district, TsDIAL, 168/1/1416; Nykonkovychi,

known, 12 were prosperous,[4] 3 middling to prosperous,[5] 4 middling,[6] 1 poor to middling (*LA* 241; when he started out in the 1840s or early 1850s) and 2 poor. The two poor peasants had secondary sources of income; one was a cobbler (*LA* 137) and the other a scribe and sometime merchant (*LA* 343). None of the peasant-activists, as far as I have been able to establish, worked as agricultural labourers on the lords' estates.[7] Even assuming that the correspondence was more likely to emphasize the wealth, rather than poverty, of activists, it is clear that the national movement within the commune was led not by the rural proletariat but by the yeoman peasantry, the rural petty bourgeoisie.[8]

As for education, the highest achievements among the peasant-activists were the acquisition of sufficient education to be a teacher in the prereform era (*LA* 343) and the completion of a four-grade school in a district capital (*LA* 231). Although considerably less educated than the priest-activists or teacher-activists, the peasant-activists were largely literate, which distinguished them from the bulk of the peasantry. It has been possible to determine that 42 or 43 of the peasant-activists were literate[9] and only 2 illiterate (*LA* 63, 171). Characteristically, as we will see, the two illiterate peasant-activists were mayors. That peasant-activists tended to be literate is confirmed by the fact, noted earlier (Table 12), that three-quarters of the members of reading clubs in 1897–1910 were literate.

Relative wealth and education approximated the peasant-activist to the notability only to a certain extent. Just as the education of a peasant-activist was primitive by comparison to that of most notables, his relative wealth was also primitive, in the sense that it was primarily based on nature rather than money. The peasant-activists also differed from the notable-activists in mobility. As has already been mentioned,[10] peasant-activists tended to live in

---

[3](continued) Lviv district, TsDIAL, 168/1/1916; Strilkiv, Stryi district, TsDIAL, 488/1/422; Zhulychi, Zolochiv district, TsDIAL, 168/1/1044). However, the percentage of landless peasants may have been considerably lower.

[4] *LA* 8, 34, 46, 63, 91, 122, 143, 207, 273, 284, 326, 367.

[5] *LA* 51, 155, 331.

[6] *LA* 3, 18, 299, 307.

[7] When Vasyl Nahirny spoke at the popular assembly in Stanyslaviv in 1892, he said that in "a well-ordered commune" (U *uporiadkovana hromada*) "a landed proprietor should not engage in wage labour." Vasyl Nahirny, "Iak maie vyhliadaty uporiadkovana hromada," *Batkivshchyna* 14, no. 29 (17 [29] July 1892): 145–6.

[8] When delegates from Dobrostany, Horodok district, attended the mass assembly sponsored by the national movement in Lviv in 1883, they were impressed by the number of educated and well-to-do peasants that they saw there. Adriian, *Agrarnyi protses*, 58–9.

[9] *LA* 1, 3 and/or 4, 36, 51, 75, 78, 90, 91, 96, 101, 117, 125, 137, 154, 155, 157, 161, 172, 177, 202, 203, 207, 215, 220, 230, 231, 246, 250, 272, 275, 284, 286, 287, 299, 306, 321, 326, 331, 343, 344, 354, 362. Included here are not only all peasant-activists whose literacy is recorded under the rubric "education" in the list of activists, but also all peasant-activists who published anything (within or outside the corpus of correspondence) or who served as cantors or scribes.

[10] See above, 114.

the community where not only they, but also their ancestors were born. Very few travelled any distance. In our list of activists, three peasants were reported to have travelled: two served in the army (*LA* 231, 362) and the third (*LA* 265) was said to have been "out in the world." The limits of most peasants' travel would be to the small nearby market towns and the district capital.

Another way in which the peasant-activists differed sharply from notables was the importance of family ties within the national movement. Of the priests, only 4 (8 per cent) had family connections with other activists;[11] of the teachers—only 2 (9 per cent);[12] and of the cantors—5 (17 per cent).[13] Of the peasant-activists, however, 41 (19 per cent) were related to other activists.[14] The notables thus displayed more individualized behaviour, while the peasants were more strongly influenced by traditional family ties. The cantors in this respect were closer to the peasants than were the other notables. Of course, to a large extent, this difference is explained by the difference in mobility. Priests and teachers, and cantors in so far as they were itinerant, lived apart from their siblings, cousins and, generally, in-laws; peasants did not.

In sum, the peasant-activists were recruited from the more prosperous and literate peasantry. With their higher economic and cultural positions, these peasants resembled the activist notability. However, by comparison with the latter, the peasant-activists were still economically and culturally primitive, trapped in their villages and traditional in outlook.

Commune and Manor

The conflict between peasant and landlord was intense in the era of serfdom and in the decades of the servitude disputes. As the agrarian strikes of 1900, 1902 and 1906 show, the peasant-landlord conflict was also intense in the period immediately following the one we are investigating. It would seem, therefore, that the peasant-landlord conflict should also have been important in the intervening decades, when the national movement was penetrating the countryside. It would also seem that the national movement of the late 1860s–1900 should have followed the pattern of 1848–9, when the peasantry understood the Ukrainian-Polish conflict as primarily a new formulation of the peasant-landlord conflict. Finally, when one considers that the landlords' economic domination of the peasantry did not cease with the abolition of serfdom,[15] that over 40 per cent of the agricultural and forest

---

[11] *LA* 244, 323, 324, 332.

[12] *LA* 83, 178.

[13] *LA* 3, 168, 264, 306, 344.

[14] *LA* 3, 4, 9, 10, 35, 36, 37, 63, 64, 65, 84, 89, 90, 107, 108, 171, 177, 180, 181, 229, 230, 236, 237, 262, 263, 270, 271, 272, 273, 306, 307, 312, 313, 316, 317, 344, 345, 350, 351, 366, 368. This list includes all peasant-activists with the same last names in the same villages.

[15] I have argued this in "The Background to Immigration," 12–13. The situation was correctly characterized by a Jewish historian: "The peasants had indeed been freed from *panshchyna* [serfdom], but not from the *pany* [lords]." Tenenbaum, *Galitsye*, 122.

land of Galicia was still demesnal in the late 1880s and early 1900s[16] and that
nearly half of all Galician peasant households in 1902 earned part of their
income from agricultural labour on someone else's (usually the landlord's)
land,[17] one has all the more reason to expect that the peasant-landlord conflict
would be a prominent issue in the rural national movement during the late
nineteenth century. However, as our corpus of correspondence testifies, the
socio-economic antagonism between Polish landlords and Ukrainian peasants
was a subsidiary theme in the national ideology of rural activists, including
peasant-activists. It is not that the struggle between commune and manor
finds no reflection whatsoever in the correspondence—it does. But that reflection is weaker than one might expect and weaker than the reflection of other
issues, such as Ukrainian-Jewish antagonism and conflicts between reading
clubs and communal governments.

The strongest statement of a correspondent against the landlords referred
to the situation in Shydlivtsi, Husiatyn district: "Our peasants are still dependent on the many and unjust whims of landlords.... As it was in the
miserable past, when people bore the yoke of serfdom, so it is even now; while
in other villages people have long ago forgotten how biting was the steward's
lash, in our Shydlivtsi serfdom has not ceased" (*CC* 129). This bitter
characterization of post-emancipation agrarian relations as still essentially
feudal is unique in the corpus of correspondence. Its significance, however, is
considerably reduced when we examine its context. The author stressed the
uniqueness of the Shydlivtsi situation. Shydlivtsi was a border village and the
peasants' farmland was entirely on the other side of the border, in the
Russian empire. For centuries, the Shydlivtsi peasants had worked this land
and also had performed corvée labour for nearby estates. With the
emancipation of the Russian serfs, the Shydlivtsi labour dues ceased, but so
did their legal rights to their rustical land. In order to continue farming, they
had to rent from the nobles what was traditionally their own land. At best, all
that emancipation meant for the Shydlivtsi peasants was the conversion of
labour rents into money rents. In practice, however, since money could only
be earned on the estates, little had changed since the abolition of serfdom.
Thus here *exceptionally* "serfdom has not ceased."

The Shydlivtsi case was extreme, but—in a mitigated form—all of Galicia
was a Shydlivtsi. The emancipation from serfdom in Austria had included no
land reform and the large estates remained intact. As under serfdom, the
landlords needed peasant labour to work the estates. Although violent
compulsion—the hallmark of feudalism—could no longer be used to generate
this labour, economic compulsion could. This is why the nobility made a point
of robbing the peasantry of forests and pastures in the aftermath of the

---

[16] Pilat, *O stosunkach własności tabularnej*, 5. Sviezhynsky, *Ahrarni vidnosyny*, 19.

[17] In 1902 there were 653,802 peasant households in Galicia; 334,109 of them earned income
from something other than working their own land: 268,472 in agriculture and 12,943 in industry
(52,694 did not specify the sector). Kravets, *Selianstvo*, 70, 74–5.

abolition of serfdom—to keep it working on the estates. This is why the nobility in the Galician diet opposed credit institutions for the peasantry—so that peasants would borrow from landlords and repay their debts in labour.[18] This is why the nobility that controlled the government of Galicia made no effort to industrialize the crownland—so that rural overpopulation would force the peasantry to work cheaply on the demesnes. This is why the nobility not only demanded cash compensation for the abolition of serfdom, but was not unhappy to see the banks which mediated the peasants' payments take a scandalously high proportion as interest[19]—that the peasants might have an ever greater need for money, which they could only earn as agricultural labourers. With half the peasants working, reluctantly,[20] on the landlords' estates in the twentieth century, what was the meaning of emancipation? When the beating of agricultural workers was sanctioned by Austrian law and was a shamefully common practice,[21] why does only one correspondent—and then in exceptional circumstances—equate the post-emancipation landlord-peasant relationship with serfdom?

Before attempting to answer this question, and the larger question of the apparently anomalous underrepresentation of the landlord-peasant theme in the correspondence, let us examine all the other references to socio-economic antagonism between the Ukrainian commune and the Polish manor. There are not many. Resentment of labour on the estates as such is not expressed in the correspondence, although one item censures a particular case in which the peasants of Brodky, Lviv district, worked on the estate on Sunday, for which they accepted liquor and hired musicians as payment (*CC* 117). The correspondent was as indignant at the peasants as he was at the landlord (Emil Torosiewicz, a deputy to the Galician diet). (Actually, censure of agricultural labour on Sundays and holy days is found in several other items

---

[18] Erazm Wolański in the Galician diet in 1881, speaking against the establishment of a crownland bank: "I am convinced from long association with the peasantry that they do not need [such] a bank—that banks are the ruination of the peasantry. For what does he need capital? His best capital are his hands which are with him always and for which he is not obliged to pay interest. Let him only work—estates are suffering from a lack of labor supply; they can supply the capital he may need in return for his work if only there is an honest desire for employment. Loans [from banks] induce laziness, for why should he work if he can borrow...." Cited in Murdzek, *Emigration*, 88.

[19] The scandal is clearly explained in Franko, "Halytska indemnizatsiia," *Tvory*, 19: 456–87. See also above, 28–9.

[20] The distaste with which peasants regarded work on the estates is made clear by a Galician emigrant to America who, shortly after arriving in New York, celebrated in verse that he would no longer have "to work for the lords as in the old country" (U *Oi Nioiorku* [sic], *slavne misto, budu v tobi zhyty / Ta ne budu, iak u kraiu, na paniv robyty*). Interestingly, after working for a while in the Pennsylvania coal mines, he idealized his life back in Galicia, where "I had no boss above me" (U *Takoi tam nad sobov ia basa ne mav, / Koly tudy khtiv—sam sy rozkazav*). Oliinyk, *Emihrantski virshi*, 42, 49.

[21] Sviezhynsky, *Ahrarni vidnosyny*, 63. My grandmother earned the money to pay her passage to America in 1909 by working on the landlord's estate in Khlivchany, Rava Ruska district. She and her coworkers frequently felt the lash on their backs.

of correspondence [*CC* 237, 241, 251, 264], but only in connection with
Jewish estate owners and estate lessees; for the moment, we are abstracting
from the question of the identification of the manor with Jews in order to
focus exclusively on peasant-landlord antagonism that had a Ukrainian-Polish
dimension.) Another item, from Spasiv, Sokal district, mentioned in passing
that "...our village is poor; it has no forest because we sold it to the
lords..." (*CC* 87). Here, laconically, are references to the nobles' control of
the forests as well as to the manor's ability to exploit the peasantry's
impoverishment for the acquisition of peasant land.[22] The nobility's profit
from propination (the monopoly over alcoholic beverages) was decried by a
peasant correspondent:

> Come Sunday or a holy day, and sometimes on a work day, the taverns [in
> Ivachiv Dolishnii, Ivachiv Horishnii and Plotycha, Ternopil district] are full of
> people, men and women. This is a joy to the side-curled [i.e., Jewish]
> tavernkeepers and to our landlord [Juliusz] Korytowski.... Mr. Korytowski is
> the peasant deputy to the diet [i.e., he was elected from the fourth—primarily
> peasant—curia], but if he cared more about our peasant welfare, he
> would...try to educate us ignorant ones and not, as in Plotycha, build taverns
> like palaces and enrich himself and the Jews by our peasant labour (*CC* 77).

It is characteristic, as we will see, that this item of correspondence has a directly political message (Korytowski, like Torosiewicz in *CC* 117 cited above,
is singled out as a deputy to the diet) and lumps the landlord together with
Jews.

Only two other items of correspondence relate to the traditional sphere of
commune-manor antagonism and these concern what might be classified as
subsidiary rather than fundamental issues of peasant-landlord conflict. One
reports the statement of a peasant from Siltse, Kalush district, at a public
meeting arranged by the national populists (*CC* 93). The peasant spoke out
against the hunting laws, which forbade peasants to shoot the wild boars that
destroyed their crops, but were much prized as game by the Polish nobility.
The manor officials

> make fun of us, saying we should go out at night into the fields with bells and
> ring them at the beast or drive it off with a rock. But how can a man, after
> working hard all day, not sleep at night and go to work again the next day?
> And how can we confront a wild boar with a rock when even the forest warden,
> often armed with a gun, climbs up a tree?

The same peasant went on to complain about the manor's conduct during
road repairs (U *sharvarok*). The commune was supposed to furnish the
labour and the manor the materials, but the question of who was responsible
for delivering the materials to the work site was disputed.[23]

---

[22] On the latter point, see Sviezhynsky, *Ahrarni vidnosyny*, 15.

[23] The Galician crownland administration decided that the commune was obliged to deliver the
materials, but on 19 April 1884 (N.S.) an administrative tribunal in Vienna decided that this
was the manor's responsibility.

The last item of correspondence to mention conflict with the manor reported that the lady of Khylchychi, Zolochiv district, fell seriously ill and vowed, if she survived, to perform the pious act of building a church where presently stood the tavern. When she recovered, the tavern-keeper convinced her to forego her oath and "make various difficulties for the commune."

> So, in order to punish the Jew, the commune decided not to buy anything more in the tavern. It has now founded its own store and for the third week is holding firm in its boycott. The Jew is yelling, the lady of the manor is lamenting and threatening (*CC* 268).

Characteristically, a Jew is both blamed and punished for the landowner's offense.

And this is all our correspondence has to say about socio-economic conflict between the Polish manor and Ukrainian commune. Not only is the conflict underplayed in the correspondence, but the correspondence praises individual landlords, the "good lords"[24] who supported the Ukrainian movement. The reading club in Dobrostany, Horodok district, was supported by the forest warden (!) and the estate manager Mroczkowski, "whom the members of the commune love very much" (*CC* 100).[25] The Polish landlord of Ripniv, Kaminka Strumylova district, donated 300 gulden to the reading club's building fund; "glory to such a good lord," exulted the correspondent who reported this (*CC* 159). Manor officials in Lopatyn, Brody district, let the peasants put on a play inside a manor hall to raise money for the reading club (*CC* 200). Leopold Obertyński, lord of Utishkiv, Zolochiv district,

> donated a lot for a community hall and a building, at our request drove the Jew from the tavern and put in his place one of our men.... Heartfelt thanks to a man who, in contrast to neighbouring lordlings and guided by healthy views, contributes to our welfare and thus to the welfare of the crownland (*CC* 216).

The Countess Sofia Starzeńska, owner of the estate of Hnizdychiv, Zhydachiv district, donated 7,000 bricks to the reading club so that it could build its own premises (*CC* 234).

The correspondence leaves the objectively false impression that there was no fundamental socio-economic conflict between the Polish landed nobility and the peasants in the Ukrainian national movement. The Polish landlords here appear to be analogous to the Greek Catholic priests, whom we have already examined, and to the village governments, who will be treated below, i.e., they seem to occupy an ambiguous position vis-à-vis the national movement: good landlords, like good priests and good mayors, support the movement, while bad ones do not.

In attempting to explain this anomaly, it is first necessary to consider whether we can entirely trust the testimony of the correspondence in this instance. The national populists, unlike their Russophile rivals, at several

---

[24] On the myth of the good lords, see Burszta, *Społeczeństwo i karczma*, 157–61.

[25] This throws more light on why some peasants in Dobrostany believed that the reading club was a step in the direction of a return to serfdom. See above, 95–6.

junctures from the late 1860s to the early 1890s eagerly sought a *modus vivendi* with the Polish nobility. Thus the editors of *Batkivshchyna* may have considered it politic to mute the sensitive socio-economic conflict in order to leave the door open for future concessions in the strictly national-cultural sphere. I have not, however, been able to find direct evidence in support of such a hypothesis.[26] Although I think certain aspects of the correspondence—the cult of "good lords" and the deliberate channelling of socio-economic resentment against Jews—does reflect the national populists' hesitation to champion the peasantry's socio-economic grievances against the Polish nobility, I cannot accept this as the major reason for the correspondence's relative silence on the peasant-landlord conflict. Against this thesis is a strong argument: analogous correspondence in the *radical* newspaper *Khliborob* in 1892–4 is also relatively silent on the landlord-peasant conflict. The radicals, of course, had no interest in or hope for reaching an accommodation with the Polish noble ruling class. (Characteristically, however, no "good lords" appeared in the radical correspondence.)

Although we must dismiss the hypothesis that national populist politics were primarily responsible for the lack of strong statements against Polish landowners in the correspondence, we must also consider whether there was external pressure to moderate the correspondence. This would have affected all correspondence to popular newspapers, of whatever political persuasion. There certainly was such pressure. The Polish nobility, ever since the peasant revolt of 1846, was extremely sensitive to any anti-landlord agitation among the peasantry. It is unlikely that the Galician authorities would have allowed a paper to flourish that deliberately fanned animosity to the nobility. It was, in fact, against the law to publish anything encouraging "enmity against the legally recognized estate of the nobility."[27] The practice of Galician censors was to expurgate even relatively mild denunciations of the nobility. For instance, the following passage was censored out of the editorial in *Batkivshchyna*, 1881, no. 16, as promoting enmity to the noble estate:

> Our Ruthenian people in Galicia—and the situation is even worse in Bukovyna—make the least use of their rights and their power of all the peoples of Austria. Because our people do not elect for themselves the sort of deputies who would do their will, but rather elect mainly Polish lords and government officials, who do the complete opposite of what the people want and need.[28]

In the editorial of *Batkivshchyna*, 1881, no. 19, the following sentence was censored for its antagonism to Polish lords: "Oppressed by all manner of burdens, we cannot extricate ourselves from our poverty, but Polish lords,

---

[26] One would expect the radical Pavlyk to have castigated the national populists for suppressing anti-landlord correspondence.

[27] TsDIAL, 152/2/15011, p. lv.

[28] *Ibid.*, p. 3.

Jewish usurers and all sorts of banks get rich from Ruthenian labour."[29] As these censored passages make clear, Ukrainian popular newspapers could not print much against the landlords without risking confiscation. Unfortunately, it is impossible to determine to what extent Galician censorship discouraged the editors of Ukrainian popular newspapers from publishing correspondence with a strong anti-landlord thrust.

Thus far we have considered editorial policy as a factor distorting the correspondence on the landlord question. We must also remember, however, that the authors of the correspondence themselves were not entirely typical of the Galician Ukrainian peasantry as a whole. The peasants who submitted correspondence were, as previously indicated, economically better off than most of their class.[30] They did not have to work on the landlords' estates. They were a rural petty bourgeoisie, relatively independent of the manor, and not, like much of the peasantry, only formally emancipated serfs and rural proletarians. Therefore they would be less than typically concerned with the landlord-peasant problem. If we assume that with time the national movement penetrated not only into more villages (horizontally) but also into lower strata of the peasantry (vertically), then the influx of poorer peasants into the movement would explain why the landlord-peasant conflict erupted with such power in the early twentieth century (the agrarian strikes of 1900 and, particularly, 1902 and 1906).

In sum, as far as the trustworthiness of the correspondence is concerned, the correspondence underplays the conflict between Polish landlord and Ukrainian peasant because of both the censorship of anti-landlord sentiments by the Galician authorities and the economic status of the peasant correspondents, which placed them on the periphery of the peasant-landlord struggle.

The socio-economic conflict between the Polish manor and Ukrainian commune was not only understated in the correspondence, but also transformed. The transformation was of two varieties: the socio-economic conflict appeared as a political conflict and the Polish manor appeared as a Jewish manor.

The national movement politicized the landlord-peasant conflict. While under feudalism individual communes confronted individual manors over economic issues, the national movement strove to have the Ukrainian peasantry as a whole oppose the Polish nobility as a whole, during elections. The most important message *Batkivshchyna* sought to convey to the peasants was: vote for the Ukrainian candidate. The correspondents had no illusions about the political sympathies and antipathies of the Polish nobility. The nobles in the correspondence were depicted as opponents of the Ukrainians' political aspirations who used bribery and pressure to make Ukrainian

---

[29] TsDIAL, 152/2/15013, p.2.

[30] There is no reason to believe that the radical correspondents of the early 1890s were derived from a much lower stratum of the peasantry than the *Batkivshchyna* correspondents of the mid-1880s.

peasants vote against their interests and for Polish noble candidates. The nobility's influence over elections was particularly effective because of the curial system of elections to the diet and parliament.[31] The population was divided into four electoral curiae: of the landowners, of the chambers of commerce, of the large cities and of everyone else (mainly the peasantry). In the fourth, peasant curia elections were indirect. Every five hundred rural inhabitants elected one elector to vote for the deputy to the diet. Thus the landlords' pressure ultimately had to be brought to bear against only a relatively few peasant electors in each electoral district. Also, the balloting in the fourth curia was open, not secret, so the landlord (as well as activists of the national movement) knew for whom an elector had cast his vote.

The correspondence records that Polish landlords bribed electors. In Ivachiv Horishnii and Dolishnii and Plotycha, Ternopil district, the owner of the estate, Juliusz Korytowski, effectively bought himself a seat in the diet by bribing peasant electors with "sausages, cigars, liquor and so forth" (*CC* 77).[32] In Radekhiv, Kaminka Strumylova district, the mayor and a councilman were chosen as electors in the parliamentary elections of 1885. They promised "to stand for all of Rus', because this is our fatherland." But "when they [the Polish nobles or their agents] began to give out liquor and sausages and, moreover, began to light cigars, the councilman and mayor completely forgot about Rus', their fatherland, because both cast their vote for Mr. Kielanowski." Electors from Mukan, a village near Radekhiv, "sold their votes for a thousand bricks" (*CC* 222). At a pre-election meeting in Zhovkva, a landlord (U *didych*) drove up to promise access to forests and pastures to compliant electors; he also distributed bribes in money, of 15–20 gulden, to lure votes away from the Ukrainian candidate (*CC* 225). In Lviv district a number of Ukrainian peasant electors voted for the conservative landlord Dawid Abrahamowicz, "some for a pasture, some for fir trees, some for money" (*CC* 242).[33] In addition to bribes, landlords used the threat of refusing loans of seed grain to sway electors (*CC* 211).[34]

Ukrainian peasant electors who submitted to the bribes or threats of landlords were dubbed *Mykyty Khruni* or simply *khruni* by the national

---

[31] The curial system with respect to parliamentary elections was reformed in 1897 and replaced by universal manhood suffrage in 1907. Elections to the Galician diet retained the curial system until 1914.

[32] Stanisław Madeyski, later prime minister of Austria, spent 400 gulden on banquets and drinks for peasant electors in order to become a deputy to parliament in 1879. Radzyner, *Stanisław Madeyski*, 59–60.

[33] Among the papers of the Potocki estates is a letter to Count Roman Potocki from a peasant elector, Maciej Czajkowski (10 December 1900). Czajkowski wrote that as an elector he had always voted for Count Potocki as a deputy to the diet. Furthermore, "having influence and popularity among the peasantry, I have also agitated during elections among the peasant electors with the best effect for His Excellency." He promised to campaign for the Count in the 1901 diet elections. He concluded the letter with a request for one oak and fourteen softwood trees to build a farm building as well as four cartloads of firewood. LNB, Pot., No. 292, pp. 7–8v.

[34] See also Julian Marchlewski [J. Karski], "Galizien," *Neue Zeit* 20 (1902), Bd. 2, pp. 748–9.

movement (*CC* 56, 77, 211). A *khrun* was literally an "oinker," i.e., a pig. *Khruni* were also sometimes called *kovbasnyky*, i.e., sausagists, because they accepted "electoral sausage"[35] as a bribe (*CC* 56, 212). The national movement tried to shame electors into holding firm and voting for the Ukrainian candidates. Electors who sold their votes in Rava Ruska district were jeered at in rhyme: "*To Mykyta Khrun, Khrun, iemu v ochi pliun, pliun*" (That's Mykyta Khrun, Khrun; spit, spit in his eyes) (*CC* 211). Thus the electoral conflict with the Polish nobility also had ramifications within the commune.

The electoral conflict between the Ukrainian national movement and the Polish nobility also involved the Jewish minority in Galicia. Jews were often used by the Polish nobility as instruments of electoral chicanery (*CC* 166, 182, 203, 204, 225, 239). Jewish tavernkeepers were used to bribe and confuse peasant electors, Jews of the manor were used to apply economic pressure and Jewish thugs—recruited from the Jewish lumpenproletariat in the towns—were sent to steal the precious legitimation cards from peasant electors.

Bribery, as has already been seen, was commonplace during elections. It was rumoured that Krizer, a Hungarian Jew engaged in the lumber business in Perehinsko, Dolyna district, hosted the Perehinsko electors at "Rubin's Restaurant" prior to polling (*CC* 203). In the hill region in the south of Galicia, peasant electors were said to have allowed themselves to be bribed by Jews "with liquor and sausages to our shame and detriment" (*CC* 182). A peasant who served as an elector several times reported to *Batkivshchyna* a practice that he had heard of from other electors:

> It would happen that when an elector would come to town, the Jews would lie in wait for him as a cat for a mouse, they would surround him like crows, drag him to the tavern and tell him that the electors from all the villages had already gathered there. All the while they would speak to him smoothly. Before long they would drag in a second and third elector and whisper to each that all had already agreed to vote for the Polish candidate, that there was nothing he himself could do about it and that he would do better to eat and drink his fill rather than listen to the priest[36] and vote in vain for a Ruthenian (*CC* 166).

Another elector reported that votes were bought with money: "Like black crows, Jews in caftan robes and suits wove their way among us and traded in votes as if at a bazaar" (*CC* 225).

A further electoral abuse documented in our correspondence (and elsewhere)[37] was the theft of peasant electors' legitimation cards. In Sokal

---

[35] U *vyborcha kovbasa*, G *Wahlwurst*.

[36] Another elector reported: "I heard a Jew approach our peasant [at the polling place,] and say: 'So you listen to the priests, but they fleece you' (P *To wy księży słuchacie a oni was drą*)" (*CC* 204).

[37] *Die Reichsratswahlen in Ostgalizien im Jahre 1897*, verfasst vom Ausschusse des ruthenischen Landeswahlkommitees (Vienna: 1898), 52, cited in Staruch, "Der Kampf der galizischen Ukrainer," 69. Olesnytsky, *Storinky*, 2:104, 113–14.

district, according to one elector, "the [electoral] commission was composed exclusively of landlords and they did not allow two peasants to vote without their legitimation cards, which Jews had torn from their hands, and the gendarmes even arrested one elector because he wanted to hold on to the arm of a Jew who grabbed his card" (*CC* 204). The elector who reported that Jews were buying votes with money went on to say: "When [the Jews] did not succeed in buying off a peasant, they distributed money among Jewish thugs and criminals like Symkhe Bart or Shmaie Grintal and others, and these leapt on us like wolves...and grabbed our legitimation cards" (*CC* 225).

Ultimately it was the Polish nobility who assigned Jews their role as instruments of electoral chicanery. A clear example of this subordination appears in an item of correspondence from Lviv district. Dawid Abrahamowicz, a wealthy landowner and prominent Polish conservative politican of Armenian extraction, sold Jews in the lumber business the right to cut trees from his forest. Peasants from Dmytrie drove to Abrahamowicz's woods, hoping to earn money by hauling lumber. But the Jews could not hire them—Abrahamowicz had forbidden hiring peasants from Dmytrie, because the village had voted against him in the parliamentary elections a few weeks earlier (*CC* 242). Thus Jews were used to execute the economic punishment dictated by a Polish landlord for a political offence.

Since Jews figured as the nobility's agents during elections, the national movement's political struggle against the Polish nobility frequently had an anti-Jewish component. Moreover, the *socio-economic* conflict between commune and manor was frequently expressed as a Ukrainian-Jewish rather than Ukrainian-Polish conflict.

The identification of Jews and the manor was primarily a phenomenon of the constitutional era. For almost the whole first century of Austrian rule in Galicia, the stewards, mandators and leaseholders had been recruited largely from the Polish gentry. Jews were expressly forbidden to engage in such occupations until their emancipation in 1868. They had also been forbidden, as a rule, to own estates. Beginning in the late 1860s, the impoverished Polish gentry that had managed the demesnal estates found new careers in government service[38] and their places on the estates were taken by Jews. Also, many traditional noble landowners did not adjust to the new economic conditions of the late nineteenth century, particularly the absence of serfdom and the transition to a money economy;[39] they were inclined to leave the management of their estates to a people accustomed to a money economy, the Jews, or to lease and even sell their estates to them.

---

[38] Rudolph Kurzweil, the tax collector who came to Dobrotvir in 1873, was a retired manorial steward (see above, 48). Judging by his name, however, Kurzweil was a German, not a Pole.

[39] The deepening crisis of the noble estates is reflected in the fact that in all of Galicia in 1881–1900 there were 1,618 cases of purchase and sale of tabular land, while in 1900–7 there were 2,326 such cases. Sviezhynsky, *Ahrarni vidnosyny*, 19–20.

Rural Jews represented a sizable portion of Galicia's Jewish population (36.6 per cent in 1910). As the Jewish demographer Jacob Lestschinsky noted, the weight of rural Jewry in Galicia was anomalous in comparison to Jewish settlement patterns elsewhere: "Except for Bukovyna, Galicia is the only land in the whole world where such a large percentage of Jews lives in villages."[40] The legislation of Joseph II had forbidden Jews who were not registered as farmers to live in the countryside.[41] Although the ban was poorly enforced, the late eighteenth and early nineteenth centuries witnessed an exodus of Galician Jews from village to town, and the emancipation of the Austrian Jews in the 1860s brought a reimmigration into the countryside. The correspondence published in *Batkivshchyna* records an influx of Jews into the village. One correspondent wrote ironically that "the people of Mshanets [Staryi Sambir district] are very fortunate, because they have as many as seven friends of the Jewish faith in their village, where once, some thirty years ago, there were only two Jewish families" (*CC* 66). Another correspondent noted that in the village of Perehinsko, Dolyna district, there were only two Jewish families in the 1840s, but by 1885 the village had seven hundred Jews (*CC* 257).[42]

In the late nineteenth and early twentieth centuries, Jews were prominent as estate officials (stewards, overseers, labour recruiters and the like). In 1794 the emperor had prohibited the employment of Jews in any clerical capacity on estates;[43] the law was poorly enforced and altogether invalidated by the full emancipation of the Jews in 1868. In 1900 there were 1,495 Jewish estate officials in Galicia. There were almost three and one-half times as many Jewish as Ukrainian officials, although there were thirty-four times as many Ukrainians as Jews engaged in agriculture.[44] Almost all the officials on estates owned by Jews were Jewish,[45] and Jewish officials also worked on Polish estates. It was customary for Polish nobles to keep

> Jewish factors, factotums and familiars, popularly known as "Moszki." Their task was to supply the "the Honourable Lord" with news, gossip, information and advice on prices, characterizations of merchants and lessees of taverns and mills, and so forth. These familiars perforce had enormous influence on events in the demesnes, among Jewish merchants and even among the authorities,

---

[40] Lestschinsky, *Dos idishe folk in tsifern*, 99.

[41] Tenenbaum, *Galitsye*, 122. Friedman, "Landvirtshaft," 135–6.

[42] The census of 1880 recorded 548 Jews in Perehinsko; the total population of the village was 4,294. *Spec. Orts-Rep. 1880.*

[43] Mahler, *History*, 334.

[44] Buzek, *Stosunki zawodowe i socyalne.* Since Ukrainains here are calculated by language and Jews by religion, and since 5 per cent of the Jews listed Ukrainian as their language, a significant proportion of the 429 Ukrainian officials may have been Jewish. Friedman ("Landvirtshaft," 140) states that Jews made up 30 per cent of the 4,000 agricultural administrators in Galicia in 1902 and that Jewish estate officials were concentrated in Ukrainian-inhabited Eastern Galicia.

[45] Kofler, "Żydowskie dwory," 3. "Juden als Ackerbauer," *Der Israelit*, no. 20 (30 October 1885): 6.

depending on how much they were trusted by their masters. And for the most part they were trusted 100 per cent. This guaranteed the "Moszko" a comfortable and even ample living.[46]

Estate officials were in a very exposed position, between landlord and peasant, and could easily replace the landlord as the object of the peasants' hatred. An item of correspondence in *Batkivshchyna* illustrates this:

> In the neighbourhood of Bovshivets, in Kukilnyky, Medukha, Slobidka, Iabloniv, Zahirie, Dytiatyn, Byblo and other villages, wherever you turn, there is such poverty that one is overcome by sadness. Jewry has settled in the region and conquered it as speargrass does an empty field. The villages mentioned above are the property of the Latin-rite archdiocese. So all of them have lessees (U *posesory*), who bring with them a whole gang of sublessees (U *pakhtiari*), tavern-lessees (U *arendari*), mill-lessees (U *miroshnyky*), stewards (U *faktory*), dairy-lessees (U *vydiinyky*), familiars (U *povirnyky*) and whatever else they're called. Those who are best at dealing with peasant skin become officials (U *zhondtsi*). And wherever there's one of these caftan-garbed officials, a Christian is fortunate if he is left with his shirt (*CC* 264).

Another statement of peasant hatred for Jewish estate officials is contained in a leaflet confiscated by the police during an agricultural labourers' strike in Borshchiv district in 1900. The leaflet was handwritten, obviously by a peasant, on the back of a printed invitation to join the Prosvita society. The leaflet urged peasants to stop working on the estates because wages were so low.

> Look! The lord is ashamed to cheat you [himself], so he keeps Jews to cheat you. Because the Jew is a devil. He'll even swindle the lord![47]

Jews acted as labour recruiters, both for local estates[48] and for estates abroad. Several items of correspondence complain about the practices of Jews who recruited peasants to work in Bessarabia and Moldavia. A correspondent from the town of Lysets, Bohorodchany district, wrote:

> Jews also deal in labourers; they send them by the hundreds to work in the fields of Bessarabia. The Jew receives 3,000 gulden a year to supply a certain number of workers. During the winter he gives [peasants] an earnest of a dozen or so gulden. Whoever takes it must go where the Jew tells him. The most important dealer in people is named Moshko Shporn (*CC* 62).

The correspondent went on to describe the terrible working conditions in Bessarabia. Another correspondent from Lysets also registered complaints about Shporn (*CC* 82). The correspondent from Kiidantsi, Kolomyia district, wrote that some of his impoverished fellow villagers went to work in

---

[46] Kofler, "Żydowskie dwory," 3.

[47] TsDIAL, 146/4/2209, p. 38.

[48] Referring to the town of Sighet, in a Ukrainian-inhabited region of Hungary, a journalist observed: "If the peasant wants to be hired, he usually goes not directly to the farmer, but to the Jew, who at daybreak is arranging his terms in the large central market-square and in the court-yards surrounding it." Pennel, *The Jew at Home*, 33-4.

Moldavia. "When they didn't work off the money they took in advance and escaped home, the Jew who recruited them brought the runaways to court and during the autumn before last the court auctioned off their property" (*CC* 165).

Jews invested in the appurtenances of the manor: stands of wood, lumber mills, pastures, hayfields, grain mills and ponds. In old Poland, renting such appurtenances from the manor provided a major source of livelihood for rural Jews, who would then charge the villagers for their use.[49] Joseph II had prohibited Galician Jews from leasing mills and similar sources of revenue in 1785, but enforcement of his legislation, especially after his death, was lax.[50] After emancipation Jews openly returned to their old occupation of leaseholding and sometimes bought, rather than leased, a specific manorial appurtenance.

Renting or owning the appurtenances brought Jews into direct conflict with peasants. Especially after the bitter struggle over servitudes, peasants resented having to pay for wood or grazing rights. Rights to hayfields and ponds were also contested. Grain mills seem to have been more clearly associated with the manor, but peasants were nonetheless resentful of the nobles' monopoly. Inasmuch as Jews rented or bought these contested appurtenances from the nobles, they deflected the peasants' enmity to themselves.

Jews had been involved in the lumber trade in Eastern Galicia since at least the seventeenth century.[51] Emancipation and the economic decline of the Polish nobility allowed Jews to purchase 7.4 per cent of Galicia's forest land by 1902.[52] A correspondent from Zhuzhil, Sokal district, felt that Jewish ownership of forests meant higher prices for wood:

> In the village of Zhuzhil neither the manor nor the peasants have even a bit of woodland, therefore wood for fuel and construction are purchased from Jewish retailers who bought up the larger tracts of forests from the neighbouring landlords. It is no wonder that wood bought at second or third hand is very expensive.... The Jews set whatever price they like just to extract the greatest profit from our Christian (*CC* 261).

A correspondent from Perehinsko, Dolyna district, reported that Jews paid 100 gulden for 1,600 trees from a village-owned forest and then sold the wood back to the peasants for 2,000 gulden (*CC* 258). (On Jews in the lumber trade, see also *CC* 1, 33, 107, 203, 242, 258.)

The leasing of pastures and hayfields by Jews is also mentioned in the correspondence (*CC* 92, 101, 107, 151). In Drozdovychi, Horodok district, the Jewish tavernkeeper rented a meadow from the landlord and charged the

---

[49] Jews also sometimes leased feudal rents in nature (chickens, capons, geese, thread and the like), as was the case in the Komarno region in 1822. *Klasova borotba*, 132.

[50] Mahler, *History*, 327–8.

[51] Rawita Gawroński, *Żydzi... na Rusi*, 106.

[52] Rosenfeld, *Die polnische Judenfrage*, 111.

peasants three or four times as much as he paid to lease it (*CC* 101). Jewish mill owners and lessees also figure in the correspondence (*CC* 66, 151, 257).

Control of the manorial appurtenances could occasion more than purely economic conflict between peasants and Jews. A peasant from Verbiv, Pidhaitsi district, wrote to *Batkivshchyna* to complain of a Jew who used his control of the mill and hayfield to discourage peasants from joining the village reading club. The correspondent urged his fellow villagers to boycott the Jew's mill and hayfield until he mended his ways. The proposed boycott also had an economic aspect, however. Currently, when the peasants cut hay for the Jew, they received only every sixth haystack; after the boycott they should be able to receive every fourth (*CC* 151; see also *CC* 242).

In old Poland Jews had frequently leased the estates themselves from the nobility. Ineffective Josephinian and subsequent legislation had prohibited this leaseholding,[53] but after emancipation Jews again openly leased estates. The correspondence accuses Jewish lessees of expropriating peasant cattle that had either strayed or been driven by a lackey of the estate onto the manorial pasture (*CC* 107, 110).

Actual Jewish ownership of estates was an innovation of Austrian rule. Some exceptional Jews with the rights of *Hofjuden* were allowed to acquire estates in the late eighteenth and early nineteenth centuries.[54] The revolution of 1848 removed restrictions on Jewish acquisition of real estate and some Jews then purchased tabular land. Jews were prohibited from buying estates in October 1853,[55] but were allowed to do so again in 1860. They very quickly acquired a significant share in the ownership of estates. By 1902 Jews owned 18.5 per cent of the tabular land in private estates in Eastern Galicia. In all of Galicia there were 543 Jewish-owned estates, averaging 555 hectares each.[56] Jewish estate ownership was concentrated in Eastern, Ukrainian-inhabited Galicia.[57] To purchase an estate required considerable wealth, which might have derived from trade,[58] tavernkeeping or usury.[59] Jewish estate-owners are mentioned in the correspondence three times: for influencing village politics (*CC* 58), for underpaying labourers (*CC* 251) and for polluting the village water supply with a distillery and cattle (*CC* 265).

The Money Economy and Its Representatives

Aside from the reasons already adduced, there is one more very important reason why the correspondence is relatively silent on the conflict between

---

[53] Mahler, *History*, 327–8.

[54] Kofler, "Żydowskie dwory," 17–18.

[55] Friedman, "Landvirtshaft," 132–3.

[56] Rosenfeld, *Die polnische Judenfrage*, 111; see also Sviezhynsky, *Ahrarni vidnosyny*, 20.

[57] Rosenfeld, *Die polnische Judenfrage*, 111. Friedman, "Landvirtshaft," 141.

[58] Kofler, "Żydowskie dwory," 17.

[59] Max Zetterbaum, "Klassengegensätze bei den Juden," *Neue Zeit* 11, Bd. 2 (1893): 36–7. Zetterbaum estimated that a usurer had to foreclose on thirty to fifty peasant farms in order to buy an estate; or a noble debtor might lose his estate directly to a Jewish creditor.

manor and commune: it was no longer the primary and exclusive socio-economic issue for the post-emancipation peasantry. To some extent from the abolition of serfdom in 1848, but much more intensively after the 1860s, the peasantry suffered above all from the penetration of a money economy and the concomitant destruction of the traditional natural economy. With this shift in the terrain of socio-economic tension came also a shift in the terrain of national conflict: under feudalism the Polish-Ukrainian conflict, not yet perceived as a national conflict, was the dominant polarity for the Ukrainian peasantry; but with the penetration of the money economy, coinciding with the penetration of the national movement, Ukrainian peasant antagonism was directed more against the representatives of the money economy—the Jews. This explains why, even in correspondence concerned with manor-commune antagonism, anti-Jewish sentiments are prominent.

With the emancipation from serfdom in 1848, the Galician peasant became a petty, independent farmer.[60] His independence was threatened from two directions: from the past and from the future. The past was represented by the feudal landlord, who, with his large estate intact, sought to render the abolition of corvée labour merely formal. This was the meaning of the landlords' expropriation of forests and pastures during the servitudes struggle (and explains why the landlord-peasant conflict was still so intense for the first two decades after emancipation). The threat from the future was the development of capitalism which "must . . . always and everywhere fight a battle of annihilation against every form of natural economy [and independent petty production] that it encounters."[61]

The economy of serfdom was largely natural.[62] As already noted, the greatest part of the serf's rents—94 per cent—was paid in labour or nature. The serf's own needs (as opposed to rents) required very little money (liquor and salt were the major expenses). The abolition of serfdom created a self-sufficient farmer who primarily needed money to pay taxes (including the compensation to the nobility for the cessation of corvée labour) and to fight the servitudes battle. In his domestic and economic life, he had little use for it and might hoard it.[63] Evhen Olesnytsky, in his memoirs, recalled the natural peasant economy of his youth (the 1860s):

---

[60] "Free self-managing peasant proprietorship . . . is found among modern nations as one of the forms arising from the dissolution of feudal landownership." Marx, *Capital*, 3:806.

[61] Luxemburg, *Accumulation of Capital*, 369.

[62] On the great problems the natural economy of Austrian serfdom posed for the Josephine civil service in attempting to calculate the net profit of peasant agriculture, see Rosdolsky, *Die grosse Steuer und Agrarreform*, 44–5.

[63] " . . . In every Rusniak [i.e., Galician Ukrainian] household will be found [in the early 1840s] a little box, to which the master of the house alone has the key, where he deposits his savings, often a considerable sum, with whose amount, however, not even his wife or children are acquainted." Kohl, *Austria*, 434–5: "The less advanced is the production of commodities, the more important is hoarding—the first form in which exchange-value assumes an independent existence as money—and it therefore plays an important role among ancient nations, in Asia up to

Farming (U *hospodarstvo*) was, especially in the older times I can remember, more natural than money-based. The farm produce was used at home. People wove cloth at home, even dipped [their own] candles. Hired hands were also usually paid not in money, but in kind. They received clothing, linen (U *billia*), boots and also grain. Work at harvest-time was paid in kind as well.... [64]

Jan Słomka of Dzików provided similar testimony in his memoirs for the same period: "We ate what the land gave us, and our clothing was of homespun.... The turnover of money in the villages was still trifling in my early days."[65]

In general, the economy of Galicia on the eve of the constitutional era was dominated by petty producers—the peasant proprietor in the countryside and the small craftsman in the city.[66] In the era of rapidly expanding capitalist relations, this was an unstable and unviable economic complex. It was undermined by the rapid penetration of a money economy, especially from the 1860s on.

Before outlining how the money economy in Galicia destroyed the petty producers' society, with its natural economy in the countryside, it is necessary to clarify some terminology and conceptualizations. In Soviet historiography on Galicia, the year 1848 divides the feudal from the capitalist era. While this is a handy and in some respects justifiable simplification, it does not elucidate the real relations of production in late-nineteenth century Galicia. Nor is it consistent with Marx's view of economic history, which held that "wherever [capitalism] appears, the abolition of serfdom has been long effected."[67] At least from 1848 until the turn of the century, capitalism as such did not exist in Galicia. Instead, the economy was based on petty producers,[68] and therefore a fundamental precondition of capitalism—the separation of the labourer from the means of production—was lacking. This economy was transitional, at least in the abstract, between feudalism and capitalism,[69] but it did not correspond to either. Also, when speaking of the

---

[63](continued) now, and among contemporary agrarian nations, where exchange-value has not yet penetrated all relations of production.... Where the bourgeois mode of production has reached an advanced stage the formation of hoards is reduced to the minimum.... " Marx, *Contribution to the Critique of Political Economy*, 134, 151.

[64] Olesnytsky, *Storinky*, 1:22.

[65] Slomka, *From Serfdom to Self-Government*, 12, 84.

[66] On artisanal production, see Himka, *Socialism*, 3, 13, 80–2.

[67] Marx, *Capital*, 1:715 (and see 1:717).

[68] Analogously, "through much of Western Europe, notably much of France, serfdom had been succeeded not by capitalism, but by an economy dominated by what were essentially peasant freeholders." Brenner, "Origins," 73.

[69] It is difficult to speak of the late nineteenth century as concretely transitional to capitalism, since a very weak capitalism lasted such a short time in Galicia—from sometime in the early twentieth century (I would propose 1918 as a convenient marker) until 1939. In this context, the

dissolution of the petty producers' society, I prefer to speak of its penetration by a *money*, rather than capitalist, economy. By this I mean to stress that what initially entered Galicia were not capitalist relations, but precapitalist relations. Marx made a sharp distinction between "money as money" and "money as capital."[70] This distinction, like all of Marx's categories, is not only logical, but historical.[71] By a money economy, therefore, I understand an economy based on exchange, with money as a universal equivalent, but in which the fundamental feature of capitalism, the self-expansion of value, is still absent. A money economy paves the way for capitalism, both by destroying the natural economy of petty producers in the countryside and by propagating exchange value.

For the moment it is necessary to focus on the money economy's destructive aspect, i.e., the money economy as a solvent of the natural economy. It was this aspect, incidentally, which most interested the traditional landowning class, which viewed the money economy as an excellent mechanism for breaking down the self-sufficiency of the peasantry and inducing it to return to work on the estates for very low wages.

The most naked confrontation between money and the natural economy was usury, here understood in the technical, Marxist sense of precapitalist moneylending. The high rates of interest characteristic of usury cannot be compared to capitalist interest rates; usury in precapitalist modes of production can assimilate almost *all* of the surplus product of an independent producer, while interest under capitalism is only a part of surplus value. The ruinous *effect* of usury—the separation of the labouring producer from his means of production—was the *starting point* of capitalism.[72]

---

[69](continued) few decades of capitalism can be viewed as part of a transition directly from feudalism into a Soviet-style formation.

[70] From Marx's *Grundrisse* (p. 251): "In any case, *money as capital* is distinct from *money as money*. The new aspect is to be developed." The clearest development of this aspect is in Marx, *Capital*, 1:146–54 (see also 1:94–145).

[71] This is exceptionally well argued by Rosdolsky, *The Making of Marx's "Capital"*, 114–15, 118, 167.

[72] Usury is the precapitalist loan of money to landowners and "to small producers who possess their own conditions of labour—this includes the artisan, but mainly the peasant, since particularly under pre-capitalist conditions, in so far as they permit of small independent individual producers, the peasant class necessarily constitutes the overwhelming majority of them." But to what extent the ruin of landowners and small producers "does away with the old mode of production, as happened in modern Europe, and whether it puts the capitalist mode of production in its stead, depends entirely upon the stage of historical development and the attendant circumstances.... In the form of interest, the entire surplus above the barest means of subsistence...can be consumed by usury..., and hence it is highly absurd to compare the level of *this* interest, which assimilates *all* the surplus-value excepting the share claimed by the state, with the level of the modern interest rate, where interest constitutes at least normally only a part of the surplus-value.... Under the capitalist mode of production usury can no longer separate the producer from his means of production, for they have already separated." Where the means of production are dispersed, usury "does not alter the mode of production, but attaches itself firmly to it like a parasite and makes it wretched. It sucks out its blood, enervates it and compels reproduction to proceed under ever more pitiable conditions. Hence the popular hatred against

Usury, a marginal but indispensable component of the feudal economy, was transformed by the 1860s into the vanguard of the young and rising money economy. The abolition of serfdom was a precondition for the proliferation of usury. Under feudalism, the usurer could not aim at the total expropriation of the peasant, because the landlord, who required landed serfs to work his estate, would not allow it. But when the former serf became an independent producer, the usurer could, and did, aim at the total expropriation of the peasant farm. The usurer's aim was consonant with the interests of the post-feudal landlord, who now had to hire labour and therefore welcomed the creation of a reserve of landless peasants. The Austrian economic reforms of the 1860s gave a further impetus to usury. In 1868, as part of the triumph of constitutionalism and strategy for economic development, peasants were permitted to divide their lands for sale; the traditional moneylenders of Galicia, the Jews, were legally allowed to engage in lending after nearly a century of formal prohibition; and all restrictions on interest rates were abolished. In the immediate aftermath of these reforms, Galician peasants began borrowing money at the rates of 52 and 104 per cent. The pace of ruination of the Galician (and Bukovynian) peasantry was so swift that a special law of 1877 attempted to reimpose interest limits in Galicia and Bukovyna.[73]

The nationality most prominent in usury in Galicia was the Jews.[74] In feudal Poland Jews had lent peasants money and sold them alcoholic beverages on credit, but from the beginning of Austrian rule in Galicia a series of laws limited both peasant indebtedness and Jewish lending.[75] The legislation of 1868 allowed Jews to return to usury, and under much more favourable circumstances than feudalism had permitted. Although, as we will see, usury was not an exclusively Jewish occupation in post-feudal Galicia, Jews were dominant. In the 1880s nearly nine out of ten persons convicted in Galicia of exceeding the interest limits established in 1877 were Jews.[76] Most Ukrainian peasants tended to identify usury with the Jews; as a proverb had it, "every Jew is a usurer" (U *Shcho zhyd, to lykhvar*).[77]

Resentment of "Jewish usury" was expressed by many correspondents (*CC* 1, 6, 26, 33, 48, 67, 77, 107, 111, 148, 184). According to a peasant from the Carpathians,

---

[72](continued) usurers.... Only where and when the other prerequisites of capitalist production are present does usury become one of the means assisting in establishment of the new mode of production.... " Marx, *Capital*, 3:594–7. As is clear from the foregoing (and see Marx, *Grundrisse*, 535), the flourishing of usury in late-nineteenth-century Galicia indicates that capitalism did not exist there and further justifies the distinction between a money and capitalist economy. See also Leon, *The Jewish Question*, 143–4.

[73] Caro, "Lichwa," 125–238.

[74] On Jews and usury in Western Galicia, see Slomka, *From Serfdom to Self-Government*, 84–8.

[75] Mahler, *History*, 318. Rosdolsky, *Stosunki poddańcze*, 1:96–7, 226.

[76] More accurately, for seven consecutive years sometime between 1877 and 1892, 87.5 per cent of all persons so convicted in Galicia were Jews. Ivan Franko, "Żydzi o kwestji żydowskiej," *Tydzień. Dodatek literacki Kurjera Lwowskiego* 1, no. 6 (6 February 1893): 42.

[77] Franko, *Halytsko-ruski narodni prypovidky*, 113.

there are villages where out of a hundred households it is hard to find a single landed peasant who is not in debt—to the Jews, of course. . . . In almost every one of the local towns, such as Stare Misto [Staryi Sambir], Khyriv, Dobromyl, Ustrzyki and others, there is some rich Jew who has [peasant land] under his control, i.e., in his pocket. . . . Often on a single day he will summon from ten to a hundred of his debtors to court for their debts; and he does not usually do so in vain (*CC* 141).

Another correspondent summarized the situation as follows: "It's often the case that someone borrows a dozen or so gulden from the Jew for some requirement and after that can't get the Jew off his back; he pays and works off the debt, but still ends up losing his land" (*CC* 30).

Land was the penalty or reward for borrowing or lending:

Some of these Jews came naked to Mshanets [Staryi Sambir district], but today they all have their own houses and plots of land which they bought and snatched away from people. One of them, Abramko, took a house and land away from a certain widow for a debt of 25 gulden (*CC* 66).

A correspondent from Chortovets, Horodenka district, reported:

Several years ago he [Ivan Lubyk] borrowed 100 gulden from the Jew Shulim Naiberger. He gave him one *Joch* of arable land as collateral and worked off 60 gulden by carting. But Mr. Shulim counted these 60 gulden as interest and in the end, after several years, the 40 gulden [debt] grew to 400 gulden of interest. [Allegedly] as insurance, the Jew tried to convince Ivan to sign a promissory note in court for 400 gulden, which the Jew [said he] would keep until death. Ivan, through his ignorance, let himself be talked into it by the Jew, not foreseeing that it would be his ruin. And in Obertyn he signed a promissory note in court for 400 gulden. Now the Jew is driving poor Lubyk off his land and from his house! Ivan, grab your sack and go begging! (*CC* 2).

Sometimes the credit was extended in liquor rather than money, but with the same result:

Ten years ago the lessee Khaim Breslier came here [Kryve, Berezhany district]. And there was a landed peasant here named Nykola Pytel, number one in the village, but also number one in the tavern. He had twelve *Joch* of land, a house, a garden and a fine orchard. When his wife died and his children went to live with other families, Nykola took to drink until all he had left was four *Joch* of land, the garden and the house. One day Khaim said to him: "Listen, Nykola, you're always drinking, but you never give me any money. Let's reckon it up: I'll pay you the difference and you sign over to me the house with the land and garden." Nykola agreed and the Jew reckoned the debt at 160 gulden. They went to a notary in Kozova and signed a document which said that the Jew could keep Nykola's property for ten years as interest. If by that time Nykola hadn't paid up, the arrangement would become permanent. It wasn't easy for Nykola to earn 160 gulden to pay the Jew, so he decided to sell the property. A certain landed peasant offered him 200 gulden just for the house and garden, but the Jew didn't want to give up the property until the ten years had passed. When the alotted time had expired and Nykola didn't return the money, the

Jew took over all the property. Nykola's son Stefan had meanwhile earned some money and wanted to pay the debt, but the Jew wouldn't take the money. The matter went to court, where it is still being contested (*CC* 281).

In addition to Jewish usurers, there were also some Ukrainian usurers in the Galician countryside. Some priests (e.g., *LA* 70) lent money to the peasantry at high interest, and some rich peasants also engaged in usury.[78] A peasant from Olesha, Tovmach district, reported on a peasant usurer in his village:

> We still have one evil, and that is usury. And it is not only Jewry that fleeces the poor peasant, but—what is more saddening—one peasant flays another through usury. In our village there is the rich peasant Tymko Kuzma. He does not come from a wealthy family, but, having some money, he began to loan it to peasants on provision (U *na proviziiu*) [i.e., the debtor offered as collateral for the loan a piece of land; the creditor had full usufruct of the land until the loan was paid off]. Thus he gradually accumulated much property. But even now, although he is already rich, he doesn't give up his custom. He lent the local proprietor Onufrii Lazoruk 100 gulden and now for the fourth year he is keeping on provision 5 *Joch* of good arable land. Just from the provision of this land he has taken much more than 100 gulden.... Of course, the communal government, although well aware of these extortions, keeps silent[79] ... (*CC* 78).

A nonpeasant complained that many peasant-run loan associations displayed less "brotherly Christian love" than a desire for "Jewish usury" (*CC* 111).

The pervasive usury led to large-scale auctioning of peasant land to pay debts. Between 1873 and 1894 there were 49,823 such auctions ordered by Galician courts, over two thousand a year.[80] Although land was the most important of the means of production from which usury separated the peasant, livestock also changed hands through debt.[81]

With the encouragement of the national populists, the peasants took a number of measures to combat usury. They founded reading clubs, which raised their educational level and thus, as some believed (*CC* 6), indirectly helped them in the contest with usurers. They also founded their own loan associations to compete with private lenders. The village of Korchyn, Stryi district, planned such a loan fund "which would do much to rescue us. Instead of going to the Jew to borrow money at high interest, we'd prefer to borrow from ourselves at lower interest" (*CC* 107). A peasant from Strilkiv, Stryi district, boasted that "no one goes to the Jew to borrow, only to the communal fund" (*CC* 34). Similarly, in Kolodribka, Zalishchyky district, "no one has to go to the Jew anymore to borrow, because there is our own fund. In this way we have driven out of our village one enemy—Jewish usury" (*CC* 67). Loan associations were founded throughout Galicia and some were

---

[78] Peasant usury is mentioned in a novel by Ivan Franko set in the early 1880s. Franko, "Perekhresni stezhky," *Zibrannia tvoriv*, 20:296.

[79] See below, 175–89.

[80] Kravets, *Selianstvo*, 103–4.

[81] Oliinyk, "V Amerytsi spomyny pro staryi krai," *Emihrantski virshi*, 38–9.

affiliated with various national institutions. Prosvita was the patron of 257 credit unions in 1912.[82]

A close cousin of the loan association was the communal granary, which also competed with usurers. Particularly in the spring before sowing and in the lean months preceding the harvest, peasants could feel an acute shortage of grain. To avoid borrowing either cash or grain from usurers, peasants set up communal granaries to take care of their needs: "Let's establish...a communal granary so that in case of need we won't go to the Jew to borrow grain or money" (CC 2). Some granaries worked out well, such as the one in Korchyn:

> We have a lot of people who sometimes run out of grain either for sowing or for bread, and straightaway they go to the Jew, borrow money at usurious interest and pay dearly. But now it's completely different. Now if they borrow from the communal granary, they don't have to pay anything back until after the harvest; and if they contribute more, it remains theirs in the future (CC 107).

Other communal granaries, like one in Kiidantsi, Kolomyia district, had trouble accumulating a sufficient fund of grain to perform their function:

> For eight years now we've had a granary,...but what good does it do us if it's empty! That's a great pity, because thanks to our carelessness the Jews clean us out every time. And they have plenty of time to clean us out, because it's a long time from Christmas to the fall and it's a rough stretch before the harvest. No one is able to remedy this evil, except for the granary. So to work, landed peasants! (CC 185).

Both the loan association and the communal granary meant competition for the Jewish lenders in the village. It is not surprising, then, that they opposed these institutions. As one correspondent wrote: "The priest...advised us.... [to establish] a communal granary: but this too is somehow not in the Jews' and mayor's interest" (CC 265). Thus usury engendered conflict not only between Ukrainian peasant debtors and Jewish creditors, but also between peasant lending institutions and private Jewish lenders.

The loan associations and more sophisticated credit institutions contributed to the economic decline of Galician Jews by restricting their opportunities to engage in usury. According to Raphael Mahler, by the turn of the century "the development of modern banking, mortgage banks, and savings and loan associations practically did away with private moneylending, which had become particularly widespread among Galician Jews, especially among the village shopkeepers, after the abolition of serfdom in 1848."[83]

Jews themselves, however, particularly petty shopkeepers and artisans, also suffered from Jewish usurers. To combat usury, the Jewish Colonization Association founded loan associations in Galicia where Jewish tradesmen could obtain loans at 6 per cent. Six associations had been established by

---

[82] *Entsyklopediia Ukrainoznavstva*, pt. 1, 3:1118–20.

[83] Mahler, "Economic Background," 260.

1903. According to a contemporary account, the Jewish credit associations were also undermining the usurers.[84]

Related to usury was Jewish investment in peasant property, e.g., livestock. Jews frequently bought young animals which they gave to peasants to tend and feed. When the animal matured and was sold, the original Jewish investor and the peasant who raised the animal would divide the money received from the sale. There are relatively many references to this practice in the correspondence, all of them negative (*CC* 1, 26, 30, 33, 141, 178). A clear and full statement of the dissatisified peasant viewpoint was provided by a correspondent from Vyktoriv, Stanyslaviv district:

> And now [the Jews] have started buying small bull calves with their own money and giving them to the poorer peasants to feed for several years. After two or three years the bull calves become oxen. The Jew then says to take them to the marketplace and they both [the Jew and the peasant] sell them. From the money they get for the oxen, the Jew takes as much as he paid for the bull calves, and the rest they divide in half. If this went fairly, perhaps there would be some benefit for the peasant, but the Jew isn't stupid! He makes an arrangement in the marketplace with the Jewish merchants, and the latter, speaking aloud, name a price that is lower than what they whispered into the ear of the Jew [the investor]. As a result, there is less money to split after the sale, and the peasant is cheated. Sometimes, if the Jew is very fortunate, a peasant will only receive a few gulden for several years' feeding; and sometimes a peasant even ends up paying the Jew. If a peasant runs out of fodder during the second winter, he returns the oxen to the Jew: the Jew takes them, but the first winter's feeding is unrecompensed and the peasant loses his right to the oxen (*CC* 30).

A peasant from the Carpathian foothills complained that twenty or thirty years earlier, i.e., before Jewish emancipation,

> every farmer had his own cart and horses or oxen, but today perhaps in every tenth household someone has oxen, and rarely his own, because most of the cattle is owned jointly with Jews, which had not been the case in the past.... Now the Jews not only invest in cattle, but in our region they even invest in pigs, although they don't eat them themselves (*CC* 178).[85]

Some Jews invested in peasant grain. They could buy it relatively cheaply in the fall after the harvest and sell it back to the peasants at higher prices in the spring, when peasants were most in need of it. A peasant from the town of Zboriv, Zolochiv district, wrote:

> Mr. Berko runs the granary[86].... He is a very obliging man and therefore only takes very low interest. For example, if someone sells him a bushel of rye for 5 gulden in the fall, he will take for the same grain, but a skimpier measure, only twice as much, i.e., 10 gulden, in the spring (*CC* 112).

---

[84] Pappenheim and Rabinowitsch, *Zur Lage der jüdischen Bevölkerung*, 30, 73–4. For more on Jewish credit institutions, see Rosenfeld, *Die polnische Judenfrage*, 120–1.

[85] On Jewish investment in peasant livestock, see also Hryniuk, "A Peasant Society," 313.

[86] The correspondent is using irony in referring to Berko's investment as a granary. He also calls the tavern a reading club and the usurer a loan association.

The natural economy was also broken down by the expansion of commerce; this too drew the Ukrainian peasantry into antagonistic relations with sectors of the Jewish population. New needs and new products entered the peasant household and enlarged the role of money. Again, the emancipation of the peasantry from serfdom was a precondition for this process, which accelerated only from the 1860s on. Austrian reform legislation, such as the industrial law of 1859, and especially the development of transportation (Lviv was linked by railway with the Viennese and Bohemian industrial centres in 1861)[87] brought the cheap and new factory-made goods into the countryside.[88]

In the corpus of correspondence there is a very interesting item defending the natural economy against the influx of commodities:

Everywhere in our villages around Stanyslaviv the old way of life—our own Ruthenian way of life—is dying out; in its place, bad customs from the outside are being introduced. Maybe these customs are fine for someone else, but they do not suit the Ruthenian—unless they are invented to make the Ruthenian the object of scorn and ridicule. It's not so much the vests, which a lot of peasants have now started to wear, but isn't it ridiculous when a peasant buys himself an umbrella so that people would think he's a gentleman on his way to town: otherwise they'd think him a peasant. I once had to feel shame when I saw a formerly well-off proprietor from Pavelche, now down on his luck; he was walking to town all puffed up beneath his umbrella and a Jew called to him in mockery: "Mister Nykola, come on to my place! I have some rum fit for gentlemen." The bait, God knows, was attractive, and Nykola would have stopped for a little drink, but apparently he had not a kreuzer; because poor old Nykola runs around to his neighbours asking for a quart of flour to make a thin gruel for his children. And don't think he's the only one who has bought an umbrella, because there are many like him. And all of this is introduced by all kinds of railway workers, brakemen and watchmen. From the wives of these watchmen, from the Polish women of the small towns or from women who once worked as servants in the cities, some of our farm women have learned to make *kutia* [a ceremonial pudding] out of rice. Don't you see, grand ladies, that that's not *kutia* at all, but rice porridge? The old home cooking isn't good enough anymore. Bah, even the *paska* [Easter bread] is no longer baked from domestic flour, but from the whitest flour, the kind gentlemen use for their delicate pastries. This is improper, farmers and wives! People will laugh and you will reduce your children to begging (*CC* 250).

This correspondent, who was most likely a peasant, resented having to acquire articles of clothing (umbrellas, vests) that could only be bought, not made, just as he resented having to acquire food (white flour, rice) that could only be bought, not produced on his own homestead. His argument against commodities had a political-moral as well as economic edge: every purchased

---

[87] The line was extended to Brody, on the Russian border, and to Zolochiv by 1869. *Rocznik Statystyki Galicyi* 3 (1889–91): 218–19. For a map of the railway system in 1889, see *Artaria's Eisenbahn u. Post-Communications-Karte*. By 1910 Galicia had 4,117 kilometres of railway. *Oesterreichisches statistisches Handbuch ... 1911*, 213. A map of the development of the railway system in Galicia through 1914 can be found in *Historia Polski*, vol. 3, pt. 1, *Mapy*.

[88] Himka, *Socialism*, 14–15. Himka, "Voluntary Artisan Associations," 180.

innovation was not only a source of economic ruin, but a betrayal of the traditional Ukrainian way of life. For him, the national movement represented the preservation of the natural economy. (*CC* 254 contained a reponse arguing that progress is inevitable, that not all the old ways are the best and that no harm can derive from umbrellas, rice and white flour. Judging by the style, the author was a nonpeasant.)

Another item of correspondence also expressed opposition to commodities. Describing the activities of the late pastor of Khotin, Kalush district—the priest-activist Hnat Rozhansky—it praised Rozhansky's efforts to preserve traditional crafts and discourage the purchase of ready-made goods. Rozhansky

> wanted to have everyone try to make their own cloth, because these two villages [Khotin and Zahirie] and the city [of Kalush] annually spend more than 2,000 gulden on that stupid calico for [sewing] shirts, aprons, skirts and kerchiefs; and this all is flimsy and tears quickly, so one has to buy again. But if one has one's own domestic cloth (whether hemp or fustian), one shirt will last for three years, but for those others you have to buy three times in one year.

Father Rozhansky "had [also] abolished the practice of giving engaged couples wreaths of feathers,[89] which cost 4 gulden from the Jews, as well as other idiocies, for which unintelligent people give the Jews considerable profits and destroy [the fruits of] their labour without the slightest need or benefit" (*CC* 31). The peasant correspondent believed that the traditional wedding wreaths, plaited by peasant women from flowers or periwinkle, were both more fitting and more economical than the store-bought variety. Here again tradition and the natural economy are opposed to innovation and the money economy, and *Jews* are seen as the agents of the destructive process of innovation. These same points were also made by an English traveller to Galicia: "...The average Jew all over the southeastern part of the Continent is doing his best to crush out all artistic sense in the peasants by supplanting their really good handiwork with the vilest machine-made trash that he can procure."[90]

The preeminence of Jews in trade was reflected in Galician Ukrainian folk proverbs: "Without a Jew, there's no trade" (U *Bez zhyda i torhu nema*) and "From infancy a Jew has his own bazaar within" (U *Zhyd z malenku v seredyni svii iarmarok maie*), i.e., he is an inveterate merchant.[91] In 1900 over a third of Galicia's Jews were engaged in or supported by trade and communications, making up over two-thirds of all Galicians in that occupational sector.[92] The census, however, understated Jewish involvement in

---

[89] It was customary in the Ukrainian marriage ritual to crown the couple with wreaths during the church service, whence one of the Ukrainian words for marriage, *vinchannia* (from *vinets*, wreath).

[90] Pennel, *The Jew at Home*, 56.

[91] Franko, *Halytsko-ruski prypovidky*, 106–7.

[92] Buzek, *Stosunki zawodowe i socyalne*.

commerce, since many of those who listed no profession probably engaged in jobbing, and retail trade could often complement another primary occupation such as tavernkeeping[93] (which in Austrian statistics was included in the industrial sector). By contrast, Ukrainians were almost absent from the sphere of commerce. This was part of the legacy of serfdom, and it began to change, very slowly, only after emancipation in 1848. There is a telling letter from the Ternopil Ruthenian council to the Supreme Ruthenian Council, dated 30 September 1848 (O.S.), in which the Ternopil council made a number of propositions for a Ukrainian economic programme. "As for commerce and industry," wrote the Ternopil Ukrainians, "the local council can offer no advice, because it has no merchants and people who understand commerce among its members; one can only hope that, with the freedom now emerging, the Ruthenian people will want to think also about commerce."[94] Thinking, and some action, did indeed begin, but by 1900 only 20,029 Ukrainian-speakers (at most) were employed in or dependents of persons employed in trade and communication. This was 0.7 per cent of the total Ukrainian-speaking population and about one-fourteenth of the number of Jews in the commercial sector (279,571).[95]

This social imbalance greatly disturbed the leaders of the Ukrainian national movement in Galicia, who sought to develop a more diversified Ukrainian society. They therefore advocated a markedly different response to the proliferation of commodity exchange than did some of the peasants and rural notability who joined their movement. Instead of sharing the universal peasant distrust of the merchant as such, instead of identifying the natural economy with Ukrainian tradition and instigating a boycott of the money economy, the leadership of the national movement urged the peasants and rural notability, especially the cantors, to *take part* in the developing money economy by establishing and managing Ukrainian stores, whether cooperative or private.[96]

The notion, radical in its time, that not only Jews, but also Ukrainians could operate stores intensified and, in a certain sense, modernized Ukrainian-Jewish antagonism in the village. It was no longer merely a phenomenal expression of the conflict between the peasant and the representative of the money economy. Under the influence of the national movement, more conscious villagers began to abandon their traditional distrust of commerce and expressed their dissatisfaction that only Jews

---

[93] "Our village [Bereziv, Kolomyia district] had ... two Jewish stores, and besides them every tavernkeeper ... retails all sorts of things at a good price" (*CC* 168).

[94] *Klasova borotba*, 434.

[95] Buzek, *Stosunki zawodowe i socyalne*, "Tablice." Since 5 per cent of all Jews were, for census purposes, Ukrainian-speakers, it is possible that in reality there were only about six thousand Ukrainians engaged in or dependent on trade and communication.

[96] Nonetheless Vasyl Nahirny, in the same speech in which he said that every village should have a Ukrainian-run store, urged peasants to wear traditional clothing instead of city-style clothing. Vasyl Nahirny, "Iak maie vyhliadaty uporiadkovana hromada," *Batkivshchyna* 14, no. 29 (17 [29] July 1892): 145–6.

engaged in it. A Ukrainian storekeeper in Barani Peretoky, Sokal district, urged his conationals: "Establish stores in the villages and towns while there is still time..., because if Jewry makes its nest in the villages and establishes its own stores, then it will be too late for us" (*CC* 3). In response to frequent exhortations in *Batkivshchyna* to establish Ukrainian shops, a correspondent from Kostarowce, Sanok district, wrote:

> You say we should set up shops in the village, and really: Why shouldn't our peasant draw the profit which [now] goes into a Jewish pocket? We will heed your advice and will try to set them up. Maybe it's not such a big deal to run a shop if even an ignorant, shaggy Jew can do it (*CC* 254).

Already in this item of correspondence one can detect more contempt for Jews as such than in previously cited items referring to more traditional spheres of conflict. Also, one hears the voice of an embryonic shopkeeper breaking through. Both of these notes are sounded more clearly in another item of correspondence:

> In our land Jews have taken over commerce to such an extent that it seems no one else can have a store or state concession [to sell tobacco or salt], only a Jew.... In Bereziv [Kolomyia district] it happened that a Jew did not sell tobacco honestly and in accordance with regulations, so his concession was revoked and given to a Ruthenian merchant [the author?].... Over a dozen times already it's happened that a travelling Jew, seeing the eagle [i.e., the state emblem, signifying a state concession] displayed on the building, entered it with the certainty that he would find one of his own people; and he was very amazed when he saw not a Jew sitting there but a Christian. One such Jew drove up to the concession and even unhitched his horse, thinking he would spend some time there; but when he entered inside and saw images of the saints on the walls, he became so frightened that he immediately fled, and didn't look back. If only in all our villages the Jews would flee so! (*CC* 174).

We attend here the birth of shopkeepers' anti-Semitism in Ukrainian Galicia.

To emphasize their non-Jewish character, the new Ukrainian-owned stores were sometimes referred to as "Christian stores" (*CC* 33, 206, 207). One store, in Stariava, Mostyska district, was actually founded by the church committee to raise money for the church. The manager of the store wrote to *Batkivshchyna*: "...People have recognized the Jewish trap set for them, and they remember the beautiful aim of our commerce, so their pious hearts do not permit them to go to the Jews, but draw them instead to the church store" (*CC* 116).

The item just quoted implies that the Ukrainian shopkeeper, unlike his Jewish rival, entered business for disinterested motives. The same point was made by a correspondent from Bereziv, Kolomyia district: "Good people have opened a Ruthenian variety store, not so much for their own profit as in order to prevent the Jewish shopkeepers from fleecing [people] completely" (*CC* 168). The rest of the article concerned the false weights and inflated prices to be found in Jewish stores.

There is frequent mention in the correspondence of competition between Ukrainian and Jewish shops (*CC* 36, 80, 86, 189), as well as Jewish opposition to the Ukrainian-owned stores (*CC* 30, 78, 118, 207, 265). A correspondent from Vyktoriv, Stanyslaviv district, described the ruin of a community-owned store because of opposition from Jewish competitors:

> There was a communal shop, the only one, and it was developing very nicely; the whole village shopped there. But the Jews were resolved against it. They tied the mayor's hands in the way they know how, and set up no less than four of their own shops. The communal store collapsed and today barely manages to stay in existence (*CC* 30).

A less successful, but more colourful, attack on a commune-owned store is described at greater length by a correspondent from Trybukhivtsi, Husiatyn district:

> When the communal council resolved to establish a communal store and the Jews learned of it, they at first did not want to believe that peasants could do such a thing; but when they found out it was the honest truth, they became very alarmed. One Jew who had his own store came to the communal office and said: "Listen, what do you need stores for, who's going to tend it [sic]? And even if you find someone, you will have to pay him well, so that you will have nothing left of your profits. It would be best if I gave you 400 gulden; don't set up the shop and you will save yourself much trouble." But the councillors saw what lay behind this offer; they would have returned the 400 gulden with usurious interest....

The store was established and in its first week it had a turnover of 150 gulden. "When the Jews saw there was nothing they could do about it, four of them rode to the rabbi in Husiatyn to request him to curse Mr. Pynkovsky and Mr. Cherevatiuk [the shop managers]; but they, as faithful Christians, were not afraid even of this curse" (*CC* 207).[97]

The correspondence also mentions the traditionalist peasant reaction to the innovation of Ukrainian-owned stores. Some peasants continued to prefer shopping at the familiar Jewish-owned stores. A correspondent from Dmytriv, Kaminka Strumylova district, stated that the newly opened Ukrainian store had lower prices than the local Jewish store:

> But there are still people who go to Radekhiv, buy salt at the same price [as in the Ukrainian store, but] from the Jews and carry it a mile [7.6 kilometres] home. When will they get some sense! (*CC* 269).

Some Ukrainian peasants simply could not be persuaded to get involved in commerce. The memoirs of the pastor of Manaiv, Zboriv district, quote a peasant, c. 1897, who was reluctant to contribute his share to a cooperative store: "That's Jewish stuff and what does a peasant know about it? It requires a Jew's head for that business, not a peasant's."[98] The mayor of

---

[97] The "curse" referred to here must have been the *kheyrem* (excommunication), which placed a person and his business under a ban.

[98] Tarnavsky, *Spohady*, 174–5. "Peasants had nothing to do with trade, holding it to be a Jewish enterprise, for which only Jews (the saying was) were fitted." Slomka, *From Serfdom to Self-Government*, 81.

Novytsia, Kalush district, built a store at his own cost and refused to rent the building to Jews, even when they offered 120 gulden. He wanted to rent it to a Ukrainian for 50 gulden and even offered to give the shopkeeper a piece of land and the right to graze a cow along with the mayor's cattle. But no Ukrainian was willing to take up his offer, although, according to the correspondent, the village had a population of three thousand (*CC* 155).[99]

Yet in spite of the initial peasant reluctance to break with tradition, the Ukrainian cooperative movement was flourishing by the eve of World War I. A central commercial cooperative organization, Narodna torhovlia (National Commerce), was founded in Lviv in 1883. In addition to its central warehouse in Lviv, Narodna torhovlia had 10 branches with warehouses in 1894 and 19 in 1913. In 1894 the organization had 314 stores; in 1896–7—346. By 1913 the Ukrainians in Galicia had 92 consumer cooperatives with 12,500 members. The famous dairy cooperative Maslosoiuz, so prominent in the interwar era, started in Stryi in 1907; by 1911 it had united 75 dairies.[100] The real development of the Ukrainian cooperative movement came in the decade preceding the First World War, as is indicated by the appearance at that time of a series of economic-cooperative periodicals including *Ekonomist* (1904–14), *Samopomich* (1909–14) and *Torhovi visty* (1914).[101] The Ukrainians' initial involvement in commerce in the late nineteenth century should be viewed as a pioneering stage.

A particular branch of commerce was tavernkeeping. It was particular as being more than an outpost of the money economy. It represented also the influence of the manor, since the landlord owned the tavern; furthermore, as promoter of feudal-rooted alcoholism, it was bitterly opposed by the Ukrainian national movement, especially its clerical contingent. Although ownership of taverns in Galicia was the hereditary privilege of the Polish nobility (the so-called right of propination), beginning in the seventeenth century Jews rented this right.[102] Although early Austrian legislation forbade Jews to engage in tavernkeeping,[103] the prohibition was frequently evaded.[104]

---

[99] The census of 1880 recorded a total population of 2,382, of whom 2,247 were Greek Catholics and 78 Jews. *Spec. Orts-Rep. 1880.*

[100] Bujak, "Rozwój gospodarczy Galicji," 382–3. Rosenfeld, *Die polnische Judenfrage,* 119. Kravets, *Selianstvo,* 64–5.

[101] Ihnatiienko, *Bibliohrafiia ukrainskoi presy.* Magocsi, *The Peter Jacyk Collection.*

[102] Rawita Gawroński, *Żydzi ... na Rusi,* 104. See also Levine, "Gentry, Jews, and Serfs," 233–50.

[103] Mahler, *History,* 326. Rosdolsky, *Stosunki poddańcze,* 1:98.

[104] Mahler, *History* 339–40. See TsDIAL, 146/64b/3219, pp. 71–2; 146/87/1126, p. 105; 146/87/1130, p. 18. " ... If we consider that the Jews in these times were almost the exclusive representatives of merchants' and usurers' capital in Galicia as well as almost the only purchasers of the peasants' products, then we will not wonder that—with the exception perhaps of the last three years of Joseph II's rule—the legislation concerning Jewish leaseholds remained largely on paper and that in spite of legal prohibitions Jewish tavernkeepers in the villages of Galicia continued to ply their trade under the most diverse pretenses.... " Rosdolsky, *Stosunki poddańcze,* 1:99.

In 1900 Jews made up over 80 per cent of all Galicians involved in any way in the liquor trade.[105]

In the correspondence referring to Jewish tavernkeeping the theme most often repeated is that Jews grew rich from the peasants' drunkenness (*CC* 27, 62, 66, 67, 77, 87, 157, 254, 278, 281). A peasant from Ivachiv Dolishnii, Ternopil district, wrote: "The tavernkeepers, even though they pay thousands for propination, still grow rich from it and all of this they take from our stupid goy-peasant.... Through liquor the Jewish tavernkeepers have become lords, while we Ruthenian peasants are becoming beggars" (*CC* 77). The correspondent from Kostarowce, Sanok district, in arguing the need for Ukrainian-owned stores, also spoke of the tavern:

> If only we were allowed to establish stores with concessions, where peasants could buy tobacco and snuff from their own people, then the sun would shine in the villages and the Iudky and Mekhli would slowly have to retreat from them! Take us, for example, in Kostarowce: over half the village no longer ... drinks liquor, and more than one of us would not so much as look at the tavern, were it not for the need to go in and buy tobacco or snuff, without which it is hard to get by once you get the habit. So, you go into the tavern for tobacco, and the Jew begins to talk smoothly, he begins to praise his liquor and make fun of [the] sobriety [movement] and the apostles of sobriety [i.e., priests active in the temperance campaign]. Before you know it, you've had one drink, then another, though you promised yourself to flee from the tavern with your tobacco and not so much as look at the liquor! In more than one case, someone has just begun to abstain from alcohol, but his will is weak. Because of tobacco or snuff, he goes on such a binge again that he sells his boots for liquor and pays double for whatever he drinks.[106] And Iudka just puts his hands in his pockets, jingles his money, laughs and makes fun of the drunk (*CC* 254).

The correspondents' tales about the tavernkeepers' easily acquired wealth were exaggerated. Leases on propination were high, not only because of the avarice of the nobles, but because so many Jews sought to obtain them.[107] At the turn of the century, Galicia had 17,277 taverns, i.e., one for every 420 inhabitants. This was an improvement over the 1850s–70s, when there was a tavern for every two to three hundred inhabitants.[108] A reading club member from Fytkiv, Nadvirna district, reported that this village with a hundred households[109] had four taverns (*CC* 22). Another correspondent, from Mshanets, Staryi Sambir district, wrote that some Jews who did not legally lease the right of propination nonetheless sold liquor to supplement their incomes (*CC* 66).[110] As Raphael Mahler has noted: "The exceptionally large number of taverns and saloons, reflecting the frightful extent of alcoholism in

---

[105] Buzek, *Stosunki zawodowe i socyalne*, "Tablice."

[106] Galician tavernkeepers understood "the art of watering schnapps, and of doubling the chalked score of anyone who went upon the tick." Franzos, *The Jews of Barnow*, 321.

[107] Franko, "Żydzi o kwestji żydowskiej," *Tydzień* 1, no. 5 (30 January 1893): 35.

[108] Wyka, *Teka Stańczyka*, 51–6.

[109] The census of 1880 recorded 567 inhabitants in Fytkiv. *Spec. Orts-Rep 1880.*

[110] See also Slomka, *From Serfdom to Self-Government*, 78, 80–1.

the country, could nevertheless not provide a livelihood for the considerable number of Jews in the villages and towns who were engaged in this deplorable occupation, because of the terrific competition existing in the field."[111] To all this must be added the effects of the sobriety movement, which also contributed to the economic decline of the Galician tavernkeeper.[112] In 1900 the weekly income of an average tavernkeeper was estimated at 1.2 to 2.2 gulden (in Pechenizhyn, a district capital).[113]

The tavernkeeper's poverty only exacerbated Ukrainian-Jewish conflict. If the tavernkeeper wanted to pay his rent and make something for himself, he had no choice but to foster the alcoholism of the peasants and to extract as much as possible from them in payment by employing sharp practices or by encouraging them to drink on credit. *This* is why the Jewish tavernkeeper, the agent of demoralization and economic ruin, was such a hated figure to representatives of the Ukrainian national movement.

As we know, the national movement through the clergy called on peasants to abstain from alcohol. Two items of correspondence mention that the sobriety movement was directed against the Jews (*CC* 12, 158) and two others that Jews opposed the sobriety movement (*CC* 67, 254). During a temperance mission held in Kolodribka, Zalishchyky district,

> The Jews walked about in the distance, for some reason saddened. They looked and listened, shaking their heads, even tearing their beards. "Ei, *gvalt!* What are those lads doing, what do they need this for? Why are they spending money [on the pageantry of the mission]? We told them, but did they listen?" And the bolder ones stole into Andrii Mehera's orchard near the church, set a little table with bottles of liquor and glasses under a cherry tree and kept calling out from behind the fence: "Gentlemen, ladies, good liquor! Please, we invite you!" But no one even looked in that direction (*CC* 67).

In order for the national movement to combat the tavern's influence, it had to develop an alternative institution that would assume the tavern's social functions. The reading club became this rival institution: "What a great thing the reading club is in a village; it is education, recreation and life. We no longer need taverns" (*CC* 153). "...Better our own reading club than the Jewish tavern" (*CC* 42). In Vynnyky, Zhovkva district, the church fraternities and sororities had traditionally celebrated their feast days in the tavern; but when a reading club was established in Vynnyky, the celebrations were transferred to its premises (*CC* 5, 153).

Sometimes the commune would continue to frequent the tavern and content itself with putting the tavern under Ukrainian control. The Ukrainian-managed tavern was analogous to the Ukrainian-owned store. The

---

[111] Mahler, "Economic Background," 258.

[112] Kohos Leib Szparer, tavernkeeper of Pidhorodyshche, Bibrka district, petitioned the administration of the Potocki estates in 1884 to lower the cost of the propination lease. Among the reasons he cited for his request was that "almost the entire village, bound by an oath, has stopped drinking vodka." LNB AN URSR, Viddil rukopysiv, Pot., No. 272, p. 15.

[113] N. Blickstein, "Die Lage der Juden Galiziens," *Die Welt*, no. 18 (4 May 1900): 6.

change in management may have been accompanied by a reform of the functions of the tavern. In Utishkiv, Zolochiv district, the landlord Leopold Obertyński ousted the Jewish tavernkeeper at the commune's request and replaced him with "our man." The new tavernkeeper transformed the tavern into a combination of reading club and store by subscribing to the popular press for his customers and offering for sale "the most necessary and inexpensive things" (*CC* 216). In Kurivtsi, Ternopil district, the commune itself leased the right of propination from the landlord. The priest who reported this to *Batkivshchyna* commented: "Thus the inhabitants of Kurivtsi have shown that where the commune is conscious and sober, it does not allow an unbaptized one to rake in money from the commune and to exact such high tribute for spreading demoralization" (*CC* 44). It is difficult, however, to see how Ukrainian-owned taverns could survive for long as "reform taverns," given the high costs of propination leases.[114]

In light of the preceding it should be clear why there was such a pronounced anti-Jewish component in the Ukrainian national movement, especially its rural variety, in late nineteenth-century Galicia. The economic antagonism between Jews and Ukrainians had its roots deep in the feudal era, when Ukrainians were, broadly speaking, serfs and Jews were representatives of merchants' and usurers' capital as well as middlemen between nobles and peasants. The abolition of serfdom in 1848 and the constitutional and economic reforms of the 1860s (including the emancipation of the Austrian Jews in 1868) did not mitigate the economic antagonism inherited from feudalism, but in fact exacerbated it. Such, for example, was the effect of repealing Austrian legislation aimed at limiting traditional Jewish economic activities in the village. More important, however, were two other moments. First, the abolition of serfdom and other restraints on modern economic development pushed the formerly marginal sphere of the money economy into the foreground and afforded its representatives, the Jews, opportunities in the sphere of usury and commerce that did not exist, and could not exist, under feudalism. Secondly, the great reforms of the mid-nineteenth century also created new opportunities for the Ukrainians. Freed from serfdom and with more access to education than ever in the past, the Ukrainians became interested in engaging in economic activities that hitherto had been pursued almost exclusively by Jews (commerce, lending, even tavernkeeping). In the late nineteenth century Ukrainians became for the first time economic rivals of the Jews.

The Challenge to Traditional Authority in the Commune

The coming of the national movement had profound implications for local self-government. Municipal government had been undergoing a continual, but

---

[114] In Pidhorodyshche (see above, note 112) a peasant was given the lease of the tavern in 1872. He could not make the payments on the lease and was removed after seven years. LNB AN URSR, Viddil rukopysiv, Pot., No. 272, p. 17.

never thorough, democratization from above on the eve of the penetration of the national movement into the village. The major moments in this process were the attempts to curtail seigneurial domination of local administration when Galicia came under enlightened Austrian rule, the reforms of municipal administration attendant upon the abolition of serfdom and the extensive municipal autonomy introduced in connection with the constitutional restructuring of Austria in the 1860s. These reforms were never intended to institute a radically democratic system of self-government in the commune, and the weight of tradition in the Galician countryside was such as to inhibit even the full implementation of what was intended. The national movement, however, gave impetus to a more far-reaching democratization of local self-government and therefore challenged traditional authority in the commune.

The importance of local government in the national movement is signalled both by the list of activists (34 activists, i.e., 9.2 per cent of all activists, held a position in municipal government)[115] and by the corpus of correspondence (73 items, i.e., 26.0 per cent of the total, referred to municipal government). The correspondents of *Batkivshchyna* presented a very ambiguous picture of local self-government in relation to the national movement, much as they had done in the case of the clergy.[116] Of the 73 items referring to communal government, the vast majority (70.0 per cent) described the government in a negative way,[117] and only a minority (28.8 per cent) described it positively.[118] This mixed view of communal government[119] corresponded to contradictory attitudes of the local governments to the national movement, which in turn corresponded to contradictory and conflicting forces in the make-up of the governments themselves. The roots of these contradictions lie in the feudal era.

The basic offices of local self-government—those of the mayor[120] and aldermen[121]—went back to the late fourteenth and fifteenth centuries, to the introduction of German law in Galician villages as a result of German

---

[115] *LA* 11, 16, 46, 51, 53, 63, 70, 90, 92, 107, 122, 171, 197, 199, 246, 266, 268, 276, 285, 288, 292, 301, 303, 304, 307, 327, 328, 331, 334, 337, 343, 348, 350, 362.

[116] See above, 133–42.

[117] *CC* 1, 10, 13, 16, 23, 25, 30, 33, 36, 49, 54, 58, 60, 61, 62, 68, 77, 78, 84, 86, 87, 106, 112, 118, 125, 141, 143, 151, 169, 173, 197, 199, 206, 211, 214, 217, 222, 224, 231, 232, 235, 236, 237, 241, 249, 257, 258, 263, 265, 270, 278.

[118] *CC* 2, 32, 34, 52, 69, 74, 95, 105, 114, 115, 121, 137, 155, 161, 188, 201, 216, 223, 240, 260, 276. One item, *CC* 123, was too mixed to classify; it was negative in relation to the former government and positive in relation to the new government.

[119] Noted also by Hryniuk, "A Peasant Society," 420–2.

[120] U *viit*; P *wójt*; G *Vogt, Ortsrichter, Dorfrichter, Gemeinderichter*; L *praetor*.

[121] U *prysiazhni*, P *przysiężni*, G *Geschworene*, L *jurati*.

colonization.[122] The local self-government of that period had independence from the seigneurs as well as a fairly wide competence. But with the advent of "second serfdom," the autonomy of peasant self-government was severely restricted. In most villages the seigneurs "succeeded in making the mayors their creatures,"[123] while in others the organs of local self-government were altogether eradicated. It was primarily on royal estates that the traditional, autonomous village government was preserved into the Austrian era.[124]

The historical mixture of village autonomy and seigneurial influence was codified and made uniform for all of Galicia by Joseph II's patent of 13 April 1784 (N.S.). While certainly an improvement in the status of the communal governments in most of Galicia,[125] the Austrian reform still allowed considerable legal leeway for the lord to make his influence felt. The law established that each village would have its own mayor and from two to twelve aldermen, depending on the size of the locality. The mayor was to be chosen by the landlord from three candidates elected by the commune. The aldermen were to be elected by the commune alone, but in agreement with the mayor (G *mit Einverständniss des Richters*). After election, the mayor and aldermen had to take an oath to the landlord that they would perform their functions loyally and conscientiously. The government held office for three years, but any officer who merited it could be approved by the landlord (G *Grundobrigkeit*) and commune for another term. In the reactionary 1830s, laws were issued that allowed the landlords themselves to exercise the functions of any communal officer guilty of not reporting to the manor, or embezzling, fines imposed on the villagers.[126]

The functions of communal self-government under feudalism were very limited, since much of the local administration was simply entrusted to the manor and its appointees, particularly the mandator. The mayor and aldermen heard cases of disputes between serfs, but their decisions could be appealed to the manor; they also had the obligation to administer communal property, but under the strict control of the manor. In the main, the communal governments were only executive and auxiliary organs of the demesnes.[127] Characteristically, a folk song considered the mayor as much a manorial official as the steward.[128]

The legal influence of the feudal landlord on communal government was thus not insignificant. In practice, however, his influence was much greater than the law envisaged or permitted. For example, the village governments

---

[122] See Kaindl, *Beiträge zur Geschichte des deutschen Rechtes.*

[123] Blum, "The Rise of Serfdom," 824.

[124] Grodziski, *Historia ustroju*, 78, 80–1.

[125] In spite of Joseph's distrust of communal autonomy, mentioned in Rosdolsky, *Die grosse Steuer und Agrarreform*, 75.

[126] Klunker, *Die gesetzliche Unterthans-Verfassung*, 1:261–2.

[127] Rosdolsky, *Stosunki poddańcze*, 1:69–70.

[128] See above, 16.

traditionally held their sessions in taverns, which were owned by the
landlords; the tavernkeeper, by skillful distribution of alcohol and banter,
could influence the proceedings.[129] Other abuses, though, were far more
egregious. There were cases where the landlord, following the old Polish
custom, simply appointed the mayor without the nicety of an election of three
candidates by the commune. A peasant grievance from the Komarno region
in 1822 noted that "those mayors, who according to the patent are supposed
to be elected by the commune of each village, have been deposed by the
lords."[130] The peasant rebels of the Chortkiv circle in 1838 demanded the
replacement of village officers who were devoted to the landlords with elected
officials who would defend the communes' interest;[131] this demand implies
that the communes' rights to elect village officers had been rendered
ineffective. That the landlords were abusing their legal role in the selection of
communal officers is also indirectly confirmed by a reform of 1846, i.e., in
response to the jacquerie of that year: the landlords from then on were to
send the three mayoral candidates to the circle authorities, who would choose
one of them and administer the oath.[132]

Since the village government represented a combination of manorial
influence, recognized in law and dominant in practice, with the influence of
the serf commune, dominant in law but weaker in practice, it is only natural
that, in the struggle between landlords and serfs, officers of the village
government could be found on both sides of the conflict, and somewhat more
often on the side of the landlords.

A documentary collection on antifeudal struggle in the Galician
countryside (*Klasova borotba*) mentions five instances in which members of
the communal government led or supported peasant resistance[133] and eight
instances in which they sided with the landlords.[134] The same source shows a
basic continuity during the revolutionary years 1848–9, when one mayor led
an attack on the landlords and steward,[135] but the Supreme Ruthenian
Council received four complaints of the anti-Ukrainian and pro-landlord
biases of the communal governments.[136]

Communal administration was somewhat reformed in the wake of the
revolution, but the far-reaching reforms legislated by the Kroměříž

---

[129] See the "amusing" account by Prince Betański in his memorial of 1773: "Ces jugements se
font ordinairement au cabaret chez le juif . . . , une dose plus ou moins d'eau de vie influe dans les
procédures et quelque fois les juges et les parties se rossent mutuellement d'importance."
Rosdolsky, *Stosunki poddańcze*, 2:44. Of course, the prince here neglects to mention any benefit
to the landlord deriving from this particular venue.

[130] *Klasova borotba*, 134.

[131] *Ibid.*, 207.

[132] Grodziski, *Historia ustroju*, 78–9.

[133] *Klasova borotba*, 52–3, 67, 71, 237–8, 281.

[134] *Ibid.*, 101, 184, 187–8, 190, 207, 237, 299–300, 304–5.

[135] *Ibid.*, 388–9.

[136] *Ibid.*, 424, 430–1, 473, 500.

parliament were not implemented at all in Galicia. During the decade of centralist reaction, manorial control of the local government was weakened, but the manor's influence was replaced by that of the central bureaucracy rather than by that of the commune.[137] The bureaucracy rather than the manor often appointed the mandators in the early 1850s, and the mandators disappeared altogether in 1854–6 when the whole demesnal apparatus of local administration was dismantled.[138] Thus during the period when the servitude commissions were most active in Galicia, communal governments were influenced by the central bureaucracy; this may have weakened the determination of village councils to support the communes' claims against the decisions of the commissions. As has already been shown in the case of Dobrotvir,[139] even after the autonomy of communal government was augmented (1866), a government could earn the enmity of the commune by accepting an unfavourable settlement of a servitudes dispute.

The Austrian constitutional reforms of the 1860s, which heralded the beginning of the penetration of the national movement into the villages, included a fundamental restructuring of municipal government that granted considerable autonomy to the communes. The municipal reforms were characterized by the principle of duality in administration, i.e., alongside the various gradations of the central bureaucracy, which reached down to the district level, authority at the municipal level rested in the hands of autonomous, elected organs of self-government. Although in Galicia the influence of the district captaincies over the communal governments was somewhat stronger than elsewhere in Austria, the basic principle of autonomy was instituted here as well. The Polish nobility as a class had influence over the communes in so far as the district captaincies, which represented its interests, had an influence, but otherwise there was no formal connection between the manor and the commune as a self-governing unit. Since 1851 manor and commune had been separated as administrative entities in Galicia (as well as Bukovyna), and the municipal reform of 1866 retained this administrative division. Thus the landlord in Galicia neither paid taxes to the communal government nor voted in communal elections.

The manor still retained an informal, general influence over village affairs, but judging by the paucity of references to it in the correspondence, it was

---

[137] By law, the commune elected three candidates for mayor and the circle authorities made the final selection. In memoirs referring to the early 1860s, Evhen Olesnytsky recalled the practice in his village which differed from the legal norm and gave the commune decisive power. A circle commissioner would simply come to the village, assemble the commune and ask whom it wanted to be mayor. The villagers shouted their choice unanimously and the commissioner officially conferred office on the man they so chose. Olesnytsky, *Storinky*, 1:30. Olesnytsky did not venture to assess whether this practice was exceptional or common. Obviously, this method could only have been employed when the commune was not divided over its choice.

[138] The dissolution of the demesnal apparatus began several years earlier elsewhere in Austria. On the general structure of municipal government, 1848–1918, see Grzybowski, *Galicja*, 227–89; Klabouch, "Die Lokalverwaltung"; Klabouch, *Die Gemeindeselbstverwaltung*.

[139] See above, 45–8.

not very strong. The corpus of correspondence contains only two passing references to this influence, in both of which the manor in question was in Jewish hands. The mayor of Fytkiv, Nadvirna district, was said to have a special understanding "with the landlord Khaskel and other Jews" (*CC* 58), while the mayor of Berezhnytsia, Kalush district, was reputed to "cling to the Jew like a burr to a sheepskin coat, and whatever Iudka [the lessee of the estate] says, the mayor considers sacred" (*CC* 173). Jewish manorial influence on the village government is corroborated, and assessed more sympathetically, outside the corpus of correspondence, in the memoirs of the son of a Jewish estate owner.[140] A brief notice in *Batkivshchyna* from 1884 mentions the influence of landlords in general: "In the village of Kalynivshchyna [Chortkiv district], the mayor is illiterate, he knows no regulation or law, he only knows how to ingratiate himself with the lords."[141]

Although general manorial influence on village government was weak in the post-reform era, one specific outpost of this influence remained strong: the tavern. The practice, instituted under serfdom, of running communal affairs from the tavern continued into the late nineteenth century. With the manor's loss of formal mechanisms of control over the village government and in the context of distrust between manor and autonomous commune, the indirect influence of the tavern, which had played a subsidiary role in the early nineteenth century, swelled in importance. A village priest observed, with reference to the period after 1866:

> The peasants made a village parliament out of the tavern, where all local affairs were decided in accordance with the advice of the Jewish tavernkeeper, with liquor. The Jewish tavernkeeper had orders from the lord, the owner of the manor, how to decide each communal matter.... The lord, the owner of the village, instructed the Jewish tavernkeeper who should be elected as mayor and who as councilmen, who should be scribe...and member of the communal directorate.[142]

The corpus of correspondence records several instances of communal business being conducted regularly in the tavern. In Dynyska, Rava Ruska district, "the mayor and the whole communal council meet in the tavern with a bottle at hand..." (*CC* 231). In Tsvitova, Buchach district, the mayor conducted village business in the tavern, because "he likes to drink one glass after another..." (*CC* 16). In Turia Velyka, Dolyna district, "the communal government drinks its fill of beer in the tavern, sometimes from evening all the way to midnight" (*CC* 33). In the small town of Khrystynopil, Sokal district, the tavernkeeper "daddy Ioso" (U *tatko Ioso*) made the decisions.

The influence of the tavern on village politics is also implied in the frequent complaints in the correspondence about communal officers who drank. A correspondent from Peremyshliany district complained that ignorant

---

[140] Kofler, "Żydowskie dwory," 91.

[141] S.T., "...vid Chortkova," *Batkivshchyna* 6, no. 16 (18 [6] April 1884): 100.

[142] Tarnavsky, *Spohady*, 41.

people, succumbing to pressure from landlords and Jews, elected "drunkards" to communal councils (*CC* 241). A correspondent from Radvantsi, Sokal district, charged that the mayor of the village encouraged the commune to drink (*CC* 106). In Perviatychi, Sokal district, the former mayor allegedly "from time to time sat in the tavern and drank away people's labour," i.e., he spent communal money on drink (*CC* 87). The municipal government of Liubycha Kameralna, Rava Ruska district, was accused of unnecessarily selling communal timber in order to pay for drinks; commune members could only receive wood if they bribed the councilmen, usually with liquor (*CC* 49). A correspondent for Ivachiv Dolishnii, Ivachiv Horishnii and Plotycha, Ternopil district, wrote: "Our famous councilman Vasyl Dobosh not long ago spent three days in jail in Ternopil for drunkenness, and now he's going to jail for eight days because of some rowdy stunts he pulled in the tavern one night" (*CC* 77). Correspondents reserved special ridicule for mayors who took a sobriety oath, but then invoked a rustic casuistry to justify backsliding. In November 1883 the mayor of Spasiv, Sokal district, swore off vodka (U *horilka*), but within a year he was allegedly the largest consumer of arrack (U *arak*) in the village (*CC* 87). A correspondent from Berezhnytsia, Stryi district, wrote much the same about the former mayor Ivan Sachavsky: "He doesn't even give a good example to the commune, because he'll look into the tavern and, even though he's taken an oath to abstain from vodka, he won't forget to drink some arrack or plum brandy or at least some beer; sometimes he even spends the night at Khaskel's [i.e., the tavern], because he's still a bit ashamed to lie in the ditch" (*CC* 236).

The correspondents' opposition to the tavern's influence on communal government does not seem to have been motivated primarily by the tavern's connection with the manor. Rather, the prime motivations for the opposition appear to be rooted in complexes already described: the general antagonisms between the Ukrainian national movement and the Jews,[143] between the sobriety movement and the tavernkeepers, and between the reading clubs and taverns.[144] The many motivations of the Ukrainian national movement's opposition to the tavern's influence on village government account for the prominence this theme is given in the correspondence.

The transformation of manorial influence into "Jewish" influence is analogous to the previously discussed transformation of the socio-economic conflict between commune and manor into Ukrainian-Jewish antagonism. There is also an analogy to the transposition of manor-commune conflict from the socio-economic to the political sphere. The influence of the Polish nobility as a class on the mayors of peasant communes was very much in evidence, if

---

[143] For an overview of this antagonism in the sphere of local government, see Himka, "Ukrainian-Jewish Antagonism."

[144] "So you see, good people," wrote the correspondent from Tsvitova, "we draw people to the reading club while the mayor draws them to liquor" (*CC* 16). In Hlubichok Velykyi, Ternopil district, "the communal officers don't care about the reading club, only about the tavern and drinking parties...." "Z pid Ternopolia," *Batkivshchyna* 6, no. 34 (22 [10] August 1884): 212.

we are to believe the correspondence, during elections to the diet and parliament. Mayors were frequently chosen as electors for these elections (in the peasant curia the elections were indirect). The corpus of correspondence mentions several cases of mayors selling their votes to the Polish candidate (*CC* 217, 222), including that of the former mayor of Berezhnytsia, Stryi district, "who even brought home the sausage which he had acquired for his efforts" (*CC* 236).[145] In Rava Ruska district, the communal scribes, in fear of losing their jobs, were said to have convinced the mayors to vote for the Polish candidate (*CC* 211). The mayor of Hora, Sokal district, even gave a speech in the district capital in which he "very maliciously" opposed the Ukrainian candidate (*CC* 235). In Svystilnyky, Rohatyn district, the lessee of the estate wanted to be an elector; when he was not chosen, the mayor tried to have the initial results of the primary election nullified (*CC* 199).[146]

Already from some of the correspondence cited, it should be clear that there was bound to be frequent conflict between the rural national movement and village officers who continued to function in ways more proper to the period preceding the emancipation from serfdom, the reform of municipal government and the penetration of the national movement. The conflict between the correspondents and the tavern-frequenting communal officers was also a conflict between a new way of doing things and traditionalism. It has already been shown[147] that the national movement engendered tension between the older, largely illiterate, traditionalist peasants, who opposed such innovations as reading clubs, and the younger, often literate peasants who were more open to change. At least before the national movement was able to alter the situation, the village governments, and the mayors in particular, were recruited from the milieu of the traditionalist peasantry. The electoral law for communal government excluded from a formal voice in communal affairs, either as electors or officers, anyone under twenty-four years of age and anyone who did not pay taxes (hence all "lads," who were by definition landless). Thus young people, who formed about a quarter of the reading clubs' membership,[148] were not represented in the communal government. Custom even more than law ensured that older peasants dominated the village government, since in a culture only just emerging from an exclusively oral tradition, wisdom was associated with experience and age rather than with knowledge gained through some other means.[149] Hence the mayors tended to be older peasants and, much more often than not, illiterate. A

---

[145] See also Himka, *Socialism*, 214 note 72.

[146] See also Hryniuk, "A Peasant Society," 419.

[147] See above, 92–9.

[148] See above, 97.

[149] "...High authority [was] vested in the main carriers and transmitters of traditional culture. Clearly, the most influential were the old people, whose long life and numerous contacts with people permitted them not only to accumulate the greatest amount of traditional knowledge, but also to gain the richest experiences through economic and social practice." Dobrowolski, "Peasant Traditional Culture," 287.

contributor to *Batkivshchyna* in 1884 complained that there were only two literate mayors in all of Stanyslaviv district.[150] In 1886 only one out of seven mayors in Galicia could read and write.[151] A survey conducted by the Galician crownland administration in 1888 showed that of 5,933 mayors, 4,743 (86 per cent) were illiterate.[152] It was only natural therefore that the domination of the highest village offices by illiterate old men would be challenged by the national movement, whose adherents in the countryside, as represented by the membership of the reading clubs, were generally younger as well as literate (see Table 12). It was also only natural that mayors could be found in the forefront of the traditionalist opposition to reading clubs.[153] As the correspondent from Korelychi, Peremyshliany district, wrote: "We also, sad to say, have enemies of the reading club; it is all the sadder that these people are older and members of the council" (*CC* 84).

There were also economic motivations for the communal officers' opposition to reading clubs. The reading clubs often started communal loan funds, communal granaries and stores and generally raised the socio-economic consciousness of the peasantry. These developments were patently unwelcome from the point of view of landlords, estate lessees, moneylenders and tavernkeepers. Hence, to the extent that mayors and other communal officers were under the influence of the manor or its agents, they would oppose the establishment of reading clubs. However, even independently of direct or indirect manorial influence, the communal governments would tend to oppose the economic activities of the reading clubs, since the governments were dominated by the richest strata of the peasantry.[154]

The domination of the rich was a deliberate consequence of the communal electoral law introduced in the 1860s. The central Austrian government sought to avoid a radical democratization of the commune and to ensure that propertied and wealthier citizens held sway. The law excluded from the franchise all members of the commune who did not pay taxes, thus all landless peasants. Furthermore, since the electoral law was based on the Prussian "three-class" franchise, the votes of the richest members of the commune counted for much more than the votes of the middling and poor proprietors. The taxpayers of a village were divided into three electoral circles[155] according to the amount of tax each elector paid. The circles were

---

[150] Roz., "...z-pid Halycha," *Batkivshchyna* 6, no. 23 (6 June [30 (sic; should be 25) May] 1884): 140.

[151] "Oplata shkilna," *Batkivshchyna* 8, no. 28 (16 [4] July 1886): 171.

[152] "Sprava pysariv hromadskykh," *Batkivshchyna* 10, no. 39 (16 [28] September 1888): 238–9.

[153] See above, 94.

[154] Interestingly, mayor Jan Słomka of Dzików benefited indirectly from Jewish usury: "About 1874 I got hold of five acres from neighbours whose places had gone to ruin either in part or altogether from drunkenness or from borrowing off Jews. I got part of this direct from the owner, the rest by redeeming it from the moneylender." Slomka, *From Serfdom to Self-Government*, 174.

[155] If the commune had fifty or fewer electors, there were only two circles.

equal only in the total amount of taxes paid by each; the number of electors in each circle differed. The first circle had the least, but wealthiest, electors; the third circle had the most, but poorest, electors. Because each circle elected one-third of the members of the communal council, the richest peasants had a disproportionate say in who was elected. Further aspects of the electoral law that favoured the richest peasants were the provisions that the first circle (i.e., the circle of the richest peasants) voted last, after the results of the elections in the other circles had been made public, and that the mayor, a strong and relatively independent executive, was elected by the councilmen rather than by the commune as a whole. Hence, the communal officers tended to be well-to-do peasants.[156]

That communal officers tended to be richer than the peasantry as a whole and even richer than the peasant-activists as a whole finds corroboration in the list of activists. Of four mayor-activists who can be classified by economic status, three were wealthy (*LA* 46, 63, 122) and only one middling (*LA* 307). In the corpus of correspondence we find confirmation as well, both sympathetically expressed (the mayor in Fytkiv, Nadvirna district, was said to be "wealthy and hard-working" [*CC* 58]) and unsympathetically expressed (in Korelychi, Peremyshliany district, the councilmen were identified with "our rich guys" [U *nashi bohachyky*] [*CC* 237]). Confirmation, from diverse perspectives, is also to be found outside the corpus of correspondence. For example, the radical newspaper *Khliborob* wrote in 1892:

> The result of this [the communal electoral law] is that in all communes a few rich men in the village always control the communal council. And since now the communal councils pick the mayors from among their own members, it is, of course, a rich man or someone who is in service to the rich that is elected mayor. And once such a rich man's party gets together, it does what it wants to, how it wants to, in the commune.[157]

A member of one of the rich families in the village of Nysmychi, Sokal district, recalled in her memoirs that the thirteen richest families controlled village politics even into the interwar period. Representatives of the thirteen families, who were nicknamed "the Habsburgs," always dominated the communal council.[158]

The correspondence often linked the wealth of the village officers with their opposition to manifestations of the national movement. A particularly full account comes from Uvysla, Husiatyn district:

> In our village only rich men are respected; only those who have a dozen or so *Joch*, "wise heads," though more than one of them perhaps cannot understand

---

[156] It should be noted that the weighting of the electoral law in favour of the rich peasantry was simultaneously a weighting in favour of the older peasantry.

[157] *Khliborob* (1 August 1892), cited in Kravets, *Selianstvo*, 131.

[158] Kimpinska-Tatsiun, *Rik u zhytti ukrainskoi zhinky-hospodyni*, 93–4. In the interwar era women were enfranchised. On the eve of World War I Nysmychi had a population of 467, thus about ninety-three families. Chanderys, *Kompletny skorowidz* (1911), 115.

as much as a poor cottager; because they acquired their property not by their own intelligence, but because their daddies left it to them. Nonetheless such a person is more likely to become mayor and councilman and who knows what else.... This year a dozen or so poorer people announced that they wanted to establish a loan fund.... But when the mayor heard of it, he told these poor people: "Well, well! You will yet, each of you, go to jail!" And he has altogether 40 *Joch* of farmland. And...a councilman...said: "What good is a loan fund to me?" (*CC* 68).

In Mshana, Zolochiv district, the new reform mayor, Iosyf Skochylias, founded a loan fund; the correspondent noted: "It would have been possible to have established a fund twenty years ago, but the former rich mayors didn't try to..." (*CC* 123). In Novosilka Iazlovetska, Buchach district, the pastor founded a loan association, but the communal government refused to use the commune's bonds as capital for the association. "...We still have plenty of people who always say: 'We didn't have that in the past and things were good!' This is because they are rich, you see, and the satisfied man does not know the hungry one" (*CC* 48). In Korelychi, Peremyshliany district, "the reading club members again advised the commune to collect a few bushels of grain from each member and in this manner to establish a [communal] granary; and again our rich guys [i.e., the councilmen] said: 'The best granary is to have grain in your own storehouse [U *komora*]" (*CC* 237). As if generalizing the above experiences, a correspondent from Tetevchytsi, Kaminka Strumylova district, advised peasants:

> ...When our people elect their representatives, they only make sure that these are well-to-do proprietors and do not consider whether they will defend the rights of the whole commune as well.... During the coming communal elections..., one should not look to those who are well-to-do and care only about their own good, but to those who would care for the good of the whole commune (*CC* 214).

The complaint that village officers used their powers to promote their own interests, and the interests of those who had special protection, is frequently met in the correspondence.[159] A number of peasants in Turia Velyka, Dolyna district, registered a grievance with the district captaincy that their mayor "perpetrates various extortions and abuses his powers" (*CC* 33). More specific charges were raised against the mayor of Olesha, Tovmach district: "Wood from the communal forest is cut down without informing and obtaining permission from the communal council; wood provided by the manor to repair the bridges went to build a storehouse for the mayor, though on the bridges you can break your leg in broad daylight" (*CC* 118). The communal governments assigned members of the commune for various communal duties, including much-hated road work (U *sharvarok*);[160] according to a number of correspondents (*CC* 33, 86, 107, 110, 118, 257), the governments exempted

---

[159] See also Klabouch, *Die Gemeindeselbstverwaltung*, 50.

[160] On the resistance to road work, which led to mass arrests in 1887, see Kravets, "Dzherela," 65.

certain groups in the commune from these onerous duties: the Jews,[161] the rich and the Ukrainian petty gentry (the so-called [U] *shliakhta khodachkova*, to be discussed later). The correspondence mentions embezzlement quite frequently, by scribes (*CC* 13, 23, 141),[162] mayors (*CC* 235, 236) and councils as a whole (*CC* 33, 241). The correspondents also criticized village governments for poor management of village property (*CC* 16, 143, 231, 265). The bridges with holes, impassable roads, treeless forests and empty treasuries described by the correspondents imputed to the village governments incompetence at best and peculation at worst. That the reading clubs and correspondents brought such matters to public attention further soured relations between the municipal governments and the national movement.

The national movement created a peasantry that sat in judgment on the village governments, much as it sat in judgment on the clergy.[163] The national movement gave the affected peasantry a new self-confidence and a new set of criteria for assessing village affairs. Members of the reading clubs felt justified in demanding mayors who voted for the Ukrainian candidate in the same way that they felt justified in demanding pastors who promoted enlightenment. But there was a major difference between the criticism of the village officers, on the one hand, and of the pastors, on the other: village officers were chosen by the commune itself, by the *hromada*, and it was possible for enlightened communes to replace undesirable officers with reform candidates. Thus the village activists' criticism of their governments had a much more concrete intent than their criticism of the clergy.[164]

The reading clubs were in the forefront of reforming village government. The correspondent from Olesha, Tovmach district, announced to the readers of *Batkivshchyna* that "the reading club will protect the commune from the extortions and arbitrary rule of the government officers" (*CC* 60). The chief proponent of the reading club in Olesha was the scribe, Mykhailo Diakon (*LA* 53); the chief opponents were the mayor and councilmen. The council fired Diakon as scribe, and Diakon led a campaign against the mayor, even organizing the commune to submit grievances against the mayor to all branches of the state bureaucracy (*CC* 118). In Volia Iakubova, Drohobych district, the reading club led by Panas Melnyk (*LA* 215) waged a bitter struggle against the communal government and ran its own slate of

---

[161] For a fuller treatment, see Himka, "Ukrainian-Jewish Antagonism."

[162] In 1884 Danylo Klub, the scribe in Kaminka Voloska, Rava Ruska district, was tried in Lviv for embezzling taxes, interest on communal bonds and money from the loan fund as well as for accepting bribes. In two years he acquired about 2,300 gulden. He was ostentatious with his new wealth, even purchasing 26 *Joch* of land. Klub pleaded innocent at the trial and "appealed to the fact that during elections he always agitated for the Polish candidate." In spite of his protestations, he was sentenced to three years of severe imprisonment. "Spravy sudovi," *Batkivshchyna* 7, no. 2 (9 January 1885 [28 December 1884]): 15.

[163] See above, 135–7, 139.

[164] In this light, the longstanding demand of the national movement that the communes, not the landlords, confirm pastors in their appointments had a radical subtext that is generally overlooked.

candidates in the communal elections of 1885.[165] In Berezhnytsia, Stryi district, the reading club campaigned against the long-term mayor, Ivan Sachavsky. At last, in 1885, "our commune...came to its senses" and elected two of the founders of the reading club to the council. One of the reading club activists was even chosen mayor by the other councilmen (the vote was almost unanimous; only one councilman, "who is rarely ever sober," voted against the reading club's candidate) (*CC* 236). In Shliakhtyntsi, Ternopil district, the mayor and scribe, "obedient to what the Jew [the tavernkeeper] whispered," had persecuted the reading club; the reading club avenged itself in the 1885 communal elections: the old mayor was replaced by the vice-president of the reading club and the secretary of the reading club became deputy mayor (*CC* 249). Thus the reading club could act much like a political party in the village, contesting seats in local government. The national movement created village politics.

In addition to running reform candidates for council, the national movement also attempted to reform the one appointed office in the village government: that of scribe. The scribe was hired by the council, not elected by the commune; in theory the scribe was merely a subordinate, the council's clerk, but in practice, given the illiteracy of the mayors, he was a crucial figure in village government, its *éminence grise*.[166] The national movement advocated that its own local activists, particularly cantors,[167] be hired as scribes; after all, they were literate and devoted to the good of the commune. The worst thing for a commune, according to the movement, was to hire a nonlocal scribe recommended by the nationally and socially hostile district captaincy.

The correspondence explained in detail the advantages of the local scribe over the nonlocal scribe. In the Dobromyl-Staryi Sambir region the district authorities strongly recommended certain individuals as scribes, but these "imposed scribes," warned a correspondent, were likely to embezzle and demand high salaries; where a cantor might charge 12 gulden a year for serving as scribe, a nonlocal scribe would charge from 60 to 100. The nonlocal scribes were "a cause of poverty" not only for the above-mentioned reasons, but also because they necessitated expensive travel for the commune.

> Sometimes it happens that several people travel several miles [1 Austrian mile = 7.6 kilometres] in some minor matter to such a scribe, and they sometimes waste two days and quite a bit of money, especially when, as is the custom, they stop at every tavern along the road there and back and moreover must treat the scribes and themselves [when they arrive]. In fact, it even

---

[165] Himka, *Socialism*, 131–2.

[166] The crownland administration came to the conclusion that, since 86 per cent of the mayors were illiterate, communal affairs were actually managed by the scribes, opening the door to many abuses. "Sprava pysariv hromadskykh," 238. A case of an illiterate mayor being "led by the nose" by the scribe and the dissatisfaction this caused in the village is mentioned by Kofler, "Żydowskie dwory," 91.

[167] See above, 112, 130.

happens that people come from afar and do not find the scribe in. They wait a second day, and, if he does not return, they start home on the third day (*CC* 141).

A similar tale was told by a correspondent from the Burshtyn area in Rohatyn district (*CC* 13).

The nonlocal scribe in Kiidantsi, Kolomyia district, was not so much an inconvenience as a menace to the commune:

> ...We have no educated people in our communal government. In our village the scribe is a very important gentleman. Our communal scribe comes from the city, he is not a Ruthenian, and, as is generally true of such scribes, he does the commune more harm than good. In our village the scribes, as prominent people, led the communal officers to the tavern and thus ruined our communal officers, who are sometimes such as have never given a thought to the commune's good (*CC* 169).

In sum, to quote a contributor to *Batkivshchyna* in 1884: "No commune should accept as scribe any vagrant (U *proidysvit*); it is best that one's own literate proprietor or cantor do the work of scribe, either by himself or under the supervision of the priest. The most swindling (U *tsyhanstvo*) is perpetrated by those scribes who are scribes for several villages.... "[168]

Although the grounds for conflict between communal governments and the rural national movement were many, and although the majority of items of correspondence that mentioned village government presented it in a negative fashion, there were nonetheless instances of cooperation between the village governments and the national movement.[169] These instances admit of a number of explanations. The most obvious one is that sometimes overall class and communal solidarity took precedence over the particular interests of municipal officers. Then too, as in the case of priests, village officers might have originally supported reading clubs without yet realizing the full implications of their activities. Perhaps something like this occurred in Berezhnytsia, Kalush district. According to Aleksii Maneliuk, a member of the reading club, the scribe in Berezhnytsia was secretary of the club and even read his own verses at the club's opening in the fall of 1884.[170] But four months later Maneliuk portrayed the same scribe and the mayor as the chief enemies of the reading club and allies of the tavernkeeper and the Poles (*CC* 173). The list of activists offers evidence that some of the cooperation between the village governments and reading clubs rested on delicate foundations: some activists who held office in the village government had opponents as well as supporters in the national movement[171] and others found

---

[168] Roz., "...z-pid Halycha," *Batkivshchyna* 6, no. 23 (6 June [30 sic; should be 25) May]): 140.

[169] See above, note 118.

[170] A[leksii] M[aneliuk], "...vid Kalusha," *Batkivshchyna* 6, no. 45 (7 November [26 October] 1884): 285.

[171] *LA* 63, 70, 199, 304, 331.

themselves in a minority within their communal governments.[172] Cooperation between the village government and the national movement was probably never fully assured until a reform mayor, who accepted the principles of the national movement, was elected.[173]

In conclusion, the national movement pressed for a new type of village government, free of influences that were socially and nationally alien, responsive to the needs of the commune as a whole, not just to the desires of an elite, and supportive of the institutions of the movement. It brought to the villages a struggle for the democratization of the commune that went beyond the limits of the democratization from above that had been implemented by the Austrian government. The national movement did not, however, demand a thorough democratization. One does not find in *Batkivshchyna*, for example, an explicit call for the abolition of the three-class franchise or any call, even implicit, for the extension of the franchise to women. These limitations reflected the national leadership's deliberate policy of courting the more prosperous, male peasantry. Nonetheless, what the movement demanded was enough to unsettle communal governments throughout Eastern Galicia and to create a new politics in the villages. Communal solidarity, which had played such a prominent part in the resistance to serfdom before 1848, was now to be harnessed to the national cause.

The Transformation of Peasant Culture

The peasantry played an unconscious role in the national awakening as the preserve, so to speak, of ethnicity, as the guardian of the sacred legacy of folk songs, popular customs and vernacular language, all of which the intelligentsia appropriated and mythologized in order to canonize them in the national ethos and ideology.[174] Indeed, this cultural borrowing from the peasantry constituted a major component of the initial, romantic (heritage-gathering) phase of national revivals throughout Eastern Europe. In characterizing the peasantry's role as "unconscious," there is no intention to minimize the creativity of the peasantry in developing songs, fables, proverbs and rituals. But in this activity, the peasantry was not consciously participating in a national movement; rather, it was meeting its own cultural needs and only inadvertently creating the *ethnos* that the educated classes would later use as a primary element in the national idea.

Ironically, simultaneously with the penetration of the national movement into the countryside, the traditional peasant culture that was the repository of ethnicity was undergoing a profound transformation. Beginning in the last third of the nineteenth century[175] the peasants' cultural experience was

---

[172] *LA* 53, 343.

[173] *LA* 288, 304.

[174] See Hofer, "The Creation of Ethnic Symbols."

[175] See above 59, 63, 159–62, 167. The same dating has also been applied to Polish Galicia: "Generally it may be said that the peasant culture of Southern Poland [Western Galicia] showed a preponderance of the traditional elements until the emancipation of the peasants in 1848, and even beyond that to about 1870." Dobrowolski, "Peasant Traditional Culture," 297.

changing as the countryside moved from a natural to a money economy and as a print culture began to supplement and then supplant the traditional oral culture in the village. These changes were epoch-making and heralded the extinction of cultural patterns and skills dating back centuries, perhaps millennia. The relationship between these cultural changes and the progress of the national movement was that each spurred the other on.[176]

The penetration of the money economy has already been described, particularly in relation to the destruction of the natural economy.[177] In addition to this destructive aspect, however, there was also a constructive aspect that touched off a tremendous cultural metamorphosis in the countryside. As noted by the Polish ethnographer Kazimierz Dobrowolski, some aspects of the money economy contributed to the strengthening of a "forward-looking perspective among the peasantry." Among these features were: "the growing infiltration into the villages of products demanding higher technical skill and knowledge about how to use them" as well as "a more intensive exchange of goods between town and country and the breaking up of the spacial isolation of the countryside."[178]

A comprehensive analysis and catalogue of the changes wrought by money cannot be included in this study. Still, it is possible to indicate the extent of the change by briefly considering how the money economy was altering the way in which peasants satisfied their basic needs for food, clothing and shelter, or—to rephrase this in more clearly cultural terms—how the money economy transformed the folk cuisine, costume and architecture of Ukrainian Galicia.

"As for articles of food," wrote Jan Słomka of the 1860s, when the natural economy was still dominant, "only salt and beverages were bought in the shops. Village folk lived mostly on what they themselves sowed and planted on their own land."[179] By the mid-1880s the situation was already quite different. The inventory of a village store in Kolodribka, Zalishchyky district, in 1884 included the traditionally bought salt, but it also included an array of other food items that had already been part of the peasant diet: honey, vinegar, fish, yeast and nuts. The presence of fish and nuts in the store reflected the fact that ponds and forests were largely expropriated by the landlords as private property in the two decades following the abolition of serfdom. The sale of honey, vinegar and yeast suggests that these items were

---

[176] Among the factors which Dobrowolski isolated (*ibid.*, 297–8) as initiating the disintegration of traditional peasant culture was "the wider connexion of village populations with social, political and cultural movements on a national scale."

[177] See above, 158–75.

[178] Dobrowolski, "Peasant Traditional Culture," 297. For some concrete aspects, see Hryniuk, "A Peasant Society," 238–43.

[179] Slomka, *From Serfdom to Self-Government*, 26.

now less often produced domestically. Food items new to the peasant diet and offered for sale by the store included pepper and other spices, tea and its necessary complement, sugar, and buns made from white flour (U *bułky*) (*CC* 73). Writing in 1912 and comparing the foodstuffs available then with what had been available in the 1860s, Słomka stated: "Coffee, tea, sugar, rice, raisins, almonds, oranges, lemons—things sold today in every store with other articles of food—were virtually unknown in the village."[180] In 1885 a Ukrainian peasant from the Stanyslaviv region wrote of rice and white flour as superfluous innovations introduced to the villages by, among others, the wives of railway workers.[181] The extent of the change is perhaps best illustrated by the cabbage roll (U *holubets*), popularly considered very traditional ethnic food. The cabbage roll as we know it is stuffed with rice, yet rice does not grow in Galicia. Therefore it had to be imported and purchased; it could only have entered the West Ukrainian diet in a significant way after the 1860s. But it caught on to such an extent that today only students of the history of diet would think of a cabbage roll filled with the truly traditional millet, maize or buckwheat.

In costume the changes were even more far-reaching. The handmade national costumes could barely withstand the competition of the cheap, colourful textiles coming from foreign factories. To quote again from Słomka:

> Our clothing was for each whatever could be made at home.... Until well after 1860 folk dressed in white both summer and winter, both on workdays and holidays; and all home-spun materials tended to stay that colour. More dressy women and girls, however, were already putting on bright coloured skirts and girdles of bought materials, as well as kerchiefs, shawls and stays from the stores.... With the years, clothing made of bought stuffs became the regular thing; and about 1870 the new fashion caught on.[182]

The village store in Kolodribka sold linen, ready-made kerchiefs, yarn, cotton material and thread (*CC* 73). The peasant from the Stanyslaviv region who complained about rice and white flour also felt that the umbrellas coming into the villages ("introduced by all kinds of railway workers, brakemen and watchmen") were expensive and useless novelties; but even he had reconciled himself to "the vests, which many peasants have now started to wear." Peasants in the Kalush area in 1884 were buying what one peasant characterized as "stupid calico" to make shirts, aprons, skirts and kerchiefs, even though "this all is flimsy and tears quickly so one has to buy again." They preferred buying the calico to making their own cloth, although their home-made hemp shirts lasted nine times as long.[183] Obviously, to buy a

---

[180] *Ibid.*, 29.

[181] See above, 167.

[182] Słomka, *From Serfdom to Self-Government*, 21, 23–4.

[183] See above, 168.

cheap, short-lived, factory-produced textile meant that one would not waste labour embroidering it.[184]

The construction and furnishings[185] of the peasant cottage were also modified under the impact of the all-pervading money economy. The thatched roof—the very symbol of the Ukrainian village—began to give way to roofs covered with sheets of tin.[186] Other metal[187] and glass[188] (neither of which could be produced by a peasant household) found increasing application in the Ukrainian peasant cottage.

Although none of the changes noted above constituted by itself a revolution in lifestyle, the sum total of all such changes did. In the late nineteenth century, Ukrainian peasants entered the world of commodities. As a result, their specific material culture began to alter in conformity with the much more general, in fact universalized, material culture of industrial Europe.

In West European history the transition from feudalism to capitalism occurred simultaneously with the employment of the printing press. The widespread exchange of commodities characteristic of capitalism, and of its predecessor, the money economy, was ideally suited to the dissemination of printed material. National networks of commodity exchange served also as the networks for the distribution of the printed word. The printed book was itself a commodity, in fact "the first modern-style mass-produced industrial commodity";[189] the same can by no means be said of the oral creation or even of the manuscript. Thus historically (and for more reasons than can be developed here) there has been a close link between an economy based on exchange and a culture based on print, and it is not unusual that a money economy and a print culture penetrated the Galician countryside at the same time.

The Galician Ukrainian peasantry had preserved an almost exclusively oral culture into the late nineteenth century. Wisdom was passed from generation to generation and from village to village in the form of proverbs, songs and

---

[184] On the impact of factory-made textiles, see also Hryniuk, "A Peasant Society," 304.

[185] A traveller in the early 1840s reported: "The Rusniak peasant, like those of Little Russia, makes all his furniture and household utensils himself: he is his own architect, carpenter, coachmaker, and shoemaker." Kohl, *Austria*, 434.

[186] Insurance companies, concerned about fires, were the chief promoters of tin roofs. According to insurance-company statistics, the peasants of Volhynia gubernia, the region of Russian-ruled Ukraine bordering Galicia, spent over 120,000 rubles on 762,631 kilogrammes of tin in just nine months of 1913. "Prodazh bliakhy," *Rada* 9, no. 2 (3 [15] January 1914): 3.

[187] The store in Kolodribka sold nails (*CC* 73). They would have been used primarily to attach shingles and to hang objects of domestic use.

[188] The home of a well-off peasant in Kamianka Lisna, Rava Ruska district, in 1884 was distinguished by its "large windows" and by the presence of a bookcase "with glass doors" (*CC* 53). See also *LA* 343. "The board-covered window was very rare by the end of the nineteenth and beginning of the twentieth century. It consisted of thinly whittled boards that covered the elongated window openings and the window itself which was filled either with cow-stomach lining or many pieces of glued-together glass of different colours, sizes and thicknesses." Chomiak, "Vernacular Architecture," 65.

[189] Anderson, *Imagined Communities*, 38.

tales. In an oral culture it is difficult to maintain continuity and therefore to accumulate knowledge, especially precise knowledge. By contrast, a culture based on literacy fixes the knowledge of previous generations and of diverse peoples, thus making the accumulation of knowledge more efficient.[190] The benefits of a literate culture are accelerated by the use of print. The print culture, by diffusing knowledge quickly to many people, allows more rapid development and greater participation in the expansion of human understanding. It was the print culture that made possible the scientific advances on which the industrial and subsequent technological revolutions have been based. In a wider sense, print culture includes not only the production and distribution of printed matter, but also the knowledge and theories shared by those participating in the print culture.

Ukrainian peasants in Galicia were introduced to the print culture through the school system established at the end of the 1860s. Under serfdom the peasants had been kept ignorant deliberately. But as we have seen, about half the children of Galicia were attending school by the 1880s, and on the eve of the First World War elementary education became quite widespread in Galicia.[191] Corresponding to the increase in school attendance was a slow, steady increase in the literacy rate. By 1914 the majority of young peasants in Galicia could read. In addition to the school system, the Ukrainian national movement also did much to promote literacy and reading among the peasantry, particularly by establishing reading clubs and publishing a popular press. The reading clubs, furthermore, spread the message of the print culture to illiterates, since public readings were an important component of their activities and undoubtedly the clubs' influence extended beyond the dues-paying membership.

One inevitable result of the introduction of a print culture into the village was a certain displacement of the traditional oral culture. This is strikingly, but unconsciously, revealed in a passage from Słomka's memoirs:

> Parties would be arranged evenings in the winter from house to house. In the summer folk would gather in groups on Sundays or holidays on the lawns, or indeed anywhere in the open, to gossip about the lately abolished serfdom, or the campaigns the older ones had seen.... In general, stories were popular, or jokes, riddles and prophecies; as well as news from afar, or incidents of interest from the villages. *In other days these things counted for what the reading of books or papers does now* [1912].[192]

The introduction of the print culture effected changes in almost all aspects of peasant life and folk ways. It meant, for example, that theatre was added to the peasants' entertainments,[193] that clock time was starting to replace solar

---

[190] See Dobrowolski, "Peasant Traditional Culture," 279.

[191] See above, 62–4.

[192] Emphasis added. Slomka, *From Serfdom to Self-Government*, 102. See also Dobrowolski, "Peasant Traditional Culture," 285.

[193] Peasants in Lopatyn, Brody district, staged an amateur theatrical performance in 1885 to raise money for the reading club and its library (*CC* 200).

and stellar time,[194] that traditional religious and seasonal feasts were now supplemented by new print-culture holidays (e.g., the annual commemorations of national poet Taras Shevchenko in March[195] and of the abolition of serfdom in May),[196] that lines from the poet Shevchenko were sometimes used by peasants in place of traditional folk sayings,[197] that traditional folk medicine was now being denounced as harmful and stupid superstition by reading peasants,[198] that the icons hanging on the walls of a peasant cottage were now more likely to have been printed rather than painted and that they had to share space with secular portraits.[199] The print culture also drastically altered the peasant world-view: the reading peasant developed a modern national consciousness, political opinions and, in some cases, a more critical attitude to the church.

To illustrate the type of changes implicit in the diffusion of the print culture we might focus briefly on the impact of the print culture on folk music. The folk songs of Ukrainian Galicia were recorded by representatives of the print culture, i.e., by professional and amateur folklorists, who subsequently published collections of these songs. At least among the more democratic folklorists, there was a desire to make these published collections available to the peasantry,[200] and some collections did indeed reach the reading clubs.[201] In such cases the oral creativity of the peasants was transformed

---

[194] The well-to-do peasant of Kamianka Lisna had "a beautiful clock" against one of the walls of his home (*CC* 53). On traditional methods of timekeeping and the introduction of the clock, see Slomka, *From Serfdom to Self-Government*, 18–19. And cf. above, 5.

[195] For a description of a Shevchenko commemoration in Zakomarie, Zolochiv district, see *CC* 29. Hundreds of peasants attended the Shevchenko concert in the city of Ternopil in 1884 (*CC* 19, 44).

[196] See above, 57–8.

[197] "In every commune let there be a reading club, a communal granary, a loan fund, a store, unity as well, and all kinds of economic associations. Then we will not give in to anyone, then we will show our enemies who we are, whose children, of what parents (U *khto my, chyi syny, iakykh batkiv)*" (*CC* 110).

[198] *CC* 50, 78, 181, 274. See also: [Hryhorii] R[ymar], "Pysmo z-pid Drohobycha," *Batkivshchyna* 4, no. 18 (16 [4] September 1882): 144. Himka, *Socialism*, 132.

[199] The wealthy peasant of Kamianka Lisna decorated his walls with "images of the saints, of the baptism of Rus', and portraits of our Ruthenian personalities" (*CC* 53).

[200] Dei, *Ukrainska revoliutsiino-demokratychna zhurnalistyka*, 82.

[201] Vasyl Fedorovych, librarian of the reading club in Dobrostany, Horodok district, came upon a collection of Bukovynian folk songs compiled by Hryhorii Kupchanko. He was so impressed that he wrote to the editors of *Batkivshchyna*: "After reading that book, I came up with the suggestion: We have a lot of reading clubs, and we have enough literate members, and we gather in the reading clubs to sing and enjoy ourselves; and we even have literate young people who recently finished school. It would do no harm, therefore, if some of them took up this task energetically and in their free moments copied down the secular [i.e., nonliturgical] carols, songs, tales and sayings; if they described the customs at weddings, feast days, burials and christenings; and if they sent off all that they had written to Lviv. ... Then they ["those learned Ruthenians who best understand such things"] would publish new collections of folk literature and folk customs. ... In this way we peasants would get to know one another more intimately; we would get to know our cultural life and our history" (*CC* 146).

into an object of the print culture and returned to them in this new form.[202]
The school system also influenced the musical culture of the village.
Elementary schools were expected to teach singing,[203] and songbooks for
Ukrainian schools in Austria were prepared by the Bukovynian composer
Sydir Vorobkevych (who studied at the conservatory in Vienna in 1868).[204]
Thus peasant children were exposed to non-folk music and to folk music that
had been arranged by a highly educated, professional musician. Finally, the
national movement encouraged the development of choirs in the villages,
generally in association with the reading clubs. Already by 1884 national
populist students had counted 68 choirs in Galicia and Bukovyna, 48 of which
were attached to reading clubs.[205] The choirs often made a point of singing
from notes (a great fad at least in the 1880s), and introducing polyphony.[206]
Some, such as the famous choir of Denysiv, Ternopil district, became
accomplished enough to appear on stage in the cities (*CC* 19).[207] The founder
of the choir in Dobrostany, Horodok district, not only attended Anton
Bruckner's lectures at the conservatory in Vienna, but sang in the chorus of a
leading Viennese operatic house (*LA* 245).

All of this intervention by the print culture began to alter the character of
peasant music. In an oral culture the words to songs undergo continual
modification, but once they are printed they are relatively fixed. Exactly the
same applies to melodies. The fluidity and spontaneity of folk culture does
not easily survive imprisonment in print. With the dissemination of songbooks
and choirs, moreover, the repertoire of peasants' songs expanded to include
songs composed outside the villages, within the context of the print culture.
This would imply some displacement of the authentic folk music, especially
since the folk songs would be competing with songs that had lyrics by
talented poets (a number of Shevchenko's works, for instance, were set to
music) and melodies by professional composers (such as Vorobkevych).
Finally, the sound of the music itself began to change, and not simply
because of the introduction of novel harmonic techniques in the choirs. The
change was more complex. Once peasant music was captured by notation and

---

[202] Exactly the same thing happened in Hungary. Hofer, "The Creation of Ethnic Symbols," 142.

[203] Sirka, *The Nationality Question in Austrian Education*, 77–8.

[204] *Entsyklopediia Ukrainoznavstva*, s.v. "Vorobkevych Sydir." *Narysy z istorii Pivnichnoi Bukovyny*, 237.

[205] [Mykhailo], "Spravy ruskykh chytalen. III," *Batkivshchyna* 6, no. 49 (5 December [23 November] 1884).

[206] Danylo Saikevych of Radvantsi, Sokal district, was agitating for "enlightenment" in his village, but was opposed by traditionalist peasants under the mayor's leadership. He then recruited twenty-eight boys and girls and "began to teach them notes, then divided them up into voices; this pleased them so much that even adult peasants joined the singing group" (*CC* 106). See also *CC* 15 and *LA* 164. "The first modern musical club was formed in 1881 in Miechocin, the school teacher there being the leader. It was composed of pupils, and had ten boys in it. They played from notes. . . . " Slomka, *From Serfdom to Self-Government*, 114–15.

[207] The choir was directed by Father Iosyp Vitoshynsky who was a professional enough director to open a school for directors. *Entsyklopediia Ukrainoznavstva*, s.v. "Vitoshynsky Iosyp."

choirs began to sing in accordance with the notation, some of the very important tones of Ukrainian folk music disappeared. The musically illiterate, traditional singer deliberately sang some tones flatter or sharper than can be conveyed by standard notation. These shades of difference were lost in notation, and when notation superseded oral tradition the original sound was lost. Traditional peasant singing can be compared with a violin, an unfretted instrument on which any interval between tones can be played. The new, notation music was like a piano, with its limited set of predetermined tones. Also, standard musical notation does not encompass nuances that were very important in traditional singing: quavers, wails, shouts, timbre. Notation tended not only to abstract from such nuances, but to minimize their importance and eradicate them. Thus pre- and post-notation music (oral and literate-print music) sounded very different.[208]

Such changes as have been described for music affected all aspects of peasant culture to a greater or lesser extent, depending on the degree to which the print culture had fastened on to a particular aspect.

In the late nineteenth century the money economy and print culture were only beginning to effect a sea-change in peasant cultural life. Some isolated Galician localities would be but little or late affected, while others would be experiencing rapid change. The extent of the changes among the peasantry was also determined by generational, gender and economic differences. At this time, then, the Ukrainian peasant in Galicia still lived in two worlds, the traditional world of the natural economy and oral culture and the "modern" world of the money economy and print culture.

A more subtle change was also occurring in peasant culture under the influence of the national movement. Elements of peasant culture were acquiring new significance as *self-differentiating symbols*, i.e., as symbols marking one nation off from another.[209] This accretion of symbolic meaning to cultural elements that had hitherto been "unconscious" in relation to the national movement[210] was the result of an exchange (via print) between the peasantry and the intelligentsia: the peasants developed and created a culture with no *national* purpose in mind; the intellectuals codified the culture and endowed it with political, self-differentiating symbolism; then they returned it to the peasants who integrated this revised and symbolized culture into their own. This was the general process implied by the specific phenomenon previously noted in regard to folk songs, i.e., the peasantry's own songs, collected, codified, annotated and printed by the intelligentsia, were returned to it in new form.

Let us look at the symbolic transformation of the two most salient cultural markers of the Ukrainian nation in Galicia: language and religion.

---

[208] I am grateful to Andrij Hornjatkevyč for discussing these problems with me.

[209] See the perceptive remarks in Connor, "Nation-Building or Nation-Destroying?" 337–8.

[210] See above, xxii, 189.

Language is one of the most important—perhaps, as some argue,[211] *the most important*—of the cultural elements in national movements, since submerged nationalities strive to make their language the accepted medium of communication. It might be thought that in the case of the peasantry, the linguistic issue assumed its most pragmatic aspect, that here the language question was a question of comprehension. The peasant, one might argue, was disadvantaged because he did not understand the foreign language of the administration and other higher spheres; so he was drawn into the national movement in order to make the language he understood the language of modern communication. Although the problem of comprehension was a serious one before the late 1860s, when German was frequently used in the administration,[212] it was not so in the era of the national movement, dominated by Polish-Ukrainian linguistic rivalry. In the corpus of correspondence proper, no item treats the Polish-Ukrainian language question from the practical viewpoint of comprehensibility. However, a brief notice in *Batkivshchyna* in 1884 does mention this problem as an afterthought:

> On 23 and 24 October [1884] elections to the communal council were held in [Nyzhniv, Tovmach district]. On the first day few of our people showed up, because not everyone knew about the elections. True, announcements were posted near the church, but few of our people know how to read and those announcements were written only in Polish.[213]

That this part of the language question had little urgency for the Ukrainian peasantry is perhaps not as strange as it first appears. First, the lexical overlap in Polish and Ukrainian, especially its Galician dialects, as well as the centuries of Poles' and Ukrainians' cohabitation in this region made the Polish language a relatively comprehensible idiom. The mutual comprehensibility was strengthened by the educational system; the Polish language was taught in elementary schools, especially after 1892.[214] Secondly, the Ukrainians in Galicia did enjoy certain linguistic rights already, significant ones by comparison with Ukrainians in the Russian empire; in Galicia use of the Ukrainian language in the press, public life and administration was tolerated. And thirdly, the major barrier between the peasantry and the modern means of communication was not so much the Polish language as illiteracy; as the quoted passage specified in the first place, "few of our people know how to read." Linguistic comprehensibility, then, did not figure prominently in the peasantry's motivation for participating in the national movement.

It would be a mistake, however, to go one step further and conclude that comprehensibility played no part at all in the way the peasantry's national awakening took shape. It did play a role as a limiting or excluding factor. If

---

[211] See especially: Stokes, "Cognition and the Function of Nationalism," esp. 536–7; Stokes, "The Undeveloped Theory of Nationalism," 155–7; and Gellner, *Thought and Change*, 146–78.

[212] See above, 15.

[213] Chytalnyk, "... z Nyzhneva," *Batkivshchyna* 6, no. 47 (21 [9] November 1884): 297.

[214] Sirka, *The Nationality Question in Austrian Education*, 80.

the nationally conscious intelligentsia were to address the peasantry, orally or in print, it had to do so in the peasant vernacular, not in Polish and not in any other language. This precluded, or at least hindered, the development of a *Polish* national movement in the Ukrainian village.[215]

This follows logically from what the correspondence suggests about the limits to Russophilism's popularity in the village. Russophilism, the orientation on Russian culture and the Russian state, had a linguistic aspect. Russophiles wrote either in "attempted Russian" or—more commonly in this period—in an artificial amalgam of Russian, Ukrainian and Church Slavonic. What happened when Russophile publications fell into the hands of the peasants? Vasyl Fedorovych, who read a book of folk songs collected by the Bukovynian Russophile, Hryhorii Kupchanko, complained: "I did not understand very well the introduction to this book, because it was written in some sort of hard[216] language" (*CC* 146).[217] The introduction the peasant refers to was written for the intelligentsia and therefore it was composed in the "high" literary style of Russophilism, which was difficult for the peasant to understand. In their popular, peasant-oriented publications, such as *Nauka* or *Ruska rada*, the Russophiles did attempt to write in a more popular idiom, closer to the Ukrainian vernacular. But even so, it was hard to compete with the national populist newspaper *Batkivshchyna*, which was published completely in the vernacular with many dialectical features preserved. Consider the words of a man who referred to himself as "a simple peasant from the village of Rudno," Lviv district:

Dear Sirs:
I first became acquainted with this paper, yours and ours, when it came to the reading club, when our founding members subscribed to it for us. At first we had only read *Nauka* and *Ruska rada* from Kolomyia, and we did not know that there was yet something as good for us as the paper *Batkivshchyna*. But now, even if no one else read it, I would continue to read it until my dying day. Because it has become for me like my own dear mother *on account of its easily understood language*,[218] its advice and counsel, and other things useful for peasants (*CC* 240).

---

[215] Although Polish was *relatively* comprehensible to the peasantry (see above, 30), it was not perfectly comprehensible. This was noted by the Galician police chief Leopold von Sacher-Masoch (not to be confused with his son, the writer). He submitted a memorandum to the governor's office in 1846 urging that all decrees relating to the East Galician peasantry be promulgated also in the Ukrainian vernacular, lest linguistic misinterpretation give rise to false rumours and social unrest. TsDIAL, 146/87/1122, pp. 123–4.

[216] By "hard" Fedorovych does not mean "difficult," but Russophile. The word (U) *tverda*, in the sense of uncompromising or rigid, was frequently used—and not only by peasants—to describe the language of the Russophiles and Russians. According to a Hutsul peasant, the Russian Orthodox religion was also a "hard" religion, "harder" than Greek Catholicism (U *to tverda vira, tverdsha vid nashoi*); the connotation here is positive. For the Hutsul's views on the "hardness" of the Russian faith, see Pavlyk, *Moskvofilstvo*, 9–10.

[217] This same Fedorovych delivered a lecture on the Ukrainian language in the reading club in Dobrostany, Horodok district (*CC* 245).

[218] Emphasis added.

It seems not unreasonable therefore to suppose that if linguistic comprehensibility was not a primary issue drawing the peasant into the national movement, it nonetheless could influence the specific orientation of the peasantry within the movement.

The most interesting aspect of the role of language in the peasant awakening, however, is the extent to which language figured as a *symbol*, as an extension of identity. In an item of correspondence from Uhniv, Rava Ruska district, a small agricultural town that held bazaars, the inhabitants complained about the high-handed ways of the local gendarme, who ripped up horse licences written in the Ukrainian language and demanded that the licences be written in Polish. The item of correspondence was in the form of a petition to the viceroy of Galicia. In it there was not one word about the incomprehensibility of Polish-language licences; instead, the emphasis was on the inconvenience caused by the gendarme's behaviour. There was also mention, however, of the *dishonour* done to the Ukrainian language, and this theme ran implicitly through the whole account:

Inhabitants of Uhniv presented the following letter to the imperial-royal viceroyalty in Lviv:
  Excellent imperial-royal viceroyalty!
  Inhabitants of Uhniv, Rava Ruska district, bring a complaint against the gendarme Rejowski posted at Uhniv, because at the Uhniv bazaar he rips up all horse licences issued in the Ruthenian language. He explains to those who have such licences that he rips them up because only Polish-language licences are supposed to be displayed. A witness to the above-mentioned arbitrary behaviour of the said gendarme is Ivan Petrovsky, proprietor from Shchepiatyn, whose Ruthenian-language licence the gendarme tore up on 15 May of this year with these words: It is forbidden to write licences in Ruthenian (P *po rusku paszportów nie wolno pisać*). He also ripped up the licence of Vasyl Partysovsky of Novosilky Peredni with the same words; this was on 30 October 1884 [N.S.] on the feast of St. Luke. He tore up the licence of a man from Shchepiatyn and wrote on the other side: A licence must be displayed in Polish, not in Ruthenian (P *paszport ma się wystawiać po polsku, a nie po rusku*). He has destroyed the licences of still more peasants, and all because they are written in Ruthenian. And a few people, hearing such words from the gendarme, hid their licences and hid themselves with their horses in corners, being afraid lest the gendarme confiscate their horses. Hryn Kushnir from Novosilky Kardynalski had two licences written in Ruthenian; afraid because it was forbidden to possess Ruthenian licences, he harnessed his horses to his cart and fled from the horse market. We only mention these three proprietors because we were eyewitnesses and we know their names; but we refrain from mentioning people from other local villages because we do not know their names.
  The high-handed ways of gendarme Rejowski went much beyond this, because he even ordered all people with Ruthenian licences to leave the bazaar at once together with their livestock; otherwise he would confiscate their animals. Thus, terror overcame both bazaars, the one on 30 October 1884 as well as the one on 15 May 1885. There was weeping and grumbling, because these people had come to sell their livestock precisely in order to pay the taxes they owed to the emperor and, in some cases, in order to pay a debt to the Jew

and meet various domestic expenses. And here Rejowski deprived them of this one possibility. Through Rejowski's arbitrary conduct our Ruthenian writing was dishonoured, because after ripping up the licences he cast them under his feet. But leaving that aside, we ask the excellent imperial-royal viceroyalty to consider the loss that people endured as a result of this: they lost the day and their expenses, but gained nothing. We are of the opinion that the gendarmes should serve the public, not bring it to loss. In this most unpleasant situation of ours, we ardently ask the excellent imperial-royal viceroyalty to kindly instruct the subordinate authorities to be alert for similar instances of the gendarmes' high-handed conduct and to punish the disobedient accordingly (*CC* 205).

Similar in spirit was an item of correspondence from Strilkiv, Stryi district, complaining that the district council refused to accept Ukrainian-language documents. Once again, it was linguistic pride rather than the functional purpose of language that was at issue:

Our scribe presented papers written in Ruthenian to the district council, but some new gentleman there did not accept them and, in agitation, refused to sign them. He said that we do not accept Ruthenian papers and that they will be returned to the mayor. But the one who brought the papers (?; U *torbar*) said: "Excuse me, sir, but our scribe has been writing everywhere in Ruthenian for two years now and everywhere what he writes is accepted, and here too, previously, the other gentleman who was secretary accepted it!" To this the gentleman had no answer (*CC* 34).

The following item of correspondence is yet more explicit in its equation of the use of one's native language with the preservation of one's dignity. The author, from the district capital of Zbarazh, may not have been a peasant himself; he took the village governments to task for their lack of concern with the language question:

Many of our Ruthenian communes, by the very fact that they conduct their correspondence in Polish, bring shame upon themselves before the whole world. Because why not write in their own Ruthenian script and in their own native language, when the community officers and the whole commune are all Ruthenians and when the emperor also gives us Ruthenians the right to write everywhere in our Ruthenian script and in our language? And how a commune that writes like this dishonours itself:

[There follows an official letter from the Ukrainian commune of Klymkivtsi, Zbarazh district. The letter is written in Polish so overladen with Ukrainianisms, so ungrammatical and so misspelled that it is difficult to make sense of it.]

Now really, honourable readers, this is a dandy letter, isn't it? Do you understand what the letter is about? Because I, to tell the truth, do not understand what the communal government in Klymkivtsi tried to express by its strange and stupid letter. If, then, some authority or anybody at all reads this monstrosity from a Ruthenian commune, what will he think about such a commune?

Is it any wonder than anyone in gabardine [i.e., a Jew], any tramp has contempt for our peasant, calls him a goy or a boor (U *kham*), has no good word for him? Our peasant at the very entrance to some government building doffs his cap; during the winter he stands for hours in the vestibule with a bared head; he licks the hand of any scrivener or clerk. Is this the sort of behaviour proper for the free citizen of a constitutional state? It is right to give honour to whom honour is due, but to debase oneself in this way is unworthy of a free man; it is shameful and disgusting. Only slaves act like that, but in our land—praise the Lord!—slavery has already perished forever. Let us, then, respect ourselves, our human dignity, our very own ancestral Ruthenian language, our Ruthenian script, our Ruthenian faith; then others too will respect us. Why should we, so to say, yearn after foreign gods, use the Polish script and the Polish language, when we have our own, native, beautiful, Ruthenian language, which the emperor allows us to use everywhere? We should not disdain this favour of the emperor, because by doing so we offend the emperor himself. On the contrary, we should everywhere take grateful advantage of this favour, by which we will earn for ourselves honour and glory among people and the emperor's love, and we will become worthy of further favour from the emperor. Because the emperor sees that we Ruthenians do not want to take advantage of his favour, do not want to use our language and our script everywhere, and so he thinks us unworthy of any further favours. That is why things are so bad for us and everywhere we are on the bottom. Now we see where our carelessness has led us and will lead us (*CC* 147).

In a similar vein, a correspondent from Tsvitova, Buchach district, asked: "Why is the sign near the communal chancery written in Polish and not in Ruthenian?" (*CC* 16).

A peasant correspondent discussing the newly established Crownland Bank also linked language with pride. He noted that the new bank would start making mortgage loans, but the lowest amount that could be borrowed was 500 gulden. This was too high for peasants, so the author decided that the bank had been established in the interests of the large estate owners. He went on to make a telling point about language:

And something else goes to show that this bank is only supposed to be for lords. The bank issues mortgage certificates just as the Rustical Bank used to issue. The certificates of the Rustical Bank were written also in the Ruthenian language, but the certificates of the Crownland Bank are only in Polish, German and French without a word of Ruthenian, although there are Ruthenians too in the crownland and the bank was established also with Ruthenian money. Is this just? Is this proper, gentlemen? Is it that our peasant Ruthenian money is good, but our Ruthenian language bad? When it is election time they speak to us so enchantingly and sweetly in Ruthenian, but after the elections Ruthenian is a "vulgar, peasant" language—and the peasants are shown the door (*CC* 51).

Here the symbolic import of language—as an extension of identity—finds full expression in an injured pride. What is noteworthy about this piece of correspondence, in addition to the explicitness of expression, is the nature of the pride, the identity, that is injured. It was not just the Ukrainian language that the Crownland Bank held in contempt: it was the *peasant* language. And the disdain the bank showed for the peasants' language was the same as the disdain in which the bank and all "gentlemen" ("lords") held the Ukrainians as *peasants*. The content of the language-symbol is here revealed to be social as well as national.[219]

Peasant attitudes toward religion were also transformed during the rural awakening. It has already been noted that the progress of the national movement in the village could sometimes lead peasants to a criticism of the clergy and even of religious traditions.[220] It would have been surprising had this not happened, given the tremendous impact the new cultural movement must have had on the way the peasantry related to religion. In traditional peasant culture, magical beliefs and practices played a great role,[221] but this magic was anathema to the new culture associated with the national movement.[222] It is reasonable to suppose, therefore, that the peasantry was evolving from a superstitious form of religion to a more rational form of religion during this period. One might even say that there was a small-scale Reformation underway in the Ukrainian village in the late nineteenth and early twentieth centuries which was to produce radicalism in Galicia[223] and Protestantism and a Protestant-like Orthodoxy among Galician emigrants to Canada.[224]

Although the tendencies imputed above find little direct confirmation in the correspondence (just what has already been noted), they find fairly strong confirmation in the complete absence in the correspondence of religious expression that has neither a formulaic nor a symbolic character. There are, that is, no reflections on divine providence, God's mercy, the effective intercession of the saints or other topics that one might expect to be discussed by people steeped in a religious world-view. Perhaps, one might argue, the absence of religious writing in the correspondence says nothing against the heartfelt religiosity of the Ukrainian peasant, but only indicates that *Batkivshchyna* was not the place for religious discussion as such. But this is much my point: Religion as such and the national movement were very

---

[219] Cf. this reaction to the performance of the Denysiv choir at the Ternopil Shevchenko commemoration: The choir was composed of "*'serdaky'* and *'kozhukhy'* just like us.... With their wonderful singing they enchanted everyone; they proved to everyone that our Ruthenian people, which some call a nation of 'peons,' has a heart and a sensitivity to the exalted and beautiful, that it has healthy buds of humanity, that it has the full right to be respected *as a nation equally with other nations*.... No pen can describe, no tongue can express the impression that each individually and all together experienced" (*CC* 19). A (U) *serdak* was a peasant coat of coarse cloth and a (U) *kozhukh* the characteristic sheep-skin coat of West Ukrainian peasants.

[220] See above, 137–9.

[221] Dobrowolski, "Peasant Traditional Culture," 289.

[222] See above, note 198.

[223] The overt links between radicalism and Protestantism were manifold. For example, the main theoreticians of radicalism, Drahomanov and Pavlyk, popularized the Stundist movement in publications for the Galician peasantry, Drahomanov wrote a number of popular works on Protestantism and Drahomanov asked to be buried by Protestant ministers.

[224] Martynowych, *The Ukrainian Bloc Settlement*, 170–88. Pavlyk hoped that tensions between Latin- and Greek-rite Catholics in America in the late 1880s would lead to a schism and the formation of an independent Ukrainian church with Protestant characteristics. Pavlyk, *Perepyska*, 5:289, 292.

distinct modes, and the peasantry was learning to make all manner of judgments—on behaviour, on ideas, on people (including people in authority in the communal government or parish)—on the basis of a *secular world-view*.[225]

Two "religious" themes do crop up in the correspondence, but in both themes religion already figures as a symbol, much as language figured as a symbol. The first theme is the renovation of village church structures. Numerous communes renovated their churches or built new churches in the 1880s and then reported on this to *Batkivshchyna*.[226] Here the renovation of the church building figured as a sign that a particular commune was on the move, the church project being conceived of as one more aspect of the (U) *novi poriadky*, new order, which included temperance brotherhoods, reading clubs and cooperatives.[227]

In the second theme religion figures much more unequivocally as a symbol and moreover as a *self-differentiating* symbol; this was the issue of the so-called "three-armed cross" (U *tryramennyi krest*), popularly known in English as the three-barred or Orthodox cross. In the late nineteenth century many Ukrainian Greek Catholics began to emphasize their distinctiveness from the Polish Roman Catholics by the increasing and prominent display of three-armed crosses. Polish civil and ecclesiastical authorities opposed the display of crosses of this type, arguing that they were schismatic (i.e., Orthodox) and Russian. The civil authorities frequently removed or performed "amputations" on these crosses and in doing so provoked the indignant resentment of the Ukrainian peasantry.[228] The theme figures three times in the corpus of correspondence (twice in relation to newly renovated churches). In Tysmenytsia, Tovmach district, the commune intended to put three-armed crosses on its newly renovated church, but the district authorities prohibited this on the grounds that "the erection of three-armed crosses spreads alarm...and...can...even disturb the peace and public order" (*CC* 113). In Kniahynychi, Bibrka district, a three-armed cross was erected on the cupola of the newly renovated church. Gendarmes and a commission were sent from the district capital to discover who was responsible for this. "...The frightened Father Administrator denied everything even before the cock crowed" (*CC* 117). The officers of the reading club in Dobrostany, Horodok district, wrote: "...Now it's come to this, that when they see a three-armed cross in the village, they immediately cry out: There's schism here! And it may in the end come to such a pass that when they see you, brother, cross yourself three times [as is the custom among Ukrainian Greek

---

[225] On the wider ramifications of this, see Himka, "The Greek Catholic Church," 442–52.

[226] See, for example, *CC* 23, 67 and 279; this is not a complete list.

[227] Thus I disagree with Stella Hryniuk, who interprets the building and renovation of churches in this period as an expression of the peasantry's "deep-rooted attachment to religion." "A Peasant Society," 413.

[228] This partly lay behind an upsurge of naive tsarism in Galicia in the mid-1880s. Himka, "Hope in the Tsar," 134.

Catholics and other Eastern Christians], they'll say: You're a schismatic, you're a Russian (U *moskal*), you accept rubles!"[229] (*CC* 122). Both when the communes erected them and when the district authorities removed them, the three-armed crosses had already lost all religious significance; they were political, national symbols.

Class and Nation

An important question to consider in a study of the *national* movement among the peasant *class* is to what extent the movement was national and to what extent social.[230] This is a very difficult question to answer in any case, but particularly in a study that concentrates its focus on a specific historical moment (1884–5). Yet it is possible to put forward some propositions and provide information that points toward answers.

From what has already been said, several relevant points should be clear. In the pre-emancipation period, which was also prior to the period when the national movement began to seek a mass base in the peasantry, the movement of the peasantry was entirely social, i.e., class-based, without a national dimension. During the revolution of 1848–9 the still pre-eminently social movement of the peasantry acquired temporarily a thin national veneer, a very primitive national dimension, in which the abstract national goals were conflated with concrete socio-economic objectives such as access to a particular pasture. The primary cause of the emergence of this national aspect was the establishment of a national leadership (the Supreme Ruthenian Council) that championed the peasantry's class interests. During the following decade or so, i.e., during the most intense period of struggle over servitudes and before the constitutional reforms again permitted a linkage between a national leadership and the peasantry, the social aspect of the peasant movement overshadowed the national aspect even more than it had during the revolution. In the whole period prior to the 1860s, then, the peasantry was engaged in a socio-economic struggle that only briefly and tenuously acquired a national character.

Beginning with the last third of the nineteenth century, however, the national aspect grew in prominence, as evidenced, of course, by the penetration of the national movement into the countryside. One might identify two broad reasons behind this change: 1) the strengthening of the national aspect, owing to the re-establishment of a linkage between the leadership of the national movement and the peasantry; this linkage, moreover, was stronger than it had been in 1848–9 owing to both the duration of the Austrian reforms permitting it (1867–1914) and the cultural revolution in the countryside which facilitated the diffusion of the national idea; and 2) the weakening of the social aspect, owing to the abatement of

---

[229] A reference to tsarist Russian subsidies for Russophiles in Galicia.

[230] To use the more precise terminology developed by Józef Chlebowczyk: To what extent was the movement reflective of "horizontal integration" and to what extent of "vertical integration"? *On Small and Young Nations*, esp. 11, 15.

the acute manor-commune antagonism that had forged the highly developed class consciousness of the Galician peasantry and to the transformation of serfs into independent petty producers.[231]

Granted the emergence of the national aspect to the foreground in the late nineteenth century, it is nonetheless not entirely clear to what extent the national movement of the peasantry did not remain merely *a phenomenal form of a socio-economic, i.e., class-based, movement.* It must be remembered that post-feudal Eastern Galicia was characterized by a general congruence of social and national groups. The nobility was largely Polish, the representatives of the money economy largely Jewish and the peasantry largely Ukrainian. This is a fact so fundamental that it might easily be overlooked. However, the effect of this circumstance is to make it very difficult, perhaps impossible, to gauge the proportions of "national" and "social" in the peasants' national movement. For indeed the national ideology, with its opposition to everything Polish and Jewish, could have appealed to the peasantry primarily because this was also opposition to landlords, usurers, merchants and tavernkeepers; yet the original motivation of the peasantry—national or social—need not have been expressed, since the sophisticated distinction was not one the peasantry necessarily understood.[232] The ideology of the Ukrainian *national* movement was simultaneously the most radical *social* ideology to which the peasantry had access (at least prior to the diffusion of radicalism proper in the 1890s).

The importance of the socio-economic dimension of the national movement, at least into the mid-1880s, is evident from items of correspondence linking participation in the national movement to an improvement of the peasantry's socio-economic condition. In fact this linkage is implicit in every item of correspondence boasting of or agitating for communal granaries, cooperative stores or loan funds, but explicit "theoretical" statements to this effect can also be found.[233]

Typical were the words of a correspondent from Mshanets, Staryi Sambir district, who said that the impoverishment of the Ukrainian peasantry was "the result of our ignorance, the lack of enlightenment." The correspondent also alluded to historical factors: "Those who started our people's misery have

---

[231] One should not make too much of it, but Marx certainly had a point when he wrote: "The small peasant proprietors form an immense mass, the members of which live in the same situation but do not enter into manifold relationships with each other. Their mode of operation isolates them instead of bringing them into mutual intercourse.... Each individual peasant family is almost self-sufficient; it directly produces the greater part of its own consumption and therefore obtains its means of life more through exchange with nature than through intercourse with society. The smallholding, the peasant, and the family; next door, another smallholding, another peasant, and another family. A bunch of these makes up a village, and a bunch of villages makes up a department. Thus the great mass of the French nation is formed by the simple addition of isomorphous magnitudes, much as potatoes in a sack form a sack of potatoes." Marx, "The Eighteenth Brumaire of Louis Bonaparte," *Surveys from Exile*, 238–9. Marx went on to argue that in some respects peasants do not even form a class. See above, 20 note 133.

[232] See my remarks in "Hope in the Tsar," 138.

[233] *CC* 25, 32, 72, 77, 123, 161, 164.

long been rotting in the damp grave..." (*CC* 72). A peasant correspondent from Korchyn, Stryi district, told a similar story: "In ancient times, our Rus' was distinguished by prosperity, wealth and courage. [But] terrible hordes of Tatars and Turks descended on our land, wreaking devastation, burning and butchering...." He went on to recommend "enlightenment" as the antidote to poverty and the curse of history: "Let us all go to the reading club, let us learn, let us become enlightened, and a new era of wellbeing will arise and the new glory of Rus' will shine forth" (*CC* 32). What is interesting about these items of correspondence is that they overtly connected the whole national "enlightenment" movement and the national historical myth with the concrete economic struggle against what they perceived as pervasive poverty.[234]

Very similar points, without the same historical emphasis, were made by other correspondents. A peasant writing from Ivachiv Dolishnii, Ivachiv Horishnii and Plotycha, Ternopil district, also linked enlightenment (and national politics) with the improvement of the peasantry's economic situation: "...As long as we peasants remain ignorant, know nothing and read nothing, the landlords and Jews will have it good, because an ignorant peasant...will not eat, but will drink, and will even elect a landlord as deputy" (*CC* 77). A correspondent from Mshana, Zolochiv district, asked: "Why are Czech and German peasants much better off than ours?" His answer: "Because they are all literate and enlightened..." (*CC* 123). The correspondent from Mshanets, Staryi Sambir district, charged the Ukrainian intelligentsia to rescue the peasantry economically through enlightenment: "Educated Ruthenian people should help [the Ukrainian poor] in everything, draw them to themselves, teach them and show them the way to a better life, help them achieve a better lot" (*CC* 25).

In sum, peasants saw the "enlightenment" aspect of the national movement (reading clubs, newspapers) to be related to the pursuit of economic improvement.

Further confirmation of the deep social roots of the peasantry's national movement emerges from an exploration of the borders between the social and the national in the movement. Specifically, we will look here at three "borderline" cases: 1) relations between peasants and nonpeasants in the Ukrainian movement, 2) relations between (U) *latynnyky*, i.e., Ukrainian-speaking peasants of the Latin rite, and the Ukrainian movement, and 3) relations between the Ukrainian petty gentry (U *shliakhta khodachkova*) and the national movement.

To some extent, the first of these topics has already been explored in the section on tensions between priest and peasant.[235] To summarize and rephrase

---

[234] Stella Hryniuk has written of the Galician peasants that "they were not in general the cruelly impoverished population of the literature that purports to deal with them." Hryniuk, "Peasant Agriculture in East Galicia," 243. However, the peasants' own perception would seem to deny this claim.

[234] See above, 133–42.

the findings of that section: tensions between the peasantry and the three strata of the notability increased with the social distance of each notable stratum from the peasantry (thus the cantors and peasants came into conflict the least, the priests and peasants the most). There was also some distrust between peasants and Ukrainian burghers, as evidenced by the following letter to *Batkivshchyna* from a peasant who served on the district council of Kaminka Strumylova:

> In our district council of Kaminka [Strumylova] we Ruthenians have a majority, because in addition to twelve councilmen from the villages three Ruthenians from the city were elected (from Busk, Father Petrushevych and burgomaster Vano were elected). But what good is this if we don't hold together and don't make use of our majority. It's a pity that we peasants have no one to depend on; in particular, some of our burghers pretend that they are really friends of the people, but when something actually comes up, they mostly look the other way. The peasant councilmen in the district council wanted to have Father Krasitsky elected marshall, but our other councilmen were frightened that the choice would not be confirmed. So Count Badeni was elected marshal.... [236]

Trust between the urban secular intelligentsia, i.e., the leadership of the Ukrainian national movement, and the peasantry was, of course, a precondition for the spread of the movement in the countryside, and this trust was implied in every item of correspondence submitted by a peasant to *Batkivshchyna*'s editors in Lviv. The importance of this trust (and the absence of it in the traditionalist peasantry) is well brought out by a peasant correspondent from Verbiv, Pidhaitsi district:

> I, as a simple peasant, appeal to you, brother peasants: Let us cast off once and for all the dishonesty that became rooted in us while we yet lived under serfdom; let us listen to the voice of our learned patriots who work through the night to enlighten us. Don't say that they write the newspapers only to make money, because the money they make is barely enough for paper and printing. For them the only reward is to see that their teaching has warmed our stony hearts, to wait for the moment when we will take the road that our learned friends tell us to take. Then the officials, the priests and the teachers will no longer be ashamed of us; they will no longer call us dissimulators who more than once repaid their good advice with ingratitude (*CC* 151).

Yet in spite of the presence and necessity of such trust among all peasant activists of the national movement, it is still possible to detect a point of difference between the peasants and the intelligentsia. The cantor Luka Tomashevsky (*LA* 328) of Novosilky Kardynalski, Rava Ruska district, gave expression to a resentment on the part of the peasantry that only members of the intelligentsia and clergy were put forward as candidates in elections to the diet and parliament:

---

[236] Radnyi, "...vid Buska," *Batkivshchyna* 6, no. 23 (6 June [30 (sic); should be 25 May] 1884): 139.

I would think and advise (because I hear this from the people) that the Supreme Ruthenian Committee in Lviv should—where it is most difficult to bring about the election of a member of the Ruthenian intelligentsia, a priest, professor, lawyer or official—put forward the candidacy of a good, honest peasant. Certainly a peasant would more eagerly elect another peasant, and perhaps he would be less greedy for sausages, jellied meats and cigars. Because during the elections one can hear the voices of peasants: "Hey, if only we could elect a peasant!" I know that perhaps the educated Editorial Board or someone else will laugh at this idea and say: "What can a peasant do in parliament when he doesn't know German? He will sit or stand, blink his eyes and gape and will be an object of laughter for the Germans, Czechs, lawyers and professors."[237] I myself admit this, but I say that at least a peasant will occupy the place our enemy would otherwise have taken, and [the peasant elector] would still be voting for a Ruthenian candidate (CC 191).

Shades of 1848! Indeed, the idea Tomashevsky put forward so hesitantly in 1885 became a reality in 1889 when two peasant deputies, Oleksa Barabash and Iosyf Huryk, were elected to the diet.[238] The peasantry thus had an interest in *self*-emancipation,[239] and some chafed under the paternalism of the intelligentsia.[240]

It is impossible to formulate anything more than a tentative generalization on the relations between peasants and nonpeasants in the Ukrainian movement on the basis of the fragmentary evidence available. However, it does seem fair to say that the peasants in the national movement, in addition to acquiring a sense of vertical integration into a nation that included notables, burghers and urban intelligentsia, retained a sense of horizontal, class separateness characteristic of the traditional peasantry.

We are on surer ground in examining the second of our "borderline" cases, the more discrete one of the *latynnyky*. Here the evidence is relatively more plentiful, if still not free of contradictions. *Latynnyky* were peasants who belonged to the Latin rite rather than to the Greek rite, but who spoke the Ukrainian language. With whom would their sympathies lie, with the Polish "gentlemen," whose religion they shared, or with the Ukrainians, whose language and social position they shared? And if they sided with the Ukrainians, on what grounds did they do so—linguistic or social, or both? In our corpus of correspondence, only one item was submitted by a *latynnyk*, but it is a very interesting one:

In our village I heard more than enough from our priests (may they be healthy!) about the Ruthenians, that they are like this and like that; I heard so much that

---

[237] It sounds as if for Tomashevsky lawyers and professors were as alien to the Ukrainian peasantry as Germans and Czechs.

[238] "Posly seliane," *Batkivshchyna* 11, no. 26 (30 June [12 July] 1889): 325–6.

[239] An item of correspondence from Brovary, Buchach district: "...Although a few members of our intelligentsia went hand in hand with the people, nonetheless the actual idea [to establish a reading club] came from the peasants themselves, who felt the need for enlightenment and solidarity" (CC 75). On the striving for *self*-emancipation on the part of the peasantry, see also the excellent observations in Hryniuk, "A Peasant Society," 424–5, 428–9.

[240] For a good example of this paternalism, see Kyrylo Kakhnykevych's remark above, 102.

I was bewildered. Because you see, Mr. Editor, I am of the Latin rite. The Latin-rite priests speak about the celebration of the third of May [O.S.; i.e., the commemoration of the abolition of serfdom], and they say that the Ruthenians are introducing a schismatic holiday (P *szyzmatyckie święto zaprowadzają*). Well, I by chance attended just such a celebration in the neighbouring village of Roznoshyntsi [Zbarazh district]; and I so feasted my eyes on that Ruthenian ritual and on the Ruthenian people that I will never forget it and will tell everyone about it.

[Here the *latynnyk* author describes the festivities connected with the commemoration of the abolition of serfdom; his account has already been quoted *in extenso*.][241]

Later I also went to the church for a service and then to a grave-side commemorative service (U *parastas*) for the souls of the departed who with such difficulty bore the yoke of serfdom's slavery. Finally, I attended a dinner at the cemetery, where the whole village sat together on the lawn. There was everything there—bread, meat, sausages, eggs, all sorts of things, only instead of liquor they drank beer (each had contributed 12 kreuzer for a whole barrel). During the dinner they conversed soberly, intelligently and sincerely; they sang all sorts of Ruthenian songs, and then once again the bells were rung and the mortars set off. Thus they enjoyed themselves late into the night.

I stayed overnight there, and the next day I went to my own village and was telling our *latynnyky* about the Ruthenian celebration and the Ruthenian people. I even composed this verse:

O you peasants, you Poles, stick with the Ruthenians;
When you're voting at elections, don't side with the lords!
Because if you send those *liashenky* to the diets,
You will live in even worse poverty;
Because the *liashenky* never have and never will do you any good,
They will just laugh at us poor and ignorant peasants! (*CC* 94).[242]

The (U) *liashenky* that the peasant refers to are Polish lords. ([U] *Liakh* was a derogatory name for Poles, *liashenky* a diminutive form of *liakh*.) The author distinguishes between these *liashenky* and himself and his fellow villagers, to whom he refers as *latynnyky* or (U) *poliaky* (Poles). Because of the religious difference, he also distinguishes between his own people, the *latynnyky-poliaky*, and the Ukrainians (Ruthenians, [U] *rusyny*). The distinctions he makes, then, are based on social position and religion, and he takes no account of the linguistic connection. His unequivocal solidarity with the Ukrainians derives not from a shared language, but from a shared

---

[241] See above, 58.

[242] The text of the verse in transliteration:

Oi vy khlopy, vy poliaky, trymaitesia rusyniv!
Pry holosakh, pry vyborakh ne khapaitesia paniv!
Bo iak budete liashenkiv do soimiv posylaty,
To budete ieshche tiazhche v sviti biduvaty;
Bo liashenky dlia vas dobra ne robyly i ne budut,
A z nas bidnykh, temnykh khlopiv posmikhatysia budut!

experience of suffering at the hands of the lords. It is the *social* bond, including the *historical* social bond, that determines his attitude.

Aside from this item of correspondence contributed by a *latynnyk*, other items of correspondence also document solidarity between Ukrainian and *latynnyk* peasants and the participation of the latter in the Ukrainian national movement. Two items of correspondence mention that *latynnyky* voted for the Ukrainian candidate in the 1885 parliamentary election, in spite of special pressures to show solidarity with the Poles. According to a peasant correspondent, at the polling place in the district capital of Terebovlia,

> there was also one *latynnyk* elector, Vavryk Mazur [*LA* 211], and they called him aside for a confidential discussion, but this honest soul did not allow himself to be confused and gave his vote to the Ruthenian candidate. Because, indeed, both in Strusiv and in Darakhiv there are reading clubs, and our people there know that just because someone is of the Latin rite he need not be a Pole, but can be a Ruthenian of the Latin rite (*CC* 220).

Another peasant reported:

> During the elections to parliament, all three electors from Kryve [Berezhany district], including the Pole Ioan Liagotsky, voted solidly for the Ruthenian candidate, which made the Latin-rite priest from Kozova very angry (*CC* 281).

A third item of correspondence (*CC* 279) stated that the *latynnyky* in Ostriv, Sokal district, helped the Ukrainians build a new stone church of the Greek rite.

The solidarity between *latynnyk* and Ukrainian peasants in the national movement also finds abundant confirmation in the list of activists. It seems that the officers of the Ukrainian reading club in Kutkivtsi, Ternopil district, were largely *latynnyky*,[243] while individual *latynnyky* held posts in reading clubs in widely scattered districts of Eastern Galicia.[244]

Thus, overall, in spite of the religious difference between *latynnyk* and Ukrainian peasants (and in spite of the great importance in Galicia of rite as an ethnic marker),[245] both united, as peasants, in the Ukrainian national movement in the mid-1880s. The recognition of this fact probably led the cantor Luka Tomashevsky to offer this advice to the national populists at the same time that he suggested running Ukrainian peasant candidates for elections: "It would also be good to write an appeal to Western Galicia, to the Mazurs [i.e., ethnically Polish peasants], so that they would not elect lords but peasant-Mazurs, because these latter would surely be in solidarity with the Ruthenian deputies" (*CC* 191). In other words, Tomashevsky thought it was still possible in the mid-1880s to resurrect the alliance of West Galician

---

[243] *LA* 16, 186, 212, 356.

[244] *LA* 80, 211, 261, 289.

[245] See Himka, "Greek Catholic Church," 434–5.

Polish peasants with the Ukrainian national movement as it had existed during the revolution of 1848–9.[246]

The general picture of *latynnyk*-Ukrainian peasant solidarity is not invalidated by two items of correspondence that do present a contradictory view. The first of these was submitted by a priest:

> There [in Tsebriv, Ternopil district] . . . a third [of the population] is comprised of *latynnyky*,[247] for whom sobriety and learning are some sort of marvel, and who look unfavourably on all endeavours in this sphere (*CC* 44).

There are problems with accepting this item as a genuine description of the attitudes of the *latynnyky* in Tsebriv. First of all, it was written by a priest. For a priest, much more than for any other stratum, the religious difference was paramount. Previously cited items of correspondence have already shown Latin-rite priests opposing the Ukrainian movement with which their parishioners sympathized. Secondly, this particular priest was religiously narrow-minded. It is characteristic that he first mentioned "sobriety," the clerical specialty in the national movement, as something to which the *latynnyky* of Tsebriv were allegedly indifferent. Moreover, this same priest was one of no more than three authors in the entire corpus of correspondence to refer to Jews by the religious epithet "the unbaptized ones."[248] Thus it seems reasonable to assume that this priest was merely blaming the slow development of the national movement in Tsebriv on the strong presence of a religiously alien element, the *latynnyky*. His testimony may therefore be discounted.

The second item (*CC* 90), from Husiatyn district, mentioned how Polish landlords tried to Polonize the *latynnyky* and use them politically; according to the correspondent, the landlords were enjoying some success. This cannot be discounted, because this in fact is what happened on a large scale by the turn of the century. In reaction to the rise of the Ukrainian movement in the countryside and under the impact of Polish integral nationalist ("national democratic") ideology, the Polish nobility exerted influence to Polonize the *latynnyky*. Individual landlords would offer special privileges to *latynnyky* (e.g., the right to manage the tavern in place of a Jew or employment in the forestry service), the Galician government would offer other advantages (e.g., Polish schools or subsidies for Polish agricultural societies) and Polish nationalist organizations would collect money to further the establishment of Polish institutions (e.g., Roman Catholic churches or Polish reading clubs) in Eastern Galicia.[249] The Polish nobility and the Polish national movement were able to weaken the solidarity of the *latynnyk* peasantry with the Ukrainian

---

[246] See above, 27, 31 note 185.

[247] In 1880 the commune had 1,085 inhabitants. There were 386 Roman Catholics, 671 Greek Catholics and 28 Jews; there were 91 Polish-speakers and 991 Ukrainian-speakers. *Spec. Orts-Rep. 1880*.

[248] See Himka, "Ukrainian-Jewish Antagonism."

[249] For a programme aimed at the maintenance and expansion of the Polish element in Eastern Galicia, see Głąbiński, *Ludność polska*, 58–9.

peasantry only to the extent that they were successful in creating a privileged position for *latynnyky*. This was not yet generally the case in the mid-1880s.

The third "borderline" case worth examining is that of the Ukrainian petty gentry.[250] There were a few ten thousand of this stratum in Galicia, with a large concentration in the region of Sambir.[251] The Ukrainian petty gentry was Ukrainian by language and by religion,[252] although it did have some of its own ethnographic peculiarities, particularly in manner of dress. There was some intermarriage between the Ukrainian petty gentry and peasantry; particularly, peasant grooms would take petty noble brides. Although Ukrainian petty nobles and peasants would socialize together in the villages, the peasants thought that the titles and noble posturings of the petty gentry were ridiculous, especially since the petty nobles had the reputation of being poorer, through sheer laziness, than the peasantry.

The socio-economic difference between the Ukrainian petty gentry and peasantry was quite great prior to 1848, because the gentry was not enserfed. It did not own estates, so it never became the object of the peasantry's intense class hatred in the way that the landed nobility did. Yet, since it did not experience serfdom, it also did not share the peasantry's feelings toward the landed nobility. With the abolition of serfdom in 1848, the socio-economic difference between the petty gentry and the peasantry disappeared.

A political difference between the petty gentry and the peasantry was in evidence even before the advent of the national movement in the countryside. During the Polish insurrections of the nineteenth century, the petty gentry sympathized with the insurgents, while the peasantry only wished them evil. In 1848 the petty gentry volunteered for the *Polish* national guard, and in 1863 the petty gentry took up collections for the insurgents in the Russian partition.[253]

Behind this political difference ultimately lay the difference between the traditionally free and the former serfs. The Austrian reforms were experienced quite differently by the petty gentry and the peasantry. For the peasantry, the abolition of serfdom, for all its half-measures, was a giant step forward. For the petty gentry, however, the abolition of serfdom meant equalization with the peasantry. This was a step backward, even if there were no concrete economic losses resulting from the reform (such as the landed nobility suffered). The reforms, moreover, did involve at least one concrete disadvantage. Under serfdom, the petty gentry in a village was not under the jurisdiction of the manor-dominated mayor and aldermen; instead, it elected

---

[250] U *khodachkova shliakhta* (derogatory), *zahonova shliakhta*; P *szlachta chodaczkowa* (derogatory), *szlachta zaściankowa, szlachta zagrodowa*; G *Rustikaledelleute, Kleinedelleute*.

[251] In 1849 Hipolit Stupnicki estimated that there were 32,200 nobles in Galicia, of whom 8,468 inhabited twenty-one villages in the Sambir region. Kozik, *Ukraiński ruch narodowy*, 69 note 10.

[252] Soter Ortynsky, the first Ukrainian Greek Catholic bishop in America (1907–16), was a member of the Sambir region petty gentry.

[253] Franko, "Znadoby.... I. Deshcho pro shliakhtu khodachkovu," *Zibrannia tvoriv*, 26: 180–5.

its own prefect and governed itself autonomously.[254] The petty gentry was not obliged to perform road work and other communal duties imposed on the serfs. All this changed between 1848 and 1867. Not only was the petty gentry now socio-economically the equal of the peasantry, but it also had exactly the same legal rights and obligations, with no special privileges. It had to join the same administrative commune as the peasantry and be liable for the same obligations. Not surprisingly, the petty gentry in the late 1860s made a number of unsuccessful appeals to the crownland government for the erection of separate communes for the gentry,[255] and, as our corpus of correspondence mentions, sometimes the petty gentry managed to evade such onerous communal obligations as road work (*CC* 110).

In sum, then, the Ukrainian petty gentry occupied a very peculiar place on the socio-national borderline. Ethnically, this stratum was Ukrainian, much more unequivocally so than the *latynnyky*. Socially, in the late nineteenth century, the petty gentry consisted of petty independent producers, the same as the peasantry, yet it had a highly developed sense of distinctiveness from the peasantry owing to historical social differences. The sense of separateness from the peasantry went hand in hand with an ideology, also rooted in the feudal era, of solidarity with the Polish nobility. With whom would these amphibians side in the national rivalry in late-nineteenth-century Galicia?

For the mid-1880s, the answer, in general, was: with the Polish nobility and against the Ukrainian national movement. This circumstance demonstrates how crucial the feudal era was in determining the political alignments of the post-emancipation period.

The correspondence depicted the petty gentry as being, on the whole, opposed to the reading club movement. Ivan Mikhas (*LA* 220), the radicalized peasant from Morozovychi, Sambir district, wrote:

> ... In our region of Sambir there are many gentry villages which don't consider peasants creatures of God and which fraternize with the Poles, because, as they say, "Rus' has no significance." Of these gentry villages there is a reading club only in Stupnytsia, ... but even that reading club has its local enemies (*CC* 130).

Among the signatories of a petition against the radical reading club in Volia Iakubova, Drohobych district, were two members of the petty gentry (*CC* 92).[256]

The correspondence has more to say about how the petty gentry behaved during elections. The above-cited Ivan Mikhas, in reporting on elections to the district council, wrote that "of all the gentry villages only the commune of Siltse stood on the side of the Ruthenians" (*CC* 130). Two items of

---

[254] *Ibid.*

[255] In 1870 the crownland administration ruled definitively that there could be no separate gentry communes. Grzybowski, *Galicja*, 276.

[256] Although radicals were involved in both cases, I have the impression that this is merely accidental.

correspondence mentioned members of the petty gentry agitating for the Polish candidate during the 1885 parliamentary elections; one, called Mykyta Khodakovsky[257] by the correspondent, allegedly purchased votes for the Polish candidate at 30 gulden apiece, while the other was a priest of petty gentry origin (*CC* 220). A correspondent from the Bovshivets region of Rohatyn district had this to say:

> ... Here in the villages the village gentry, the so-called *shliakhta khodachkova*, has a considerable majority. This gentry is cunning, vociferous, arrogant and is constantly repeating [the saying]: A noble with a garden is the equal of a palatine (P *szlachcic na zagrodzie równy wojewodzie*).[258] And it is all the more arrogant, since at all elections (but *only* at elections) it is reminded with sausages of this equality. On other occasions all sorts of lordlings (U *panky*) are always inciting in it a consciousness of superiority to the peasant, and because of this it is much quicker to trust the first lord's lackey (U *pidpanok*) or Jew that comes along rather than the best-disposed friend of the people (*CC* 264).

Some activists of the rural national movement did not even consider the petty gentry to be of Ukrainian nationality (*CC* 133).[259] Conflict between the Ukrainian petty gentry and peasantry is also documented in *Batkivshchyna* in the mid-1880s outside the corpus of correspondence.[260]

The evidence of the corpus of correspondence is thus quite unanimous in depicting the Ukrainian petty gentry, in contrast to the *latynnyky*, as being outside and opposed to the national movement. The evidence of the list of activists corroborates this. Only two of the activists (*LA* 83, 84) have been identified as belonging to the petty gentry. These were the brothers Kyrylo and Stefan Genyk-Berezovsky. Kyrylo, the more active of the two, was a teacher by profession and had been influenced by Ukrainian radicals, especially Ivan Franko, whom he met during the course of his studies in Lviv.

Although the petty gentry was not drawn to the Ukrainian national movement in the mid-1880s, it seems that with the passage of time, as one moved away from the feudal era and as the Ukrainian movement grew more differentiated, the petty gentry also found a place in the movement. By the early twentieth century there was an Association of the Ruthenian Gentry in Galicia (U *Tovarystvo ruskoi shliakhty v Halychyni*) which was allied with the national movement, especially its conservative and clerical-conservative tendencies: in 1908 its executive invited Bishop Soter Ortynsky to be its patron and in 1909 it sent a special note of thanks to Viacheslav Lypynsky, the future ideologue of Ukrainian conservatism, for writing on the history of

---

[257] See above, 152–3.

[258] A reference to the entirely theoretical equality of all nobles, from petty gentry to magnates, in the old Polish-Lithuanian commonwealth.

[259] See also Iosyf z Khmelivky, "...vid Burshtyna," *Batkivshchyna* 6, no. 26 (27 [15] June 1884): 159.

[260] Prytomnyi, "...vid Kalusha," *Batkivshchyna* 6, no. 24 (13 [1] June 1884): 144. Ivan Mikhas [Ivan z-nad Dnistra], "Pysmo z Sambirshchyny," *Batkivshchyna* 8, no. 3 (22 [10] January 1886): 17.

the Ukrainian gentry. The association survived into the interwar era.[261] In the 1920s there was at least one distinctly gentry reading club associated with Prosvita (U *Shliakhotska chytalnia Prosvity*). In the 1930s the Polish government, in its efforts to divide the Ukrainian population and polonize whom it could, founded its own Ukrainian petty gentry movement with polonophile tendencies (the so-called [P] *Koła szlacheckie*). A representative of the former Polish administration admitted during World War II, in a confidential memorandum to the London government, that the movement was farcical (P *nasz operetkowy ruch szlachty zagrodowej*).[262]

From all that has been said in this section, it is clear that the social, "horizontal" aspect of the national movement was still dominant in the mid-1880s. Whether it continued to be as dominant thereafter is, of course, a question for further research to decide. Key moments to investigate would include the interrelation of the social and national during the West Ukrainian revolution of 1918–19, as well as the social aspects of the popularity of the radical-right Organization of Ukrainian Nationalists in the Galician village in the 1930s and early 1940s. One is tempted to proffer some speculations and perspectives, but this would carry us much too far afield.

---

[261] Fylypchak, "Tovarystvo 'Ruskoi shliakhty.'" Unfortunately, I only had access to a single installment (the fourth) of a series of articles on the history of the association.

[262] "Kwestia ukraińska," 4, 10. I am grateful to Dr. Paweł Korzec for providing me with a copy of this interesting document.

Conclusions

On the eve of the First World War, the Austrian social democrat Otto Bauer penned some lines that summarize the main theme of the foregoing study. He wrote of "a portentous advancement, the awakening of millions who until now had been poor, powerless and meek, but who at present are climbing onto the stage of history."[1]

> The Galician peasant is awakening. In the east of the crownland the peasant is a Ruthenian, while the landlord, the official and the city-dweller are Poles. As long as the peasant was poor, uncultured and powerless, the small Polish minority ruled the great Ruthenian peasant mass. Now, as the peasant economy is strengthened[2] and the peasants' self-consciousness awakened, the peasant carries his nationality forward with him.... This is ... something great—to see a people of three and a half million all at once awaken from centuries-long numbness, awaken to its own powerful will.[3]

The revolution of 1848 had liberated the peasantry from an extremely oppressive variety of serfdom; it had turned what nonpeasants had regarded as beasts into people, a precondition for them to be turned into Ukrainians. The great reforms of the 1860s, which continued the work of 1848, afforded the civil freedoms, particularly the freedom of the press and of association, that allowed the peasantry to be drawn into national politics. With the aid of village priests, teachers and cantors—these midwives of national-cultural rebirth—nationally oriented institutions, especially the popular press and reading clubs, penetrated the countryside and carried the national message to the peasants. The national idea found a strong resonance in the East Galician village because of the virtual identity of national and social conflict. The result, by the turn of the century, was that the peasantry was integrated into the Ukrainian nation in Galicia and furnished it with a strong backbone.

---

[1] Otto Bauer, "Erwachende Völker," *Der Kampf* 7, no. 4 (1 January 1914): 146.

[2] The Galician peasantry's economic circumstances improved considerably in the period 1900–14, primarily owing to mass emigration, which both alleviated population pressure on the land and provided the countryside with an important new source of income. Stella Hryniuk ("A Peasant Society," "Peasant Agriculture") argues, unconvincingly in my opinion, that the improvement was already well under way in the period 1880–1900.

[3] Bauer, "Erwachende Völker," 147.

Thus summarized, our story was, after all, a simple one and perhaps even well known. However, the purpose of this study has not been to demonstrate *that* the process outlined above took place, but *how* it took place. This has been a study of the mechanics of rural nation-building with close attention to the social intricacies of the process. There is no need here to march past for review the general conclusions arrived at in the text concerning generational conflict, the ambiguous positions of certain social strata or the impact of certain institutions. Indeed, a capsule summary of these points would run counter to the purpose of a study aimed at presenting a particular social process with as much precision and complexity as the sources allow.

The results of our investigation would be enriched by similar analyses, using a related or improved methodology, of other East European peasantries during the era of the development of rural national movements. The Polish peasantry of Western Galicia would make a particularly fruitful study.[4] Here much of the social and political background would be identical to that of the present study, with the crucial and intriguing difference that both the peasantry and the landed nobility were of the same nationality. This circumstance certainly delayed the formation of a Polish national consciousness among the West Galician peasantry, but it did not in the end prevent it. Another useful study would be a comparison of the Ukrainian and Romanian national movements in rural Bukovyna. This would allow investigation of much the same theme as in the case of the Polish peasantry of Galicia, since the landlord class in Bukovyna was in great part Romanian. Further afield, it would be enlightening to study the national integration of the peasantry in the independent Balkan states. Would it follow patterns more akin to those of France, where the state purposely and crucially intervened to accomplish rural nation-building,[5] or more akin to the grass-roots movement as described for Galicia; or would it be a hybrid of these two? Would it even be possible to perform a similar investigation concerning East European peasantries such as the Slovak or Dnieper-Ukrainian peasantries, which had the full force of the state turned against the formation and development of a rural national movement?

In addition to methodologically related comparative studies, it would be instructive to return to Eastern Galicia in later periods. Even the late 1880s and 1890s as a point of focus could provide significant differences in perspective. The national movement continued to expand after the mid-1880s. Not only were more villages, and presumably more strata of the peasantry, drawn into the movement, but the institutional infrastructure grew ever more sophisticated, moving beyond the basic reading clubs and cooperatives to include everything from insurance agencies to paramilitary gymnastic societies. The *modus operandi* of the national movement also grew more refined.

---

[4] Archival sources for the West Galician peasantry are much more accessible than for the East Galician peasantry.

[5] See Weber, *Peasants into Frenchmen.*

Beginning in 1886, thus immediately after the narrowest period on which this study is focussed, the national movement made ever more frequent and expert use of mass peasant assemblies (U *vicha*) held in district capitals. The assemblies, even more concretely than the newspapers, broke down the isolation of individual communes, brought Ukrainian rural activists from various villages into contact with one another and encouraged a free flow in the exchange of ideas and information.[6] Closely connected to the burgeoning of mass assemblies was the growth in importance after the mid-1880s of the Ukrainian intelligentsia, particularly lawyers, in cities outside Lviv. The small-town intelligentsia organized the mass assemblies and also aided local reading clubs intellectually and even materially. This intelligentsia was an important intermediary step between the village notables and the national leadership in Lviv.[7] Thus the national movement not only expanded after 1885, but it developed certain refinements and additional complexities. It also grew more politically differentiated with the emergence of the radical party in 1890. It would be useful to undertake a comparative study of the national populist and radical movements in the countryside in the 1890s, just as it would be interesting to compare the Russophile movement in the countryside with its rivals. The era of the agrarian strikes, 1900–6, could also be explored with profit using the methodology developed in this study; so could the Galician village on the eve of World War I, in the 1920s and in the 1930s. The list of what could be done to deepen our understanding of rural nationalism in Eastern Europe in general or Eastern Galicia in particular is, as can be seen, quite long.

But is our ultimate conclusion only to be that further research is necessary? I would hope not. I would hope that certain things have been demonstrated clearly by this study, at least within the geographical and chronological limitations stated at the outset.

For one thing, the study confirms the general perspective advanced by Bauer, that is, that it was the *peasantry*, a social class, which awoke and which carried its nationality forward with it. The strong social component in the rural national movement had two aspects, one connected with the peasantry's immediate past (the era of serfdom and servitudes), the other with its present (the penetration of the money economy). The era of serfdom, together with its epilogue in the period of struggle over servitudes, had a profound impact on the shaping of the Ukrainian peasantry's consciousness. The memory of serfdom was kept alive throughout the late nineteenth century; the national movement consciously sought to overcome the deleterious results of serfdom, particularly ignorance, but also alcohol

---

[6] On the mass peasant assemblies, see Kravets, "Masovi selianski vystupy"; Hryniuk, "A Peasant Society," 424–5; Himka, *Socialism*, 149–52, 172.

[7] In our list of activists, there was only one example of this intermediary group (*LA* 67). For accounts of the role of the small-town intelligentsia, see Himka, *Socialism*, 148–52; Hryniuk, "A Peasant Society," 417–18; Olesnytsky, *Storinky*; Franko, "Perekhresni stezhky" (fiction), *Zibrannia tvoriv*, 20.

addiction; and the experience or lack of experience of serfdom was a critical element in determining whether a particular group participated in the national movement or not (the *latynnyky* and the Ukrainian petty gentry). In the late nineteenth century, after the abolition of serfdom and the general settlement of the servitude disputes, manor-commune conflict abated, even if it did not disappear. In that period, the new money economy was the chief concern of the peasantry and the pressing social conflict was that between the representatives of the money economy in the villages and small towns, on the one hand, and the peasants as independent petty producers, on the other. This took the national form of a Ukrainian-Jewish conflict. Owing, furthermore, to the increasing role of Jews in manorial management and ownership, the lingering class conflict between landlords and peasants in the post-emancipation era was often transformed in the peasants' consciousness from a Polish-Ukrainian to a Jewish-Ukrainian conflict.[8] (In the cities, particularly Lviv, the Ukrainian national movement remained primarily directed against the Poles rather than the Jews.)

As intense as were the feelings of Ukrainian peasants against those whom they perceived to be their socio-national enemies, there was no outbreak of mass violence against Jews or Poles in Eastern Galicia during the entire period of Austrian constitutional rule. This is in sharp contrast to the frequent and savage pogroms that occurred at that time in Ukrainian territory under Russian rule, just across the border from Galicia;[9] it is also in sharp contrast to the jacquerie that swept across Romania in 1907 and to the pogrom that broke out in otherwise so similar Western Galicia in 1897. The major difference between tranquil Eastern Galicia and these other regions was that in Eastern Galicia, thanks to the development of a strong national movement in the countryside, the socio-national conflict was almost completely politicized and channelled into nonviolent venues such as elections, strikes and boycotts. The national movement provided a lightning rod against peasant violence, but by no means left the peasantry defenceless; in fact, the Galician Ukrainian peasant was better armed with a newspaper he could read than any of his fellows with a straightened-out and sharpened scythe. And when it would prove necessary, i.e., during the revolutionary years, the Galician Ukrainian peasantry would not shrink from violence, albeit not the wild violence of a peasant rebellion, to accomplish its political aims.

These reflections on the politicization of the Galician Ukrainian peasantry bring us to a consideration of the precondition for such politicization: the great Austrian reforms of the 1860s, particularly the restoration of a parliament, the introduction of compulsory education and the guarantee of

---

[8] *Mutatis mutandis* this may be the key to understanding how the Polish, Romanian and Magyar peasantries were integrated into nations that included a nobility: by a shared antagonism to the Jews. This would help explain the relatively large role played in these nationalisms by anti-Semitism.

[9] Similarly, during the revolutionary years following the First World War, Ukrainian peasants in Galicia (and Bukovyna) abstained from the sort of jacqueries and pogroms in which their counterparts in Dnieper Ukraine engaged.

basic civil liberties such as freedom of the press and freedom of association. The democratization of political life afforded by the Austrian reforms both turned the attention of the national leadership to the peasantry, its only source of the votes required to enter parliament, and allowed the national movement to penetrate into the villages. Otto Bauer wrote that "in the growth of democracy on Austrian soil, the most important event today is perhaps the awakening of the Galician peasant."[10] Whether the Galician peasant awakening was as important to the consolidation of Austrian democracy as Bauer opined is an open question, but that the converse was true cannot be doubted. Where would the Ukrainian national movement have been without peasants who could read, newspapers like *Batkivshchyna* and institutions like the reading clubs?

The answer to that question, unfortunately, is not at all abstract, since Ukrainian peasantries shorn of education and rights existed in Hungary (Transcarpathia) and in the Russian empire. In both these peasantries national consciousness was very weak. In the case of the Ukrainian peasantry in Transcarpathia, its national awakening only began when the region passed from Hungarian to democratic Czechoslovakian rule in 1918. The delay had no serious consequences for Ukrainian history, because the Ukrainians of Transcarpathia were numerically small, geographically peripheral and an object rather than a subject in the revolutionary years following the First World War. The same, however, cannot be said of the Ukrainians of the Russian empire, who constituted the vast majority of the Ukrainian nation, inhabited large, historically hallowed territories and occupied the centre of the historical stage during the Ukrainian revolution. The retarded national consciousness of the Dnieper Ukrainian peasantry—largely illiterate, with almost no political and institutional experience—proved the greatest obstacle to the successful establishment of an independent Ukrainian state (Bolshevik or anti-Bolshevik) in 1917–20. The effects of the enforced slumber of the Ukrainian village in the former Russia are still felt today in the weaker sense of national identity in Dnieper Ukraine compared to Western Ukraine.

Otto Bauer, like many other contemporary observers, was keenly aware of the great differences between Austrian- and Russian-ruled Ukraine and noted that "the awakening of the Galician peasant has an effect beyond Austria's boundaries; it creates new points of friction between Austria and Russia...."[11] The tsarist government was indeed extremely disturbed by the flourishing of a Ukrainian national movement on its borders; the movement, thanks to its mass base in the peasantry, was very strong and helped to keep alive the persecuted and small, but surviving and potentially dangerous, Ukrainian movement in Russia itself. The desire of the Russian government to crush the Ukrainian movement in Galicia was one of the manifold causes of World War I. Within the same year that Bauer published his article, the Russian army invaded Galicia and the tsarist administration began a

---

[10] Bauer, "Erwachende Völker," 146.

[11] *Ibid.*, 151.

systematic and draconian programme to eradicate the Ukrainian movement. Russia lost the First World War and had to withdraw from Galicia. But almost exactly twenty-five years after the first Russian invasion of Galicia, a new Russia—not tsarist but Stalinist, yet still disturbed by the power of the Ukrainian movement in Galicia—invaded the region again. Once again, Russia's desire to crush the national movement in Galicia was one of the manifold causes of a world war. Thus the modest actions of modest people—the reading of newspapers and the formation of associations by peasants and rural notables—had, in the end, very grave implications. Once the rural masses of Eastern Europe took up national politics, these politics became much more serious and explosive than they had ever been in the past.

Appendices

I. Archival Sources

Archival research for this monograph was conducted in Lviv, the former capital of Galicia, in 1983. To orient myself in the rich archival holdings of this city, I benefitted from the unpublished manuscript of Patricia K. Grimsted's forthcoming guide to Soviet Ukrainian archives and manuscript repositories[1] as well as from a number of published works.[2] Plans to use archives in Ternopil and Ivano-Frankivsk were frustrated, as was the plan to use the manuscript collection of the Institute of Literature of the Academy of Sciences of the Ukrainian SSR (in Kiev). Work in the Austrian archives in 1982 did not uncover sources of direct relevance to the subject of this monograph, but the Viennese archives remain an important and little-explored repository of historical documentation on Galician history.

The richest collection of unpublished sources on the history of Galicia during the Austrian period is located in the Central State Historical Archives of the Ukrainian SSR in Lviv (U *Tsentralnyi derzhavnyi istorychnyi arkhiv URSR u m. Lvovi*; abbreviated as TsDIAL). The Central Archives have inherited the papers of various Galician government institutions and major civic organizations. Unfortunately, there is no published guide to these archives, although a number of articles describe aspects of their holdings.[3]

The papers of the Presidium of the Galician Viceroy's Office (U *Halytske namisnytstvo, m. Lviv. Prezydiia*) are contained in TsDIAL, fond 146, opysy 4–8 (and presumably others). Particularly valuable for this study were documents dealing with the publication and confiscation of political brochures and periodicals, including

---

[1] Patricia K. Grimsted, *Archives and Manuscript Repositories in the USSR: Ukraine and Moldavia* (Princeton, NJ: Princeton University Press, forthcoming).

[2] V. Borys, "Dokumentalni materialy pro stavlennia selian Halychyny do ahrarnoi reformy 1848 r.," *Arkhivy Ukrainy*, no. 1 (1966): 56–63. *Derzhavni arkhivy Ukrainskoi RSR. Korotkyi dovidnyk* (Kiev: Naukova dumka, 1972). Stanisław Franciszek Gajerski, "Źródła do dziejów południowo-wschodniej Polski w bibliotekach i archiwach Lwowa," *Studia Historyczne* 20, no. 2 (77) (1977): 295–302. Patricia Kennedy Grimsted, "Lviv Manuscript Collections and Their Fate," *Harvard Ukrainian Studies* 3–4 (1979–80): 348–75. N.F. Vradii, "Arkhivni dokumenty pro pidnesennia revoliutsiinoho rukhu v Halychyni na pochatku XX st.," *Arkhivy Ukrainy*, no. 5 (1973): 56–60. S. Zlupko, "Materialy lvivskykh arkhivoskhovyshch z istorii ukrainskoi ekonomichnoi dumky epokhy kapitalizmu," *Naukovo-informatsiinyi biuleten Arkhivnoho upravlinnia URSR*, no. 5 (55) (1962): 65–9.

[3] See especially: Kravets, "Dzherela." N.F. Vradii, "Tsentralnyi derzhavnyi istorychnyi arkhiv URSR u m. Lvovi," *Arkhivy Ukrainy*, no. 4 (132) (July-August 1975): 41–7.

Batkivshchyna, 1877–85 (opys 7, odynytsi zberezhennia [od. zb.], 4149, 4220, 4240, 4276, 4278, 4320, 4352). These included correspondence with the Austrian ministry of the interior and quarterly reports prepared by the Lviv police on the press run of political periodicals. The materials were in Polish and German.

Also among the materials of the Galician Viceroy's Office, fond 146, opysy 64, 64a and 64b, were the documents of the so-called servitudes commission, officially known as the Crownland Commission on the Redemption and Regulation of Land Obligations (U *Halytske namisnytstvo, m. Lviv. Kraiova komisiia u spravakh vykupu i vrehuliuvannia pozemelnykh povynnostei*; G *Grundlasten-Ablösungs- und Regulierungs Landes Kommission*). These acts deal with disputes between the manor and peasant commune over rights to forests and pastures. The acts form an exceedingly large corpus of documentation. Generally, a single servitudes case, encompassing one or more villages, takes up about five folders of over a hundred leaves each. Each individual act (od. zb.) is labelled, with some variations, The Case of Servitude Disputes over the Right to Use Forests and Pastures of the Inhabitants of the Village of..., ...Circle (U *Sprava pro servitutni superechky za pravo korystuvannia lisamy i pasovyskamy zhyteliv s.... ...okruhu*). The arrangement of the individual cases within opysy 64 and 64b (the status of 64a is not clear to me) is by a combination of geographical, alphabetical, chronological and thematic criteria. After an initial section in opys 64 containing the general papers of the servitudes commission, the individual cases are segregated by district, although this is not indicated on the covers of the folders, which provide only the name of the village and its circle. The districts follow one another in Ukrainian alphabetical order. Within each district, cases are again ordered alphabetically according to the name of the principal village involved. The folders (od. zb.) within each case appear in roughly chronological order, but with some thematic divisions as well. Chronologically, the documentation focuses on the period from the mid-1850s to the early 1870s, although many documents from the late eighteenth and early nineteenth centuries are included in the folders as well as a few copies of documents of even earlier provenance; later documents can also be found, some even from the 1920s. The languages of the servitude documents are primarily German and Polish, but some older documents are in Latin and there is some use of Ukrainian; more rarely, only in signatures, Yiddish appears.

The main thematic focus of the servitude documents is, of course, the servitude disputes proper. But in addition to illuminating the struggle for forests and pastures between landlords and peasants, the servitude acts contain an untapped treasury of information on other topics, ranging from the occupation of village Jews under serfdom to the history of vernacular architecture and construction in late-nineteenth-century Galicia. For the purposes of this monograph, however, these sources have been used to learn about serfdom and the servitudes struggle as well as to acquire information on the family background, mobility, age and civic involvement of the peasant-activists of the mid-1880s.

Related to the servitude documents are the Materials concerning Property Disputes of Peasants with Landowners in Galicia (R *Materialy ob imushchestvennykh sporakh krestian s zemlevladeltsami v Galitsii*). They were originally the papers of the Tenth Department of the Galician Gubernium, which dealt with the so-called "matters concerning subjects [i.e., serfs]" (G *Unterthanssache*) or "public-political matters" (L *Publico-Politica*). Now they are housed in TsDIAL, fond 146 (Galician Viceroy's Office), opys 87. I was able to consult fifteen of these folders (od. zb. 1116–30), each of which consisted of about 180 leaves. The acts emanated from 1847 and early 1848 (before the revolution); the primary language of the documents was German, and

TABLE 15 TsDIAL, 146/64–64b (Servitudes Commission): Holdings Consulted

Fond	Opys	Od. zb.	Village(s)	Circle	District
146	64	1–6	General papers of the commission, 1855–64		
146	64	37–42	Baznykivka, Saranchuky	Berezhany	Berezhany
146	64	197–200	Mechyshchiv	Berezhany	Berezhany
146	64	605, 609	Hrabivets, Pakhivka, Sadzhava	Stanyslaviv	Bohorodchany
146	64	637	Solotvyna	Stanyslaviv	Bohorodchany
146	64	656–61	Solotvyna, Maniava, Markiv	Stanyslaviv	Bohorodchany
146	64	676	Solotvyna, Khmelivka	Stanyslaviv	Bohorodchany
146	64	735–43	Hlubichok, Lanivtsi, Tsyhany	Chortkiv	Borshchiv
146	64	1031	Hai Smolenski	Zolochiv	Brody
146	64	1123–5	Mykolaiv	Zolochiv	Brody
146	64	1153–5	Nakvasha	Zolochiv	Brody
146	64	1189	Rudenko Liatske	Zolochiv	Brody
146	64	1190–2	Smorzhiv, Stremilche	Zolochiv	Brody
146	64a	1–12	Hanusivtsi	Stanyslaviv	Stanyslaviv
146	64a	467–9	Lanchyn	Stanyslaviv	Nadvirna
146	64a	972–3	Nahuievychi	Sambir	Drohobych
146	64b	578–9	Zhydiatychi	Lviv	Lviv
146	64b	1119–22	Fytkiv	Stanyslaviv	Nadvirna
146	64b	2285–96	Dobrianychi, Korelychi	Berezhany	Peremyshliany
146	64b	2800	Verkhrata	Zhovkva	Rava Ruska
146	64b	2936	Novosilky Kardynalski	Zhovkva	Rava Ruska

Fond	Opys	Od. zb.	Village(s)	Circle	District
146	64b	2974–5	Uhniv	Zhovkva	Rava Ruska
146	64b	3212–19	Kunashiv	Berezhany	Rohatyn
146	64b	4244	Vydyniv	Kolomyia	Sniatyn
146	64b	4247–8	Demyche	Kolomyia	Sniatyn
146	64b	4249	Dzhuriv	Kolomyia	Sniatyn
146	64b	4359–73	Korchyn, Rozhdzhaliv	Zhovkva	Sokal
146	64b	4437–46	Pozdymyr, Radvantsi, Skomorokhy	Zhovkva	Sokal
146	64b	4843–50	Volytsia, Vivnia, Dobriany	Stryi	Stryi
146	64b	4940–4	Lysiatychi	Stryi	Stryi

Polish figured only secondarily. These materials are difficult to use because the arrangement of the acts is chronological, as the viceroy's office took up each case, with no provision for geographic and thematic organization. In addition to providing information on property disputes between lord and peasant, the acts also document excessive physical abuse of serfs by the manor (G *Misshandlungen*). The coverage of incidents is far from exhaustive, since these documents only register abuse that a peasant reported, the circle authorities confirmed and the manor then appealed. Still, the documents record a great number of cases and afford an important insight into the workings of the feudal system on the eve of the abolition of serfdom. On the whole, however, the Materials concerning Property Disputes did not prove very useful for this monograph.

Of more relevance were the papers of the Criminal Division of the Crownland Court in Lviv (U *Kraiovyi sud, m. Lviv. Kryminalnyi viddil*), which are in TsDIAL, fond 152, opys 2. I used documents relating to the confiscation of the newspaper *Batkivshchyna*, 1879–81 (od. zb. 14789–90, 14898–903, 15007–13). The documents, which are largely in Polish, include the often interesting justification for confiscation as well as copies of the confiscated issues.

Confiscations of *Batkivshchyna*, 1879–80, are also documented in the papers of the Supreme State Prosecutor's Office in Lviv (U *Vyshcha derzhavna prokuratoriia, m. Lviv*; P *C.k. Nadprokuratoria Państwa we Lwowie*; G *Die k.k. Oberstaat-sanwaltschaft in Lemberg*) in TsDIAL, fond 156, opys 1 (od. zb. 545). Also among these papers are reports of local prosecutors concerning illegal actions undertaken by peasants to regain forests and pastures that the servitudes commission had decided belonged to the manor. These colourful documents are mainly in Polish and German, but quotes from the peasantry are often given in Ukrainian, in Polish transcription. Each individual case is labelled, with some variations, Reports of the Prosecutor of the City of . . . concerning Anti-Landlord Actions by the Inhabitants of the Village . . . (U *Donesennia prokurora m. . . . pro antypomishchytski vystupy meshkantsiv s. . . .*). I had access to a dozen of these cases.

A source consulted, but abandoned as insufficiently productive, was the so-called Crownland Tabula (U *Kraiova tabulia*) or Books for the Registration of Property Acts (U *Knyhy zapysu mainovykh dokumentiv*), known in Latin as *Libri Instrumentorum*. They are housed in TsDIAL, fond 166, opys 1. I surveyed books from

Zymna Voda and Rudno, Lviv circle, 1860s–80 (od. zb. 1168–71);

Hai Starobridski, Zolochiv circle, 1799–1879 (od. zb. 1383);

Liubycha Korolivska, Zhovkva circle, 1831–61 (od. zb. 1778);

Potelych, Zhovkva circle, 1821–70 (od. zb. 1898–9);

Uhniv, Zhovkva circle, 1820–83 (od. zb. 2234);

Khrystynopil, Zhovkva circle, 1841–83 (od. zb. 2555–7);

Berezhany circle, 1834–89 (od. zb. 3028, 3042, 3053, 3055–6, 3059–62, 3064, 3066, 3068–9, 4094–7, 4099–111);

and Zhovkva circle, 1834–63 (od. zb. 4158).

The acts recorded in the books are (chronologically) in Latin, German and Polish. Although occasionally one can find in them information on peasants, if their inheritance affairs became unduly entangled or if they played a role in local government, generally these books deal with demesnal property. They would be an excellent source for studying the mounting debts of the nobility in the nineteenth century.

TABLE 16 TsDIAL, 156/1 (Supreme State Prosecutor's Office in Lviv, Illegal Servitude Actions): Holdings Consulted

Fond	Opys	Od. zb.	Village	Local Prosecutor	Year(s)
156	1	28	Nyzhni Hai	Lviv	1870
156	1	29	Chekhy	Zolochiv	1870
156	1	59	Dobrotvir	Zolochiv	1872–3
156	1	60	Knihynychi	Zolochiv	1872–3
156	1	61	Kniahynychi	Ternopil	1872
156	1	62	Dobrotvir	Zolochiv	1872–3
156	1	63	Biliavtsi	Zolochiv	1872
156	1	64	Cholhany	Sambir	1872
156	1	65	Holhoche	Zolochiv	1872–3
156	1	99	Verbytsia	Lviv	1873
156	1	100	Zaszkowce (Zashkivtsi)	Przemyśl	1873–5
156	1	142	Borky Dominikanski	Lviv	1874–5

An outstanding source on the nature of feudal obligations in Galicia, on differentiation in the peasant community in the mid-nineteenth century and on the status and wealth of individual peasants in the decade after emancipation are the papers of the so-called indemnization commission, officially known as the Ministerial Commission on the Emancipation from the Obligations of Serfdom (U *Ministerska komisiia po zvilnenniu vid panshchynnykh povynnostei*, R *Ministerskaia kommissiia po delam osvobozhdeniia ot krepostnykh povinnostei*). I used the Lists of Subjects with an Inventory of Obligations of Serfdom Abolished by Redemption (U *Spysky piddanykh s....z perelikom skasovanykh za vykup panshchynnykh povynnostei...okruhu*), which are housed in TsDIAL, fond 168, opysy 1 and 2, and fond 488, opys 1. For each village, the indemnization commission prepared a concise inventory of all the feudal obligations that were being abolished as well as a list of all former serfs and their holdings, usually divided into four economic strata. The provenance of the documents is the 1850s; the languages used are German and Polish, and only very rarely Ukrainian. The lists are arranged geographically, by circle, and the circles are placed in Ukrainian alphabetical order. Fond 168, opys 1, contains the circles through Stanyslaviv; fond 488, opys 1, from Stryi on. (The status of fond 168, opys 2, is not clear to me.) Within each circle, the Lists are arranged by village in Ukrainian alphabetical order.

Similar information, only more relevant to the peasant-activists of the mid-1880s, should have been provided by the cadastral records of 1865 and 1880. The cadastral records of 1865 are housed in TsDIAL, fond 186, opys 3, and originate from the Crownland Land-Tax Commission of the Ministry of Agriculture and Agrarian Reforms in Lviv (U *Kraiova zemelno-podatkova komisiia Ministerstva zemlerobstva ta ahrarnykh reform, m. Lviv*). Most of the materials I had access to were summary land statistics with the individual village (and not the individual peasant household) as the smallest unit on which information was provided. I looked at cadastral records from Sambir circle (od. zb. 1754–65) and Ternopil and Chortkiv circles (od. zb. 2201–4). The records were in German. In only one instance did I have the cadastral records of an individual village (G *Steuergemeinde*), Khryplyn, Stanyslaviv circle (od. zb. 1855). Its cover bore the title Summary Inventory of Taxes Collected from Communities of Stanyslaviv Circle in 1865 (U *Pidsumkovyi perelik stiahnenykh podatkiv z hromad za 1865 rik Stanislavskoho okruhu*). Unfortunately, this particular village did not figure as the home of any of the known village activists of the mid-1880s and so did not prove relevant to this study. From this specimen, however, it was evident that such village cadastres for 1865, and especially 1880, would have provided detailed information on the economic status and, indirectly, age of the village activists. The staff of TsDIAL told me that the individual village cadastres for 1865 and 1880 have not been preserved in those archives. (I also looked for landholding records from 1880 in the Lviv Oblast State Archives; see below.)

The papers of the Prosvita society (U *Tovarystvo "Prosvita", m. Lviv*) are preserved in TsDIAL, fond 348. In opys 1 are the reports of individual reading clubs to the central Prosvita offices in Lviv, 1896–1939. Individual folders are labelled Reports, Minutes, Correspondence and Other Materials on the Activity of the Reading Club in the Village of ... (U *Zvity, protokoly, lystuvannia ta inshi materialy pro diialnist chytalni v s.... *). They are arranged in Ukrainian alphabetical order by the name of the individual village, irrespective of district. This documentation is in Ukrainian. The reports were used for this study to gain a better understanding of reading clubs as well as to collect biographical information on the village activists of the mid-1880s. For the latter task, the reports to which I had access, selected geographically, were sufficient; however, more extensive access to the early Prosvita

TABLE 17 TsDIAL, 168/1–2 and 488/1 (Indemnization Commission): Holdings Consulted

Fond	Opys	Od. zb.	Village	Circle
168	1	126	Ozeriany [originally spelled Iezeriany?]	Berezhany
168	1	198, 259	Kryve	Berezhany
168	1	228	Mechyshchiv	Berezhany
168	1	302	Pukiv	Berezhany
168	1	327	Saranchuky	Berezhany
168	1	421–5	Batiatychi	Zhovkva
168	1	483–5, 571	Vynnyky	Zhovkva
168	1	612	Korchyn	Zhovkva
168	1	633	Kulykiv	Zhovkva
168	1	1016	Dmytriv	Zhovkva
168	1	1039	Zheniv	Zolochiv
168	1	1044	Zhulychi	Zolochiv
168	1	1074	Zozulia	Zolochiv
168	1	1183	Nestanychi (Nestanyshche)	Zolochiv
168	1	1193	Ohliadiv	Zolochiv
168	1	1197–8	Olesko	Zolochiv
168	1	1222	Polove	Zolochiv
168	1	1253	Polonychna, Chanyzh	Zolochiv
168	1	1340	Trudovach	Zolochiv

Fond	Opys	Od. zb.	Village	Circle
168	1	1416	Balyntsi	Kolomyia
168	1	1503	Kiidantsi	Kolomyia
168	1	1759	Zahorodky	Lviv
168	1	1764	Zapytiv	Lviv
168	1	1916	Nykonkovychi	Lviv
168	1	1946	Pisky	Lviv
168	1	1959	Rudno	Lviv
168	1	3729	Strachocina (Strakhotyna)	Sanok
168	1	3891	Vyktoriv	Stanyslaviv
168	1	3954	Drohomyrchany	Stanyslaviv
168	1	4087	Nadorozhna	Stanyslaviv
168	1	4099	Olesha	Stanyslaviv
168	2	100	Mechyshchiv	Berezhany
168	2	147	Saranchuky	Berezhany
488	1	11	Berezhnytsia	Stryi
488	1	61–2	Volytsia	Stryi
488	1	11	Tovstenke	Stryi
488	1	213–19	Korchyn	Stryi
488	1	277	Mizun	Stryi
488	1	290	Nyniv Horishnii	Stryi
488	1	347	Rozhniativ	Stryi
488	1	422	Strilkiv	Stryi
488	1	464	Tukholka	Stryi

Fond	Opys	Od. zb.	Village	Circle
488	1	538	Vorobiivka	Ternopil
488	1	612	Ivachiv Horishnii	Ternopil
488	1	613	Ivachiv Dolishnii	Ternopil
488	1	652–3	Kutkivtsi	Ternopil
488	1	673	Mykulyntsi	Ternopil
488	1	756	Zbarazh Staryi [originally spelled Staryi Zbarazh?]	Ternopil
488	1	1070–1	Trybukhivtsi	Chortkiv
488	1	1093–4	Khorostkiv	Chortkiv
488	1	1123–4	Iabluniv	Chortkiv

reports, which I was denied, would have provided a surer picture of trends in the development of reading clubs. It should be noted that the documentation from the interwar period, which I only glanced at, contains more detailed information about individuals in local reading club administrations than do the prewar reports.

(The holdings of TsDIAL, fond 488, have already been discussed in connection with TsDIAL, fond 168 [the lists of former serfs prepared by the indemnization commission in the 1850s].)

Important sources in TsDIAL to which I was altogether denied access, probably because they are not yet well catalogued, are the metric books (U *Metrychni knyhy*), that is, books originating in the parish chancery and registering births and baptisms, marriages and deaths. Even selectively consulted, these books would have allowed me to determine the age and family background of peasant-activists with more precision than I have.

The Lviv Oblast State Archives (U *Lvivskyi oblasnyi derzhavnyi arkhiv*; abbreviated as LODA) concentrate more on the interwar period of Polish rule in Galicia than on the Austrian period.[4] But LODA does have some government records from before the First World War. I used records of the Zhovkva magistrate (R *Magistrat g. Zholkvy*), LODA, fond 10, which included documents relating to the real estate owned by the city of Zhovkva, 1869–1928 (opys 1, od. zb. 13, 18, 29, 33, 48–9, 81–3, 99, 114–15, 129, 149). It was possible to find some information here on peasants who were local activists of the Ukrainian movment in Vynnyky, a suburban village incorporated into the city of Zhovkva.

There was another Vynnyky, in Lviv district, which was the seat of a district court (R *Povetovyi sud v Vinnikakh*). Its papers are housed in LODA, fond 102. They provided no information directly relevant to this study, but they did contain four items that would have been extremely useful had they concerned the right villages. These were the Minutes of the Commission [of the district court] on Entering Registration into the Land (Hypothecary) Books (R *Protokoly kommissii o vnesenii zapisei v zemelnye [ipotechnye] knigi*) of the villages of Vovkiv, Zhyravka, Zahirie and Pidtemne for 1880 (opys 1, od. zb. 1–4). For each village there was a book listing every parcel of rustical land, its size, its former owner (in 1865) and its current owner. The parcels of land were numbered, and the order of the entries follows their numeration. This source, had it extended to villages for which I had recorded activists, would have provided exact information on the economic status of peasant-activists and indirect information on their age. The staff of LODA informed me that only these four books had somehow been preserved in the archives.

The records of the Directorate of the Lviv Police (R *Direktsiia politsii v Lvove*) are in LODA, fond 350. The few papers to which I had access (opys 1, od. zb. 2706–7, 2806, 4916–7, 4920) proved of little relevance to this study.

Valuable unpublished sources were found in the Manuscript Division (U *Viddil rukopysiv*) of the V. Stefanyk Lviv Scientific Library of the Academy of Sciences of the Ukrainian SSR (U *Lvivska naukova biblioteka im. V. Stefanyka Akademii nauk URSR*; abbreviated as LNB AN URSR).[5] The Ivan Omelianovych Levytstky

---

[4] See the published guide to these archives: *Lvivskyi oblasnyi derzhavnyi arkhiv. Putivnyk* (Lviv: Kameniar, 1965).

[5] P.H. Babiak, "Avtohrafy ukrainskykh pysmennykiv u viddili rukopysiv," in *Skarbnytsia znan. Tematychnyi zbirnyk naukovykh prats*, ed. V.V. Mashotas *et. al.* (Lviv: Akademiia nauk Ukrainskoi RSR, Lvivska naukova biblioteka im. V. Stefanyka, 1972), 78–82. O.O. Dzioban, *Osobysti arkhivni fondy viddilu rukopysiv. Anotovanyi pokazhchyk* (Lviv: Akademiia nauk

TABLE 18 TsDIAL, 348/1 (Prosvita, Reports from Reading Clubs); Holdings Consulted

Fond	Opys	Od. zb.	Village	District	Years
348	1	1050	Bereziv Nyzhnii	Kolomyia/Pechenizhyn	1902–37
348	1	1297	Brovary	Buchach	1901–37
348	1	1319	Briukhovychi	Peremyshliany	1896–1939
348	1	1479	Vydyniv	Sniatyn	1899–1938
348	1	1498	Vysloboky	Lviv	1896–1936
348	1	1624	Volytsia	Zhovkva	1903–38
348	1	1627	Volytsia	Sanok	1903–35
348	1	2439	Zhuzhil	Sokal	1901–39
348	1	2846	Kiidantsi	Zbarazh	1898–1939
348	1	2900	Kovalivka	Kolomyia/Pechenizhyn	1900–37
348	1	2936	Kolodribka	Zalishchyky	1897–1938
348	1	3031	Korelychi	Peremyshliany	1896–1938
348	1	4914	Saranchuky	Berezhany	1902–39
348	1	4921	Svarychiv	Dolyna	1897–1936
348	1	5874	Khorostkiv	Husiatyn	1901–37
348	1	6127	Iabloniv	Kolomyia/Pechenizhyn	1892–1937
348	1	6169	Iazhiv Staryi	Iavoriv	1897–1939

collection (U *fond I.O. Levytskoho*), sprava 6, papka 2, contained the unpublished continuation for 1894 of Levytsky's detailed bibliography of Ukrainian publications appearing in Austria-Hungary (U *Materialy do ukr[ainskoi] bibliohrafii Avstro-Uhorshchyny, 1894*; abbreviated as Lev3).

Also among his papers, sprava 290, papka 1, was a notebook labelled an Alphabetical List of Ukrainian Authors (U *Alfavitnyi spysok ukrainskykh avtoriv, skladenyi za danymy halytskoi presy za 1863–1895 rr., 'Istorii literatury' Ohonovskoho ta in. dlia biohrafichnoho slovnyka*). The list is not limited to authors at all, and I suspect that it represents an attempt by Levytsky to establish who should have been included in his massive, never-completed biographical dictionary.

Levytsky's biographical dictionary (U *Materialy do biohrafichnoho slovnyka*) is housed not with his own papers, but with the papers of the Shevchenko Scientific Society: LNB AN URSR, Viddil rukopysiv, fond 1 (NTSh), sprava 493 (abbreviated as Lev493). The energetic Levytsky had decided to compile a biographical dictionary of Ukrainians in the Habsburg empire, but, after collecting numerous autobiographical letters, press clippings, portraits and other materials, he abandoned his labours.[6] What he did collect has been preserved and arranged in modern Ukrainian alphabetical order. Levytsky gathered information on many lesser figures in the Ukrainian movement, including dozens of the village activists of the 1880s. The language of the documentation is almost exclusively Ukrainian. I did not have access to the entire collection, but had to request individual files by name. This is why I had to rely on the names listed in the Alphabetical List of Ukrainian Authors mentioned above.

Also in the manuscript division of the LNB AN URSR are the archives of the Counts Potocki of Łańcut (U *Arkhiv hrafiv Pototskykh z Lantsuta* or simply *fond Pototskykh*).[7] I used materials on leaseholding (U *orenda*), which revealed the close political links between landlords and tavernkeepers (no. 277, 292). The materials are primarily in Polish with some German.

Very useful were the papers of the Zaklynsky family (U *fond Zaklynskykh*), also in the manuscript division of the LNB AN URSR. Especially interesting were the letters of the teacher-activist Maksym Krushelnytsky to Leonid Zaklynsky (no. 192, papka 31), in which various activists and activities of the reading clubs were discussed frankly. The Zaklynsky papers also contain a few letters from the seminarian-activist Bohdar Kyrchiv (no. 193, papka 31). The letters are in Ukrainian.

---

[5](continued) Ukrainskoi RSR, Lvivska naukova biblioteka im. V. Stefanyka, 1977). Patricia Kennedy Grimsted, "The Stefanyk Library of the Ukrainian Academy of Sciences: A Treasury of Manuscript Collections in Lviv," *Harvard Ukrainian Studies* 5, no. 2 (June 1981): 195–229.

[6] Ia.R. Dashkevych, "Materialy I.O. Levytskoho iak dzherelo dlia biohrafichnoho slovnyka," *Istorychni dzherela ta ikh vykorystannia*, vyp. 2 (Kiev: Naukova dumka, 1966): 35–53. See also Magocsi, "Nationalism and National Bibliography," 95–100.

[7] Ie. Humeniuk, "Arkhiv Pototskykh," *Naukovo-informatsiinyi biuleten Arkhivnoho upravlinnia URSR* 17, no. 4 (60) (July-August 1963): 57–65.

II. Corpus of Correspondence

Batkivshchyna 6 (1884)

no. 1 (4 January 1884 [23 December 1883])

1. Ilko Sheshor, "Pysmo z Bohorodchanskoho," 4–5.
2. Pryiatel, "Pysmo vid Obertyna," 5.
3. Ivan Ivanets, "Pysmo vid Sokalia," 6.
4. [Mykolai] Basaichuk, "Pysmo vid Nadvirnoi," 6.

no. 2 (11 January 1884 [30 December 1883])

5. Chlen chytalni, "Pysmo vid Zhovkvy," 10.
6. Chlen chytalni, "Pysmo vid Khorostkova," l0.
7. Tanas, "Pysmo vid Zalozets," 11.

no. 3 (18 [6] January 1884)

8. Myroliub, "Pysmo z mistochka," 16.
9. Nykolai, "Pysmo z Komarna," 16–17.
10. Chlen chytalni, "Pysmo vid Iarychova," 18.

no. 4 (25 [l3] January 1884)

11. Avksentii, "Pysmo z Ternopolia," 22.
12. Z vydilu chytalni, "Pysmo vid Nadvirnoi," 22.

no. 5 (1 February [20 January] 1884)

13. Radnyi, "Pysmo z-pid Burshtyna," 27.
14. Luka Tomashevsky, diak i pysar, "Pysmo vid Uhnova," 27–8.
15. Maksym Krushelnytsky [Andriichuk], "Pysmo z Horodenky," 28.
16. Svii, "Pysmo vid Buchacha," 28–9.

no. 6 (8 February [27 January] 1884)

17. V.V., starshii brat, "Pysmo vid Zhydacheva," 34.
18. Kamianetskii Bobroid, "Pysmo z Ravskoho," 34–5.

no. 7 (15 [3] February 1884)

19. M. Seliukh, "Pysmo z-pid Zborova," 40–1.
20. Selianyn, "Pysmo vid Berezhan," 41.
21. Iurii Kekosh z Khorostkova, "Pysmo z Khorostkova," 41–2.

no. 8 (22 [10] February 1884)

22. Chytalnyk, "Pysmo vid Nadvirnoi," 46.
23. Radnyi, "Pysmo vid Rohatyna," 46.
24. Radnyi, "Pysmo vid Zabolotova," 46–7.

no. 9 (29 [17] February 1884)

25. O.I., "Pysmo z Staromiskoho povitu," 52–3.
26. Ilko Sheshor, "Pysmo z Bohorodchanskoho," 53.
27. [Kost Vykhtorivsky], "Pysmo vid Halycha. I," 53–4.

no. 10 (7 March [24 February] 1884)

28. I.V., "Pysmo vid Rozdolu," 58.
29. Hromadiane Zakomarski, "Pysmo vid Ozhydova," 58–9.

no. 11 (14 [2] March 1884)

30. Kost Vykhtorivsky, "Pysmo vid Halycha. II," 64.
31. Selianyn, "Pysmo vid Kalusha," 64–5.
32. Kost Kyrchiv, selianyn, "Pysmo vid Skoleho," 65.
33. Susid, "Pysmo vid Dolyny," 65–6.

no. 12 (21 [9] March 1884)

34. Stryian, "Pysmo z Stryiskoho," 69–70.
35. Radnyi, "Pysmo vid Shchyrtsia," 70.
36. Selianyn, "Pysmo vid Zolocheva," 70.

no. 13 (28 [16] March 1884)

37. Tymkovych, "Pysmo z Ravskoho," 75.
38. "Pysmo z-nad Dnistra. I," 76.
39. Iu.M., "Pysmo vid Rohatyna," 76.
40. Iliarion Sichynsky, "Pysmo z Stryiskoho," 76–7.
41. Chytalnyk, "Pysmo z-pid Zalozets," 77.

no. 14 (4 April [23 March] 1884)

42. Ivan Petryshyn [Liubomir Seliansky], "Pysmo z Zolochivskoho," 82.
43. Andrii Bolekhivsky, "Pysmo vid Zhuravna," 82–3.

no. 15 (11 April [30 March] 1884)

44. Ks[ondz], "Pysmo z Ternopilshchyny," 89–90.
45. "Pysmo z-nad Dnistra. II," 90.
46. K.K.H., chleny chytalni, "Pysmo z Dolynskoho," 90.

no. 16 (18 [6] April 1884)

47. Pidhirianyn, "Pysmo z sela," 97–8.
48. Susid, "Pysmo z Iazlivtsia," 98.
49. Vasylii Holovka, "Pysmo z Ravskoho," 98.
50. K.V., "Pysmo vid Kalusha," 99.

no. 17 (25 [13] April 1884)

51. Pavlo Pidrichny, z-nad Solokii, "Pysmo vid Ravy-ruskoi," 102–3.

no. 18 (2 May [20 April] 1884)

52. Chlen chytalni, "Pysmo vid Radekhova," 106.

no. 19 (9 May [27 April] 1884)

53. Chlen chytalni v Vynnykakh, "Pysmo z Zhovkvy," 112.
54. Pysmennyi, "Pysmo vid Burshtyna," 112–13.
55. Seliukh, "Pysmo vid Nadvirnoi," 113–14.

no. 20 (16 [4] May 1884)

56. Vl.R., "Pysmo z Zhydachivskoho," 118.
57. "Pysmo vid Peremyshlian," 118–19.
58. Oden, "Pysmo vid Nadvirnoi," 119.

no. 21 (23 [11] May 1884)

59. Ochevydets, "Pysmo vid Belza," 128.
60. Pravdoliub [=Hospodar], "Pysmo vid Tovmacha," 128–9.
61. "Pysmo z Rohatynskoho povitu," 129–30.

no. 22 (30 [18] May 1884)

62. Zar., "Pysmo vid Stanyslavova," 130 [sic; pages repeated].
63. Kls., "Pysmo vid Drohobycha," 130.
64. K.Kh., "Pysmo vid Kalusha," 131.

no. 23 (6 June [30 (sic; should be 25) May] 1884)

65. Vl.R., "Pysmo z Zhydachivskoho," 136.
66. "Pysmo vid Staroho-mista. I," 136–7.
67. [Hryhorii Tymchuk], "Pysmo vid Zalishchyk. I," 137–8.
68. Sm., "Pysmo vid Khorostkova," 138.

no. 24 (13 [1] June 1884)

69. Val., "Pysmo vid Ternopolia," 142–3.
70. Bohdan z-nad Okopu, "Pysmo vid Stryia," 143.
71. Susid, "Pysmo z Bridshchyny," 143.

no. 25 (20 [8] June 1884)

72. "Pysmo vid Staroho mista. II," 148.
73. [Hryhorii Tymchuk], "Pysmo vid Zalishchyk. II," 148–9.
74. "Pysmo vid Ravy," 149.
75. Zhychlyvyi, "Pysmo z Buchatskoho," 149–50.

no. 26 (27 [15] June 1884)

76. Hryhorii Tymchuk, uchytel i radnyi, "Pysmo vid Zalishchyk. III," 156.
77. Trokhym, hospodar, "Pysmo vid Ternopolia," 156–7.
78. Pravdoliub [=Hospodar], "Pysmo vid Tovmacha," 157–8.
79. Oden z chleniv [rady povitovoi], "Pysmo z Ravskoho," 158.

no. 27 (4 July [22 June] 1884)

80. Ivan Tverdyi, "Pysmo vid Zbarazha," 164.
81. Iakov Loza, "Pysmo z Ravskoho," 164–5.
82. I.K., "Pysmo vid Strusova," 165.
83. "Pysmo vid Iarycheva," 165–6.

no. 28 (11 July [29 June] 1884)

84. M[ykhailo] S[yvy], chytalnyk, "Pysmo z Peremyshlianskoho," 172.
85. I. Zvarych, dvernyk ruskoi seminarii dukhovnoi, "Pysmo zi Lvova," 172–3.
86. R., "Pysmo vid Stanislavova," 173.
87. Svii, "Pysmo vid Tartakova," 173.
88. Roz., "Pysmo z Bohorodchanskoho," 173–4.

no. 29 (18 [6] July 1884)

89. Pravdoliub, "Pysmo z pid Horodka," 181–2.

no. 30 (25 [13] July 1884)

90. "Pysmo z Husiatynskoho," 186–7.

no. 31 (1 August [20 July] 1884)

91. Vyborets, "Pysmo vid Kalusha. I," 192–4.
92. [Atanas Melnyk], "Pysmo z pid Drohobycha," 194.

no. 32 (8 August [27 July] 1884)

93. Vyborets, "Pysmo vid Kalusha. II," 198–9.

no. 33 (15 [3] August 1884)

94. "Pysmo zi Zbarazhskoho," 204.
95. "Pysmo z Kolomyishchyny," 204–5.
96. Druh naroda, "Pysmo z Mykulynets," 205.
97. Ochevydets, "Pysmo vid Borshcheva," 205–6.

no. 34 (22 [10] August 1884)

98. I.I.V., "Pysmo z Zhydachivskoho," 210–11.

no. 35 (29 [17] August 1884)

99. Iosyf Byliv, pivets z Burkanova, "Pysmo z Zhydachivskoho," 216–17.
100. "Pysmo vid Horodka," 217.
101. Drozdivets, "Pysmo vid Horodka," 217–18.

no. 36 (24 August [5 September] 1884)

102. I.I.V., "Pysmo z Zhydachivskoho," 222–3.

(no. 37 contained no items of correspondence)

no. 38 (19 [7] September 1884)

103. Iosyf Byliv, pivets z Burkanova, "Pysmo vid Pidhaiets," 232.
104. K.A. Lisovyk, "Pysmo vid Buchacha," 233.
105. Hryhorii Senyshyn, "Pysmo vid Shchyrtsia," 233.
106. Danylo Saikevych, "Pysmo z Sokalshchyny," 233–4.

no. 39 (26 [14] September 1884)

107. Selianyn, "Pysmo vid Skoleho. I," 240–1.
108. Chytalnyk, "Pysmo vid Ternopolia," 241–2.
109. Pravdoliub, "Pysmo z-pid Radekhova," 242.

no. 40 (3 October [21 September] 1884)

110. Selianyn, "Pysmo vid Skolioho. II," 245.

no. 41 (10 October [28 September] 1884)

111. I.I.V., "Pysmo z Zhydachivskoho," 253–4.
112. Ivan Pidhliadaiko, hospodar, "Pysmo z Zborova," 254.
113. M.V., "Pysmo z Tysmenytsi," 255.

no. 42 (17 [4] October 1884)

114. Pravdoliub, "Pysmo vid Radekhova," 261–2.

no. 43 (24 [12] October 1884)

115. Teofan Hlynsky [Oden z prytomnykh], "Pysmo z Husiatynskoho," 267.

no. 44 (31 [19] October 1884)

116. [Mykhailo Pikh], "Pysmo vid Mostysk. I," 274–5.
117. O.T.P., "Pysmo z sela," 275–6.
118. Hospodar [=Pravdoliub], "Pysmo vid Tovmacha," 276.

no. 45 (7 November [26 October] 1884)

119. Mykhailo Pikh, provizor tserkovnyi i zastupnyk korporatsii tserkovnoi do provadzhenia torhovli, "Pysmo vid Mostysk. II," 282–3.
120. Nadsianenko, "Pysmo vid Peremyshlia," 283.
121. Kalushanyn, "Pysmo vid Kalusha," 283–4.

no. 46 (14 [2] November 1884)

122. Vid vydilu chytalni "imeny Shevchenka" v Dobrostanakh; Ivan Khoma, sekretar, Petro Forlita, zastupnyk holovy, Hryhorii Andriyshyn, zastupnyk sekretaria, "Pysmo vid Horodka," 291.
123. Pryiatel, "Pysmo vid Zborova," 291–2.

124. Prokip Zeleny, "Pysmo z Chortkivskoho," 292.
125. Hospodar, "Pysmo vid Rozdolu," 292–3.

no. 47 (21 [9] November 1884)

126. Teodor Ianishevsky, predsidatel tymchas[ovoho] komitetu, "Pysmo z Zolocheva," 296.
127. N., "Pysmo vid Krystynopolia," 296.

no. 48 (28 [16] November 1884)

128. I.I.V., "Pysmo vid Zhydacheva," 301–2.
129. "Pysmo vid Husiatyna," 302–3.
130. Ivan Mikhas [Ivan z nad Dnistra], "Pysmo z Sambirshchyny," 303.
131. Nykyta, chlen chytalni, "Pysmo z Sokalshchyny," 303–4.

no. 49 (5 December [23 November] 1884)

132. Susid, "Pysmo vid Rohatyna," 308–9.

no. 50 (12 December [30 November] 1884)

133. Ivan Mikhas [Ivan z nad Dnistra], "Pysmo z Sambirshchyny. I," 312–13.

no. 51 (19 [7] December 1884)

134. Ivan Mikhas [Ivan z-nad Dnistra], "Pysmo z Sambirshchyny. II," 317–18.
135. Toi sam, "Pysmo z Zolocheva," 318.
136. N., "Pysmo vid Krystynopolia," 318–19.
137. M[ykolai] L[un] i A[ntin] H[avlytsky], "Pysmo z Ravskoho," 319.

no. 52 (26 [14] December 1884)

138. Osnovateli, "Pysmo vid Kolomyi," 324.

Batkivshchyna 7 (1885)

no. 1 (2 January 1885 [21 December 1884])

139. Vyborets, "Pysmo z Bobretskoho," 4.
140. Ochevydets, "Pysmo vid Mykulynets," 5.

no. 2 (9 January 1885 [28 December 1884])

141. Hospodar oden v imeny mnohykh, "Pysmo vid Dobromylia," 11–12.
142. Chlen chytalni, "Pysmo z Iavorova," 12.
143. Chlen chytalni, "Pysmo vid Halycha," 12–13.

no. 3 (16 [4] January 1885)

144. Toi sam, "Pysmo z-nad Buha. I," 19–20.
145. Atanas Melnyk [Chytalnyky], "Pysmo vid Drohobycha," 20–21.
146. Vasyl Fedorovych, "Pysmo vid Horodka," 21.

no. 4 (23 [11] January 1885)

147. Oleksa Zhuk, "Pysmo vid Zbarazha," 28–9.
148. Toi sam, "Pysmo z-nad Buha. II," 29.
149. Oden z prytomnykh, "Pysmo z Stryiskoho," 29–30.

no. 5 (30 [18] January 1885)

150. Teofan Hlynsky [Sviashchenyk], "Pysmo vid Horodenka," 36.
151. Hospodar, "Pysmo vid Pidhaiets. I," 36–7.
152. Diak, "Pysmo vid Buchacha," 37.

no. 6 (6 February [25 January] 1885)

153. Chlen chytalni, "Pysmo z-pid Zhovkvy," 44–5.
154. S[tefan] L[esiuk], "Pysmo vid Zolocheva," 45.
155. Pryiatel, "Pysmo vid Kalusha," 45–6.

no. 7 (13 [1] February 1885)

156. Ochevydets, "Pysmo z Ternopilshchyny," 52–3.
157. N.-i, "Pysmo z Dolynskoho," 53.
158. Narodovets, "Pysmo vid Kalusha," 53–4.
159. Oden z hostei, "Pysmo z Kamenetskoho," 54.

no. 8 (20 [8] February 1885)

160. Sviashchenyk T[eofan] H[lynsky], "Pysmo vid Horodenky," 60–1.
161. Pastukh z-nad Limnyts, "Pysma vid Kalusha. I," 61.
162. Havriyl Posatsky, diak, pysar i holova chytalni, "Pysma vid Kalusha. II," 61.

no. 9 (27 [15] February 1885)

163. Matvii [Kamianetsky], "Pysmo z Ravskoho," 68–9.
164. "Pysma z Kolomyishchyny. I," 69.
165. [Kr.], "Pysma z Kolomyishchyny. II," 69.

no. 10 (6 March [22 February] 1885)

166. Vasyl, hospodar, "Pysmo z Pidhaiechchyny," 75–6.
167. Druh dobrykh liudei, "Pysmo z-pid Karpat," 76–7.
168. N.Iu.S., "Pysmo z-za Kolomyi," 77.
169. [Kr.], "Pysma z Kolomyishchyny. III-IV," 77–78.

no. 11 (13 [1] March 1885)

170. N., "Pysmo z Sokalshchyny," 83–4.
171. Ochevydets, "Pysmo z Kamianetskoho," 84.
172. [Kr.], "Pysmo z Kolomyishchyny. V-VI," 84–5.
173. Aleksii Maneliuk, chlen chytalni, "Pysmo vid Kalusha," 85.
174. N.Iu.S., "Pysmo z-za Kolomyi," 85–6.

no. 12 (20 [8] March 1885)

175. [K.S.T.A.Kh.Zh.], "Pysmo z Ternopilshchyny. I," 92–3.
176. Ihnat Polotniuk, diak i uchytel spivu, "Pysmo z Krystynopolia," 92–3.
177. [Kr.], "Pysma z Kolomyishchyny. VII," 93–4.

no. 13 (27 [15] March 1885)

178. Selianyn, "Pysmo z Pidhiria. I," 99–100.
179. Chlen Tovarystva rybatskoho, "Pysmo z Podillia," 100.
180. [K.S.T.A.Kh.Zh.], "Pysmo z Ternopilshchyny. II," 100.
181. [Kr.], "Pysma z Kolomyishchyny. VIII," 101.

no. 14 (3 April [22 March] 1885)

182. Selianyn, "Pysmo z Pidhiria. II," 109.
183. [Kr.], "Pysma z Kolomyishchyny. IX," 109–10.

no. 15 (10 April [29 March] 1885)

184. K.S.T.A.Kh.Zh., "Pysmo z Ternopilshchyny. III," 114–15.

no. 16 (17 [5] April 1885)

185. [Kr.], "Pysma z Kolomyishchyny. X," 119–20.
186. Ivan Korchemny, "Pysmo vid Brodiv," 120.
187. Teodor Ianishevsky, Iliia Menchakevych, Stefan Monchalovsky, "Pysmo vid Zborova," 120–1.
188. Susid, "Pysmo z Sokalshchyny," 121.

no. 17 (24 [12] April 1885)

189. "Pysmo z Ternopilshchyny," 128.
190. Kr., "Pysma z Kolomyishchyny. XI-XIII," 128–9.

no. 18 (1 May [19 April] 1885)

191. Luka Tomashevsky vid Uhnova, "Pysmo z Ravskoho," 137–8.
192. Symeon Tsypivko, pysar i diak, "Pysmo z Iavorivskoho," 138.

no. 19 (8 May [26 April] 1885)

193. Nkch., "Pysmo z Sokalshchyny," 146.
194. Chytalnyk, "Pysmo z Verkhovyny," 146.

no. 20 (15 [3] May 1885)

195. Iliia Boikevych, pivets z Rohatyna, "Pysmo z Rohatyna," 151.

no. 21 (22 [10] May 1885)

196. V., "Pysmo z Zhovkivskoho," 155.
197. M.S., K.P., R.L., mishchane, "Pysmo z Radekhova," 156.
198. Susid, "Pysmo z Bridshchyny," 156–7.

no. 22 (29 [17] May 1885)

199. Pravyborets, "Pysmo z Rohatynskoho," 162–3.

no. 23 (5 June [4 May] 1885)

200. "Pysmo z Bridshchyny," 168–9.
201. Oden z prysutnykh, "Pysmo z pid Brodiv," 169–70.
202. Mishchanyn iazlovetskii, "Pysmo vid Buchacha," 170.

no. 24 (12 June [31 May] 1885)

203. Pryiatel narodu i buvshii vyborets, "Pysmo z Dolynshchyny," 175–6.
204. Vyborets, "Pysmo z Sokalshchyny," 177.
205. "Pysmo z Ravskoho," 177–8.
206. Prysutnyi, "Pysmo z kolomyiskoho Pidhiria," 178.
207. Susid, "Pysmo z-nad Zbrucha," 178–9.

no. 25 (19 [7] June 1885)

208. Vyborets, "Pysmo z Bobretskoho," 183.
209. H., "Pysmo vid Horodenky," 183–4.
210. Luka Tomashevsky z Novosilok, "Pysma z Ravskoho. I," 184.
211. Matvii Kamianetsky, "Pysma z Ravskoho. II," 184.
212. Ivan Svii, "Pysmo z Belzkoho," 184–5.

no. 26 (26 [14] June 1885)

213. Vyborets, "Pysmo vid Drohobycha," 191–2.
214. Pravdoliub, "Pysmo z-pid Radekhova," 192.
215. Teodor Ianishevsky, ispytovanyi pivets tserk[ovnyi] v Zborovi, "Pysmo vid Zborova," 192.
216. Zemliak, "Pysmo z nad Buha," 192–3.
217. "Pysmo vid Iarycheva," 193.

no. 27 (3 July [21 June] 1885)

218. Skalatskii mishchanyn, "Pysmo z Skalatshchyny," 197–8.
219. Atanas Melnyk [Chytalnyk], "Pysmo vid Drohobycha," 198.

no. 28 (10 July [28 June] 1885)

220. Hospodar, "Pysmo z-pid Terebovli," 203.
221. Vyborets, "Pysmo z-pid Hrymalova," 203.
222. Mishchanyn, "Pysmo z Radekhova," 203–4.
223. "Pysmo vid Stanislavova," 204.
224. Pryiatel prosvity, "Pysmo z Zolochivskoho," 204–5.

no. 29 (17 [5] July 1885)

225. "Pysmo z Zhovkvy," 211–12.
226. Vyborets, "Pysmo z pid Sokalia," 212.
227. Vyborets Sava Spravedlyvyi, "Pysmo z Ravskoho," 212.
228. Staryi znakomyi, "Pysmo vid Kalusha," 212–13.

no. 30 (24 [12] July 1885)

229. "Pysmo z Stanyslavova. [I]," 219.

no. 31 (19 [31] July 1885)

230. "Pysmo z Stanyslavova. [II]," 222.
231. P. Shchyryi, "Pysmo z Ravskoho," 222.

no. 32 (26 July [7 August] 1885)

232. "Pysmo z Kopechynets," 225–6.
233. Staryi znakomyi, "Pysmo vid Kalusha," 226.
234. "Pysmo z Hnizdycheva," 226.

no. 33 (2 [14] August 1885)

235. V[asyl Chernetsky], "Pysmo z Sokalshchyny," 230–1.
236. Chytalnyk, "Pysmo z Berezhnytsi," 231.

no. 34 (9 [21] August 1885)

237. Andrunyk z Chytalni, "Pysmo z Korelych," 234–5.
238. Roman Iskra, hospodar, "Pysmo z Piznanky," 235.

no. 35 (16 [28] August 1885)

239. Skalatskii mishchanyn, "Pysmo z Skalatshchyny," 238.
240. Petro Pravdoliub, "Pysmo z Rudna," 238–9.

no. 36 (4 September [23 August] 1885)

241. Chytalnyk, "Pysmo z Peremyshlianskoho," 242.
242. Ivan P., "Pysmo z Lvivskoho," 242.

no. 37 (11 September [30 August] 1885)

243. Dmytro Maksymovych, kasiier chytalni, "Pysmo z-pid Lvova," 249.
244. Iosyf Byliv, pivets z Burkanova, "Pysmo vid Pidhaiets," 249–50.

no. 38 (18 [6] September 1885)

245. I.Iu. z Voli-dobrostanskoi, "Pysmo vid Horodka," 256–7.
246. Mishchanyn, chlen upavshoi chytalni, "Pysmo z Horodenky," 257.

no. 39 (25 [13] September 1885)

247. Ivan Mikhas [Ivan z-nad Dnistra], "Pysmo z Sambirshchyny," 264–5.
248. Vid vydilu Chytalni ruskoi: Iliia Myroniuk, Vasyl Kovbuz, Petro Kotyk, "Pysmo z Horodenky," 265.

no. 40 (2 October [20 September] 1885)

249. Mishchanyn Ternopilskii, "Pysmo z Ternopolia," 272.
250. Blyzkii, "Pysmo z-pid Stanislavova," 272–3.

no. 41 (9 October [27 September] 1885)

251. Hospodar, "Pysmo z Skalatshchyny," 279–80.
252. Chytalnyky, "Pysmo z Sokalshchyny," 281.

no. 42 (16 [4] October 1885)

253. Volod[ymyr] Maksymovych, "Pysmo z sela. I," 288.
254. T.P., "Pysmo z Sianitskoho," 288–9.
255. V[asyl Chernetsky], "Pysmo z Sokalshchyny," 289.

no. 43 (24 [12] October 1885)

256. Volod[ymyr] Maksymovych, "Pysmo z sela. II," 296–7.
257. [B.T.N.], "Pysmo z Dolynskoho. I," 297.

no. 44 (30 [18] October 1885)

258. B.T.N., "Pysmo z Dolynskoho. II," 304–5.
259. Iliia Boikevych, sekretar zboru, "Pysmo z Rohatyna," 305.
260. Chytalnyk i buvshii hromadianyn Kovalivskii, "Pysmo z Kolomyiskoho Pidhiria," 305–6.

no. 45 (6 November [25 October] 1885)

261. S., "Pysmo z-pid Belza," 310.
262. Danylo Taniachkevych, "Pysmo z sela," 310–11.

no. 46 (13 [1] November 1885)

263. Chytalnyk, "Pysmo z Kolomyiskoho Pidhiria," 317.
264. Kop., "Pysmo z-pid Halycha," 317–18.
265. Maksym Zukh, "Pysmo vid Berezhan," 318.

no. 47 (20 [8] November 1885)

266. "Zi Lvova," 324–5.
267. Ivan S., "Pysmo z Peremyshlianskoho," 325.
268. Ivan Petryshyn [Liubomir Seliansky], "Pysmo z Zolochivskoho," 325–6.

no. 48 (27 [15] November 1885)

269. Dmytrovets, "Pysmo vid Radekhova," 330.
270. --i --i, "Pysmo vid Kalusha," 330.

no. 49 (4 December [27 (sic; should be 22) November] 1885)

271. Luka Pavliv, chlen chytalni, "Pysmo z-pid Brodiv," 337.
272. Pravdoliub, "Pysmo z Mykulynets," 337–8.
273. Ivan Mikhas [Ivan z-nad Dnistra], "Pysmo z Sambirshchyny," 338.
274. --i --i, "Pysmo vid Kalusha," 338.

no. 50 (11 December [29 November] 1885)

275. Ivan Petryshyn [Liubomir Seliansky], "Pysmo z-nad Buha," 342–3.
276. Hist, "Pysmo z Sokalshchyny," 343.

no. 51 (18 [6] December 1885)

277. Holovchuk, sekretar chytalni, "Pysma z Sokalshchyny. I. Z Ordova," 348.
278. "Pysma z Sokalshchyny. II. Z Krystynopolia," 348–9.
279. "Pysma z Sokalshchyny. III. Z Ostrova," 349.
280. Mishchanyn, "Pysmo z Buska," 349.

no. 52 (25 [13] December 1885)

281. L-k-v, selianyn, "Pysmo z Berezhanshchyny," 354–5.

III. Correspondence by Occupation of Authors

1. Teacher
3. Merchant
4. Teacher
11. Burgher
14. Cantor and scribe (one author)
15. Teacher
20. Peasant
21. Peasant and cobbler (one author)
26. Teacher
31. Peasant
32. Peasant
34. Peasant
36. Peasant
38. Peasant
40. Priest
42. Teacher
43. Teacher
44. Priest
45. Peasant
47. Peasant
49. Peasant
60. Peasant
67. Teacher
73. Teacher
76. Teacher
77. Peasant
78. Peasant
81. Scribe
84. Peasant
85. Cantor
92. Peasant and cantor (one author)
94. Peasant
96. Burgher
99. Cantor

103. Cantor
105. Peasant
106. Cantor
107. Peasant
110. Peasant
112. Peasant
115. Priest
116. Merchant
118. Peasant
119. Merchant
122. Cantor and two peasants (three authors)
125. Peasant
126. Cantor
130. Peasant
133. Peasant
134. Peasant
137. Peasant and teacher (two authors)
141. Peasant
146. Cantor and peasant (one author)
150. Priest
151. Peasant
152. Cantor
154. Priest
160. Priest
161. Priest
162. Cantor and scribe (one author)
166. Peasant
167. Peasant
173. Peasant
176. Cantor
178. Peasant
182. Peasant
186. Cantor
187. Cantor
191. Cantor and scribe (one author)
192. Cantor, scribe and peasant (one author)
195. Cantor
197. Burgher
199. Peasant
202. Burgher
210. Cantor and scribe (one author)
215. Cantor
218. Burgher
220. Peasant
222. Burgher
235. Priest
237. Peasant
238. Peasant
239. Burgher
240. Peasant
243. Peasant

244. Cantor
246. Burgher
247. Peasant
248. Peasant
249. Burgher
251. Peasant
255. Priest
259. Cantor
262. Priest
268. Teacher
271. Peasant
273. Peasant
275. Teacher
280. Burgher
281. Peasant

Peasants

20, 31, 32, 34, 36, 38, 45, 47, 49, 60, 77, 78, 84, 94, 105, 107, 110, 112, 118, 125, 130, 133, 134, 141, 151, 166, 167, 173, 178, 182, 199, 220, 237, 238, 240, 243, 247, 248, 251, 271, 273, 281

(More than one occupation or more than one author)

21. (and cobbler, one author)
92. (and cantor, one author)
122. (two peasants and cantor, three authors)
137. (and teacher, two authors)
146. (and cantor, one author)
192. (and cantor and scribe, one author)

Cantors

85, 99, 103, 106, 126, 152, 176, 186, 187, 195, 215, 244, 259

(More than one occupation or more than one author)

14. (and scribe, one author)
92. (and peasant, one author)
122. (and two peasants, three authors)
146. (and peasant, one author)
162. (and scribe, one author)
191. (and scribe, one author)
192. (and scribe and peasant, one author)
210. (and scribe, one author)

Teachers

1, 4, 15, 26, 42, 43, 67, 73, 76, 268, 275

(More than one author)

137. (and peasant, two authors)

Burghers and Artisans
11, 96, 197, 202, 218, 222, 239, 246, 249, 280

(More than one occupation)

21. (and peasant)

Priests
40, 44, 115, 150, 154, 160, 161, 235, 255, 262

Scribes
81.

(More than one occupation)
14.   (and cantor)
162. (and cantor)
191. (and cantor)
192. (and cantor and peasant)
210. (and cantor)

Merchants
3, 116, 119

IV. List of Activists

LOCATION: The main centre of the individual's activities, 1884-5.

OCCUPATION: This refers to occupations in 1884–5. Occupations appearing in parentheses signify that the given occupation is presumed rather than determined with certainty.

POSITION IN RC: Position in the reading club, 1884-5.

AUTHOR: Refers only to contribution of items of correspondence included in the corpus of correspondence.

POSITION IN LOCAL GOVT: Position in the communal (municipal) government.

DISTINGUISHING FEATURES: Such as *latynnyk*, *shliakhta khodachkova* or non-Ukrainian nationality.

FAMILY BACKGROUND.

FAMILY CONNECTIONS: With other activists.

ECONOMIC STATUS.

EDUCATION.

AGE: In the case of teachers, twenty-two is taken to be the most common age to begin teaching (see below *LA* 14, 29, 83, 178, 256, 340). In the case of peasants, twenty is taken to be the minimum age to come into land and twenty-five the most common age to marry and come into land.

DEATH.

MARITAL STATUS: Only for priests.

MOBILITY.

PUBLICATIONS: Refers only to items outside the corpus of correspondence.

OTHER ACTIVITIES: Refers to activities not included under other rubrics.

Amvrosii de Krushelnytsky

Danylo Taniachkevych (younger)

Kyrylo Genyk

Sylvester L. Drymalyk

Antin Rybachek

1. **Andriishyn, Hryhorii**

   LOCATION: Dobrostany, Horodok district. OCCUPATION: (Peasant). POSITION IN RC: Deputy administration (*CC* 100, 122). AUTHOR: *CC* 100 (coauthor). OTHER ACTIVITIES: Presented lecture in the reading club on Volodymyr Barvinsky, 1885 (*CC* 245).

2. **Andrukhovych**

   LOCATION: Tsvitova, Buchach district. OCCUPATION: (Peasant). AGE: Referred to as "young Andrukhovych" (*CC* 16). OTHER ACTIVITIES: Singled out as the main reformer in the village and backbone of the reading club.

3. **Andrunyk, Hrynko**

   LOCATION: Korelychi, Peremyshliany district. OCCUPATION: (Peasant, perhaps cantor). AUTHOR: *CC* 37 (signed only "Andrunyk z Chytalni"; the author may have been *Andrunyk, Ivan*). ECONOMIC STATUS: In 1864 he paid taxes of 4.9 gulden, which differed little from the average tax paid by the Greek Catholic parishioners of Korelychi, 4.7 gulden.[1] AGE: In 1864 he was already listed among the tax-paying Greek Catholic parishioners of Korelychi. Thus he had already come of age, which suggests that he was born in 1839 or earlier.[2] OTHER ACTIVITIES: Directed the reading club's choir in 1884.[3]

   1) TsDIAL, 146/64b/2294, pp. 54–61. *2) Ibid.*, p. 56v. *3)* Chytalnyk, "...vid Peremyshlian," *Batkivshchyna* 6, no. 46 (14 [2] November 1884): 294.

4. **Andrunyk, Ivan**

   LOCATION: Korelychi, Peremyshliany district. OCCUPATION: Peasant. POSITION IN RC: Librarian (*CC* 84). AUTHOR: *CC* 237 (possibly; see *Andrunyk, Hrynko*). ECONOMIC STATUS: Proprietor (*CC* 84). AGE: Probably born after 1839, since he had not come of age in 1864 (see *Andrunyk, Hrynko*).

5. **Antoniv, Martyn**

   LOCATION: Pochapy, Zolochiv district. OCCUPATION: (Peasant). POSITION IN RC: Secretary (*CC* 268).

6. **Babiak, Andrii**

   LOCATION: Kolodribka, Zalishchyky district. OCCUPATION: (Peasant). POSITION IN RC: Deputy administration (*CC* 76).

7. **Babynets, Ivan**

   LOCATION: Fytkiv, Nadvirna district. OCCUPATION: Nonpeasant (*CC* 58). POSITION IN RC: Treasurer (*CC* 58).

8. **Bakuska, Vasyl**

   LOCATION: Mykolaiv, Brody district. OCCUPATION: Peasant. ECONOMIC STATUS: A wealthy[1] proprietor (*CC* 198). AGE: Mentioned as a relatively new property-owner in a document from 1859, thus probably born c. 1834.[2] OTHER ACTIVITIES: Vice-president of Pravda society, 1884–5 (*CC* 71, 198).

   1) Tarnavsky, *Spohady*, 32. *2)* TsDIAL, 146/64/1124, p. 139v.

9. **Balaban, I.**

   LOCATION: Shliakhtyntsi, Ternopil district. OCCUPATION: (Peasant). POSITION IN RC: Librarian (*CC* 108).

10. **Balaban, R.**

    LOCATION: Shliakhtyntsi, Ternopil district. OCCUPATION: (Peasant). POSITION IN RC: Treasurer (*CC* 108).

11. **Balandiuk, Pavlo**

LOCATION: Utishkiv, Zolochiv district. OCCUPATION: Teacher, retired. POSITION IN RC: President (*CC* 216). POSITION IN LOCAL GOVT: Scribe. AGE: He had been teaching since at least the early 1870s and he retired by the 1880s.[1] He was therefore probably born sometime before 1850. MOBILITY: He was a teacher in the parish school in Kupche, Kaminka Strumylova district, in the early 1870s,[2] then moved to Obelnytsia, Rohatyn district,[3] and finished the 1870s teaching in Kozara, Rohatyn district.[4] He came to Utiskiv in March 1885 (*CC* 216). OTHER ACTIVITIES: Within three months of his arrival in Utishkiv he founded the reading club there (*CC* 216).

1) Szem. kr. Gal. 1871, 405; he is not listed in *ibid. 1881, 1884* or *1885*. *2) Ibid. 1871*, 405; *ibid. 1872*, 392; *ibid. 1873*, 396; *ibid. 1874*, 427. *3) Ibid. 1874*, 443 (he is listed twice in the 1874 schematism). *4) Ibid. 1877*, 435; *ibid. 1878*, 424; *ibid. 1879*, 417.

12. **Balias, Havrylo (Havrykh)**

LOCATION: Dobrostany, Horodok district. OCCUPATION: Peasant. POSITION IN RC: Treasurer (*CC* 100, 245). ECONOMIC STATUS: Proprietor. OTHER ACTIVITIES: He hosted the reading club in his home for at least a year (*CC* 100, 245).

13. **Balytsky, Aleksander**

LOCATION: Kolodribka, Zalishchyky district. OCCUPATION: Priest. POSITION IN RC: President (*CC* 76). ECONOMIC STATUS: Assistant in the parish of Synkiv, which had a daughter church in Kolodribka; together they had 3,728 members.[1] AGE: Born 1858, ordained 1879.[1] MARITAL STATUS: Married.

1) Shem. Lviv. 1884, 250.

14. **Banakh, Mykhail**

LOCATION: Rudno, Lviv district. OCCUPATION: Teacher. POSITION IN RC: Secretary (*CC* 243). FAMILY BACKGROUND: Son of peasants of moderate means (10 *Joch*).[1] EDUCATION: He finished the first three grades of elementary school in his native Vynnyky, Lviv district, where he was taught by a cantor. He finished the fourth grade and began attending gymnasium in Lviv. At that time instruction at the gymnasium was in German. During the fifth class of gymnasium he quit his studies in order to work as a teacher.[1] AGE: Born 13 November 1850 (O.S.).[1] DEATH: 24 March 1888 (O.S.); he died of typhus.[1] MOBILITY: Born in Vynnyky and educated in Lviv, he taught in Biała, Rzeszów district, for six or seven years and then in Vorotsiv, Horodok district, for three or four years. He came to Rudno in 1883 and stayed there until his death.[1] PUBLICATIONS: He contributed frequently to the pedagogical periodicals *Hazeta shkolna*, 1877–9,[2] and *Shkolna chasopys*, 1881–2, 1884–5.[3] He published new-year carols (U *shchedrivky*) from Rudno in *Zoria* in 1885[4] and articles on conservation in *Hospodar i promyshlennyk* in 1887.[5] He also sent items of correspondence to *Slovo*, 1881,[6] and *Novyi prolom*.[1] The Kachkovsky society published his booklet *Khlib nash nasushchnyi*[1] and the Vydavnytstvo narodne his *Velyki hroshi z maloho zakhodu* (Lviv, 1888).[7] OTHER ACTIVITIES: In the late 1870s, he taught in Biała, a Ukrainian village near Rzeszów. Here he acted as a missionary of Ruthenianism among the local Lemko population.[1] In 1877 he contributed an article to *Hazeta shkolna* on "The Ruthenians near Rzeszów."[8] He was one of the founders of the reading club in Rudno (*CC* 240).

1) Lev493, B-34. *2)* Lev1, no. 1654IV, 1787I, 1787IV, 1919I, 1919III. *3)* Lev1, no. 2362, 2520, 2881, 3114. *4)* Lev1, no. 2954I. *5)* Lev2, no. 64. *6)* Lev1, no. 2330VIII. *7)* Lev2, no. 416. *8)* Mykhail Banakh, "Rusyny pid Reshovom," *Hazeta shkolna*, 1877, no. 11, cited in Lev1, no. 1654IV.

15. **Barnych, Kornylo**

LOCATION: Kadobna, Kalush district. OCCUPATION: (Peasant). POSITION IN RC: Administration (*CC* 121).

16. Bartetsky, Roman

LOCATION: Kutkivtsi, Ternopil district. OCCUPATION: Peasant. POSITION IN RC: Vice-president (*CC* 69). POSITION IN LOCAL GOVT: Mayor (*CC* 69). DISTINGUISHING FEATURES: Bartetsky was probably a *latynnyk*. His name is typically Polish rather than Ukrainian. When *Batkivshchyna* took to task five mayors in Ternopil district for using Polish-language community seals, Bartetsky was not singled out—as were two others—as a Ruthenian.[1] The commune of Kutkivtsi in 1880 had a community of about 160 *latynnyky* in a total population of 701.[2] FAMILY BACKGROUND: A Stefan Bartetsky was listed among the peasants of Kutkivtsi in 1854–6. Along with three other peasants, he shared a half-peasant holding of under 13 *Joch*; the average holding was under 15 *Joch* and holdings ranged from 290 square *Klafter* to 39 *Joch* 1078 square *Klafter*. Stefan was himself a quarter peasant in a village that roughly broke down into 13 per cent whole peasants, 37 per cent half peasants, 25 per cent quarter peasants and 25 per cent gardeners. Thus Stefan, who was probably Roman's father, was a middling peasant of just below average status.[3] MOBILITY: The Bartetsky family had been in Kutkivtsi at least since 1854.[3]

1) Rozhnivanyi, "...z Ternopilshchyny," *Batkivshchyna* 6, no. 45 (7 November [26 October] 1884): 286. *2) Spec. Orts-Rep. 1880*, 426. *3)* TsDIAL, 488/1/653, p. 12v and page facing p. 79v.

17. Basaichuk, Mykola (Nykola[i], Michał)

LOCATION: Hvozd, Nadvirna district. OCCUPATION: Teacher. POSITION IN RC: President.[1] AUTHOR: *CC* 4. ECONOMIC STATUS: He was an "assistant teacher" (but there was no other teacher in Hvozd) in an "unreorganized" school, i.e., one that had not been fully integrated into the standard school system.[2] Thus he did not receive the standard teacher's salary. AGE: He began teaching in 1879[2] and therefore was born c. 1857. PUBLICATIONS: He published an obituary of another activist teacher in *Shkolna chasopys* in 1885 (see *Vidlyvany, Nykyfor*). OTHER ACTIVITIES: His wife, who was Polish, was also active in the Hvozd reading club; she read aloud to the peasants.[1] Mykola Basaichuk helped establish the reading club in Fytkiv, Nadvirna district (*CC* 22).

1) Nadvirnianskii, "Pysmo vid Nadvirnoi," *Batkivshchyna* 5, no. 52 (28 [16] December 1883): 310. *2) Szem. kr. Gal. 1879*, 411; *ibid. 1881*, 425; *ibid. 1885*, 405; neither Basaichuk nor a school in Hvozd are mentioned in *ibid. 1873, 1877* or *1878*.

18. Berbeka, Levko

LOCATION: Dmytriv, Kaminka Strumylova district. OCCUPATION: Peasant. POSITION IN RC: Treasurer (*CC* 52). ECONOMIC STATUS: A Levko Berbeka had the middling holding of 10 *Joch* 578 square *Klafter* in the mid-1850s.[1] However, four Berbeka households were in Dmytriv at that time[2] and it is difficult to be certain that this was the same Levko Berbeka. AGE: If Levko Berbeka held land in 1855,[1] he was probably born in 1830 or earlier and no later than 1835. MOBILITY: The Berbeka family had long been in Dmytriv, since they had established four households there by the 1850s.[2]

1) TsDIAL, 168/1/1016, p. 16v. *2) Ibid.*, pp. 16v, 26v, 36v; see also p. 78.

19. Bernyk, Andrukh (Andrus)

LOCATION: Lysiatychi, Stryi district. OCCUPATION: Peasant and merchant. POSITION IN RC: Administration (*CC* 70). FAMILY BACKGROUND: The Bernyk family was prominent in village affairs since at least 1846, when Ivan Bernyk served as plenipotentiary.[1] A Tymko Bernyk was plenipotentiary in 1853,[2] a Stefan Bernyk was an alderman (P *przysiężny*) in 1861[3] and a Iats Bernyk was plenipotentiary and mayor in 1865.[4] AGE: Andrukh Bernyk was not yet mentioned in a list of villagers claiming servitude rights in 1870.[5] Hence, he had probably not yet come of age and was born after 1845. MOBILITY: The Bernyk family was well established in Lysiatychi by the 1840s.[1] PUBLICATIONS: A speech of his was published in *Batkivshchyna* in 1892.[6] OTHER ACTIVITIES: He participated in the movement to establish Ukrainian stores, worked closely with the priest-activist *Hrynevetsky, Apolinarii*, and was an active member of the reading club administration (*CC* 70). In 1892 he spoke at a national populist political meeting in Stryi, where he emphasized the importance of reading clubs and urged that reading clubs concern themselves more with economic matters, such as the founding of communal granaries.[6] On the eve of the notorious Badeni elections of 1895, Bernyk was arrested and detained until the elections were over; he was not even interrogated, simply kept in custody to prevent him from agitating for the Ukrainian candidate.[7]

1) TsDIAL, 146/64b/4940, p. 92 (see also p. 107v). *2) Ibid.*, 4941, p. 36. *3) Ibid.*, 4943, p. 50. *4) Ibid.*, 4944, p. 26. *5) Ibid.*, pp. 63–5, 98–9. *6)* [Andrukh] Bernyk, "Z Lysiatych," *Batkivshchyna* 14, no. 27 (3 [15] July 1892): 136. *7)* Olesnytsky, *Storinky*, 2:100–1.

20. Bilan, Oleksa

LOCATION: Olesha, Tovmach district. OCCUPATION: (Peasant). POSITION IN RC: Deputy administration (*CC* 60). MOBILITY: The Bilan family had been in Olesha since at least the 1850s.[1]

1) TsDIAL, 168/1/4099, pp. 70v, 85v.

21. Bilevych, Konstantyn

LOCATION: Utishkiv, Zolochiv district. OCCUPATION: Priest. ECONOMIC STATUS: Pastor of Utishkiv, which had 1,318 parishioners, an endowment of 87 *Joch* of arable land and 64 *Joch* of meadow and a *congruum* of 128 gulden 62 kreuzer.[1] EDUCATION: He attended normal school in Zhovkva and gymnasium in Lviv; he studied philosophy and theology at Lviv University. He knew, in addition to Ukrainian, Old Church Slavonic, Polish, German and Latin.[2] AGE: Born 1823, ordained 1847.[1] MARITAL STATUS: Widowed.[1] MOBILITY: He was educated in Zhovkva and Lviv. Utishkiv, where he became pastor in 1872,[2] was not his first posting. OTHER ACTIVITIES: He was a founder of the reading club in Utishkiv (*CC* 216). He was the administrator of the Busk deanery from 1868 and dean from 1872 (even though he lived in the Olesko deanery). He was named a (U) *kryloshanyn* in 1883, but turned down the appointment.[3]

1) Shem. Lviv. 1884, 116. *2)* Lev493, B-145. *3) Ibid.*; see also *Shem. Lviv. 1884*, 51.

22. Bilevych, Mykhailo

LOCATION: Kukyziv, Lviv district. OCCUPATION: (Peasant). POSITION IN RC: Secretary (*CC* 10).

23. Bilokha, Vasyl

LOCATION: Buzhok, Zolochiv district. OCCUPATION: (Peasant). POSITION IN RC: Deputy administration (*CC* 42). OTHER ACTIVITIES: He served on the administration of the Buzhok reading club at its founding in 1881.[1]

1) Ivan Petryshyn [Liubomyr Seliansky], "Pysmo z Hlukhoho Kuta," *Batkivshchyna* 3, no. 10 (16 May 1881): 80.

24. Bilynsky, Pankratii

LOCATION: Toky, Zbarazh district. OCCUPATION: Priest. POSITION IN RC: President (*CC* 80). ECONOMIC STATUS: Pastor of a parish with 1,650 members, an endowment of 100 *Joch* of arable land and 105 *Joch* of meadow and a *congruum* of 17 gulden 97 kreuzer.[1] AGE: Born 1839, ordained 1864.[1] MARITAL STATUS: Married. OTHER ACTIVITIES: He helped found a granary and loan association (*CC* 80).

1) Shem. Lviv. 1884, 79.

25. Boichuk, Vasyl

LOCATION: Liucha, Kolomyia district. OCCUPATION: (Peasant). POSITION IN RC: Deputy administration (*CC* 206).

26. Boikevych, Iliia

LOCATION: Rohatyn (district capital). OCCUPATION: Cantor. AUTHOR: *CC* 195, 259. PUBLICATIONS: Numerous contributions on the cantors' movement to *Batkivshchyna*, 1884,

1886–7, 1890;[1] *Dilo*, 1885–6;[2] *Myr*, 1885–6;[3] *Novyi prolom*, 1885;[4] and *Slovo*, 1885.[5] OTHER ACTIVITIES: He was a major activist in the cantors' movement and in 1885 represented the cantors to the metropolitan (*CC* 195). In 1887 he was secretary of the cantors' committee.[6]

1) Iliia Boikevych, "Vidozva do ruskykh diakiv Halychyny i Bukovyny," *Batkivshchyna* 6, no. 35 (29 [17] August 1884): 213–14 (an eloquent programmatic statement of the cantors' movement); Iliia Boikevych, "Pysmo z Rohatyna," *ibid.* 8, no. 5 (5 February [24 January] 1886): 29; Iliia Boikevych, "Pysmo z Rohatyna," *ibid.* 9, no. 1 (7 January 1887 [26 December 1886]): 4; Iliia Boikevych, "Pysmo vid Rohatyna," *ibid.* 9, no. 19 (13 [1] May 1887): 112–13; Iliia Boikevych, "Sprava diakivska," *ibid.* 12, no. 9 (23 February [7 March] 1890): 115. *2)* Lev1, no. 2943IX, 2943X, 3163IX, 3163X. *3)* Lev1, no. 2997IX, 3223IX. *4)* Lev1, no. 3016IX. *5)* Lev1, no. 3074IX. *6)* Boikevych, "Pysmo vid Rohatyna," *Batkivshchyna* 9 (1884): 112–13.

27. Boiko, Iurko

LOCATION: Darakhiv, Terebovlia district. OCCUPATION: Peasant. ECONOMIC STATUS: Proprietor (*CC* 82). OTHER ACTIVITIES: Founder of reading club (*CC* 82).

28. Bokii, Kyrylo

LOCATION: Bilyi Kamin, Zolochiv district. OCCUPATION: Burgher (*CC* 148). POSITION IN RC: Administration (*CC* 275).

29. Bolekhivsky, Andrei I.

LOCATION: Chertezh, Zhydachiv district. OCCUPATION: Teacher. AUTHOR: *CC* 43. FAMILY BACKGROUND: His father, Ioann Bolekhivsky, lived in the circle capital of Kolomyia and combined farming with trading in pottery at markets in Bukovyna, Podillia, Pokuttia, Hungary and Romania. The Bolekhivsky family claimed to be of boyar descent. Andrei's mother Anna (maiden name: Melnyk) was the daughter of a Kolomyia burgher. Both the father and mother had priests in their family.[1] EDUCATION: He attended the normal school (G *K.k. Kreis-Hauptschule*) in Kolomyia, 1860–4, and then gymnasium in the same city, 1865–9. In 1870 he set off on a journey through Hungary, traversing nearly half the country on foot. He planned to continue his education there, but the Magyar language of instruction proved an impediment. From 1871 to 1873 he attended the teachers' seminary in Lviv.[1] AGE: Born 6 December 1851 (O.S.).[1] DEATH: 21 February 1897 (O.S.).[1] MOBILITY: Educated in his native Kolomyia and Lviv, he travelled outside Galicia as a youth, accompanying his father to market towns in Russian Ukraine, Romania and the eastern Austro-Hungarian empire. He also travelled through Hungary in 1870. Chertezh was at least his second posting as a teacher; he taught there from 1883 to 1891. From 1895 until his death he was the principal of the school in Rozvadiv, Zhydachiv district.[1] PUBLICATIONS: He contributed riddles and puzzles as well as items of correspondence to: *Narodna shkola* (Kolomyia), 1875; *Russkaia rada*, c. 1875–7; *Hazeta shkolna*, 1876–39; *Dilo*, 1880; *Vesna* (Kolomyia), 1880; *Priiatel ditei*, 1882; *Przyjaciel Domowy*, 1882–34; *Różowe Domino*, 1882; *Szczutek*, 1882; *Głos Nauczycielski* (Kolomyia), 1883; *Przedświt* (Chernivtsi), 1883–4; *Swiat Illustrowany* (Vienna), 1883; *Novyi prolom*; *Besida* (Lviv), 1887; *Novyi halychanyn*, 1889; *Szkoła* (Lviv), 1893.[1] OTHER ACTIVITIES: In Rozvadiv he established a reading club and store.[1]

1) Lev493, B-244.

30. Borys, Hr[yhorii]

LOCATION: Iavoriv (district capital). OCCUPATION: Burgher (*CC* 142). POSITION IN RC: Administration (*CC* 142). AGE: Elder brother in church brotherhood (*CC* 142).

31. Borys, P.

LOCATION: Iavoriv (district capital). OCCUPATION: Burgher (*CC* 142). POSITION IN RC: Deputy administration (*CC* 142).

32. Brateiko, Luka

LOCATION: Makhniv, Rava Ruska district. OCCUPATION: (Peasant). POSITION IN RC: Librarian (*CC* 137).

33. Brytan, Antin

LOCATION: Iavoriv (district capital). OCCUPATION: Burgher (*CC* 142). POSITION IN RC: Administration (*CC* 142). AGE: Born c. 1835.[1] DEATH: 1 July 1890 (O.S.).[1] OTHER ACTIVITIES: He donated a subscription to one periodical to the reading club in Iavoriv, 1885 (*CC* 142).

Together with his brother Ostap, Antin Brytan was arrested in early 1888. In December 1887 the brothers had allegedly stated that "the Russians (U *moskali*) will come and slaughter the Poles and Jews." This was at a time of Austro-Russian tension, when naive tsarist sentiments flourished in Galicia and many of the common people awaited a Russian invasion that would bring justice and a bloody vengeance.[2] The brothers' statement was denounced to the authorities, who ordered their arrest. According to *Batkivshchyna* (1888, no. 7), the arrest was primarily motivated by considerations of local ethnic politics. Iavoriv had just had elections in which twenty-four Ukrainians and only twelve non-Ukrainians were elected to city council. The non-Ukrainians contested the result and new elections were expected. The arrest of the Brytan brothers was intended to neutralize their considerable influence among Iavoriv burghers. A court in Przemyśl sentenced Antin Brytan to two months' imprisonment, but a tribunal of cassation in Vienna revoked the sentence. The Ukrainian press (see *Chervonaia Rus'*, 1890, no. 141) reported that the arrest and trial undermined Antin Brytan's health and was the indirect cause of his death.

1) Lev493, B-322. *2)* See Himka, "Hope in the Tsar," 133–4.

34. Buchma, Stefan

LOCATION: Kamianka Lisna, Rava Ruska district. OCCUPATION: Peasant. POSITION IN RC: Vice-president.[1] ECONOMIC STATUS: Wealthy peasant (*CC* 53). OTHER ACTIVITIES: Patron of the reading club (*CC* 53).

1) "Ot Ravy russkoi," *Slovo* 24, no. 46 (26 April [8 May] 1884): 2.

35. Burak, Ilko

LOCATION: Vynnyky, Zhovkva district. OCCUPATION: Peasant. ECONOMIC STATUS: Proprietor (*CC* 262). OTHER ACTIVITIES: Administration of the Pravda society (*CC* 262).

36. Burak, Lev (Leon)

LOCATION: Vynnyky, Zhovkva district. OCCUPATION: Peasant. POSITION IN RC: Treasurer (*CC* 5, 153). FAMILY BACKGROUND: His father, Danko Burak, was a middling peasant with 10 *Joch* 860 square *Klafter* of land. He served as alderman (P *przysiężny*) in 1854 and was illiterate.[1] ECONOMIC STATUS: Proprietor (*CC* 262). EDUCATION: Literate.[2] AGE: Born c. 1850.[3] MOBILITY: His grandfather, Lesko Burak, had also lived in Vynnyky.[2] OTHER ACTIVITIES: Treasurer of the reading club from 1883.[4] Cofounder of the reading club, loan fund (Pravda society) and communal granary.[5] On the administration of the Pravda society in 1885 (*CC* 262) and still treasurer in 1894.[6]

1) TsDIAL, 168/1/484, pp. 1v, 36v, 79v. *2)* LODA, 10/1/18, p. 15. *3)* LODA, 10/1/49, p. 40. *4)* Vynnychanyn, "Pysmo vid Zhovkvy," *Batkivshchyna* 5, no. 50 (14 [2] December 1883): 301. *5)* "Pysmo vid Zhovkvy," *Batkivshchyna* 10, no. 14 (6 April [25 March] 1885): 85. *6)* Sylvester Drymalyk, "Pysmo z Zhovkvy," *Batkivshchyna* 16, no. 6 (16 [28] March 1894): 45.

37. Burak, Semko

LOCATION: Vynnyky, Zhovkva district. OCCUPATION: (Peasant). POSITION IN RC: Librarian (*CC* 153). OTHER ACTIVITIES: Secretary of the Pravda society, 1894.[1]

1) Sylvester Drymalyk, "Pysmo z Zhovkvy," *Batkivshchyna* 16, no. 6 (16 [28] March 1894): 45.

38. **Burnadz, Semen (Symeon)**

LOCATION: Horodenka (district capital). OCCUPATION: Priest. POSITION IN RC: President, early 1884 (*CC* 15). ECONOMIC STATUS: Assistant in a parish of 4,862; salary of 210 gulden.[1] AGE: Born 1856, ordained 1883.[1] DEATH: 8 November 1914.[2] MARITAL STATUS: Married.[1] MOBILITY: Born in Serafyntsi, Kolomyia circle, and certainly educated in Lviv, he served as an assistant in Horodenka and Repuzhyntsi, Horodenka district, and as pastor in Oliieva-Korolivtsi, Horodenka district.[2] OTHER ACTIVITIES: In 1883 he organized a collection to acquire premises for the reading club.[3] He was mentioned as still a member of the Horodenka reading club in the late winter of 1886,[4] but he was no longer active by the late summer of that year.[5] He was an outspoken opponent of the radical movement in rural Horodenka district at the turn of the century.[6]

1) Shem. Lviv. *1884*, 214. *2)* Iashan and Marunchak, "Pomianyk peredovykh sviashchenykiv Horodenshchyny," 661. *3)* Maksym Krushelnytsky [Andriichuk], "Pysmo z Horodenky," *Batkivshchyna* 5, no. 49 (7 December [25 November] 1883): 295. *4)* K.L.S., "Pysmo z Horodenky," *Batkivshchyna* 8, no. 11 (19 [7] March 1886): 65. *5)* Pravdoliub, "Pysmo z Horodenky," *Batkivshchyna* 8, no. 35 (17 [5] September 1886): 208. *6)* "Novynky. Pip—voroh prosvity!," *Hromadskyi holos*, no. 16 (1900): 135.

39. **Byliv, Iosyf**

LOCATION: Burkaniv, Pidhaitsi district. OCCUPATION: Cantor. AUTHOR: *CC* 99, 103, 244. ECONOMIC STATUS: Poor. Byliv had to supplement his income by working as an agricultural labourer (*CC* 99). MOBILITY: Before moving to Burkaniv, he had been cantor in Mozalivka, also in Pidhaitsi district (*CC* 99). PUBLICATIONS: He contributed articles on the cantors' movement to *Batkivshchyna*, 1885;[1] *Slovo*, 1886;[2] *Halychanyn*, 1894;[3] and *Russkoe slovo*, 1894. OTHER ACTIVITIES: In 1879, as cantor in Mozalivka, he agitated for the Ukrainian candidate in parliamentary elections. The landlord became angry, had the gendarmes search his home and put pressure on the pastor to have him fired within a year (*CC* 99). The village of Burkaniv had a choir in 1884,[5] which was probably established and directed by Byliv.

1) I[osyf] B[yliv], "V spravi diakivskii," *Batkivshchyna* 7, no. 4 (23 [11] January 1885): 31. *2)* Lev1, no. 3285IX. *3)* Lev3, no. 3504. *4)* Lev3, no. 3937. *5)* "Ruski selianski i mishchanski spivni khory v Halychyni," *Batkivshchyna* 6, no. 35 (29 [17] August 1884): 215.

40. **Chemerynsky, Antonii**

LOCATION: Tsebriv, Ternopil district. OCCUPATION: Priest. ECONOMIC STATUS: Pastor of Vorobiivka, Ternopil district, with the daughter church in Tsebriv; together, the two congregations numbered 1,971. The endowment in arable land was 135 *Joch* and in meadow 5 *Joch*. The *congruum* was 90 gulden 36 kreuzer.[1] AGE: Born 1833, ordained 1858.[1] MARITAL STATUS: Married.[1] OTHER ACTIVITIES: Proponent of enlightenment in Tsebriv (*CC* 44).

1) Shem. Lviv. *1884*, 159.

41. **Chepil, Konstantyn**

LOCATION: Kadobna, Kalush district. OCCUPATION: Priest. POSITION IN RC: President (*CC* 121). ECONOMIC STATUS: Pastor of Kropyvnyk, Kalush district, with 2,062 parishioners, an endowment of 56 *Joch* of arable land, 135 *Joch* of meadow and a *congruum* of 143 gulden 53 kreuzer.[1] AGE: Born 1829, ordained 1859.[1] MARITAL STATUS: Married.

1) Shem. Lviv. *1884*, 94.

42. Cheredarchuk, Vasyl

LOCATION: Nakvasha, Brody district. OCCUPATION: Teacher. POSITION, IN RC: Treasurer (*CC* 201). AGE: Began teaching in 1878,[1] therefore born c. 1856. MOBILITY: He first taught in Pidkamin in 1878,[1] then in Ruda Bridska from 1879 until the early 1880s,[2] and finally in Nakvasha;[3] all these localities were in Brody district. OTHER ACTIVITIES: He was one of the founders of the reading club and director of the village choir (*CC* 201).

1) He is not mentioned in *Szem. kr. Gal. 1877*, but figures as junior teacher (P *nauczyciel młodszy*) in *ibid. 1878*, 387. *2) Ibid. 1879*, 382; *ibid. 1881*, 392. *3) Ibid. 1884*, 372; *ibid. 1885*, 372.

43. Cherevatiuk

LOCATION: Trybukhivtsi, Husiatyn district. OCCUPATION: Cantor and merchant (*CC* 207). MOBILITY: No Cherevatiuk family is mentioned in the records of Trybukhivtsi in 1854. OTHER ACTIVITIES: Comanager of community store (*CC* 207).

44. Chernetsky, Vasyl

LOCATION: Silets Belzkyi, Sokal district. OCCUPATION: Priest. POSITION IN RC: President, 1884 (*CC* 127); administration, 1885 (*CC* 278). AUTHOR: *CC* 235, 255. FAMILY BACKGROUND: Son of a priest.[1] ECONOMIC STATUS: He spent nineteen years as chaplain in Stroniatyn, Lviv district, until on 20 May 1884 he was made pastor of Silets Belzkyi.[1] In 1880 Silets Belzkyi had 2,315 Greek Catholics.[2] EDUCATION: He attended normal school together with the future Cardinal Sylvester Sembratovych in Jasło (circle capital) in 1844–7; lower gymnasia in Rzeszów, Przemyśl and Nowy Sącz (all circle capitals); and higher gymnasia in Prešov, Košice and Uzhhorod (all in Hungary). He studied theology in Lviv and Przemyśl, 1859–62.[1] AGE: Born 7 January 1837 (O.S.), ordained 7 December 1862 (O.S.).[1] DEATH: 1900.[3] MOBILITY: Born in the Carpathian village of Tarnawka (Tarnavka), Sanok circle, he was educated in several central Galician circle capitals (today all in Poland), in several towns in Slovakia and Transcarpathia and in Lviv. For almost two decades he was chaplain in Stroniatyn, near Lviv, and spent the last sixteen years of his life as a priest-activist in Sokal district.[1] PUBLICATIONS: He first contributed to the press in 1862 and was a prolific contributor thereafter. His works include articles in *Strakhopud*, 1864, 1867, 1869, 1872, 1880; *Slovo*, 1866–8, 1871–6, 1878–80; *Batkivshchyna*, 1884–91; and *Dilo*, 1886–9. Memoirs of his student years were published in *Dilo*, 1886–9. He also published a series of brochures on the local history of East Galician towns and villages.[1] OTHER ACTIVITIES: He had been president of the reading club in Zapytiv, Lviv district, while still chaplain of Stroniatyn.[4] He was reputed to have founded fourteen reading clubs by the spring of 1885,[5] but in an autobiographical letter to Ivan Omelianovych Levytsky (13 February 1896 [O.S.]) he only mentioned twelve.[1] In 1885 he founded a loan association in Khrystynopil, Sokal district,[5] and in 1895 a political society, Ruska rada, in Sokal.[1] He was active in the cantors' movement;[1] he chaired a cantors' convention in Khrystynopil in 1885 (*CC* 193) and pleaded the cantors' cause in the press.[6] In 1892 the Przemyśl eparchy named him censor of religious books and titular councillor. In 1893 the Lviv metropolitan also named him titular councillor. In 1897 he was made dean of Belz.[1]

He served on the administration of the Sokal district council.[1]

1) Lev493, Ch-33. *2) Spec. Orts-Rep. 1880. 3) Ukrainska Zahalna Entsyklopediia*, s.v. "Chernetsky." *4)* K., "...vid Iarycheva," *Batkivshchyna* 6, no. 18 (2 May [20 April] 1884): 107. *4)* "Dribni visty," *Batkivshchyna* 7, no. 10 (6 March [22 February] 1885): 80. *5)* V. Chernetsky, "Pysmo z Krystynopolia," *Batkivshchyna* 8, no. 30 (3 August [22 July] 1886): 186. Vasyl Chernetsky, "Pysmo z Krystynopolia," *Batkivshchyna* 9, no. 7 (1887), cited in Lev2, no. 15II.

45. Cherniak, Petro

LOCATION: Chekhy, Brody district. OCCUPATION: Peasant. POSITION IN RC: Treasurer (*CC* 271). ECONOMIC STATUS: Proprietor (*CC* 262). OTHER ACTIVITIES: Founder of the Pravda society (*CC* 262).

46. Chornobai, Aleksander

LOCATION: Makhniv, Rava Ruska district. OCCUPATION: Peasant. POSITION IN RC: Vice-president (*CC* 137). POSITION IN LOCAL GOVT: Mayor (*CC* 137). ECONOMIC STATUS: A proprietor wealthy enough to have purchased a four-room home built by a retired civil servant (*CC* 137). OTHER ACTIVITIES: Donated part of his home for the use of the reading club and promised to provide the fuel to heat it. A member of the Rava Ruska district council (*CC* 137).

47. Chuba, Maksym

LOCATION: Ordiv, Sokal district. OCCUPATION: (Peasant). OTHER ACTIVITIES: Donated part of his home as premises for the reading club (*CC* 272).

48. Chypchar, Vasyl

LOCATION: Dmytriv, Kaminka Strumylova district. OCCUPATION: Teacher. POSITION IN RC: Vice-president (*CC* 52). AGE: He started teaching c. 1880 and was therefore born c. 1858.[1] MOBILITY: He first taught in Neslukhiv, Kaminka Strumylova district,[1] and came to Dmytriv in the early 1880s.[2]

1) He is not mentioned in *Szem. kr. Gal. 1879*; he is, however, in *ibid. 1881*, 408. *2) Ibid. 1884*, 387; *ibid. 1885*, 387.

49. Dachynsky, Iarema

LOCATION: Nakvasha, Brody district. OCCUPATION: (Peasant). POSITION IN RC: Secretary (*CC* 201).

50. Danyliv, Iliarii (Ilko)

LOCATION: Briukhovychi, Peremyshliany district. OCCUPATION: Cantor (*CC* 84). OTHER ACTIVITIES: He was a founder of the reading club in Briukhovychi (*CC* 57) and spoke at the opening of the reading club in Korelychi, Peremyshliany district (*CC* 84).

51. Derkach, Panko

LOCATION: Vynnyky, Zhovkva district. OCCUPATION: Peasant. POSITION IN RC: Secretary (*CC* 153). POSITION IN LOCAL GOVT: A member of the Zhovkva city council in 1900.[1] ECONOMIC STATUS: Proprietor (*CC* 262). He seems to have been prosperous by the turn of the century. He bid on land at an auction held by the city of Zhovkva in 1890.[2] EDUCATION: Literate (by 1901).[3] MOBILITY: The Derkach family had been in Vynnyky since at least the 1850s.[4] OTHER ACTIVITIES: He had been secretary of the reading club since 1883.[5] In the early and mid-1880s he was cofounder of the reading club, loan fund (Pravda society) and communal granary.[6] In 1885 he was on the administration of the Pravda society (*CC* 262) and in 1894 he was its vice-president.[7]

1) LODA, 10/1/83, p. 31. *2)* LODA, 10/1/49, pp. 3–3v. *3)* LODA, 10/1/115, pp. 21, 24. *4)* TsDIAL, 168/1/484, p. 16v. *5)* Vynnychanyn, "Pysmo vid Zhovkvy," *Batkivshchyna* 5, no. 50 (14 [2] December 1883): 301. *6)* "Pysmo vid Zhovkvy," *Batkivshchyna* 10, no. 14 (6 April [25 March] 1885): 85. *7)* Sylvester Drymalyk, "Pysmo z Zhovkvy," *Batkivshchyna* 16, no. 6 (16 [28] March 1894): 45.

52. Diakiv, Danylo

LOCATION: Korelychi, Peremyshliany district. OCCUPATION: Peasant. POSITION IN RC: Deputy administration (*CC* 84). ECONOMIC STATUS: Proprietor (*CC* 84). MOBILITY: The Diakiv family had been registered in the Greek Catholic community of Dobrianychi (near Korelychi), Peremyshliany district, in 1864.[1] OTHER ACTIVITIES: He recited verse at the opening of the Dobrianychi reading club in 1884.[2]

*1)*TsDIAL, 146/64b/2294, p. 59v. *2)* Chytalnyk, " ...vid Peremyshlian," *Batkivshchyna* 6, no. 46 (14 [2] November 1884): 294.

53. Diakon, Mykhail

LOCATION: Olesha, Tovmach district. OCCUPATION: Scribe. POSITION IN RC: Secretary (*CC* 60). POSITION IN LOCAL GOVT: Scribe, but fired in 1884 (*CC* 60, 78, 118). EDUCATION: In an advertisement seeking employment, Diakon described his qualifications as follows: "A trained scribe with experience in the courts, as a notary, in the political administration and, above all, in local government; perfectly acquainted with the laws of local government and with the management of village affairs.... "[1] MOBILITY: The Diakon name does not appear in the lists of villagers from 1850–5.[2] OTHER ACTIVITIES: He founded the reading club in Olesha (*CC* 60) and tried to found a store (*CC* 78). He led a campaign against the mayor, which resulted in the community suing the mayor and Diakon being fired as scribe.[3]

1) [Mykhail Diakon], "Pysar," *Batkivshchyna* 7, no. 2 (9 January 1885 [28 December 1884]): 16. *2)* TsDIAL, 168/1/4099. *3)* "...z Tovmatskoho," *Batkivshchyna* 7, no. 1 (2 January 1885 [21 December 1884]): 6.

Didukh, Ivan

LOCATION: Utishkiv, Zolochiv district. OCCUPATION: Cantor (*CC* 216). POSITION IN RC: Vice-president (*CC* 216). OTHER ACTIVITIES: A founder of the reading club, he was described as "an ardent patriot" (*CC* 216).

55. Dmyterko, Semen

LOCATION: Ninovychi, Sokal district. OCCUPATION: Peasant. ECONOMIC STATUS: Proprietor (*CC* 188). OTHER ACTIVITIES: A founder of the reading club (*CC* 188).

56. Dnistriansky, Lev

LOCATION: Ozeriany, Borshchiv district. OCCUPATION: Priest. POSITION IN RC: President (*CC* 97). ECONOMIC STATUS: Pastor of a parish with 1,390 members, an endowment of 80 *Joch* of arable land and a *congruum* of 148 gulden 37 kreuzer.[1] AGE: Born 1836, ordained 1860.[1] MARITAL STATUS: Widowed.[1] PUBLICATIONS: He wrote a report for *Ruskii Sion* in 1884 on a mission held in Ozeriany.[2] OTHER ACTIVITIES: A proponent of enlightenment (*CC* 97).

1) Shem. Lviv. 1884, 265. *2)* Lev1, no. 2834.

57. Dobriansky, Hnat

LOCATION: Shliakhtyntsi, Ternopil district. OCCUPATION: (Peasant). POSITION IN RC: Deputy administration (*CC* 9).

58. Dobrovolsky, Ivan

LOCATION: Komarno, Rudky district. OCCUPATION: (Artisan). POSITION IN RC: Deputy administration (*CC* 9).

59. Dolnytsky

LOCATION: Ripniv, Kaminka Strumylova district. OCCUPATION: Priest (*CC* 159). OTHER ACTIVITIES: Promoter of reading club (*CC* 159).

60. Dolnytsky, Andrei

LOCATION: Pochapy, Zolochiv district. OCCUPATION: Priest. POSITION IN RC: President (*CC* 268). ECONOMIC STATUS: Pastor of a parish with 1,260 members, an endowment of 55.5 *Joch* of arable land and 31 *Joch* of meadow and a *congruum* of 180 gulden 56 kreuzer.[1] AGE: Born 1829, ordained 1852.[1] MARITAL STATUS: Married.[1] OTHER ACTIVITIES: Dean of Zolochiv.[2]

1) Shem. Lviv. 1884, 89. *2)* Ibid., 85.

61. Domsky, Toma

LOCATION: Kukyziv, Lviv district. OCCUPATION: (Peasant). POSITION IN RC: Vice-president (*CC* 10).

62. Dorozhynsky, Vladyslav

LOCATION: Voltsniv, Zhydachiv district. OCCUPATION: Priest. ECONOMIC STATUS: Pastor of a parish with 1,026 members, an endowment of 24 *Joch* of arable land and 12 *Joch* of meadow and a *congruum* of 217 gulden 21 kreuzer.[1] AGE: Born 1840, ordained 1864.[1] MARITAL STATUS: Widowed.[1] OTHER ACTIVITIES: Proponent of a cooperative store and enlightenment (*CC* 17). Commissar of school affairs, Rozdil deanery.[1]

1) Shem. Lviv. 1884, 135–6.

63. Dragan, Iurko

LOCATION: Khotin, Kalush district. OCCUPATION: (Peasant). POSITION IN RC: Vice-president (*CC* 121). POSITION IN LOCAL GOVT: Long-term mayor.[1] ECONOMIC STATUS: Wealthy.[2] EDUCATION: Illiterate.[3]

OTHER ACTIVITIES: A founder of the reading club,[4] he donated part of his home for it to use as premises (*CC* 121).

In 1885, Khotin elected two Jews to the village council. One contributor to *Batkivshchyna* addressed the villagers of Khotin as follows: "... You would do better, gentlemen of the community, to listen to your honourable mayor, Mr. Iurko Dragan, and vote for your own people; then you wouldn't have brought such shame upon yourselves."[5] A response to this was submitted by four peasants of Khotin, including *Kushchak, Fedor,* the reading club's treasurer: "It is not true that the mayor Iurko Dragan counselled us to elect honest Christian peasants. He was not sure he himself would be elected and in order to ensure this he surrounded himself with his lackeys, to whom do not at all belong the best proprietors of Khotin; and he conducted the election with various irregularities. That Jews now make up almost half the village is no one's fault; if anyone is to blame it is the aforementioned mayor, since during his three terms as mayor most of them settled in our village."[6] (In 1880 there were 69 Jews in the commune of Khotin, which had a total population of 1,071.)[7]

Dragan was a member of the Khotin church committee in 1889.[8] In the face of community opposition and other difficulties, he led a campaign to build a new church. He received a certificate of commendation (U *hramota pokhvalna*) from the metropolitan for his efforts.[9]

In 1893 a correspondent accused Dragan of opposing the revived reading club, which was headed by *Kendiukh, Hnat* and composed mainly of younger and poorer peasants. Dragan also allegedly attacked with a cudgel members of the administration of a loan association, also composed of younger and poorer peasants.[2] Dragan denounced both the reading club and the loan association to the district authorities. He himself, however, was under investigation by the district council for "diverse abuses and crimes."[10] On 8 December 1893 (N.S.) he was removed from office for embezzlement and nearly all of his property was confiscated.[3]

1) He had been mayor for a number of years already in 1885 and remained mayor until almost the end of 1893. Ivan Dovbenka, Iurko Voletsky, Zakhar Posatsky, Fedor Kushchak, "... vid Kalusha pro vybory do rady hromadskoi v Khotini," *Batkivshchyna* 7, no. 48 (27 [15] November 1885): 332. M.D., "Visty z kraiu," *Batkivshchyna* 11, no. 25 (23 June [5 July] 1889): 318–20. L.K., "Pysmo z Kalushchyny," *Batkivshchyna* 15, no. 2 (16 [28] January 1893): 12. Chlen chytalni, "Pysmo vid Kalusha," *Batkivshchyna* 15, no. 24 (16 [28] December 1893): 188–9. *2)* L.K., "Pysmo z Kalushchyny," *Batkivshchyna* (1893): 12. *3)* Chlen chytalni, "Pysmo vid Kalusha," *Batkivshchyna* (1893): 188–9. *4)* Hp., "Nova chytalnia," *Batkivshchyna* 6, no. 26 (27 [15] June 1884): 159. *5)* M., "... vid Kalusha," *Batkivshchyna* 7, no. 45 (6 November [25 October] 1885): 312. *6)* Dovbenka *et al.*, "... vid Kalusha," *Batkivshchyna* (1885): 332. *7) Spec. Orts-Rep. 1880. 8)* "Zaprosyny," *Batkivshchyna* 11, no. 19 (12 [24] May 1889): 252. *9)* M.D., "Visty z kraiu," *Batkivshchyna* (1889): 318–20. *10)* "Z Kalushchyny," *Batkivshchyna* 15, no. 15 (1 [13] August 1893): 116.

64. Dragan, Konstantyn

LOCATION: Khotin, Kalush district. OCCUPATION: Peasant.[1] POSITION IN RC: Secretary (*CC* 121). OTHER ACTIVITIES: A founder of the reading club.[1]

1) Hp., "Nova chytalnia," *Batkivshchyna* 6, no. 26 (27 [15] June 1884): 159.

65. Dragan, Nykola

LOCATION: Khotin, Kalush district. OCCUPATION: (Peasant). POSITION IN RC: Librarian (*CC* 121).

66. Dron, Teodor

LOCATION: Fytkiv, Nadvirna district. OCCUPATION: Priest. POSITION IN RC: President (*CC* 58). ECONOMIC STATUS: Administrator of a parish of 657 members, an endowment of 10 *Joch* of arable land and 30 *Joch* of meadow and a *congruum* of 210 gulden 78 kreuzer.[1] AGE: Born 1839, ordained 1879.[1] MARITAL STATUS: Celibate.[1]

1) Shem. Lviv. *1884*, 256.

67. Drymalyk, Sylvester L.

LOCATION: Vynnyky, Zhovkva district. OCCUPATION: Physician. POSITION IN RC: President (*CC* 153). FAMILY BACKGROUND: His father, Lavrentii Drymalyk (died 1896), was a priest.[1] EDUCATION: He attended the Ukrainian gymnasium in Lviv, 1865–73, and studied medicine at the University of Vienna, 1876–9.[1] AGE: Born 11 January 1855 (O.S.).[1] DEATH: 1923.[2] MOBILITY: He was born in the village of Olszany (Olshany), Przemyśl circle, and educated in Lviv and Vienna. He set up his medical practice in Zhovkva,[1] and stayed there until 1914, when he directed a free medical clinic in Lviv.[2] PUBLICATIONS: He wrote popularly on medicine for the calendars of the Kachkovsky Society, 1887, 1889–91. He wrote a popular booklet on children's diseases, published by the Kachkovsky Society; a revised edition appeared in 1901. He was also author of other popular booklets, such as *Likarskyi poradnyk*[2] and (on venereal diseases) *Pro polovi khvoroby*.[3] He contributed professional articles to Viennese medical journals and to the Ukrainian journals *Zdorovlie* and *Likarskyi visnyk*.[2] He wrote on enlightenment work among the peasantry in a brochure, *O selskykh chytalniakh poluchennykh s kasamy pozhychkovymy* (Lviv, 1889);[1] also in *Batkivshchyna* and *Dilo*, 1894.[4]

OTHER ACTIVITIES: He was a founder of the reading club[1] and choir in Vynnyky, 1882 (*CC* 53), also cofounder of the loan fund (Pravda society), 1885, and communal granary.[5] He presided over the reading club and Pravda society in Vynnyky at least through 1896.

In 1876–9, as a student in Vienna, he was president of the Russophile student society Russkaia osnova; in 1879 he was made an honourable member of the national populist student society in Vienna, Sich.

He served in the district administration of Zhovkva from 1880 until at least 1896. In 1885 he was elected to the Zhovkva district council, but resigned along with eleven other Ukrainian members (including *Tarchanyn, Amvrosii*) to protest city elections.

In 1892, together with the lawyer Mykhail Korol, he founded the political association Ruska rada in Zhovkva.[1] From 1914 on, he served as the director of the Narodnia lichnytsia, a free medical clinic, in Lviv.[3]

1) Lev493, D-160. *2)* *Ukrainska Zahalna Entsyklopediia,* s.v. "Drymalyk." *3) Entsyklopediia Ukrainoznavstva,* s.v. "Drymalyk Sylvester." *4)* Lev3, no. 3446, 3615. *5)* Vynnychanyn, "Pysmo vid Zhovkvy," *Batkivshchyna* 7, no. 14 (6 April [25 March] 1885): 85.

68. Dubovy, Ivan

LOCATION: Kukyziv, Lviv district. OCCUPATION: (Peasant). POSITION IN RC: Librarian (*CC* 10).

69. Dushansky, Dymytrii

LOCATION: Berezyna, Zhydachiv district. OCCUPATION: Peasant. ECONOMIC STATUS: Proprietor (*CC* 28). OTHER ACTIVITIES: Reading club activist (*CC* 28).

70. Dutkevych (Dudkevych), Evhenii

LOCATION: Rudno, Lviv district. OCCUPATION: Priest and landowner. POSITION IN LOCAL GOVT: Scribe, 1882.[1] ECONOMIC STATUS: Owned the estate of Rudno, which he turned into a health resort.[2] Also pastor of Rudno, with 924 parishioners, an endowment of 79 *Joch* of arable land and 34 *Joch* of meadow and a *congruum* of 45 gulden 39 kreuzer.[3] He lent money to peasants and demanded healthy repayment in kind.[1] An obituary in *Halychanyn*, no. 200 (1897), described him as "an altogether enterprising and energetic man, and at the same time cautious."[2] AGE: Born 1836, ordained 1858.[3] DEATH: 13 September 1897 (O.S.).[2] MARITAL STATUS: Married.[3]

OTHER ACTIVITIES: He was apparently indifferent to the enlightenment movement at first. A parishioner complained in 1882: "Father D[utkevych] in Rudno indeed receives something like ten Ruthenian and four Polish newspapers *for himself*, and that not at his own cost; but how does that benefit the people?...Our reverend father is our priest and landlord and scribe. He thus has all authority in his hands and could easily bring the community to order and prosperity. But what sort of order and prosperity do we have?!...And if our reverend father helps someone with a loan, with money, then he says to pay him back well in kind. Therefore the people has no attachment to and trust in its pastor, which are so necessary, in fact indispensable, for the Ruthenian cause."[1] But in 1885, Dutkevych was a founder of the reading club (*CC* 240); he was also active in its revival in 1890.[4]

He was a founder of the cooperative commercial association Narodna torhovlia, and headed it for twelve years, until 1896. He was also a founder of the insurance company Dnister. He was commissioner of servitude affairs in the Lviv archeparchy[3] and later a councillor of the metropolitan consistory.[2] He was a member of the Lower Austrian bee-keeping society and the Lviv city gardening society.[3] PUBLICATIONS: *Novyi prolom*, 1884, published a speech he gave on the occasion of the opening of a branch store of Narodna torhovlia in Przemyśl.[5]

1) Khv., "Pysmo z-pid Lvova," *Batkivshchyna* 4, no. 10 (16 [4] May 1882): 78. *2)* Lev493, D-191. *3)* *Shem. Lviv. 1884*, 104. *4)* "Zahalni zbory chytalni v Rudni," *Batkivshchyna* 12, no. 20 (11 [23] May 1890): 258. *5)* Lev1, no. 2799III.

71. Dyhdalevych, Ivan

LOCATION: Kukyziv, Lviv district. OCCUPATION: Priest. POSITION IN RC: President (*CC* 10). AGE: Born 1821, ordained 1846.[1] OTHER ACTIVITIES: Founder of the reading club (*CC* 10).

1) *Catalogus...cleri Dioeceseos Premisliensis...1848*, 64.

72. Dykevych (Dzykevych), Pavlo

LOCATION: Bilyi Kamin, Zolochiv district. OCCUPATION: Burgher (*CC* 148). POSITION IN RC: Administration (*CC* 275).

73. Dylynsky, Volodymyr

LOCATION: Liashky Dolishni and Horishni, Bibrka district. OCCUPATION: Priest. ECONOMIC STATUS: Pastor of a parish with 1,006 members, an endowment of 65 *Joch* of arable land and 6 *Joch* of meadow and a *congruum* of 184 gulden 16 kreuzer.[1] AGE: Born 1848, ordained 1871.[1] MARITAL STATUS: Married.[1] OTHER ACTIVITIES: Proponent of enlightenment (*CC* 139).

1) *Shem. Lviv. 1884*, 180.

74. Dynsky, Toma

LOCATION: Kolodribka, Zalishchyky district. OCCUPATION: Peasant. POSITION IN RC: Treasurer (*CC* 76; actually referred to as Tymish, but this seems to be an error for Toma, correctly named later in *CC* 76). ECONOMIC STATUS: Proprietor (*CC* 76). OTHER ACTIVITIES: Treasurer of the reading club in 1890.[1]

1) "Chytalnia v Kolodribtsi," *Batkivshchyna* 12, no. 24 (8 [20] June 1890): 311.

75. Fedorovych, Vasyl

LOCATION: Dobrostany, Horodok district. OCCUPATION: Cantor (*CC* 245) and peasant (*CC* 100). POSITION IN RC: Librarian, 1884–5 (*CC* 100, 146); secretary, 1885 (*CC* 245). AUTHOR: *CC* 146. ECONOMIC STATUS: Proprietor (*CC* 100). OTHER ACTIVITIES: He spoke at the opening of the reading club in 1884 (*CC* 100) and gave a lecture on the Ukrainian language in 1885 (*CC* 245).

76. Fedun, I.

LOCATION: Bila, Ternopil district. OCCUPATION: (Peasant). POSITION IN RC: Secretary (*CC* 69).

77. Filvarkiv

LOCATION: Horodenka (district capital). OCCUPATION: (Peasant). POSITION IN RC: Administration (*CC* 15).

78. Forlita, Petro

LOCATION: Dobrostany, Horodok district. OCCUPATION: (Peasant). POSITION IN RC: Vice-president, 1884 (*CC* 100, 122); auditor, 1885 (*CC* 245). AUTHOR: *CC* 122 (coauthor).

79. Fyniak, Dmytro

LOCATION: Korelychi, Peremyshliany district. OCCUPATION: Peasant. POSITION IN RC: Deputy administration (*CC* 84). FAMILY BACKGROUND: In 1864 a Mykhailo Fyniak, presumably Dmytro's father, paid taxes of 6.7 gulden, which was higher than the average tax paid by the Greek Catholic parishioners of Korelychi, 4.7 gulden.[1] ECONOMIC STATUS: Proprietor (*CC* 84). MOBILITY: The Fyniak family had been in Korelychi since at least 1864.[1]

1) TsDIAL, 146/64b/2294, p. 55v.

80. Gabrysh (Gabrysz), Liudvyk (Ludwik)

LOCATION: Nykonkovychi, Lviv district. POSITION IN RC: President (*CC* 105). DISTINGUISHING FEATURES: He was of the Latin rite,[1] either a *latynnyk* or a Pole.[2] MOBILITY: The Gabrysh family was not recorded among the former serfs of Nykonkovychi in 1852–5.[3] OTHER ACTIVITIES: He was a founder of the reading club, which met in his home (*CC* 105). His son was a student in Lviv (*CC* 105).

1) "Novi chytalni," *Batkivshchyna* 6, no. 20 (16 [4] May 1884): 120. *2)* The commune of Nykonkovychi in 1880 had 34 Roman Catholics, 393 Greek Catholics, 5 Jews and 11 of other religions (probably Evangelicals); there were 28 German-speakers, 13 Polish-speakers and 402 Ukrainian-speakers. *Spec. Orts-Rep. 1880.* If we assume that the Jews and Evangelicals spoke German, then 12 of the Roman Catholics were German-speakers. Thus 22 of the Roman Catholics were either Polish-speaking (Poles) or Ukrainian-speaking (*latynnyky*). There were 13 Polish-speakers recorded in the census, thus leaving 9 Ukrainian-speaking Roman Catholics. The latter figure corresponds to the 9 Ukrainian-speakers who were not Greek Catholics. Hence it is most probable that the village had 13 Poles proper and 9 *latynnyky*. *3)* TsDIAL, 168/1/1916.

81. Galat (Halat), Roman

LOCATION: Brovary, Buchach district. OCCUPATION: Cantor (*CC* 75). POSITION IN RC: Secretary (*CC* 75). OTHER ACTIVITIES: He was a founder of the original reading club

(*CC* 75) and then of the revived reading club in 1901. He was president of the revived reading club from 1901 until at least 1903. At that time Galat was an agent for the insurance company Dnister.[1]

1) TsDIAL, 348/1/1297, pp. 21, 24–5, 31v.

82. Gelmas, Ivan

LOCATION: Nykonkovychi, Lviv district. OCCUPATION: Peasant. POSITION IN RC: Treasurer (*CC* 105). MOBILITY: The Gelmas family had already established six peasant households in Nykonkovychi by 1852–5.[1] OTHER ACTIVITIES: A founder of the reading club (*CC* 105).

1) TsDIAL, 168/1/1916, pp. 1v, 11v, 16v, 21v.

83. Genyk (Genik, Genig) (-Berezovsky), Kyrylo (Cyril, Charles)

LOCATION: Bereziv Nyzhnii, Kolomyia district. OCCUPATION: Teacher. DISTINGUISHING FEATURES: *Shliakhta khodachkova.*[1] FAMILY BACKGROUND: Descended from the large and ancient Berezovsky clan of Bereziv, Ukrainian nobility that gradually became impoverished after the occupation of Galicia by Poland in the fourteenth century.[1] The Berezovsky family bore the Sas coat-of-arms.[2] "This group multiplied profusely and formed a large settlement of free yeomanry who jealously guarded their patents of nobility as a safeguard against falling into servitude."[1] His father Ivan was mayor and the wealthiest farmer in the village.[3] FAMILY CONNECTIONS: Brother of *Genyk, Stefan* (*CC* 206); married the daughter of *Tsurkovsky, Ihnatii.*[1] ECONOMIC STATUS: According to another teacher-activist (*Krushelnytsky, Maksym*), Genyk used to boast of his wealth.[4] EDUCATION: He received his primary education in Liucha, Kolomyia district, where he took private lessons from Andrii Nykorovych (probably a cantor). He finished five grades of the Polish gymnasium in Kolomyia,[3] attended the teachers' seminary in Stanyslaviv, and after graduating, finished the academic gymnasium in Lviv.[1] In the mid-1880s he wanted to study law at Chernivtsi University but failed the entrance examination.[5] AGE: Born 1857.[1] DEATH: 12 February 1925 (N.S.).[1] MOBILITY: He was born in his ancestral village of Bereziv Nyzhnii and educated in Kolomyia, Stanyslaviv and Lviv.[1] He first taught in Kaminne, Nadvirna district, in 1879,[6] but returned to Bereziv Nyzhnii, where he established a school in 1882 and taught in it.[7] He later opened a store in Iabloniv, Kolomyia district. In June 1896 he emigrated to Canada, where he lived mainly in Winnipeg, Manitoba. In his later years he moved to the United States, but died in Winnipeg.[1] PUBLICATIONS: He contributed an item of correspondence concerning emigration to Canada to *Dilo* in 1896. He wrote on Ukrainian immigrant life in Canada for the American paper *Svoboda*, 1897 and after. He also contributed to *Kanadiiskyi farmer*, 1903 and probably after.[8]

OTHER ACTIVITIES: He was a founder of the reading clubs in Bereziv Nyzhnii and Liucha (*CC* 206); he attended the inauguration of the reading club in Stopchativ (*CC* 263) and spoke on Shevchenko at the opening of the reading club in Kovalivka (*CC* 260). All these villages were in Kolomyia district.

Other teacher-activists found him pretensious about his petty noble origins. *Krushelnytsky, Maksym* described him as follows in 1885: "He's a materialist and one can see in him the arrogance of the nobility. He likes to brag about his wealth and we talk little about education."[4] Mykola Koltsuniak referred to him as "Korol,"[9] which is Ukrainian for "king" and a pun on the name Kyrylo.

In spite of these pretensions, Genyk had socialist leanings. He became acquainted with the Ukrainian radicals Ivan Franko and Ostap Terletsky in the late 1870s and distributed socialist literature to the peasants.[10] In early March 1880 Franko, who had already been tried as a socialist, came to Bereziv Nyzhnii allegedly to help Genyk prepare for his *matura* examination. The police were following Franko at the time and suspected that Franko had come to Kolomyia district on socialist business. On 9 March Genyk was arrested, along with peasants in whose possession socialist literature had been discovered (including *Hladii, Porfyr*). Genyk was never put on trial and was released from prison on 6 June.[11] (The dates here are in new style.) Genyk remained close to Franko and other

Ukrainian radicals as long as he remained in Galicia. His political affiliations prevented his appointment as a postal clerk in Galicia, even though he had passed the civil service examination. In 1892 Franko and Genyk established a local organization of the Ruthenian-Ukrainian Radical Party in Bereziv Nyzhnii.[12]

In the mid-1880s he became interested in business. He bought a mill in Iabloniv. In 1886, also in Iabloniv, he founded and directed an enterprise called "The Carpathian Store" (U *Karpatska kramnytsia*), which bought up Hutsul craft products for sale in Podillia. In 1889 a Carpathian Store also opened in Kolomyia, and Genyk travelled around the villages of Kosiv district to raise shares to open branches in Kosiv and Horodenka. He served on the auditing commission of the Hutsul Industrial Cooperative (U *Hutsulska spilka promyslova*), founded April 1888, and on the administration of the People's Cooperative (U *Narodna spilka*), founded in Kolomyia at the end of 1890. In 1890 he was elected to Kolomyia district council.[13]

Genyk took an interest in the mass emigration then underway from Galicia. He collaborated with Dr. Iosyf Oleskiv (Josef Oleskow) in advocating Canada as the country for the settlement of Ukrainian immigrants and attended the conference on emigration that Oleskiv convened in Lviv on 14 November 1895 (N.S.). On Oleskiv's urging, Genyk emigrated to Canada as the leader of the second group of emigrants assembled by Oleskiv in June 1896.[1] In Canada, Genyk was prominent in civic affairs. He was the first Ukrainian to enter Canadian government service, working as an immigration officer from early 1897[14] to March 1911.[1] While retaining his Ukrainian radical sympathies, he worked with the Liberal Party in Canada.[15] He founded a reading club in Winnipeg in 1899 and helped establish the newspaper *Kanadiiskyi farmer* (Winnipeg) in 1903[16] and the radically oriented, Protestant-leaning Independent Greek Church in 1903–4.[17]

1) Kaye, *Early Ukrainian Settlements*, 381–2. *2)* Kaye, *Dictionary of Ukrainian Canadian Biography*, 134. *3)* Kravchuk, *Kanadskyi druh*, 7. *4)* Letter of Maksym Krushelnytsky to Leonid Zaklynsky, 5 January 1885, in LNB AN URSR, Viddil rukopysiv, fond Zaklynskykh, 192/31, p. 147. *5)* Kravchuk, *Kanadskyi druh*, 8. *6)* *Szem. kr. Gal. 1879*, 411. *7)* Kravchuk, *Kanadskyi druh*, 7–8. *8)* Ibid., 45, 52, 56. *9)* Letter of Mykola Koltsuniak to Kornylo Hnatovych Zaklynsky, 8 July 1883, in LNB AN URSR, Viddil rukopysiv, fond Zaklynskykh, 192/31, p. 121. *10)* Kravchuk, *Kanadskyi druh*, 10. *11)* Kalynovych, *Politychni protsesy*, 106–16. *12)* Kravchuk, *Kanadskyi druh*, 23. *13)* Ibid., 8–9. *14)* Kaye and Swyripa, "Settlement and Colonization," 45. *15)* Martynowych and Kazymyra, "Political Activity in Western Canada," 91. *16)* Kalynovych, *Politychni protsesy*, 152. *17)* Yuzyk, "Religious Life," 152 (with dates corrected on the basis of information provided by Frances Swyripa).

84. **Genyk (-Berezovsky), Stefan**

LOCATION: Bereziv Nyzhnii, Kolomyia district. OCCUPATION: (Peasant). DISTINGUISHING FEATURES: *Shliakhta khodachkova*.[1] FAMILY BACKGROUND: See *Genyk, Kyrylo*. FAMILY CONNECTIONS: Brother of *Genyk, Kyrylo* (*CC* 206). AGE: He was older than *Genyk, Kyrylo*,[1] and was therefore born in 1856 or earlier. MOBILITY: Bereziv Nyzhnii was the Genyk ancestral home.[1] OTHER ACTIVITIES: He was a founder of the reading club in Bereziv Nyzhnii (*CC* 206). The writer Ivan Franko stayed with him on visits to Bereziv Nyzhnii between 1900 and 1913.[2]

1) Kaye, *Early Ukrainian Settlements*, 381–2. *2)* Kravchuk, *Kanadskyi druh*, 24.

85. **Gurnytsky (Hornytsky), Iosyf**

LOCATION: Korelychi, Peremyshliany district. OCCUPATION: Peasant. POSITION IN RC: Auditor (*CC* 84). ECONOMIC STATUS: Proprietor (*CC* 84). MOBILITY: Two Gurnytsky households were included in the list of Greek Catholic parishioners in Korelychi, 1864.[1] OTHER ACTIVITIES: He was one of the founders of the revived reading club in 1896 and was elected to its administration in 1897.[2]

1) TsDIAL, 146/64b/2294, p. 58. *2)* TsDIAL, 348/1/3031, pp. 3, 18v.

86. Halapats, Ivan

LOCATION: Vynnyky, Zhovkva district. OCCUPATION: (Peasant). POSITION IN RC: Vice-president (*CC* 5, 153). OTHER ACTIVITIES: Vice-president of the reading club from 1883.[1]

1) Vynnychanyn, "Pysmo vid Zhovkvy," *Batkivshchyna* 5, no. 50 (14 [2] December 1883): 301.

87. Havlytsky, Antin

LOCATION: Liubycha Kniazi, Rava Ruska district. OCCUPATION: Teacher. POSITION IN RC: Vice-president (*CC* 137). AUTHOR: *CC* 137 (coauthor). AGE: He was teaching from at least 1871[1] and was therefore born by 1849. MOBILITY: He taught in Liubycha Kniazi from at least 1871 until at least 1885.[1]

1) *Szem. kr. Gal. 1871*, 418; *ibid. 1885*, 410.

88. Herynovych, Petro

LOCATION: Khrystynopil, Sokal district. OCCUPATION: (Burgher). POSITION IN RC: Administration (*CC* 278).

89. Hetman, Iosyf

LOCATION: Nakvasha, Brody district. OCCUPATION: Peasant. POSITION IN RC: Deputy administration (*CC* 201). ECONOMIC STATUS: Proprietor (*CC* 201). AGE: He already held a representative function in the village by 1872[1] and was thus probably born before 1847. OTHER ACTIVITIES: A founder of the reading club, he also presented a talk on history at its inaugural meeting (*CC* 201). In 1872 he had been a plenipotentiary of the commune in servitude affairs.[1]

1) TsDIAL, 146/64/1154, p. 108.

90. Hetman, Stefan

LOCATION: Nakvasha, Brody district. OCCUPATION: Peasant. POSITION IN RC: Vice-president (*CC* 201). POSITION IN LOCAL GOVT: In 1867 he was a councilman.[1] ECONOMIC STATUS: Proprietor (*CC* 201). EDUCATION: Literate by 1867.[1] AGE: He was already a councilman in 1867,[1] so he was born before 1842. OTHER ACTIVITIES: He was a founder of the reading club (*CC* 201). In 1872 he had been a plenipotentiary of the commune in servitude affairs.[2]

1) TsDIAL, 146/64/1154, p. 2. *2) Ibid.*, p. 108.

91. Hladii, Porfyr(ii)

LOCATION: Bereziv Vyzhnii, Kolomyia district. OCCUPATION: Cantor,[1] peasant (*CC* 206) and merchant (*CC* 206). ECONOMIC STATUS: Proprietor of land (*CC* 206) and of a store.[2] AGE: Described as "young" (*CC* 206). PUBLICATIONS: Possible author of an item of correspondence in *Batkivshchyna*, 1883.[1]

OTHER ACTIVITIES: He was the founder of a reading club in Bereziv Vyzhnii in 1883, against the opposition of the mayor Iurko Genyk and the scribe.[1] Described as "an ardent Ruthenian patriot," he read aloud from books at the inauguration of reading clubs in Liucha (*CC* 206) and Kovalivka (*CC* 260) and also spoke at the inauguration of the reading club in Bereziv Nyzhnii.[2] All these villages were in Kolomyia district.

Earlier, on 9 March 1880 (N.S.), he had been arrested along with other peasants as well as Ivan Franko and *Genyk, Kyrylo* on suspicion of distributing socialist propaganda. A search of his home led to the discovery of socialist literature, but he was released without being brought to trial on 6 June (N.S.).[3]

In 1887 he and other peasants tried to organize a concert in the village, but the district authorities prohibited it. In the same year the mayor had him arrested in the course of a conflict over the reading club.[4]

1) P[or]F[y]R [Hladii?], "Pysmo z Kolomyishchyny," *Batkivshchyna* 5, no. 4 (26 [14] January 1883): 23. *2)* "O nashykh chytalniakh," *Batkivshchyna* 7, no. 23 (5 June [24 May] 1885): 172. *3)* Kalynovych, *Politychni protsesy,* 106–16. *4)* Kravchuk, *Kanadskyi druh,* 8–9.

92. Hladun, Nykola

LOCATION: Mizun, Dolyna district. OCCUPATION: Peasant. POSITION IN RC: Vice-president.[1] POSITION IN LOCAL GOVT: Mayor.[1] FAMILY BACKGROUND: Andrei Hladun, presumably Nykola's father, paid average annual taxes to the manor of 1.9 gulden on cattle and 10.1 gulden on sheep and swine, 1836–45; the average peasant of Mizun paid 1.1 gulden on cattle and 0.1 gulden on sheep and swine. Thus Andrei Hladun was exceptionally wealthy in livestock. In 1852 he owned 26 *Joch* 938 square *Klafter,* which made him one of the richest 10 per cent of peasant landholders in the village.[2] MOBILITY: The Hladun family had been settled in Mizun since at least 1836.[2] OTHER ACTIVITIES: He was described as "a patriot known throughout the region."[1] During the 1885 parliamentary elections, he alone of the mayors of his electoral district voted for the Ukrainian candidate (*CC* 203). In 1886 he took a leading role in plans to build a new stone church in Mizun. The Russophile paper that reported on these activities of "the fine mayor" nonetheless regretted that "he corresponds with the authorities in Polish."[3]

1) Kh., "...vid Dolyny," *Batkivshchyna* 6, no. 36 (24 August [5 September] 1884): 224. *2)* TsDIAL, 488/1/277, pp. 25v, 84v–85, 91. *3)* Exc., "Iz dolynskoho povita," *Novyi prolom* 4 (6), no. 356 (26 July [7 August] 1886): 2.

93. Hlibovytsky, Aleksander

LOCATION: Nakvasha, Brody district. OCCUPATION: Priest. POSITION IN RC: President (*CC* 201). ECONOMIC STATUS: pastor of a parish with 1,266 members, an endowment of 52 *Joch* of arable land and 14 *Joch* of meadow and a *congruum* of 185 gulden.[1] AGE: Born 1835, ordained 1862.[1] MARITAL STATUS: Married.[1] OTHER ACTIVITIES: He was a founder of the reading club, temperance society, communal granary and loan association; he also had the parish buildings restored (*CC* 201). In 1875–6 he had been involved in a servitudes dispute with the manor over pasturing.[2]

1) *Shem. Lviv. 1884,* 49–50. *2)* TsDIAL, 146/64/1155.

94. Hlibovytsky, Konstantyn

LOCATION: Briukhovychi, Peremyshliany district. OCCUPATION: Priest. ECONOMIC STATUS: Chaplain of a Greek Catholic community with 344 members, an endowment of 35 *Joch* of arable land, 6 *Joch* of meadow and 40 square metres of wood for fuel and a *congruum* of 87 gulden.[1] AGE: Born 1837, ordained 1864.[1] MARITAL STATUS: Married.[1] OTHER ACTIVITIES: He was a founder of the reading club and proponent of enlightenment (*CC* 57). He was prefect of the archeparchal widows' and orphans' fund.[1]

1) *Shem. Lviv. 1884,* 106.

95. Hlynsky, Teofan

LOCATION: Horodnytsia, Horodenka district. OCCUPATION: Priest. AUTHOR: *CC* 115,[1] 150, 160. ECONOMIC STATUS: Pastor of a parish with 1,516 members, an endowment of 116 *Joch* of arable land and 0.67 *Joch* of meadow and a *congruum* of 143 gulden 26 kreuzer.[2] He was also an avid bee-keeper.[3] AGE: Born 1806, ordained 1829.[2] DEATH: 17 April 1893 (N.S.).[4] MARITAL STATUS: Married.[2] PUBLICATIONS: An obituary mentioned that he was a frequent contributor of correspondence and practical, didactic articles to the Ukrainian press.[4] Several articles in *Hospodar i promyshlennyk,* 1881, and *Zoria,* 1882, attest to his interest in bee-keeping.[3]

OTHER ACTIVITIES: In two of the items of correspondence contributed to *Batkivshchyna* (*CC* 150, 160), Hlynsky argued for a radical revision and expansion of popular education as well as for participatory democracy based on a system of popular tribunes.

Hlynsky was a long-time veteran of the Ukrainian movement. In June 1848 he was elected secretary of the Ruthenian Council in Bohorodchany.[5] He took part in the congress of Galician-Ruthenian scholars convened in Lviv in October 1848; he was a member of the sections on theology and elementary education and delivered a lecture on language.[6] He was then and remained throughout his life a consistent advocate of phonetic orthography.[4] He subscribed to the literary almanach *Zoria halytskaia* in 1860.[7] He was a member of Prosvita in 1868–74[8] and later, as well as a member of Narodnyi dim[2] and the Shevchenko society. He promoted sobriety in his parish.[6] He was a titular councillor of the metropolitan consistory with the designation *kryloshanyn*.[2]

1) Authorship determined on the basis of a letter of Maksym Krushelnytsky to Leonid Zaklynsky, 8 March 1885, in LNB AN URSR, Viddil Rukopysiv, fond Zaklynskykh, 192/31, p. 150. *2) Shem. Lviv. 1884,* 214. *3)* Lev1, no. 2251, 2406I. *4)* "Posmertni opovistky. Teofan Hlynsky," *Zoria* 14, no. 8 (15 [27] April 1893): 164. *5) Klasova borotba,* 401–2. *6)* Lev493, H-121. *7)* "Spys vpcht. prenumerantov," *Zoria halytskaia...1860*; this should not be confused with the newspaper bearing a similar title. *8)* "Chleny tovarystva 'Prosvita'," *Spravozdaniie z dilanii "Prosvity"* (1874), 26–32

96. Holodryha (Holodryga), Mykola

LOCATION: Mykolaiv, Brody district. OCCUPATION: Peasant.[1] PUBLICATIONS: Coauthor of a denunciation of the teacher *Medynsky, Ivan*[2] and of an item of correspondence describing Mykolaiv's celebration of the anniversary of the abolition of serfdom (3 May 1888 [O.S.]).[1] OTHER ACTIVITIES: He served on the deputy administration of the Pravda society, 1884–5 (*CC* 71, 198).

1) Vasyl Iakubiv, Mykola Martyshuk, Mykola Holodryga, "Pysmo z Brodskoho," *Batkivshchyna* 10, no. 22 (1 June [20 May] 1885): 135. *2)* Mykola Holodryha *et al.,* "Dopysy 'Dila'. Mykolaiv v poviti bridskim," *Dilo* 8, no. 92 (20 August [1 September] 1887): 2.

97. Holoiad, Adam

LOCATION: Piznanka Hnyla, Skalat district. OCCUPATION: Peasant. POSITION IN RC: Treasurer (*CC* 238). ECONOMIC STATUS: Proprietor (*CC* 238).

98. Holovatsky, Danylo

LOCATION: Bilyi Kamin, Zolochiv district. OCCUPATION: (Burgher). EDUCATION: Literate (*CC* 262). OTHER ACTIVITIES: He served on the deputy administration of the Pravda society (*CC* 262).

99. Holovchuk

LOCATION: Ordiv, Sokal district. POSITION IN RC: Secretary (*CC* 277). AUTHOR: *CC* 277.

100. Holovinsky, Stefan

LOCATION: Fytkiv, Nadvirna district. OCCUPATION: Cantor.[1] POSITION IN RC: Secretary (*CC* 58). OTHER ACTIVITIES: He was still secretary of the reading club in 1886.[1]

1) M. Ianevorihvash, "Pysmo z Nadvirnianskoho," *Batkivshchyna* 8, no. 13 (2 April [21 March] 1886): 77.

101. Holovka, Vasyl(ii)

LOCATION: Liubycha Kniazi, Rava Ruska district. OCCUPATION: (Peasant). POSITION IN RC: Deputy administration (*CC* 137). AUTHOR: *CC* 49. FAMILY BACKGROUND: A Hrynko Holovka had been mayor in 1847–51.[1] AGE: A "young man" (U *molodets*) (*CC* 137). MOBILITY: The Holovka family had been in Liubycha Kniazi since at least the 1840s.[1] OTHER ACTIVITIES: He declaimed verse at the inauguration of the reading club in Makhniv, Rava Ruska district (*CC* 137).

1) TsDIAL, 166/1/1778, pp. 16, 18, 39, 67, 79.

102. Horak, Ivan

LOCATION: Shliakhtyntsi, Ternopil district. OCCUPATION: (Peasant). POSITION IN RC: Deputy administration (*CC* 108).

103. Horbachuk, Pavlo

LOCATION: Khrystynopil, Sokal district. OCCUPATION: (Burgher). POSITION IN RC: Administration (*CC* 278).

104. Horodysky, Iakiv

LOCATION: Stupnytsia, Sambir district. OCCUPATION: Teacher. AGE: He began teaching in the mid-1870s,[1] and hence was born in the early 1850s. MOBILITY: He first taught in Rudky (district capital) until 1877,[1] then in Dubliany, Sambir district, from 1878 to c. 1879,[2] and later in Stupnytsia, from c. 1881.[3] OTHER ACTIVITIES: He was a cofounder of one of the few reading clubs in a village inhabited almost exclusively by *shliakhta khodachkova* (*CC* 130).

1) He is not mentioned in *Szem. kr. Gal. 1874*, but is in *ibid. 1877*, 436. *2) Ibid. 1878*, 427; *ibid. 1879*, 419. *3) Ibid. 1881*, 434; *ibid. 1885*, 414.

105. Horutsky, Oleksander P.

LOCATION: Strilkiv, Stryi district. OCCUPATION: Teacher. POSITION IN RC: President (*CC* 149). AGE: He began teaching in 1878,[1] which would suggest he was born c. 1858. However, his first contributions to the Ukrainian press appeared in 1870,[2] which would suggest that he was at least five years older, thus born c. 1853. MOBILITY: He first taught in Sholomyia, Bibrka district, from 1878 until the early 1880s;[3] he then taught in Strilkiv.[4] PUBLICATIONS: He contributed verses to the national populist children's magazine *Lastivka*, 1870 and 1872;[2] and to the pedagogical journals *Hazeta shkolna*, 1879, and *Shkolna chasopys*, 1880.[5] He published a short novel, *Kryvoprysiaha*, as a Prosvita booklet in 1883.[6] OTHER ACTIVITIES: He was a member of Prosvita at some time during the period 1868–74.[7]

1) He is not mentioned in *Szem. kr. Gal. 1873* or *1877*; he first appears in *ibid. 1878*, 385. *2)* Lev1, no. 954I and 1145I. *3) Szem. kr. Gal. 1878*, 385; *ibid. 1881*, 389. *4) Ibid. 1884*, 420; *ibid. 1885*, 420. *5)* Lev1, no. 1919II, 2215. *6)* Lev1, no. 2549. *7)* "Chleny tovarystva 'Prosvita'," *Spravozdaniie z dilanii "Prosvity"* (1874), 26–32.

106. Hrabovetsky, Ivan

LOCATION: Olesha, Tovmach district. OCCUPATION: Peasant. POSITION IN RC: Deputy administration. MOBILITY: Four Hrabovetsky households lived in Olesha in 1850–5.[1]

1) TsDIAL, 168/1/4099, pp. 1v, 88v.

107. Hrabovetsky, Lavrentii

LOCATION: Balyntsi, Kolomyia district. OCCUPATION: Peasant. POSITION IN LOCAL GOVT: Mayor (*CC* 95). ECONOMIC STATUS: Proprietor (*CC* 95). MOBILITY: There were seven Hrabovetsky households in Balyntsi, 1837–46.[1] OTHER ACTIVITIES: He was a founder of the reading club (*CC* 95).

1) TsDIAL, 168/1/1416, pp. 84v–92.

108. Hrabovetsky, Mykhailo

LOCATION: Balyntsi, Kolomyia district. OCCUPATION: Peasant. ECONOMIC STATUS: Proprietor (*CC* 95). MOBILITY: There were seven Hrabovetsky households in Balyntsi, 1837–46.[1] OTHER ACTIVITIES: He was a founder of the reading club (*CC* 95). In 1893 he was a member of the radical political association Narodna volia.[2]

1) TsDIAL, 168/1/1416, pp. 9v, 45v, 58v, 84v–92. *2)* "Spys chleniv 'Narodnoi Voli'," *Khliborob* 3, no. 20 (15 October 1893): 144.

109. Hrabovych, Ioann

LOCATION: Stopchativ and Kovalivka, Kolomyia district. OCCUPATION: Priest. POSITION IN RC: President in both Stopchativ (*CC* 263) and Kovalivka (*CC* 260). ECONOMIC STATUS: Pastor of Stopchativ and its daughter church in Kovalivka, with 2,891 members and an endowment of 24 *Joch* of arable land, 155 *Joch* of meadow (U *sinozhatiie*), 7 *Joch* 850 square *Klafter* of forest, 107 *Joch* of pasture (U *pasovysko*) and 52 square metres of beechwood; instead of a *congruum*, he paid 30 gulden 51 kreuzer to the treasury.[1] Stopchativ had the reputation of being a lucrative parish.[2] AGE: Born 1824, ordained 1848.[1] MARITAL STATUS: Married.[1] OTHER ACTIVITIES: He was a founder of the reading club in Stopchativ (*CC* 263). He was administrator of the Pistyn deanery and titular councillor of the metropolitan consistory with the rank of *kryloshanyn*.[3]

1) Shem. Lviv. 1884, 261. *2)* Olesnytsky, *Storinky*, 240. *3) Shem. Lviv. 1884*, 256.

110. Hrynevetsky, Apolinarii

LOCATION: Lysiatychi, Stryi district. OCCUPATION: Priest. ECONOMIC STATUS: Assistant in a parish of 2,840 members.[1] AGE: Born 1850, ordained 1877.[2] MARITAL STATUS: Married.[1] MOBILITY: He was an assistant in Lysiatychi for several years, but was transferred by 1884 (*CC* 70). OTHER ACTIVITIES: He was active in the reading club and a founder of other village institutions (*CC* 70).

1) Shem. Lviv. 1883, 154. *2) Ibid. 1884*, 66.

111. Hrynkiv, Ivan

LOCATION: Dobrostany, Horodok district. OCCUPATION: Peasant. POSITION IN RC: Auditor, 1884 (*CC* 100); vice-president, 1885 (*CC* 245). ECONOMIC STATUS: Proprietor (*CC* 245). OTHER ACTIVITIES: He was a trustee (U *provizor*) of the church (*CC* 100). In the late 1860s and early 1870s he was active in Dobrostany's conflict with the manor over servitudes; he, along with other peasants, pastured cattle on what had legally been declared demesnal land. A hundred hussars quelled the resistance in 1871. In 1872 Hrynkiv was sentenced to sixteen days in jail and a fine of 260 gulden.[1]

1) Adriian, *Agrarnyi protses*, 48.

112. Hrytsyna, Teodor

LOCATION: Horodnytsia, Husiatyn district. OCCUPATION: Priest. ECONOMIC STATUS: Pastor of a parish with 1,240 members, an endowment of 116 *Joch* of arable land and a *congruum* of 140 gulden 55 kreuzer.[1] AGE: Born 1826, ordained 1852.[1] DEATH: 1894.[2] MARITAL STATUS: Married.[1] MOBILITY: He had been administrator of Tsyhany and Zhelentsi, Chortkiv circle, in 1864.[3] OTHER ACTIVITIES: He was a founder of the reading club (*CC* 115). In 1864 he had been involved in a servitudes dispute with Prince Adam Sapieha.[4]

1) Shem. Lviv. 1884, 219. *2)* Lev493, H-258. *3)* TsDIAL, 146/64/738, p. 6. *4) Ibid.*, and TsDIAL, 146/64/741, p. 33.

113. Hunkevych, Hrynko

LOCATION: Bilyi Kamin, Zolochiv district. OCCUPATION: (Burgher). POSITION IN RC: Deputy administration (*CC* 275).

114. Hunkevych, Klym

LOCATION: Bilyi Kamin, Zolochiv district. OCCUPATION: (Burgher). EDUCATION: Literate (*CC* 262). OTHER ACTIVITIES: He served in the administration of the Pravda society (*CC* 262).

115. Hupalo, Stefan

LOCATION: Kukyziv, Lviv district. OCCUPATION: (Peasant). POSITION IN RC: Deputy administration (*CC* 10).

116. Hysovsky, Ioann

LOCATION: Zhuravtsi, Rava Ruska district. OCCUPATION: Priest (*CC* 137). POSITION IN RC: Vice-president (*CC* 137). OTHER ACTIVITIES: He attended the inauguration of the reading club in Makhniv, Rava Ruska district (*CC* 137).

117. Iakoba, Aleksander

LOCATION: Olesko, Zolochiv district. OCCUPATION: (Peasant). FAMILY BACKGROUND: Pavlo Iakoba, presumably Aleksander's father, had the third largest holding in the village, 1852–5.[1] EDUCATION: Literate (*CC* 262). MOBILITY: The Iakoba family had been in Olesko since at least 1852.[1] OTHER ACTIVITIES: He served on the administration of the Pravda society (*CC* 262).

118. Ianishevsky, Teodor

LOCATION: Zboriv, Zolochiv district. OCCUPATION: Cantor. AUTHOR: *CC* 126, 187 (coauthor), 215. EDUCATION: An "examined cantor" (U *ispytovanyi pivets*) (*CC* 215). PUBLICATIONS: He contributed a brief note on the cantors' movement to *Batkivshchyna*, 1885.[1] OTHER ACTIVITIES: He was president of the temporary cantors' committee, 1884 (*CC* 126).

1) Teodor Ianishevsky, "V spravi diakivskii," *Batkivshchyna* 7, no. 8 (20 [8] February 1885): 64.

119. Iarema, Ivan

LOCATION: Mykulyntsi, Ternopil district. OCCUPATION: (Artisan or peasant). POSITION IN RC: President (*CC* 96). FAMILY BACKGROUND: A Kindrat Iarema, presumably Ivan's father, was a quarter-peasant in 1852–5. He had 7 *Joch* 769 square *Klafter* of land in a town where the holdings of the agricultural households averaged just under 8 *Joch*. He was, then, a middling peasant. MOBILITY: The Iarema family had lived in Mykulyntsi since at least 1852.[1] OTHER ACTIVITIES: Ivan Iarema remained active in the reading club. He was still president in 1890[2] and vice-president in 1895.[3]

1) TsDIAL, 488/1/673, p. 6v. *2)* "Nashi chytalni," *Batkivshchyna* 12, no. 38–9 (21 September [3 October] 1890): 492. *3)* "Visty z kraiu," *Batkivshchyna* 17, no. 8 (16 [28] April 1895): 60.

120. Iasenytsky, Mykhail

LOCATION: Kutkivtsi, Ternopil district. OCCUPATION: Priest. POSITION IN RC: President (*CC* 69). ECONOMIC STATUS: Pastor of a parish with 902 members, an endowment of 118 *Joch* of arable land and 31 *Joch* of meadow and a *congruum* of 31 gulden 25 kreuzer.[1] AGE: Born 1832, ordained 1858.[1] MARITAL STATUS: Married.[1] OTHER ACTIVITIES: In 1886 he signed a protest against an attempt by the national populists to gain entry into Narodnyi dim in Lviv.[2]

1) Shem. Lviv. 1884, 162. *2)* R.M., "Ot Ternopolia," *Slovo* 26, no. 33 (26 March [7 April] 1886): 2. For the background to this matter, see Olesnytsky, *Storinky*, 1:202–3.

121. Iaskuliak, I.

LOCATION: Bila, Ternopil district. OCCUPATION: (Peasant). POSITION IN RC: Vice-president (*CC* 69).

122. Iasynsky, Vasyl

LOCATION: Kovalivka, Kolomyia district. OCCUPATION: (Peasant). POSITION IN RC: Vice-president (*CC* 260). POSITION IN LOCAL GOVT: Mayor (*CC* 260). FAMILY BACKGROUND: His father Mykhailo had been mayor in the past (*CC* 260). ECONOMIC STATUS: He was probably prosperous, since the room of his house that he let the reading club use was described as "beautiful and spacious" (*CC* 260). MOBILITY: His father was already well established in Kovalivka (*CC* 260). OTHER ACTIVITIES: He was a founder of the reading club, which he hosted in his home. Regularly chosen as an elector, he cast his votes for Ukrainian candidates (*CC* 260).

123. Iavorsky, Aleksander

LOCATION: Stupnytsia, Sambir district. OCCUPATION: Seminarian (*CC* 130). AGE: Born 1854, ordained 1885.[1] MOBILITY: In 1900 he was pastor of Lopushanka Khomyna, Staryi

Sambir district.[1] OTHER ACTIVITIES: He was a founder of one of the few reading clubs in a village inhabited almost exclusively by *shliakhta khodachkova* (*CC* 130).

1) Schematismus... cleri dioeceseos... Premisliensis... 1900, 149.

124. Iavorsky, Ivan

LOCATION: Stupnytsia, Sambir district. OCCUPATION: Seminarian (*CC* 130). AGE: Born 1858, ordained 1884.[1] DEATH: 1930.[2] MOBILITY: In 1900 he was pastor of Strilbychi, Staryi Sambir district. OTHER ACTIVITIES: He was a founder of one of the few reading clubs in a village inhabited almost exclusively by *shliakhta khodachkova* (*CC* 130). Later he was active in the Ukrainian National Democratic Party. He served as a deputy to the Galician diet, fought for the expansion of Ukrainian education and organized agricultural labourers' strikes in 1902.[2]

1) Schematismus... cleri dioeceseos... Premisliensis... 1900, 151. *2) Ukrainska Zahalna Entsyklopediia*, s.v. "Iavorsky."

125. Iskra, Roman

LOCATION: Piznanka Hnyla, Skalat district. OCCUPATION: Peasant. AUTHOR: *CC* 238. ECONOMIC STATUS: Proprietor (*CC* 238). PUBLICATIONS: He contributed an item of correspondence on the opening of the reading club in Piznanka Hnyla to *Slovo* in 1885.[1]

1) Roman I[skra], "Ot Skalata," *Slovo* 25, no. 86 (10 [22] August 1885): 3.

126. Iurkiv, Roman

LOCATION: Darakhiv, Terebovlia district. OCCUPATION: Peasant. POSITION IN RC: President (*CC* 82). ECONOMIC STATUS: Proprietor (*CC* 82). OTHER ACTIVITIES: He was a founder of the reading club (*CC* 82).

127. Iuzkiv, Iliia

LOCATION: Utishkiv, Zolochiv district. OCCUPATION: (Peasant). POSITION IN RC: Deputy administration (*CC* 216).

128. Iuzvak, Semen

LOCATION: Mykolaiv, Brody district. OCCUPATION: Peasant. AGE: He was registered as a landholder in a document from 1859; the document implies that he only very recently had come into the land.[1] He was therefore born c. 1834. OTHER ACTIVITIES: He was an auditor of the Pravda society (*CC* 198).

1) TsDIAL, 146/64/1124, p. 145v.

129. Ivanets, Ivan

LOCATION: Barani Peretoky, Sokal district. OCCUPATION: Merchant. AUTHOR: *CC* 3. OTHER ACTIVITIES: He established a store in Barani Peretoky in 1882. In his item of correspondence he urged more Ukrainians to establish stores (*CC* 3).

130. Ivantsiv, Avksentii

LOCATION: Utishkiv, Zolochiv district. OCCUPATION: (Peasant). POSITION IN RC: Deputy administration (*CC* 216).

131. Kalynsky, Iosyf

LOCATION: Kukyziv, Lviv district. OCCUPATION: (Peasant). POSITION IN RC: Treasurer (*CC* 10).

132. Kamianetsky, Matvii

LOCATION: Rava Ruska district. AUTHOR: *CC* 163, 211.

133. Kamynsky, Ivan

LOCATION: Darakhiv, Terebovlia district. OCCUPATION: Teacher. POSITION IN RC: Secretary (*CC* 82). AGE: He began teaching in 1871[1] or earlier and was therefore born before 1849. MOBILITY: He taught in Darakhiv from at least 1871 until at least 1885.[1]

1) Szem. kr. Gal. 1871, 427; *ibid. 1885*, 424.

134. Karp, Kost

LOCATION: Makhniv, Rava Ruska district. OCCUPATION: (Peasant). POSITION IN RC: Deputy administration (*CC* 137).

135. Karp, Vasyl

LOCATION: Bilyi Kamin, Zolochiv district. OCCUPATION: (Burgher). EDUCATION: Literate (*CC* 262). OTHER ACTIVITIES: He served in the deputy administration of the Pravda society (*CC* 262).

136. Kavchynsky, Stefan

LOCATION: Kadobna, Kalush district. OCCUPATION: Teacher. POSITION IN RC: Vice-president (*CC* 121). AGE: He began teaching in 1871[1] or earlier and was therefore born before 1849. MOBILITY: He taught in Krushelnytsia, Stryi district, in 1871;[1] in Kavsko, Stryi district, in 1872;[2] in Voleniv, Zhydachiv district, from 1873 until at least 1874;[3] in Berezyna, Zhydachiv district, from at least 1877 until at least 1879;[4] in Veldizh, Dolyna district, in 1881 at least;[5] and in Kadobna at least in 1884–5.[6]

1) Szem. kr. Gal. 1871, 424. *2) Ibid. 1872*, 411. *3) Ibid. 1873*, 425; *ibid. 1874*, 459. *4) Ibid. 1877*, 455; *ibid. 1879*, 436. *5) Ibid. 1881*, 399. *6) Ibid. 1884*, 387; *ibid. 1885*, 387.

137. Kekosh, Iurii

LOCATION: Khorostkiv, Husiatyn district. OCCUPATION: Peasant and cobbler (*CC* 21). AUTHOR: *CC* 21. ECONOMIC STATUS: He was a small-holder, with only a "string" (U *shnur*)[1] of arable land. He worked in the winter and part-time in the spring as a cobbler (*CC* 21).

1) A *shnur* was a unit of length, 44.665 metres. It was used particularly in areas, like Husiatyn district, where repartitional land communes had existed until the early nineteenth century. In these areas all the holdings in a village had the same width (generally one *shnur*) and the size of a particular holding was determined by its length. See Rosdolsky, *Wspólnota gminna*, 1–9, 19–36. A *shnur* was also a unit of area. According to Ihnatowicz, *Vademecum*, it was equal to 0.199499 hectares; according to a Ukrainian-German dictionary from the mid-1880s, however, it was larger than a *Joch*.

138. Kendiukh, Hnat

LOCATION: Khotin, Kalush district. OCCUPATION: Peasant.[1] POSITION IN RC: Deputy administration (*CC* 121). OTHER ACTIVITIES: He was a founder of the reading club in 1884;[1] when the reading club was revived in 1892, he was unanimously elected president.[2] He was re-elected president in 1893.[3] He had been a member of the Khotin church committee in 1889[4] and supported the mayor *Dragan, Iurko* in his campaign to build a new church.[5] As an elector in the elections to the diet in 1895, he voted for the Ukrainian candidate.[6]

1) Hp., "Nova chytalnia," *Batkivshchyna* 6, no. 26 (27 [15] June 1884): 159. *2)* "Z Khotina kolo Kalusha," *Batkivshchyna* 14, no. 31 (31 July [12 August] 1892): 153. *3)* "Z Kalushchyny," *Batkivshchyna* 15, no. 15 (1 [13] August 1893): 116. *4)* "Zaprosyny," *Batkivshchyna* 11, no. 19 (12 [24] May 1889): 252. *5)* M.D., "Visty z kraiu," *Batkivshchyna* 11, no. 25 (23 June [5 July] 1889): 319. *6)* Iaroslav Korytovsky, "Iak perevodyly sia vybory v Kalushchyni," *Batkivshchyna* 17, no. 19 (1 [13] October 1895): 146.

139. Kharambura, Ivan

LOCATION: Iavoriv (district capital). OCCUPATION: Burgher (*CC* 142). POSITION IN RC: Deputy administration (*CC* 142).

140. Kharambura, Stefan

LOCATION: Iavoriv (district capital). OCCUPATION: Burgher (*CC* 142). POSITION IN RC: President (*CC* 142). OTHER ACTIVITIES: He donated a periodical subscription to the reading club (*CC* 142).

141. Kholevchuk, Dmytro

LOCATION: Liucha, Kolomyia district. OCCUPATION: (Peasant). POSITION IN RC: Secretary (*CC* 206).

142. Khoma, Ivan

LOCATION: Dobrostany, Horodok district. OCCUPATION: Cantor (*CC* 100). POSITION IN RC: Secretary (*CC* 100, 122). AUTHOR: *CC* 122 (coauthor). PUBLICATIONS: He contributed a brief note on the reading club's activities to *Batkivshchyna* in 1885.[1]
OTHER ACTIVITIES: He sang a baritone solo at the reading club's commemoration of the twenty-fourth anniversary of Shevchenko's death (1885)[2] and also presented a talk on Shevchenko in the reading club (*CC* 245).

Dobrostany had a history of conflict with the authorities and was reluctant to recognize laws and institutions that originated from the imperial, crownland and district administrations. In 1886–7 the commune of Dobrostany refused to recognize the state school system and set up its own school in the reading club, with Ivan Khoma as cantor-teacher (U *diakouchytel*). The Horodok district authorities summoned the mayor to court three times and ordered him either to close down or to regularize the school. But the mayor declared in the name of the commune that the commune had its own school and teacher and that no other school would be accepted. The district authorities also took Khoma to court in 1887 and prohibited him from teaching under the threat of severe punishment.[3]

1) Ivan Khoma, "...vid Horodka," *Batkivshchyna* 7, no. 4 (23 [11] January 1885): 31. *2)* "O nashykh chytalniakh," *Batkivshchyna* 7, no. 12 (20 [8] March 1885): 95. *3)* Pidhorodchuk, "Pysmo z pid Horodka," *Batkivshchyna* 9, no. 47 (25 [13] November 1887): 280.

143. Khudoba, Vasyl

LOCATION: Mykolaiv, Brody district. OCCUPATION: Peasant.[1] ECONOMIC STATUS: Wealthy.[1] OTHER ACTIVITIES: He served in the deputy administration of the Pravda society in 1884 (*CC* 71) and as auditor in 1885 (*CC* 198).

1) Tarnavsky, *Spohady*, 32.

144. Klymivsky, Pavlo

LOCATION: Bilyi kamin, Zolochiv district. OCCUPATION: (Burgher). POSITION IN RC: Administration (*CC* 275).

145. Kmet, Matvii

LOCATION: Tsebriv, Ternopil district. OCCUPATION: (Peasant). POSITION IN RC: Deputy administration (*CC* 44).

146. Koliankovsky, Volodymyr

LOCATION: Chekhy, Brody district. OCCUPATION: Priest. POSITION IN RC: President (*CC* 271). ECONOMIC STATUS: Pastor of a parish with 1,300 members, an endowment of 28 *Joch* of arable land and 18 *Joch* of meadow, compensation for servitudes of 8 *Joch* of meadow and 20 *Klafter* of wood, and a *congruum* of 147 gulden 29 kreuzer.[1] AGE: Born 1846, ordained 1880.[1] MARITAL STATUS: Married.[1] OTHER ACTIVITIES: He was a founder of the Pravda society (*CC* 262).

1) Shem. Lviv. 1884, 116.

147. **Koltsuniak (Kovtsuniak), Vasyl**

LOCATION: Kovalivka, Kolomyia district. OCCUPATION: (Peasant). POSITION IN RC: Treasurer (*CC* 260). FAMILY BACKGROUND: A Semen Koltsuniak had been a respected mayor of Kovalivka. His son Mykola became a teacher in Iabloniv, Kolomyia district, and was very active in the reading club movement in Kolomyia district.[1]

1) K., "Rukh v nashykh chytalniakh. Chytalni v Kovalivtsi i Stopchatovi," *Dilo* 6, no. 120 (31 October [12 November] 1885): 3.

148. **Koltuniak, Nykolai**

LOCATION: Komarno, Rudky district. OCCUPATION: Priest. POSITION IN RC: Treasurer (*CC* 9). ECONOMIC STATUS: Assistant (*CC* 9) in a town that had 1,995 Greek Catholics in 1880.[1] AGE: Born 1857, ordained 1882.[2] MARITAL STATUS: Married.[2] MOBILITY: He was transferred from Komarno to Steniatyn, Sokal district, in 1884;[3] in 1900 he was pastor of Tarnawka (Tarnavka), Łańcut district.[2] OTHER ACTIVITIES: He was a member of the supervisory board of the Komarno loan fund until he was transferred.[4]

1) Spec. Orts-Rep. 1880. 2) Schematismus...cleri dioeceseos...Premisliensis...1900, 61. *3)* [Dmytro?] Vilkhovy, "Dopysy. Z Komarna," *Dilo* 6, no. 75–6 (11 [23] July 1885): 3. *4)* "Dopysy. Z Komarna," *Dilo* 7, no. 62 (7 [19] June 1886): 4.

149. **Komarensky, Kuzma**

LOCATION: Bilyi Kamin, Zolochiv district. OCCUPATION: (Burgher). POSITION IN RC: Deputy administration (*CC* 275).

150. **Konashevych, Teodor**

LOCATION: Bilyi Kamin, Zolochiv district. OCCUPATION: Burgher (*CC* 148). POSITION IN RC: Administration (*CC* 275).

151. **Korchemny, Ivan**

LOCATION: Hai Starobridski, Brody district. OCCUPATION: Cantor (*CC* 186). AUTHOR: *CC* 186. OTHER ACTIVITIES: He was an elected representative of the Brody deanery cantors in 1885 (*CC* 186). He was a candidate during elections to the Brody district council in July 1885.[1]

1) "...vybory do rady povitovoi," *Batkivshchyna* 7, no. 28 (10 July [28 June] 1885): 206.

152. **Kormyliuk, Ivan**

LOCATION: Mykolaiv, Brody district. OCCUPATION: (Peasant). POSITION IN RC: Deputy administration (*CC* 198).

153. **Kostelnytsky, Kazymir**

LOCATION: Kolodribka, Zalishchyky district. OCCUPATION: Peasant. POSITION IN RC: Librarian (*CC* 76). ECONOMIC STATUS: Proprietor (*CC* 76). OTHER ACTIVITIES: He was librarian of the reading club in 1890[1] and one of the founders of the revived reading club in 1897.[2]

1) "Chytalnia v Kolodribtsi," *Batkivshchyna* 12, no. 24 (8 [20] June 1890): 311. *2)* TsDIAL, 348/1/2936, p. 40.

154. **Kostetsky, Ivan**

LOCATION: Olesko, Zolochiv district. OCCUPATION: (Peasant or artisan). FAMILY BACKGROUND: A Vasyl Kostetsky, presumably Ivan's father, was a small-holder with only 2 *Joch* 595 square *Klafter* in 1852–5.[1] He probably combined farming with a trade. EDUCATION: Literate (*CC* 262). MOBILITY: The Kostetsky family had lived in Olesko since at least 1852.[1] OTHER ACTIVITIES: He served on the administration of the Pravda society (*CC* 262).

1) TsDIAL, 168/1/1197, p. 27v.

155. **Kostiv, Ivan**

LOCATION: Vistova, Kalush district. OCCUPATION: Peasant. POSITION IN RC: Secretary (*CC* 161). ECONOMIC STATUS: It was said that "he farms well" (U *dobre hospodariuie*) (*CC* 161). EDUCATION: He loved books and was said to know Ukrainian history (*CC* 161). AGE: A young man (U *molodets*) (*CC* 161).

156. **Kotovy, F.**

LOCATION: Kutkivtsi, Ternopil district. OCCUPATION: (Peasant). POSITION IN RC: Deputy administration (*CC* 69).

157. **Kotyk, Petro**

LOCATION: Horodenka (district capital). OCCUPATION: (Peasant). POSITION IN RC: Administration (*CC* 15, 248). AUTHOR: *CC* 15 (coauthor).

158. **Koval, Ivan**

LOCATION: Zapytiv, Lviv district. OCCUPATION: Peasant. POSITION IN RC: Treasurer.[1] ECONOMIC STATUS: Proprietor (*CC* 217). MOBILITY: There were already five Koval households in Zapytiv in 1854–5.[2] OTHER ACTIVITIES: He voted for the Ukrainian candidate during the 1885 parliamentary elections (*CC* 217).

1) K., "...vid Iarycheva," *Batkivshchyna* 6, no. 18 (2 May [20 April] 1884): 107. *2)* TsDIAL, 168/1/1764, pp. 1v, 9v, 17v, 33v.

159. **Kovalsky, Emilii**

LOCATION: Turia Velyka, Dolyna district. OCCUPATION: Priest. ECONOMIC STATUS: Administrator of a parish with 2,314 members.[1] AGE: Born 1844, ordained 1866.[1] MARITAL STATUS: Married.[1] OTHER ACTIVITIES: He was a founder of the reading club, communal granary and loan fund; he also agitated for a Ukrainian store (*CC* 33). However, after he left Turia Velyka and the teacher Nakonechny died, the reading club and granary collapsed.[2]

1) *Shem. Lviv. 1884*, 46. *2)* "Nashi narodni chytalni," *Batkivshchyna* 11, no. 2 (14 [26] January 1889): 20.

160. **Kovalsky, Mykhailo**

LOCATION: Strilkiv, Stryi district. OCCUPATION: Peasant. POSITION IN RC: Secretary (*CC* 149). MOBILITY: Three Kovalsky households lived in Strilkiv, 1852–5.[1]

1) TsDIAL, 488/1/422, p. 1v.

161. **Kovbuz, Vasyl**

LOCATION: Horodenka (district capital). OCCUPATION: Peasant. POSITION IN RC: Administration (*CC* 15, 248). AUTHOR: *CC* 15 (coauthor). ECONOMIC STATUS: Proprietor.[1] OTHER ACTIVITIES: Described as a "sober and very honest proprietor"; along with *Kurovytsky, Atanazii*, he was "the soul of our reading club."[1]

1) Maksym Krushelnytsky [Andriichuk], "Pysmo z Horodenky," *Batkivshchyna* 5, no. 49 (7 December [25 November] 1883): 295.

162. **Koziuk, Pavlo**

LOCATION: Dmytriv, Kaminka Strumylova district. OCCUPATION: Priest. POSITION IN RC: President (*CC* 52). ECONOMIC STATUS: Administrator of a parish with 1,450 members.[1] AGE: Born 1851, ordained 1880.[1] MARITAL STATUS: Married.[1] OTHER ACTIVITIES: He was the main founder of the reading club (*CC* 52). When he was about to be transferred, the parishioners protested and wanted him to stay on instead of the old priest offered the parish in 1885 (*CC* 114).

1) *Shem. Lviv. 1884*, 184.

163. Krupnytsky, Antin

LOCATION: Nakvasha, Brody district. OCCUPATION: Peasant. POSITION IN RC: Deputy administration (*CC* 201). ECONOMIC STATUS: Proprietor (*CC* 201). OTHER ACTIVITIES: He was a founder of the reading club (*CC* 201).

164. Krushelnytsky, Amvrozii de

LOCATION: Bila, Ternopil district. OCCUPATION: Priest. POSITION IN RC: President (*CC* 69). FAMILY BACKGROUND: The name indicates noble ancestry. His father was a priest.[1] ECONOMIC STATUS: Pastor of a parish with 1,404 members, an endowment of 159 *Joch* of arable land and 25 *Joch* of meadow and no *congruum*.[2] He had an orchard and bee-hives. As the father of eight children (six daughters and two sons), he found it difficult to make ends meet. In the 1870s and 1880s he could afford a private tutor for his children. But when his daughter, the famous Ukrainian singer Solomiia Krushelnytska (1872–1952), went to study at the Lviv conservatory in 1890, he went into debt to pay for her education. He had not paid off the debt several years later.[3] EDUCATION: He was well read in world literature (Goethe, Schiller, Shakespeare) and in Ukrainian literature (Shevchenko, Franko), and knew foreign languages.[4] AGE: Born 1841, ordained 1867.[2] DEATH: January 1903.[5] MARITAL STATUS: Married.[2] MOBILITY: Prior to becoming pastor of Bila, he served in Petlykivtsi, Buchach district; Biliavyntsi, Buchach district; Tysiv, Dolyna district; and Osivtsi, Buchach district. In 1893 he accompanied his daughter Solomiia to Milan, and in 1894 he visited her there. In 1895 he visited his daughter in Vienna.[6] OTHER ACTIVITIES: He was a founder of the reading club (*CC* 69), and donated many books to it. In 1894 he was active in trying to revive the reading club, which had been dormant for six years.[7]

He had been a member of Prosvita, 1868–74.[8] He was sympathetic to the radicals Ivan Franko and Mykhailo Pavlyk; his progressive views may account for his frequent transfers in the 1870s. He was popular with the peasants, whom he encouraged to send their children to school.

He played violin and piano and was the first singing instructor of his daughter Solomiia. He organized a choir in Bila, in which Solomiia also sang. On special occasions he directed the choir of the Ruska besida society in Ternopil.[9] In 1885 he offered a five-month course in singing from notes and playing the violin.[10]

1) Holovashchenko, *Solomiia Krushelnytska*, 1:49. *2) Shem. Lviv. 1884*, 159. *3)* Holovashchenko, *Solomiia Krushelnytska*, 1:10, 12, 50, 54, 75. *4) Ibid.*, 1:50, 69. *5) Ibid.*, 1:72. *6) Ibid.*, 1:9, 49, 55–6, 69. *7) Ibid.*, 1:75, 2: 205. *8)* "Chleny tovarystva 'Prosvita'," *Spravozdaniie z dilanii "Prosvity"* (1874), 26–32. *9)* Holovashchenko, *Solomiia Krushelnytska*, 1:9, 50–1, 69, 75. *10)* "...nauku spivu z not z naukoiu hry na skrypkakh," *Batkivshchyna* 6, no. 51 (19 [7] December 1884): 321.

165. Krushelnytsky, Maksym

LOCATION: Horodenka (district capital). OCCUPATION: Teacher. AUTHOR: *CC* 15.[1] ECONOMIC STATUS: He was fired from his job in Horodenka in 1885[2] and only found steady employment in 1887.[3] In 1903, when he was planning to retire, he wrote to a friend: "I live in poverty."[4] AGE: He began teaching c. 1876[5] and was therefore born c. 1854. DEATH: 1904 or after.[6] MOBILITY: He lived in Horodenka in the mid-1880s; in 1887 he was hired to teach in Kotykivka, a suburb of Horodenka.[3] PUBLICATIONS: He contributed pedagogical articles to *Shkolna chasopys* in 1882–4[7] and items of correspondence in 1885[8] and 1886.[9] He published items of correspondence on the Horodenka reading club in *Batkivshchyna*, 1883[10] and 1886.[11] He contributed to *Dilo* in 1885[8] and 1890,[12] and to the *Zapysky NTSh* in 1899.[13] OTHER ACTIVITIES: He was active in the Horodenka reading club and this cost him his job when the pastor mounted a campaign against the club.[8] He spoke at the opening of reading clubs in Kovalivka, Kolomyia district,[2] and in Horodnytsia, Horodenka district. He agitated for the founding of a reading club in Dzhuriv, Sniatyn district.[8]

1) Authorship established on the basis of Dei, *Slovnyk ukrainskykh psevdonimiv*, 56. *2)* Letter of Maksym Krushelnytsky to Leonid Zaklynsky, 10 September 1885, in LNB AN

URSR, Viddil rukopysiv, fond Zaklynskykh, 192/31, p. 154. *3)* Letter to Leonid
Zaklynsky, 6 February 1882, *ibid.*, p. 158. *4)* Letter to Roman Zaklynsky, 25 January
1903, *ibid.*, p. 170. *5)* Letter to Leonid Zaklynsky, 25 January 1888, *ibid.*, p. 159. *6)* His
last letter to Roman Zaklynsky was dated 2 July 1904, *ibid.*, p. 171. *7)* Lev1, no. 2520,
2684, 2881. *8)* LNB AN URSR, Viddil rukopysiv, fond Zaklynskykh, 192/31, p. 150. *9)*
Maksym Krushelnytsky [Hist, chlen chytalni], "Dopsy. Z Horodenky," *Shkolna chasopys*
6, no. 6 (16 [28] March 1885): 45–6. *10)* Maksym Krushelnytsky [Andriichuk], "Pysmo z
Horodenky," *Batkivshchyna* 5, no. 49 (7 December [25 November] 1883): 295. *11)*
Maksym Krushelnytsky [Horodensky], "Pysmo z Horodenky," *Batkivshchyna* 8, no. 10 (12
March [28 February] 1886): 58. *12)* Dei, *Slovnyk ukrainskykh psevdonimiv*, 290. *13)*
Ibid., 194.

166. Kryshtalovych, Petro

LOCATION: Horodnytsia, Husiatyn district. OCCUPATION: Peasant. POSITION IN
RC: Secretary (*CC* 115). ECONOMIC STATUS: Proprietor (*CC* 115). OTHER ACTIVITIES: He
was a founder of the reading club (*CC* 115).

167. Kryzhanovsky, Roman

LOCATION: Korchyn, Stryi district. OCCUPATION: Priest. ECONOMIC
STATUS: Administrator of a parish with 1,111 members.[1] AGE: Born 1844, ordained
1870.[1] MARITAL STATUS: Married.[1] MOBILITY: He spent the first sixteen years of his
priesthood wandering from parish to parish as an administrator
(U *admynystrator-skytalets*).[2] OTHER ACTIVITIES: He was a strong supporter of the reading club (*CC* 194). A Russophile newspaper published this description of him in 1886:
"While absolutely strict in the fulfillment of his priestly duties, Father Kryzhanovsky has
that gift of heaven which makes one loved and popular after short acquaintance. Accessible
to everyone, humane and modest, he has quickly become the outstanding favourite of his
parishioners.... A strict ritualist, a precise celebrant of the liturgy and
preacher-instructor...."[2]

1) Shem. Lviv. 1884, 30–1. *2)* B. Pod., "Ot Skoleho," *Novyi prolom* 4 (6), no. 309 (8 [20]
February 1886): 2.

168. Kukhar, Antin

LOCATION: Piatnychany Volytsia, Stryi district. OCCUPATION: Cantor (*CC* 70). FAMILY
CONNECTIONS: Son-in-law of *Kurylyshyn, Hryhorii*. MOBILITY: Two Kukhar farmers lived
in Volytsia in 1820.[1] OTHER ACTIVITIES: He formerly held public readings (*CC* 70).

1) TsDIAL, 146/64b/4845.

169. Kulyk, Fedko

LOCATION: Nykonkovychi, Lviv district. OCCUPATION: Peasant. POSITION IN
RC: Administration (*CC* 105). MOBILITY: Five Kulyk households had been established in
Nykonkovychi by 1852–5.[1]

1) TsDIAL, 168/1/1916, pp. 1v, 16v, 21v.

170. Kurovytsky, Atanazii

LOCATION: Horodenka (district capital). OCCUPATION: Cantor.[1] POSITION IN
RC: Vice-president (*CC* 15). OTHER ACTIVITIES: *Krushelnytsky, Maksym* thought highly
of him, calling Kurovytsky and *Kovbuz, Vasyl* the "soul" of the Horodenka reading club.[2]
"...A very sincere man, he is very active in the reading club, and sometimes up to two
hundred people are in the club and he reads to them."[1]

1) Letter of Maksym Krushelnytsky to Leonid Zaklynsky, 30 December 1883, in LNB AN
URSR, Viddil rukopysiv, fond Zaklynskykh, 192/31, p. 142. *2)* Maksym Krushelnytsky
[Andriichuk], "Pysmo z Horodenky," *Batkivshchyna* 5, no. 49 (7 December [25
November] 1883): 295.

171. **Kurylyshyn, Hryhorii**

LOCATION: Piatnychany Volytsia, Stryi district. OCCUPATION: Peasant. POSITION IN LOCAL GOVT: Long-term mayor (*CC* 70). FAMILY CONNECTIONS: Father-in-law of *Kukhar, Antin.* EDUCATION: Illiterate (*CC* 70). AGE: He had been mayor for thirty-four years in 1884 (*CC* 70) and was therefore born in 1825 at the latest.

172. **Kushchak, Fedor**

LOCATION: Khotin, Kalush district. OCCUPATION: (Peasant). POSITION IN RC: Treasurer, 1884 (*CC* 121). PUBLICATIONS: In 1885 he was coauthor of a denunciation of *Dragan, Iurko,* vice-president of the reading club and mayor.[1]

1) Ivan Dovbenka, Iurko Voletsky, Zakhar Posatsky and Fedor Kushchak, "...vid Kalusha pro vybory do rady hromadskoi v Khotini," *Batkivshchyna* 7, no. 48 (27 [15] November 1885): 332.

173. **Kushniryk, Dmytro**

LOCATION: Olesha, Tovmach district. OCCUPATION: Miller (*CC* 60). POSITION IN RC: Vice-president (*CC* 60). ECONOMIC STATUS: He was wealthy enough to erect a cross in the village in honour of the reading club (*CC* 60). OTHER ACTIVITIES: He had been vice-president of the first reading club in Olesha, which had been set up in affiliation with the Kachkovsky Society.[1] He was a founder of the revived reading club in 1884 (*CC* 60).

1) Kukhnii, "Olesha," 915.

174. **Kuzma, Kyrylo**

LOCATION: Bilyi Kamin, Zolochiv district. OCCUPATION: Burgher (*CC* 262). POSITION IN RC: President (*CC* 148, 262, 275). EDUCATION: Literate (*CC* 148). OTHER ACTIVITIES: He served on the administration of the Pravda society (*CC* 148).

175. **Kvasnytsia, Vasyl**

LOCATION: Utishkiv, Zolochiv district. OCCUPATION: (Peasant). POSITION IN RC: Secretary (*CC* 216).

176. **Kyrchiv, Bohdar (Bohdan, Teodor)**

LOCATION: Korchyn, Stryi district. OCCUPATION: Seminarian (*CC* 32, 57). FAMILY BACKGROUND: He was the son of a peasant from Korchyn.[1] In addition to *Kyrchiv, Kost* and *Kyrchiv, Pavlo* other members of the Kyrchiv clan were prominent as enlighteners. A Toma Kyrchiv was a teacher in Korchyn in 1871[2] and an Oleksa Kyrchiv, a literate peasant, was the first president of the Korchyn reading club.[3] Oleksa was probably the father of both Bohdar and Pavlo Kyrchiv, perhaps also of Kost. FAMILY CONNECTIONS: Presumably the brother of *Kyrchiv, Pavlo* and perhaps of *Kyrchiv, Kost.* ECONOMIC STATUS: He studied theology only because he lacked the money for a secular education at the university.[1] EDUCATION: He finished gymnasium in Lviv,[1] where he also studied theology (*CC* 32, 57). AGE: Born 1856, ordained 1886.[4] DEATH: November 1900.[1] MOBILITY: He was born in Korchyn and educated in Lviv. After ordination he was an assistant in Lysiatychi, Stryi district, and later pastor in Dovhe, Stryi district, where he remained until his death. In 1899 he had undertaken a journey to Istanbul, Egypt and Palestine, returning by way of Russia.[1] PUBLICATIONS: He published poems and short stories in *Zoria* and other periodicals[1] (including two verses in *Zoria* in 1882).[5] As a fourth-year theology student in 1885, he was a member of a committee planning to publish music booklets.[6] He contributed many items of correspondence to *Dilo,* especially after ordination.[1]

OTHER ACTIVITIES: He was a founder of the reading club in Korchyn (*CC* 32) and signed the statutes of the reading club in Briukhovychi, Peremyshliany district, where *Kyrchiv, Pavlo* was a teacher (*CC* 57).

In the seminary he was distinguished by his defence of seminarians' rights and he campaigned for more secular education for future priests.[1] He was expelled from the seminary, but readmitted—after defending himself before the bishop—in the fall of 1884.[7]

He was a member of Prosvita, Narodna rada and Pidhirska rada in the late 1890s.[4]

His friend Ivan Franko wrote his obituary: "He had a passionate nature and pure and uncompromising character. He stood out both as a speaker at meetings of the youth and as an organizer.... " As a priest, "he was able to win the love of the peasants because of his sincere, brotherly conduct toward them and the courage with which he stood in their defence. But all the same he felt profoundly unhappy in his situation. Only more wide-ranging literary and civic work could have satisfied his nature. In rural seclusion, without educated company, in the midst of constant troubles and worries, he became depressed and languished. Later would come moments when he once again threw himself into work—agitating, writing stories, preparing and delivering public lectures; but after some time he would once again drop everything and give way to discouragement."

His health began to decline. His trip to the Orient momentarily revived good health and spirits, but back in the village he underwent a rapid decline. A short and painful illness carried him off.[1]

1) I[van] F[ranko], "Nekrology. O. Bohdar Kyrchiv," *Literaturno-naukovyi vistnyk*, richnyk IV, tom XIII (1901), [second part], pp. 66–7. *2) Szem. kr. Gal. 1871*, 424. *3)* F.P., "Pysmo vid Skoloho," *Batkivshchyna* 5, no. 30 (27 [15] July 1880): 190. *4) Shem. Lviv. 1900*, 171. *5)* Lev1, no. 2406I. *6)* "Zaprosheniie do peredplaty," *Batkivshchyna* 7, no. 13 (27 [15] March 1885): 104. *7)* Letter of Bohdar Kyrchiv to Leonid Zaklynsky, 1884, in LNB AN URSR, Viddil rukopysiv, fond Zaklynskykh, 193/31, p. 109.

177. Kyrchiv, Kost

LOCATION: Korchyn, Stryi district. OCCUPATION: Peasant (*CC* 32). AUTHOR: *CC* 32. FAMILY BACKGROUND: See *Kyrchiv, Bohdar*. FAMILY CONNECTIONS: Perhaps the brother of *Kyrchiv, Bohdar* and *Kyrchiv, Pavlo*.

178. Kyrchiv, Pavlo

LOCATION: Briukhovychi, Peremyshliany district. OCCUPATION: Teacher (*CC* 57). FAMILY BACKGROUND: See *Kyrchiv, Bohdar*. FAMILY CONNECTIONS: Probably the brother of *Kyrchiv, Bohdar*, perhaps also of *Kyrchiv, Kost*. AGE: Born 1862.[1] DEATH: 1916.[1] MOBILITY: He was probably born in Korchyn, Stryi district; he taught in Briukhovychi in the mid-1880s; he worked as an editor in Chernivtsi in 1888;[2] he lived in Lviv in the early 1890s;[3] he was married in Prysivtsi, Zolochiv district, in 1896.[4] PUBLICATIONS: He was a prolific author, whose writings included: a translation in a collection of short novels published by Ivan Belei in 1885;[5] fiction and nonfiction in *Shkolna chasopys*, 1886–8;[6] contributions to *Uchytel*, 1889–94;[7] a story and verse in *Batkivshchyna*, 1890–2; verse in the children's magazine *Dzvinok* (Lviv), 1892[4] and 1894;[8] a translation from Polish which appeared as a booklet in 1892; literary translations from German and French and a story in *Dilo*, 1893;[4] and a story in *Chytalnia*, 1894.[9] OTHER ACTIVITIES: He was a founder of the reading club in Briukhovychi (*CC* 57) and spoke at the inauguration of the reading club in Korelychi, Peremyshliany district (*CC* 84). He was editor of *Bukovyna* in 1888[2] and of *Pravda* in 1891 (through May).[10]

1) Entsyklopediia Ukrainoznavstva, s.v. "Kyrchiv Pavlo." *2) Ibid.*, s.v. "'Bukovyna'." *3)* Himka, *Socialism*, 166. *4)* Lev493, K-88. *5)* Lev1, no. 2955. *6)* Lev1, no. 3331; Lev2, no. 398II, 796. *7)* Lev2, no. 1070, 1414, 1780, 2119, 2484; Lev3, no. 3984. *8)* Lev3, no. 3571. *9)* Lev3, no. 4015. *10)* "Vid vydavnytstva," *Pravda* 2, no. 5 (May 1891): 344.

179. Kyzhyk, Pavlo

LOCATION: Bilyi Kamin, Zolochiv district. OCCUPATION: Burgher (*CC* 148). EDUCATION: Literate (*CC* 262). OTHER ACTIVITIES: He served on the administration of the Pravda society (*CC* 262).

180. Kyzyk, Ivan

LOCATION: Dobrostany, Horodok district. OCCUPATION: Peasant. POSITION IN RC: Deputy secretary (*CC* 245). ECONOMIC STATUS: Lad (U *parubok*), and thus had not yet come into any land. AGE: Lad (U *parubok*), and thus was born after 1860.

181. Kyzyk, Mykola

LOCATION: Dobrostany, Horodok district. OCCUPATION: Peasant. POSITION IN RC: Deputy librarian (*CC* 245). ECONOMIC STATUS: Lad (U *parubok*), and thus had not yet come into any land. AGE: Lad (U *parubok*), and thus was born after 1860.

182. Lapchynsky, Iosyf

LOCATION: Tsebriv, Ternopil district. OCCUPATION: (Peasant). POSITION IN RC: Deputy administration (*CC* 44).

183. Lazor, Ioan

LOCATION: Liubycha Kniazi, Rava Ruska district. OCCUPATION: Priest. POSITION IN RC: President (*CC* 137). ECONOMIC STATUS: Pastor (*CC* 137) in a small town with 1,342 Greek Catholics in 1880.[1]

1) Spec. Orts-Rep. 1880.

184. Leshnovsky, Stefan

LOCATION: Bilyi Kamin, Zolochiv district. OCCUPATION: (Burgher). EDUCATION: Literate (*CC* 262). OTHER ACTIVITIES: He served on the administration of the Pravda society (*CC* 262).

185. Lesiuk, Stefan

LOCATION: Bilyi Kamin, Zolochiv district. OCCUPATION: Priest. POSITION IN RC: Secretary (*CC* 275). AUTHOR: *CC* 154. ECONOMIC STATUS: Assistant (*CC* 144) in a parish of 650 members.[1] AGE: Born 1851[2] or 1852,[3] ordained 1882.[2] DEATH: 1891.[4] MARITAL STATUS: Married.[1] MOBILITY: He was in Bilyi Kamin in the mid-1880s, but died as pastor of Zaliztsi Novi, Brody district, in 1891.[3] OTHER ACTIVITIES: He was a supporter of the reading club and enlightenment in Bilyi Kamin (*CC* 144), "the soul of the reading club" (*CC* 275). He was president of the local Pravda society (*CC* 262). He established (*CC* 148) and directed a burgher choir in Bilyi Kamin. He attended the general meeting of the reading club in Buzhok, Zolochiv district, in 1885.[5] Together with *Taniachkevych, Danylo (younger)*, he was one of the two priests who attended the Olesko deanery's cantors' convention in 1885 (*CC* 154).

1) Shem. Lviv. 1884, 112. *2) Ibid.*, 188. *3) Ibid. 1891*, 51. *4)* Lev493, L-123. *5)* "O nashykh chytalniakh," *Batkivshchyna* 7, no. 9 (27 [15] February 1885): 71.

186. Levandovsky, Valentii

LOCATION: Kutkivtsi, Ternopil district. OCCUPATION: (Peasant). POSITION IN RC: Treasurer (*CC* 69). DISTINGUISHING FEATURES: Kutkivtsi had a sizable *latynnyk* population (see *Bartetsky, Roman*), and the name Levandovsky has a distinctly Polish ring to it. OTHER ACTIVITIES: He was one of the main activists in the reading club (*CC* 69). In 1886 he signed a protest against an attempt by the national populists to gain entry into Narodnyi dim in Lviv.[1]

1) R.M., "Ot Ternopolia," *Slovo* 26, no. 33 (26 March [7 April] 1886): 2. For the background to this matter, see Olesnytsky, *Storinky*, 1:202–3.

187. Levytsky, Pavlo

LOCATION: Khrystynopil, Sokal district. OCCUPATION: (Burgher). POSITION IN RC: Administration (*CC* 278).

188. Lishchynsky, Havrylo

LOCATION: Komarno, Rudky district. OCCUPATION: (Artisan). POSITION IN RC: Deputy administration (*CC* 9).

189. **Lisovyk, K.A.**

LOCATION: Trybukhivtsi, Buchach district. AUTHOR: *CC* 104.

190. **Liubynetsky, Ivan**

LOCATION: Brovary, Buchach district. OCCUPATION: (Peasant). POSITION IN RC: Librarian (*CC* 75).

191. **Lopatynsky, Vasylii Slepovron**

LOCATION: Berezyna, Zhydachiv district. OCCUPATION: Priest. POSITION IN RC: President (*CC* 28). FAMILY BACKGROUND: The name indicates noble ancestry. ECONOMIC STATUS: Pastor of Rozdil, with a daughter church in Berezyna; the parish had 2,620 members, an endowment of 49 *Joch* of arable land and 46 *Joch* of meadow and a *congruum* of 72 gulden 95 kreuzer.[1] AGE: Born 1838, ordained 1862.[1] DEATH: 1888, of typhus.[2] MARITAL STATUS: Widowed.[1] OTHER ACTIVITIES: He was a member of Narodnyi dim and other Ukrainian organizations. He took an active part in the 1885 parliamentary elections; at one point a gendarme dispersed an election meeting in his home, where peasants and priests had gathered. He was the second marshal of the district council in Zhuravno.[2] In the mid-1880s he was vice-dean[3] and later dean of Rozdil.[2]

1) *Shem. Lviv. 1884*, 138. *2)* "O. Vasyl Lopatynsky," *Batkivshchyna* 10, no. 19 (11 May [29 April] 1888): 120. *3)* *Shem. Lviv. 1880*, 135.

192. **Lototsky, Iurii**

LOCATION: Tsebriv, Ternopil district. OCCUPATION: (Peasant). POSITION IN RC: Secretary (*CC* 44).

193. **Loza, Iakiv**

LOCATION: Tenetyska, Rava Ruska district. OCCUPATION: Scribe.[1] AUTHOR: *CC* 81. POSITION IN LOCAL GOVT: Scribe.[1] PUBLICATIONS: He sent a brief notice on horse thievery to *Batkivshchyna* in 1884[2] and an item of correspondence on the need to regulate village scribes in 1886.[1]

1) Iakiv Loza, "Pysmo z Ravskoho," *Batkivshchyna* 8, no. 21 (28 [16] May 1886): 125. *2)* Iakov Loza, "...z Ravskoho," *Batkivshchyna* 6, no. 23 (6 June [30 (sic; should be 25) May] 1884): 140.

194. **Lun, Mykolai**

LOCATION: Liubycha Kniazi, Rava Ruska district. OCCUPATION: (Peasant). POSITION IN RC: Librarian (*CC* 137). AUTHOR: *CC* 137 (coauthor). OTHER ACTIVITIES: He was an activist in the reading club (*CC* 137).

195. **Lutsyk, Iuvenal**

LOCATION: Piznanka Hnyla, Skalat district. OCCUPATION: Priest. POSITION IN RC: President (*CC* 238). ECONOMIC STATUS: Pastor of a parish with 1,122 members, an endowment of 141 *Joch* of arable land and 12 *Joch* of meadow and a *congruum* of 168 gulden 76 kreuzer.[1] AGE: Born 1835, ordained 1858.[1] MARITAL STATUS: Married.[1] PUBLICATIONS: He was coauthor of a brief note on the reading club.[2] OTHER ACTIVITIES: He was a founder of the reading club (*CC* 238).

1) *Shem. Lviv. 1884*, 143–4. *2)* Iuvenal Lutsyk and Ivan Pundo, "Vydil chytalni v Piznantsi," *Batkivshchyna* 7, no. 32 (26 July [7 August] 1885): 228.

196. **Lypak, Petro**

LOCATION: Kamianka Lisna, Rava Ruska district. OCCUPATION: Peasant. POSITION IN RC: Administration (*CC* 53). ECONOMIC STATUS: He was a lad (U *parubok*) (*CC* 53), and therefore he had not yet come into land. AGE: He was described as a "young lad" (*CC* 53), and therefore was born c. 1864. OTHER ACTIVITIES: He recited Shevchenko's and his own poetry at the reading club's inauguration (*CC* 53).

197. Maievsky, Hryhorii

LOCATION: Nykonkovychi, Lviv district. OCCUPATION: Peasant. POSITION IN RC: Vice-president (*CC* 105). POSITION IN LOCAL GOVT: Mayor (*CC* 105). MOBILITY: Three or four Maievsky households were already living in Nykonkovychi by 1852–5.[1]

1) TsDIAL, 168/1/1916, pp. 1v, 11v.

198. Makohonsky, Stefan

LOCATION: Horodenka (district capital). OCCUPATION: Priest. POSITION IN RC: President (*CC* 15). ECONOMIC STATUS: At first administrator of this parish of 4,862;[1] then assistant,[2] with a salary of 210 gulden.[1] AGE: Born 1856, ordained 1882.[1] MARITAL STATUS: Married.[1] MOBILITY: After leaving Horodenka he became pastor in Potochyshche, Horodenka district, where he remained until at least 1918.[3] OTHER ACTIVITIES: He founded a choir that sang from notes (*CC* 15). After a conflict between the pastor of Horodenka and the reading club, Makohonsky stopped being active in the club.[4] He contributed much to the national development of Potochyshche. He was later a dean.[5]

1) *Shem. Lviv. 1884*, 214. *2*) *Schem. Leop. 1885*, 186. *3*) Ivanochko, "Natsionalne vidrodzhennia sela Potochyshche," 514. *4*) Pravdoliub, "Pysmo z Horodenky," *Batkivshchyna* 8, no. 35 (17 [5] September 1886): 208. *5*) Iashan and Marunchak, "Pomianyk peredovykh sviashchenykiv Horodenshchyny," 666.

199. Maksymovych, Dmytro

LOCATION: Rudno, Lviv district. OCCUPATION: Peasant. POSITION IN RC: Treasurer (*CC* 243). AUTHOR: *CC* 243. POSITION IN LOCAL GOVT: Mayor (elected fall 1885).[1] FAMILY BACKGROUND: A Mykola Maksymovych, presumably Dmytro's father, was a half peasant with 25 *Joch* 1563.5 square *Klafter* in 1851–5. This was the largest holding in a village consisting of 73 per cent half-peasant households and the rest quarter-peasant; the average holding was just under 10 *Joch*.[2] MOBILITY: The Maksymovych family had been in Rudno since at least 1851–5.[3] PUBLICATIONS: He defended his honour in an article in *Slovo*, 1886.[3] OTHER ACTIVITIES: He was accused in *Slovo* of having been the tavernkeeper's candidate for mayor in 1885 (when he replaced *Olynets, Mykhailo*).[1] Maksymovych denied the allegation and said that the denunciation reflected division and rivalry in the reading club.[3]

1) "Iz pod Lvova," *Slovo* 26, no. 37–8 (5 [17] and 8 [20] April 1886): [1] supplement. *2*) TsDIAL, 168/1/1959, p. 1v. *3*) Dmytrii Maksymovych, "Iz Rudna pod Lvovom," *Slovo* 26, no. 54 (17 [29] May 1886): 2.

200. Maksymovych, Volodymyr

LOCATION: "A village" (*CC* 253, 256). AUTHOR: *CC* 253, 256 (on fruit trees and gardens).

201. Mandii, Danylo

LOCATION: Utishkiv, Zolochiv district. OCCUPATION: (Peasant). POSITION IN RC: Treasurer (*CC* 216).

202. Mandiuk, Vasyl

LOCATION: Olesko, Zolochiv district. OCCUPATION: (Burgher or peasant). FAMILY BACKGROUND: A Vasyl Mandiuk was a literate plenipotentiary to the indemnization committee and an Ivan Mandiuk was mayor in 1854.[1] EDUCATION: Literate (*CC* 262). MOBILITY: The Mandiuk family was well established in Olesko by 1854.[1] OTHER ACTIVITIES: He served on the administration of the Pravda society (*CC* 262).

1) TsDIAL, 168/1/1197, pp. 76–76v.

203. Maneliuk, Aleksii

LOCATION: Berezhnytsia, Kalush district. OCCUPATION: (Peasant). AUTHOR: *CC* 173.
PUBLICATIONS: He contributed a brief notice to *Batkivshchyna* in 1884.[1] OTHER
ACTIVITIES: He was a member of the reading club (*CC* 173).[1]

1) A[leksii] M[aneliuk], chlen chytalni, "...vid Kalusha," *Batkivshchyna* 6, no. 45 (7
November [26 October] 1884): 285.

204. Manila, Fedko

LOCATION: Nykonkovychi, Lviv district. OCCUPATION: (Peasant). POSITION IN
RC: Administration (*CC* 105).

205. Markevych, Ivan (Ioann)

LOCATION: Khreniv, Kaminka Strumylova district. OCCUPATION: Priest. ECONOMIC
STATUS: Chaplain of a Greek Catholic community with 580 members; an endowment of
34 *Joch* of arable land and 9 *Joch* of meadow; compensation for servitudes (U *ekvyvalent*)
of 5 *Joch*, presumably of pasture; and a *congruum* of 93 gulden (93 *kreuzer* in the source,
but this is clearly an error).[1] AGE: Born 1849, ordained 1875.[1] MARITAL
STATUS: Married.[1] MOBILITY: He came to Khreniv in 1881;[2] in 1902 he was a priest in
Iunashiv, Rohatyn district, about to be transferred to Darakhiv, Terebovlia district.[3] OTHER
ACTIVITIES: "Honest, ardent and a true father to his [spiritual] children," he campaigned
for sobriety in Khreniv in the early 1880s.[2] In 1884 he was active in the reading club (*CC*
83). In 1891 he was the main initiator of the branch office of Prosvita in Rohatyn. He was
an expert on bee-keeping and orchards.[3]

1) Shem. Lviv. 1884, 56. *2)* Khrenevets, "Pysmo vid Iarycheva," *Batkivshchyna* 5, no. 17
(27 [15] April 1883): 105. *3)* Lev493, M-70.

206. Martyniuk (Martynek), Vasyl

LOCATION: Horodnytsia, Husiatyn district. OCCUPATION: Teacher. AGE: He began
teaching c. 1882–4,[1] and was therefore born c. 1860–2. OTHER ACTIVITIES: He was a
founder of the reading club (*CC* 115).

1) He was not mentioned in *Szem. kr. Gal. 1881*; he is listed as a younger teacher
(*P n[auczyciel] mlod[szy]*) in Horodnytsia in *ibid. 1884*, 383, and *ibid. 1885*, 383.

207. Martyshuk, Pavlo

LOCATION: Mykolaiv, Brody district. OCCUPATION: Peasant. ECONOMIC
STATUS: Wealthy.[1] EDUCATION: He was already literate in 1866.[2] AGE: He had come of
age by 1866,[2] and thus was probably born in 1841 or earlier. OTHER ACTIVITIES: He was
auditor of the Pravda society in 1884 (*CC* 71) and served on its administration in 1885
(*CC* 198). In 1866–8 he had served as plenipotentiary in a servitudes dispute.[2]

1) Tarnavsky, *Spohady*, 32. *2)* TsDIAL, 146/64/1124, pp. 42, 44 and *passim.*

208. Matsiakh, Mykola

LOCATION: Dmytriv, Kaminka Strumylova district. OCCUPATION: Peasant. POSITION IN
RC: Librarian (*CC* 52). MOBILITY: Four or five Matsiakh households farmed in Dmytriv
in the early 1850s.[1]

1) TsDIAL, 168/1/1016, pp. 6v, 16v.

209. Matviishyn, Ivan

LOCATION: Buzhok, Zolochiv district. OCCUPATION: (Peasant). POSITION IN RC: Treasurer
(*CC* 42).

210. Matviishyn, Petro

LOCATION: Chekhy, Brody district. OCCUPATION: Peasant. POSITION IN
RC: Vice-president (*CC* 271). ECONOMIC STATUS: Proprietor (*CC* 262). OTHER
ACTIVITIES: He was a founder of the Pravda society (*CC* 262).

211. Mazur, Vavryk

LOCATION: Darakhiv, Terebovlia district. OCCUPATION: (Peasant). POSITION IN RC: Deputy administration (*CC* 82). DISTINGUISHING FEATURES: *Latynnyk* (*CC* 220). OTHER ACTIVITIES: As an elector in the 1885 parliamentary elections, he could not be persuaded to vote against the Ukrainian candidate (*CC* 220).

212. Mazurchak, Tymko

LOCATION: Kutkivtsi, Ternopil district. OCCUPATION: Peasant. POSITION IN RC: Secretary and deputy administration (*CC* 269). DISTINGUISHING FEATURES: The last name suggests he was a *latynnyk*, which would not have been unusual for the Kutkivtsi reading club (see *Bartetsky, Roman*). FAMILY BACKGROUND: A Tymko Mazurchak was a quarter peasant in Kutkivtsi in 1854–6, with 10 *Joch* 684 square *Klafter* of land. This would have made him a middling peasant of just below average status (see *Bartetsky, Roman*). He was in the village government in 1854.[1] The possibility exists that the T. Mazurchak of the 1884 reading club and the Tymko Mazurchak of the 1854 village government were the same person, but I think it more likely that the first is the son and the second the father. To complicate matters, there were two people named Tymko Mazurchak in Kutkivtsi in 1886.[2] MOBILITY: The Mazurchak family was established in Kutkivtsi by 1854.[1] OTHER ACTIVITIES: In 1886 he (actually, both Tymko Mazurchaks) signed a protest against an attempt by the national populists to gain entry into Narodnyi dim in Lviv.[2]

1) TsDIAL, 488/1/653, pp. 27v, 79v. *2)* R.M., "Ot Ternopolia," *Slovo* 26, no. 33 (26 March [7 April] 1886): 2.

213. Mazykevych, I.

LOCATION: Makhniv, Rava Ruska district. OCCUPATION: Priest. POSITION IN RC: President (*CC* 137). ECONOMIC STATUS: Pastor (*CC* 137) in a village that had 753 Greek Catholics in 1880.[1]

1) Spec. Orts-Rep. 1880.

214. Medynsky (Medynski), Ivan (Jan)

LOCATION: Mykolaiv, Brody district. OCCUPATION: Teacher. DISTINGUISHING FEATURES: When opponents wrote about him, they used the Polish first name Jan;[1] this may have been done, however, to discredit or insult him. AGE: He had been teaching since at least 1877,[2] and was therefore born in 1855 or earlier. MOBILITY: He taught in Mykolaiv since at least 1877[2] until 1887–8, when he moved to Korsiv, Brody district.[1] OTHER ACTIVITIES: He was secretary of the Pravda society in 1884 (*CC* 71) and also in the administration in 1885 (*CC* 198). In 1887 he came into conflict with the other members of the Pravda society and with the reading club. *Holodoryha, Mykola*; *Pylypchuk, Hryhorii*; *Shostak, Semen*; and others censured him in the press for maltreatment of his pupils and opposition to the reading club. Medynsky was accused of denouncing the reading club before the district authorities and circuit court. In the winter of 1887 he was said to have pulled a window out of a house where a party was being held and to have dispersed the guests by force.[1]

1) Mykola Holodryha *et al.*, "Dopysy 'Dila'. Mykolaiv v poviti bridskim," *Dilo* 8, no. 92 (20 August [1 September] 1887): 2. Vasyl Iakubiv, Mykola Martyshuk, Mykola Holodryga, "Pysmo z Brodskoho," *Batkivshchyna* 10, no. 22 (1 June [20 May] 1888): 135. *2)* Szem. kr. Gal. 1877, 399.

215. Melnyk, Atanas(ii) (Panas)

LOCATION: Volia Iakubova, Drohobych district. OCCUPATION: Peasant and cantor.[1] POSITION IN RC: President (*CC* 92). AUTHOR: CC 92, 145, 219. POSITION IN LOCAL GOVT: Councilman, 1885.[1] FAMILY BACKGROUND: The Melnyk family had been involved in peasant disturbances in Volia Iakubova in 1819 (over servitudes) and 1843 (over taxes).[1] ECONOMIC STATUS: He was still a lad (U *parubok*) in 1884, and so had not yet come into land (*CC* 92). AGE: Born c. 1860.[1] DEATH: Late 1880s.[1] PUBLICATIONS: He contributed correspondence on developments in Volia Iakubova to *Batkivshchyna*, 1881–2, and *Gazeta Naddniestrzańska*, 1885.[1] He contributed an article on the treatment of distemper to *Hospodar i prosmyshlennyk*, 1883.[2] OTHER ACTIVITIES: He was the leader of a reading club that attempted radical reform in the village and so encountered serious opposition from the village government and pastor. His friends included the Ukrainian radical Ivan Franko and the Polish socialist Ignacy Daszyński. Together with other radically inclined village leaders (such as *Mikhas, Ivan*), Melnyk held secret meetings where socialist and anticlerical ideas were promulgated. He was arrested in March 1886 along with other reading club activists from Volia Iakubova and nearby Dobrivliany. Imprisoned in Sambir, they were charged with blasphemy and belonging to a secret socialist organization. They were tried *in camera* before a jury in Sambir, 31 May–3 June 1886 (N.S.). Melnyk was only convicted of publicly reading forbidden books and sentenced to six days in jail or a fine of 30 gulden. However, the three months he spent in confinement in Sambir proved adequate time for him to contract a lung disease; he died within the next few years.[1]

1) Himka, *Socialism*, 130–8, 216–18. *2)* Lev1, no. 2550.

216. Melnyk, Ivan

LOCATION: Kovalivka, Kolomyia district. OCCUPATION: (Peasant). POSITION IN RC: Deputy administration (*CC* 260). OTHER ACTIVITIES: He was among the founders of the revived reading club in 1901.[1]

1) TsDIAL, 348/1/2900, p. 27.

217. Melnyk, Petro

LOCATION: Liucha, Kolomyia district. OCCUPATION: (Peasant). POSITION IN RC: Treasurer (*CC* 206).

218. Melnyk, Tymko

LOCATION: Dmytriv, Kaminka Strumylova district. OCCUPATION: (Peasant). POSITION IN RC: Secretary (*CC* 52).

219. Menchakevych, Iliia

LOCATION: Zolochiv district? OCCUPATION: Cantor. AUTHOR: *CC* 187. OTHER ACTIVITIES: He was active in the cantors' movement (*CC* 187).

220. Mikhas (Mykhas), Ivan

LOCATION: Morozovychi, Sambir district. OCCUPATION: Peasant. AUTHOR: *CC* 130, 133, 134, 247, 273.[1] POSITION IN LOCAL GOVT: Mayor (at least from 1893[2] through 1899).[3] PUBLICATIONS: He published an item of correspondence in *Batkivshchyna* in 1884[4] and wrote for the radical newspaper *Khliborob* in 1893.[2] OTHER ACTIVITIES: In the mid-1880s he was already connected with the radical and anticlerical movement as a participant in clandestine meetings involving Ivan Franko, *Melnyk, Atanas* and others.[5] In 1893 he was elected to the administration of the Prosvita branch in Sambir, but declined to accept, because it meant working with priests who opposed the radical version of enlightenment.[6] He then came out publicly as a radical, claiming that his conversion had only occurred in the previous year. In his confession of radicalism in 1893, he wrote: "... I went deeply into the teachings of Jesus Christ, analyzed his life and compared it to our life. Because of this I began to stand up for the poor, wronged man."[7] In 1899 he told a radical assembly (U *viche*) in Morozovychi: "Jesus Christ sated five thousand people with five loaves and two fishes, while today five thousand people can't sate one priest."[3]

1) Authorship established on the basis of Dei, *Slovnyk ukrainskykh psevdonimiv*, 179. *2)* Ivan Mikhas [Ivan z nad Dnistra], "Iak viit prystav do radykaliv," *Khliborob* 3, no. 10 (15 May 1893): 66. Ivan Mikhas, "Prosvita narodu i pevni ruski ottsi dukhovni v Sambirshchyni," *Khliborob* 3, no. 21–3 (October 1893): 153–5. *3)* Uchasnyk, "Vicha v seli Morozovychakh," *Hromadskyi holos*, no. 3 (1899): 19–21. *4)* Ivan Mikhas [Ivan z-nad Dnistra], "Pysmo z Sambirshchyny," *Batkivshchyna* 8, no. 3 (22 [10] January 1886): 17.

5) Himka, *Socialism*, 135–6. 6) Mikhas, "Prosvita," 153–5. 7) Mikhas, "Iak viit prystav," 66.

221. Mocherniuk, Iura (Iurii)

LOCATION: Kovalivka, Kolomyia district. OCCUPATION: (Peasant). POSITION IN RC: Librarian (*CC* 260). FAMILY BACKGROUND: A Petro Mocherniuk had been mayor until he died in 1883 (*CC* 260). OTHER ACTIVITIES: He was among the founders of the revived reading club in 1901. He was president in 1901–4 and 1908; secretary in 1906 and 1910.[1]

1) TsDIAL, 348/1/2900, pp. 3, 4, 27, 34v, 35v, 36v, 37v, 40, 42v, 43.

222. Monchalovsky, Stefan

LOCATION: Sasiv, Zolochiv district. OCCUPATION: Cantor. AUTHOR: *CC* 187 (coauthor). OTHER ACTIVITIES: He was elected the representative of the Olesko deanery cantors in 1885 (*CC* 154).

223. Mostovyk, Hrynko

LOCATION: Buzhok, Zolochiv district. OCCUPATION: (Peasant). POSITION IN RC: Secretary (*CC* 42). OTHER ACTIVITIES: He was on the first administration of the reading club in 1881.[1]

1) Ivan Petryshyn [Liubomyr Seliansky], "Pysmo z Hlukhoho Kuta," *Batkivshchyna* 3, no. 10 (16 May 1881): 80.

224. Mozola, Vasyl

LOCATION: Berezyna, Zhydachiv district. OCCUPATION: Peasant. ECONOMIC STATUS: Proprietor (*CC* 28). OTHER ACTIVITIES: He was an activist in the reading club (*CC* 28).

225. Mudrak, Mykhail

LOCATION: Hvozd, Nadvirna district. OCCUPATION: Priest. ECONOMIC STATUS: Pastor of a parish with 1,498 members, an endowment of 46 *Joch* of arable land and 27 *Joch* of meadow and a *congruum* of 191 gulden 89 kreuzer.[1] AGE: Born 1812, ordained 1846.[1] MARITAL STATUS: Married.[1] OTHER ACTIVITIES: He was a proponent of the reading club and of sobriety in Hvozd (*CC* 55).

1) Shem. *Lviv. 1884*, 252–3.

226. Muzh, Petro

LOCATION: Khrystynopil, Sokal district. OCCUPATION: (Burgher). POSITION IN RC: Administration (*CC* 278). FAMILY CONNECTIONS: He may have been related to *Polotniuk, Ihnatii*.

227. Mykhalevych, Symeon

LOCATION: Liubycha Kniazi, Rava Ruska district. OCCUPATION: (Peasant). POSITION IN RC: Secretary (*CC* 137). OTHER ACTIVITIES: He was an activist in the reading club (*CC* 137).

228. Mykhaliuk, Mykhail

LOCATION: Dmytriv, Kaminka Strumylova district. OCCUPATION: (Peasant and) merchant (*CC* 52). FAMILY BACKGROUND: An Ilko Mykhaliuk, presumably Mykhail's father, was a half peasant with 8 *Joch* 1434 square *Klafter* in the early 1850s.[1] OTHER ACTIVITIES: He was a member of the reading club. He established a store that obtained its wares from Narodnia torhovlia (*CC* 52).

1) TsDIAL, 168/1/1016, p. 26v.

229. Mykuliak, Hryhorii

LOCATION: Brovary, Buchach district. OCCUPATION: (Peasant). POSITION IN RC: Treasurer (*CC* 75). OTHER ACTIVITIES: He was among the founders of the revived reading club in 1901.[1]

1) TsDIAL, 348/1/1297, p. 21.

230. Mykuliak, Petro.

LOCATION: Brovary, Buchach district., OCCUPATION: Peasant. POSITION IN RC: President (*CC* 75). ECONOMIC STATUS: Proprietor (*CC* 75). EDUCATION: Literate (*CC* 75). AGE: He was an elder brother of the church brotherhood (*CC* 75). OTHER ACTIVITIES: He was a founder of the reading club, which met in his home (*CC* 75).

231. Myroniuk, Iliia

LOCATION: Horodenka (district capital). OCCUPATION: Soldier, peasant. POSITION IN RC: Vice-president, 1884;[1] administration, 1885 (*CC* 248). AUTHOR: *CC* 248 (coauthor). FAMILY BACKGROUND: Son of a peasant from Horodenka.[1] ECONOMIC STATUS: A lad (U *parubchak*),[2] and thus still landless. EDUCATION: He finished the four-grade school in Horodenka. Interested in books since childhood, he used his free time while stationed as a soldier in Vienna to read. In the army he earned the rank of corporal (U *kapral*).[1] AGE: He was still serving in the army at the end of 1883,[3] but had returned to Horodenka by the end of 1884.[2] Thus he was probably drafted in 1881 and born in 1861. DEATH: 1886 (funeral, 8 February 1886 [O.S.]).[1] MOBILITY: He spent most of his life in his native Horodenka, but his service in the army took him to Vienna.[1] PUBLICATIONS: He published an item of correspondence from Vienna in *Batkivshchyna*, 1884.[1] OTHER ACTIVITIES: While stationed in Vienna in 1883, he corresponded with the teacher-activist *Krushelnytsky, Maksym*, who gave him a letter of recommendation to the Ukrainian student society Sich. He subscribed to *Batkivshchyna* and read it aloud to the other soldiers.[3] Back in Horodenka in 1884, he took an active part in the reading club, on one occasion presenting a talk on the need for enlightenment.[2] His work in Horodenka, however, was short-lived. In the army he had caught a lung disease from which he never fully recovered. He died after several months of illness.[1]

1) Maksym Krushelnytsky [Horodensky], "Pysmo z Horodenky," *Batkivshchyna* 8, no. 10 (12 March [28 February] 1886): 58. *2)* Maksym Krushelnytsky [Chlen chytalni], "Dopysy. Z Horodenky," *Shkolna chasopys* 6, no. 6 (16 [28] March 1885): 46. *3)* Letter of Maksym Krushelnytsky to Leonid Zaklynsky, 30 December 1883, in LNB AN URSR, Viddil rukopysiv, fond Zaklynskykh, 192/31, p. 142.

232. Nahirny, Andrei

LOCATION: Ninovychi, Sokal district. OCCUPATION: (Peasant). POSITION IN LOCAL GOVT: Mayor (*CC* 188). OTHER ACTIVITIES: He was a founder of the reading club (*CC* 188).

233. Navrotsky, Ivan

LOCATION: Brovary, Buchach district. OCCUPATION: (Peasant). POSITION IN RC: Vice-president (*CC* 75).

234. Navrotsky, Severyn

LOCATION: Shliakhtyntsi, Ternopil district. OCCUPATION: Priest. POSITION IN RC: President (*CC* 108). ECONOMIC STATUS: Pastor of a parish with 901 members, an endowment of 81 *Joch* of arable land and 4 *Joch* of meadow and a *congruum* of 135 gulden 77 kreuzer.[1] AGE: Born 1843, ordained 1869.[1] MARITAL STATUS: Celibate.[1] MOBILITY: He was an assistant in Ternopil in the mid-1870s before becoming pastor of Shliakhtyntsi.[2] OTHER ACTIVITIES: He was a founder of the reading club (*CC* 108). He was vice-dean of Ternopil and commissar of school affairs for Ternopil circle.[3] Evhen Olesnytsky, who knew him in the mid-1870s, characterized him as "not very energetic."[2]

1) Shem. Lviv. 1884, 164. *2)* Olesnytsky, *Storinky,* 1:102. *3) Shem. Lviv. 1884,* 157.

235. Novosad, Semko

LOCATION: Makhniv, Rava Ruska district. OCCUPATION: (Peasant). POSITION IN RC: Deputy administration (*CC* 137).

236. Nychyk, Dmytro

LOCATION: Darakhiv, Terebovlia district. OCCUPATION: Peasant. POSITION IN RC: Treasurer (*CC* 82). ECONOMIC STATUS: Proprietor (*CC* 82). OTHER ACTIVITIES: He was a founder of the reading club (*CC* 82).

237. Nychyk, Maksym

LOCATION: Darakhiv, Terebovlia district. OCCUPATION: Peasant. ECONOMIC STATUS: Proprietor (*CC* 82). OTHER ACTIVITIES: He was a founder of the reading club (*CC* 82).

238. Oleiniuk, Oleksa

LOCATION: Tsebriv, Ternopil district. OCCUPATION: (Peasant). POSITION IN RC: Librarian (*CC* 44).

239. Olenchyn, Andrii

LOCATION: Korelychi, Peremyshliany district. OCCUPATION: Peasant. POSITION IN RC: Treasurer (*CC* 84). MOBILITY: The Olenchyn family name was very common among the Greek Catholic parishioners of Korelychi in 1864.[1]

1) TsDIAL, 146/64b/2294, pp. 54–61.

240. Oliinyk, Iu[rii]

LOCATION: Kutkivtsi, Ternopil district. OCCUPATION: (Peasant). POSITION IN RC: Administration (*CC* 69).

241. Olynets, Mykhail

LOCATION: Rudno, Lviv district. OCCUPATION: Peasant. POSITION IN LOCAL GOVT: Mayor (*CC* 240) until 1885;[1] then from 1888 until at least 1890.[2] FAMILY BACKGROUND: Mykhail was descended from Hryhorii Olynets, who in 1820 had 10 *Joch* 1414.75 square *Klafter* of land. This was inherited by Mykhail's father, who died in 1841, and then by Mykhail's older brother Dmytro, with the stipulation that he provide for all the siblings. Dmytro inherited some land from his wife and gave the original Olynets holding in 1856 to the youngest of the three brothers, Stefan. Stefan, in return for the holding, was obliged to provide the youngest sibling, Anna, when she came of age, with a pair of draught oxen and a cow; he also had to pay for her wedding. The land Stefan inherited—only a little larger than the average holding in the village in the 1850s, but encumbered by obligations *vis-à-vis* his sister—was confiscated by the Credit-Anstalt bank to pay for debts in 1869.[3] ECONOMIC STATUS: His father was a middling peasant with three sons and a daughter, so Mykhail probably started off quite modestly in the 1840s or early 1850s.[3] AGE: In 1856 Mykhail Olynets had a younger brother who had come of age to inherit.[3] Therefore Mykhail was born in 1835 or earlier. OTHER ACTIVITIES: He was a founder of the reading club in the mid-1880s (*CC* 240); he was also active in reviving the defunct club in 1890.[2] As mayor, he allegedly forbade the villagers to spend Sundays and holidays in the tavern and preferred that they spend their leisure time in the reading club. He was not re-elected mayor in the fall of 1885, supposedly because of the tavernkeeper's agitation. (He was replaced by *Maksymovych, Dmytro*.)[1]

1) "Iz pod Lvova," *Slovo* 26, no. 37–8 (5 [17] and 8 [20] April 1886): [1] supplement. *2)* "Chytalnia v Rudni," *Batkivshchyna* 12, no. 18 (27 April [9 May] 1890): 238. *3)* TsDIAL, 166/1/1168, pp. 475–83; TsDIAL, 166/1/1170, pp. 260–1.

242. **Onyshkevych, Onufrii**

LOCATION: Liubycha Kniazi, Rava Ruska district. OCCUPATION: (Peasant). POSITION IN RC: Treasurer (*CC* 137). OTHER ACTIVITIES: A Stefan Onyshkevych, a seminarian, spoke at the inauguration of the reading club (*CC* 137).

243. **Osmilovsky, L.**

LOCATION: Khrystynopil, Sokal district. OCCUPATION: Priest (*CC* 278). POSITION IN RC: Administration (*CC* 278).

244. **Pachovsky, Ivan**

LOCATION: Dobrostany, Horodok district. OCCUPATION: Priest. POSITION IN RC: President (*CC* 100, 245). FAMILY CONNECTIONS: Father of *Pachovsky, Mykhailo.*[1] ECONOMIC STATUS: Pastor of a parish with 2,007 members and an endowment of 105 *Joch* of arable land and 35 *Joch* of meadow; he had to pay an assistant 179 gulden 80 kreuzer.[2] He had three sons and seven daughters and was unable to pay for the education of two of his sons.[1] AGE: Born 1814, ordained 1837.[2] MARITAL STATUS: Married.[2] MOBILITY: He had been pastor in Dobrostany since at least 1861.[1]

1) Lev493, P-62. *2) Shem. Lviv. 1884*, 58–9.

245. **Pachovsky, Mykhailo**

LOCATION: Dobrostany, Horodok district. OCCUPATION: University student.[1] FAMILY BACKGROUND: His father was a priest with three sons, of whom Mykhailo was the youngest, and seven daughters.[1] FAMILY CONNECTIONS: He was the son of *Pachovsky, Ivan.* ECONOMIC STATUS: He struggled with poverty as a student. Beginning in the second grade of gymnasium he gave lessons to pay for his own and an older brother's education. In 1887 material considerations led him to interrupt his university education in Vienna and take work as a gymnasium teacher in Lviv.[1] EDUCATION: He attended the academic gymnasium in Lviv, 1875–82, and then studied in the philosophy faculty at the University of Vienna, 1882–7. He first specialized in classical philology, but changed to Slavistics; among his teachers were Franz Miklosich and Vatroslav Jagić. He loved music and attended Anton Bruckner's lectures at the conservatory. He received a doctorate from the University of Chernivtsi in 1895.[1] AGE: Born 20 September 1861 (O.S.).[1] DEATH: 1933.[2] MOBILITY: He was born in Dobrostany and educated in Lviv and Vienna. He taught the Ukrainian language in gymnasia in Lviv, 1887–93 and 1897–1911?; and in Kolomyia, 1893–7.[1] He was director of the private gymnasium in Dolyna, 1911–22.[2] PUBLICATIONS: He wrote the novel *Vechornytsi* and several scholarly and popular-scholarly works, including: *Pro ruski byliny i dumy* (1895), *Pokhoronnyi obriad na Rusy* (1903), *Iliustrovane ukrainsko-ruske pysmenstvo v zhyttiepysakh* (1909), *Vyimky z ukrainskoho pysmenstva XI–XVIII st.* (1911) and essays on Ivan Kotliarevsky, Markiian Shashkevych and Taras Shevchenko. He also compiled textbooks and composed songs for a mixed choir.[2] OTHER ACTIVITIES: He was the main founder of the reading club[3] and also established a choir in Dobrostany (*CC* 245). While a student in Vienna in the mid-1880s, he was a member of the Ukrainian student society Sich and of the Slavonic singing association; he also sang in the chorus of Vienna's leading operatic house, the Theater an der Wien. In 1902 he edited the children's magazine *Dzvinok.*[1] During the Ukrainian revolution of 1918 he was a member of the Ukrainian National Council of the West Ukrainian People's Republic.

1) Lev493, P-62. *2) Entsyklopediia Ukrainoznavstva*, s.v. "Pachovsky Mykhailo." *3)* "Novi chytalni," *Batkivshchyna* 6, no. 22 (30 [18] May 1884): 131–2.

246. **Parii, Vasyl**

LOCATION: Dmytriv, Kaminka Strumylova district. OCCUPATION: (Peasant and) scribe (*CC* 52). POSITION IN RC: Vice-president.[1] POSITION IN LOCAL GOVT: Scribe (*CC* 52). MOBILITY: Seven Parii households lived in Dmytriv in the 1850s.[2] OTHER ACTIVITIES: He was an activist in the reading club (*CC* 52).

1) "O nashykh chytalniakh," *Batkivshchyna* 7, no. 16 (17 [5] April 1885): 122. *2)* TsDIAL, 168/1/1016, pp. 11v, 21v, 26v, 84v.

247. Pashkovsky, Atanazii

LOCATION: Olesko, Zolochiv district. OCCUPATION: Priest. ECONOMIC STATUS: Pastor of a parish with 2,927 members, an endowment of 119 *Joch* of arable land and 27 *Joch* of meadow and a *congruum* of 10 gulden 98 kreuzer.[1] AGE: Born 1822, ordained 1848.[1] MARITAL STATUS: Widowed.[1] OTHER ACTIVITIES: He was president of the Pravda society in Olesko (*CC* 262).

1) Shem. Lviv. 1884, 113.

248. Pashkovsky, Iuliian

LOCATION: Iuzkovychi and Olesko, Zolochiv district. OCCUPATION: Teacher. AGE: He began teaching c. 1878,[1] and was therefore born c. 1856. MOBILITY: He first taught in Slobidka Ianivska, Ternopil district, in 1878;[1] he taught in Dobromirka, Zbarazh district, in 1881,[2] in Ihrovytsia, Ternopil district, in 1884,[3] and in Iuzkovychi, Zolochiv district, in 1885.[4] OTHER ACTIVITIES: He served in the administration of the Pravda society in Olesko (*CC* 262).

1) He is not mentioned in *Szem. kr. Gal. 1873, 1874* or *1877*, and first appears in *ibid. 1878*, 437; but he is not mentioned in *ibid. 1879*. *2) Ibid. 1881*, 447. *3) Ibid. 1884*, 422. *4) Ibid. 1885*, 428.

249. Patsahan, Pavlo

LOCATION: Olesha, Tovmach district. OCCUPATION: Peasant. POSITION IN RC: Librarian (*CC* 60). MOBILITY: Three peasant households with the name of Patsahan lived in Olesha in 1850–5.

1) TsDIAL, 168/1/4099, pp. 20v, 35v.

250. Pavliv, Luka

LOCATION: Chekhy, Brody district. OCCUPATION: (Peasant). POSITION IN RC: Librarian (*CC* 271). AUTHOR: *CC* 271.

251. Pavlychko, Ivan

LOCATION: Stopchativ, Kolomyia district. OCCUPATION: (Peasant). POSITION IN RC: Deputy administration (*CC* 263).

252. Pelekhaty, Fedor

LOCATION: Darakhiv, Terebovlia district. OCCUPATION: (Peasant). POSITION IN RC: Deputy administration (*CC* 82).

253. Pelensky, Oleksa

LOCATION: Komarno, Rudky district. OCCUPATION: Burgher.[1] POSITION IN RC: Librarian (*CC* 9). ECONOMIC STATUS: Judging by his publications, he had an orchard.[2] PUBLICATIONS: He contributed two articles on orchards to *Hospodar i promyshlennyk* in 1886.[2] OTHER ACTIVITIES: He was elected to the supervisory council of the loan association in Komarno in 1886.[1]

1) "Dopysy. Z Komarna," *Dilo* 7, no. 62 (7 [19] June 1886): 4. *2)* Lev1, no. 3154.

254. Petriv, Lev

LOCATION: Utishkiv, Zolochiv district. OCCUPATION: (Peasant). POSITION IN RC: Librarian (*CC* 216).

255. Petrovych, Emyliian

LOCATION: Korchyn, Stryi district. OCCUPATION: Priest. ECONOMIC STATUS: Pastor of a parish with 1,167 members, no endowment in land and a *congruum* of 254 gulden 21 kreuzer.[1] AGE: Born 1842, ordained 1871.[1] MARITAL STATUS: Married.[1] OTHER ACTIVITIES: He was active in the reading club (*CC* 32).

1) Shem. Lviv. 1884, 147.

256. Petryshyn, Ivan

LOCATION: Pochapy, Zolochiv district. OCCUPATION: Teacher. POSITION IN RC: Librarian (*CC* 268). AUTHOR: *CC* 42, 268, 275. AGE: Born 1850.[1] DEATH: 1913.[1] MOBILITY: He first taught in Kruhiv, Zolochiv district,[2] before moving to Pochapy in 1878.[3] PUBLICATIONS: He was a prolific writer who frequently used the pseudonym Liubomyr Seliansky. He contributed to *Batkivshchyna*, 1881–2,[4] 1890;[5] *Dzvinok*, 1890–1910;[6] *Uchytel*, 1892–3;[7] *Dilo*, 1898; *Haidamaky*, 1902; *Zoria*, 1910;[6] *Komar, Zerkalo, Khlopska pravda, Zoria* and the calendar *Zaporozhets*.[1] He was also the author of popular books: *U piatdesiatu richnytsiu znesenia panshchyny i vidrodzhenia halytskoi Rusy*, Knyzhochky 'Prosvity', no. 215–16 (Lviv, 1898);[8] *Hostynets z Ameryky, abo Nauka pro se, iak u sviti zhyty* (1906). He wrote several historical operas, including *Iasne sonichko Rusy-Ukrainy* (1911) and *Orleanska divchyna* (1912).[1] OTHER ACTIVITIES: He was active in the reading club in Buzhok. He attended its inauguration in 1881,[9] gave instruction to its members,[10] joined it and lectured at its general meeting in 1885 (*CC* 42). He also lectured on Shevchenko at the reading club in Bilyi Kamin (*CC* 275). These localities were in Zolochiv district. He married into the priestly Tarnavsky family and was one of the few in the family to use the Ukrainian language at home.[11] From 1908 to 1912 he edited the teachers' journal *Prapor*, which came out in Kolomyia.[1]

1) Entsyklopediia Ukrainoznavstva, s.v. "Petryshyn...Ivan." *2)* He is not mentioned in *Szem. kr. Gal. 1874*; he is in *ibid. 1877*, 453. *3) Ibid. 1878*, 442. *4)* Lev1, no. 2229, 2371. *5)* Ivan Petryshyn [L. Seliansky], "Praznyk svobody," *Batkivshchyna* 12, no. 21 (18 [30] May 1890): 273. Ivan Petryshyn [Liubomyr Seliansky], "Podorozh v krai Darmoidiv," *Batkivshchyna* 12, no. 34–5 (24 August [5 September] 1890): 446–9 (a translation from German). *6)* Dei, *Slovnyk ukrainskykh psevdonimiv*, 344. *7)* Lev2, no. 2119, 2484. *8)* "...A kind of apologia for the Austrian regime." Magocsi, *Galicia*, 137. *9)* Ivan Petryshyn [Liubomyr Seliansky], "Pysmo z Hlukhoho Kuta," *Batkivshchyna* 3, no. 10 (16 May 1881): 80–1. *10)* "O nashykh chytalniakh," *Batkivshchyna* 7, no. 9 (27 [15] February 1885): 71. *11)* Tarnavsky, *Spohady*, 24.

257. Pidgursky, Antin

LOCATION: Kolodribka, Zalishchyky district. OCCUPATION: (Peasant). POSITION IN RC: Deputy administration (*CC* 76).

258. Pidrichny, Pavlo

LOCATION: Rava Ruska district. AUTHOR: *CC* 51.

259. Pikh, Mykhailo

LOCATION: Stariava, Mostyska district. OCCUPATION: Merchant. AUTHOR: *CC* 116, 119. PUBLICATIONS: He contributed correspondence to *Batkivshchyna* in 1886.[1] OTHER ACTIVITIES: He was the manager of the church store and trustee of the church (*CC* 116, 119).

1) Lev1, no. 3122.

260. Pochapsky, Vasyl

LOCATION: Pochapy, Zolochiv district. OCCUPATION: (Peasant). POSITION IN RC: Treasurer (*CC* 268). FAMILY BACKGROUND: A Mykhalko Pochapsky was mayor in 1882.[1]

1) Ivan Petryshyn [Liubomyr Seliansky], "Pysmo z Zolochivskoho," *Batkivshchyna* 4, no. 24 (16 [4] December 1882): 192.

261. Poliak, Iosyf (Iuzio)

LOCATION: Strilkiv, Stryi district. OCCUPATION: Peasant. POSITION IN RC: Librarian (*CC* 149). POSITION IN LOCAL GOVT: Councilman (*CC* 34). DISTINGUISHING FEATURES: His first and last names indicate Polish origin. In 1880 the village had 14 Polish-speaking Roman Catholics (i.e., Poles) and 2 Ukrainian-speaking Roman Catholics (i.e., *latynnyky*).[1] It is possible that the Polish-speaking Roman Catholics were, in fact, *latynnyky*, since the census-takers tended to favour the Polish nationality and were not always above tampering with the census results.[2] The first names recorded for the Poliak family in the 1850s, however, were decidedly Greek Catholic and Ukrainian (Iwan, Dmytro, Olexa).[3] MOBILITY: Four Poliak households were recorded in Strilkiv in 1852–5.[3] OTHER ACTIVITIES: He was a founder of the reading club (*CC* 34).

1) Spec. Orts-Rep. 1880. 2) The Ukrainian parliamentary deputy Vasyl Kovalsky protested the abuses of the 1880 census in an interpellation to Austrian minister of the interior Count Eduard Taaffe on 1 February 1881 (N.S.). "Iak perevedena konskryptsiia v Halychyni?" *Batkivshchyna* 3, no. 4 (16 February 1881): 25–6. *3)* TsDIAL, 488/1/422, pp. 1v, 21v.

262. Polishchuk, M.

LOCATION: Bila, Ternopil district. OCCUPATION: (Peasant). POSITION IN RC: Deputy administration (*CC* 69).

263. Polishchuk, P.

LOCATION: Bila, Ternopil district. OCCUPATION: (Peasant). POSITION IN RC: Librarian (*CC* 69).

264. Polotniuk, Ihnatii (Hnat)

LOCATION: Khrystynopil, Sokal district. OCCUPATION: Cantor. AUTHOR: *CC* 176. POSITION IN LOCAL GOVT: He was a councilman and assessor in 1880 in Kliusiv, Sokal district.[1] FAMILY BACKGROUND: He stemmed from an old Khrystynopil burgher family, but his grandfather Iosyf had been left an orphan and went to work as an agricultural labourer for peasants (serfs). Iosyf married a woman from Novyi Dvir, a suburb of Khrystynopil. He became a fairly well-to-do peasant and served as mayor for over twenty-five years. He abstained from alcohol, had eight children and died at the age of eighty-five. Ihnatii's father, Ivan, was a peasant with a holding of 18 *Joch*. He served as a councilman for many years. He himself was literate and was the main founder of a school in Kliusiv. He loved music (singing) and passed this on to his son. Ihnatii's mother's maiden name was Muzh. Ihnatii was the oldest of five children still living in 1896.[1] FAMILY CONNECTIONS: Through his mother's family he may have been related to *Muzh, Petro.* EDUCATION: In 1864 he began attending the normal school in Khrystynopil, where he finished three grades. He transferred to Kliusiv in 1868, when a school was opened with the cantor Symeon Rybak as instructor. He finished the fourth grade in Kliusiv and also studied singing under Rybak. The Basilian fathers who taught him catechism wanted him to be sent for higher education, but his mother would not allow it. He followed his old teacher Rybak to nearby Boratyn, also in Sokal district, to continue his education; sometimes he took Rybak's place as instructor. While a cantor in Khrystynopil, 1872–6, he studied ritual and church singing with the Basilians. In 1876–9 he served in the army; while stationed in Lviv he prepared to take a teacher's examination and passed a cantor's examination at St. George's Cathedral on 18 March 1878 (O.S.). In 1891 he passed the sixth-grade examination of a district administration school (U *vydilova shkola*) and continued studying.[1] AGE: Born 29 December 1856 (O.S.).[1] DEATH: 1903.[2] MOBILITY: Until 1876, when he was drafted into the army, he spent his life in Khrystynopil and nearby villages. While in the army, 1876–9, he was stationed both outside of Ukrainian territory and in Lviv. He was cantor in Khrystynopil from 1880 to 1887, when he moved to Stanyslaviv. Here he worked as a cantor in the cathedral until his death.[1] PUBLICATIONS: He published notes on the cantors' movement in *Dilo*, 1885;[3] *Slovo*, 1885;[4] and *Halychanyn*, 1900.[1] He published a collection of church songs, *Napivnyk tserkovnyi*.[2]

OTHER ACTIVITIES: As a youth in 1870 he became a teacher in Bendiuha, Sokal district. He received the position because the founder of the school, a repentant horse-thief, had stipulated that the teacher be an expert at church singing. In a neighbouring village was the teacher Tymofei Khomyn, originally from Khlivchany, Rava Ruska district, who was the founder and director of several village choirs. With his help, Polotniuk established a choir in Bendiuha; it made its first public appearance in the Khrystynopil church on Easter Sunday. In the spring of 1871 Polotniuk and his choir took the place of the Khrystynopil cantor for six weeks and in 1872—at the age of sixteen—Polotniuk became the cantor of Khrystynopil.

While serving in the army, 1876–9, he filled twenty-one notebooks with church music. In 1880 he rescued the declining communal granary in his native Kliusiv.

As cantor of Khrystynopil again in 1880–7, he began to take pupils to study the cantor's art. In 1885 he founded a cantors' school, which lasted into the late 1890s, at first based in Khrystynopil, then in Stanyslaviv. By the end of 1896, ninety-eight students had passed through his school, fifty of whom subsequently passed a cantor's examination. In the period 1874–8 he founded twelve choirs in villages.[1] At the inauguration of the reading club in Zhuzhil, Sokal district, he directed the choir (*CC* 212).

Polotniuk was a leading activist of the cantors' movement. He proposed the establishment of a cantors' association for Przemyśl eparchy (*CC* 176) and initiated its first convention on 30 April 1885 (O.S.) (*CC* 193). He was a cantors' deputy to the bishops in 1881, 1885 and 1886. On 14 June 1887 (O.S.) the Lviv metropolitan consistory convoked a cantors' convention with the aim of founding a cantors' association for all of Galicia; Polotniuk was elected secretary of the committee to carry on further action. From 30 August 1889 (O.S.) he served as treasurer of the Stanyslaviv eparchy cantors' association. In October 1895 he founded the cantors' monthly *Diakivskii hlas* in Stanyslaviv,[1] and edited it until his death in 1903.[5] In June 1901 he led a deputation of cantors and organists to the Galician diet.

In 1902 he founded the association Ruska khata in Stanyslaviv, for burghers and the middle-level intelligentsia.[1]

1) Lev 493, P-164. *2) Ukrainska Zahalna Entsyklopediia*, s.v. "Polotniuk." *3)* Lev1, no. 2943. *4)* Lev1, no. 3074VIII. *5) Entsyklopediia Ukrainoznavstva*, s.v. "Polotniuk Hnat."

265. Popovych, Fedir

LOCATION: Fytkiv, Nadvirna district. OCCUPATION: Peasant. POSITION IN RC: Librarian (*CC* 58). ECONOMIC STATUS: Proprietor (*CC* 58). AGE: Young (*CC* 22). MOBILITY: "A man who has been out in the world" (U *buvalyi v sviti cholovik*) (*CC* 22). OTHER ACTIVITIES: He was active in the founding of the reading club; once he hosted forty people in his home to discuss the matter (*CC* 22). The reading club met in his home in 1885 (*CC* 58). In 1886 he was still librarian of the reading club.[1]

1) M. Ianevorihvash, "Pysmo z Nadvirnianskoho," *Batkivshchyna* 8, no. 13 (2 April [21 March] 1886): 77.

266. Posatsky, Havrylo (Havryil)

LOCATION: Khotin, Kalush district. OCCUPATION: Cantor (*CC* 121) and scribe.[1] POSITION IN RC: President (*CC* 121). AUTHOR: *CC* 162. POSITION IN LOCAL GOVT: Scribe.[1] OTHER ACTIVITIES: He was a founder of the reading club in 1884[1] and a member of the church committee in 1889.[2]

1) Hp., "Nova chytalnia," *Batkivshchyna* 6, no. 26 (27 [15] June 1884): 159. *2)* "Zaprosyny," *Batkivshchyna* 11, no. 19 (12 [24] May 1889): 252.

267. Proskurok, M.

LOCATION: Bila, Ternopil district. OCCUPATION: (Peasant). POSITION IN RC: Deputy administration (*CC* 69).

268. Prukhnytsky, Mykhailo

LOCATION: Komarno, Rudky district. OCCUPATION: Weaver.[1] POSITION IN RC: President (*CC* 9). POSITION IN LOCAL GOVT: Councilman for many years, also mayor.[1] AGE: Born c. 1850.[1] DEATH: 27 December 1901 (O.S.).[1] OTHER ACTIVITIES: He served on the administration of the loan association and as secretary of the weavers' association in Komarno.[1]

1) Lev493, P-225.

269. Pryhodsky, Emil

LOCATION: Stopchativ, Kolomyia district. OCCUPATION: (Peasant). POSITION IN RC: Treasurer (*CC* 263). OTHER ACTIVITIES: He was a founder of the reading club (*CC* 263).

270. Pukhalsky, H.

LOCATION: Darakhiv, Terebovlia district. OCCUPATION: (Peasant). POSITION IN RC: Librarian (*CC* 82).

271. Pukhalsky, Ivan

LOCATION: Darakhiv, Terebovlia district. OCCUPATION: Peasant. ECONOMIC STATUS: Proprietor (*CC* 82). OTHER ACTIVITIES: He was a founder of the reading club (*CC* 82).

272. Punda (Pundo), Ivan

LOCATION: Piznanka Hnyla, Skalat district. OCCUPATION: Peasant. POSITION IN RC: Secretary (*CC* 238). ECONOMIC STATUS: Proprietor (*CC* 238). PUBLICATIONS: Coauthor of a brief note on the reading club.[1]

1) Iuvenal Lutsyk and Ivan Pundo, "Vydil chytalni v Piznantsi," *Batkivshchyna* 7, no. 32 (26 July [7 August] 1885): 228.

273. Punda (Pundo), Lesko

LOCATION: Piznanka Hnyla, Skalat district. OCCUPATION: Peasant. ECONOMIC STATUS: Rich peasant (*CC* 85). OTHER ACTIVITIES: He was a founder and member of the reading club (*CC* 238). He also started a loan fund and communal granary (*CC* 85).

274. Pundyk, Ivan

LOCATION: Pochapy, Zolochiv district. OCCUPATION: (Peasant). POSITION IN RC: Deputy administration (*CC* 268).

275. Pylypchuk, Hryhorii (Hrytsko)

LOCATION: Mykolaiv, Brody district. OCCUPATION: (Peasant). PUBLICATIONS: Coauthor of a denunciation of the teacher *Medynsky, Ivan.*[1] OTHER ACTIVITIES: He was secretary of the Pravda society in 1884 (*CC* 71) and also served in its administration in 1885 (*CC* 198).

1) Mykola Holodryha et al., "Dopysy 'Dila'. Mykolaiv v poviti bridskim," *Dilo* 8, no. 92 (20 August [1 September] 1887): 2.

276. Pynkovsky

LOCATION: Trybukhivtsi, Husiatyn district. OCCUPATION: Merchant. POSITION IN LOCAL GOVT: Scribe (*CC* 207). FAMILY BACKGROUND: A Mykyta Pynkovsky, presumably the merchant's father, was a half peasant with 14 *Joch* 646 square *Klafter* in 1854.[1] The village then consisted of 3 per cent whole-peasant, 43 per cent half-peasant and 54 per cent quarter-peasant and gardener households, with an average holding of 13 *Joch*.[2] Thus Mykyta Pynkovsky was a middling peasant only slightly better off than average. MOBILITY: The Pynkovsky family had been in Trybukhivtsi since at least 1854.[1] OTHER ACTIVITIES: He was comanager of the community store (*CC* 207).

1) TsDIAL, 488/1/1071, p. 11v. *2) Ibid.*, and TsDIAL, 488/1/1070.

277. **Ripchuk, Ivan**

LOCATION: Kovalivka, Kolomyia district. OCCUPATION: (Peasant). POSITION IN RC: Deputy administration (CC 260).

278. **Romaniv, Ivan**

LOCATION: Kukyziv, Lviv district. OCCUPATION: (Peasant). POSITION IN RC: Deputy administration (CC 10).

279. **Romanyk, Petro**

LOCATION: Ozeriany, Borshchiv district. OCCUPATION: (Peasant). POSITION IN RC: Secretary (CC 97).

280. **Rybachek (Rybachyk), Antin M.**

LOCATION: Mykulyntsi, Ternopil district. OCCUPATION: Teacher. FAMILY BACKGROUND: He was the son of a peasant.[1] ECONOMIC STATUS: In addition to teaching, he tended an orchard and bee-hives.[1] EDUCATION: He finished the lower real school in Brody. He served in the Austrian army in 1854–64, fighting in the Italian war of 1859 and earning the rank of sergeant (U *feldfebl*) as well as decorations. He completed his education after leaving the army.[1] AGE: Born 22 June 1832 (O.S.).[1] DEATH: 13 April 1895 (N.S.).[2] MOBILITY: He was born in Lozivka, Ternopil circle (later Zbarazh district), and educated in the district capital of Brody. His ten years in the Austrian army took him abroad. He taught in Palchyntsi, Zbarazh district; Stryivka, Zbarazh district[1] (1871),[3] and Orikhovets, Skalat district, before he became the principal (U *upravytel*) of the four-grade school in Mykulyntsi. He stayed in the latter town until his death.[1] PUBLICATIONS: He contributed to *Hazeta shkolna*, 1879;[4] *Vesna*, 1879;[5] *Shkolna chasopys*, 1881–2 and 1884–5;[6] *Batkivshchyna*, 1882;[7] and *Uchytel*, 1892–3.[8] OTHER ACTIVITIES: He was a founder of the reading club in Mykulyntsi and attended the inauguration of the reading club in Darakhiv, Terebovlia district (CC 82). His activities in the Mykulyntsi reading club had gotten him into trouble with the crownland school council in 1882. The council censured him, but Rybachek fought the censure by appealing to higher authorities and had it revoked. He founded a loan association attached to the reading club and a special reading club for school-age youth. He was vice-president of the Mykulyntsi reading club in 1890[9] and president in 1895.[10] He belonged to Prosvita and the Ruthenian pedagogical society;[1] he was also president of the teachers' circle of the Polish pedagogical society (P *Towarzystwo Pedagogiczne*) in Mykulyntsi.[11] A member of the United Galician association for Gardening and Bee-keeping, he set up a model fruit orchard and apiary in Mykulyntsi.[1]

1) Lev493, R-48. *2)* "Posmertni vistky," *Ucytel* 7, no. 9 (5 May 1895): 144. *3)* *Szem. kr. Gal. 1871*, 430. *4)* Lev1, no. 1919III. *5)* Lev1, no. 1910IV. *6)* Lev1, no. 2362, 2881, 3114. *7)* A.M. Rybachyk, upravytel shkoly, "Pysmo z Mykulynets," *Batkivshchyna* 4, no. 3 (1 February 1882): 22. *8)* Ant[in] Rybachek, "Dopys," *Uchytel* 4, no. 22 (15 [27] November 1892): 355. Lev2, no. 2484. *9)* "Nashi chytalni," *Batkivshchyna* 12, no. 38–9 (21 September [3 October] 1890): 492. *10)* "Visty z kraiu," *Batkivshchyna* 17, no. 8 (16 [28] April 1895): 60. *11)* Odyn z hostei, "Dopys," *Shkolna chasopys* 7, no. 6 (16 [28] March 1886): 45. Rybachek, "Dopys," *Uchytel* (1892): 355.

281. **Sadovy, Ivan**

LOCATION: Berezyna, Zhydachiv district OCCUPATION: Peasant. ECONOMIC STATUS: Proprietor (CC 28). OTHER ACTIVITIES: He was an activist in the reading club (CC 28).

282. **Saikevych, Danylo**

LOCATION: Radvantsi, Sokal district. OCCUPATION: (Cantor, former or aspiring) (CC 106). AUTHOR: CC 106. OTHER ACTIVITIES: A musician who taught the village youth to sing from notes, he was a proponent of enlightenement and sobriety and an opponent of the mayor (CC 106).

283. Salitra, Oleksa

LOCATION: Olesha, Tovmach district. OCCUPATION: Peasant. POSITION IN RC: Treasurer (*CC* 60). MOBILITY: Four Salitra peasant households lived in Olesha in 1850–5.[1]

1) TsDIAL, 168/1/4099, pp. 6v, 25v.

284. Semotiuk, Stefan

LOCATION: Balyntsi, Kolomyia district. OCCUPATION: Peasant. POSITION IN RC: President (*CC* 95). ECONOMIC STATUS: An "affluent proprietor" (U *hospodar zazhytochnyi*).[1] EDUCATION: Literate.[1] MOBILITY: The Semotiuk name was very common in the village by 1837.[2] OTHER ACTIVITIES: He was a founder of the reading club (*CC* 95).

1) "Otkrytiie chytaln [sic]," *Russkaia rada* 14, no. 10 (15 [27]May 1884): 82. *2)* TsDIAL, 168/1/1416, pp. 84v–91, 94–7.

285. Seniuk, Mykhail (Nykola)

LOCATION: Torky, Sokal district. OCCUPATION: (Peasant). POSITION IN RC: Secretary (*CC* 276). POSITION IN LOCAL GOVT: Mayor (*CC* 276). OTHER ACTIVITIES: As mayor in 1887 he was among the main initiators of the community's purchase of 108 *Joch* of forest.[1]

1) V.K., "Pysmo z Sokalshchyny," *Batkivshchyna* 9, no. 17 (29 [17] April 1887): 100.

286. Senyshyn, Hryhorii

LOCATION: Nykonkovychi, Lviv district. OCCUPATION: Peasant. POSITION IN RC: Secretary (*CC* 105). AUTHOR: *CC* 105. FAMILY BACKGROUND: A Petro Senyshyn, presumably Hryhorii's father, was a full peasant with 14 *Joch* 1555.2 square *Klafter* in 1852–5. This was the largest holding in a village where the average holding for full peasants was under 11 *Joch*. The village consisted of 56 households: 75 per cent full-peasant, 7 per cent quarter-peasant and gardener (both categories had less than 1 *Joch*) and 18 per cent landless cottager.[1]

1) TsDIAL, 168/1/1916, p. 16v.

287. Serbyn, Ivan

LOCATION: Vyktoriv, Stanyslaviv district. OCCUPATION: Peasant. FAMILY BACKGROUND: He was presumably the son of Danylo Serbyn, a half peasant with 15 *Joch* 559 square *Klafter* in 1852–9, who paid an average annual tax of 2.5 gulden on cattle, 1836–45. The village consisted of 2 per cent three quarter peasants, 84 per cent half peasants, 3 per cent quarter peasants, less than 2 per cent gardeners and serfs who paid money rent (P *czynszownicy*), 5 per cent cottagers and 4 per cent tenants. The average holding in the village was under 16 *Joch*, but some peasants had holdings in the 60s and one had over 98 *Joch*. The average annual cattle tax in 1836–45 was 1.6 gulden. Thus Danylo Serbyn was a middling peasant. Danylo Serbyn was a plenipotentiary to the indemnization committee in the 1850s.[1] He was also a member of the church brotherhood and helped initiate church renovations. He was no longer alive by 1884 (*CC* 27). MOBILITY: Danylo Serbyn was already in Vyktoriv by 1836.[1] PUBLICATIONS: Ivan Serbyn wrote an article for *Batkivshchyna* urging peasants to vote for Ukrainian candidates in the 1889 elections to the diet.[2] OTHER ACTIVITIES: He was elected to the auditing committee and reading club committee of the Stanyslaviv branch of Prosvita in 1885 (*CC* 230). He was vice-president of the reading club in Vyktoriv in 1889.[2]

1) TsDIAL, pp. 1v, 94, 99v–100. *2)* Ivan Serbyn, "Holos selianyna do brativ selian," *Batkivshchyna* 11, no. 19 (12 [24] May 1889): 237–8.

288. Serediuk, Ivan

LOCATION: Shliakhtyntsi, Ternopil district. OCCUPATION: Peasant. POSITION IN RC: Vice-president (*CC* 108). POSITION IN LOCAL GOVT: Mayor (elected as reform mayor in 1885) (*CC* 249).

289. Serenetsky, Karol

LOCATION: Fytkiv, Nadvirna district. OCCUPATION: Peasant. POSITION IN RC: Vice-president (*CC* 58). DISTINGUISHING FEATURES: Judging by his name, especially his first name, he might have been one of 24 *latynnyky* inhabiting Fytkiv in 1880.[1] ECONOMIC STATUS: Proprietor (*CC* 58). MOBILITY: The Serenetsky family name is not included in a list of all the peasants of Fytkiv, 1868.[2]

1) Spec. Orts-Rep. 1880. 2) "Konsygnacyia wszystkich gospodarzy gruntowych, iako też zagrodników i chałupników w gminie Fytków znajdujących się w roku 1868," in TsDIAL, 146/64b/1120, pp. 61–4.

290. Serkes, Tymofii

LOCATION: Nykonkovychi, Lviv district. OCCUPATION: Teacher.[1] POSITION IN RC: Librarian (*CC* 105).

1) "Novi chytalni," *Batkivshchyna* 6, no. 20 (16 [4] May 1884): 120.

291. Shchyrba, Hr[yhorii]

LOCATION: Iavoriv (district capital). OCCUPATION: Burgher (*CC* 142). POSITION IN RC: Administration (*CC* 142).

292. Shchyrba, Luka

LOCATION: Nakvasha, Brody district. OCCUPATION: Peasant. POSITION IN RC: Librarian (*CC* 201). POSITION IN LOCAL GOVT: Mayor (*CC* 201). ECONOMIC STATUS: Proprietor (*CC* 201). AGE: He had come of age by 1867,[1] and was therefore born by 1847 and probably by 1842 or earlier. OTHER ACTIVITIES: He was a founder of the reading club (*CC* 201).

1) TsDIAL, 146/64/1153, p. 101.

293. Sheshor, Ilko (Iliia)

LOCATION: Khmelivka, Bohorodchany district.[1] OCCUPATION: Teacher.[1] AUTHOR: *CC* 1, 26. AGE: He began teaching in the early 1880s,[1] and was already contributing to the Ukrainian press by 1878.[2] He was probably born in the late 1850s. PUBLICATIONS: He contributed three articles to *Pysmo z "Prosvity"* in 1878[2] and an article to *Batkivshchyna* in 1890.[2]

1) He is not mentioned in *Szem. kr. Gal. 1881*; he is referred to as a teacher in the "unorganized school" (P *szkoła niezorganizowana*) in Khmelivka in *ibid. 1884*, 371, and *ibid. 1885*, 371. *2)* Levl, no. 1856. *3)* Iliia Sh[eshor], "Z Bohorodchanskoho pyshut," *Batkivshchyna* 12, no. 38–9 (21 September [3 October] 1890): 488–9.

294. Shkraba, Vavryk

LOCATION: Dmytriv, Kaminka Strumylova district. OCCUPATION: (Peasant). OTHER ACTIVITIES: He was an activist in the reading club and treasurer of the church committee (U *kasiier provizorochnoho vydilu*) (*CC* 52).

295. Shostak, Semen

LOCATION: Mykolaiv, Brody district. OCCUPATION: Cantor.[1] AGE: He was drafted in the 1870s,[2] and therefore was born in the 1850s. MOBILITY: He served over three years in the army; he was stationed in Hungary.[2] PUBLICATIONS: He was coauthor of a denunciation of the teacher *Medynsky, Ivan*.[3] OTHER ACTIVITIES: He was an auditor of the Pravda society in 1884 (*CC* 71) and also served on the administration in 1885 (*CC* 198). He spoke at an evening to commemorate the abolition of serfdom, 3 May 1888 (O.S.).[1] In the 1870s, as an assistant cantor (U *piddiachyi*), he had held public readings for the peasants.[2]

1) Vasyl Iakubiv, *et al.*, "Pysmo z Brodskoho," *Batkivshchyna* 10, no. 22 (1 June [20 May] 1888): 135. *2)* Tarnavsky, *Spohady*, 36. *3)* Mykola Holodryha *et al.*, "Dopysy 'Dila'. Mykolaiv v poviti bridskim," *Dilo* 8, no. 92 (20 August [1 September] 1887): 2.

296. Shpytko, Ivan (Ioann)

LOCATION: Mizun, Dolyna district. OCCUPATION: Priest. ECONOMIC STATUS: Administrator of a parish with 1,867 members.[1] AGE: Born 1853, ordained 1878.[1] MARITAL STATUS: Married.[1] MOBILITY: When transferred from Mizun in 1884 (*CC* 46), he became administrator in Voltsniv, Zolochiv district.[2] OTHER ACTIVITIES: He was a founder of the reading club in Mizun in 1883 (*CC* 46).

1) *Shem. Lviv. 1884*, 119. *2)* O-y, "Ot Dolyny," *Slovo* 24, no. 90 (18 [30] August 1884): 2.

297. Shvets, Luts

LOCATION: Liubycha Kniazi, Rava Ruska district. OCCUPATION: (Peasant). POSITION IN RC: Deputy administration (*CC* 137).

298. Sichynsky, Iliarion

LOCATION: Strilkiv, Stryi district. OCCUPATION: Priest. POSITION IN RC: President (*CC* 149). AUTHOR: *CC* 40. ECONOMIC STATUS: Administrator of a parish with 615 members.[1] AGE: Born 1853, ordained 1878.[1] MARITAL STATUS: Married.[1] MOBILITY: He was about to be transferred in early 1885 (*CC* 149). OTHER ACTIVITIES: He helped establish the reading club (*CC* 34).

1) *Shem. Lviv. 1884*, 156.

299. Sirko, Antin

LOCATION: Korchyn, Sokal district. OCCUPATION: Peasant. POSITION IN RC: President (*CC* 252). POSITION IN LOCAL GOVT: He was mayor in 1872–3[1] and in 1885.[2] ECONOMIC STATUS: He owned a half-peasant holding in 1859, when 85 per cent of the households in Korchyn were half-peasant.[3] EDUCATION: Literate by 1865.[4] AGE: He was not a landholder in 1855,[5] but had come into land by 1859.[3] He was thus probably born between 1830 and 1834 and no later than 1839. MOBILITY: Four Sirko households lived in Korchyn in 1852–5.[5] OTHER ACTIVITIES: He had been a plenipotentiary in servitude affairs, 1865–6 and 1872–3.[6] Apparently, he gained enough experience in this position to qualify him for membership in the district estimating commission (P *komisja szacunkowa*) of Sokal in (at least) 1872–4, 1877 and 1881.[7] He was also a member of the district council, as a representative of the village communes (P *z grup gmin wiejskich*) in (at least) 1874, 1877, 1881 and 1885.[8] As mayor of Korchyn he "did much to improve the community"; "by his ardent and decisive actions he cleansed the village of drunkenness."[2]

1) TsDIAL, 146/64b/4372, p. 57; TsDIAL, 146/64b/4373, p. 75. *2)* "...vid Sokalia," *Batkivshchyna* 7, no. 25 (19 [7] June 1885): 186. *3)* TsDIAL, 146/64b/4361, pp. 57–9. *4)* TsDIAL, 146/64b/4363, p. 122. *5)* TsDIAL, 168/1/612. *6)* TsDIAL, 146/64b/4363, p. 134; TsDIAL, 146/64b/4369, p. 6v; TsDIAL, 146/64b/4372, p. 2; TsDIAL, 146/64b/4373, p. 50. *7)* He is not mentioned in *Szem. kr. Gal. 1871*. His membership in the commission is mentioned in *ibid. 1872*, 205; *ibid. 1873*, 203; *ibid. 1874*, 227; *ibid. 1881*, 265; but not in *ibid. 1884* or *1885*. *8)* *Ibid. 1874*, 298; *ibid. 1877*, 281; *ibid. 1881*, 268; not mentioned *ibid. 1884*; mentioned *ibid. 1885*, 249.

300. Skobelsky, Ioann

LOCATION: Lishnia, Drohobych district. OCCUPATION: Priest. OTHER ACTIVITIES: He was a founder[1] and promoter of the reading club (*CC* 63) who let the club meet in his home, provided the meetings with lighting and explained what was read to the members.[1] He was president of the local branch of the Kachkovsky Society and a member of the Drohobych district council (*CC* 63).

1) I. Sosiuk and — Zakhariuk, "Dopysy. Ot Drohobycha," *Russkaia rada* 15, no. 23 (2 [14] December 1885): 184.

301. Skochylias, Iosyf

LOCATION: Mshana, Zolochiv district. OCCUPATION: (Peasant). POSITION IN LOCAL GOVT: (Reform) mayor (*CC* 123). OTHER ACTIVITIES: He used money from fines imposed

by the village government to help pay for a subscription to *Batkivshchyna* for the village.
He also founded a loan association (*CC* 123).

302. Skrehunets, Semen

LOCATION: Stopchativ, Kolomyia district. OCCUPATION: (Peasant). POSITION IN
RC: Deputy administration (*CC* 263).

303. Sliusarchuk, Nykola

LOCATION: Stopchativ and Liucha, Kolomyia district. OCCUPATION: Scribe. POSITION IN
RC: Secretary in Stopchativ (*CC* 263). POSITION IN LOCAL GOVT: Scribe in Liucha (*CC*
206, 263). AGE: Young.[1] MOBILITY: He lived in Stopchativ, but was scribe in Liucha (*CC*
263). OTHER ACTIVITIES: Described as "our young patriot,"[1] he was a founder of the reading clubs in Liucha (*CC* 206) and Stopchativ (*CC* 263) and read aloud at the inauguration
of the reading club in Kovalivka, also in Kolomyia district (*CC* 260).

1) K., "Rukh v nashykh chytalniakh. Chytalni v Kovalivtsi i Stopchatovi," *Dilo* 6, no. 120
(31 October [12 November] 1885): 3.

304. Sliuzar, Mykhailo

LOCATION: Kadobna, Kalush district. OCCUPATION: Cantor.[1] POSITION IN RC: Secretary
(*CC* 121). POSITION IN LOCAL GOVT: Scribe.[2] PUBLICATIONS: He contributed to *Hazeta
shkolna* in 1876.[3] OTHER ACTIVITIES: He was denounced in *Batkivshchyna* as a Polonizer
and opponent of enlightenment,[1] but subsequently defended as a Ukrainian patriot.[2]

1) "Vid Kalusha," *Batkivshchyna* 6, no. 33 (15 [3] August 1884): 208. *2)* "...vid
Kalusha," *Batkivshchyna* 6, no. 38 (19 [7] September 1884): 235. *3)* Lev1, no. 1521I.

305. Smolynsky, Vasyl

LOCATION: Pochapy, Zolochiv district. OCCUPATION: (Peasant). POSITION IN RC: Deputy
administration (*CC* 268).

306. Soltys, Hryn

LOCATION: Strilkiv, Stryi district. OCCUPATION: Cantor (*CC* 149) (and peasant). POSITION
IN RC: Treasurer (*CC* 149). MOBILITY: Three Soltys full-peasant households lived in
Strilkiv in 1852–5.[1] OTHER ACTIVITIES: He was a founder of the reading club (*CC* 34).

1) TsDIAL, 488/1/422, pp. 1v, 13v.

307. Soltys, Onofer (Onufer)

LOCATION: Strilkiv, Stryi district. OCCUPATION: Peasant. POSITION IN RC: Vice-president
(*CC* 149). POSITION IN LOCAL GOVT: Mayor (*CC* 34). ECONOMIC STATUS: In 1852–5 he
was a full peasant with 7 *Joch* 461 square *Klafter*;[1] this made him a middling peasant.
AGE: Since he had come of age by 1852,[1] he was born in 1832 or earlier and probably by
1827. OTHER ACTIVITIES: He was a founder of the reading club (*CC* 34).

1) TsDIAL, 488/1/422, p. 1v.

308. Spolitakevych, Ioan (Ivan)

LOCATION: Ninovychi, Sokal district. OCCUPATION: Cantor (*CC* 188). OTHER
ACTIVITIES: He was a founder of the reading club (*CC* 188). In 1897 he was a founder
and the vice-president of the revived reading club.[1]

1) Hist, "Dopysy. Z Sokalshchyny," *Svoboda* 1, no. 20 (15 [27] May 1897): 155–6.

309. Stadnyk, Andrei

LOCATION: Berezyna, Zhydachiv district. OCCUPATION: Peasant. ECONOMIC
STATUS: Proprietor (*CC* 28). OTHER ACTIVITIES: He was an activist in the reading club
(*CC* 28).

310. Staryk, I.

LOCATION: Darakhiv, Terebovlia district. OCCUPATION: (Peasant). POSITION IN RC: Vice-president (*CC* 82).

311. Stashkiv, Aleksander

LOCATION: Makhniv, Rava Ruska district. OCCUPATION: (Peasant). POSITION IN RC: Secretary (*CC* 137).

312. Stefanko, Hryts

LOCATION: Liucha, Kolomyia district. OCCUPATION: (Peasant). POSITION IN RC: Librarian (*CC* 206).

313. Stefanko, Petro

LOCATION: Liucha, Kolomyia district. OCCUPATION: (Peasant). POSITION IN RC: Vice-president (*CC* 206).

314. Stupnytsky, Havryil

LOCATION: Kolodribka, Zalishchyky district. OCCUPATION: Priest. ECONOMIC STATUS: Assistant[1] in a parish (Synkiv and Kolodribka) with 3728 members.[2] AGE: Born 1848[3] or 1849, ordained 1876.[1] MARITAL STATUS: Married.[3] MOBILITY: He spent six years in Kolodribka before being transferred in 1883 (*CC* 73). In 1884 he was administrator in Silets, Stanyslaviv district.[3] OTHER ACTIVITIES: He was a founder of the reading club (*CC* 73).

1) Schem. Leop. 1882, 183. *2) Shem. Lviv. 1884*, 250. *3) Ibid.*, 212.

315. Susiak, Vasyl

LOCATION: Lishnia, Drohobych district. OCCUPATION: Peasant (*CC* 63). POSITION IN LOCAL GOVT: Former mayor (*CC* 63). OTHER ACTIVITIES: He was a founder of the reading club (*CC* 63).

316. Svidersky, Ios[yf]

LOCATION: Buzhok, Zolochiv district. OCCUPATION: (Peasant). POSITION IN RC: Deputy administration (*CC* 42).

317. Svidersky, Ivan

LOCATION: Buzhok, Zolochiv district. OCCUPATION: Peasant;[1] aspiring merchant and innkeeper (*CC* 42). POSITION IN RC: Vice-president (*CC* 42). ECONOMIC STATUS: Proprietor.[1] OTHER ACTIVITIES: He hosted the inauguration of the reading club and served on its administration in 1881.[1] He had plans to open a Ukrainian store and an inn (*CC* 42).

1) Ivan Petryshyn [Liubomyr Seliansky], "Pysmo z Hlukhoho Kuta," *Batkivshchyna* 3, no. 10 (16 May 1881): 80.

318. Sych, Irynei

LOCATION: Ninovychi, Sokal district. OCCUPATION: Peasant. ECONOMIC STATUS: Proprietor (*CC* 188). OTHER ACTIVITIES: He was a founder of the reading club (*CC* 188).

319. Sych, Stefan

LOCATION: Makhniv, Rava Ruska district. OCCUPATION: (Peasant). POSITION IN RC: Deputy administration (*CC* 137).

320. Sydorko, Aleksii

LOCATION: Makhniv, Rava Ruska district. OCCUPATION: (Peasant). POSITION IN RC: Treasurer (*CC* 137).

321. Syvy, Mykhailo

LOCATION: Korelychi, Peremyshliany district. OCCUPATION: Peasant. POSITION IN RC: Vice-president (CC 84). AUTHOR: CC 84. ECONOMIC STATUS: Proprietor (CC 84). MOBILITY: The Syvy family name was common among the Greek Catholic parishioners of Korelychi in 1864.[1] OTHER ACTIVITIES: He spoke at the opening of the reading club in nearby Dobrianychi, Peremyshliany district, in 1884.[2]

1) TsDIAL, 146/64b/2294, pp. 54–61. *2)* Chytalnyk, "...vid Peremyshlian," *Batkivshchyna* 6, no. 46 (14 [2] November 1884): 294.

322. Tanchakovsky, Aleksander

LOCATION: Novosilka Iazlovetska, Buchach district. OCCUPATION: Priest. ECONOMIC STATUS: He was an assistant in Iazlovets, Buchach district, with a daughter church in Novosilka Iazlovetska; the parish had 2,940 members (according to the 1885 schematism)[1] and the assistant had 47 *Joch* of arable land and 5 *Joch* of pasture (U *pasovysko*) at his disposal.[2] AGE: Born 1849, ordained 1873.[3] MARITAL STATUS: Married.[2] MOBILITY: In the fall of 1884 he was made pastor of Dunaiv, Peremyshliany district.[4] OTHER ACTIVITIES: He was the main founder of the reading club and a loan association; he personally taught a peasant to read (CC 48). In 1868–74 he was a member of Prosvita.[5]

1) Shem. Lviv. 1885, 300. *2)* Ibid. 1884, 295. *3)* Ibid. 1885, 110. *4)* Ibid., 303. *5)* "Chleny tovarystva 'Prosvita'," *Spravozdaniie z dilanii "Prosvity"* (1874), 26–32.

323. Taniachkevych, Danylo (elder)

LOCATION: Mykolaiv, Brody district. OCCUPATION: Priest. FAMILY BACKGROUND: He was descended from an old priestly family; his father was a priest.[1] FAMILY CONNECTIONS: Father of *Taniachkevych, Danylo (younger)* (CC 71). ECONOMIC STATUS: Chaplain of a Greek Catholic community of 1,318, with an endowment of 46 *Joch* 663 square *Klafter* of arable land, 17 *Joch* of meadow, 3 *Joch* 1447 square *Klafter* of pasture and 18 *Klafter* of wood as well as a *congruum* of 58 gulden 31 kreuzer.[2] EDUCATION: He was well read. His library contained the works of Shevchenko and Panteleimon Kulish as well as books in Polish, German and French.[3] AGE: Born 1817, ordained 1842.[2] MARITAL STATUS: Married.[2] MOBILITY: He had been in Mykolaiv since at least 1868.[4] "...He never went anywhere."[3]

OTHER ACTIVITIES: He presided over the local Pravda society in 1884 (CC 71) and 1885 (CC 198). He opened the evening to commemorate the abolition of serfdom on 3 May 1888 (O.S.).[5]

In 1868–77 he had had a dispute with the manor over servitudes.[4]

In the 1870s he was "a conscious Ukrainian in a sea of Ruthenians, Russophiles and Polonophiles." His home was decorated with portraits of Shevchenko, Kulish, Marko Vovchok and Bohdan Khmelnytsky. He founded a communal granary in the village and took an interest in the school. He fought against alcoholism; when his sermons failed to introduce sobriety, he took a stick and chased the musician and drinkers from the tavern. He also engaged in philanthropic activities, including the adoption of orphans.[3]

1) Lev493, T-8, pp. 36–36v. *2)* Shem. Lviv. 1884, 186. *3)* Tarnavsky, *Spohady*, 29, 33, 35–6. *4)* TsDIAL, 146/64/1123. *5)* Vasyl Iakubiv et al., "Pysmo z Brodskoho," *Batkivshchyna* 10, no. 22 (1 June [20 May] 1888): 135.

324. Taniachkevych, Danylo (younger)

LOCATION: Zakomarie, Zolochiv district. OCCUPATION: Priest. AUTHOR: CC 262. FAMILY BACKGROUND: He was descended from an old priestly family; his grandfather and father were priests.[1] FAMILY CONNECTIONS: Son of *Taniachkevych, Danylo (elder)* (CC 71). ECONOMIC STATUS: He was chaplain of a Greek Catholic community of 501 members, with an endowment of 14 *Joch* of arable land and 17 *Joch* of meadow and a *congruum* of 115 gulden 48 kreuzer.[2] He was poor and deeply in debt. The captain of Zolochiv district, in a confidential letter to the presidium of the viceroy's office, 6 November 1879 (N.S.), described Taniachkevych's material situation: "The main cause of his current critical economic situation, close to complete ruin, is the circumstance that, to his own detriment, he saved his brother-in-law who had fallen gravely ill; because of this he went into debt to Jews. As a man engaged in intellectual work and impractical, he has been unable to cope with the loan he took out, which, augmented now by interest and additional loans, has grown to dimensions almost exceeding what it is possible for him to pay."[3] When his father-in-law died, Taniachkevych took in his six children, including three sons whom he sent to school. "Therefore poverty crept into his house, so that often enough the whole family went hungry."[4] EDUCATION: He attended elementary school in the small town of Vytkiv, Zolochiv circle, and in Lviv. He finished gymnasium and theology in Lviv.[5] AGE: Born 6 November 1842 (O.S.), ordained 1867.[5] DEATH: 1906.[6] MARITAL STATUS: Widowed.[2] MOBILITY: He was born in Didyliv, Zolochiv district, where his grandfather was pastor. He was educated in nearby Vytkiv and in Lviv. Except for his first year after ordination, he was stationed in Zakomarie for all of his priestly career.[5] He knew Vienna, however, since he served as a deputy to parliament in 1897–1900.[6] PUBLICATIONS: He was a prolific author. Under various pseudonyms, including Budevolia (=There will be freedom),[7] he contributed as a seminarian in the 1860s to the early national populist press: *Vechernytsi*, *Meta* and *Nyva*.[8] He wrote the first manifesto of the national populist movement, *Pysmo narodovtsiv ruskykh do redaktora politychnoi chasopysi "Rus'", iako protest i memoriial* (1876).[9] Among his numerous brochures was also a guide to founding Pravda societies.[10] OTHER ACTIVITIES: He was the inventor of the Pravda societies and active in them not only in his own parish, but in that of his father (Mykolaiv, Brody district) (*CC* 71, 198). He founded a reading club in Zakomarie (*CC* 28). In 1885 he presided over the cantors' convention in Olesko, Zolochiv district (*CC* 154).

As a seminarian in the 1860s he had been close to the leaders of the fledgling national populist movement and set up an informal national populist circle in the Lviv seminary. Through extensive correspondence, he spread the ideas of national populism among the Galician youth.[11] He was a member of Prosvita, 1868–74,[12] and later an honorary member of that society.[6] In matters of ritual he was close to the Easternizing tendency in the Greek Catholic church.[13]

As a deputy to the Austrian parliament, 1897–1900, he belonged to the opposition[8] and defended peasant interests.[14] In parliament in 1897 he said: "Today they call us radicals. If by this is meant the tendency to elevate the popular masses, then I agree with this name."[15]

1) Lev493, T-8, pp. 36–36v. *2) Shem. Lviv. 1884*, 112–13. *3)* TsDIAL, 146/7/4149, pp. 182–3. *4)* Tarnavsky, *Spohady*, 39. *5)* Lev493, T-8, p. 36v. *6) Ukrainska Zahalna Entsyklopediia*, s.v. "Taniachkevych." *7)* Lev493, T-8, p. 27. *8) Ibid.*, p. 37v. *9) Entsyklopediia Ukrainoznavstva*, s.v. "Taniachkevych Danylo." *10)* Lev1, no. 2665. *11)* Lev493, T-8, pp. 37–37v. *12)* "Chleny tovarystva 'Prosvita'," *Spravozdaniie z dilanii "Prosvity"* (1874), 26–32. *13)* TsDIAL, 146/7/4149, p. 180. *14)* Lev493, T-8. *15) Ibid.*, 19.

325. Tarchanyn, Amvrosii

LOCATION: Vynnyky, Zhovkva district. OCCUPATION: Priest. ECONOMIC STATUS: Hegumen of the Basilian monastery in Zhovkva.[1] MARITAL STATUS: Celibate. MOBILITY: Before coming to Zhovkva, he had been a teacher in Lavriv, Staryi Sambir district (1868).[2] OTHER ACTIVITIES: He was vice-president of the Pravda society (*CC* 262). In 1885 he was elected to the Zhovkva district council, but along with eleven other Ukrainian members (including *Drymalyk, Sylvester L.*), he resigned to protest Zhovkva city elections.[3]

1) "Vybory do rad povitovykh," *Batkivshchyna* 7, no. 42 (16 [4] October 1885): 286. *2) Skhymatism shkol narodnykh . . . 1868*, 53. *3)* Lev 493, D-160.

326. Tarnavsky, Vasyl

LOCATION: Pochapy, Zolochiv district. OCCUPATION: Peasant. POSITION IN RC: Vice-president (*CC* 268). ECONOMIC STATUS: He was a wealthy peasant involved in

1882 in a business venture of purchasing and leasing forest from the manor.[1]
EDUCATION: Literate.[1]

1) Ivan Petryshyn [Liubomyr Seliansky], "Pysmo z Zolochivskoho," *Batkivshchyna* 4, no. 24 (16 [4] December 1882): 192.

327. Tetorniuk, Hryhorii

LOCATION: Ozeriany, Borshchiv district. OCCUPATION: (Peasant). POSITION IN RC: Vice-president (*CC* 97). POSITION IN LOCAL GOVT: Mayor (*CC* 97). OTHER ACTIVITIES: He was a member of the Borshchiv district council (*CC* 97).

328. Tomashevsky, Luka(sh)

LOCATION: Novosilky Kardynalski, Rava Ruska district. OCCUPATION: Cantor and scribe (*CC* 149). POSITION IN RC: Vice-president.[1] AUTHOR: *CC* 14, 191, 210. POSITION IN LOCAL GOVT: Scribe in three villages (*CC* 14) and deputy mayor in Novosilky Kardynalski (*CC* 79). ECONOMIC STATUS: He wrote that he was not poor (*CC* 14). OTHER ACTIVITIES: He was a plenipotentiary for the village in servitude matters in 1879.[2] He was a founder of and activist in the reading club (*CC* 74). He may have done some teaching, since he was referred to as a cantor-teacher (U *diako-uchytel*). He was elected to the Rava Ruska district council and served on its administration (*CC* 79). "At a session of the district council he spoke fervently against excessive and unnecessary expenditures that overly burden our poor farmer. So now the Rava district authorities are expelling him from the council, because, they say, as a village scribe he has no right to sit on the council." But in the past, three scribes had belonged to the council (*CC* 163).

1) "O chytalniakh," *Batkivshchyna* 7, no. 7 (13 [1] February 1885): 56. *2)* TsDIAL, 146/64b/2936, pp. 6–6v.

329. Tomyn, Oleksa

LOCATION: Stopchativ, Kolomyia district. OCCUPATION: (Peasant). POSITION IN RC: Vice-president (*CC* 263). OTHER ACTIVITIES: He was a founder of the reading club (*CC* 263).

330. Tsaryk, Fed

LOCATION: Vynnyky, Zhovkva district. OCCUPATION: Peasant. ECONOMIC STATUS: Proprietor (*CC* 262). OTHER ACTIVITIES: He served in the deputy administration of the reading club in 1883[1] and in the administration of the Pravda society in 1885 (*CC* 262).

1) Vynnychanyn, "Pysmo vid Zhovkvy," *Batkivshchyna* 5, no. 50 (14 [2] December 1883): 301.

331. Tsipyvko, Symeon (Semen)

LOCATION: Iazhiv Staryi, Iavoriv district. OCCUPATION: Cantor, scribe (*CC* 192) and peasant.[1] POSITION IN RC: Secretary.[2] AUTHOR: *CC* 192. POSITION IN LOCAL GOVT: Scribe, from c. 1860[1] until at least 1899.[3] ECONOMIC STATUS: He did not consider himself well off, but hired a farm hand to pasture his horses at an estimated cost of 120 gulden a year.[1] PUBLICATIONS: He contributed short notes to *Batkivshchyna* in 1884[2] and 1887 (on the two-hundred-fiftieth anniversary of the erection of Iazhiv Staryi's church).[4] He also published an article in *Svoboda* in 1897.[1] OTHER ACTIVITIES: When a revived, Prosvita-affiliated reading club was established in 1897, Tsipyvko joined. Soon, however, he had a falling out with the administration and went on to found an independent reading club with its own store. Tsipyvko said the reason for the conflict and split was that he objected to the strict regulations on abstinence from alcohol imposed by the administration of the Prosvita reading club.[3] (Tsipyvko himself, however, had abstained from hard liquor [U *horivka*] since 1867 and from all alcoholic beverages since 1881.)[1] The real cause of the split probably lay elsewhere, since Tsipyvko's reading club was composed of wealthier proprietors and supported by the mayor.[3] Both sides denounced each other in the press[5] and in letters to the Prosvita administration in Lviv. The situation lasted until at least 1899.[3]

1 Symeon Tsipyvko, "Slovo pro viitiv okruzhnykh," *Svoboda* 1, no. 9 (27 February [11 March] 1897): 66–7. *2)* Sem[en Tsipyvko], "...vid Iavorova," *Batkivshchyna* 6, no. 22 (30 [18] May 1884): 132. *3)* TsDIAL, 348/1/6169, pp. 13–27. *4)* Symeon Tsipyvko, "...z Iazhova-staroho (v Iavorivshchyni)," *Batkivshchyna* 9, no. 9 (4 March [20 February] 1887): 55. *5)* Tsipyvko (not by name) and his reading club are denounced in: Chytalnyky, "Dopysy. Z Iavorivshchyny," *Svoboda* 3, no. 3 (7 [23] January 1899): 20.

332. Tsurkovsky, Ihnatii (Hnat)

LOCATION: Liucha, Kolomyia district. OCCUPATION: Priest. POSITION IN RC: President (*CC* 206). FAMILY CONNECTIONS: Father-in-law of *Genyk, Kyrylo*.[1] ECONOMIC STATUS: He was pastor of a parish with 1,065 members, an endowment of 6 *Joch* of arable land, 77 *Joch* of meadow, 22 *Joch* of pasture, 51 cubic metres of wood and a 3 gulden redemption-payment for milling privileges; he had a *congruum* of 227 gulden 57 kreuzer.[2] The parish was considered a "poor" (U *uboha*) parish. Tsurkovsky had spent more than two decades as an assistant and administrator, allegedly only because he refused to beg for a decent post.[3] When *Krushelnytsky, Maksym* met him in the mid-1880s, he wrote to Leonid Zaklynsky: "I liked Father Tsurkovsky very much, only it's obvious that he's depressed by want" (U *prydavlenyi rizhnoiu bidoiu*).[4] AGE: Born 1820, ordained 1846.[2] DEATH: 9 September 1889 (O.S.).[3] MARITAL STATUS: Widowed.[2] MOBILITY: He served in various parishes from 1846 to 1868, and in Liucha from 1868 until his death.[3] OTHER ACTIVITIES: He founded the reading club in Liucha (*CC* 206) in 1884. A national populist, he was a member of the organizations Prosvita, Narodna rada and Shkilna pomich. In spite of his poverty he donated to the national populist periodicals *Pravda*, *Dilo* and *Zoria*. "He treated the people humanely."[3]

1) Kaye, *Early Ukrainian Settlements*, 381–2. *2)* *Shem. Lviv. 1884*, 259. *3)* ...i ... [hard sign]," "O. Hnat Tsurkovsky," *Batkivshchyna* 11, no. 41 (13 [25] October 1889): 506–7. *4)* Letter of 5 January 1885, in LNB AN URSR, Viddil rukopysiv, fond Zaklynskykh, 192/31, p. 147.

333. Turkevych, Nykolai

LOCATION: Korelychi, Peremyshliany district. OCCUPATION: Priest. POSITION IN RC: President (*CC* 84). ECONOMIC STATUS: Pastor of a parish with 1,747 members, an endowment of 87 *Joch* of arable land, 13 *Joch* of meadow and 12 *Joch* of pasture and a *congruum* of 51 gulden 14 kreuzer.[1] AGE: Born 1848, ordained 1872.[1] MARITAL STATUS: Married.[1]

1) *Shem. Lviv. 1884*, 108.

334. Tymchuk, Hryhorii

LOCATION: Kolodribka, Zalishchyky district. OCCUPATION: Teacher. POSITION IN RC: Vice-president (*CC* 76). AUTHOR: *CC* 67, 73, 76. POSITION IN LOCAL GOVT: Councilman (*CC* 76). AGE: He had been teaching in Kolodribka since 1865 (*CC* 76), and hence was born c. 1843. MOBILITY: He had lived in Kolodribka since at least 1865 (*CC* 76). OTHER ACTIVITIES: He was vice-president of the reading club in 1890.[1]

1) "Chytalnia v Kolodribtsi," *Batkivshchyna* 12, no. 24 (8 [20] June 1890): 311.

335. Tytsieiko, Hrynko

LOCATION: Dobrostany, Horodok district. OCCUPATION: (Peasant). POSITION IN RC: Librarian, 1885 (*CC* 245).

336. Vandrovych, Iosyf

LOCATION: Berezyna, Zhydachiv district. OCCUPATION: Peasant. ECONOMIC STATUS: Proprietor (*CC* 28). OTHER ACTIVITIES: He was an activist in the reading club (*CC* 28).

337. Vandych, Prokip

LOCATION: Kiidantsi, Kolomyia district. OCCUPATION: Peasant. POSITION IN LOCAL GOVT: Deputy mayor (*CC* 190). ECONOMIC STATUS: Proprietor (*CC* 190). MOBILITY: Two Vandych households lived in Kiidantsi in 1851–5.[1] OTHER ACTIVITIES: He donated a room in his home to the reading club (*CC* 190).

1) TsDIAL, 168/1/1503, pp. 5v, 44v, 68v.

338. Vasyliuk, Dmytro

LOCATION: Piznanka Hnyla, Skalat district. OCCUPATION: Peasant. POSITION IN RC: Deputy administration (*CC* 238). ECONOMIC STATUS: Proprietor (*CC* 238).

339. Vertiukh, Oleksa

LOCATION: Tsebriv, Ternopil district. OCCUPATION: (Peasant). POSITION IN RC: Administration (*CC* 44).

340. Vidlyvany, Nykyfor

LOCATION: Fytkiv, Nadvirna district. OCCUPATION: Teacher. ECONOMIC STATUS: He had been a teacher at a better school (U *etatova posada*), but for his activities in the Ukrainian movement he was transferred to a worse position (U *filiialna*) in Fytkiv.[1] He was a bee-keeper.[2] AGE: Born c. 1850.[1] DEATH: 18 (30) April 1885.[1] MOBILITY: He had originally taught in Pererisl, Nadvirna district, in the early 1870s.[3] He did not teach in the late 1870s.[4] In the early 1880s he taught in Kaminne, Nadvirna district,[5] and in the mid-1880s he taught in Fytkiv,[6] where he died.[1] OTHER ACTIVITIES: For being active in the Ukrainian movement he ran into trouble with the school board in the early 1880s.[1] "An ardent enlightener of the people," he was active in establishing the reading club in Fytkiv (*CC* 22).

1) Mykola Basaichuk, "Posmertni zhadky i podiaka," *Shkolna chasopys* 6, no. 15–16 (16 [28] August 1885): 124. *2)* "Umerly," *Batkivshchyna* 7, no. 40 (2 October [20 September] 1885): 275. *3)* *Szem. kr. Gal. 1871*, 414; *ibid. 1873*, 406; *ibid. 1874*, 437. *4)* He is not listed in *ibid. 1877, 1878* or *1879*. *5)* *Ibid. 1881*, 425. *6)* *Ibid. 1884*, 405; *ibid. 1885*, 405.

341. Vilkhovy, Dmytro

LOCATION: Komarno, Rudky district. OCCUPATION: (Artisan). POSITION IN RC: Secretary (*CC* 9). AGE: He is referred to as "the younger" (*CC* 9). PUBLICATIONS: He probably wrote an item of correspondence for *Dilo*, 1885.[1] OTHER ACTIVITIES: He was an amateur poet (*CC* 9).[2]

1) [Dmytro?] Vilkhovy, "Dopysy. Z Komarna," *Dilo* 6, no. 75–6 (11 [23] July 1885): 3. *2)* "Dopysy. Vid Komarna," *Dilo* 5, no. 19 (16 [28] February 1884): 2.

342. Vilkhovy, Mykhailo

LOCATION: Komarno, Rudky district. OCCUPATION: (Artisan). POSITION IN RC: Vice-president (*CC* 9).

343. Voinarovsky, Symeon (Semen)

LOCATION: Kovalivka, Kolomyia district. OCCUPATION: Peasant. POSITION IN RC: Secretary (*CC* 260). POSITION IN LOCAL GOVT: Scribe in 1885 (*CC* 260). In the 1870s he had served as councilman, treasurer and tax-assessor (U *taksator*); the community wanted to elect him mayor, but he declined the nomination.[1] ECONOMIC STATUS: After working for twelve years as a teacher, he began farming in the 1870s[2] with 2 *Joch* of land and a house in poor condition left to him by his father-in-law. He had a debt to pay off as well as the obligation to marry off his wife's sister. These burdens, the construction of a new house with two large rooms (U *s dvoma svitlytsiamy*) and double windows (U *podviini vikna*) and the acquisition of 5 more *Joch* of land and five cattle put him deeper into debt. He had the additional misfortune of sowing too early one year and reaping a miserable crop. After six years of farming, he was still deeply in debt. He had sold some books in the village both to enlighten his neighbours and to earn money, and in 1876 he was considering peddling New Testaments from village to village throughout Galicia.[1] AGE: He began teaching c. 1864,[2] and therefore was born c. 1842. PUBLICATIONS: He contributed to the Russophile publications *Russkaia rada*, 1875[3] and 1878,[4] *Nauka*, 1877,[1] and *Slovo*, 1877.[2] OTHER ACTIVITIES: He had been a plenipotentiary in servitude affairs in the 1870s. He was the first peasant in Kovalivka to join the brotherhood of holy sobriety, in 1874–5, and he agitated against alcohol in his village[1] and in the press.[2] He worked closely with the pastor in the sobriety campaign and incurred some enmity in his own and the local Jewish community for his efforts.[1] In 1877 he came into conflict with the mayor, Semen Koltsuniak, over anti-alcohol reforms that he, as a councilman, wanted to introduce; Koltsuniak took Voinarovsky to court before the district authorities, for slander.[2] He sold books in his village in 1874 and in 1876 dreamed of selling New Testaments throughout Ukrainian Galicia.[1]

At least in the late 1870s he had strong Russophile convictions. After he had read an issue of the national populist journal *Pravda*, he stamped on it. He considered the editors "a fanatical, separatist, petty party infected with the disease of Ukrainomatism [sic]." Addressing the editors, he wrote: "... You won't fool us with the poems of Shevchenko, for they appeal only to the youth, but proprietors find in them neither counsel nor salvation.... We are Galician, not Ukrainian, Ruthenians...."[4] He was a member of the Kachkovsky Society.[2]

In 1906 he was vice-president of the revived, Prosvita-affiliated reading club in Kovalivka.[5]

1) Symeon Voinarovsky, "Dopysy. Pysmo iz Kovalivky," *Nauka* 6, no. 1 (1 January 1877): 16–17. *2)* Semen Voinarovsky, "Iz Kovalevky," *Slovo* 17, no. 67 (18 [30] June 1877): 2–3. *3)* Semen Voinarovsky, "Pysmo dlia vsikh selian umiiushchykh chytaty!," *Russkaia rada* 5, no. 8 (15 April 1875): 60–1. *4)* Semen Voinarovsky, "Dopysy. Z-nad Pruta," *Russkaia rada* 8, no. 9 (1 May 1878): 71–2. *5)* TsDIAL, 348/1/2900, p. 42v.

344. Vozniak, Ivan

LOCATION: Chekhy, Brody district. OCCUPATION: Cantor (*CC* 271) and peasant. POSITION IN RC: Secretary (*CC* 271). ECONOMIC STATUS: Proprietor (*CC* 262). PUBLICATIONS: He contributed an item of correspondence to *Russkaia rada*, 1885.[1] OTHER ACTIVITIES: He was a founder of the Pravda society (*CC* 262).

1) I[van] V[ozniak], "Dopys. Chekhy kolo Brodiv," *Russkaia rada* 15, no. 22 (16 [28] November 1885): 170.

345. Vozniak, Mykhailo

LOCATION: Chekhy, Brody district. OCCUPATION: Peasant. ECONOMIC STATUS: Proprietor (*CC* 262). OTHER ACTIVITIES: He was a founder of the Pravda society (*CC* 262).

346. Vyntoniak, Karpo

LOCATION: Buzhok, Zolochiv district. OCCUPATION: Priest. POSITION IN RC: President (*CC* 42). ECONOMIC STATUS: He was chaplain of a community with 650 members, an endowment of 36 *Joch* of arable land and 10 *Joch* of meadow and a *congruum* of 103 gulden 31 kreuzer.[1] EDUCATION: He was well read, had an impressive personal library and maintained an interest in contemporary European intellectual trends.[2] AGE: Born 1848, ordained 1872.[1] MARITAL STATUS: Widowed.[1] OTHER ACTIVITIES: He was a founder of the reading club (*CC* 42) and served on its first administration in 1881.[3] He spoke at the second annual general meeting of the reading club in Bilyi Kamin, Zolochiv district, in 1885 (*CC* 275). He was elected to the Zolochiv district council (*CC* 135).

1) *Shem. Lviv. 1884*, 112. *2)* Tarnavsky, *Spohady*, 62. *3)* Ivan Petryshyn [Liubomyr Seliansky], "Pysmo z Hlukhoho Kuta," *Batkivshchyna* 3, no. 10 (16 May 1881): 80.

347. Vyshensky, Iakiv

LOCATION: Iavoriv (district capital). OCCUPATION: Burgher (*CC* 142). POSITION IN

RC: Administration (*CC* 142). AGE: He was an elder brother in the church brotherhood (*CC* 142).

348. Vyshynsky, Ioan

LOCATION: Kolodribka, Zalishchyky district. OCCUPATION: Scribe and builder (U *reientyi i budivnychyi*) (*CC* 73). POSITION IN RC: Secretary (*CC* 76). POSITION IN LOCAL GOVT: Scribe (*CC* 73).

349. Zablotsky (Zabłocki), Feliks

LOCATION: Khrystynopil, Sokal district. OCCUPATION: Painter (U *maliar*) and scribe.[1] POSITION IN RC: Administration (*CC* 278). DISTINGUISHING FEATURES: His first and last names are typically Polish. No *latynnyk* community was recorded in Khrystynopil in 1880.[2] OTHER ACTIVITIES: He was denounced in the Ukrainian press in 1888 for abusing his position as scribe in Khrystynopil to issue a building permit to a Jew in Silets Belzkyi, Sokal district, who had bought land from a drunk. The district court in Sokal sentenced him to 14 days in prison and a 5 gulden fine.[1]

1) "Novynky. Z Krystynopolia," *Dilo* 9, no. 218 (1 [13] October 1888): 2. *2) Spec. Orts-Rep. 1880.*

350. Zabolotny, Mykhail

LOCATION: Piznanka Hnyla, Skalat district. OCCUPATION: Peasant. POSITION IN RC: Librarian (*CC* 238). POSITION IN LOCAL GOVT: Deputy mayor (*CC* 238). ECONOMIC STATUS: Proprietor (*CC* 238).

351. Zabolotny, Pavlo

LOCATION: Piznanka Hnyla, Skalat district. OCCUPATION: Peasant. POSITION IN RC: Deputy administration (*CC* 238). ECONOMIC STATUS: Proprietor (*CC* 238).

352. Zaiachuk, Vasyl

LOCATION: Stopchativ, Kolomyia district. OCCUPATION: (Peasant). POSITION IN RC: Librarian (*CC* 263).

353. Zakharchuk, Kindrat

LOCATION: Liatske Male, Zolochiv district. OCCUPATION: Peasant. ECONOMIC STATUS: Proprietor (*CC* 36). OTHER ACTIVITIES: He was one of the founders of the reading club in 1884[1] and allowed it to meet in his home (*CC* 36). After the 1885 parliamentary elections, he took the viceroy's office to court for electoral chicanery (allowing more so-called [U] *virylisty* to vote than the law permitted). He won his case at an administrative tribunal in Vienna. Not long after this, on 11 November 1885 (N.S.), he spoke in Lviv at the general meeting of the Russophile political association Russkaia rada.[2] The main thrust of his speech was that the Ukrainian intelligentsia should not divide into factions, but should be united (*CC* 268). "We are all," said Zakharchuk, "as sturdy [U *tverdyi*; an allusion to the division into "hard" (Russophile) and "soft" (national populist) Ruthenians] as an oak and no one can knock us over. If from us, from that oak, grows a branch, then it will not be an oak, but a branch, which does no harm to the oak, but it itself cannot exist without the oak."[2] Zakharchuk was especially disturbed by the burial of a young radical (Adolf Narolsky) without clergymen officiating (*CC* 268) and by the national populist satirical journal *Zerkalo*, which "slings mud at our most outstanding patriots and at our Ruthenian institutions."[2] By 1887 he was running a store in Liatske.[3] In the late 1890s he was a prominent Russophile agitator.[4] In 1901 he was arrested on the eve of elections as part of the usual Galician government policy of hindering Ukrainian electoral activity.[2]

1) "Iz Zolochevskoho," *Novyi prolom* 2, no. 190 (17 [29] November 1884): 3. *2)* Lev493, Z-57. *3)* "Poriadky v Liadskom," *Slovo* 27, no. 35–6 (9 [21] and 11 [23] April 1887): 2. *4)* Tarnavsky, *Spohady*, 212.

354. Zanevych, Iosyf

LOCATION: Korelychi, Peremyshliany district. OCCUPATION: Peasant. POSITION IN RC: Secretary (*CC* 84). ECONOMIC STATUS: Proprietor (*CC* 84). EDUCATION: Literate by 1897.[1] MOBILITY: Two Zanevych families were listed among the Greek Catholic parishioners of Korelychi in 1864.[2] OTHER ACTIVITIES: He was among the founders of the revived reading club in 1896. He served on the administration in 1897–8 (in both years as secretary), 1905 (as vice-president) and 1906.[1]

1) TsDIAL, 348/1/3031, pp. 3, 18v, 23, 25v, 50v, 53. *2)* TsDIAL, 146/64b/2294, pp. 55v, 56v.

355. Zarivny, Petro

LOCATION: Horodnytsia, Husiatyn district. OCCUPATION: Peasant. POSITION IN RC: President (*CC* 115). ECONOMIC STATUS: Proprietor (*CC* 115). OTHER ACTIVITIES: He was a founder of the reading club (*CC* 115).

356. Zarytsky, D.

LOCATION: Kutkivtsi, Ternopil district. OCCUPATION: (Peasant). POSITION IN RC: Librarian, but not on the administration (*CC* 69). DISTINGUISHING FEATURES: His last name could be Polish; he may have been a *latynnyk*, since Kutkivtsi had a sizable *latynnyk* population (see *Bartetsky, Roman*).

357. Zavidovsky, O.

LOCATION: Bila, Ternopil district. OCCUPATION: (Peasant). POSITION IN RC: Treasurer (*CC* 69).

358. Zelenko, Hnat

LOCATION: Khotin, Kalush district. OCCUPATION: (Peasant). POSITION IN RC: Deputy administration (*CC* 121).

359. Zeleny, Prokip

LOCATION: Chortkiv district. AUTHOR: *CC* 124.

360. Zhmur, Klymentii

LOCATION: Mykulyntsi, Ternopil district. OCCUPATION: Master chimney-sweep.[1] POSITION IN RC: Secretary (*CC* 96). ECONOMIC STATUS: He was evidently a prosperous master artisan, since he could donate the whole of a "spacious" house for the use of the reading club. The house was remodelled on the inside to suit the purposes of the reading club (furnished with benches, tables and a bookcase; decorated with images of the saints and portraits); and there were plans to set up a stage in the house.[1] AGE: He was a "young master."[1] OTHER ACTIVITIES: He was librarian of the reading club in 1890.[2]

1) "Dopysy. Z-nad Sereta," *Dilo* 5, no. 71 (21 June [3 July] 1884): 2. *2)* "Nashi chytalni," *Batkivshchyna* 12, no. 38–9 (21 September [3 October] 1890): 492.

361. Zhuk, Oleksa

LOCATION: Zbarazh district. AUTHOR: *CC* 147.

362. Zhybchyn, Petro

LOCATION: Horodenka (district capital). OCCUPATION: (Peasant). POSITION IN RC: Administration (*CC* 15). POSITION IN LOCAL GOVT: City treasurer.[1] EDUCATION: "He is an educated man—he possesses quite a bit of knowledge, writes well, a reader, he was a non-commissioned officer [U *zastupnyk ofitsera*].... "[1] AGE: Young.[1] MOBILITY: He had served in the army.[1] OTHER ACTIVITIES: *Krushelnytsky, Maksym* thought he would be a good candidate to run for deputy to the diet.[1]

1) Letter of Maksym Krushelnytsky to Leonid Zaklynsky, 9 February 1886, in LNB AN URSR, Viddil rukopysyv, fond Zaklynskykh, 192/31, p. 155.

363. Ziembitsky, Hryhorii

LOCATION: Zhuravtsi, Rava Ruska district. OCCUPATION: Nonpeasant (CC 137). POSITION IN RC: President (CC 137).

364. Zukh, Maksym

LOCATION: Berezhany district. AUTHOR: CC 265.

365. Zvarych, Havryshko

LOCATION: Dmytriv, Kaminka Strumylova district. OCCUPATION: Peasant. MOBILITY: Five Zvarych households lived in Dmytriv in the early 1850s.[1] OTHER ACTIVITIES: A former vice-president of the church committee (U provizorochnyi vydil), he was an activist in the reading club (CC 52).

1) TsDIAL, 168/1/1016, pp. 11v, 31v, 36v, 84v.

366. Zvarych, Hryhorii

LOCATION: Piznanka Hnyla, Skalat district. OCCUPATION: Blacksmith and peasant (CC 238). POSITION IN RC: Vice-president (CC 238). ECONOMIC STATUS: Proprietor (CC 238). OTHER ACTIVITIES: He was briefly arrested while agitating for the Ukrainian candidate during the 1885 parliamentary elections (CC 218, 239).

367. Zvarych, Hrynko

LOCATION: Tsebriv, Ternopil district. OCCUPATION: Peasant. POSITION IN RC: Vice-president and treasurer (CC 44). ECONOMIC STATUS: He was a fairly prosperous proprietor, judging by the largess he displayed toward the reading club (CC 44). OTHER ACTIVITIES: He hosted the inauguration of the reading club and sent horses to Ternopil to pick up the guest speakers (CC 44).

368. Zvarych, I.

LOCATION: Piznanka Hnyla, Skalat district. OCCUPATION: Cantor (former); custodian (U dvernyk) at the Ukrainian seminary in Lviv (CC 85). AUTHOR: CC 85. MOBILITY: He was cantor in Piznanka Hnyla until 1883, when he started working at the seminary in Lviv (CC 85). PUBLICATIONS: He contributed a brief note to Batkivshchyna in 1885 urging the cantors of Skalat deanery to become active in the cantors' movement.[1]

1) I. Zvarych, "V spravi diakivskii," Batkivshchyna 7, no. 2 (9 January 1885 [28 December 1884]): 14.

V. Activists by Occupation

Peasants

1. Andriishyn, Hryhorii
2. Andrukhovych
4. Andrunyk, Ivan
5. Antoniv, Martyn
6. Babiak, Andrii
8. Bakuska, Vasyl
9. Balaban, I.
10. Balaban, R.
12. Balias, Havrylo
15. Barnych, Kornylo
16. Bartetsky, Roman
18. Berbeka, Levko
20. Bilan, Oleksa
22. Bilevych, Mykhailo
23. Bilokha, Vasyl
25. Boichuk, Vasyl
27. Boiko, Iurko
32. Brateiko, Luka
34. Buchma, Stefan
35. Burak, Ilko
36. Burak, Lev
37. Burak, Semko
45. Cherniak, Petro
46. Chornobai, Aleksander
47. Chuba, Maksym
49. Dachynsky, Iarema
51. Derkach, Panko
52. Diakiv, Danylo
55. Dmyterko, Semen
57. Dobriansky, Hnat
61. Domsky, Toma
63. Dragan, Iurko
64. Dragan, Konstantyn
65. Dragan, Nykola

68. Dubovy, Ivan
69. Dushansky, Dymytrii
74. Dynsky, Toma
76. Fedun, I.
77. Filvarkiv
78. Forlita, Petro
79. Fyniak, Dmytro
82. Gelmas, Ivan
84. Genyk, Stefan
85. Gurnytsky, Iosyf
86. Halapats, Ivan
89. Hetman, Iosyf
90. Hetman, Stefan
92. Hladun, Nykola
96. Holodryha, Mykola
97. Holoiad, Adam
101. Holovka, Vasyl
102. Horak, Ivan
106. Hrabovetsky, Ivan
107. Hrabovetsky, Lavrentii
108. Hrabovetsky, Mykhailo
111. Hrynkiv, Ivan
115. Hupalo, Stefan
117. Iakoba, Aleksander
121. Iaskuliak, I.
122. Iasynsky, Vasyl
125. Iskra, Roman
126. Iurkiv, Roman
127. Iuzkiv, Iliia
128. Iuzvak, Semen
130. Ivantsiv, Avksentii
131. Kalynsky, Iosyf
134. Karp, Kost
138. Kendiukh, Hnat
141. Kholevchuk, Dmytro
143. Khudoba, Vasyl
145. Kmet, Matvii
147. Koltsuniak, Vasyl
152. Kormyliuk, Ivan
153. Kostelnytsky, Kazymir
155. Kostiv, Ivan
156. Kotovy, F.
157. Kotyk, Petro
158. Koval, Ivan
160. Kovalsky, Mykhailo
161. Kovbuz, Vasyl
163. Krupnytsky, Antin
166. Kryshtalovych, Petro
169. Kulyk, Fedko
171. Kurylyshyn, Hryhorii
172. Kushchak, Fedor

175. Kvasnytsia, Vasyl
177. Kyrchiv, Kost
180. Kyzyk, Ivan
181. Kyzyk, Mykola
182. Lapchynsky, Iosyf
186. Levandovsky, Valentii
190. Liubynetsky, Ivan
192. Lototsky, Iurii
194. Lun, Mykolai
196. Lypak, Petro
197. Maievsky, Hryhorii
199. Maksymovych, Dmytro
201. Mandii, Danylo
203. Maneliuk, Aleksii
204. Manila, Fedko
207. Martyshuk, Pavlo
208. Matsiakh, Mykola
209. Matviishyn, Ivan
210. Matviishyn, Petro
211. Mazur, Vavryk
212. Mazurchak, Tymko
216. Melnyk, Ivan
217. Melnyk, Petro
218. Melnyk, Tymko
220. Mikhas, Ivan
221. Mocherniuk, Iura
223. Mostovyk, Hrynko
224. Mozola, Vasyl
227. Mykhalevych, Symeon
229. Mykuliak, Hryhorii
230. Mykuliak, Petro
232. Nahirny, Andrei
233. Navrotsky, Ivan
235. Novosad, Semko
236. Nychyk, Dmytro
237. Nychyk, Maksym
238. Oleiniuk, Oleksa
239. Olenchyn, Andrii
240. Oliinyk, Iurii
241. Olynets, Mykhail
242. Onyshkevych, Onufrii
249. Patsahan, Pavlo
250. Pavliv, Luka
251. Pavlychko, Ivan
252. Pelekhaty, Fedor
254. Petriv, Lev
257. Pidgursky, Antin
260. Pochapsky, Vasyl
261. Poliak, Iosyf
262. Polishchuk, M.
263. Polishchuk, P.

265. Popovych, Fedir
267. Proskurok, M.
269. Pryhodsky, Emil
270. Pukhalsky, H.
271. Pukhalsky, Ivan
272. Punda, Ivan
273. Punda, Lesko
274. Pundyk, Ivan
275. Pylypchuk, Hryhorii
277. Ripchuk, Ivan
278. Romaniv, Ivan
279. Romanyk, Petro
281. Sadovy, Ivan
283. Salitra, Oleksa
284. Semotiuk, Stefan
285. Seniuk, Mykhail
286. Senyshyn, Hryhorii
287. Serbyn, Ivan
288. Serediuk, Ivan
289. Serenetsky, Karol
292. Shchyrba, Luka
294. Shkraba, Vavryk
297. Shvets, Luts
299. Sirko, Antin
301. Skochylias, Iosyf
302. Skrehunets, Semen
305. Smolynsky, Vasyl
307. Soltys, Onofer
309. Stadnyk, Andrei
310. Staryk, I.
311. Stashkiv, Aleksander
312. Stefanko, Hryts
313. Stefanko, Petro
315. Susiak, Vasyl
316. Svidersky, Iosyf
318. Sych, Irynei
319. Sych, Stefan
320. Sydorko, Aleksii
321. Syvy, Mykhailo
326. Tarnavsky, Vasyl
327. Tetorniuk, Hryhorii
329. Tomyn, Oleksa
330. Tsaryk, Fed
335. Tytsieiko, Hrynko
336. Vandrovych, Iosyf
337. Vandych, Prokip
338. Vasyliuk, Dmytro
339. Vertiukh, Oleksa
343. Voinarovsky, Symeon
345. Vozniak, Mykhailo
350. Zabolotny, Mykhail

351. Zabolotny, Pavlo
352. Zaiachuk, Vasyl
353. Zakharchuk, Kindrat
354. Zanevych, Iosyf
355. Zarivny, Petro
356. Zarytsky, D.
357. Zavidovsky, O.
358. Zelenko, Hnat
362. Zhybchyn, Petro
365. Zvarych, Havryshko
367. Zvarych, Hrynko

With more than one occupation
3. Andrunyk, Hrynko (and perhaps cantor)
19. Bernyk, Andrukh (and merchant)
75. Fedorovych, Vasyl (and cantor)
91. Hladii, Porfyr (and cantor and merchant)
119. Iarema, Ivan (or artisan)
137. Kekosh, Iurii (and cobbler)
154. Kostetsky, Ivan (or artisan)
202. Mandiuk, Vasyl (or burgher)
215. Melnyk, Atanas (and cantor)
228. Mykhaliuk, Mykhail (and merchant)
231. Myroniuk, Iliia (and soldier)
246. Parii, Vasyl (and scribe)
306. Soltys, Hryn (and cantor)
317. Svidersky, Ivan (and aspiring merchant-innkeeper)
331. Tsipyvko, Symeon (and cantor and scribe)
344. Vozniak, Ivan (and cantor)
366. Zvarych, Hryhorii (and blacksmith)

Priests

13. Balytsky, Aleksander
21. Bilevych, Konstantyn
24. Bilynsky, Pankratii
38. Burnadz, Semen
40. Chemerynsky, Antonii
41. Chepil, Konstantyn
44. Chernetsky, Vasyl
56. Dnistriansky, Lev
59. Dolnytsky
60. Dolnytsky, Andrei
62. Dorozhynsky, Vladyslav
66. Dron, Teodor
70. Dutkevych, Evhenii
71. Dyhdalevych, Ivan
73. Dylynsky, Volodymyr
93. Hlibovytsky, Aleksander
94. Hlibovytsky, Konstantyn
95. Hlynsky, Teofan
109. Hrabovych, Ioann

110. Hrynevetsky, Apolinarii
112. Hrytsyna, Teodor
116. Hysovsky, Ioann
120. Iasenytsky, Mykhail
146. Koliankovsky, Volodymyr
148. Koltuniak, Nykolai
159. Kovalsky, Emilii
162. Koziuk, Pavlo
164. Krushelnytsky, Amvrosii de
167. Kryzhanovsky, Roman
183. Lazor, Ioan
185. Lesiuk, Stefan
191. Lopatynsky, Vasylii Slepovron
195. Lutsyk, Iuvenal
198. Makohonsky, Stefan
205. Markevych, Ivan
213. Mazykevych, I.
225. Mudrak, Mykhail
234. Navrotsky, Severyn
243. Osmilovsky, L.
244. Pachovsky, Ivan
247. Pashkovsky, Atanazii
255. Petrovych, Emyliian
296. Shpytko, Ivan
298. Sichynsky, Iliarion
300. Skobelsky, Ioann
314. Stupnytsky, Havryil
322. Tanchakovsky, Aleksander
323. Taniachkevych, Danylo (elder)
324. Taniachkevych, Danylo (younger)
325. Tarchanyn, Amvrosii
332. Tsurkovsky, Ihnatii
333. Turkevych, Nykolai
346. Vyntoniak, Karpo

Burghers and Artisans

28. Bokii, Kyrylo
30. Borys, Hryhorii
31. Borys, P.
33. Brytan, Antin
58. Dobrovolsky, Ivan
72. Dykevych, Pavlo
88. Herynovych, Petro
98. Holovatsky, Danylo
103. Horbachuk, Pavlo
113. Hunkevych, Hrynko
114. Hunkevych, Klym
135. Karp, Vasyl
139. Kharambura, Ivan
140. Kharambura, Stefan
144. Klymivsky, Pavlo

149. Komarensky, Kuzma
150. Konashevych, Teodor
173. Kushniryk, Dmytro (miller)
174. Kuzma, Kyrylo
179. Kyzhyk, Pavlo
184. **Leshnovsky, Stefan**
187. Levytsky, Pavlo
188. Lishchynsky, Havrylo
226. Muzh, Petro
253. Pelensky, Oleksa
268. Prukhnytsky, Mykhailo (weaver)
291. Shchyrba, Hryhorii
341. Vilkhovy, Dmytro
342. Vilkhovy, Mykhailo
347. Vyshensky, Iakiv
360. Zhmur, Klymentii (chimney-sweep)

With more than one occupation
119. Iarema, Ivan (or peasant)
137. Kekosh, Iurii (cobbler; and peasant)
154. Kostetsky, Ivan (or peasant)
202. Mandiuk, Vasyl (or peasant)
348. Vyshynsky, Ioan (builder; and scribe)
349. Zablotsky, Feliks (painter; and scribe)
366. Zvarych, Hryhorii (blacksmith; and peasant)

Cantors

 26. Boikevych, Iliia
 39. Byliv, Iosyf
 50. Danyliv, Iliarii
 54. Didukh, Ivan
 81. Galat, Roman
100. Holovinsky, Stefan
118. Ianishevsky, Teodor
142. Khoma, Ivan
151. Korchemny, Ivan
168. Kukhar, Antin
170. Kurovytsky, Atanazii
219. Menchakevych, Iliia
222. Monchalovsky, Stefan
264. Polotniuk, Ihnatii
282. Saikevych, Danylo (former or aspiring)
295. Shostak, Semen
304. Sliuzar, Mykhailo
308. Spolitakevych, Ioan

With more than one occupation
  3. Andrunyk, Hrynko (perhaps; and peasant)
 43. Cherevatiuk (and merchant)
 75. Fedorovych, Vasyl (and peasant)
 91. Hladii, Porfyr (and peasant and merchant)

215. Melnyk, Atanas (and peasant)
266. Posatsky, Havrylo (and scribe)
306. Soltys, Hryn (and peasant)
328. Tomashevsky, Luka (and scribe)
331. Tsipyvko, Symeon (and scribe and peasant)
344. Vozniak, Ivan (and peasant)
368. Zvarych, I. (former; and custodian at Lviv seminary)

Teachers

11. Balandiuk, Pavlo (retired)
14. Banakh, Mykhailo
17. Basaichuk, Mykola
29. Bolekhivsky, Andrei I.
42. Cheredarchuk, Vasyl
48. Chypchar, Vasyl
83. Genyk, Kyrylo
87. Havlytsky, Antin
104. Horodysky, Iakiv
105. Horutsky, Oleksander P.
133. Kamynsky, Ivan
136. Kavchynsky, Stefan
165. Krushelnytsky, Maksym
178. Kyrchiv, Pavlo
206. Martyniuk, Vasyl
214. Medynsky, Ivan
248. Pashkovsky, Iuliian
256. Petryshyn, Ivan
280. Rybachek, Antin M.
290. Serkes, Tymofii
293. Sheshor, Ilko
334. Tymchuk, Hryhorii
340. Vidlyvany, Nykyfor

Scribes

53. Diakon, Mykhailo
193. Loza, Iakiv
303. Sliusarchuk, Nykola

With more than one occupation
246. Parii, Vasyl (and peasant)
266. Posatsky, Havrylo (and cantor)
328. Tomashevsky, Luka (and cantor)
331. Tsipyvko, Symeon (and cantor and peasant)
348. Vyshynsky, Ioan (and builder)
349. Zablotsky, Feliks (and painter)

Merchants

129. Ivanets, Ivan
259. Pikh, Mykhailo
276. Pynkovsky

With more than one occupation
19. Bernyk, Andrukh (and peasant)
43. Cherevatiuk (and cantor)
91. Hladii, Porfyr (and cantor and peasant)
228. Mykhaliuk, Mykhailo (and peasant)
317. Svidersky, Ivan (aspiring; and peasant)

Seminarians

123. Iavorsky, Aleksander
124. Iavorsky, Ivan
176. Kyrchiv, Bohdar

University Student

245. Pachovsky, Mykhailo

Physician

67. Drymalyk, Sylvester L.

Soldier (with additional occupation)

231. Myroniuk, Iliia (and peasant)

Custodian (with additional occupation)

368. Zvarych, I. (and former cantor)

Unidentified

7. Babynets, Ivan (nonpeasant)
80. Gabrysh, Liudvyk
99. Holovchuk
132. Kamianetsky, Matvii
189. Lisovyk, K.A.
200. Maksymovych, Volodymyr
258. Pidrichny, Pavlo
359. Zeleny, Prokip
361. Zhuk, Oleksa
363. Ziembitsky, Hryhorii (nonpeasant)
364. Zukh, Maksym

Bibliography

Contemporary Press and Serials Consulted

Batkivshchyna (Lviv) 1879–96.

Biblioteka Warszawska (Warsaw) 1843.

Catalogus universi venerabilis cleri Dioeceseos Premisliensis graeco-catholica pro anno Domini . . . (Przemyśl) 1848.

Dilo (Lviv) 1884–8.

Halychanyn (Lviv) 1901.

Hromada (Geneva) 1881.

Hromadskyi holos (Lviv) 1899–1900.

Der Israelit (Lviv) 1885.

Der Kampf (Vienna) 1914.

Khliborob (Lviv and Kolomyia) 1892–4.

Kurjer Lwowski (Lviv) 1889.

Literaturno-naukovyi vistnyk (Lviv) 1901.

Nauka (Kolomyia) 1874, 1877.

Die Neue Zeit (Stuttgart) 1893, 1902.

Novyi prolom (Lviv) 1884, 1886.

Oesterreichisches statistisches Handbuch (Vienna) 1882, 1884, 1891, 1895–6, 1900–1, 1906–7, 1910–11.

Pravda (Lviv) 1874, 1891.

Rada (Kiev) 1914.

Rocznik Statystyki Galicyi (Lviv) 1889–91.

Ruskii Sion (Lviv) 1877.

Ruslan (Lviv) 1905, 1908.

Russkaia rada (Kolomyia) 1875, 1878, 1884–5.

Schematismus universi venerabilis cleri Archidioeceseos Metropolitanae graeco-catholicae Leopoliensiis pro anno Domini . . . (Lviv) 1882, 1885.

Schematismus universi venerabilis cleri dioeceseos gr.-cath. Premisliensis pro anno Domini . . . (Przemyśl) 1900.

Shematyzm vsechestnoho klyra Mytropolytalnoi arkhidietsezii hreko-katolycheskoi Ivovskoi na rik . . . (Lviv) 1880, 1883–5, 1891.

Shkolna chasopys (Lviv) 1885–6.

Skhymatism shkol narodnykh upravliaiemykh ruskoiu ep. konsistoriieiu peremyskoiu na hod . . . (Przemyśl) 1868.

Slovo (Lviv) 1861, 1875, 1877, 1884–7.

Statistische Monatsschrift (Vienna) 1878.

Svoboda (Lviv) 1897, 1899.

Szematyzm Królestwa Galicyi i Lodomeryi z Wielkim Księstwem Krakowskiem na rok . . . (Lviv) 1871–4, 1877–9, 1881, 1884–5.

Tafeln zur Statistik der österreichischen Monarchie (Vienna) 1846.

Tydzień. Dodatek literacki Kurjera Lwowskiego (Lviv) 1893.

Uchytel (Lviv) 1892, 1895.

Volnoe slovo (Geneva) 1883.

Die Welt (Vienna) 1900.

Wiadomości Statystyczne o Mieście Lwowie (Lviv) 1877.

Zhytie i slovo (Lviv) 1896.

Zoria (Lviv) 1893.

Other Literature

Adriian. *Agrarnyi protses u Dobrostanakh*. Lviv: Nakladom Ukrainsko-ruskoi vydavnychoi spilky, 1901.

Anderson, Benedict. *Imagined Communities: Reflections on the Origin and Spread of Nationalism*. London: Verso Editions, New Left Books, 1983.

Artaria's Eisenbahn u. Post-Communications-Karte v. Oesterreich-Ungarn 1889. Vienna: [1889].

Artaria's General-Karten der österreichischen und ungarischen Länder. Nr. 12: Galizien und Lodomerien (R.A. Schulz's General Post- und Strassenkarte des Kronlandes Galizien und Lodomerien mit Auschwitz, Zator und Krakau; so wie des Kronlandes Bukowina). Vienna: Artaria & Co., 1885.

Assonova, N.T. *Sotsialistychni pohliady ukrainskykh revoliutsioneriv-demokrativ (kinets XIX–pochatok XX st.* Kiev: Vydavnyche obiednannia "Vyshcha shkola," Vydavnytstvo pry Kyivskomu derzhavnomu universyteti, 1977.

Bartel, Wojciech M. *Zur Geschichte des galizischen Landesschulrates 1867–1918*. Sonderabdruck aus dem Anzeiger der phil.-hist. Klasse der Österreichischen Akademie der Wissenschaften, 114, Jahrgang 1977, So. 17. [Pp. 346–56.] Vienna: Verlag der Österreichischen Akademie der Wissenschaften, 1978.

Bevölkerung und Viehstand von Galizien nach der Zählung vom 31. December 1869. Herausgegeben von der k.k. statistischen Central-Commission. Vienna: 1871.

Blum, Jerome. *Noble Landowners and Agriculture in Austria, 1815–1848: A Study in the Origins of the Peasant Emancipation of 1848*. Baltimore: The John Hopkins Press, 1948.

Blum, Jerome. "The Rise of Serfdom in Eastern Europe." *American Historical Review* 62, no. 4 (July 1957): 807–36.

Bohachevsky-Chomiak, Martha. "Feminism in Ukrainian History." *Journal of Ukrainian Studies* 12 (Spring 1982): 16–30.

Bohachevsky-Chomiak, Martha. "Natalia Kobryns'ka: A Formulator of Feminism." In *Nationbuilding and the Politics of Nationalism: Essays on Austrian Galicia*, ed. Andrei S. Markovits and Frank E. Sysyn (Cambridge, MA: Harvard Ukrainian Research Institute, 1982), 196–219.

Bohachevsky-Chomiak, Martha. *The Spring of a Nation: The Ukrainians in Eastern Galicia in 1848*. Philadelphia: Shevchenko Scientific Society, 1967.

Brenner, Robert. "The Origins of Capitalist Development: A Critique of Neo-Smithian Marxism." *New Left Review*, no. 104 (July-August 1977): 25–92.

Brodowska-Kubicz, Helena. "Wizja Polski w świadomości chłopów." *Acta Universitatis Lodziensis, Folia Historica* 1 (1980): 23–39.

Bujak, Fr. *Galicya*. 2 vols. Lviv: H. Altenberg, 1908–10.

Bujak, Franciszek. "Rozwój gospodarczy Galicji (1772–1914)." In *Wybór pism*, 2 vols. (Warsaw, 1976), 2:342–97.

Bujak, Franciszek. "Wieś zachodnio-galicyjska u schyłku XIX wieku." In *Wybór pism*, 2 vols. (Warsaw, 1976), 2:279–341.

Bujwidowa, Kazimiera. *Kwestya kobieca. Czy kobieta powinna mieć te same prawa co mężczyzna?* Encyklopedya Ludowa, 4. Cracow: Nakładem tow. wydawniczego "Encyklopedyi Ludowej," 1909.

Burszta, Józef. *Społeczeństwo i karczma. Propinacja, karczma i sprawa alkoholizmu w społeczeństwie polskim XIX wieku.* Warsaw: Ludowa Spółdzielnia Wydawnicza, 1951.

Buszko, Józef. *Zum Wandel der gesellschaftsstruktur in Galizien und in der Bukowina.* Österreichische Akademie der Wissenschaften, Philosophisch-historische Klasse, Sitzungsberichte, Bd. 343. Vienna: Verlag der Österreichischen Akademie der Wissenschaften, 1978.

Buzek, Józef. *Stosunki zawodowe i socyalne ludności w Galicyi według wyznania i narodowości, na podstawie spisu ludności z 31. grudnia 1900 r.* Wiadomości Statystyczne o Stosunkach Krajowych, tom 20, zeszyt 2 (Lviv: 1905).

Caro, Leopold. "Lichwa na wsi w Galicyi," *Studya społeczne,* 2nd ed. (Cracow: Czas, 1908).

Chanderys, Szymon. *Kompletny skorowidz miejscowści w Galicyi i Bukowinie.* 2nd ed. Lviv: M.T. Krzysztofowicz, 1911.

Chlebowczyk, Józef. *On Small and Young Nations in Europe: Nation-Forming Processes in Ethnic Borderlands in East-Central Europe.* Polish Historical Library, 1. Wrocław, Warsaw, Cracow, Gdańsk: Zakład Narodowy imienia Ossolińskich, Wydawnictwo Polskiej Akademii Nauk, 1980.

Chlebowczyk, Józef. *Procesy narodotwórcze we wschodniej Europie środkowej w dobie kapitalizmu (od schyłku XVIII do początków XX w.).* Warsaw: Państwowe Wydawnictwo Naukowe, 1975.

Chomiak, Chrystia. "Vernacular Architecture and Forms and Plans of Rural Settlement, Western Ukraine, c. 1900." Manuscript prepared for the Ukrainian Cultural Heritage Village. Edmonton: 1985.

Connor, Walker. "Nation-Building or Nation-Destroying?" *World Politics* 24, no. 3 (April 1972): 319–55.

Davies, Norman. *God's Playground: A History of Poland in Two Volumes.* New York: Columbia University Press, 1984.

Dei, O.I. *Slovnyk ukrainskykh psevdonimiv ta kryptonimiv (XVI–XX st.).* Kiev: Naukova dumka, 1969.

Dei, O.I. *Ukrainska revoliutsiino-demokratychna zhurnalistyka. Problema vynyknennia i stanovlennia.* Kiev: Vydavnytstvo AN URSR, 1959.

Deutsch, Karl W. *Nationalism and Social Communication: An Inquiry into the Foundations of Nationality.* New York: The Technology Press of the Massachusetts Institute of Technology and John Wiley & Sons, Inc., 1953.

Dmytruk, V. *Narys z istorii ukrainskoi zhurnalistyky XIX st.* Lviv: Vydavnytstvo Lvivskoho universytetu, 1969.

Dobrowolski, Kazimierz. "Peasant Traditional Culture." In *Peasants and Peasant Societies: Selected Readings,* ed. Teodor Shanin (Harmondsworth: Penguin Books, 1971), 277–98.

Drahomanov, M.P. *Literaturno-publitsystychni pratsi*. 2 vols. Kiev: Naukova dumka, 1970.

Dytiachyi folklor. Kolyskovi pisni ta zabavlianky. Edited by O.I. Dei, *et al*. AN URSR, Instytut mystetsvoznavstva, folkloru ta etnohrafii im. M.T. Rylskoho. Ukrainska narodna tvorchist. Kiev: Naukova dumka, 1984.

Eley, Geoff. "State Formation, Nationalism and Political Culture in Nineteenth-Century Germany." In *Culture, Ideology and Politics: Essays for Eric Hobsbawm*, ed. Raphael Samuel and Gareth Stedman Jones, History Workshop Series (London, Boston, Melbourne and Henley: Routledge & Kegan Paul, 1983), 277–301.

Entsyklopediia Ukrainoznavstva. Edited by Volodymyr Kubiiovych. Paris: NTSh, 1949– .

"Die Ergebnisse der Volkszählung vom 31. December 1890. . . . " 1. Heft: "Die summarischen Ergebnisse der Volkszählung." *Österreichische Statistik* 32 (1892).

Franko, Ivan, ed. *Halytsko-ruski narodni prypovidky*. Vol. II, pt. 1: *(Dity-Kpyty)*. Etnografichnyi zbirnyk, 23. Lviv: NTSh, 1907.

Franko, Ivan. *Tvory*. 20 vols. Kiev: Derzhlitvydav URSR, 1950–6.

Franko, Ivan. *Zibrannia tvoriv*. 50 vols. Kiev: Naukova dumka, 1976– .

Franzos, Karl Emil. *The Jews of Barnow*. New York: D. Appleton and Company, 1883; reprint "The Modern Jewish Experience," New York: Arno Press, 1975.

Friedman, Filip. "Landvirtshaft, kolonizatsye un grundbazits bey di galitsyanishe yidn. (Arum der helft fun des 19-tn yorhundertn)." *Yunger historiker* (Warsaw) 2 (1929): 131–42.

Fylypchak, Ivan. "Tovarystvo 'Ruskoi shliakhty v Halychyni'. Istorychnyi narys." *Ukrainskyi Beskyd* (Przemyśl), no. 31 (496) (13 August 1939): 2.

Gellner, Ernest. *Thought and Change*. Chicago: Chicago University Press, 1965; reprint ed., n.p.: Midway Reprint, 1974.

Gemeindelexikon der im Reichsrate vertretenen Königreiche und Länder. Bearbeitet auf Grund der Ergebnisse der Volkszählung vom 31. Dezember 1900. Herausgegeben von der k.k. statistischen Zentralkommission. Bd. 12: *Galizien*. Vienna, 1907.

Głąbiński, Stanisław. *Ludność polska w Galicyi Wschodniej*. Lviv: Nakładem autora, 1903.

Grodziski, Stanisław. *Historia ustroju społeczno-politycznego Galicji 1772–1848*. PAN—Oddział w Krakowie, Prace Komisji Nauk Historycznych, 28. Wrocław, Warsaw, Cracow, Gdańsk: Zakład Narodowy imienia Ossolińskichich, Wydawnictwo Polskie Akademii Nauk, 1971.

Grzybowski, Konstanty. *Galicja 1848–1914. Historia ustroju politycznego na tle historii ustroju Austrii*. Polska Akademia Nauk, Komitet Nauk Prawnych, Studia nad Historią Państwa i Prawa—Seria II, tom 9. Cracow: Zakład Narodowy imienia Ossolińskich, Wydawnictwo Polskiej Akademii Nauk, 1959.

Himka, John-Paul. "The Background to Emigration: The Ukrainians of Galicia and Bukovyna, 1848–1914." In *A Heritage in Transition: Essays in the History of Ukrainians in Canada*, ed. Manoly R. Lupul; Generations: A History of

Canada's Peoples (Toronto: McClelland and Stewart Ltd. in association with the Multiculturalism Directorate, Department of the Secretary of State and the Canadian Government Publishing Centre, Supply and Services Canada, 1982), 11–31.

Himka, John-Paul. "The Greek Catholic Church and Nation-Building in Galicia, 1772–1918." *Harvard Ukrainian Studies* 8, no. 3–4 (December 1984): 426–52.

Himka, John-Paul. "Hope in the Tsar: Displaced Naive Monarchism among the Ukrainian Peasants of the Habsburg Empire." *Russian History* 7 (1980): 125–38.

Himka, John-Paul. "Polish and Ukrainian Socialism: Austria, 1867–1890." PhD dissertation: University of Michigan, 1977.

Himka, John-Paul. "Priests and Peasants: The Greek Catholic Pastor and the Ukrainian National Movement in Austria, 1867–1900." *Canadian Slavonic Papers* 21 (1979): 1–14.

Himka, John-Paul. "A Researcher's Handbook on Western Ukraine (Galicia and Bukovyna) in the Late Nineteenth and Early Twentieth Centuries." Manuscript prepared for the Ukrainian Cultural Heritage Village. Edmonton: 1985.

Himka, John-Paul. *Socialism in Galicia: The Emergence of Polish Social Democracy and Ukrainian Radicalism (1860–1890).* Cambridge, Mass.: Harvard Ukrainian Research Institute, 1983.

Himka, John-Paul. "Ukrainian-Jewish Antagonism in the Galician Countryside during the Late Nineteenth Century." In *Jewish-Ukrainian Relations in Historical Perspective*, ed. Howard Aster and Peter J. Potichnyj (Edmonton: Canadian Institute of Ukrainian Studies, forthcoming).

Himka, John-Paul. "Voluntary Artisan Associations and the Ukrainian National Movement in Galicia (The 1870s)." In *Nationbuilding and the Politics of Nationalism: Essays on Austrian Galicia*, ed. Andrei S. Markovits and Frank E. Sysyn (Cambridge, MA: Harvard Ukrainian Research Institute, 1982), 178–95.

Historia Polski. Opracowanie zbiorowe. Edited by Stanisław Arnold and Tadeusz Manteuffel. Multivolume. Polska Akademia Nauk, Instytut Historii. Warsaw: Państwowe Wydawnictwo Naukowe, 1958- .

Hladylovych, Iuryi. "Spomyny ruskoho sviashchenyka pro rizniu 1846 roku," *Zapysky NTSh*, rik V, 1896, kn. IV, tom XII, pp. 1–20 (separate pagination).

Hobsbawm, E.J. *Primitive Rebels: Studies in Archaic Forms of Social Movement in the 19th and 20th Centuries.* New York: Norton, 1965.

Hofer, Tamás. "The Creation of Ethnic Symbols from the Elements of Peasant Culture." In *Ethnic Diversity and Conflict in Eastern Europe*, ed. Peter F. Sugar, Joint Committee on Eastern Europe Publication Series, 8 (Santa Barbara, Oxford: ABC-Clio, 1980), 101–45, 463–72.

Holovashchenko, Mykhailo, ed. *Solomiia Krushelnytska. Spohady, materialy, lystuvannia.* 2 vols. Kiev: Muzychna Ukraina, 1978–9.

Homola, Irena. "Nauczycielstwo krakowskie w okresie autonomii (1867–1914)." In *Inteligencja polska XIX i XX wieku. Studia*, ed. Ryszarda Czepulis-Rastenis, Polska Akademia Nauk, Instytut Historii (Warsaw: Państwowe Wydawnictwo Naukowe, 1981), 83–130.

Hornowa, Elżbieta. *Ukraiński obóz postępowy i jego współpraca z polską lewicą społeczną w Galicji 1876–1895.* Wrocław: Zakład Narodowy im. Ossolińskich, 1968.

Hroch, Miroslav. "The Social Composition of the Czech Patriots in Bohemia, 1827–1848." In *The Czech Renascence of the Nineteenth Century,* ed. Peter Brock and H. Gordon Skilling (Toronto: University of Toronto Press, 1970), 33–52.

Hroch, Miroslav. *Die Vorkämpfer der nationalen Bewegung bei den kleinen Völkern Europas: Eine vergleichende Analyse zur gesellschaftlichen Schichtung der patriotischen Gruppen.* Acta Universitatis Carolinae Philosophica et Historica Monographia, 24. Prague: 1968.

Hryniuk, Stella. "Peasant Agriculture in East Galicia in the Late Nineteenth Century." *Slavonic and East European Review* 63, no. 2 (April 1985): 228–43.

Hryniuk, Stella M. "A Peasant Society in Transition: Ukrainian Peasants in Five East Galician Counties 1880–1900." PhD dissertation: University of Manitoba, 1984.

Ia[shan], V[asyl], and M[ykhailo] H. M[arunchak]. "Pomianyk peredovykh sviashchenykiv Horodenshchyny." In *Horodenshchyna. Istorychno-memuarnyi zbirnyk,* ed. Mykhailo H. Marunchak, NTSh, Ukrainskyi arkhiv, 28 (New York: 1975).

Iashchuk, Pavlo. *Mykhailo Pavlyk. Literaturno-krytychnyi narys.* Lviv: Knyzhkovo-zhurnalne vydavnytstvo, 1959.

Ihnatiienko, V. *Bibliohrafiia ukrainskoi presy 1816–1916.* Reprint; State College, Pa.: Vyd-vo "Ukrainska nova knyha," 1968.

Ihnatowicz, Ireneusz. *Vademecum do badań nad historią XIX i XX wieku.* 2 vols. Warsaw: Państwowe Wydawnictwo Naukowe, 1967–71.

Istoriia gorodov i sel Ukrainskoi SSR. Lvovskaia oblast. Kiev: Glavnaia redaktsiia Ukrainskoi Sovetskoi Entsiklopedii, 1978.

Istoriia mist i sil Ukrainskoi RSR. Ivano-Frankivska oblast. Kiev: Holovna redaktsiia Ukrainskoi Radianskoi Entsyklopedii, 1971.

Istoriia mist i sil Ukrainskoi RSR. Lvivska oblast. Kiev: Holovna redaktsiia Ukrainskoi Radianskoi Entsyklopedii, 1968.

Istoriia mist i sil Ukrainskoi RSR. Ternopilska oblast. Kiev: Holovna redaktsiia Ukrainskoi Radianskoi Entsyklopedii, 1973.

Istoriia selianstva Ukrainskoi RSR. 2 vols. Kiev: Naukova dumka, 1967.

Ivan Kotliarevsky u dokumentakh, spohadakh, doslidzhenniakh. Kiev: Dnipro, 1969.

Ivanochko, A. "Natsionalne vidrodzhennia sela Potochyshche." In *Horodenshchyna. Istorychno-memuarnyi zbirnyk,* ed. Mykhailo H. Marunchak, NTSh, Ukrainskyi arkhiv, 28 (New York, 1975).

Jüdische Statistik. Edited by Alfred Nossig. Berlin: Jüdischer Verlag, 1903.

Kachala, Stefan. *Shcho nas hubyt a shcho nam pomochy mozhe.* Lviv: Prosvita, 1869.

Kaindl, Raimund Friedrich. *Beiträge zur Geschichte des deutschen Rechtes in Galizien.* 3 vols. Vienna: In Kommission bei Alfred Hölder, 1906–10.

Kalendarz Nauczycielski na rok 1885. Wydany przez Redakcyę "Głosu Nauczycielskiego". Kolomyia: Nakład i druk H. Zadembskiego i A.J. Hollendra, [1884].

Kalynovych, V.I. *Politychni protsesy Ivana Franka ta ioho tovaryshiv.* Lviv: Vydavnytstvo Lvivskoho universytetu, 1967.

Kann, Robert A., and Zdeněk V. David. *The Peoples of the Eastern Habsburg Lands, 1526-1918.* A History of East Central Europe, 6. Seattle, London: University of Washington Press, 1984.

Kaye, Vladimir J. *Dictionary of Ukrainian Canadian Biography: Pioneer Settlers of Manitoba 1891-1900.* Toronto: Ukrainian Canadian Research Foundation, 1975.

Kaye, Vladimir J. *Early Ukrainian Settlements in Canada 1895-1900: Dr. Josef Oleskow's Role in the Settlement of the Canadian Northwest.* Toronto: Published for the Ukrainian Canadian Research Foundation by University of Toronto Press, 1964.

Kaye (Kysilewsky), Vladimir J., and Frances Swyripa. "Settlement and Colonization." In *A Heritage in Transition: Essays in the History of Ukrainians in Canada,* ed. Manoly R. Lupul; Generations: A History of Canada's Peoples (Toronto: McClelland and Stewart Ltd. in association with the Multiculturalism Directorate, Department of the Secretary of State and the Canadian Government Publishing Centre, Supply and Services Canada, 1982), 32–58.

Kelsiev, Vasilii. *Galitsiia i Moldaviia, putevyia pisma.* St. Petersburg: Pechatnia V. Golovina, 1868.

Khodyly opryshky. Zbirnyk. Edited by I.M. Senko. Uzhhorod: Karpaty, 1983.

Kieniewicz, Stefan. *The Emancipation of the Polish Peasantry.* Chicago: The University of Chicago Press, 1969.

Kieniewicz, Stefan, ed. *Galicja w dobie autonomicznej (1850–1914). Wybór tekstów.* Wrocław: Wydawnictwo Zakładu Narodowego im. Ossolińskich, 1952.

Kieniewicz, Stefan. *Pomiędzy Stadionem a Goslarem. Sprawa włościańska w Galicji w 1848 r.* Wrocław, Warsaw, Cracow, Gdańsk: Zakład Narodowy imienia Ossolińskich, Wydawnictwo, 1980.

Kimpinska-Tatsiun, Oleksandra. *Rik u zhytti ukrainskoi zhinky-hospodyni.* Winnipeg-Fort William: Nakladom avtorky, 1967.

Klabouch, Jiří. *Die Gemeindeselbstverwaltung in Österreich 1848–1918.* Österreich Archiv. Munich-Vienna: Verlag R. Oldenbourg, 1968.

Klabouch, Jiří. "Die Lokalverwaltung in Cisleithanien." In *Die Habsburgermonarchie 1848–1918,* ed. Adam Wandruszka and Peter Urbanitsch, Österreichische Akademie der Wissenschaften, Bd. 2: *Verwaltung und Rechtswesen* (Vienna: Verlag der Österreichischen Akademie der Wissenschaften, 1975), 270–305.

Klasova borotba selianstva Skhidnoi Halychyny (1772–1849). Dokumenty i materialy. Kiev: Naukova dumka, 1974.

Klunker, J. Ludwig. *Die gesetzliche Unterthans-Verfassung in Galizien. Aus dem Wortlaute der bis auf die neueste Zeit erflossenen Verordnungen systematisch zusammengestellt von....* 3 vols. Lviv: Verlag von Eduard Winiarz, 1845–6.

Kofler, Oskar. "Żydowskie dwory. (Wspomnienia z Galicji Wschodniej od początku XIX wieku do wybuchu I wojny światowej." Typescript at YIVO library, New York. [Poland: 1979?]

Kohl, J.G. *Austria. Vienna, Prague, Hungary, Bohemia, and the Danube; Galicia, Styria, Moravia, Bukovina, and the Military Frontier.* London: Chapman and Hall, 1844.

Korczok, Anton. *Die griechisch-katholische Kirche in Galizien.* Osteuropa-Institut in Breslau. Leipzig, Berlin: 1921.

Kosachevskaia, E.M. *Vostochnaia Galitsiia nakanune i v period revoliutsii 1848 g.* Lviv: Izdatelstvo Lvovskogo universiteta, 1965.

Kozik, Jan. *Między reakcją a rewolucją. Studia z dziejów ukraińskiego ruchu narodowego w Galicji w latach 1848–1849.* Zeszyty Naukowe Uniwersytetu Jagiellońskiego, 381, Prace Historyczne, 52. Warsaw, Cracow: Państwowe Wydawnictwo Naukowe, Nakładem Uniwersytetu Jagiellońskiego, 1975.

Kozik, Jan. "Moskalofilstwo w Galicji w latach 1848–1866 na tle odrodzenia narodowego Rusinów. (Praca magisterska)." MA dissertation: Jagellonian University, Cracow, 1958.

Kozik, Jan. *Ukraiński ruch narodowy w Galicji w latach 1830–1848.* Cracow: Wydawnictwo Literackie, 1973.

Kramarz, Henryka. "Schematyzmy galicyjskie jako źródło historyczne." *Studia Historyczne* 25, no. 1 (96) (1982): 27–48.

Kravchuk, Petro. *Kanadskyi druh Ivana Franka.* Toronto: Kobzar, 1971.

Kravets, M.M. "Dzherela z istorii selianskoho rukhu u Skhidnii Halychyni v druhii polovyni XIX st." *Arkhivy Ukrainy,* no. 4 (1977): 63–5.

Kravets, M.M. "Masovi selianski vystupy u Skhidnii Halychyni v 90-kh rokakh XIX st." *Z istorii Ukrainskoi RSR,* vyp. 8 (Kiev: 1963), 3–27.

Kravets, M.M. *Selianstvo Skhidnoi Halychyny i Pivnichnoi Bukovyny u druhii polovyni XIX st.* Lviv: 1964.

Kravets, M.M. "Servitutne pytannia v masovykh selianskykh vystupakh u Skhidnii Halychyni naprykintsi 60-kh rokiv XIX st." *Visnyk Lvivskoho... universytetu.... Seria istorychna,* vyp. 6 (Lviv: 1970), 66–72.

Kudlich, Hans. *Rückblicke und Erinnerungen.* 3 vols. Vienna: 1873.

Kukhnii, Fedir. "Olesha." In *Almanakh Stanyslavivskoi zemli. Zbirnyk materiialiv do istorii Stanyslavova i Stanyslavivshchyny,* ed. Bohdan Kravtsiv; NTSh, Ukrainskyi arkhiv, 28 (New York: 1975).

Kupchanko, Hryhorii [Gregor Kupczanko]. *Die Schicksale der Ruthenen.* Leipzig: Verlag von Wilhelm Friedrich, 1887.

Kurhansky, I.P. *Maisternist Franka-publitsysta.* Lviv: 1974.

"Kwestia ukraińska na terenie powiatu drohobyckiego." Manuscript. London, 1942.

Leon, Abram. *The Jewish Question: A Marxist Interpretation.* New York: Pathfinder Press, Inc., 1970.

Leshchenko, M.H. "Posylennia klasovoi borotby v ukrainskomu seli v 1848 r." *Ukrainskyi istorychnyi zhurnal* 16, no. 2 (143) (February 1973): 42–52.

Lestschinsky, Jacob. *Dos idishe folk in tsifern.* Berlin: Klal-Verlag, 1922.

Levine, Hillel. "Gentry, Jews, and Serfs: The Rise of Polish Vodka." *Review: A Journal of the Fernand Braudel Center for the Study of Economics* 4, no. 2 (Fall 1980): 233–50.

Levytsky, Ivan Em. *Halytsko-ruskaia bybliohrafiia XIX-ho stolitiia s uvzhliadneniiem ruskykh izdanii poiavyvshykhsia v Uhorshchyni i Bukovyni (1801–1886).* 2 vols. Lviv: Stavropyhiiskii instytut, 1888–95.

Levytsky, Iv. Em. *Ukrainska bibliografiia Avstro-Uhorshchyny za roky 1887–1900.* 3 vols. Materiialy do ukrainskoi bibliografii, Bibliografichna komisiia NTSh, 1–3. Lviv: NTSh, 1909–11.

Levytsky, Kost. *Istoriia politychnoi dumky halytskykh ukraintsiv 1848–1914.* 2 vols. Lviv: 1926–7.

Liebel-Weckowicz, Helen, and Franz J. Szabo. "Modernization Forces in Maria Theresa's Peasant Policies, 1740–1780." *Histoire sociale—Social History* 15, no. 30 (November 1982): 301–31.

Link, Edith Murr. *The Emancipation of the Austrian Peasant 1740-1798.* New York: Columbia University Press, 1949.

Lozynsky, Iosyf [L. z Peremyskoho]. *Hadky o vlasnosty.* Lviv: Typom Instytuta Stavropyhiiskoho, 1862.

Lozynsky, Mykhailo. *Sorok lit diialnosty "Prosvity)".* (*V 40-litnii iuvilei tovarystva).* Lviv: 1908.

Luxemburg, Rosa. *The Accumulation of Capital.* New York, London: Modern Reader Paperbacks, 1968.

Luzhnytsky, Hryhor. *Ukrainska tserkva mizh Skhodom i Zakhodom. Narys istorii ukrainskoi tserkvy.* Philadelphia: Nakladom Soiuzu ukraintsiv-katolykiv "Provydinnia," 1954.

Magocsi, Paul Robert. *Galicia: A Historical Survey and Bibliographic Guide.* Toronto: Published in association with the Canadian Institute of Ukrainian Studies and the Harvard Ukrainian Research Institute by University of Toronto Press, 1983.

Magocsi, Paul R. "The Language Question as a Factor in the National Movement." In *Nationbuilding and the Politics of Nationalism: Essays on Austrian Galicia,* ed. Andrei S. Markovits and Frank E. Sysyn (Cambridge, MA: Harvard Ukrainian Research Institute, 1982), 220–38.

Magocsi, Paul R. "Nationalism and National Bibliography: Ivan E. Levyts'kyi and Nineteenth-Century Galicia." *Harvard Library Bulletin* 28, no. 1 (January 1980): 81–109.

Magocsi, Paul R., comp., *The Peter Jacyk Collection of Ukrainian Serials: A Guide to Newspapers and Periodicals.* Toronto: Chair of Ukrainian Studies, University of Toronto, 1983.

Magocsi, Paul Robert. *The Shaping of a National Identity: Subcarpathian Rus',' 1848–1948.* Harvard Ukrainian Series. Cambridge, MA, London: Harvard University Press, 1978.

Magocsi, Paul R. "Vienna as a Resource for Ukrainian Studies: With Special Reference to Galicia." *Harvard Ukrainian Studies* 3–4 (1979–80): 608–26.

Mahler, Raphael. "The Economic Background of Jewish Emigration from Galicia to the United States." *YIVO Annual of Jewish Social Science* 7 (1952): 255–67.

Mahler, Raphael. *A History of Modern Jewry 1780–1815.* New York: Schocken Books, 1971.

Mannheim, Karl. *Essays on the Sociology of Knowledge.* London: Routledge & Kegan Paul Ltd., 1952.

Martynowych, Orest T., and Nadia Kazymyra. "Political Activity in Western Canada, 1896–1923." In *A Heritage in Transition: Essays in the History of Ukrainians in Canada,* ed. Manoly R. Lupul; Generations: A History of

Canada's Peoples (Toronto: McClelland and Stewart Ltd. in association with the Multiculturalism Directorate, Department of the Secretary of State and the Canadian Government Publishing Centre, Supply and Services Canada, 1982), 85–107.

Martynowych, Orest T. *The Ukrainian Bloc Settlement in East Central Alberta, 1890-1930: A History*. Historic Sites Service, Occasional Papers, 10 (March 1985). [Edmonton:] Alberta Culture, 1985.

Marx, Karl. *Capital*. 3 vols. New York: International Publishers, New World Paperbacks, 1967.

Marx, Karl. *A Contribution to the Critique of Political Economy*. New York: International Publishers, 1972.

Marx, Karl. *Grundrisse: Foundations of the Critique of Political Economy (Rough Draft)*. Translated with a foreword by Martin Nicolaus. The Pelican Marx Library. Harmondsworth: Penguin Books in association with New Left Review, 1973.

Marx, Karl. *Surveys from Exile*. Edited and translated by David Fernbach. The Pelican Marx Library, Political Writings, 2. Harmondsworth: Penguin Books in association with New Left Review, 1973.

Mises, Ludwig von. *Die Entwicklung des gutsherrlich-bäuerlichen Verhältnisses in Galizien (1772-1848)*. Wiener Staatswissenschaftliche Studien, Bd. 4, Heft 2. Vienna, Leipzig: Franz Deuticke, 1902.

Monchalovsky, O.A. *Pamiatnaia knyzhka v 25-litnii iuvylei Obshchestva imeny Mykhaila Kachkovskoho. 1874-1899*. Lviv: 1899.

Moroz, M.O., ed. *Ivan Franko. Bibliohrafiia tvoriv 1874-1964*. Kiev: Naukova dumka, 1966.

Müller, Sepp. *Schriftum über Galizien und sein Deutschtum*. Wissenschaftliche Beiträge zur Geschichte und Landeskunde Ost-Mitteleuropas herausgegeben vom Johann Gottfried Herder-Institut, 63. Marburg [Lahn]: 1962.

Murdzek, Benjamin P. *Emigration in Polish Social-Political Thought, 1870-1914*. Boulder, Colo.: East European Quarterly, 1977.

Nahirny, Vasyl. *Z moikh spomyniv*. Lviv: 1935.

Najdus, Walentyna. *Szkice z historii Galicji*. 2 vols. Warsaw: Książka i Wiedza, 1958–60.

Narysy z istorii Pivnichnoi Bukovyny. Kiev: Naukova dumka, 1980.

Naumovych, Ivan. *Sobraniie sochynenii*. 3 vols. Lviv: 1926–7.

Nechytaliuk, M.F. *Publitsystyka Ivana Franka (1875-1886 rr.). Seminarii*. Lviv: Vydavnytstvo Lvivskoho universytetu, 1972.

Olesnytsky, Evhen. *Storinky z moho zhyttia*. 2 vols. Lviv: Nakladom Vydavnychoi spilky "Dilo," 1935.

Oliinyk, Hryhorii. *Emihrantski virshi halytskoho selianyna*. Edited by Orest Zilynsky. Toronto: Kobzar, 1972.

Oliinyk, L.V. "Vidobrazhennia v radianskii istoriohrafii revoliutsiinykh podii 1848 r. na Ukraini." *Ukrainskyi istorychnyi zhurnal* 16, no. 2 (143) (February 1973): 52–8.

Orton, Lawrence D. "Polish Publications since 1945 on Austrian and Galician History, 1772-1918." *Austrian History Yearbook* 12–13 (1976–7), part 2, pp. 315–58.

Pappenheim, Bertha, and Sara Rabinowitsch. *Zur Lage der jüdischen Bevölkerung in Galizien. Reise-Eindrücke und Vorschläge zur Besserung der Verhältnisse.* Frankfurt a.M.: Neuer Frankfurter Verlag, 1904.

Pashaeva, N.M. "Galitsiia pod vlastiu Avstrii v russkoi i sovetskoi istoricheskoi literature (1772–1918 gg.). Bibliografiia." In *Mezhdunarodnye sviazi stran Tsentralnoi, Vostochnoi i Iugo-Vostochnoi Evropy i slaviano-germanskie otnosheniia* (Moscow: Nauka, 1968), 295–324.

Pavlyk, M. *Moskvofilstvo ta ukrainofilstvo sered avstro-ruskoho narodu.* Lviv: Z "Zahalnoi drukarni," 1906.

Pavlyk, Mykhailo, ed. *Perepyska Mykhaila Drahomanova z Mykhailom Pavlykom. (1876-1895).* 7 vols., numbered 2–8. Chernivtsi: Z drukarni tov. "Ruska rada," 1910–12.

Pavlyk, Mykhailo. "Pro rusko-ukrainski narodni chytalni." In *Tvory* (Kiev: Derzhavne vydavnytstvo khudozhnoi literatury, 1959), 416–549.

Pech, Stanley Z. "The Nationalist Movements of the Austrian Slavs in 1848: A Comparative Sociological Profile." *Histoire sociale/Social History* 9 (no. 18) (November 1976): 336–56.

Pelesh, Iuliian [Julian Pelesz]. *Geschichte der Union der ruthenischen Kirche mit Rom von den aeltesten Zeiten bis auf die Gegenwart.* 2 vols. Würzburg-Vienna: Leo Woerl, 1881.

Pennel, Joseph. *The Jew at Home: Impressions of a Summer and Autumn Spent with Him.* New York: D. Appleton and Company, 1892.

Pilat, Tadeusz. *O stosunkach własności tabularnej w Galicyi a w szczególności w obwodzie sądowym Tarnopolskim. Wykład na posiedzeniu XXIII Rady Ogólnej c.k. galicyjskiego Towarzystwa gospodarskiego.* Lviv: 1888.

Pipes, Richard. *Russia under the Old Regime.* Harmondsworth: Penguin Books, 1979.

Pravda pro uniiu. Dokumenty i materialy. 2nd, expanded ed. Lviv: Kameniar, 1968.

Prohramy vechernyts ustroienykh v chasi vandrivky akademykiv zakhodom komytetu vandrivnychoho i komitetiv misttsevykh. [Lviv:] Z drukarni Tovarystva imeny Shevchenka, [1885].

Radianska Entsyklopediia Istorii Ukrainy. 4 vols. Kiev: Holovna redaktsiia Ukrainskoi Radianskoi Entsyklopedii, 1969–72.

Radzyner, Joanna. *Stanisław Madeyski 1841–1910: Ein austro-polnischer Staatsmann im Spannungsfeld der Nationalitätenfrage in der Habsburgermonarchie.* Studien zur Geschichte der österreichisch-ungarischen Monarchie, 20. Vienna: Verlag der Österreichischen Akademie der Wissenschaften, 1983.

Rawita Gawroński, Fr. *Żydzi w historji i literaturze ludowej na Rusi.* Warsaw: Gebethner i Wolff, n.d.

Die Revolutionsjahre 1848/49 im Königreich Galizien-Lodomerien (einschliesslich Bukowina): Dokumente aus österreichischer Zeit. [Edited by] Rudolf Wagner. Munich: Verlag "Der Südostdeutsche," 1983.

Rosdolsky, Roman. *Die Bauernabgeordneten im konstituierenden österreichischen Reichstag 1848–1849.* Ludwig Boltzmann Institut für Geschichte der Arbeiterbewegung, Materialien zur Arbeiterbewegung, 5. Vienna: Europaverlag, 1976.

Rosdolsky, R. "The Distribution of the Agrarian Product in Feudalism." *Journal of Economic History* 11 (Summer 1951): 247–65.

Rosdolsky [Rozdolski], Roman. "Do historii 'krwawego roku' 1846." *Kwartalnik Historyczny* 65, no. 2 (1958): 403–20.

Rosdolsky [Rozdolski], Roman. *Die grosse Steuer- und Agrarreform Josefs II: Ein Kapitel zur österreichischen Wirtschaftsgeschichte.* Warsaw: Państwowe Wydawnictwo Naukowe, 1961.

Rosdolsky, Roman. *The Making of Marx's 'Capital'.* London: Pluto Press, 1977.

Rosdolsky [Rozdolski], Roman. Review of Hipolit Grynwaser, *Przywódcy i burzyciele włościan. Szkice z dziejów włościan skarbowych w Królestwie Polskim (1815–30),* Odbitka z "Przeglądu Współczesnego" (Warsaw: 1937). In *Roczniki Dziejów Społecznych i Gospodarczych* 6 (1937): 356–61.

Rosdolsky [Rozdolski], Roman. *Stosunki poddańcze w dawnej Galicji.* 2 vols. Warsaw: Państwowe Wydawnictwo Naukowe, 1962.

Rosdolsky [Rozdolski], Roman. *Wspólnota gminna w b. Galicji Wschodniej i jej zanik.* Badania z dziejów społecznych i gospodarczych, 27. Lviv: Instytut Popierania Polskiej Twórczości Naukowej, 1936.

Rosdolsky, Roman. *Zur nationalen Frage: Friedrich Engels und das Problem der "geschichtslosen" Völker.* Berlin: Olle & Wolter, 1979.

Rosenfeld, Max. *Die polnische Judenfrage: Problem und Lösung.* Vienna-Berlin: R. Löwit Verlag, 1918.

Rudnytsky, Ivan L. "The Ukrainians in Galicia under Austrian Rule." In *Nationbuilding and the Politics of Nationalism: Essays on Austrian Galicia,* ed. Andrei S. Markovits and Frank E. Sysyn (Cambridge, MA: Harvard Ukrainian Research Institute, 1982), 23–67.

Rutkowski, Alan, and Nadia Cyncar, comps. *Ukrainian Serials: A Checklist of Ukrainian Journals, Periodicals and Newspapers in the University of Alberta Library.* Research Report, 3. Edmonton: Canadian Institute of Ukrainian Studies, 1983.

Sacher-Masoch, [Leopold von]. *Galizische Geschichten.* Leipzig: Ernst Julius Günther, 1875.

Shevchenko, Taras. *Kobzar.* Kiev: Derzhavne vydavnytstvo khudozhnoi literatury, 1964.

Shevchenko [Szewczenko], Taras. *Wybór poezji.* Biblioteka Narodowa, Seria II, 178. Wrocław, Warsaw, Cracow, Gdańsk: Zakład Narodowy imienia Ossolińskich, 1974.

Simons, Jr., Thomas W. "The Peasant Revolt of 1846 in Galicia: Recent Polish Historiography." *Slavic Review* 30, no. 4 (December 1971): 795–817.

Sirka, Ann. *The Nationality Question in Austrian Education: The Case of Ukrainians in Galicia 1867–1914.* European University Studies, Publications, Series 3, History and Allied Sciences, 124. Frankfurt a.M.; Bern; Circencester, U.K.: Peter D. Lang, 1980.

Slomka, Jan. *From Serfdom to Self-Government: Memoirs of a Polish Village Mayor 1842-1927.* Translated by William John Rose, introduction by Stanislaw Kot. London: Minerva Publishing Co., Ltd., 1941.

Słownik Historii Polski. 6th ed. Edited by Tadeusz Łepkowski. Warsaw: Wiedza Powszechna, 1973.

Special-Orts-Repertorien der im oesterreichischen Reichsrathe vertretenen Königreiche und Länder. Herausgegeben von der k.k. statistischen Central-Commission. Bd. 12: *Galizien.* Vienna, 1886.

Special-Orts-Repertorien der im österreichischen Reichsrathe vertretenen Königreiche und Länder. Neubearbeitung auf Grund der Ergebnisse der Volkszählung vom 31. December 1890. Herausgegeben von der k.k. statistischen Central-Commission. Bd. 12: *Galizien.* Vienna: Alfred Hölder, 1893.

Spravozdaniie z dilanii "Prosvity" vid chasu zaviazannia tovarystva—26. lystopada 1868 roku, do nainoviishoho chasu. Lviv: 1874.

Staruch, Bohdan. "Der Kampf der galizischen Ukrainer um ihr Selbstbestimmungsrecht im alten Österreich 1772–1918." PhD dissertation: University of Innsbruck, 1948. (The Staruch family had the dissertation retyped c. 1980; this is the version to which I had access.)

[Steblii, F.I.] "Peredmova." In *Klasova borotba,* 3–32.

Stokes, Gale. "Cognition and the Function of Nationalism." *Journal of Interdisciplinary History* 4, no. 4 (spring 1974): 525–42.

Stokes, Gale. "The Undeveloped Theory of Nationalism." *World Politics* 31, no. 1 (October 1978): 150–60.

Studynsky, Kyrylo. *Lvivska dukhovna semynaryia v chasakh Markiiana Shashkevycha (1829–1843).* Zbirnyk filologichnoi sektsii NTSh, 17–18. Lviv: 1916.

Studynsky, Kyrylo. "Polski konspiratsii sered ruskykh pytomtsiv i dukhovenstva v Halychyni v rokakh 1831–46." *Zapysky NTSh* 80 (1907): 53–108 and 83 (1908): 87–177.

Styś, Wincenty. *Rozdrabnianie gruntów chłopskich w byłym zaborze austrjackim od roku 1787 do 1931.* Lviv: 1934.

Sviezhynsky, P.V. *Ahrarni vidnosyny na Zakhidnii Ukraini v kintsi XIX–na pochatku XX st.* Lviv: Vydavnytstvo Lvivskoho universytetu, 1966.

Tarnavsky, Fylymon. *Spohady. Rodynna khronika Tarnavskykh iak prychynok do istorii tserkovnykh, sviashchenytskykh, pobutovykh, ekonomichnykh i politychnykh vidnosyn u Halychyni v druhii polovyni XIX storichchia i v pershii dekadi XX storichchia.* Edited by Anatol Mariia Bazylevych and Roman Ivan Danylevych. Toronto: Dobra knyzhka, 1981.

Tenenbaum, Joseph. *Galitsye, mayn alte heym.* Dos poylishe yidntum, 87. Buenos Aires: Tsentral-farband fun poylishe yidn in Argentine, 1952.

Terletsky, Ostap [Ivan Zanevych]. *Znesenie panshchyny v Halychyni. Prychynok do istorii suspilnoho zhytia i suspilnykh pohliadiv 1830–1848 rr.* Lviv: Z drukarni Instytutu Stavropyhiishoho, 1895.

Thomas, William I., and Florian Znaniecki. *The Polish Peasant in Europe and America.* 2 vols. Reprint of 2nd ed.; New York: Dover, 1958.

Trusevych, S.M. *Suspilno-politychnyi rukh u Skhidnii Halychyni v 50–70-kh rokakh XIX st.* Kiev: Naukova dumka, 1978.

Ukraine: A Concise Encyclopedia. Edited by Volodymyr Kubiiovych [Kubijovyč]. Toronto: University of Toronto Press, 1963–71.

Ukraine and Poland in Documents 1918–1922. Edited by Taras Hunczak. 2 vols. Sources for the History of Ruś-Ukraine, 12. New York, Paris, Sydney, Toronto: Shevchenko Scientific Society, 1983.

Ukrainska Zahalna Entsyklopediia. Knyha znannia v 3-okh tomakh. 3 vols. Edited by Ivan Rakovsky. Lviv: Ridna shkola, n.d.

Verdery, Katherine. *Transylvanian Villagers: Three Centuries of Political, Economic, and Ethnic Change.* Berkeley, Los Angeles, London: University of California Press, 1983.

Vilfan, Sergij. "Die Agrarsozialpolitik von Maria Theresia bis Kudlich." In *Der Bauer Mittel- und Osteuropas im sozio-ökonomischen Wandel des 18. und 19. Jahrhunderts: Beiträge zu seiner Lage und deren Wiederspiegelung in der zeitgenössischen Publizistik und Literatur,* Studien zur Geschichte der Kulturbeziehungen in Mittel- und Osteuropa (Cologne, Vienna: Böhlau Verlag, 1973), 1–52.

Vozniak, Mykhailo. *Iak probudylosia ukrainske narodnie zhyttia v Halychyni za Avstrii.* Biblioteka "Novoho chasu," 1. Lviv: Z drukarni Vydavnychoi spilky "Dilo," 1924.

Weber, Eugen. *Peasants into Frenchmen: The Modernization of Rural France, 1870–1914.* Stanford: Stanford University Press, 1976.

Wilson, Duncan. *The Life and Times of Vuk Stefanović Karadzić 1787-1864: Literacy, Literature, and National Independence in Serbia.* Oxford: At the Clarendon Press, 1970.

Wójcik, Zbigniew. *Dzieje Rosji 1533–1801.* 2nd ed. Warsaw: Państwowe Wydawnictwo Naukowe, 1971.

Wyka, Kazimierz. *Teka Stańczyka na tle historii Galicji w latach 1849–1869.* Instytut Badań Literackich, Studia Historycznoliterackie, 4. Wrocław: Wydawnictwo Zakładu Narodowego imienia Ossolińskich, 1951.

Yuzyk, Paul. "Religious Life." In *A Heritage in Transition: Essays in the History of Ukrainians in Canada,* ed. Manoly R. Lupul; Generations: A History of Canada's Peoples (Toronto: McClelland and Stewart Ltd. in association with the Multiculturalism Directorate, Department of the Secretary of State and the Canadian Government Publishing Centre, Supply and Services Canada, 1982), 143–72.

Zabrovarnyi, S. "Sotsialna svidomist peremyskykh selian u pershii polovyni XIX stolittia (Uryvok z doktorskoi dysertatsii)." *Ukrainskyi kalendar 1972* (Warsaw), 284–5.

Zinoviiv, Klymentii. *Virshi. Prypovisti pospolyti.* Edited by I.P. Chepiha and V.P. Kolosova. Kiev: Naukova dumka, 1971.

Zoria halytskaia, iako album na hod 1860. Lviv: [1860]).

Zvarych, V.V. "Do pytannia pro hroshovyi obih u Halychyni pid panuvanniam Avstro-Uhorshchyny." *Istorychni dzherela ta ikh vykorystannia,* vyp. 2 (Kiev: Naukova dumka, 1966), 203–14.

Index

Abrahamowicz, Dawid 152, 154
America, United States of 147, 202,
    212, 271
Andriishyn, Hryhorii 257
Andrukhovych (peasant activist) 257
Andrunyk, Hrynko 257
Andrunyk, Ivan 257
Antoniv, Martyn 257

Babiak, Andrii 257
Babynets, Ivan 257
Babyntsi, Chortkiv circle 21
Bach, Alexander 26, 36
Bachynsky, Aleksander 126
Badeni (count; marshal of Kaminka
    Strumylova district) 207
Badeni, Kazimierz (early nineteenth
    century) 17
Bąkowski (count) 10
Bakuska, Vasyl 257
Balaban, I. 257
Balaban, R. 257
Balandiuk, Pavlo 258
Balias, Havrylo 258
Balyntsi, Kolomyia circle, Kolomyia
    district 233, 276, 304
Balytsky, Aleksander 258
Banakh, Mykhailo 258

Barabash, Oleksa 208
Barani Peretoky, Sokal district 170, 279
Barnych, Kornylo 258
Bart, Shymkhe 154
Bartetsky, Roman 259
Bartetsky, Stefan 259
Barvinsky, Volodymyr 73, 257
Baryliv, Brody district 112
Basaichuk, Mykola 259
Batiatychi, Zhovkva circle, Zhovkva
    district 43, 123, 232
Batiuk, Ivan 43–4, 47–8
Bauer, Otto 217, 219, 221
Baznykivka, Berezhany circle,
    Berezhany district 227
Beheka, Ivan 14
Belei, Ivan 287
Belz deanery 264
Bendiuha, Sokal district 301
Berbeka, Levko 259
Berezhany 26; circle 229; district 317
Berezhnytsia, Kalush district 188, 291
Berezhnytsia, Stryi circle, Stryi district
    180–2, 187, 233
Bereziv Vyzhnii,
    Kolomyia/Pechenizhyn district
    169–70, 236, 271–3

Kolomyia/Pechenizhyn district 169–70, 273
Berezyna, Zhydachiv district 94, 100, 269, 280, 289, 294, 303, 307, 311
Bernyk, Andrukh 259–60
Bernyk, Iats 259
Bernyk, Ivan 259
Bernyk, Stefan 259
Bernyk, Tymko 259
Bessarabia 156
Betański (prince) 178
Biała, Rzeszów district 258
Bibrka 26
Bila, Ternopil district 270, 278, 284, 300–1, 316
Bilan, Oleksa 260
Bilevych, Konstantyn 260
Bilevych, Mykhailo 260
Biliavtsi, Brody district 230
Biliavyntsi, Buchach district 284
Bilka, Lviv circle 25
Bilokha, Vasyl 260
Bilyi Kamin, Zolochiv district 261, 269, 275, 277, 280–2, 286–8, 299, 314
Bilynsky, Pankratii 260
Bohachevsky-Chomiak, Martha 101
Bohemia 4, 12, 15, 59, 62, 167
Bohorodchany, Stanyslaviv circle, district capital 10, 26, 274
Boichuk, Vasyl 260
Boikevych, Iliia 132, 260–1
Boiko, Iurko 261
Bokii, Kyrylo 261
Bolekhiv, Stryi circle 26
Bolekhivska, Anna (Melnyk) 261
Bolekhivsky, Andrei I. 261
Bolekhivsky, Ioann 261
Boratyn, Sokal district 300
Borkovsky, Oleksander 75–6, 78
Borky Dominikanski, Lviv district 230
Borshchiv district 114, 156
Borys, Hryhorii 261
Borys, P. 261
Bovshivets, Rohatyn district (region) 156, 214
Bratash, Dmytro 43
Brateiko, Luka 262
Breslier, Khaim 163
Briukhovychi, Peremyshliany district 94–5, 100, 236, 265, 274, 286–7

Brodky, Lviv district 147
Brody 26, 35, 167, 303; district 282; deanery 282
Brovary, Buchach district 141, 208, 236, 270, 289, 295
Bruckner, Anton 195, 297
Brytan, Antin 262
Brytan, Ostap 262
Buchach, Stanyslaviv circle 26
Buchma, Stefan 262
Budzynovsky, Viacheslav 80
Bukovyna 22, 24–5, 30, 49–50, 60, 62, 118, 126, 149, 155, 162, 179, 195, 218, 220, 261
Burak, Danko 262
Burak, Ilko 262
Burak, Lesko 262
Burak, Lev 262
Burak, Semko 262–3
Burkaniv, Pidhaitsi district 112, 132, 263
Burnadz, Semen 263
Burshtyn, Rohatyn district (region) 188
Busk, Kaminka Strumylova district 45–6; deanery 260
Buzhok, Zolochiv district 90, 260, 288, 291, 294, 299, 308, 314
Byblo, Rohatyn district 156
Byliv, Iosyf 132, 263

Canada 93, 202, 271–2
Catherine II 18
Chanyzh, Zolochiv circle 232
Chekhy, Brody district 230, 264, 281, 291, 298, 314
Chemerynsky, Antonii 263
Chepil, Konstantyn 263
Cheredarchuk, Vasyl 264
Cherevatiuk (cantor and merchant) 171, 264
Chernetsky, Vasyl 94, 264
Cherniak, Petro 264
Chernivtsi 261, 271, 287, 297
Chertezh, Zhydachiv district 261
Chlebowczyk, Józef 204
Cholhany, Dolyna district 230
Chornobai, Aleksander 265
Chortkiv 26; circle 4, 8, 17, 24, 174, 231; district 316
Chortovets, Horodenka district 82, 163

Chuba, Maksym 265
Chubei, Fedir 21
Chypchar, Vasyl 265
Cracow 108–9
Czajkowski, Maciej 152

Dachynsky, Iarema 265
Dalmatia 60
Danyliv, Iliarii 265
Darakhiv, Terebovlia district 99, 210,
    261, 279–80, 291–2, 296, 298,
    302–3, 308
Daszyński, Ignacy 293
David, Zdeněk V. 23
Davies, Norman 18, 36, 40
Demyche, Kolomyia circle, Sniatyn
    district 228
Denysiv, Ternopil district 195, 202
Derkach, Panko 265
Derzhiv, Stryi circle 34, 122
Diakiv, Danylo 265
Diakon, Mykhailo 186, 266
Didukh, Ivan 266
Didyliv, Zolochiv district 310
Dmyterko, Semen 266
Dmytrie, Lviv district 154
Dmytriv, Zhovkva circle, Kaminka
    Strumylova district 171, 232, 259,
    265, 283, 291, 293–4, 297, 305,
    317
Dnistriansky, Lev 266
Dobriansky, Hnat 266
Dobriany, Stryi circle, Stryi district 228
Dobrianychi, Berezhany circle,
    Peremyshliany district 111, 227,
    265, 309
Dobrivliany, Drohobych district 60, 293
Dobromirka, Zbarazh district 298
Dobromyl (district capital) 163; region
    187
Dobrostany, Horodok district 95–6,
    101, 144, 149, 194–5, 198, 203,
    257–8, 270, 277, 281, 287–8, 297,
    311
Dobrotvir, Kaminka Strumylova district
    40–9, 51, 54, 123, 154, 179, 230
Dobrovolsky, Ivan 266
Dobrowolski, Kazimierz 121
Dolnytsky (priest activist in Ripniv)
    266

Dolnytsky, Andrei 266
Dolyna (district capital) 297
Dolyna, Kaminka Strumylova district
    41
Domsky, Toma 267
Dorozhiv, Sambir circle 12, 118, 120
Dorozhynsky, Vladyslav 267
Dovhe, Stryi district 286
Dragan, Iurko 267–8, 280, 286
Dragan, Konstantyn 268
Dragan, Nykola 268
Drahomanov, Mykhailo 71, 75, 102,
    202
Drohobych 26, 140; district 306
Drohomyrchany, Stanyslaviv circle 233
Dron, Teodor 268
Drozdovychi, Horodok district 157
Drymalyk, Sylvester L. 256, 268, 310
Dubliany, Sambir district 276
Dubno, Rzeszów circle 6
Dubovy, Ivan 268
Dunaiv, Permyshliany district 309
Dushansky, Dymytrii 269
Dutkevych, Evhenii 269
Dyhdalevych, Ivan 269
Dykevych, Pavlo 269
Dylewski, Marian 29
Dylynsky, Volodymyr 269
Dyniv, Sanok circle 119
Dynsky, Toma 270
Dynyska, Rava Ruska district 180
Dytiatyn, Rohatyn district 156
Dzhuriv, Kolomyia circle, Sniatyn
    district 228, 284
Dzików, Tarnobrzeg district 56, 160,
    183

Egypt 286
Engels, Friedrich 29

Fedorovych, Vasyl 194, 198, 270
Fedun, I. 270
Ferdinand I 21, 57
Filvarkiv (peasant activist) 270
Fleischer, Siegfried 59
Forlita, Petro 270
Fraha, Rohatyn district 133
France 160, 218
Franko, Ivan 75–6, 78–9, 86, 89, 108,
    123, 164, 214, 271–3, 284, 287, 293

Franz I 11
Franz Joseph I 43
Fyniak, Dmytro 270
Fyniak, Mykhailo 270
Fytkiv, Stanyslaviv circle, Nadvirna
    district 94, 173, 180, 184, 227,
    257, 259, 268, 275, 301, 305, 313

Gabrysh, Liudvyk 270
Galat, Roman 270-1
Garbowski, Julian 41
Gdańsk 5
Gelmas, Ivan 271
Genyk, Iurko 273
Genyk, Ivan 271
Genyk, Kyrylo 214, 256, 271-3, 312
Genyk, Stefan 214, 271-2
Germany 65
Giżejewski (son of Adalbert) 17
Giżejewski, Adalbert 17
Goethe, Johann Wolfgang 284
Gołuchowski, Agenor 26, 36, 41, 48
Grimsted, Patricia K. 225
Grintal, Shmaie 154
Gurnytsky, Iosyf 272

Hai Smolenski, Zolochiv circle, Brody
    district 227
Hai Starobridski, Zolochiv circle 229,
    282
Hałajkiewicz, Wiktor 42, 44
Halapats, Ivan 273
Halych, Stanyslaviv circle 26
Hankevych, Iulian 125
Hannsmann, F. 4, 17
Hanusivtsi, Stanyslaviv circle,
    Stanyslaviv district 227
Havlytsky, Antin 273
Herynovych, Petro 273
Hetman, Iosyf 273
Hetman, Stefan 273
Hirne, Stryi district 74
Hladii, Porfyr 271, 273-4
Hladun, Andrei 274
Hladun, Nykola 274
Hladylovych, Demian 102
Hlibovytsky, Aleksander 274
Hlibovytsky, Konstantyn 274
Hlubichok, Chortkiv circle, Borshchiv
    district 227

Hlubichok Velykyi, Ternopil district
    181
Hlynsky, Teofan 274-5
Hnizdychiv, Zhydachiv district 149
Hodiv, Zolochiv district 99
Holeiko, Mykhailo 76, 79
Holhoche, Pidhaitsi district 230
Holodryha, Mykola 275, 292
Holoiad, Adam 275
Holovatsky, Danylo 275
Holovatsky, Iakiv 127
Holovchuk (activist) 275
Holovinsky, Stefan 275
Holovka, Hrynko 275
Holovka, Vasyl 275
Hora, Sokal district 182
Horak, Ivan 275
Horbachuk, Pavlo 276
Horodenka (district capital) 14, 263,
    270, 272, 283-5, 290, 295, 316
Horodnytsia, Horodenka district 274,
    284
Horodnytsia, Husiatyn district 277,
    285, 291, 316
Horodok 26, 33; district 281
Horodyshche, Ternopil district 100
Horodysky, Iakiv 276
Horoshova, Chortkiv circle 15, 20, 34
Horozhanna, Sambir circle 24-5, 29
Horutsky, Oleksander P. 276
Horutsky, Pavlo 142
Hrabiv, Stryi circle 121
Hrabivets, Stanyslaviv circle,
    Bohorodchany district 227
Hrabovetsky, Ivan 276
Hrabovetsky, Lavrentii 276
Hrabovetsky, Mykhailo 276
Hrabovych, Ioann 276-7
Hrushiv 26
Hrushka, Zhovkva district 42-3
Hryhorovych, Stefan 14
Hrymaliv, Skalat district (region) 137
Hrynevetsky, Apolinarii 259, 277
Hryniuk, Stella 203, 206, 217
Hryniv, Berezhany circle 34
Hrynkiv, Ivan 277
Hrytsyna, Teodor 277
Huliuk, Demko 12
Hungary 8, 23, 156, 195, 221, 261, 264

Hunkevych, Hrynko 277
Hunkevych, Klym 277
Hunter, New York 57
Hupalo, Stefan 277
Huryk, Iosyf 208
Hushalevych, Ivan 67
Husiatyn 171; district 114, 137, 211,
    280
Hvozd, Nadvirna district 259, 294
Hvozdets, Kolomyia district 65
Hysovsky, Ioann 277

Iabloniv, Kolomyia/Pechenizhyn
    district 236, 271–2, 282
Iabloniv, Rohatyn district 156
Iabluniv, Chortkiv circle 234
Iakoba, Aleksander 278
Iakoba, Pavlo 278
Iamnytsia, Stanyslaviv circle,
    Stanyslaviv district 18, 57, 81–2,
    140
Ianishevsky, Teodor 278
Iarema, Ivan 278
Iarema, Kindrat 278
Iasenytsky, Mykhail 102, 278
Iaskuliak, I. 278
Iasynsky, Mykhailo 278
Iasynsky, Vasyl 278
Iavoriv (district capital) 26, 261–2,
    280–1, 305, 314
Iavorsky, Aleksander 278–9
Iavorsky, Ivan 279
Iazhiv Staryi, Iavoriv district 236, 311
Iazlovets, Buchach district 309
Ihrovytsia, Ternopil district 298
Ilemnia, Stryi circle 121
Ilyntsi, Sniatyn district 83, 133
Iskra, Roman 279
Istanbul 286
Iunashiv, Rohatyn district 291
Iurkiv, Roman 279
Iuzkiv, Iliia 279
Iuzkovychi, Zolochiv district 298
Iuzvak, Semen 279
Ivachiv Dolishnii, Ternopil circle,
    Ternopil district 2, 6, 81, 136, 148,
    152, 173, 181, 206, 234
Ivachiv Horishnii, Ternopil circle,
    Ternopil district 81, 136, 148, 152,
    181, 206, 234

Ivanets, Ivan 279
Ivano-Frankivsk (formerly Stanyslaviv)
    225
Ivantsiv, Avksentii 279

Jagić, Vatroslav 297
Jarosław, Przemyśl circle 26
Jasło (circle capital) 264
Joseph II 3–4, 7–10, 16, 19–20, 23, 37,
    56, 108, 134, 155, 157, 172, 177

Kachala, Stefan 68, 125
Kadobna, Kalush district 258, 263, 280,
    307
Kakhnykevych, Kyrylo 59, 102
Kalechynsky, Iosyf 45
Kalush, Stryi circle, district capital 26,
    168; region 38, 191
Kalynivshchyna, Chortkiv district 180
Kalynsky, Iosyf 279
Kamianetsky, Matvii 279
Kamianka Lisna, Rava Ruska district
    192, 194, 289
Kaminka Strumylova 42, 48; district
    207
Kaminka Voloska, Rava Ruska district
    186
Kaminne, Nadvirna district 271, 313
Kamynsky, Ivan 279
Kann, Robert A. 23
Kapushchak, Ivan 28–9, 34, 134
Karadžić, Vuk 20
Karp, Kost 280
Karp, Vasyl 280
Karpinsky, Andrii 29
Kaunitz, Anton 2, 7
Kavchynsky, Stefan 280
Kavsko, Stryi district 280
Kekosh, Iurii 280
Kendiukh, Hnat 267, 280
Kharambura, Ivan 280
Kharambura, Stefan 281
Khlivchany, Rava Ruska district 147,
    301
Khmelivka, Stanyslaviv circle,
    Bohorodchany district 227, 305
Khmelnytsky, Bohdan 309
Khodoriv, Berezhany circle 26
Kholevchuk, Dmytro 281
Khoma, Ivan 281

Khomyn, Tymofei 301
Khorostkiv, Chortkiv circle, Husiatyn
    district 141, 234, 236, 280
Khotin, Kalush district 168, 267–8,
    280, 286, 301, 316
Khreniv, Kaminka Strumylova district
    291
Khryplyn, Stanyslaviv circle 231
Khrystynopil, Zhovkva circle, Sokal
    district 114, 180, 229, 264, 273,
    276, 288, 294, 297, 300–1, 315
Khudoba, Vasyl 281
Khylchychi, Zolochiv district 149
Khymka, Datsko 43, 45–7
Khymka, Oleksa 43
Khyriv, Staryi Sambir district 163
Kielanowski (Polish parliamentary
    candidate) 152
Kiev 74, 225
Kiidantsi, Kolomyia circle, Kolomyia
    district 95, 98–9, 137, 156, 165,
    188, 233, 313
Kiidantsi, Zbarazh district 236
Kliusiv, Sokal district 300–1
Klub, Danylo 186
Klymivsky, Pavlo 281
Klymkivtsi, Zbarazh district 200
Kmet, Matvii 281
Kniahynychi 230
Kniahynychi, Bibrka district 203
Knihynychi 230
Kobylytsia, Lukian 25, 118
Koliankovsky, Volodymyr 281
Kolodribka, Zalishchyky district 86–7,
    126, 164, 174, 190–2, 236, 257–8,
    270, 282, 299, 308, 311, 315
Kolomyia 26, 69, 92, 198, 261, 271–2,
    297, 299; district 80, 271–2, 282;
    region 94, 136
Koltsuniak, Mykola 271, 282
Koltsuniak, Semen 282, 314
Koltsuniak, Vasyl 282
Koltuniak, Nykolai 282
Komarensky, Kuzma 282
Komarno, Sambir circle, Rudky district
    12, 26, 266, 282, 288, 298, 302,
    313; region 9, 19, 21, 24, 30, 157,
    178
Komorowski (count) 17
Konashevych, Teodor 282

Koranda, Johann Christoph von 13
Korchemny, Ivan 282
Korchyn, Stryi district 164–5, 206, 233,
    285–7, 298
Korchyn, Zhovkva circle, Sokal district
    228, 232, 306
Korelychi, Berezhany circle,
    Peremyshliany district 141, 184,
    227, 236, 257, 265, 270, 272, 287,
    296, 309, 312, 316
Kormyliuk, Ivan 282
Korol, Mykhailo 268
Korsiv, Brody district 292
Korytowski, Juliusz 148, 152
Koshakivsky, Mykhailo 43
Košice 264
Kosiv 272; district 63, 272
Kostarowce, Sanok district 170, 173
Kostelnytsky, Kazymir 282
Kostetsky, Ivan 282
Kostetsky, Vasyl 282
Kostiv, Fed 10
Kostiv, Ivan 283
Kostruba, Petro 47–8
Kotliarevsky, Ivan 28, 297
Kotovy, F. 283
Kotyk, Petro 283
Kotykivka, Horodenka district 284
Koval, Ivan 283
Kovalivka, Kolomyia/Pechenizhyn
    district 99, 141, 236, 271, 273,
    276, 278, 282, 284, 293–4, 303,
    307, 313–14
Kovalsky, Emilii 283
Kovalsky, Mykhailo 283
Kovalsky, Vasyl 300
Kovbuz, Vasyl 283, 285
Kozara, Rohatyn district 258
Kozik, Jan 122
Koziuk, Pavlo 283
Kozova, Berezhany district 163, 210
Krasicki (count, owner of Monastyrets)
    52
Krasicki, Kazimierz 15
Krasitsky (priest) 207
Kravets, M.M. 49, 51
Krizer (lumber dealer) 153
Kroměříž 178
Kropyvnyk, Kalush district 263
Kruhiv, Zolochiv district 299

Krupnytsky, Antin 284
Krushelnytsia, Stryi district 280
Krushelnytska, Solomiia 284
Krushelnytsky, Amvrosii de 256, 284
Krushelnytsky, Maksym 237, 271,
    284–5, 295, 312, 316
Kryshtalovych, Petro 285
Kryve, Berezhany circle, Berezhany
    district 163, 210, 232
Kryzhanovsky, Roman 285
Kudryntsi, Borshchiv district 52
Kukhar, Antin 285–6
Kukilnyky, Rohatyn district 156
Kukyziv, Lviv district 260, 267–9, 277,
    279, 303
Kulachkivtsi, Kolomyia district 65, 133
Kulish, Panteleimon 309
Kulyk, Fedko 285
Kulykiv, Zhovkva circle 232
Kunashiv, Berezhany circle, Rohatyn
    district 3, 7, 11, 228
Kunysivtsi, Kolomyia circle 14
Kupchanko, Hryhorii 194, 198
Kupche, Kaminka Strumylova district
    258
Kurivtsi, Ternopil district 175
Kurovytsky, Atanazii 283, 285
Kurylyshyn, Hryhorii 285–6
Kurzweil, Rudolf 48, 154
Kushchak, Fedor 267, 286
Kushnir, Hryn 199
Kushniryk, Dmytro 286
Kutkivtsi, Ternopil circle, Ternopil
    district 102, 210, 234, 259, 278,
    283, 288, 292, 296, 316
Kuzma, Kyrylo 286
Kuzma, Tymko 164
Kvasnytsia, Vasyl 286
Kyrchiv, Bohdar 237, 286–7
Kyrchiv, Kost 286–7
Kyrchiv, Oleksa 286
Kyrchiv, Pavlo 286–7
Kyrchiv, Toma 286
Kyzhyk, Pavlo 287
Kyzyk, Ivan 287
Kyzyk, Mykola 288

Ladyshevsky, Mykola 46
Lanchyn, Stanyslaviv circle, Nadvirna
    district 227

Lanivtsi, Chortkiv circle, Borshchiv
    district 99, 227
Lapchynsky, Iosyf 288
Lavriv, Staryi Sambir district 310
Lazor, Ioan 288
Lazoruk, Onufrii 164
Leshnovsky, Stefan 288
Lesiuk, Stefan 288
Lestschinsky, Jacob 155
Levandovsky, Valentii 288
Levytsky, Ievhen 80
Levytsky, Iosyf 118
Levytsky, Ivan O. 74–6, 235, 237, 264
Levytsky, Kost 76
Levytsky, Pavlo 288
Levytsky, Volodymyr 76
Liagotsky, Ioan 210
Liashky Dolishni, Bibrka district 269
Liashky Horishni, Bibrka district 269
Liatske Male, Zolochiv district 315
Lishchynsky, Havrylo 288
Lishnia, Drohobych district 306, 308
Lisovyk, K.A. 289
Litynia, Drohobych district 99
Liubycha Kameralna, Rava Ruska
    district 83, 181
Liubycha Kniazi, Rava Ruska district
    273, 275, 288–9, 294, 297, 306
Liubycha Korolivska, Zhovkva circle
    229
Liubynetsky, Ivan 289
Liucha, Kolomyia district 260, 271,
    273, 281, 293, 307–8, 312
Liush, Hrynko 11–12, 18
Lolyn, Stryi district 123
London 215
Lopatyn, Brody district 149, 193
Lopatynsky, Vasylii Slepovron 289
Lopushanka Khomyna, Staryi Sambir
    district 278
Lototsky, Iurii 289
Lower Austria 269
Loza, Iakiv 289
Lozivka, Ternopil circle, Zbarazh
    district 303
Lozynsky, Iosyf 53–4, 123
Lubaczów, Zhovkva circle 26
Lubyk, Ivan 163
Lun, Mykolai 289
Lutsyk, Iuvenal 289

Lviv 5, 17, 26, 31, 35, 39, 41, 45–6, 48,
53, 67, 74, 80, 82, 90, 100, 102,
108, 113, 115–16, 121, 124, 144,
167, 186, 194, 199, 208, 214,
219–20, 225–6, 229, 231, 235, 258,
260–1, 263–4, 269–72, 275, 278,
284, 286–8, 292, 297, 300, 310–11,
315, 317; district 152; archeparchy
107, 109, 269
Lypak, Petro 289
Lypynsky, Viacheslav 214
Lysets, Bohorodchany district 156
Lysiatychi, Stryi circle, Stryi district
136, 228, 259, 277, 286

Madeyski, Stanisław 152
Mahler, Raphael 165, 173
Maievsky, Hryhorii 290
Maik, Panko 46
Maik, Petro 43, 46
Majbek, Piotr 17
Makhniv, Rava Ruska district 262, 265,
275, 277, 280, 292, 296, 308
Makohonsky, Stefan 290
Maksymovych, Dmytro 290, 296
Maksymovych, Mykola 290
Maksymovych, Volodymyr 290
Manaiv, Zboriv district 171
Mandii, Danylo 290
Mandiuk, Ivan 290
Mandiuk, Vasyl 290
Maneliuk, Aleksii 188, 291
Maniava, Stanyslaviv circle,
Bohorodchany district 227
Manila, Fedko 291
Mannheim, Karl 98
Mardarovych, Iliia 126
Maria Theresia 7, 9, 19, 37, 124
Markevych, Ivan 291
Markiv, Stanyslaviv circle,
Bohorodchany district 227
Martyniuk, Vasyl 291
Martyshuk, Pavlo 291
Marx, Karl 29, 160–1, 205
Matsiakh, Mykola 291
Matviishyn, Ivan 291
Matviishyn, Petro 291
Mauthner, Mateusz 44–5
Mazur, Vavryk 210, 292
Mazurchak, Tymko 292

Mazykevych, I. 292
Mechyshchiv, Berezhany circle,
Berezhany district 2, 227, 232–3
Medukha, Stanyslaviv district 156
Medynsky, Ivan 275, 292, 302, 305
Mehera, Andrii 174
Melnyk, Atanas 139–40, 186, 292–3
Melnyk, Ivan 293
Melnyk, Petro 293
Melnyk, Tymko 293
Melnytsia, Chortkiv circle 23
Menchakevych, Iliia 293
Mickiewicz, Adam 127
Miechocin, Tarnobrzeg district 195
Mikhas, Ivan 137–8, 213, 293–4
Miklosich, Franz 297
Milan 284
Mizun, Stryi circle, Dolyna district 233,
274, 306
Mocherniuk, Iura 294
Mocherniuk, Petro 294
Mokh, Rudolf 126
Moldavia 22, 156–7
Monastyrets, Lisko district 52
Monastyryska, Stanyslaviv circle 38
Monchalovsky, Stefan 294
Moravia 12
Morozovychi, Sambir district 65, 137,
213, 293
Mostovyk, Hrynko 294
Mozalivka, Pidhaitsi district 263
Mozola, Vasyl 294
Mroczkowski (estate manager) 149
Mshana, Zolochiv district 92–3, 185,
206, 306
Mshanets, Staryi Sambir district 155,
163, 173, 205–6
Mudrak, Mykhail 294
Mudryk, Pavlo 47–8
Mukan, Kaminka Strumylova district
152
Muzh, Petro 294, 300
Mykhalevych, Symeon 294
Mykhaliuk, Ilko 294
Mykhaliuk, Mykhailo 294
Mykolaiv, Zolochiv circle, Brody
district 227, 257, 275, 279, 281–2,
291–2, 302, 305, 309–10
Mykuliak, Hryhorii 295
Mykuliak, Petro 295

Mykulyntsi, Ternopil circle, Ternopil district 94, 102, 136, 234, 278, 303, 316
Mylkiv, Zhovkva circle 34
Mylna, Brody district 112
Myroniuk, Iliia 295

Nadorozhna, Stanyslaviv circle 233
Nahirny, Andrei 295
Nahirny, Vasyl 73–8, 80, 130, 144, 169
Nahuievychi, Sambir circle, Drohobych district 227
Naiberger, Shulim 163
Nakonechny (teacher) 283
Nakryiko, Andrei 47–8
Nakvasha, Zolochiv circle, Brody district 100, 227, 264–5, 273–4, 284, 305
Naraiv, Berezhany circle 26
Narolsky, Adolf 315
Naumovych, Ivan 69–70, 92
Navrotsky, Ivan 295
Navrotsky, Severyn 295
Neporadny, Havrylo 7
Neslukhiv, Kaminka Strumylova district 265
Nestanychi, Zolochiv circle 17, 232
New York 147
Ninovychi, Sokal district 266, 295, 307–8
Novosad, Semko 296
Novosilka Iazlovetska, Buchach district 60, 185, 309
Novosilky Kardynalski, Zhovkva circle, Rava Ruska district 97, 100, 132, 199, 207, 227, 311
Novosilky Peredni, Rava Ruska district 199
Novyi Dvir, Sokal district 300
Novytsia, Kalush district 172
Nowy Sącz (circle capital) 264
Nychyk, Dmytro 296
Nychyk, Maksym 296
Nykonkovychi, Lviv circle, Lviv district 233, 270–1, 285, 290–1, 304–5
Nykorovych, Andrii 271
Nyniv Horishnii, Stryi circle 233
Nysmychi, Sokal district 184
Nyzhni Hai, Lviv district 230

Nyzhniv, Stanyslaviv circle, Tovmach district 34, 197

Obelnytsia, Rohatyn district 258
Obertyn, Horodenka district 163
Obertyński, Leopold 149, 175
Ohliadiv, Zolochiv circle 232
Okhrymovych, Volodymyr 80
Oleiniuk, Oleksa 296
Olenchyn, Andrii 296
Olesha, Stanyslaviv circle, Tovmach district 84, 99, 140, 164, 185–6, 233, 260, 266, 276, 286, 298, 304
Oleskiv, Iosyf 272
Olesko, Zolochiv circle, Zolochiv district 26, 74, 232, 278, 282, 290, 298, 310; deanery 260, 288, 294
Olesnychi, Zhovkva circle 34
Olesnytsky, Evhen 116, 159, 179, 295
Oliieva-Korolivtsi, Horodenka district 263
Oliinyk, Iurii 296
Olszany, Przemyśl circle 268
Olynets, Anna 296
Olynets, Dmytro 296
Olynets, Hryhorii 296
Olynets, Mykhail 290, 296
Olynets, Stefan 296
Onyshkevych, Onufrii 297
Ordiv, Sokal district 265, 275
Orikhovets, Skalat district 303
Ortynsky, Soter 212, 214
Osivtsi, Buchach district 284
Osmilovsky, L. 297
Ostriv, Sokal district 74, 210
Ozerianka, Zolochiv circle 34
Ozeriany, Berezhany circle, Borshchiv district 99, 102, 232, 266, 303, 311

Pachovsky, Ivan 297
Pachovsky, Mykhailo 297
Pakhivka, Stanyslaviv circle, Bohorodchany district 227
Palchyntsi, Zbarazh district 303
Palestine 286
Pankivsky, Kost 76
Parii, Vasyl 297–8
Partysovsky, Vasyl 199
Pashkovsky, Atanazii 298
Pashkovsky, Iuliian 298
Patsahan, Pavlo 298

Pavelche, Stanyslaviv district 167
Pavliv, Luka 298
Pavlychko, Ivan 298
Pavlyk, Mykhailo 74–80, 99, 102, 130,
    149, 202, 284
Pechenizhyn 174; district 63
Pelekhaty, Fedor 298
Pelensky, Oleksa 298
Pennsylvania 147
Perehinsko, Stryi circle, Dolyna district
    23, 26, 74, 119, 121, 123, 153, 155,
    157
Peremyshliany district 180
Pererisl, Nadvirna district 313
Pergen, Anton 23
Perviatychi, Sokal district 65, 94, 181
Petlykivtsi, Buchach district 284
Petriv, Lev 298
Petrovsky, Ivan 199
Petrovych, Emyliian 298–9
Petrushevych (priest) 207
Petryshyn, Ivan 299
Piasecki, Modest 41, 45–6
Piatnychany Volytsia, Stryi district
    285–6
Pidgursky, Antin 299
Pidhaitsi, Berezhany circle 26
Pidhorodyshche, Berezhany circle,
    Bibrka district 33, 174–5
Pidkamin, Brody district 264
Pidrichny, Pavlo 299
Pidtemne, Lviv district 235
Pikh, Mykhailo 55–6, 299
Pipes, Richard 10
Pisky, Lviv circle, Lviv district 233
Pistyn deanery 277
Piznanka Hnyla, Skalat district 82, 100,
    275, 279, 289, 302, 313, 315, 317
Plotycha, Ternopil district 81, 148, 152,
    181, 206
Pobeda, Alberta 93
Poberezhzhia, Stanyslaviv district 82
Pochapsky, Mykhailo 299
Pochapsky, Vasyl 299
Pochapy, Zolochiv district 257, 266,
    299, 302, 307, 310
Podillia 261, 272
Podliashetsky, Volodymyr 73–6
Pokuttia 261
Poliak, Iosyf 300

Polishchuk, M. 300
Polishchuk, P. 300
Polonychna, Zolochiv circle 232
Polotniuk, Ihnatii 112, 114, 300–1
Polotniuk, Iosyf 300
Polotniuk, Ivan 300
Polove, Zolochiv circle 6–7, 232
Poniatowski, Ignacy 17
Popovych, Fedir 301
Posatsky, Havrylo 301
Potelych, Zhovkva circle 229
Potik, Stanyslaviv circle 30
Potochyshche, Horodenka district 290
Potocki (count; owner of Hryniv) 34
Potocki, Roman 152
Pozdymyr, Zhovkva circle, Sokal
    district 228
Prague 31
Prešov 264
Proskurniak, Onufrii 133
Proskurok, M. 301
Prots, Stefan 46
Protsian, Andrus 32–3
Prukhnytsky, Mykhailo 302
Pryhodsky, Emil 302
Prysivtsi, Zolochiv district 287
Pryslip, Sambir circle 117–18, 120
Przemyśl 8, 15, 26, 114, 116, 262, 264,
    269; circle 5, 13, 21; eparchy 109,
    301
Pukhalsky, H. 302
Pukhalsky, Ivan 302
Pukiv, Berezhany circle 232
Punda, Ivan 302
Punda, Lesko 302
Pundyk, Ivan 302
Pylypchuk, Hryhorii 292, 302
Pynkovsky (merchant activist) 171, 302
Pynkovsky, Mykyta 302
Pytel, Nykola 163–4
Pytel, Stefan 164

Radekhiv, Kaminka Strumylova
    district/district capital 152, 171
Radvantsi, Zhovkva circle, Sokal
    district 94, 98, 181 195, 228, 303
Rava Ruska district 153, 182, 265, 279,
    299, 311
Reiner, Johann 41, 46
Rejowski (gendarme) 199–200

Repuzhyntsi, Horodenka district 263
Ripchuk, Ivan 303
Ripniv, Kaminka Strumylova district 149, 266
Rivnia, Kalush district 84
Rohale, Kaminka Strumylova district 41
Rohatyn (district capital) 26, 132, 260, 291
Rokyty, Kaminka Strumylova district 41
Romanchuk, Iuliian 72–3, 75–7, 79
Romania 220, 261
Romaniv, Ivan 303
Romanyk, Petro 303
Rosdolsky, Roman 27
Rozdil, Zhydachiv district 26, 289; deanery 267, 289
Rozhansky, Hnat 168
Rozhdzhaliv, Zhovkva circle, Sokal district 228
Rozhniativ, Stryi circle 233
Roznoshyntsi, Zbarazh district 57–8, 209
Rozvadiv, Zhydachiv district 261
Ruda Bridska, Brody district 264
Rudenko Liatske, Zolochiv circle, Brody district 227
Rudky (district capital) 276
Rudno, Lviv circle, Lviv district 80, 94, 198, 229, 233, 258, 269, 290, 296
Russian empire 10, 18, 51–2, 66, 98, 192, 197, 220–2, 261, 286
Rutkowski, Mikołaj Pobóg- 13–14, 21
Rybachek, Antin M. 256, 303
Rybak, Symeon 300
Rzeszów (circle capital) 264

Sachavsky, Ivan 181, 187
Sacher-Masoch, Leopold von (police chief) 198
Sacher-Masoch, Leopold von (writer) 5, 135
Sadovy, Ivan 303
Sadzhava, Stanyslaviv circle, Bohorodchany district 227
Saikevych, Danylo 94, 98, 195, 303
Salitra, Oleksa 304
Sambir 26, 118, 293; circle 231; region 136, 212–13

Sanok 26
Sapieha, Adam 277
Saranchuky, Berezhany circle, Berezhany district 227, 232–3, 236
Sasiv, Zolochiv district 294
Savchynsky, Petro 133
Schiller, Friedrich 284
Schön, Johann 46–8, 54
Sembratovych, Iosyf 123, 126
Sembratovych, Sylvester 78, 264
Semotiuk, Stefan 304
Semyhyniv, Stryi circle 33
Seniuk, Mykhail 304
Senyshyn, Hryhorii 304
Senyshyn, Petro 304
Serafyntsi, Kolomyia circle 263
Serbyn, Danylo 304
Serbyn, Ivan 304
Serediuk, Ivan 304
Serenetsky. Karol 305
Serkes, Tymofii 305
Shakespeare, William 284
Shashkevych, Hryhorii 28, 33
Shashkevych, Markiian 31, 297
Shchepiatyn, Rava Ruska district 199
Shchyrba, Hryhorii 305
Shchyrba, Luka 305
Shekhovych, Severyn 68
Sheshor, Ilko 305
Shevchenko, Taras 28, 194–5, 271, 281, 284, 289, 297, 299, 309, 314
Shkraba, Vavryk 305
Shliakhtyntsi, Ternopil district 187, 257, 266, 275, 295, 304
Sholomyia, Bibrka district 276
Shostak, Semen 292, 305
Shporn, Moshko 156
Shpytko, Ivan 306
Shumiach, Turka district 114
Shvets, Luts 306
Shydlivtsi, Husiatyn district 146
Shyshka, Fedko 42
Sichynsky, Iliarion 306
Sighet 156
Silesia 12
Silets, Stanyslaviv district 308
Silets Belzkyi, Sokal district 264, 315
Siltse, Kalush district 148
Siltse, Sambir district 213
Sirko, Antin 306

Skalat district 70, 80, 84; deanery 317
Skobelsky, Ioann 306
Skochylias, Iosyf 185, 306–7
Skomorokhy, Zhovkva circle, Sokal
    district 228
Skrehunets, Semen 307
Sliusarchuk, Nykola 307
Sliuzar, Mykhailo 307
Slobidka, Rohatyn district 156
Slobidka Ianivska, Ternopil district 298
Słomka, Jan 56, 160, 183, 190–1, 193
Slovakia 264
Smarzowa, Tarnów circle 18
Smolynsky, Vasyl 307
Smorzhiv, Zolochiv circle, Brody
    district 227
Smytsniuk, Ivan 18, 57
Sniatyn district 63–4
Snihursky, Ivan 15, 114
Sokal 264; district 153–4, 264, 306
Solotvyna, Stanyslaviv circle,
    Bohorodchany district 227
Soltys, Hryn 307
Soltys, Onofer 307
Sosnicki, Felix 44
Spas, Stryi circle 121
Spasiv, Sokal district 82, 148, 181
Spolitakevych, Ioan 307
Stadion, Franz 22, 30–2
Stadnicki, Jan Kanty 17
Stadnyk, Andrei 307
Stanyslaviv 82, 114–16, 144, 300–1,
    304; circle 14, 38; district 183;
    eparchy 301; region 167, 191; see
    also *Ivano-Frankivsk*
Stariava, Mostyska district 55–6, 170,
    299
Staryi Sambir (district capital) 163;
    region 187
Staryk, I. 308
Starzeńska, Sofia 149
Stashkiv, Aleksander 308
Stefanko, Hryts 308
Stefanko, Petro 308
Steniatyn, Sokal district 282
Stoianiv, Belz circle 12
Stopchativ, Kolomyia district 84, 271,
    276, 298, 302, 307, 311, 315
Strachocina, Sanok circle 233
Stremilche, Zolochiv circle, Brody
    district 227

Strilbychi, Staryi Sambir district 279
Strilkiv, Stryi circle, Stryi district 82,
    164, 200, 233, 276, 283, 300,
    306–7
Stroniatyn, Lviv district 264
Strusevych, Mykhailo 76
Strusiv, Terebovlia district 210
Stryi 26, 33, 259; circle 39, 118
Stryivka, Zbarazh district 303
Stupnytsia, Sambir district 213, 276,
    278–9
Stupnytsky, Havryil 308
Suchodolski (leaseholder) 11
Susiak, Vasyl 308
Svarychiv, Dolyna district 87, 101, 141
Svidersky, Iosyf 308
Svidersky, Ivan 308
Svystilnyky, Rohatyn district 182
Switzerland 74
Sych, Irynei 308
Sych, Stefan 308
Sydorko, Aleksii 308
Symotiuk, Ivan 133
Synkiv, Zalishchyky district 258, 308
Syvy, Mykhailo 309
Szela, Jakub 18
Szparer, Kohos Leib 174

Taaffe, Eduard 300
Tanchakovsky, Aleksander 309
Taniachkevych, Danylo (elder) 309
Taniachkevych, Danylo (younger) 134,
    256, 288, 309–10
Tarchanyn, Amvrosii 268, 310
Tarnavsky, Fylymon 110, 113
Tarnavsky, Vasyl 310–11
Tarnawka, Łańcut district 282
Tarnawka, Sanok circle 264
Tenetyska, Rava Ruska district 289
Terebovlia 26, 210; district 137
Terletsky, Ostap 271
Ternopil 17, 26, 115, 130, 140, 169,
    181, 194, 202, 225, 284, 295, 317;
    circle 4, 8, 231; district 259;
    deanery 295
Tetevchytsi, Kaminka Strumylova
    district 81, 185
Tetorniuk, Hryhorii 311
Thomas, William 83

Toky, Zbarazh district 260
Tomashevsky, Luka 132, 207–8, 210, 328
Tomyn, Oleksa 311
Torky, Sokal district 304
Torosiewicz, Emil 147
Tovstenke, Stryi circle 233
Trach (priest) 141
Transcarpathia 93, 221, 264
Transylvania 32
Trościaniec, Przemyśl circle 34
Trostianets, Sniatyn district 81
Trudovach, Zolochiv circle 232
Trybukhivtsi, Chortkiv circle, Husiatyn district 102, 171, 234, 264, 289, 302
Tsaryk, Fed 311
Tsebriv, Ternopil district 211, 263, 281, 288–9, 296, 313, 317
Tsipyvko, Symeon 311–12
Tsurkovsky, Ihnatii 271, 312
Tsvitova, Buchach district 136, 180, 201, 257
Tsyhany, Chortkiv circle, Borshchiv district 227, 277
Tukholka, Stryi circle 233
Turia Velyka, Dolyna district 180, 185, 283
Turie, Zolochiv circle 12, 21, 23
Turka 26; district 63
Turkevych, Nykolai 312
Tymchuk, Hryhorii 86, 312
Tyrol 62
Tysiv, Dolyna district 284
Tysmenytsia, Tovmach district 203
Tytsieiko, Hrynko 312

Uhniv, Zhovkva circle, Rava Ruska district 199–200, 228–9
Ustie Zelene, Stanyslaviv circle 10
Ustiianovych, Mykola 31
Ustrzyki, Lviv district 163
Utishkiv, Zolochiv district 26, 60, 149, 175, 258, 260, 266, 279, 286, 290, 298
Uvysla, Husiatyn district 184
Uzhhorod 264

Vakhnianyn, Natal 59
Vandrovych, Iosyf 312
Vandych, Prokip 313
Vano (burgomaster) 207
Vasyliuk, Dmytro 313
Veldizh, Dolyna district 280
Velychkovsky, Iuliian 27
Verbiv, Pidhaitsi district 158, 207
Verbytsia, Rava Ruska district 52, 230
Verkhrata, Zhovkva circle, Rava Ruska district 227
Vertiukh, Oleksa 313
Vidlyvany, Nykyfor 259, 313
Vienna 18, 21, 26–7, 31, 42–3, 45–6, 66, 115, 124–5, 148, 167, 195, 225, 261–2, 268, 284, 295, 297, 310, 315
Vilkhovy, Dmytro 313
Vilkhovy, Mykhailo 313
Vilshanytsia, Stanyslaviv district 99
Vistova, Kalush district 283
Vitoshynsky, Iosyp 195
Vivnia, Stryi circle, Stryi district 228
Voinarovsky, Symeon 313–14
Volchukhy, Horodok district 135
Voleniv, Zhydachiv district 280
Volhynia gubernia 192
Volia Iakubova, Drohobych district 99, 117, 139–40, 142, 186, 213, 292–3
Voltsniv, Zhydachiv district 267
Voltsniv, Zolochiv district 306
Volytsia, Sanok district 100, 236
Volytsia, Stryi circle, Stryi district 3, 228, 233, 285
Volytsia, Zhovkva district 236
Vorarlberg 62
Vorobiivka, Ternopil circle, Ternopil district 234, 263
Vorobkevych, Sydir 195
Vorotsiv, Horodok district 258
Vovchok, Marko 309
Vovkiv, Lviv district 235
Vozniak, Ivan 314
Vozniak, Mykhailo (peasant activist) 314
Vydyniv, Kolomyia circle, Sniatyn district 141, 228, 236
Vyktoriv, Stanyslaviv circle, Stanyslaviv district 166, 171, 233, 304
Vynnyky, Lviv district 235, 258

Vynnyky, Zhovkva circle, Zhovkva district 3, 82–3, 90, 97, 99, 174, 232, 235, 265, 268, 273, 310–11
Vyntoniak, Karpo 314
Vyshatychi, Przemyśl circle 13–14, 23
Vyshensky, Iakiv 314–15
Vyshnevsky, I. 118
Vyshynsky, Ioan 315
Vysloboky, Lviv district 99–101, 141, 236
Vysotsko, Sambir district 26, 32
Vyspa, Rohatyn district 82, 136
Vytkiv, Zolochiv circle 310
Vyzhnie Synevidsko, Stryi circle 51

Wallachia 16
Wasilewski, Tadeusz 5, 9, 10, 22
Winnipeg, Manitoba 271–2
Wolański, Erazm 147
Wysłouch, Bolesław 78

Zablotsky, Feliks 315
Zabolotny, Mykhail 315
Zabolotny, Pavlo 315
Zagórze, Sanok circle 29, 39
Zahirie, Kalush district 168
Zahirie, Lviv district 235
Zahirie, Rohatyn district 156
Zahorodky, Lviv circle 233
Zaiachuk, Onufrii 84
Zaiachuk, Vasyl 315
Zakharchuk, Kindrat 315
Zaklynsky, Leonid 237, 312
Zakomarie, Zolochiv district 100, 194, 309–10
Zalishchyky district 63–4
Zaliztsi 26
Zaliztsi Novi, Brody district 288
Zaluche, Kolomyia circle 14
Zanevych, Iosyf 316
Zapytiv, Lviv circle 233, 264, 283
Zaremba, Erazm 42, 48
Zarivny, Petro 316
Zarvanytsia 26
Zarytsky, D. 316
Zaszkowce 230
Zavaliv, Pidhaitsi district 112–14
Zavidovsky, O. 316
Zbarazh 26, 121, 134, 200; district 316
Zbarazh Staryi, Ternopil circle 234

Zboriv, Zolochiv district/district capital 26, 166, 278; deanery 112
Zelenko, Hnat 316
Zeleny, M. 99
Zeleny, Prokip 316
Zhabie, Kolomyia circle 118
Zhelekhivsky, Markil 73, 76
Zhelentsi, Chortkiv circle 277
Zheniv, Zolochiv circle 232
Zhmur, Klymentii 316
Zhovkva 26, 152, 235, 260, 265, 268, 310; circle 229; district 310; region 122
Zhuk, Oleksa 316
Zhulychi, Zolochiv circle, Zolochiv district 60, 141, 232
Zhuravno, Zhydachiv district 26, 289
Zhuravtsi, Rava Ruska district 277, 317
Zhuzhil, Sokal district 157, 236, 301
Zhybchyn, Petro 316
Zhydachiv district 80
Zhydiatychi, Lviv circle, Lviv district 227
Zhyravka, Lviv district 235
Ziembitsky, Hryhorii 317
Ziemiałkowski, Florian 32
Znaniecki, Florian 83
Zolochiv 26, 41, 45; circle 13, 35, 167; district 134, 293, 309, 314; deanery 266
Zozulia, Zolochiv circle 232
Zukh, Maksym 317
Zurich 74
Zvarych, Havryshko 317
Zvarych, Hryhorii (Piznanka Hnyla) 317
Zvarych, Hrynko (Tsebriv) 317
Zvarych, I. 317
Zymna Voda, Lviv circle 229